D0934940

PHILOSOPHY OF EDUCATION

PHILO

OF ED

SOPHY

UCATION

Philip H. Phenix

TEACHERS COLLEGE COLUMBIA UNIVERSITY

HOLT, RINEHART AND WINSTON · NEW YORK

Library of Congress Catalog Card Number: 58-6308

6 7 8 9

2065456

Printed in the United States of America

Preface

THIS BOOK is designed as an introduction to the philosophy of education. While it is intended primarily for use in college and university courses in education, it may also prove of interest to a wider circle of readers —practicing teachers, administrators, parents, concerned citizens—who wish to engage in serious reflection about the issues of education.

The reader is not expected to bring to this study a knowledge of technical philosophy. Though prior acquaintance with that discipline may well prove helpful, the present work does not presuppose it. The necessary philosophic concepts and methods are explained and developed as and when required for the exposition of the educational analysis.

There are five distinctive features of the approach to educational philosophy presented in this book which should be noted.

First, a broad view of both education and philosophy is presented. The discussion of education is not restricted to what takes place in schools, but includes many other types of experience in which the development of human beings is intentionally guided. Thus, Part I deals with education in the school and Part II with education in such wider settings as nature, family, job, and community. The range of philosophic concerns is also wide. Sometimes educational philosophy is limited chiefly to social and political thought and to value theory. The present treatment, in addition to these, gives a prominent place to the theory of knowledge (Part III) and to fundamental questions about the nature of man and of the cosmos (Part IV).

Second, the presentation is guided by a particular conception of the philosophic task, as suggesting some of the factors and alternative possibilities which should be taken into account in an intelligent consideration of educational problems, rather than providing a definite set of solutions or a proposed system of concepts. Customary thought easily falls into patterns which are taken for granted without critical appraisal. Perhaps the chief role of the philosopher is to indicate the range of other possible views and to move thought to a deeper level by asking for the grounds on which the choice of one position rather than another rests.

Accordingly, each of the topics studied in this book is analyzed in the light of certain major variant positions with respect to it and of the considerations which enter into their acceptance or rejection. While the author's own preferences will doubtless be clearly evident in most instances, the purpose of the discussions is not to argue the case for one favored view but to illustrate how a variety of factors need to be considered in the reflective analysis of educational questions and to suggest some of the specific relevant considerations in particular issues.

These analyses should be considered chiefly as discussion outlines rather than as exhaustive treatments of the topics. The reader will gain philosophic understanding and competence only by engaging in further reflection and discussion on the materials presented and by concretely illustrating and applying them through reference to his own experience. Philosophy can be learned well only by personal participation in critical inquiry. Supplementary reading in the suggested bibliography and in related sources may also be helpful in filling in some of the details in the topics analyzed.

A third characteristic of the present approach is that it is not organized around the traditional systematic patterns of philosophy or educational thought. Thus, the various positions on any given problem are not presented in terms of such total schemes as Experimentalism, Idealism, Positivism, Essentialism, and so on. Two reasons underlie this decision not to use the system approach. The first is that most actual reflection does not follow the patterns imposed by such systems of ideas. Each problem generates its own set of possible views, and these do not necessarily fit the standard schemes. For example, there are issues raised by consideration of the problems of freedom, of administrative responsibility, and of the nature of art which are more or less specific to each of those areas of inquiry and which do not simply reflect the differences of view deduced from the various traditional philosophic systems. It seems more useful, then, to discuss the issues in their own terms rather than to ask what the respective positions of Pragmatists, Existentialists, etc., would be.

The other reason for not using the traditional systems is that they sometimes tend to arrest rather than to stimulate thought. When educational problems are analyzed in the light of certain standard philosophies, undiscriminating readers may easily confuse labels and stereotypes with real understanding. To such people, it seems necessary only to decide, for example, whether to be a Realist or an Idealist, and to deduce from this the chosen position on any educational problem. It would appear that critical inquiry requires rather that each problem be considered afresh and not merely as an opportunity to affix philosophic labels. This is not to deny the considerable merit of the treatment of educational philosophy through the standard systems—especially for promoting consistency of ideas. It is hoped, however, that the present alternative approach may prove to have its own special virtues.

A fourth distinctive feature of this text is that the ideas and the arguments are considered almost entirely without reference to the authorities who have advocated them. There is, of course, great value in knowing, for example, that a certain view was held by Plato, another by St. Thomas, and a third by Dewey. The history of ideas is of major importance in educational thought. However, the decision to omit reference to the authorities in the present book is based on the belief that there is also value in learning to follow arguments and to appraise ideas solely in the light of their intrinsic persuasiveness and relevance. The logic of a discussion is no better and no worse simply because Aristotle or anybody else, famous or obscure, used it. The authorship of an idea is in itself no proof of its validity or cogency. If a view is represented as belonging to Rousseau, for example, the student may be predisposed in his consideration of it by his general attitude toward Rousseau as a man or as a thinker. And if he knows nothing about Rousseau, he may be to some extent distracted from the central task of understanding the position by noting and remembering its connection with this authority.

Furthermore, the identification of an authority with a position on a particular problem frequently does scant justice to his thought. A man's view on a given issue cannot fairly be taken out of the context of his whole life of thought and action. Thus, if certain positions were to be indicated as belonging to Whitehead or to Maritain, for example, a misleading and one-sided impression might be gained about their total philosophical and educational standpoints.

In the absence of thorough, discriminating, and well-documented presentations of the positions held by representative persons—impossible in a book of such scope as this—it has seemed best to let the views carry their own authority and to bear no person's name. But the more important reason for this is simply the desire to simplify and concentrate the philosophic effort by considering ideas on their own terms, apart from their historic connections. Relating the various ideas with appropriate names will be a useful supplemental endeavor for the reader, in the light of his further explorations in the selected bibliography and in other sources.

A fifth feature of the book calling for special comment is the topical division and order. Each topic has been treated with a certain degree of independence, as a separable unit of study appropriate for one or more class sessions. The order of the chapters is based upon a movement from the more specific and concrete aspects of education toward the more general and abstract ones. Following the introductory chapter, the eight chapters of Part I deal with problems of school education, which are the most particular and may be the most familiar to the reader. The seven chapters of Part II examine education in a wider context and from a broader point of view. Part III considers the still more penetrating questions of knowledge, whether gained in school or in any other situation, both generally and in a number of more specific fields of experience. Finally, Part IV is devoted to the most general and searching questions of all—questions which arise out of any and all of the more specific problems earlier discussed. Included in this last part are two chapters on human nature and development, two on the nature and development of the cosmos, and two on the nature of good and evil—all in their bearing on the concerns of education.

It might be argued that from a logical standpoint the ultimate questions should be answered first, and that the more particular conclusions should then follow from these. Some users of the book may prefer on these grounds to reverse the order of the parts, dealing first with the nature of man, of reality, and of value, then with knowledge, and finally with the natural, social, and formal aspects of the educative process. There is no reason why the book may not be read in this order by those who find the logic of the development more congenial that way. This order has not been followed in arranging the book for two reasons. Most readers, especially beginners, are better able to grasp the more concrete problems initially and only after they have gained some sense of the philosophic approach are they prepared for the more fundamental questions. Second, it seems to the author that the problems of education may not fruitfully be dealt with by essentially deductive procedures, i. e., by starting with general conceptions about man and the universe and deriving from them certain consequences for topics like the study of science, education through recreation, and the professional education of teachers. The more inductive approach used in this book seems to be in better keeping with the way reflection about education actually takes place and more consonant with the psychology of the reader not already skilled in philosophic inquiry.

I am indebted to many people for their help in the preparation of this book. The immediate stimulus for it has been the students in my classes in educational philosophy at Teachers College, Columbia University. I give my particular thanks to Professor R. Freeman Butts for valuable editorial suggestions and for encouragement in undertaking the book, to Professor Lawrence A. Cremin for reading and commenting helpfully on a part of the manuscript, and to my wife and two boys for their unfailing moral support and interest. I wish also to acknowledge my special appreciation for the personal and philosophic benefit I have enjoyed during the period of writing this book from association with Professor James E. McClellan, my colleague in philosophy of education at Teachers College. Finally, I want to express my gratitude to Miss Mary Anna Aldrich, for her skillful typing of the manuscript.

P. H. P.

New York, N. Y.
October 15, 1957

Contents

Part III EDUCATION AND THE FIELDS OF KNOWLEDGE

Part IV ULTIMATE QUESTIONS IN EDUCATION

Introduction

1

Philosophy, Education, and Philosophy of Education

LET US begin our study by indicating first in a tentative way what philosophy is, next what we mean by education, and finally the nature of the resulting compound, philosophy of education.

Philosophy

The content of philosophy. What is philosophy? In Chapter 25 we shall examine the subject in some detail, but now we require only a general view. In the first place, philosophy is not a body of knowledge. The study of philosophy does not result in the accumulation of a store of facts. There is no such thing as a definite set of "philosophic truths" which emerge from the philosopher's inquiry. To be sure, one can acquire knowledge about philosophers and philosophizing, but that is not the same as engaging in the philosophic enterprise itself.

In addition, philosophy is not even primarily a way of obtaining knowledge. It is not a method of research whose objective is the discovery of new facts. Herein lies its contrast with science, the goal of which is continually to drive back the boundaries of the unknown. Philosophy is not essentially a set of special techniques which, like statistical method or the procedures of depth psychology, open new areas to the conquest of the mind.

If, then, philosophy is neither a body of knowledge nor a tool for acquiring knowledge, what is it? Is it a function of the imagination, an artistic enterprise whose fruits are the varied expressions of subjective fancy? Is the philosopher a kind of prose poet? There is indeed an element of imaginative creativity in his work; yet he is also concerned with fact and knowledge and the sober truth about things as they are. He is not first or foremost an artist, nor is he a scientist. Then what is he and what does he produce?

Philosophy is a way of looking at knowledge which we already have. It involves the organization, interpretation, clarification, and criticism of what is already within the realm of the known and the experienced. The philosopher utilizes as his data the content of the various sciences and of the arts, religion, and literature, as well as the understandings of "common sense."

Thus, the subject matter of philosophy is as wide as human experience itself. Most other studies have a particular area of concern: geology deals with the earth, and history deals with the temporal record of human affairs. Philosophy is not specialized in this fashion; there is no aspect of things animate or inanimate, terrestrial or cosmic, natural or supernatural, which is outside its province and purview. Anything and everything is food for philosophic thought. The specialization that distinguishes philosophy is not one of content area but of aim and process. It is a particular way of looking at knowledge and experience already in possession.

The way of the philosopher. How does one philosophize? What is this philosophic way of looking at things? What does the philosopher do? What tools and procedures does he employ? He does not have a laboratory nor does he conduct experiments as the scientists do. He does not use pigments, clay, or metal to fashion material forms as artists do. The instruments by which the philosopher does his work are *concepts* and *words* and their organized forms in *language*. But these are also the stock-in-trade of the orator, or the poet, or the essayist. How does the philosopher's use of concepts and words differ from their other uses? There are three aspects to be noted.

Aim. The aim of philosophic inquiry is to purify, enrich, and coordinate the language used to interpret experience. Thus in philosophy a merely customary language is not used, e.g., to express feelings, to deliver commands, or to state opinions, but the goal is the transformation and fashioning of language so as to achieve greater clarity and depth of understanding.

Method. The method by which this transformation takes place is the *dialogue*. This does not mean that philosophers can only function in pairs. It means that the sharpening and enlarging of ideas which are the aim of philosophy can only take place in the give-and-take of conversation. It is by talking that concepts are subjected to the searching test of wider application and concrete illustration. The dialogue may be within one person; the philosopher often does converse with himself. If the discourse is both solitary and silent, it becomes *reflection*. All reflective thought is an inner dialogue. Of particular importance for the philosopher is the use of questions. To ask a question is to put concepts on trial, to challenge their adequacy for the interpretation of experience. The philosophic process par excellence is a constant probing by questions which search out wider and deeper implications and meanings. Hence the philosopher's first duty is not to give answers but to raise questions, and every answer is for him the prelude and provocation for a new question.

Philosophy is thus inescapably *social*. (Even reflection is social, in that it implies prior social experience and in that it is in form an internalized dialogue.) Its life-blood is in the interplay of ideas in discussion. The student of philosophy of education must then, above all, learn to engage in "the great conversation" about the issues which concern him. He cannot expect to understand philosophy apart from becoming philosophical himself through critical discussion and serious reflection. He cannot learn philosophy merely by reading and remembering the contents of a textbook. Books on philosophy at best provide guidance and present occasions for the student to engage in the living dialogue.

Level. Philosophy is distinguished from other disciplines also by the level of concepts with which it has to do. It is the function of philosophy to deal with the most basic ideas, with those conceptions which lie at the root of the language we ordinarily use or even of technical and specialized discourse.

Two examples may help to make this clear. If one were to ask, "What makes the sun red in this evening's sky?" that would be a scientific question, and the answer (e.g., "There are molecules in the atmosphere which scatter the short wave lengths of light more than the long ones") would be a scientific answer. The philosopher might make the observation that both the scientific question and its answer are based on an idea of the world where every "effect" (e.g., sun appearing red) has a "cause" (e.g., molecules in the atmosphere). This might lead to further philosophic questions about the meaning of "cause" and "effect" and the grounds for assuming that things are related in this way.

As a second example, consider the obvious common-sense proposition, "Health is a good thing." The philosopher would not assume the obviousness of this, and would ask such questions as these: "Is 'health' a 'thing,' and if so, in what sense?" "Does the proposition hold everywhere and for all time, or does it rest upon conditions not explicitly stated?" "On what grounds is the assertion made, and what kind of evidence could be introduced in support of it?"

The business of the philosopher, then, is always to push the inquiry back to fundamental premises and underlying assumptions. His task is to survey the grounds on which beliefs in any and every field rest.

The love of wisdom. Having sketched these three distinctive features of the philosophic approach, let us now take a fresh start, looking at philosophy from a somewhat different standpoint. The literal meaning of "philosophy" is "the love of wisdom," derived from the two Greek words *philia* (love) and *sophia* (wisdom). Note that by this definition philosophy is not wisdom itself but love of wisdom. Thus, the philosopher is not so much one who has arrived, attained, or accumulated as one who is concerned and devoted. To be philosophic is to possess an attitude, a spirit, an intention, rather than a secure accomplishment. An ignorant man in search of wisdom would be more of a philosopher than a learned man satisfied with his knowledge.

The "love" in philosophy also implies that the philosopher is not one who sits in cold detachment from the world which he contemplates. He is no true philosopher who lacks deep feeling and intense personal involvement in his explorations of the deepest questions of life.

And what of the "wisdom" part of the definition? What is this that the philosopher loves? Wisdom is not the same as knowledge. It is a truism that the wisest men are not always those with the greatest store of information or the most impressive academic attainments. Wisdom implies a maturity of outlook, a penetration and grasp, which knowledge alone cannot guarantee. By way of elaborating this it may be helpful to suggest that the wisdom which the philosopher loves has four components, as follows:

Comprehension. The wise man takes a comprehensive view. He considers all the available data. He is not content with one corner or department of experience. He strives to see life whole. The philosopher thus employs concepts of great generality, such as "matter," "mind," "form," "entity," or "process" which are comprehensive in that they apply to the whole range of human experience. He also tries to discover relationships between seemingly diverse aspects of the world, and through these connections to comprehend the world as a meaningful whole. The basic concepts which he employs are the means by which he hopes to gather up the many threads into some coherent design.

Perspective. The wise man does not take a partial, narrow view. He has sufficient breadth of outlook to see things in perspective and thus to assess their true significance. He transcends the limitations of merely private interest and personal concern. He is then in a position to render critical judgment in the sense that he seeks a standpoint from which he can render intelligent judgment. For example, if someone should assert that since freedom is good, the less government the better, the philosopher might make a critical analysis of the statement by discussing the various meanings of freedom, the different kinds and functions of government, and the relationships between the two implied in the several cases. That is, he would endeavor to consider the proposition in broad enough perspective—and not merely from the view of a special pleader—so that he could make well-grounded judgments about it.

Insight. The wise man is not superficial, but has insight. He knows that things are not always what they appear to be, that the seemingly trivial and insignificant may actually be of the greatest importance or that the outwardly impressive may ultimately be of little account. He is unwilling to accept ideas at face value and insists on asking what they really mean. Thus, if it is asserted that history is a record of past events, the philosopher might inquire whether this is actually true, or whether history is not rather a record of certain observers' perceptions of special aspects of past events, and he would show the difference which such an insight might make in the understanding and use of the past. Again, the philosopher might take an apparently simple common-sense concept such as time and ask questions about it which would show the depth of mystery contained in it. (E.g., The past no longer is and the future is not yet; only the present is. But the present is only the meeting point between the past and future, and hence as a mathematical fiction has no being of its own. From this it would appear that past, present, and future are none of them actual. How, then, can we speak of the reality of time, what sort of being does it have, and how are past, present, and future related to each other?).

This search for philosophic insight is also another way of saying that the philosopher seeks to uncover the basic assumptions which underlie our views of life and the world. Insight in this sense means the recognition that the language we use presupposes certain implied but unexpressed beliefs. For example, to say "I am reading this book" implies that there is an identifiable personal entity which is designated by the word "I," that there is at least one other entity called "this book," that with this entity, the "I" can enter into a relationship called "reading," and finally that the "I" is of such a character as to be able to affirm its own being and activity. Such a set of beliefs indicates a very particular world view, by no means the only possible one. Other basic beliefs would be reflected in a different structure of language and of conduct.

Vision. The wise man is in some sense a "seer"—one who has vision. This does not mean unbridled speculation or an irrational mysticism. It means that the philosopher has a view which lifts him from purely immediate and common concerns to the wider possibilities of the world ideally and imaginatively conceived. He searches for concepts and principles which illuminate and meaningfully interpret the whole range of human experience. For example, one of the great modern visions is that all experience—that which relates not only to the behavior of material bodies but also to life and mind—can be analyzed and coordinated by the method of critical scientific intelligence. This daring outlook, based on the assumption of the universal relevance and competence of scientific method, is no less a high philosophic vision than, for example, the traditional religious vision of a world created and directed by an omnipotent deity.

Who are philosophers? Next we might ask, who philosophizes? Who are the philosophers? It is especially important for the student to attend carefully to the answer, for upon it may depend his readiness to participate in philosophic activity himself. From what has been said above it might seem that philosophy is reserved for a special class of extraordinary people—the wise men—and that ordinary people can at best only look in on what the philosophers do. It is true that there have been great men whose interpretations of the world have made them especially deserving of the name "philosopher." In addition to these, there are professional academic philosophers who practice the art or science of philosophizing and who usually give instruction in the subject in colleges and universities.

But these two groups—the philosophic greats and the professionals—are not the only ones who philosophize. Philosophy is the business of any and every person. It is not for the genius or the academician only; it is not reserved for an inner circle of initiates. For every person it is both a privilege and duty to ask fundamental questions and to make clear through dialogue and reflection the assumptions which underlie conduct and conviction. It is open to every person to fashion a comprehensive view, to strive for a perspective from which to make critical judgment, to gain insight into the deeper meanings of life, and to seek a vision of total meaning or method. Each in his own way has it within him to love wisdom.

The student of philosophy must always remember that the philosophic task is directly and vitally his own. The masters and the professors may provide suggestions; textbooks may help to clarify what others have done. But the aim of the study of philosophy ultimately is to practice philosophy oneself.

Furthermore, the practice of philosophy always begins where one is; in a sense there are no prerequisites for it, apart from the ordinary experience of life and a concern to understand it better. One cannot practice trigonometry until he has mastered arithmetic, elementary algebra, and geometry. Philosophy is not like that. To be sure, there are levels of sophistication in it. But basically philosophy is a spirit and a process which are applicable at every stage of intellectual maturity.

The motives for philosophy. We have now described something of the nature of philosophy and indicated who engages in it. It may finally be of interest to suggest some of the motives for being philosophical. What good is philosophy? Why should anyone want to practice it? What interests does it satisfy, and what benefits does it confer?

Curiosity. The most obvious answer to these questions is that man is by nature curious. Possessed of rationality, he inevitably inquires about the meaning of things. There is something inherently satisfying about understanding, and this is what philosophy ought to provide.

Symbolic interest. A second answer is that human beings are by nature concerned with symbols and the varieties of forms, patterns, and arrangements which they can assume. Especially important are linguistic symbols—the various forms of meaningful language. It is deeply satisfying to persons to talk to one another and to themselves, to try out new words and combinations of words, to probe meanings, to explore shades of difference, to feel the shock of contradiction and the harmony of synthesis. Philosophy provides an occasion par excellence for "the talking animal" to exercise this essential function.

Search for meaning. A third motive is the search for meaning. Man is set afoot in a vast and complex world. To reduce the anxiety which this creates, he tries to find ways of reducing its multiplicities to a more comprehensible pattern, to discover threads which are clues to the design of the whole, to discern in the larger scene traces of what he knows as purposes in his own conscious life. These are some of the goals of philosophy.

Drive for completion. Closely related to this is the basic human drive for completion. Many if not all persons prefer wholeness to partiality and fragmentation. They want to see the entire picture and not only a corner of it. The lure of philosophy is, at least in part, the promise of comprehensiveness—the attempt to provide a synoptic view from which the whole of things may be surveyed.

Desire to solve problems. In the fifth place, philosophy is motivated in part by the desire to solve problems. When persons are faced with perplexing situations, reflection is stimulated to find a way out. Some difficulties are a result of faulty ideas that can be corrected by analysis of underlying assumptions, which is one of the functions of philosophy. There are conflicts and contradictions of ideas that can best be overcome by the critical and clarifying functions of philosophy.

Need for inspiration. A sixth and final benefit expected from philosophy is indicated by the vague and academically suspect word inspiration. If by this is meant a glow of satisfaction resulting from pleasing but irresponsible speculation or from wishful thinking, then it is an unworthy motive. But there is a legitimate inspiration which philosophy at its best ought to provide. To understand, to gain comprehensive insights, to penetrate to the fundamental assumptions, to see relationships, to purify language, to stretch the imagination, to overcome contradictions, to be caught up in a vision of ideal possibilities—all these and the other similar fruits of philosophy tend to impart life, energy, or spirit.

Education

Having now completed this preliminary survey of the nature of philosophy, let us consider in a general way the nature of education.

The method of definition. A philosophical approach to the definition of any term such as "education" involves the determination of a pattern of concepts which will describe what is intended by the word. A definition consists of a statement of equivalence between the concept to be defined and a set of other concepts whose meaning is presumed known on other grounds. For example, the word "chair" may be defined as equivalent to the following pattern of terms: "a piece of furniture for one person to sit on, consisting of a horizontal surface raised above the floor or ground level by more or less vertical supports, and having some kind of more or less vertical surface against which the sitter may rest his back." This definition should enable one to determine whether or not the designation "chair" would be appropriate to any particular object. It would, for instance, rule out a similar piece of furniture meant for more than one person, which might be called a "couch" or a "divan." It would rule out a table, which has no back rest and is not intended for sitting purposes. This definition would of course, be meaningful only if one already understood the meanings of such concepts as "furniture," "sit," "horizontal," etc., and the significance of the grammatical conventions governing their arrangement in the definition.

The fact that the terms of the definition are presumed known on other grounds means that they must be explained by further discussion, illustration, and definition. In the case of education, we cannot simply give a definition and consider that this will impart full understanding. Each term in the definition will require clarification and exemplification in still other terms. If this were not so, a textbook on the principles of education would need only one chapter, in which the definition of education would be developed. In reality, the definition only sets the task, marking out the lines along which the further elaboration of the subject must proceed.

A critical definition is, in fact, both a statement of convention and a proposal. It is a statement of convention to the extent that it actually reflects the customary usage of language. No definition which runs completely counter to convention is a good definition, because language is meant to be understood by others and not to confuse them, and the meanings indicated in the definition ought to rest largely on common consent. But a critical definition is not merely conventional; it is also a proposal to modify ordinary usage by more precise, more profound, or more consistent use of terms. Thus, any critical definition implies a point of view and certain emphases about the subject under discussion—a reasoned intention to deal with it within a chosen framework and along certain lines considered most promising.

A definition of education. The definition of education now to be developed will thus constitute a proposal about how education may usefully be studied and at the same time should correspond in broad compass to the common understanding of the word.

A human enterprise. First, it is clear that education has to do with human beings and not, for example, with inanimate objects, plants, or animals. Thus, we may train a dog, but we do not educate it. Implicit in this is an assumption of the special nature of man, whereby he is distinguishable from all other classes of things. To distinguish human beings from other beings does not mean to deny certain continuities and relationships between them. It does imply certain real differences in kind.

A process. What has education to do with human beings? It is not, strictly speaking, a thing which persons possess or which is a part of them. One does not have education in the same way as he might have a thousand dollars or brown hair. Even knowledge or skill or good character are not in themselves education, but only evidence that one has been educated. Education is not a thing; it is a process, a kind of activity in relation to human beings. To educate is to engage in a process, and to "have an education" is to be someone who has undergone a process.

Development. Next we must ask what kind of person-related process education is. The answer is that it has to do with the development of human beings as persons. It is a process involving personal becoming. Education is thus concerned with the real and inmost nature of the person and not with those things which belong to him only by association. For example, the process of acquiring property or of becoming famous would not be education by our definition except as such happenings might actually make a difference in what the person is and not merely in what he has or how he is regarded by others. Education is a process of personal growth or learning.

Direction. But still further qualifications are necessary in the definition. Not all processes involving human development are education. It is only those which guide, direct, or fashion personal becoming. That is to say, education requires an educative agent acting upon the person to be educated. It is an interactive, bipolar process. This rules out a view of education as a process of unfolding, as the emergence in persons of powers already present but not apparent. It rules out processes of organic maturation and those which produce purely instinctive behavior.

By persons. Then what agencies for guiding or fashioning personal development are proper to education? Not every influence will qualify. Undoubtedly, pets do help to fashion children's growth as persons, yet we do not propose to include this as an example of education. The physical environment of human beings also guides their learning, and still it does not seem appropriate to regard the mountains or the weather as educational agencies. According to the proposed definition, education will be restricted to the direction, by persons, of personal development. That is to say, the only admissible agencies for education will be human beings.

Included in such personal agencies will be the self. The directing of one's own personal development is called self-education, certainly an important department of the whole enterprise of education. In the paragraph on direction it was stated that education is an interactive, bipolar process. This is not in conflict with a conception of self-education, since it is the nature of the self to be bipolar—i.e., to be able to carry on an internal dialogue, as already noted in the discussion about reflection in philosophy.

Intentional. Finally, one further qualification is necessary to complete the definition. That is that the direction which persons give be intentional or deliberate. The influence which a friend may unconsciously have on a person simply by associating with him does not count as education in the present definition. Insofar as the person intentionally uses his friend's life as a guide for his own conduct education would occur. In this case it would be self-education. The friend would become an educator only if he deliberately sought to direct his companion's development as a person.

It is important to note that not all intentional directing of persons is education. A policeman may direct the driver of an automobile to make a turn, but that is not education because the intent is not to influence the driver's growth as a person but only to get the traffic to move properly. It is only those deliberate processes of directing which are intended to influence personal growth and learning that fall within the definition of education.

The definition of education. We are now ready to state the complete definition of education which has been developed step by step in the preceding paragraphs: *Education is the process whereby persons intentionally guide the development of persons.*

Analysis and critique of the definition. It may be of interest at this point, by way of philosophic analysis, to note the method by which this definition was arrived at. A definition can be compared with a marksman's target, consisting of a series of concentric circles. The outermost circle is the largest class of things to which the entity to be defined belongs. In our case, this outer circle was the class of all human enterprises. Within this outermost circle lies the next circle, a subclass of the former one. For our definition, this was that part of the group of human enterprises called processes. Enclosed within this was the sub-subclass of person-related processes having to do with development or becoming. Successively smaller circles indicated the further subgroupings described by the qualifiers "guiding," "by persons," and "intentional." The definition may thus be represented by a pattern of six concentric circles. Each circle represents a concept which limits, restricts, or modifies the preceding one. A sharp or precise definition is one which proceeds in this fashion to a central focus—forming, as it were, a target with a bull's eye.

The chief objection which would probably be raised to the definition of education developed is that it is too narrow, and this narrowness would particularly relate to the two innermost circles. That is, some would prefer not to restrict education to the *intentional* guidance of human development, on the grounds that many of the most important lessons are learned from those who have no intention of teaching them. Similarly, some would regard non-human agencies as important educative influences and would accordingly prefer to include within the province of education the learning which occurs, for example, from association with animals or plants. With regard to the latter point, these learnings would be included under our definition if they were the result of selection by the self or someone else to provide a learning situation. The point at issue is whether or not the word "education" is appropriate where such non-human influences act without any human mediation.

No judgment of right or wrong can be rendered about such questions of breadth in definition. A certain latitude is permissible in dealing with terms which have no precise conventional meaning. We have proposed the somewhat narrower definition because it seems to provide a degree of precision without neglect of important common meanings. Actually, the definition is a middle course between narrow concepts of education (e.g., "learning at school") which omit significant analogous learning areas and broad concepts (e.g., "all of life") which are so comprehensive that they blur distinctions and obscure careful analysis.

Philosophy of Education

Thus far the meaning of philosophy and the meaning of education have been described. We are now in a position to discuss the nature of philosophy of education.

Briefly, philosophy of education is the application of philosophic method and outlook to the area of experience called education. It includes such things as the search for concepts which will coordinate various aspects of education in a comprehensive scheme, the clarification of meanings in educational terminology, the exhibiting of basic premises or assumptions upon which statements about education rest, and the development of categories which relate education to other areas of human concern.

Comparison with other ways of studying education. It may assist in understanding philosophy of education if we survey briefly some of the standard ways of studying education and compare these one by one with the philosophical approach to the subject.

History of education. First, there is the history of education, in which an attempt is made to describe as faithfully as possible what has happened in the past with respect to education. The historian's resources are a variety of records which constitute evidence of what occurred. These he sifts, compares, and analyzes in order to produce a new and more accessible report. Philosophy of education clearly also depends upon experience of the past, but its function is not primarily to portray the past but to interpret, criticize, and reconstruct the conceptual schemes in which educational experience is expressed. The historian seeks primarily to state what has happened, the philosopher to ask fundamental questions. The historian's currency is temporal events; the philosopher's is the concepts, ideas, and categories of intelligible discourse. The historian tries to tell what has occurred in education, the philosopher what is meant, implied, or presupposed when we speak in various ways about education.

Psychology of education. Second, there is the psychology of education. This is the application of the scientific study of individual human behavior to the problems of education. It involves the use of concepts and techniques which have been successful in the general study of behavior for the understanding of behavior in educational situations. Psychology of education differs from philosophy of education in two main respects. A central feature of it is systematic observation and experimentation whereby new data are collected and subjected to theoretical analysis. Philosophy, in contrast, is not a fact-gathering enterprise but deals with the coordination and clarification of data already in hand. The other main difference is one of scope. Psychology of education is the application to education of a limited set of principles which form a more or less well-defined field of research. Philosophy of education, by comparison, is more far-ranging. It aims to comprehend education in ways which cross field boundaries, to formulate concepts which will interpret education with utmost generality. Another way of saying this is that psychology is a science, while philosophy, though in some ways scientific in approach, is not.

Social science of education. A third important branch of the study of education may be called the social science of education, i.e., the application to education of the methods and concepts of the social sciences such as sociology, social psychology, anthropology, economics, and political science. The differences between these disciplines and the philosophy of education are substantially the same as in the case of the psychology of education.

Principles of education. A fourth approach to the study of education may be designated by the vague term "principles of education." This may be further subdivided into such fields as "principles of school administration," "principles of teaching," "principles of curriculum construction," "principles of guidance," etc. Such terms generally denote a systematic treatment of the main problems of education in its various phases, setting forth the best available results of research and conclusions from practical experience. The aim is chiefly to provide guidance for the active practitioners of education. The study of principles differs from educational philosophy in part by virtue of this predominately practical intent. Philosophy is primarily concerned with interpretation or understanding and only secondarily with application. Another difference is in the depth of the inquiry. Philosophy of education is the exploration of first principles through the asking of questions which probe the very foundations of the subject. The ordinary study of "principles" is concerned with *last* principles rather than with basic assumptions. That is, it deals largely with the best-attested conclusions of educational theory and practice and not with the premises upon which they rest.

Ways of studying educational philosophy. Not only are there these different approaches to the study of education, but there are also different ways of studying the philosophy of education. The following five ways may be noted.

The history of ideas. Men have always been philosophical about education, and there is a considerable body of literature which reflects this interest. One method of approaching the philosophy of education is to study the ways in which able thinkers in the course of civilization have explored the fundamental issues. Major philosophers like Plato, Aristotle, Augustine, Aquinas, Locke, Kant, Dewey, and Whitehead have written about educational problems. All of the great historic systems of thought have relevance to the questions of education. The student of educational philosophy may gain valuable insights from acquaintance with these thinkers and systems of the past.

The study of the history of ideas has the advantage of giving long-term perspective to educational problems and of showing the deep roots of present educational ideas. It has the disadvantages, especially for the beginning student, of requiring relatively greater background in history and philosophy than some of the other approaches and of appearing to be less immediately applicable to present-day needs.

Types of educational philosophy. It is possible within limits to classify educational philosophy into types or "schools of thought." For example, there is one educational philosophy called "experimentalism," reflecting chiefly the concern for scientific method and a problem-solving approach to the learning process. Another type is the Roman Catholic philosophy of education, based on the primacy of the Christian revelation as mediated through the institutional church. There is no fixed and standard way of typing the philosophies. Every writer on the subject has his own system of classification, though there are some types which have gained rather wide currency.

An advantage of the use of types in studying educational philosophy is that comparisons and contrasts may be made, thus sharpening issues and throwing main characteristics into clear relief. It also has the merit of presenting educational thought in broad outline, highlighting principal features and avoiding a mass of subordinate detail. On the other hand, type-study has the defect of sometimes glossing over important distinctions and qualifications of individual philosophies and of artificially forcing them into molds which may unfairly represent them.

Selection from general philosophy. Educational philosophy may be regarded as that portion of general philosophy which is a necessary part of the content of all teaching. For example, it may be said that every teacher inevitably teaches logic to his students. Rules of inference and principles of evidence are inherent in instruction in every subject rationally approached. Hence, it could be argued that educational philosophy should include at least the study of the principles of right thinking. Again, all educational activity involves choice between better and worse—decision between alternatives. The grounds for making such choices are the province of ethics. Therefore, it seems that educational philosophy ought to include the study of ethical principles. On the other hand, the branches of technical philosophy called metaphysics (theories about reality), esthetics (theories about the beautiful), and epistemology (theories about knowledge) would not be so directly relevant, since their content would not necessarily be included in all teaching, though some position about these things would still be presupposed.

The advantage of this method is that it provides material of some immediate practical utility in teaching. It has the disadvantage that it leaves out of account many of the most basic questions about education, from those areas of philosophy in which direct teaching content (as indicated above) is not provided.

Problems of education. Still another method of studying philosophy of education is to identify the main problems or issues in education and to study them in a philosophic manner. Typical of the central issues would be the aims or goals of education, the relation of education to church and to state, the respective functions of public and private schools, and the nature of the curriculum. Such problems may be analyzed with respect to fundamental assumptions and conceptual schemes most relevant to their clarification or solution.

The special value of this approach to educational philosophy is its clear and immediate relevance to the practical concerns of education. A disadvantage may be that it sometimes fails to give the student as clear a picture of the philosophic systems or outlooks as provided, for example, by the study of types of educational philosophy.

Systematic philosophy of education. Many books or courses on the philosophy of education are intended to present systematically only one view or standpoint. As suggested under types of educational philosophy, there are many different "schools" of educational philosophy involving different ways of asking fundamental questions and different sets of concepts in which to frame answers. Some teachers and students find it more profitable—especially if there is little time for philosophy of education in their curriculum—to deal more thoroughly with one philosophic approach than to present several philosophies superficially. Others are so convinced of the correctness of one particular position that they believe it their duty to teach it exclusively.

This method has the obvious merits of depth and coherence of treatment but lacks the breadth of perspective and critical acuteness fostered by a method which presents alternatives.

In practice, no treatment of the subject is purely of any one kind. For example, it would be hard to find a systematic philosophy of education which was not organized in part around educational problems, which took no account of other philosophies or of the history of ideas, and which did not teach some logic and ethics. Similarly, a study of the history of types of educational philosophy presupposes some systematic outlook for the selection and interpretation of these materials.

The present book is such a compound of approaches. In its organization of topics and in the methods of analysis chosen a single reasonably coherent point of view prevails, and to that extent a systematic philosophy of education is presented. But within this framework some of the major problems of education are dealt with, and in each discussion some indication of alternative types of philosophy is given. There is relatively little specific reference to the history of ideas and little attempt to present directly the principles of logic and ethics.

The value of educational philosophy. We conclude this chapter with a discussion of some of the benefits which may accrue from the study of the philosophy of education. We have already done this with respect to philosophy in general, and now we consider more particularly the fruits of a philosophic study of education.

Understanding. First, and most fundamentally, there is the reward simply of understanding better what it means to be engaged in the process of education. No person who is intellectually alive can fail to be inquisitive about basic human activities, especially ones in which he is himself most intimately involved.

Seeing relationships. Second, the philosophy of education ought to enable one to see the educational task in its wholeness and in relation to other aspects and concerns of life. Particularly in this modern era of specialization it is easy for one to become so engrossed in his own profession or area of special interest within the profession that he loses a conception of the place he occupies within the larger scheme of things. Such a narrowing of outlook frequently breeds a sense of futility in the task because there is no sense of relatedness, meaning, and direction in the work done. One product of educational philosophy should be a kind of exhilaration and satisfaction in seeing one's own work as integral and contributory, not only to the grand scheme of education in all its phases, but also to the far grander human and cosmic drama.

Removing inconsistencies. A less exalted but none the less important result of educational philosophy is the provision of means for recognizing and eliminating conflicts and contradictions in the theory and practice of education. Through discussion about educational experience, concepts are clarified and criticized so as to yield coherent schemes of interpretation. It is also the faith of the philosopher of education that dialogue between persons of different persuasions about the subject will yield progressively more mutual understanding if not agreement.

Suggesting new developments. Another product of educational philosophy is the suggesting of new lines of educational development, research, and action. From any comprehensive and critical scheme of interpretation it is possible to deduce certain theoretical consequences which may be tested in practice. For example, a philosophy in which education is defined as we have done earlier in this chapter would suggest the value of studies in which the distinctive characteristics of human beings as compared with lower animals would be investigated, and it would encourage the shaping of educational practice so as to keep those unique functions central, subordinating the purely animal-training aspects of human growth.

Raising questions. Finally, it bears repeating that the main business of philosophy—including philosophy of education—is not so much to give answers as to raise questions. One fruit of the study of educational philosophy should be the development of an attitude, capacity, and taste for asking questions. No student of this subject ought ever to be content merely to accept standard ideas and programs in education. He should always want to inquire about them: Why? On what grounds? Within what context? On the basis of what assumptions? He should never be satisfied with purely habitual or traditional modes of thought and conduct in education. He should be alert to alternative possibilities which can be tested and compared with existing patterns. It is only with such a seeking, questioning, examining attitude that education can be a vital and growing enterprise and that those who are its practitioners can fulfill their own potentialities as reflective persons.

PART I

Education in the School

2

The School

WHEN ONE thinks or talks about education, he first and most naturally has in mind the kind of activities that take place in schools. To say that a person is educated is commonly taken to mean that he has completed a course of study in school. To call someone an educator is to associate him vocationally with a school. It is appropriate, therefore, in a philosophic study of education to reflect about the school as the most immediate, definite, and obvious source of educational experience.

The Agencies of Education

A first observation emerging from reflection about the school is that there are in addition to it many other agencies of education. If education is broadly defined, as in the introductory chapter, then there are many agencies through which it is conducted. Among these, schools are certainly of central importance, but it is not only in them that the development of persons is deliberately guided. Prior to the school, and in many respects of more profound and lasting effect on personality, is the home. Religious institutions frequently exercise a significant influence. Associations with friends and fellow citizens in activities of common concern and participation in business and professional life similarly have much to do with directing human growth. Institutions such as libraries and museums, as well as schools, may serve as agencies of intellectual growth. The powerful educational effect of newspapers, magazines, radio, television, and motion pictures is clearly evident. In fact, it has often been suggested that these agencies of mass communication are far more influential in the development of persons than are the schools. Finally, the individual himself is an educative agency of fundamental importance. What a person becomes is never wholly determined by the influence of external factors, but also by his own inner power of self-direction.

Thus education takes place through many agencies and not exclusively in schools. It is this multiplicity of educative agencies which prompts the question: In what way is the school unique and distinctive among these agencies, and how is the educative work of the school related to that of the others? In the long run the school can perform its functions well only when those concerned with it are conscious of its true nature and proper mission. Hence the need for reflection about the nature and social function of the school.

Definition of the School

We begin by asking what a school is. What are its essential features, its fundamental ingredients? A school is not in essence a building, with classrooms and blackboards, a playground to one side and a flagpole in the front walk. There can be schools without any such typical physical equipment. Nor is a school necessarily a place where there are classes of students reading books. There can be schools without class groups and with no books. In structure and in types of activities schools are of the greatest variety, ranging from informal play groups in a nursery school to the association of adviser with doctoral candidate in a program of advanced research. What do all these have in common that they should fall within the same designation, "school"?

A social institution. The essential features of a school would seem to be two. First, it is a social institution, specifically recognized and designated as such and set apart for a particular objective. A social institution is a deliberate and formal social arrangement, and not merely an incidental feature of general social organization. Friendship groups, by way of contrast, are social entities, but they are not institutional in character. On the other hand, the family shares with the school an institutional nature, since it is specifically set apart and recognized by custom and law. As an institution, the school has certain rights and obligations within the total social scene, defined by a whole complex of relationships with other institutions. It is by these factors that the nature of any particular school is designated. The role of a trade school, for example, is defined by its relationship to the specific occupations for which it prepares its students, and this distinguishes it from an institution dedicated chiefly to the general education of the young for good citizenship.

Education the explicit and primary objective. Granted, then, that the school is a social institution, it still remains to specify the second essential, for there are many kinds of institutions and the unique character of the school among all of these is still to be stated. A school may be defined as a social institution whose explicit and primary objective is education. Any social institution deliberately set apart for the work of education is a school. This is not to assert that education takes place only in schools. This is evidently not the case. Often the family is educationally of even greater importance than the school. But the family is not a school because its primary social function is not education but the more fundamental one of perpetuating the species biologically. Education is a concomitant of that basic function. Nor is the church a school, though it may exercise a significant educative influence. Its primary work is the preservation, celebration, and advancement of the life of faith within the believing community, and the educative task is ancillary to that main purpose. Public libraries and museums perform valuable educational services, yet they are not schools because their central and unique functions are not to educate but to conserve the cultural heritage by maintaining collections of books and other products of human contrivance. Work in business or profession may likewise be of great educative value, but the office is not a school, since the major objective in the job is to produce goods and services and to earn a livelihood.

Just as the primacy of education in the school does not exclude other social agencies from the realm of education, so also does it not exclude the school from other than educative functions. Schools educate, but they do other things too. They may provide health services or community recreation facilities, or serve as polling places. It is characteristic of schools that these other functions appear to be secondary and incidental rather than primary. They are functions which are carried out as a matter of convenience but would be considered by many as not essential to the central task, which is education.

Not only is education the primary function of the school; it is also an explicit function. A school is recognized and acknowledged as an educative agency. It advertizes itself as a place of learning, and those who conduct it are responsible for taking thought about the best means and directions for the development of the learner. Other social agencies such as families and business enterprises, which may do great service educationally, are frequently not self-conscious in their educative intentions. A school, on the other hand, is established on the premise that educative activity is its stock in trade and that whatever is done to advance learning will be based upon responsible deliberation. In short, a school is a social institution in which some degree of specialized competence in the guidance of learning is presumed.

Components of the school. Teachers, students, and curriculum would seem to be the three fundamental components in any school. Buildings, books, classes, degrees, and all the other paraphernalia of academic life are then tools to aid in the learning process. May it not be that the heart of the school itself is none of these things, but is in the relation of teachers with pupils engaged in the deliberate pursuit of learning? The material and process of education—the manner of organization of the learning experience—is the curriculum. The simplest kind of school consists of a master and a student engaged in instructive conversation. Normally, however, the teacher has many pupils, and the curriculum is such as to require a variety of materials such as books, pictures, and laboratory equipment. But these elaborations need not obscure the fact that the basic constituents of every school are the teacher, the student, and the course of study. Obvious as this may appear, it is worth emphasizing because when one is deeply immersed in the work of education, it is easy to lose sight of the fundamentals and to act on the assumption that budgets, buildings, and books *are* the school, when they would perhaps better be assessed in relation to the three essentials.

The Need for the School

Schools do actually exist, but there is no absolute necessity for this particular type of social institution. A society without schools is possible; in the history of mankind, in fact, school-less societies have been the rule. Homes, religious organizations, and occupational associations have done the necessary work of educating the young, and in many societies no special institutions have been established for this purpose. It can be argued that the intimate connection between life and learning is best preserved when the educating is done through family, church, and craft organizations and that the setting apart of special educational institutions may lead to irrelevancy and inefficiency in learning. However, since schools have proven useful in advanced societies, it is pertinent to inquire into the basic reasons for their existence. At least five considerations may be noted.

Specialization. The passage from simple to complex forms of social organization is characterized by increasing specialization of function. In the simplest societies each person performs a great variety of tasks, and most people do substantially the same kinds of things. To be sure, there are some specialties, such as child-bearing, which are grounded in physiological necessity. Even the elementary forms of social arrangement also require some division of labor, setting apart those who primarily hunt and fight or who judge and rule. But the general principle is that each person is able to exercise a wide range of functions, making him to a considerable degree self-sufficient. In such societies education is everybody's business, and the work of guiding human development is carried on incidentally and concomitantly with other activities. Hence no schools are required.

As social organization becomes more complex the principle of generalism and self-sufficiency gives way to specialism and interdependence. Each person is held primarily responsible for a relatively narrow range of activities in which he becomes expert, rendering service to others in turn for their benefits to him. Among the resulting classes of specialists are those whose primary function is to educate. The specialists in ruling, fighting, trading, or building may be so absorbed in pursuing their calling that they are not in a position to teach their craft to the on-coming generation. Hence, a new group of specialists is necessary whose designated function is to instruct. The regularizing of this function is achieved through the establishment of schools.

Schools, then, are one consequence of the increasing complexity of social organization. In this they are like all other social institutions. Institutionalization is the means of fixing responsibility and insuring reasonable stability in a highly interdependent society. The designation of particular responsibility for the work of education in an advanced society with marked division of labor is one basic reason for the existence of schools.

Efficiency. Closely related to the principle of specialization is the principle of efficiency. There are schools because they have been found necessary for the most effective employment of available educational resources. In simple societies the knowledge and skills to be acquired are fairly limited. Every person can master with relative ease all he needs to know. Under these circumstances no special care need be taken in dispensing instruction; time and personnel for imparting whatever is required are readily available. As civilization becomes more complex, the range and variety of necessary competences greatly increase. The demand for trained manpower rises, and at the same time greater resources are requisite for producing these people. Education enters into competition with other human enterprises for a share in human and material energies. Schools are established as means for the best utilization of this allotment for education. Instead of permitting the nurture of the immature to be incidental to the work of agencies designated for other primary purposes, the responsibility for education is vested in an institution specifically created for that end. A regularized, systematic process replaces haphazard and uncoordinated instruction. As a visible social institution the school becomes subject to judgment and control by the community which it is designed to serve. It can be expected of those who conduct these schools that they will discover and apply the most efficient ways of using the limited time set apart for education.

Schools also yield an economic advantage through permitting the simultaneous instruction of many students. In a family or other institution organized for some other primary objective education is limited to those who happen to be present in that type of social arrangement. The greater efficiency of the school rests in part on the possibility of utilizing classes of appropriate size and of adjusting the student-teacher ratio, within limits, to the needs of the educational program rather than to the requirements of another activity to which education is incidental. In like manner the school because of its size can make use of specialist instructors and courses in a variety of fields and thus provide far greater scope and depth of teaching than would be possible where education is adjunct to some other primary enterprise.

Socialization. A third fundamental need served by the school is for socialization. Human nature is profoundly social, in that what a human being becomes is to a large extent affected by his interrelations with other persons. Man is a social animal; his very life and being are fashioned in the matrix of society. Personality does not develop in isolation, but largely through interaction in the human community. This development occurs, of course, in many types of association—with parents and siblings, in friendship groups, in participation as a citizen, in work, and in play. All of these relationships may have important educative effect. Ordinarily, however, they are not consciously fashioned with an eye to their influence on personal development, but in the light of other aims to which the quality of socialization is subordinate. The establishment of schools meets the need for a direct and explicit contribution to the social development of personality. It substitutes for the largely fortuitous types of association a deliberately controlled network of human interactions calculated to produce the optimum conditions for personal growth.

By establishing an appropriate human environment within which learning may take place the school promotes a sense of the personal and present relevance of what is studied. The individual gains emotional reinforcement from the realization that his efforts for mastery are matched by those of fellow students, and his own progress is often advanced through sharing in joint enterprises with them.

Cultural conservation and transmission. Societies are able to persist for long periods because the cultural treasure is preserved and handed on from each generation to the next. Knowledge and skill acquired during a lifetime of learning are not passed on to children through biological inheritance. Every person is born only with certain possibilities for cultural achievement. The actual accomplishments of civilization must be learned; they are not a part of one's genetic constitution. The continuity of civilization and the possibility of further progress depend upon the faithful conservation and the effective transmission of the funded experience of mankind embodied in the cultural tradition. New discovery and radical innovation are also essential to the advance of civilization. The present generation is not called upon merely to preserve the culture derived from the past. But this heritage is still indispensable. It is the very foundation and subject matter of any possible invention or improvement. No person or group can really begin anew and within its short span recapitulate the cultural history of mankind. Human history is cumulative, each generation building upon the structure provided by its forebears.

Two different means for the conservation and transmission of culture may be distinguished. One is by the use of various sorts of durable records which may serve as more or less permanent memorials of the past. Buildings, books and pictures, the tools and products of manufacture—any of the relatively enduring artifacts of civilization—can be gathered into such institutions as libraries and museums, if not left in their original situation, and maintained as lasting evidence of the achievements of the past.

The other means is through education, whereby the heritage is preserved not in lifeless deposits but in live people. By education contemporary persons become living embodiments of the wisdom of the past, flesh-and-blood memorials of the cultural tradition. Indeed, even the keeping of durable inanimate records of the past conserves culture only because there are educated people who have learned the meaning of these deposits. Thus, it seems that ultimately the only way of securing the gains of the past is by building them into the personalities of each successive generation. This is the fundamental task of education.

Every social institution is charged with certain responsibilities of maintaining and transmitting the culture. Governments conserve the political order. Professional organizations guard the traditions of their respective vocations. Religious societies hand on the faith once delivered to them. Each of these, however, is responsible only for those aspects of the tradition which directly relate to their own institutional interest and task. Among the institutions of society the school is the one charged with the *general* responsibility of propagating the cultural tradition. To be sure, there are specialized schools where attention is given to particular departments of culture. But the school system as a whole exists because of the need for a systematic, comprehensive, and explicit concern with the protection of the cultural capital and its reinvestment in living persons.

Transition from family to community. The process of achieving maturity as a human being requires the progressive establishment of independence. The child begins life in total dependence upon the parents. As he gains strength, knowledge, and skill he becomes more and more capable of autonomous activity. The time comes eventually when he must take his place as a member of the adult community, as a person in his own right, without recourse to parents for support and protection. Much can be done within the family itself to prepare the young for independence, but the process is greatly assisted by the work of the school. The school is an institution which stands as an intermediary between the family and the larger community. It partakes of the nature of both the family and the larger society in which the young must at length take their place as adults. In the early grades the school is conducted along family lines. The teacher is parent, and the other children are brothers and sisters. In the later years of schooling the family pattern gives way to that of the larger community, as typified in civic affairs and in the endeavors of business, profession, or trade.

The relationships of family to the wider community could be such that the transition would be made directly. But especially with the weakening of the family which has occurred in modern industrial civilization, it has seemed important to have the school as a transition agency. Concerned as it is primarily with education, the school looks backward to the beginnings of the child's life in the family and forward to his ultimate participation in the adult world and charts the best course from source to destination. It appears to be the social agency specifically designed to wean the young from family dependence to adult autonomy. Thus to a considerable extent the development of a society of responsible and independent persons is the task of the school.

The School and Society

Some of the principal reasons for the existence of the school as a social institution have now been stated. There still remains the crucial question of the relationship between the school and the society of which it is a part. Admitting the basic social needs served by the school—of specialization, efficiency, socialization, cultural conservation, and psychological transition—how are these needs best met and how should the role of the school be conceived in relation to the other activities and agencies of society? There are at least five major conceptions of the school's role which need to be considered. Each view has its characteristic implications regarding such matters as teaching, curriculum, and administration. Actual school systems generally reflect several of these positions simultaneously, with varying degrees of emphasis on one or another view.

The school as preparer. Probably the most prevalent conception of the school is as an agency charged with the responsibility of preparing the student for the activities of adult life. Especially in advanced industrial societies the tasks imposed upon their members are of great variety and complexity. To turn persons loose upon the community without careful training would, under these conditions, be to court disaster. The more complex civilization becomes the longer and more intensive must be the preparation given to those who are to be responsible participants in it.

The school is then conceived as a necessary and integral part of the social system. It is continuous with the various other agencies of society, but receives its special character from its temporal priority and contributory relation to the functions expected of the mature person. The nature of the school program is derived from the requirements of adult life, and every activity is evaluated with respect to these demands. For instance, since the responsible citizen is expected to vote, it is necessary in school to provide studies which will make informed choice possible. Since most school children will in time establish their own households, they also need to be taught the fundamentals of good home and family life.

When the school is regarded as an agency of preparation for later life, a high premium is placed on vocational education. The student's program is planned in the light of probable job demands. Those who can decide early on the line of life work they wish to undertake have a great advantage in being able to relate their studies at each stage to the prospective vocation. On the other hand, those who decide late or who change their minds about occupation suffer great disadvantages in a school oriented largely to the future.

The school does not, of course, prepare only for occupational competence. The so-called "liberal" types of education may also be regarded as preparatory, either in developing general intellectual capacities or through providing practice in rational or esthetic activity which may become the basis for enduring skills and abiding sources of enjoyment.

In a rapidly changing civilization the preparatory view may be quite inadequate if the competences required shift too quickly. In that event what the school teaches may always be behind the times. This is most likely to happen in the case of vocational education of a highly technical nature, where modification of ideas and procedures is generally continuous and swift. Even in the less obviously vocational disciplines the overturning of established patterns of thought and practice may negate the fruits of the most careful schemes of preparation.

Since the school as preparer is oriented chiefly toward the future, the present life of the child tends to be ignored. If there are disagreeable or presently meaningless activities which must be undertaken for the sake of future results, they will be imposed and the child will be expected to endure this discipline. At an age when dominant attitudes are being formed the child is led to consider everything he does with reference to later consequences rather than in the light of present satisfactions. He may even learn the habit of feeling guilty whenever he enjoys anything in and for itself and not because of its contribution to the future. He may become so accustomed to the attitude of preparation that he fails to develop a taste for fruition and fulfillment.

The program of the school as preparer may also tend to be too largely utilitarian in emphasis. Only those activities may be undertaken which promise definite and visible results. This is undesirable in view of the fact that some of the most important outcomes of the educative process are quite subtle and not susceptible of precise demonstration.

Finally, the preparatory outlook may generate in the student a sense of unreality in his school life. With a future orientation, the assumption is made that life begins when school ends, that the years of schooling are but a prelude to the real existence of adulthood. It follows further from this that once school is completed no further study is considered necessary, since the required preparation for life has been made, and why should one once in possession of life itself return to the state of merely getting ready?

In spite of these objections to the idea of preparation when pressed too far, it cannot be denied that the school is and ought to be an agency for making the young ready to assume the larger responsibilities of adult life. In work and play, in families, and in state, the person who has had the experience of schooling dedicated to the development of basic social and vocational competences will in all likelihood derive benefits measured by outward success or inner satisfaction or both.

The school as a miniature real society. Instead of regarding the school as only justified by its contribution to the life beyond itself, the school may be considered as a smaller subsociety within the larger community, with a complete life of its own paralleling as far as possible the patterns of the society which it serves. The student is given the sense that school life is real life and not merely a getting ready for adulthood. He is expected to begin at once to participate actively and meaningfully in the social order, and the school is the miniature real society in which that participation is possible. The focus of education is on the present, not the future. There is no need to postpone responsible activity until schooling is done. The school is a place where life in its fullness is to be lived now.

The program of such a school must be comprehensive. It must be dedicated to the well-rounded life and to the development of the "whole man." Not only intellectual experience but the physical, emotional, moral, and religious components of life need to be provided for, since these are integral parts of any complete society. As far as practicable, the students will have a system of government in which they take part. They will be encouraged to try their hands at organizing and conducting financial, commercial, and policing enterprises analogous to those carried on in the larger society. In addition, a variety of student clubs will give them opportunity to express their special interests.

This type of education is more feasible in residential institutions where the students actually constitute a complete community, than it is in day schools, where they divide their time between home and school. The creation of a miniature real society is also more practicable at the higher levels of education, where the students have greater maturity and hence the capacity for a wider range of responsible activity. In fact, when the students have reached the age of marriage, the school community may include family groups and thus reflect even more completely the nature of the society beyond the school than is possible when only the unmarried are admitted.

The conception of the school as a miniature real society also encourages the continuation of education beyond an initial preparatory period. Schooling is not necessarily thought of as for children only, an activity belonging solely to the early years and properly relinquished by the adult. Education is an integral part of living, and there are occasions when persons of any age may appropriately attend school.

It can even be argued that schools organized on the miniature-real-society principle are the best means of preparing the student for the future. When the emphasis is on adult life and what must be done now to get ready for it, the student's present interests and abilities are frequently not consulted and he is likely not to learn as easily or as well as when the school's concern is to provide a good and personally significant present experience. In the latter case the future is better prepared for, not through direct reference to adult needs but as a by-product of a satisfying and meaningful program at each stage of personal development.

This conception of the school is not without its limitations. The school is never truly a complete society. It is necessarily a specialized institution within the larger society. There are certain functions which are appropriate for it and others which belong to other agencies. When the school then attempts to reflect in its activities all of the aspects of community life, a degree of artificiality and a sense of play-acting are inevitable. School banks and student government are not the same as their counterparts in the larger society. School life is real, and does not derive its value solely from its consequences in the future, but it can never be considered by itself, apart from its special functions within the whole social context.

The school as an ideal community. The view of the school as a miniature real society assumes that the school should reflect as nearly as possible the prevailing outlook and organization of the larger social order. Quite different is the conception of the school as an ideal community, whose aims and functions stand in contrast with those of the larger society. The school constitutes a new order, in which undesirable features of existing social institutions are overcome.

There are two different types of ideal to be considered. The first is the ideal of simplification. Life in an advanced civilization is extraordinarily complex. The many competing demands and conflicting influences tend to distract, confuse, and dissipate energies. Under these circumstances there is need for institutions where controlled conditions permit concentration on one task at a time, where responsibility is limited to certain definite and restricted areas, with the expectation that a few things will be done well rather than many things done poorly. Usually it is to the goal of intellectual mastery that the school as a simplified community is dedicated. The academic society is set apart, released from the cares of field and market place, in order that studies may be pursued freely and intensively without the distractions of the world of affairs or the constraints of immediate practicality. Commonly accepted concepts and cherished values are subjected to criticism, and new ideas are explored at will.

Such simplification is possible only because the other institutions of society perform the functions necessary to the maintenance of life. A student may enjoy the monastic simplicity of a school of art or of pure mathematics or even of agriculture only because there are farms, factories, banks, and hospitals by which the supply of goods and services required for general social welfare is provided.

The second type of ideal is that of improvement. The school as an ideal community in this sense is intended to furnish a standard of excellence which the actual larger society does not attain and by which its shortcomings can be measured. If the social order is afflicted with destructive conflicts caused by the clash of selfish interests, the school can provide a contrasting experience of constructive cooperation. When the prevailing preoccupation is with gross sensuality, the school can dedicate itself to the development of sensitivity and refined appreciation. In societies where basic human rights are violated the school can demonstrate in its own life the method and meaning of social justice.

The school as an ideal community will generally exist within the larger social order, accepting the benefits provided by that society and deriving its support from other institutions. This fact of dependence creates a serious problem when the school acts too freely as a critic of existing conditions. A society will not continue indefinitely to maintain subgroups within itself which contradict its own nature. If, on the other hand, it can be understood that the school is a partial demonstration of what the society aims to be but has not as a whole been able to achieve, the necessary support will be gladly provided.

Sometimes the tension between the actual society and the school as an ideal community drives the school into attempted isolation, producing the so-called "ivory tower," where association with the existing larger society is minimized. This divorce may sometimes be necessary, when certain basic values must be preserved from dissolution in a hostile social order. But generally such estrangement has the effect of weakening the school by depriving it of the help and sustenance of the larger society and by rendering the school in turn ineffective as an influence for the improvement of the social order. The most desirable relationship of society and the school as ideal community seems clearly to be one of reciprocity.

The school as caretaker. A fourth view of the position of the school in society is that it should serve a caretaker function. In agrarian cultures children perform many useful tasks on the family farm. From a fairly early age they render service which makes them economic assets rather than liabilities. In industrial society this state of affairs no longer prevails. In town and city life there is little work to which young people can be assigned. Usually child labor laws prohibit their early employment in industry. Most jobs require a degree of skill and impose responsibilities beyond the capacity of the child. Furthermore, there is usually competition for employment, and such positions as are available are reserved for adults.

Under these conditions children become an economic liability. Not only do they not contribute significantly to family income, but they require the time and energy of adults to supervise their activities. This becomes a serious matter when, as is frequently the case in modern society, the mother and the father are both employed away from home and there are no grandparents, aunts, or other kinsfolk available to care for the children.

In such a society the school plays the important role of caring for the children, beginning at the very early ages in nursery schools and continuing even through the college and postgraduate levels until the time for employment is reached. Though the young are not really useful, they must be kept occupied in some way. Otherwise they will find mischief to do. Their abundant energies must be channeled into useful pursuits. Schooling provides for group supervision instead of the much more expensive method of having employable parents care only for their own children. The years of youth are, from this standpoint, in large measure a period of waiting, of marking time, of providing constructive activities and favorable associations until maturity is attained.

When the school serves as caretaker, educational activity is essentially busy-work. The basic objective is to maintain interest. Above all, the students must be kept occupied, their morale and enthusiasm sustained, and their abilities engaged. A reasonable degree of order must also be insisted upon, so that the students will learn the essentials of social propriety and so that the functions of the group may proceed as planned.

The caretaker conception of the school suffers from several defects. If the work of education is regarded as a means of killing time and as a holding operation, this attitude readily becomes apparent to the children, who resent the insignificance and triviality of the activities imposed on them. They find ways of obstructing and defeating the program because they regard its promoters as insincere and deceptive. It is also difficult in the long run to secure capable and dedicated teachers for an enterprise which is regarded as essentially a form of baby-sitting. As in the case of the view that the school is a preparer, the present concept fails to do justice to the intrinsic values in the young person's life, placing all the emphasis on the adult years. In addition, it fosters a sense of aimlessness in the learning process and the attitude that education is something imposed and to be endured during childhood.

The school as legatee. The final view of the role of school in society to be examined is a generalization of the caretaker conception. This is the idea of the school as legatee. Whenever any social agency is unable to fulfill its functions adequately and whenever there are things to be done for which no established agencies exist, the responsibility is delegated to the school. When the family ceases to provide a stable, secure, and loving experience for the child, the school is expected to become a family-substitute. If the church fails to teach ethical and religious values effectively, that task is assigned to the school. In the face of civic apathy or lawlessness the school is charged with the duty of creating responsible and loyal citizens. Where existing health services do not suffice, the school is looked to for assistance. There is scarcely any domain of human activity in which the school has not been called upon for major help.

When one considers the broad scope of education, its concern for whatever promotes the right development of persons, it is evident why the school has been called upon for such a variety of tasks. Presumably nothing human is alien to education. And so in the modern period of rapid growth and unprecedented social change the school has assumed ever increasing responsibilities. School activities, agencies, and offices have multiplied beyond counting. The school is no longer simply the pupil, the teacher, and the lesson. Now there are school psychologists, curriculum supervisors, placement services, health and recreation activities, guidance counselors, public relations experts, and a host of other school-connected people and programs, all considered essential for adequate educational service to the community.

When the school functions in these many capacities, there is a closeness of relationship to the community which is certainly desirable. The school is clearly responsive to the needs of the people and its work is relevant to the concerns of daily life. Furthermore, flexibility in social arrangements is insured when such an institution stands ready to take on whatever tasks need urgently to be done. New institutions do not need to be created because the school already possesses the essential machinery for undertaking functions of great variety.

Against the legatee conception of the school is the fact that it may not always be well fitted to perform the new duties imposed. Perhaps teachers are not and can never be sufficient substitutes for parents. School personnel may not be competent to deal with problems of serious psychological disturbance. Religious instruction may in the nature of the case not be feasible in most schools. If the school attempts to do too many different kinds of things, it may do nothing well. There is especially the danger that the basic educational work will suffer when too many services which are not explicitly educational are provided. As pointed out earlier, the school exists as a social institution primarily because of the need in advanced civilizations for the competences made possible by specialization. If the school is expected to do anything and everything, perhaps it will fail to render its maximum service as a specialized educational agency.

Delegating responsibilities too readily to the school also permits too easy an escape from responsibility for developing truly appropriate social arrangements for satisfying new requirements. A democratic social order is characterized by variety and balance in its institutions, with no one organization or type of organization having the dominant role in fashioning the life of the community. From this standpoint it is desirable that the variety of services to be performed for the citizens be allocated to the appropriate specialized agencies and not be delegated in such large measure to the school.

The Special Function of the School

In closing this discussion of the nature and roles of the school it may be appropriate to attempt a summary statement regarding the special function of the school within the social complex. Are there criteria for deciding which tasks rightly belong to the school and which are not proper to it? Three principles are here proposed for use in making such decisions.

First, it seems clear that there is no aspect of personal development which may not properly be of concern to the school. It is sometimes maintained that the school ought only to be interested in the cognitive dimension of experience and that the emotional, moral, religious, and esthetic aspects are not within its province. This position can be maintained if one is able successfully to separate these aspects into independent compartments. This appears difficult because the human personality is whole and indivisible. Cognition is influenced by and in turn influences the emotional, moral, and other dimensions of experience. From this standpoint education is also indivisible, and all facets of the development of persons need to be taken into account in the work of the school.

But it does not follow from this first principle that all educational functions within the society are the responsibility of the school. Though the school is by definition that institution whose specific and primary function is to educate, other agencies may also perform important educational work. It is suggested as a second principle that the decision as to whether the school or another institution should assume a given educational task may then be made on the basis of their respective educational efficacy.

For example, it may well be that for many types of jobs business and industry, whose primary function is not education, are in a better position through direct experience to train their workers than schools would be. Again, the benefit to a young child may be much greater if he is allowed to stay at home rather than entering the deliberate educational program of a nursery school. Once more, the learning which takes place in a period of travel or of military service could for some be far more significant than the results of an equal period of schooling.

The third principle has to do with the taking on by the school of functions which are not specifically educational. Learning cannot take place with best effect unless the students are properly nourished and housed, clean and well clothed, and in good health. Hence the school must take account of these factors and on occasion and to some extent make special provision for them, as through periodic health examinations, consultations with parents, and school lunch programs. But this may not be sufficient reason for the school to undertake major responsibility for the total welfare of the child. Can the school operate as a social service agency, a medical dispensary, a community center, and a placement service—activities which may merely serve to keep the society and individual in good running order and not to direct the person's growth—without diverting too much of its resources from the educational task? If not, a third principle may be that only those non-educational functions should be undertaken by the school which are immediately and clearly required for the fulfillment of the primary educational tasks and which cannot with reasonable facility be taken on by other appropriate agencies.

These three principles exemplify one approach to making decisions about what the school is uniquely fitted to do. They presuppose that the integrity and breadth of the educative task should be recognized, but that the relative educational effectiveness of other types of institutions and the appropriateness of other agencies for the performance of non-educational tasks also require consideration.

The School as a Problem in Philosophy of Education

In what sense is the preceding analysis of the school philosophic in character? How does it differ from a sociological description? How does such a discussion fit into the philosophy of education? What outcomes should be expected from pursuing such an inquiry?

One basic philosophic task is that of critical definition. The philosopher seeks to make as precise as possible the meaning of commonly but uncritically used concepts, of which the term "school" is one example. Consequently, the first effort in this chapter was to frame a critical definition by which a clear distinction could be made between what is and what is not a school.

Philosophic in intention is also the attempt to relate the idea of school to certain other fundamental concepts such as specialization, efficiency, socialization, culture, and maturation. By thus showing how the existence of the school presupposes certain basic factors in human nature and in the social order, a more profound insight into the nature and sources of educational institutions may be gained.

The analysis of school and society belongs to the field of *social philosophy,* which seeks to provide a critical and synoptic view of social organization and to indicate ways of justifying alternative social arrangements. Five conceptions of the relation of school to society were suggested above, and some of the factors entering into the appraisal of each were indicated. It is one of the main functions of philosophic reflection to bring to light the variety of possible positions on the subject under consideration in order that easy and thoughtless acceptance of merely traditional ideas may be replaced by better founded judgments.

What difference, then, may a consideration of alternatives such as contained in this and later chapters make in one who entertains them seriously? It will usually give neither assured educational guidance nor concrete prescriptions for action. But reflection on alternatives may result in educational judgments more securely founded and better tested. Each thinker must take the responsibility for weighing the evidence; no one can do that for him. Hence perhaps the most that the philosopher of education should do is to say, "Consider these factors." It is his assumption that thought and practice thus informed by a wide view of possibilities are to be preferred to the narrower perspective of the unexamined outlook.

3

Teaching

IT WAS SUGGESTED in the previous chapter that the essential components of the school are teachers, students, and a curriculum. Now that some attention has been given to the general nature and functions of the school in society, we turn to consider in this chapter the nature of the teaching process and in the next chapter that of the curriculum.

The teaching-learning process normally involves a teacher and a student, and the quality of the resulting educative experience is determined by the character of the relationship between these two. It is possible to conceive of teacher and student as one and the same person, and the self-taught person as one who directs his own development through an internal interaction between the self as "I" and the self as "me." On the other hand, it is usual for one teacher to teach many students simultaneously. In that event the quality of the interaction may become generalized and impersonal or it may by appropriate means retain its person-to-person character.

Whether one, two, or many persons participate in the teaching-learning relationship, there are several distinct types of teaching which can be distinguished. This chapter will consist of a treatment of each of these types in succession. They are not to be regarded as necessarily independent and mutually exclusive teaching methods. Every actual teacher doubtless combines in certain proportions several of the types to be presented. Different modes of interaction are also appropriate for different kinds of studies, and the teaching patterns employed may well vary with the age and personality characteristics of both teachers and students.

It will be seen that this analysis of ways of teaching raises certain fundamental philosophic questions about human nature, the meaning of knowledge, and the basis for values. There is no aspect of education which more directly leads to the central philosophic problems than does the teaching process.

The Making of Persons

The first conception to be considered is that of teaching as the making of persons. Perhaps the most apt figure here would be that of the skilled craftsman who fashions a statue, a vase, or a machine according to the desired pattern. So, according to this view, the business of the teacher is to shape the pliable material of the child into the ideal form of the complete and mature human being. The pupil remains passive. It is his function to respond unquestioningly to the directions of the teacher. The "good" student is the one who offers no resistance to the teacher's requirements, while the "bad" one actively rebels or fails to respond with sufficient speed and thoroughness to the instruction provided.

The teacher is here regarded as an authority, whose objectives are to be adopted by the student as his own, as true, and as right. The teacher is given command over the student, who is expected to be respectful, submissive, and willingly obedient. When the pupil does not readily conform to the demands made on him, discipline becomes necessary. By this is meant the use of coercive measures to bring about the desired behavior. Just as the craftsman must use sharp tools and appropriate force to shape resistant materials, so the teacher must skillfully exert pressures in such a way that the lazy or wayward personality is made to conform. It is hoped that in the end the person who has learned through discipline will even be superior to those who have been easily taught, in somewhat the same way as the product made from materials which are hard to work frequently has greater elegance and permanence than objects fashioned out of soft substances. In the making of persons discipline need not always entail the use of physical force. There are various kinds of social and psychological pressure which can often be even more effective than physical power.

Put thus briefly and bluntly, one might reject such a view of teaching. Yet in broad outline the case for the teacher as maker of persons seems irrefutable. A young child left to itself would die. It needs the fostering care of older and stronger people. The development of distinctively human qualities—of language, thought, and manual ability—also depends entirely upon human provision. What the child is to become is not given in the germ plasm but is a consequence of the native endowment acted upon by environmental influences, including other people. Thus, persons inevitably enter into the making of the human being. The teacher is simply one who intentionally and professionally undertakes the task of fashioning the young. Hence teaching is in essence an act of creation, and the product of this making is nothing less than the human person.

But would not only the most arrogant and self-assured take upon himself such a role? Would any modest, gentle person presume to be an authority, to exercise power over other lives, to assume the responsibility for the fashioning of other human beings? Is any man so intimately his brother's, or his child's, keeper? Though perhaps one would not wish it so, the answer to these questions seems clearly to be that the assignment to create other persons is unavoidable. The teacher does inescapably exercise a certain authority over the young. He must make decisions about how he believes they ought to develop, and he then must adopt those procedures—"disciplines"—which will be most conducive to the realization of the desired results. The teacher often tries to hide from himself and from other people the fact that he is a maker of persons. He does this because he cannot easily bear the burden of responsibility for his decisions. He does not like to play God, since he knows so well his own finitude and shortcomings. There are other teachers who too enthusiastically and uncritically accept their role as person-makers, assured that their program and pattern are beyond questioning. But whether avoided or accepted, the important fact is that teaching is in the last analysis a process of directing human growth in accordance with a chosen pattern.

On the other hand, it does not follow from this that all teaching is the same kind of making. In particular, the analogy with the craftsman is in certain respects quite inappropriate. A human being is not a chunk of marble or clay waiting to be chiseled or pressed into shape. The student is not an inert substance passively responding, with more or less resistance, to the formative influences of the teacher. He is a living, moving, originating being, who can be intelligently dealt with only when this active nature is taken into account. The teacher who treats his students like so much material to be forced into shape will achieve either or both of two results: He will fail in his teaching objectives because the pupils will not respond as he expects, or he will in effect reduce his students to subhuman status, frustrating the very qualities which give them the dignity of manhood.

The teacher's work is not like that of the sculptor or machinist because the entity fashioned is not a thing but a person. The artisan deals with materials which are merely objects. The teacher is concerned with individuals each of whom has a personal subjective life—a sense of the "I," of selfhood—of the same sort as the teacher's own. The relationship between the teacher and student should, therefore, be that of person to person and not of person to thing. The appropriate teaching attitude is based upon a recognition of essential kinship between teacher and student. The fundamental error of the craftsman conception of teaching is that the student is treated as an object, as a thing, as less than a person.

It is true that the teacher by virtue of greater experience, knowledge, and skill is generally accorded a different role and status from that of the student. But if the student's personality is to be respected, the difference ought to reflect only varieties of position within interpersonal associations. When the teacher becomes an authority whose will is to govern the lives of the students absolutely, there is no longer merely a difference of role and of human status but the presumption of essentially disparate orders of being. The student is reduced to the position of an object to be manipulated, and this in effect constitutes exclusion from the human community.

The idea of the teacher as maker of persons tends to be associated with forms of arrogance and will-to-power which would seem unfitting for finite and fallible man. Is anyone wise enough and good enough that his will should completely determine the life of another person? Each teacher must inevitably exert his influence and each must assume responsibility for what he teaches. Still, can anyone rightly insist that his way be enforced as the complete pattern for the life of others? Dare he impose by the discipline of power the form he has chosen? Questions such as these may make necessary important qualifications and reservations regarding the view of teaching as person-making and point to the need for some of the other conceptions presently to be discussed.

Verbal Transmission of Knowledge

A second view of the teacher's role is that he verbally purveys knowledge. The teacher is learned, the student is ignorant, and the process of education is the transmission of knowledge from the teacher to the student. Just as a philanthropist from his accumulation of wealth distributes benefits to the needy, so the teacher from his gathered store of knowledge provides intellectual nourishment for unenlightened pupils. The analogy is inadequate in this respect, that while giving money away diminishes the amount in possession, knowledge conveyed to another still belongs to the giver, and is even made more secure by the giving.

In this view, the method of transmission is by the spoken or written word. It is assumed that knowledge consists of true verbal propositions—affirmations of matters of fact—and that the learning process consists of fixing these propositions in memory. A well-educated person is then regarded as one who has a large store of facts in mind. The function of the teacher is to communicate to the student more and more of these truths and to make them as permanent as possible by such techniques as repetition and recitation.

In earlier times the spoken word was the most important vehicle for conveying knowledge. But the invention of printing and the present abundance and availability of printed materials of all kinds have greatly increased the relative importance of the written word as the agency for transmitting knowledge. Since reading is far more economical of time and effort than listening to lectures, it would therefore seem that in modern times teachers as transmitters of knowledge should be authors of books rather than persons giving instruction by word of mouth. The fact that oral instruction continues to occupy a major place in the work of the school suggests that teaching consists of more than purveying knowledge. Most teachers are still primarily speakers rather than writers, and this appears to mean that something educationally valuable occurs in the relation of a speaker to a hearer which does not happen when an author addresses a reader.

The transmission conception of teaching has received considerable impetus from the development of modern science. Scientific inquiry has produced an unprecedented flood of well-tested factual information. The number and variety of propositions which can and should be known have increased enormously. Never before in history has the storehouse of knowledge been so amply stocked, and never before have the requirements of civilization placed so high a premium on being well-informed. Because scientific knowledge is also relatively stable, reliable, and cumulative in nature, it can be transmitted with an assurance not possible with the ill-founded speculations of earlier ages and with nonscientific beliefs even today.

The view of teaching as verbal transmission of knowledge is based on certain assumptions about human nature and knowledge which should be made explicit. According to this position, learning consists of the passive reception of impressions. The mind is like a series of tablets upon which messages are written, and these are stored away in succession, as it were, in the record room of memory, available for recall when needed. The intellect is thought of as a receptacle, the purpose of which is to preserve the accumulated items of information received.

Against this view it may be pointed out that persons are alive and active, and that the learning process is a result of interactions in which the initiative and predispositions of the learner play an essential part. Nor is knowledge a commodity to be collected and stored away. It is an integral component of the living person, an aspect of his nature and manner of behaving.

A storehouse idea of knowledge is essentially impersonal. Facts are seen as having an existence independent of people, and as possessing significance in and of themselves. Against this it can be urged that propositions have meaning only as they are brought alive within the dynamic structure of personality. Significance is a matter of personal relevance, and information which is merely learned by rote so that it can be returned from memory in verbal form is meaningless and of no effect. Critics of this position point out that impersonal knowledge is dead, inert. They believe that knowledge worth having must be constitutive of the very being of the living knower.

Teaching regarded as the conveying of information is perhaps also too intellectualistic. Learning is more than the committing of facts to memory, and the teacher has a broader responsibility than communicating information. A human being is a living whole, with feelings, values, and goals as well as factual knowledge. Knowledge in a person is, therefore, quite different from that contained in an encyclopedia. It is to be appraised not only by criteria of true and false but also of purpose, interest, applicability, and emotional tone.

Again, it seems clear that knowledge cannot be understood rightly as a simple summation of isolated bits of information, as implied in the transmission view. To hand out facts for storage in the mind presupposes that the items are essentially independent. In actuality, knowledge is to a high degree systematic and interconnected, so that every fact is comprehended within the context of a framework of other ideas. Thus what the student learns is never a simple transcription of what the teacher says but is always that assertion as understood from the standpoint of an existing complex of previously acquired conceptions. Knowledge is never simply transmitted. It is always in the process transformed so as to find a place within the learner's prior scheme of ideas.

Finally, teaching is more than the verbal purveying of information because knowledge is more than the sum of factual propositions. There are kinds of knowledge which cannot be expressed in words. There may be ways of knowing, as in the perception of beauty or in consciousness of the infinite, which transcend ordinary literal statements of fact.

Verbal transmission of knowledge certainly does occur in teaching. This is one legitimate and necessary conception of the learning process. But as pointed out above, there are certain assumptions often associated with this conception which require examination and criticism. This analysis suggests the need for still different formulations of the teaching function.

Demonstration

Both of the first two views about teaching presuppose a passive learner. The third view, now to be stated, to some extent takes account of the student's activity. According to this position, teaching is demonstration and learning is imitation. The teacher presents some form of overt behavior for the pupil to see or hear, and the student is invited to acquire the same ability as the teacher by duplicating as nearly as possible that type of activity. This can be regarded as one way of making persons, but here the mechanism of shaping through sense perception and the active response of the learner are recognized. It is also a way of transmitting knowledge, in which the incorporation of the knowledge into the organized structure of the student's personality is taken into account.

Teaching through demonstration, like the two earlier methods, rests on the assumption that the teacher is an authority and a model and that the objective of the student is to become like the teacher. There is nothing in any of the three views recognizing the need for individuality and radical innovation by the student. The three outlooks are essentially conservative and retrospective in nature. This is not necessarily evil. Most education must be of this type, since there is so much knowledge and skill, acquired at the cost of great effort by past generations, which needs to be made available to the oncoming generation.

Teaching by demonstration is necessary in the case of the human species because it has not been provided with instinctual mechanisms whereby the necessary skills are built into the body structure. A parent bird does not need to demonstrate to the fledgling how to fly, while a human parent does instruct a child in swimming or in speaking. The human way is more difficult, but it has the great advantage of flexibility. The human organism is relatively plastic. Its behavior patterns are not fixed by the inherited body arrangements. Hence the acquisition of a great variety of skills through education is possible, and this in turn is the basis for all human cultural activity.

Teaching by demonstration is a means of economizing learning effort. As the human organism seeks to cope with its environment, there are successes and failures. The modes of behavior which are rewarded by satisfaction of desire are confirmed and repeated. Those which lead to frustration of desire tend to be discarded. Successful forms of activity can thus be acquired through a trial-and-error process. The basic function of demonstration is to reduce the number of trials required for learning by indicating which movements have been found in the past to yield satisfaction and which have not. The efficacy of the method consists in the fact that there are usually only a few ways of succeeding in any given project, while the number of ways to fail is infinite. Hence, demonstration of right procedures makes possible a spectacular short-cutting of the learning process.

Consideration of teaching by demonstration raises an interesting question about the nature of the learning process. Common sense takes it for granted that imitation is possible. But *how* is it possible? One person cannot know directly what another person's state of being actually is. All that passes between teacher and pupil in an act of demonstration are certain energy impulses, usually in the form of light or sound. Perhaps what looks like imitation is actually only a similarity of behavior due to likeness of organic structure and of specific stimuli. Imitation would then be merely a name for the *result* and not for the *method* of learning from the demonstrator. If one accepts this view, demonstration as a teaching method may be quite unreliable. The desired learning takes place only as the teacher provides a set of sense stimuli to which the given organism of the student will respond in the desired fashion. This pattern as often as not will be considerably different from that produced by a direct demonstration. To get the pupil to perform in any particular way the teacher may have to engage in activity of a very different kind. This is simply to say that it cannot be taken for granted that the most efficient way to get another person to adopt a certain type of behavior is always to give a demonstration of it. There may be other less direct approaches which are more effective because they take account of the differences between the personal characteristics of student and teacher.

On the other hand, if the foregoing stimulus-response assumptions are replaced by certain others, a good case can be made for demonstration and imitation. The preceding argument tends to underestimate the importance of pattern-perception in learning. Since it seems likely that one cannot enter into the actual subjective experience of another person, direct and complete imitation appears impossible. But it is possible to perceive forms in the manifest behavior of other people and to translate that perception of pattern into corresponding forms of conduct. To be sure, this view also presupposes a fundamental similarity between the organisms of teacher and of student. This likeness need not be so complete, however, as the view in the preceding paragraph requires. If one takes account of the human being's intellectual capacity to grasp forms, then imitation is seen as a possible and extremely important type of learning. The words and the acts of the teacher are symbols of certain meanings. These symbols, when used as means of communication between teacher and student, evoke corresponding meanings in the student, through his apprehension of their essential form. If demonstration is a useful teaching procedure and imitation is an effective way of learning, it is largely because man has the power of perceiving patterned structures and of using symbols to convey them from one person to another.

Arranging Learning Situations

Each of the three outlooks on teaching thus far considered emphasizes the direct influence of teacher on student and minimizes the independence and self-actuation of the learner. A fourth view of teaching takes account of these latter factors in holding that the student learns only what he himself determines to learn and that the teacher's role is to arrange situations in which this self-teaching can most advantageously proceed. The three previous views centered attention on the teacher and his objectives for the student. The present position is focused rather on the student, and the teacher is seen as ministering to the learner's interests and needs. This is not to deny the decisive influence of the teacher, who still helps to guide the pupil's growth through the type of situation arranged. It is simply that the influence is generally less direct than in the other methods discussed. The student fashions himself, using the resources provided by the teacher; he is not primarily expected to duplicate the ideas or actions of the teacher.

Thus, while the earlier methods lead to repetition and conformity, the present approach leaves the way open for innovation and individuality. To be sure, it is possible to set up situations which will produce fairly uniform and conservative responses in most learners. But the path is always open for the individual to make what he will out of the conditions provided and thus to respond in ways quite different from the customary ones. The special virtue of the arrangement concept is that standardization is not inherent in it; situations may be provided so as to correspond to the particular capabilities and requirements of individual learners. This approach thus tends to favor freedom and variety as against uniform adherence to traditional knowledge and behavior.

One aspect of the learning situation is the physical environment. The teacher as arranger must consider such factors as room temperature, condition of the air, light, and facilities for sitting, reading, or exercizing. By providing a comfortable physical setting the teacher may make it easy for the student to direct his undivided attention to specific learning tasks. If there are disagreeable physical conditions, the pupil will devote some of his energy to the struggle against them. The physical arrangements also include natural objects of beauty and use from which the learner can benefit. Classrooms with rock collections, miniature zoos, and growing plants, for example, give the students opportunity for direct experience of nature.

Of even greater importance than the physical setting is the cultural situation in which the learner is placed. The development of a style of life and of sensitivity in taste and discrimination depends upon habitual association with cultural excellence. Long exposure to great music, first-class paintings, and the best literature leaves its mark on the young. The problem of standards for judging excellence is, of course, a difficult one. That is not at issue here. We are only concerned to point out the crucial significance of the cultural environment which the teacher seeks to provide for the learner.

More specialized features of the man-made environment which the teacher organizes are various resources and tools such as conveniently arranged collections of books, equipment for scientific experiments, musical instruments, and proper materials for writing and drawing. Facilities do not in themselves insure good education, but they do constitute an invitation to learning to which the self-actuated student may gratefully respond.

Some of the most important arrangements the teacher makes concern the social environment. Much of the content of education relates to social conduct, and these lessons can best be learned by actually associating with other people in a variety of shared enterprises. The teacher may provide opportunities for learning by planning occasions for such social participation. The accepted customs and manners of the classroom engender certain social attitudes and habits. The use of committees encourages cooperative endeavor. Carefully planned group discussions and orderly processes of corporate decision-making may enable the students to develop skill in cooperative inquiry and judgment. Well-organized parties and games teach competence in the arts of social enjoyment.

The entire curriculum may be regarded as an organized sequence of learning situations arranged so as to be of maximum benefit to the student. From this point of view the course of study is not a blueprint showing how the student is to be formed, nor a catalogue of knowledge and skill to be acquired by him. It is seen rather as an orderly progression of physical, cultural, and social contexts in which it seems likely that the best self-teaching will take place. The instructor then works largely by indirection, providing favorable and inviting conditions and relying on the student's own urge toward self-realization to bring the learning process to fulfillment.

It should be added that the best conditions for learning may not always be pleasant and comfortable for the student. The most significant personal growth often takes place in response to circumstances of hardship and perplexity. The teacher is thus obliged to determine the types of problems and obstacles which will most effectively challenge the student and elicit his most constructive response. If the difficulties created are too great, the student will experience frustration and discouragement. If they are too slight, there will be little stimulus to achievement. The requisite level of difficulty depends upon many factors, including the age and experience of the student, the type of problem presented, and the individual's emotional nature and degree of maturity. Not only is the decision about what problems to set for the learner an extremely complex one, but there is also the ever-present danger that the teacher may consciously or unconsciously make difficulties for the student simply as a means of expressing his own hostilities and resentments. Despite these perplexities and temptations, the teacher must place appropriate obstacles in the student's way so that he may develop the inner resources and the habits of intelligence which will prepare him to solve the problems which life inevitably presents. This is an essential part of his function as arranger of learning situations.

Appraisal

There is a second indirect way of teaching which supplements and is usually interfused with the other approaches. This is the method of appraisal, wherein the teacher judges the value of the student's work. When teaching is regarded as the making of persons, the teacher as appraiser periodically rests from the making activity to measure the progress achieved, just as a painter or sculptor on occasion lays down his brush or chisel and stands aside to view the maturing product. Likewise, the teacher who purveys knowledge or demonstrates skills from time to time needs to test the student's attainment. Nor is it sufficient for the teacher to arrange learning situations without regular provision for evaluating their educational effectiveness. Only through such appraisals can the teacher discover ways of improving his instruction and of adapting it more closely to the student's requirements.

Appraisal is not merely an adjunct to the teaching process. It is itself a form of teaching. It would be possible, in fact, to make examination the sole method of instruction. The student would then seek out his own resources for learning and would discover periodically from the examiner whether his accomplishments were approved or not. The influence of the teacher would be exercised entirely through these judgments, and would depend upon the prior establishment of an authority status for the teacher. The method of teaching by examination is in effect a kind of trial-and-error process, in which success or failure is defined by the tests administered, and in which the learner's activities are directed solely toward securing favorable test results.

Testing is a powerful teaching device because human beings are by nature social. What other people think of one is an important factor in his personal well-being. Everyone enjoys and seeks acceptance and approval from others and dislikes and avoids rejection and disapproval. By making judgments about students the teacher can exercise a decisive influence on their development. They will tend to grow in ways which win favorable judgments and to relinquish forms of behavior which are disapproved.

The effect is re-enforced and magnified when the teacher's evaluations reflect the accepted standards of society, and when (through grade records and recommendations, for example) the teacher's judgment is accepted by agencies beyond the school as one measure of the student's ability and promise. One of the responsibilities which has been laid upon the teacher is that of making a preliminary appraisal of the competence of students to guide those who must make appointments to various functions within the social organism. Hence wisdom in judgment is not only essential for the proper guidance of the student but also to provide the best possible basis for assignment of social responsibilities and privileges.

Appraisal thus serves both as stimulus for the learner and as a means of social allocation. In both respects, however, serious objections may be offered to this way of teaching. When success or failure in a task is measured by the approval or disapproval of another person, attention is diverted from the satisfactions implicit in doing the job well to those derived from personal relationships. This may lead to habits of emotional dependence which render one unduly sensitive to the judgments of others. Since other people change so readily and differ so widely in their evaluations of what one is and does, dependence on their opinions may lead to inner confusion, contradiction, and frustration. Furthermore, one who always looks to other people for justification of his own life never becomes truly a person in his own right. One mark of being a person is to accept full responsibility for what one is.

Appraisal for purposes of placement in the social scheme (as for jobs, for further schooling, or for social prestige) may have the same de-personalizing effect. The student strives to fit the pattern defined by the dominant value system of society. He learns to be guided by approved social values rather than by his own real preferences. Hence he fails to become an independent and responsible person, remaining merely a unit in the social organism.

Teaching by examination is also usually associated with a system of grading which permits comparisons between students and consequently relative ranking. This stimulates a competitive spirit, feeding the ambition of the aggressive and discouraging the more timid. Some would argue that the challenge of competition is a valuable form of motivation. Others would insist that the challenge should come from the work to be done and not from one's rank in relation to others. Rank grading does tend to externalize motivation and to direct attention to other people rather than to the activity at hand. Yet it can be urged on the other side that more successful competitors do help one to see what can be done and thus to strive for excellence which he would not aspire to on his own.

These difficulties encountered in teaching by appraisal need not be decisive. They suggest the importance of relating the evaluation process to the student himself and of connecting it as directly and integrally as possible to the work itself. Thus, the motive for acquiring competence in reading or writing ought not to be merely to win the teacher's approval, to get promoted, or to excel in a contest, but to experience the satisfaction of understanding and communicating through the use of language. The student may, with the teacher's help, formulate his own goals (e.g., to read a particular book on a subject of interest) and test himself with respect to them by objective and impersonal means (e.g., by consulting an encyclopedia).

Another problem in connection with teaching by appraisal is the nature of the standards used for evaluation. Every test is necessarily only a modest sample of the student's achievement. It is important that the sample be large enough and representative enough to give a fair picture of accomplishment. Furthermore, each type of examination measures only certain abilities. It is necessary to recognize this limitation and not to rely on any single test to appraise the person as a whole. That is to say, standards and the corresponding judgments are specific and partial rather than general and total and should always be used with this in mind. This points to the need for a great variety of appraisal standards and warns against the use of vague and comprehensive judgments of approval or disapproval of the student by the teacher. The careful construction of many specific tests further helps to relate appraisal directly and objectively to the task to be learned rather than to the personal favor or disfavor of the teacher as an authority figure.

Finally, teaching as appraisal raises insistently and immediately questions which are implicit in all education, concerning the nature, source, and justification for values. Appraisal is evaluation, and the teacher can make judgments about the student only on the basis of a system of values. Are these values objective and absolute, so that the teacher can say with assurance "This is always right and that is always wrong," or are values relative to the person and to the situation, so that all evaluations must be provisional and individual? In the latter case is appraisal justified at all? Can one person ever judge another? Where do the teacher's values come from—his own personality, society, nature, or God? How does he support them—intuitively, by reason, through scientific method, or by revelation? These fundamental questions are discussed in some detail in later chapters on moral values (Chapter 16) and on the aims of education (Chapter 30).

Participation

Each of the preceding conceptions of the teacher's role has presupposed a considerable degree of separateness between teachers and students. The makers stand over against what is made, as active agents to passive objects. The wise hand down knowledge to the ignorant or provide examples for imitation. The arrangers set up favorable learning situations for the self-actuated students and periodically sit in judgment on their progress. The view of the teacher's function now to be described places the emphasis on participation rather than on separateness. The teacher engages in various sorts of coordinate activity with the student, and it is through this interactive process that the desired learning takes place. The direction of the pupil's growth is influenced by the character of the interpersonal associations experienced with the teacher.

This method of teaching is based on a recognition of the essentially social nature of man and of education. What a human being becomes is a consequence of the kinds of encounters he has had with other persons. Therefore, it would seem that the teacher can really make a difference in the lives of his students only as he is related to them in personally significant ways. Implied in this idea of personal significance is the recognition that the student is a fully human individual in his own right and that in this respect, at least, teacher and student are equals. The teacher and the pupil are participants in a common activity, and both learn something from it. In this sense the distinction between teaching and learning is overcome, and it becomes clear that both parties to the interaction teach and learn from one another within the shared experience.

Probably the most important kind of personal interaction between teacher and student is conversation. Participation in conversation implies genuine communication. It is not a monologue in which the teacher gives forth truth which the student passively absorbs. It is not mere one-way transmission of information. It is a living dialogue, in which each member through the medium of words enters into the very life of the other. In such dialogue there is communication not only of concepts but also of emotion. The entire person, in his totality of idea, feeling, and intention, makes himself known to the other. In many cases the attitudes and values expressed are even more significant than the literal content of what is said. In true interpersonal communication the speaker does not regard the hearer as an object, but as a subject like himself, not as a thing to be manipulated, but as a person with whom one can experience community of understanding.

The teacher may also be associated with the student other than through conversation. There are everyday tasks relating to the order and cleanliness of the classroom in which all may participate. Various forms of recreation bring teachers and students into relationship as teammates, as contestants, or as those who watch or individually engage in the same activity. Shared observation of nature, of man, and of culture, work in laboratories and shops, and common enjoyment or production of things of beauty are further occasions in which teachers and pupils establish person-to-person associations with one another. Whatever type of activity is engaged in, the essential point is that teacher and student grow and learn together. The teacher is not regarded as one who has arrived at his destination and who now shows the young how he must proceed in order to reach the same place. Teacher and pupil are both en route. It may be that of the two the teacher has journeyed the longer and has acquired experience helpful to his companion, but during their association they travel the road together, and each instructs and learns from the other.

The method of instruction by participation often requires that the teacher play many different roles. In some situations he may need to act in place of the parents, seeking to give sympathy, support, admonition, or counsel as the case may be. In other circumstances the teacher may have to relate himself to the student as ruler to subject, exercizing authority and rendering judgment. Again, the teacher will often relate himself to the student as a playmate, companion, or colleague. By taking on these different roles the competent and sensitive teacher can help the student to establish more mature relationships with the actual people whose role is assumed. For example, a teacher who understands the desirable parent-child relationship can by playing a parental role when appropriate re-enforce good actual home relationships and help to counteract bad ones. Similarly, the teacher in the capacity of a good ruler can help to create desirable attitudes and responses toward actual governmental authorities. Once again, a teacher's constructive association with the student as a friend or co-worker can help to create good peer relationships in actual life. On the other hand, defective interpersonal associations between teacher and student correspondingly work against healthy relationships in social life beyond the school.

It requires a teacher of unusual ability to relate himself wisely to the student in these several roles. Teachers like everyone else have limitations which need to be recognized and accepted. They cannot be all things to all students. Hence the expectation that the teacher will be an expert in the many kinds of interpersonal association for which the student needs to be prepared is a counsel of perfection. It is in most cases at best an ideal to be striven for. Despite these limitations, every teacher does have the opportunity to direct the growth of the learner by those types of person-to-person relationships in which he has skill.

The above discussion of roles in teaching serves to qualify the earlier statements in this section about the equality of teacher and student. In true interpersonal activity there is an essential equality inherent simply in being human. But superimposed upon this essential equality there may be inequalities of contribution and of function. Some educational theorists have been so deeply impressed with the idea that the teacher and pupil share as partners in learning experiences that they have ignored or denied any real distinction of function. In general, the whole point in having teachers is that they possess special maturity, knowledge, and skill which make it appropriate and desirable for them to guide and direct the students' work and play. Put in terms of roles, this is simply to say that the teacher does not only associate with the students as companion, friend, and fellow learner, but also as adviser, judge, and in some degree as authority.

Mediation

In this final section an outlook on teaching will be discussed which combines several features of the earlier views and also adds a new dimension. It may be called teaching as mediation.

There are three elements in the teaching-learning process: the student, the teacher, and that which is to be learned (the content). All of the conceptions of teaching outlined in this chapter can be characterized by the interplay of these three elements. Teaching as the making of persons presupposes the teacher as dominant and student and content as subordinate. In teaching as transmission of knowledge or as demonstration content is paramount and teacher and student are less important. Teaching as provision of learning experience is student-centered, the teacher sinking into the background and content becoming less definite. Appraisal restores the priority of content but now indirectly as it is embodied in the standards of judgment. The autonomy of the student and the authority of the teacher are also emphasized in the appraisal process, but student, teacher, and content are not knit together in a unitary occasion of learning. Participation emphasizes student and teacher, and content is subsumed under the relationship between them.

The aim of teaching as mediation is to bring these three elements into simultaneous focus. Student and teacher are united in the common apprehension of what is true and good. The teacher is the mediator of excellence. Through his agency the student is enabled to realize goals otherwise unknown or inaccessible to him. At the same time the teacher finds new satisfaction in what he mediates. Student and teacher are related as person to person but always in the consciousness of their common privilege in sharing something of value.

Teaching as mediation starts from the conviction that there are truths to be understood and values to be acknowledged, which constitute the definite content of education, and that this content is not merely the result of personal wish or striving. Thus there is a certain objectivity in what is to be learned. Furthermore, these truths and values have the power of forming human beings and the purpose of education is to get them embodied in persons. The function of the mediating teacher is to effect this personal actualizing of ideal possibility.

Perhaps some better sense of what mediation in teaching means can be gained by indicating four components of it. The first is *imagination*. The subject to be taught is vivified by the imagination of the teacher. Ideas are not simply passed on unchanged, but are transformed into living truth through the teacher's own keen sense of their relevance to himself and to others. He puts ideas to use in new ways, relating, combining, and recombining them so that they become vivid and capable of kindling the imagination of the student.

The second ingredient is *inspiration*. This does not mean simply a vague feeling of enthusiasm, though it may include that. It means that one has the sense of new sources of personal energy and insight having been opened up for personal appropriation. Truth is grasped as *my* truth, and values as worthful *for me*. The mediator inspires his students with the good news that the whole world of knowledge is their own treasure. Though they have made but a beginning in learning, inspiration enables them to live in confident faith that they are heirs of the truth.

A third element in mediation is *love*. The teacher loves the truth and he loves the student in and for the truth. The teacher has found his own deepest satisfaction in learning, and he seeks to lead others to the same sources of refreshment. He desires to communicate his own sense of the worth of life to others still in search of meaning. He wants to open up for others sources of power with which his understanding has furnished him.

Finally it may be suggested that teaching as mediation has in it an aspect of *worship*. In his treatment of what he understands to be the truth the teacher requires a sense of reverence. It is as though he were a priest charged with administering the sacred mysteries. The truth is not of his own making, and he is entrusted with caring for it and helping others to participate in it. Teacher and student are then as it were lifted up to share the vision of that Presence which is at once infinitely beyond and above them and yet seen as the primal source and end of their own being.

4

Curriculum

The Nature of Curriculum

Having now considered the school and its teachers, we turn next to the curriculum, or course of study. The term curriculum is simply a name for the organized pattern of the school's educational program. A complete description of the curriculum has at least three components: (1) *what* is studied—the "content" or "subject matter" of instruction—(2) *how* the study and teaching are done—the "method" of instruction—and (3) *when* the various subjects are presented—the order of instruction.

The first of these components—the content—includes the whole range of matters in which the student is expected to gain some competence. There are the obvious academic subjects which are customarily associated with the idea of curriculum, such as language and literature, mathematics, the several natural sciences, history and the social sciences, and the fine arts. All of these are primarily intellectual in character. The curriculum may also include practical studies which develop skill in the manual arts and crafts either for personal enjoyment or more often for vocational purposes. Other studies combine the practical and intellectual, in preparation for service in the learned professions, such as law, medicine, or the ministry. Still another group of studies, neither primarily intellectual or practical, may best be described as personal in orientation. In this category would fall provisions for physical and mental health education, for development of mature human relationships, and for growth of desirable attitudes and values.

In the following pages we shall be chiefly concerned with the philosophy of curriculum as content or subject matter, with brief reference also to the order and units of instruction. The question of method has been taken up in the preceding chapter. It should be stated, however, that this separation between content and method is artificial and to a certain extent misleading. The possibility of separation presupposes a certain view of the relation between truth and personality. If truth is regarded as having an existence independent of persons, and if it is thought to be more or less faithfully embodied in books and other cultural artifacts, then subject matter is a definite body of material to be acquired, and the question of how it is made available has no relation to the content.

The opposite view is that truth has meaning only as known by persons, and that the way of knowing enters into the very nature of the truth. Hence the content of what a person learns is determined by the complete nature of the experiences in which the learning takes place. Since the methods of teaching are an integral part of these experiences, content and method cannot be separated. The strength of this position is particularly evident in those studies referred to above as "personal." Here the method of teaching (e.g., in matters of human relationships) is of the very essence of what is taught. In the more traditional academic subjects the independence of the subject matter can be more easily defended. The practical subjects lie in between the personal and academic. This suggests that the possibility of separating content from method may be a function of the subject studied, being most feasible in the purely intellectual disciplines and least so in such personal matters as emotional and moral instruction.

Curriculum as a Problem

It is obvious that the school must have a curriculum, for without a course of instruction it would not be an educational institution. Is it equally obvious what the curriculum should be? Does the curriculum present a problem? Under certain cultural and social conditions there is no problem in deciding what to teach. If there is a limited body of knowledge and a definite set of skills which constitute the basic cultural capital of a society, these are the necessary and appropriate subjects of study. When the student has mastered them, he is an educated person; he has completed the course. Again, in a society where to each person certain fixed and circumscribed functions are assigned, the course of study is easily prescribed. Nor is there any appreciable problem in deciding what shall be taught when the time and resources for schooling are extremely meager. In such cases instruction must clearly center about those elementary competences required for social intercourse and making a living.

Curriculum is a problem only in advanced, relatively free societies where considerable opportunities for schooling are available. It is a problem because a choice must be made among a great variety of different possibilities. In modern civilization the cultural inheritance is no longer a circumscribed, standard, and relatively stable body of content. It has become enormous in size and profoundly complex. It continually undergoes revision and receives accessions at an accelerating rate. It is not possible now, as it once was, for even an exceptionally able person to obtain a reasonable mastery of all the major fields of learning. For each individual a choice must be made from the virtually unlimited store of materials to be learned. Assuming that society is organized so that choice is possible, and assuming that schooling is provided, the problem of curriculum is to make the wisest decision about which few things among the many valuable subjects should be studied.

Essentially curriculum is a problem of economy. Unfortunately, the capacity of the human being to learn is limited. No person can learn everything that now waits to be known. If one spent a whole lifetime in study it would not suffice to produce universal competence; life is too short, and forgetting takes its toll. Many people are not endowed with more than modest learning capacities. Furthermore, there are many things to be done with life besides acquiring new knowledge; most people spend most of their time in these other pursuits. All of these limiting factors increase the disproportion between the vast cultural capital available and the limited learning capacity of the individual person. The problem of curriculum is to economize scarce learning potential by making the most judicious and appropriate selection of study content. Human intelligence is too rare and precious a thing to squander on a haphazard program of instruction.

Curriculum and Values

The choice of what shall be taught requires a principle of selection. There must be a measure of which subjects are more important than others, indicating which ones can be sacrificed—since not everything can be mastered—and which ones are absolutely essential. Criteria are needed to decide the optimum proportion of available school time to be devoted to the various studies selected. Such standards presuppose a scale of values. The central problem in all education is that of values. The educator must choose the direction in which he believes the student's growth may best proceed. He can make no decision whatever without a conviction that in that instance one way is preferable to all other possible paths. Now beliefs about what is best or preferable imply a scale of values. Hence all educational activity drives one to the question of underlying values.

The curriculum is a schedule of proposed instruction embodying the preferred direction of student development. It rests upon and manifests a certain system of values. These values constitute the aims, objectives, or purposes of education, and the curriculum is the means by which the aims are achieved, the objectives realized, and the purposes fulfilled.

Oftentimes the educator is not aware of the values which are implicit in his chosen curriculum. This may result in inconsistency and indecisiveness because the foundation for choice is not clear and explicit. One important function of educational philosophy is to promote reflection on curricular offerings in order to reveal what educational values or purposes are presupposed by them. Furthermore, certain aims may be affirmed and sincerely espoused and yet be quite at odds with the objectives implied in the curriculum. For example, the teacher may honestly desire to promote a scientific outlook and yet by the choice of study materials in fact encourage passive acceptance of authoritative pronouncements. Philosophic analysis of the curriculum may help to overcome such incongruities, bringing convictions about the purposes of education into closer accord with the aims embodied in the curriculum, through a revision of stated goals, of the course of study, or of both.

In the following paragraphs some of the classes of component values which enter into the determination of the curriculum, together with illustrations of the corresponding subjects of instruction, will be discussed. Every person and every society gives a characteristic weight to the several types of general objectives, and the relative importance assigned to each of them determines the curriculum selected. This process of assigning relative degrees of importance to general educational goals in turn rests upon the application of a still more ultimate system of values, such as that contained in a personal "philosophy of life," in a religious faith, or in the ideology of a community. Some of these ultimate values are discussed in Chapter 30, which may profitably be consulted in relation to the problem of values in the curriculum. Our purpose in what follows is merely to indicate some of the kinds of general but less than ultimate factors which must be considered in deciding the content of the course of study.

Basic Human Nature

The first requirement of any education is that it answer the basic need to be human. In constructing the curriculum the starting point is to make provision for developing those capacities which are fundamental to man as man. Just as reflection on the curriculum raises the central question of values in education, so also does it require a consideration of this other root issue—the nature of man. If there are certain features which are humanly essential—i.e., without which one would not truly be a person—the recognition and development of these should clearly be the primary objective of the curriculum. Chapter 26 deals in some detail with the nature of man, and the application of the considerations introduced there would make possible a fuller treatment of the curricular question. A briefer selection of fundamentals will have to suffice for illustration here. Following are six suggested constituents of a curriculum for essential humanity.

Elementary physical skills. The young child must learn to perform the usual physical functions of eating, walking and running, manipulating, and observing. He must develop muscular coordination and habits of sense perception which will preserve him from danger and enlarge his powers of enjoyment and control of the environment. Most of these abilities are acquired automatically as the child matures, and it is generally necessary only to provide a safe yet appropriately challenging environment, together with older persons to demonstrate what is to be learned.

Basic social skills. A person is inescapably social. His satisfaction and effectiveness in living depend upon developing productive relationships to other people. The child must early learn that there are persons besides himself with feelings and demands like his own, and that he must govern his conduct to take account of them. Hence the necessity for opportunities for planned social activity, with lessons in sharing and experience of the resulting satisfactions, instruction in manners and courtesies which make social existence more pleasant, as well as teaching of the sterner disciplines of making one's way properly in a world where injustice and deceit often prevail.

Use of symbols. Man's most notable possession is his intelligence. This power of mentality is manifest most clearly in the use of symbols, especially in the form of language. Intelligence is based upon the ability to utilize ideas or concepts, which embody the sense of meaning, and symbols to express and communicate these meanings. The ability to use language to speak, to read, and to write is therefore necessary to the achievement of essential humanity. Mathematics is another form of symbolic activity, in some ways even more powerful and more perfectly an expression of human reason than language. "The three R's" (the symbolic disciplines) have traditionally and rightly been regarded as basic to the curriculum because they help man realize his essential rationality.

Constructive activity. Human reason finds expression not only in language and mathematics, but also in various constructive activities. Man is not only a thinker and speaker, but also a maker. He fashions objects of beauty and use. He employs tools to do what his unaided hands cannot accomplish. He invents and builds. He puts his creative imagination to work in conceiving and embodying ideas in a variety of material forms. It is to supply these basic human needs that programs of arts and crafts are included in the curriculum.

Play. It is perhaps not widely enough appreciated that play is also a fundamental human function. In play a person participates in a world fashioned by the free imagination, orderly yet unconstrained by the ordinary rules of social existence, and serious yet not directed to the long-term purposes of vocational life. Learning to play is a vital part of the educational process. School recreational activity is not merely recess from the real business of learning. It is itself an essential factor in the development of freedom, imagination, and perspective.

Moral responsibility. A final constituent of basic human nature is the ability to make wise and responsible choices. It is of the essence of manhood to be able to decide between alternative courses of action. The curriculum, therefore, should provide ample opportunities for the student to exercise intelligence in choosing and opportunities to assume responsibility for his decisions. This moral instruction is generally not provided in specific segments of the curriculum, as the other five elements to a considerable extent are, but may be an ingredient in every type of activity. Its efficacy depends upon preserving the right balance, at every stage of maturity, between freedom and authority, so that the student has enough guidance to give him some foundation for choice yet enough liberty to make the alternatives genuine and the responsibility his own.

Demands of the Actual Society

The course of study clearly ought to be designed to serve the basic human needs. These are the fundamental values, but they are by no means the only ones which enter into curriculum decision. Human development goes beyond growth in basic human competences, and it is in relation to these further elaborations that other claims are advanced and other values affirmed. The present section and the four to follow describe the general nature of five such types of claims.

Language, geography, and history. First, there are the educational demands created by the special character of the actual society. For example, the language usually taught first and most intensively is the one which is in actual use in the society where the school is situated. Instruction in arithmetic employs the customary number system and usual designations of weight, length, volume, and monetary value. In the teaching of geography, attention is directed primarily to the features of the student's own state and country which he may need to know in order to be an intelligent citizen. For the same reason, in the study of history major emphasis is placed on those events which were most relevant to the making of the civilization in which the student shares.

Manners and customs. The actual society also determines the nature of the manners and customs which are taught. Such matters as clothing styles, eating habits, common courtesies, patterns of relation between the sexes, and types of recreation engaged in are of great interest to the young and are of major significance in achieving a sense of belonging in his society. The curriculum necessarily includes instruction in these concerns, usually informally and implicitly, but sometimes in regular courses of study.

Occupations. The claims of the existing social order are advanced with particular insistence in relation to education for the occupations. Society needs workers to fill its jobs. The structure of the society is reflected in part in the kinds and relative numbers of available positions, and thus pressures tend to be exerted on the school to emphasize particular types of vocational preparation. For example, a highly industrialized society can exist only as it is provided with a constant supply of scientific and technical personnel. This demand forces the schools to offer a full complement of courses in mathematics, the basic sciences, and the various technical disciplines. Again, a predominantly religious society requires a ready supply of priests and teachers, and the educational system must accordingly give major attention to instruction in the beliefs and practices of the faith. Political conditions make it expedient for many nations to advance or defend their interests by force of arms and hence to include military training in the instruction of the young, whether in the civil schools or in the military establishment itself. In each of the above examples the emphasis given to the respective studies in the curriculum depends to a large extent upon how insistent the social demand is and how critical the respective competences appear to be for the health and security of the society.

Common values. Perhaps the most fundamental demand made by the actual society is that the young be given a clear awareness of the common values upon which the society rests. An English child is nurtured in the traditions of his people. A child in the Soviet Union is taught how to be a loyal Communist. In the United States the curriculum conveys a sense of what America stands for, including such values as freedom, equality, individual dignity, enterprise, cooperation, and the special meanings given to these in American culture. One of the ways of teaching the main common values of a people is to provide courses which trace the development of the civilized heritage from its sources. Thus, an American student can learn the values of his culture through the study of the great men and movements in Western civilization from its ancient roots in Greece, Palestine, and Rome down to the present day.

Ideal Social Needs

A curriculum designed in response to the demands of the actual society subserves conformity and adjustment to what now is. The school fits the child for the existing society. No challenge is provided for the improvement of the social order, and the individual is regulated by society rather than society being dedicated to the service of the individual. Against these tendencies reformers and individualists champion other types of values which need to be considered in determining the curriculum.

In a changing and forward-looking social order there is concern not only for adjustment to existing conditions, but also for the creation of a better society. Since the school may be an important means of effecting the desired improvements, the curriculum may be expected to include elements of response to the claims of the social ideal. The course of study will then be designed to prepare the student for participation in the society that ought to be rather than for conformity to the world as it is.

There is, of course, the question as to how far the educator's ideal should depart from what now exists. If the student were prepared for life in a perfect world, he would probably be unable to participate effectively in any actual society. Education for social perfection thus appears to be irrelevant. Perhaps the rule is that the social ideal embodied in the curriculum should be an advance over what now is, but should not be so radical a departure that all connection with the imperfect conditions of actual life is lost. By this principle the social order for which the student is prepared should be reasonably possible to attain, and not a visionary utopia.

Transcending the particular culture. As pointed out above, the study of one's native language, history, and geography reflects the claims of the actual society. Mastering other languages and learning about other cultures may also prove of use in adjusting to existing conditions, as in travel or international trade. But such broadening of horizons may better be justified as a general practice by appeal to the claims of the ideal, in which purely national and ethnic loyalties will be transcended and other people and their ways will be understood and appreciated in and for themselves rather than for any practical use they may now serve.

Social cohesion. An example of appeal to the ideal is the case of a heterogeneous nation made up of peoples with many different dialects seeking through education to unify the society by teaching everyone a common language. Again, a study of the main ideas and practices of the major religious groups in a plural culture is a means of furthering mutual understanding and acceptance. More generally, the entire curriculum of public schools, as contrasted with private ones, is designed to advance the ideal of inclusive social cohesion rather than of solidarity within special groups of the society.

The ideal of social unity also underlies the consideration of controversial issues in the schools. Differences of economic, political, moral, and religious belief and practice often seriously interfere with the harmony and efficiency of society. The informed discussion of such problems in schools, under expert guidance and by students who are sufficiently mature, may contribute to the ideals of greater mutual understanding, respect for differences, and the use of constructive means for resolving conflicts.

When the accepted mark of success in a given society is power over other people, the school in response to the ideal of a cooperative commonwealth may give less weight to preparation for the competitive struggle, and more to mutual assistance, than sole concern for social adjustment would dictate. Again, where military necessity requires that the young be taught how to kill, the educator may feel a duty to supplement that demand by studies which will prepare the pupil to heal, construct, and conciliate, even though the occasion for such peaceful pursuits is not yet within sight.

Occupational balance. Consideration of the ideal society prevents the school from responding too directly to appeals for narrow vocational preparation. While the efficiency of the social mechanism may in the short run depend upon the preparation of highly trained specialists, the long-term goal of society may better be served by broadly educated citizens. If this is so, the curriculum will not only reflect the immediate demands but will also take due account of the needs of the better society that may yet come. Furthermore, when the distribution of occupations in the actual society lacks proper balance, the educational institutions by encouraging students to prepare themselves for those callings which ideally need larger representation can contribute to a more satisfactory condition.

The question of weighing ideal social needs against the demands of the actual society in the determination of curriculum is another form of the issue discussed in Chapter 2 concerning the relation of the school to the rest of society. If the school is regarded as servant and tool of the community, its curriculum will reflect the claims of the actual society. If, on the other hand, the school is considered at least in some degree as leader and molder of the community, then its curriculum will be fashioned in the light of practicable but as yet unrealized social ideals.

Demands of the Actual Individual

Since individual persons always develop within a social context and societies are made up of individuals, it is not possible entirely to separate personal and social values. There are, however, legitimate differences of emphasis which in practice make it useful to distinguish the one from the other. In particular, decisions about curriculum must take account of personal as well as of group demands. The unique qualities and capabilities of each person are values to be weighed along with those which measure the well-being of the community as a whole.

Individuation. One of the characteristic features of living things is the tendency toward individuation. Every organism is a unique integration of specialized parts. The more complex the organism, the greater is the variety of possible organized wholes. In the human being, with his amazing brain and nerve structure, and with the resulting capacity to learn from experience rather than to behave largely according to instinctive patterns, individuation reaches its highest level. Most things are best described by indicating the classes of objects to which they belong. Their nature is defined by what they have in common with other members of their kind. Though this sort of description is possible with human beings, perhaps such classification obscures the most important aspect of the person, namely, his uniqueness; the special significance of human life may rather lie in individuality.

Obviously a curriculum dedicated to the development of individuals differs considerably from one designed to produce certain classes of persons prepared to exercise specified functions within the society. The primary fact is that a curriculum which seriously takes account of individual differences cannot be a standarized course of study but must be specially constructed for each person. The same sequence of instruction cannot be used for all. Each student engages in those studies which are most consonant with his interests and abilities.

Such individual curricula are, of course, expensive. A high ratio of teachers to students must be maintained to insure the requisite individual attention. Ideally, a tutorial rather than a class system of instruction is called for, though group activities, planned with individual needs in mind, may well be part of the study program. When economic considerations make class instruction necessary, the needs of the individual may still be taken into account by grouping students of similar interests and capacities and by making allowance in the work of the class for personal choice and maximum flexibility. In fact, the whole system of grouping students into grades is a method of doing maximum justice to individual needs within the limits set by economic considerations.

Exceptional students. Concern for the individual underlies the provision of special curricula for exceptional students. The great majority of pupils can be given a reasonably standard course of instruction designed for persons of average ability. This curriculum is not, however, suitable for the relatively small proportion of exceptional persons who have unusual talent or who are markedly deficient in ability. The very able ones are not sufficiently stimulated by the average curriculum, and the slow learners are discouraged and confused by it. To care for these unusual individuals special courses of study may be designed, based upon the particular capabilities of the students. These programs may or may not call for the separation of the exceptional students into special classes or tutorial sessions, depending upon the extent of the individual's needs for social interaction with persons of different abilities and upon the possibilities for variation of assignment within a heterogeneous group.

Testing. Curriculum planning in the light of the actual individual's demands calls for a well-developed system of counseling and testing. By a variety of psychological tests the student's interests and abilities can be assessed, and in the counseling process he may be directed into the program of study which best fits him. The fundamental assumption on which the entire guidance and psychological service program of the school is based is the value of adjusting the educational program as far as possible to the unique characteristics of the individual.

Ideal Individual Needs

There is another dimension of individuality beyond that of the actual person, just as there are social needs which transcend the demands of the existing community. This is the dimension of ideal individual needs. The educator is concerned with what the person now is, but only as this bears upon what he may become. The existing individual has capabilities which may or may not be worthy of development. The demands which the person makes and the needs which he feels may or may not be worthy of affirmative response. The present characteristics of the student do not provide a complete guide to what he ought to become. Granted that what the person now desires and can do should be considered in organizing his course of study, these factors do not in themselves answer the question of what direction development should take. It may well be that some present interests should be left unsatisfied and new ones encouraged, that certain abilities should be ignored and other ones cultivated.

The ideal person. Accordingly, the curriculum maker needs some conception of the ideal individual to guide his selection of teaching materials. He must have an idea of what the good man, the complete person, the mature individual is like. Value systems differ, and no single definitive and universally accepted set of ideals can be stated. For some the ideal would be the kingly man, combining knowledge, practicality, strength, and justice. For others the goal would be the saint, with his humility, holiness, compassion, and reverence. Still another objective would be the sage, endowed with intellectual power, penetrating insight, and breadth of perspective.

The claims of the ideal individual as they are usually reflected in the curriculum can be summarized under four headings.

Intellectual. First, there are the requirements of intellectual excellence. The pupil at the beginning is ignorant and perhaps quite uninterested in acquiring knowledge. Nevertheless, truth has a claim on him, and the course of study should help to stimulate the spirit of inquiry and the love of knowledge. The standard academic fields—mathematics and the natural sciences, psychology and the social sciences, history, philosophy, and literature—are the customary means of intellectual discipline. It is not ultimately a question of whether or not the student is interested in such knowledge. He ought to know, he would be a better person through knowing; therefore, the curriculum should be designed to generate intellectual interests and then to satisfy them.

Moral. A second set of claims is ethical in nature. The ideal individual is not only intelligent; he is also morally good. Moral standards differ, of course, but every curriculum must include some instruction about right conduct. Whether these moral concepts are based upon custom, upon revelation, or upon rational or empirical inquiry is at this point irrelevant. In whatever way derived and sanctioned, ideas of right and wrong are an important element in the curriculum. Whether or not the student wishes to do right, the moral code makes its claim, and the course of instruction ought to create the desire for and achievement of goodness.

Esthetic. Third, there are esthetic claims. The individual ideally should have well-developed tastes for what is beautiful. The esthetic sensibilities of the immature are not trustworthy guides to the development of higher appreciations. There are ideals of balance, harmony, and fitness which serve as values to be grown toward and not as enjoyments in possession. The curriculum should therefore make provision both through courses in the arts and perhaps even more through incidental and informal means for habituating the student to things of beauty.

Religious. A fourth component in the ideal for the individual is the religious claim. This is difficult to define and takes many different forms, but essentially has to do with the person's basic outlook on the meaning of life and with his ultimate loyalties and commitments. Religious faith is not a simple extension of immediate interest. It comes from instruction in an ideal which has taken root in those of spiritual maturity. By means of specific courses in religion and more informally through the perspective of teachers in other subjects the religious ideal may be given its place in the curriculum. (This will be more fully treated in the following chapter.)

Claims of the Cultural Tradition

In the preceding five sections the types of values entering into determination of curriculum have had specific reference to societies or to individuals, in both cases either actual or ideal. There is, finally, a kind of value which really belongs to all five of the above categories and yet deserves special reference. This sixth type of value is based on the claims of the cultural tradition. Some things are learned by some people not because they meet any actual or ideal demand of persons singly or in association but simply to preserve and extend the cultural heritage. There is a great and growing body of knowledge much of which cannot be shown to contribute directly to human well-being but which is treasured for its own sake.

This work of conserving and augmenting the cultural capital is primarily the task of the scholarly community. The scholar is one who devotes himself to caring for and improving the received store of knowledge regardless of whether or not it has any demonstrated individual or social use. There are ancient civilizations which he seeks to keep alive, long unused languages which he explores, and curious skills which he cultivates. These things the scholar does because he believes that there is intrinsic worth in the hard-won creations of the race, which should not be allowed to fall into oblivion for lack of clear present or future relevance.

In the light of these claims, certain courses of study are designed for the express purpose of perpetuating the scholarly tradition. Often such studies can also be justified on grounds of social and personal needs, but it seems worth while to draw special attention to the trans-personal dimension in the ideal of pure scholarship and to set this off as a specific kind of value in the determination of curriculum.

The Determination of Content

In the above sections six types of value have been suggested as relevant to decisions concerning the course of instruction. Generally all of these kinds enter in some degree into the construction of any actual curriculum. Every maker of the school's program to some extent adjusts the course to the needs of society and of the individual and never wholly neglects the lure of the ideal nor the integrity of the tradition. The application of these values differs, however, from one case to another, and their respective weights vary widely. In one situation the immediate demands of society are most insistent, in another interest in perfecting the individual predominates, in still a third the preservation of the heritage seems most crucial. Where the balance falls depends upon prevailing conditions, personal, social, and cultural, and upon the pattern of ultimate values which at the deepest level govern the educator's decisions.

In determining curriculum content the educator must translate the value types into specific study units which will serve to realize them. A rough numerical weight must then be assigned to each value, and from this the school time and teaching resources must be proportionately allocated to the various units. Curriculum is, of course, primarily a matter of quality, but there must finally also be a quantitative rating of the various qualities, since a decision has to be reached on how the limited available study time shall be distributed among them.

The Problem of Timing

Decisions about when each subject is to be taught also enter into the construction of the curriculum. The course of study is not determined solely by reference to content, that is, to the distribution of subject matter, but also involves the distribution of study units in time. There are three types of factors which govern the decision about timing. These are respectively developmental, logical, and personal-social factors.

Developmental. The human being grows in accordance with an orderly plan. Beginning with a single fertilized cell at the time of conception, a definite process of development ensues. Following the pattern determined by the original germ-cell genes, a step by step progression of cell multiplication, differentiation, and organization occurs, resulting eventually, if all goes well, in the mature individual. Environment decisively influences this development, but always in accordance with the given hereditary potentials and the laws of organic growth. The person cannot learn to perform any activity for which the requisite physical organs, nervous structures, and emotional patterns have not yet matured. For example, it is futile to try to teach a two year old how to write poetry, drive a car, or decide political issues. The developmental sequence imposes a certain order upon the learning process. What can be taught at any given time is subject to the limitation that the organism must be in readiness for the learning to occur.

Hence, the curriculum must be organized in such a way that the order of studies does not conflict with the order of development. To give instruction in any subject prior to the time when it can possibly be learned is to invite failure, frustrate the student, and waste precious learning time. To teach a subject much later than the time when it can first be learned may unnecessarily retard personal growth. Yet knowledge of development stages is not a sufficient basis for curriculum determination, since at any point much more could in principle be taught then there is in fact time to learn. Hence, further principles of selection are required.

One important developmental principle is that the growth of intellectual powers increases the ability to think in abstractions. Instruction must begin on the level of the concrete, with specific situations and objects of immediate sense perception. As the person matures, generalizations and abstract processes of reasoning can be introduced in greater measure. The temptation of the adult is to impose his own relatively abstract ways of thought on the child for whom only the particular has any vivid meaning.

Another illustrative principle of development is that proper maturation involves a movement from emotional dependence, to growing independence, into eventual fruitful interdependence. The school program should, therefore, provide ample emotional support in the early years, recognize the need for enlarged autonomy as the child develops, and finally give opportunity for truly responsible social participation in the years of maturity. The stages of emotional growth are particularly important also in providing the clue to motivation. The student may be intellectually capable of mastering certain materials but emotionally apathetic to them. If intellectual capacities can be linked with emotional drive, the most efficient learning occurs. Curriculum timing should take account of the interplay of these factors in development.

Logical. In addition to the patterns of organic development, there are logical structures within the subject matter of the curriculum which may further affect the sequence of studies. Knowledge is to some extent, and especially in certain of its branches, cumulative in nature. Each item depends upon the establishment of a connected series of previous ones and cannot be understood until these prior elements have been assimilated. Algebra as usually taught presupposes familiarity with arithmetic, and success in analytic geometry similarly depends upon a prior mastery of algebra and the elements of geometry. To understand American government there must be some basic knowledge of American history, and the latter in turn requires some insight into the European roots of American civilization. Again, one cannot usefully study the principles or the philosophy of education in the absence of a prior acquaintance with the elementary facts of educational practice.

In general, the logical order and the developmental sequence are compatible. Both proceed from the simpler to the more complex, from concrete particulars to abstract generalizations. However, a distinction may usefully be made between the psychological and the formal logical sequence for the teaching of a given body of organized knowledge. The strict logic of the subject sometimes dictates its formulation in a pattern which presupposes considerable familiarity with its facts and principles. For example, formal logical exposition of a system in mathematics might begin with definitions and axioms, the reasons for which would not be clear to the novice. In such a case the teacher might better adopt a psychological presentation, that is, one which would start where the student is and build the system inductively with ample use of illustrative instances, diagrams, and applications. In decisions about timing in the curriculum it is this *psycho*-logical rather than the *formal* logical order which should be primary. Only after the subject has become familiar can the student be introduced to the strictly formal structure.

Personal-social. A third complex of factors in curriculum timing are the demands and expectations of the individual and society. A student who has unusual interests or talents in a certain type of endeavor may well be advised to apply himself to it early. Abilities which society requires of everyone must be taught from the beginning. Thus, in an urban society of highly literate people whose life is largely governed by written symbols, the child must be taught to read early. In an agrarian civilization the priority would probably be given to learning the manual skills necessary for successful farming; reading could be deferred indefinitely.

The several types of values—personal and social—entering into decisions about content are also relevant to timing. Within the limits set by developmental and logical factors, the temporal priority will generally be given to those subjects which are most valued and the subjects considered less important will be postponed.

The Organization of Instruction

Even after the problems of general curriculum content and timing have been settled, there still remains the task of organizing the materials of instruction. Assuming, for example, that the student is to be taught to read, beginning at age six, how does one select from the virtually unlimited stock of reading materials those which will be most effectively learned? Given the political system of the nation as the subject of instruction, how does the educator decide in what form to teach it? What criteria of choice will insure the maximum economy of learning resources and the greatest teaching efficiency? Three main ways of organizing instruction will now be described.

Systems of ideas. One time-honored way of organizing what is to be learned is around systems of concepts. This is the traditional "academic" approach. Knowledge is divided into definite subjects or departments, each of which has its characteristic ideas. Arithmetic is a distinct and separate kind of study, with its own set of meanings and methods; language is another well-defined subject; and art is a third. From the multitude of ideas contained in each field the teacher chooses those which best typify the whole subject. These central or key ideas, once well understood, provide a basic grasp of the entire field of study and enable the student with relative ease to acquire further detailed knowledge of the subject.

As the student becomes more advanced in knowledge the subjects often become more specialized in nature and the idea-systems more limited and intensive. On the other hand, it becomes increasingly important to establish connections between the special departments of study, and for this purpose "bridge" subjects like biochemistry or art history are created. In addition to these, as the student matures intellectually, he may be taught to consider all of his knowledge philosophically, critically examining assumptions, noting the structure and interrelations of ideas, and even creating tentative syntheses including hierarchies of organizing concepts with all grades of generality.

For extended discussions of the various fields of knowledge, including analysis of the key ideas, Part III of this book should be consulted.

Things. A second approach to organization is through actual things rather than through systems of ideas. The fields-of-knowledge approach is essentially abstract. It introduces the student to the end-products of scholarship, reflection, and research. Many people do not respond readily to such an approach. They live in the world of concrete things rather than of logic and abstraction. Hence they learn better if their study is organized around real objects, and if ideas are employed for the purpose of understanding these things. For example, if a study were organized around "American Indians," it would be useful to introduce ideas from such fields as geography, history, religion, and anthropology to understand the subject well. A study of "trees" could utilize concepts from such fields as biology, physics, chemistry, economics and history. In each case the abstractions would not be studied systematically or for their own sakes but would be selected for their relevance to the concrete object being considered.

The approach through things has the great advantage of vividness. Human experience is founded upon perception of the concrete, from which abstractions are drawn. Things are in this sense closer to reality than idea-systems. Concrete things also provide immediately and naturally for the interconnections of ideas. Concepts are most clearly linked together not in chains of systems, but in their common relevance to actual things. On the other hand, the concepts employed in the description of concrete things have been developed through the efforts of systematic thinkers, and the student should not be without understanding for these abstract modes of thought. Hence the curriculum should generally include both types of organization, the proportion of each depending largely upon the maturity and abstractive power of the student.

Problems. The first type of organization discussed above was idea-centered. The second type was thing-centered. The third is centered on the student and his problems. This approach is based on the theory that effective thinking occurs only when the person is faced with a problematic situation—a real difficulty to be overcome, an obscurity to be clarified, or a confusion to be resolved. The problem then becomes the focus of study, and ideas and things are investigated only as they provide assistance in reaching a solution. A student may see no point in studying arithmetic for its own sake, and he may have no interest whatsoever in learning about trees, for their sake, but if he has an opportunity to earn some spending money by working in an orchard, he may eagerly learn whatever is necessary about trees and arithmetic in order to do the job and calculate his earnings. The basis for study is then an activity or project motivated by a need felt as such by the student.

Problem-organization shares with thing-organization the virtues of vividness and concreteness, and it has the further merit of obvious personal relevance. Its use raises the question as to whether "natural" problems, arising out of the student's immediate perplexities, are to be the basis for inquiry, or whether the function of the teacher may not be to create other "artificial" problems for the student which in the long run will lead him to more valuable learnings than the largely fortuitous natural problems would provide. Furthermore, things and systems of ideas in themselves present challenges to the student's intelligence. For many students the motive of intellectual curiosity and the desire for clarity and completeness of comprehension are sufficient stimulus for learning. When that is the case, the idea-centered or thing-centered approach suffices, and there is no need to organize the curriculum around the student's immediate problems. In any event, a broad conception of "problem" extending beyond purely material or practical interests, seems necessary.

Problems are particularly useful in taking account of individual needs. By the same token they may require more ample teaching resources than would be required if the course of study were organized around concept systems or things.

Finally, the basic assumption of the problem approach needs to be critically examined. Do students think only when they face difficulties? May not learning also occur as students participate in any sort of experience, of satisfaction as well as frustration, of illumination as well as perplexity, of assurance as well as uncertainty?

Uses of the three approaches. There are special advantages and defects in all these major types of curriculum organization. Normally it would be wise in constructing any course of study to make use of all three as they seem respectively appropriate to age level, personality characteristics, and types of knowledge to be acquired.

For example, the program of young children may properly emphasize things, with less concern for problems and still less for systems of ideas, while for adolescents problems are the most appropriate approach in many cases, and for advanced graduate students the systematic method is most fitting. Some persons learn best through things, others are of more practical bent and need the challenge of problems, while still other personalities are gifted with abstractive power and are better served by a systematic approach. Finally, the three types of organization will clearly receive different weight depending upon whether the knowledge sought is primarily descriptive, prescriptive for practice, or theoretical.

Religion and the School

RELIGION is one possible subject of school instruction which calls for special discussion. As a matter of historical fact, the role of religion in the school has been a problem of peculiar difficulty. Long-established traditions and deep commitments generally characterize religious faith, and these concerns seek expression and implementation in the educational system. Education is necessarily grounded upon values, and sincere religious conviction reflects supreme or ultimate values. Hence religious belief is intimately connected with educational ideals and practices.

Religion in the school is a problem because of wide and continuing diversity of beliefs, which results in corresponding conflicts of educational goals. It has never proven possible to arrive at any stable concensus about the meaning and content of religious faith. These disagreements have been reflected in persistent perplexities about the place of religion in the curriculum of the school.

Religion is, of course, not the only matter on which there have been long-standing differences of belief. Cleavages of political, economic, and social conviction have perennially existed, and there are even some sharp conflicts about natural science theories. All of these diversities, as well as the specifically religious ones, are expressed in differences of school program. An analysis of religion in the school thus serves to illustrate the kinds of issues which arise whenever controversial matters of any sort are introduced into the course of instruction. Religion is concerned with the most comprehensive and most deeply rooted value systems and therefore is the crucial case for the study of value conflicts in education.

The discussion which follows is supplemented by the treatment in Chapter 25 of religion as one of the fields of knowledge. The analysis there may throw further light on the problems of religion in the schools.

Three Views of Religion

One's view about the place of religion in the school depends upon what he understands religion to be. There are three general positions that can be taken, each of which provides a distinctive answer to the problem of religion in education.

Religion as superstition. There are many who regard religion as essentially a collection of superstitions. Man lives in a difficult and mysterious world. In times past he was surrounded by forces which he did not understand and could not effectively control. He did not know whence he came at birth nor whither he would go at death. Life was brief and precarious. There were evidently powers in his environment working for his benefit and others threatening disaster. Not knowing how otherwise to deal with them, he imagined that they were spirits, invisible beings with mind and will like his own, to whom he could appeal on a personal basis. By prayers and offerings he could seek their favor and could invoke the aid of the friendly against the hostile powers.

Later the idea developed that there was only one supreme spiritual being to whom all things owed their existence. This divinity was credited with having created the universe and with continually sustaining it in being, as omnipotent and omniscient ruler of all things. He was also regarded as concerned with morality, as the giver of laws, the rewarder of well-doers, and the punisher of sinners.

This religious world view, it is argued, has been completely discredited by the rise of modern science and technology. It is still true that human existence is somewhat precarious. But the way to make it less so is not by propitiating imaginary spirits. We now understand that everything happens according to impersonal natural law and not by caprice, and it is possible to discover these principles of nature and by taking account of them to utilize the forces of the environment to serve human purposes. Disease is cured not by prayers but by medicine. Famine is conquered not by ritual sacrifices but by scientific agriculture, efficient transportation facilities, and population control.

Nor do the scientific-minded, it is claimed, look to any supernatural agency to explain the existence of the universe. Nature simply is, and one adds nothing to the knowledge of reality by the hypothesis of a deity, who in any case could be meaningfully described only in terms of natural experiences. The principles of morality also are human and natural. There is no supramundane sanction for the moral law. It is to be justified, if at all, solely on the basis of empirical social and individual interests rationally criticized and coordinated.

From this standpoint, religious ideas in the modern world are lingering superstitions from a by-gone age. In earlier times of ignorance about natural causes it was to be expected that man would invent personalistic explanations and systems for coping with the imagined powers. In the light of present knowledge this resort to mythology is evidence of psychological immaturity and intellectual irresponsibility.

If religion is superstition, it obviously does not belong in the curriculum of the school. If religious groups wish to continue indoctrinating the young with prescientific beliefs, they may perhaps be permitted to do so on the grounds that to deny them such freedom would do more harm than the error propagated by them, which will eventually be overcome anyway by the superior persuasiveness of scientific truth. But if religion is superstition, religious teaching has no place in any school which is anything more than a propaganda instrument of a religious organization. The schools today do not teach alchemy or astrology, which have long since been supplanted by genuine sciences. The influence of these earlier misconceptions may be treated in historical studies, but they are not presented as part of the living texture of contemporary thought. In the same manner, religion may be studied as an outgrown way of dealing with human problems, as an interesting phenomenon of a prescientific era. The major purpose of any such study of religion would be to show a vivid contrast to modern ways of thinking and thus to enhance appreciation for the intellectual and moral emancipation effected by the scientific revolution.

Religion as a special type of valid act and belief. A second view of religion, the most commonly held of the three to be examined, is that it is a special type of valid act and belief. It is true that much in religious life has been unintelligent and even superstitious. Perhaps these tendencies will continue. Yet credulity is not peculiar to religion; there is no phase of human life, including scientific beliefs, from which it is wholly absent. It is one function of education to help place convictions in whatever field on a solid foundation through the persistent application of intelligence.

Religious understanding has advanced along with other aspects of cultural life. The crudities of earlier religious systems have been progressively eliminated. Wherever necessary, ways of expressing religious ideas have been modified so as not to contradict well-established scientific findings. Through all the changes that have taken place, religion itself has remained as a legitimate and to all appearances permanent human concern. Customs related to eating and ways of speaking have been continuously modified, too, but no one doubts the permanence of these activities. So it is with religion. Under many forms religion holds its place as a persistent, perhaps even essential, field of interest.

A central feature of the view now being described is the *special* character of religion. That is to say, religion is seen as occupying a distinct compartment of experience parallel to such activities as having friends or studying physics. Some people are religious and others are not. Religion is one kind of experience among many which can be either chosen or avoided. There are special institutions in which religion is carried on, just as there are schools for teaching, country clubs for playing golf, and courts for adjudication. For each such institution there are experts who are responsible for the management of the respective activities.

Such religion has to do primarily with the special being called "God" and with such special activities as attending religious services, praying, and obeying the sacred law. There are ministers who superintend these functions and saints who are distinguished for their excellence in them. The latter correspond to musical virtuosi or champion athletes in their own special fields of endeavor.

When religion is regarded in this way, its proper place in the program of the school is evident. As one kind of cultural activity it deserves appropriate consideration along with other concerns, such as marriage, baseball, and painting. It should be recognized as one of the abiding constituents in the living complex of civilization and given weight in the curriculum in accordance with the governing scale of values. Individual or social needs may suggest more attention to religion in one case, less in another, and perhaps virtually none at all in a third. Some courses may be designed for the preparation of religious specialists, while others may be designed only to acquaint the student with the basic facts of religion as one cultural phenomenon among many.

While religion might thus properly have a place in the school curriculum, it can also be argued that, apart from treatment of religion as a fact of culture, instruction in this subject belongs in the home and in the religious institutions rather than in the school, particularly when there are several different faiths competing for the student's allegiance. As a specialized type of activity, religion has no necessary place in the curriculum, and nothing essential is lost when the school omits it from the course of instruction. The various churches can present their own faiths with full clarity and conviction, and parents may supplement this instruction by precept and example.

Religion as comprehensive life-orientation. According to a third view, religion is neither superstition nor merely a special form of valid act and belief, but is the total scheme of orientation around which a person's life is organized. Such religious faith refers to that which commands supreme devotion, that to which one is ultimately committed. The evidence of anyone's real faith is found in observing what he dedicates himself to with his whole heart, mind, and strength. The religious object is that which a person regards as of highest worth. The supreme value thus indicated is the source of life's meaning. It is one's God. This God of a person's real devotion is not necessarily the God of the religious tradition nor even of the faith one professes. The believer may not be fully aware of what he actually worships. The test of his actual deity is the choices he makes, the values he passionately defends, and the goals toward which he most sincerely strives.

Religious faith conceived as comprehensive life-orientation can be expressed in various creeds and rites, as symbols of the object of supreme devotion. The core of the faith, however, is not in these outward expressions but in the inward dedication. Behind and beneath the outward forms is a governing system of values, which determine the order of relative worth in every experience. That is what life-orientation means: a scale of value-priorities which govern all decision and conduct.

From this functional standpoint everyone has a faith of some sort. It is merely a question of what kind of faith. Every person has a scheme of values in which his life is grounded. For one whose God is love, everything he does aims at the realization of sensitivity to others and concern for their welfare. One who worships power as God is governed by the passion to dominate and control. Another may be supremely devoted to the God of truth, finding his life's meaning and purpose in the pursuit of knowledge. Normally one's faith is a compound of many values, fused into a unique pattern of ultimate commitment. It is also usual for a scheme of life-orientation to undergo modification through the years, in the light of new experiences and the evidence of how actual outcomes have compared with expectations.

When religion is conceived as ultimate commitment, it is obvious that the nature of the faith determines the nature of education. Every curriculum reflects a series of decisions about the relative values of different possible courses of study. The educator has to choose between the better and the worse. If one's religion manifests his basic value system, then the curriculum will necessarily reflect the educator's religious faith. The scheme of life-orientation becomes the system of life-direction, that is, the general aim of instruction. The ideals to which the educator is devoted are the goals of education as he sees them. The curriculum chosen may in turn be regarded as a clue to the teacher's real faith. It reflects what he truly values most and hence intimates the object of his actual devotion.

This comprehensive conception of religion stands in sharp contrast to the special view of the preceding section. Religious concerns in the present sense cannot be avoided. One has no choice as to whether or not he will deal with religion, for the very act of choosing, no matter what the object, presupposes a guiding faith. Religion is no particular subject, alongside other special interests, which can be elected if one has a taste for it. Rather is it manifested in the relative importance and interrelationships of all special concerns. Religion is the principle of order and preference implicit in the organization of life, including the program of education. Therefore, no department or form of educational endeavor is free of religious meaning. Nor can religious instruction be relegated wholly to special institutions. The school inescapably operates according to some pattern of commitments, engendering in the students some kind of total life-orientation. Consequently, the school, like the home, the church, and every other agency through which education occurs, assumes responsibility for fundamental systems of belief which are communicated through its program.

Appraisal of the three views. In the foregoing paragraphs three major general conceptions of religion have been described and the consequences of each for the problem of religion and the school have been indicated. Religion as superstition has no place at all in the course of study. Religion as a special form of valid act and belief may or may not belong in the school curriculum, depending on individual and social circumstances and upon the role of the home and the church in providing such instruction. Finally, religion as comprehensive life-orientation not only belongs in the school but is by definition an inescapable factor in every educational endeavor as its governing principle.

What are the respective values in these three positions? The merit of the first is that it calls into question religious ideas which are immature, intellectually indefensible, and out of accord with the best-attested knowledge. Its weakness is that it may too completely negate and too narrowly construe an aspect of human experience which has been and still is of incalculable importance to mankind and in which many intelligent and critically minded persons still find meaning and value.

The second position is probably the most widely held of the three and is the one which is presupposed in most discussions of the problems of religion and the school. Its value is in its clarity and definiteness. God is a specific being, and religion is concerned with certain particular sacred acts and concepts which can be handled in the appropriate institutions and by specified persons and methods. This view has the defect that it leads to a separation of sacred and secular and tends to render religion both trivial and irrelevant to the other concerns of life.

The third view is the one to which most competent scholars in the field of religion would give assent. It also represents the stated meaning and intent of all the major religions of mankind. The really serious believer never conceives of his faith merely as a special department of his life but always as that which gives meaning and purpose to the whole of personal existence. Thus, the third position best insures the relevance of religion to all the special concerns of life. Against this view it may be urged that it is too vague and too sophisticated, since the average person thinks of religion primarily as consisting of definite things like churches, creeds, and sacraments.

The Plurality of Religions

The fact of plurality. One of the noteworthy facts about religion is the plurality of faiths. There is no doctrine to which all believers give assent, no rule of life nor group loyalty which all share. This pluralism holds for all three conceptions of religion described above. The tangle of hoary superstitions, according to the first of the views, is only too evident. The fertile imagination of man, subject to no check by reality, invents divinities, composes sacred lore, and ordains creeds and codes at will to satisfy particular sets of desires. Each social group, seeking means of strengthening its coherence, employs religious rites and symbols to sanctify the way of life peculiar to it. Every person invents or adopts the religious ideology which best neutralizes the fears and threats that most severely beset him.

The same plurality holds for religion as a valid special concern. There are ten or more major Protestant Christian denominations, and smaller sects number in the hundreds. Catholics are divided among Roman, Orthodox, and several minor types. Jews are Orthodox, Conservative, or Reform. Besides these three groups there are the Hindu, Buddhist, and Islamic faiths, each containing distinctive subtypes. All of these well-established historic religions of mankind have their characteristic institutions, belief systems, moral codes, and ritual practices, providing support and fellowship for like-minded people, ideas about sacred things, and prescriptions for conduct and celebration. For most adherents of these faiths the religious concepts and practices fulfill a relatively independent function in the total scheme of life, generally parallel to but interacting at occasional points with such other functions as earning a living, raising a family, and investigating the causes of things. The ways of faith are as manifold as these other special interests. Just as there are many patterns of livelihood, family structure, and scientific inquiry, so there are many kinds of special religious beliefs and expression.

In the third place, there are many varieties of religion defined as comprehensive life-orientation. In the last analysis there are as many such religions as there are individual people, for every person has his own unique way of organizing his existence, his own special hierarchy of values. Yet there are also groups of people with substantially similar ultimate loyalties, made up of the most committed members of the historic faiths or constituting functional analogues of the traditional religious bodies. There are Christians whose whole life is controlled by faith in Jesus, Jews fully dedicated in all they do to God and his righteous law, Buddhists completely devoted to the way of emancipation and enlightenment. For others the object of supreme concern may be the state, mankind, money, sensation, power, or knowledge. Though such dominant and all-controlling values are not ordinarily designated as religious, they do operate as comprehensive principles of life-organization and therefore may be included within the functional definition of religion.

The problem of social coherence. The plurality of religions creates difficult problems of social coherence. Every society is based upon certain accepted modes of behavior, which in turn reflect an accepted system of values. Every subgroup within the society, whether a family, a club, a labor union, a business organization, or a religious community, is defined by its special code, which generally makes prescriptions of a more detailed nature than those pertaining to membership in the larger society. Furthermore, each individual has his own unique values and patterns of conduct. Now a stable and harmonious social order can exist only if the regulating principles of individuals and subgroups are not too largely at odds with the standards which govern membership in the society as a whole, since these standards are the basis for coordination among the diverse elements constituting society. For example, every society must have certain accepted juridical principles and procedures by which conflicts among disputants can be resolved. This implies a common rule to which all members of the community must be subject, regardless of their private or smaller group preferences.

Religious faiths provide a crucial test of social coordination. The problem is less serious when religion is defined as a special type of belief and act than when it is taken as comprehensive life-orientation. In the former case it is usual for religion to specialize in beliefs that do not affect the larger social and political life. The affairs of religion are regarded as "spiritual," having nothing to do with the temporal concerns of state and business. Occasionally, however, there are special beliefs that may contravene public policy, as for example in matters of military service, marriage customs, and health regulations. In these cases there are four possible ways of resolving the conflict: (1) The faith may be modified to agree with public policy;

(2) public policy may be modified so as to permit the practice in question, either as a general rule or on the basis of special dispensation; (3) the offenders may be expelled, imprisoned, or otherwise punished for their nonconformity; or (4) the social order may in the respect in question break down, and partial or total anarchy ensue. All four of these ways of dealing with dissident persons and groups have been followed in the turbulent history of mankind. No one approach is always to be preferred. Even social breakdown is sometimes necessary as a prelude to social reconstruction.

As already mentioned, the problem of social coherence is most acute when there are different systems of total life-organization within the same society, because under this definition of religion no aspect of life, including concerns of business, school, government, family, or recreation, falls beyond its purview. Thus, there can be no matters of public policy which are outside of and irrelevant to the system of actual religious faith. When there are conflicts between public policy and the belief system of groups or individuals, one or more of the modes of resolution stated in the preceding paragraph must be followed. However, instead of these adjustments being occasional and marginal, as in the case of religion as a special activity, the entire dynamics of social change and adjustment comes into play. It involves the construction and reconstruction of a common faith in respect to those matters of belief and practice which apply to all members of the body politic. For example, the principles of justice and the procedures by which the society is to be governed must become articles within the real faith of every member of the community.

Religious pluralism and the schools. We are now in a position to consider the consequences of religious pluralism for the schools. The school, like the whole society, must have certain reasonably unified policies and objectives. There must be some degree of consistency in aims and coherence in program. To the fulfillment of these requirements the variety of faiths presents considerable difficulties. There are three ways in which the unity of the school can be maintained. These constitute the three possible general solutions to the problem of religion in the schools.

Segregation of religions. The conflict of faiths in the schools can be avoided by assigning students to separate schools according to their religious affiliation. Instruction can be provided in the special features of the particular belief system without giving offense to anyone, and the curriculum can be organized according to the basic value system of the religion in question. These one-faith schools are normally conducted under the auspices of the pertinent religious institutions, and are considered as their educational arm.

Segregation by religion provides the most simple and definite solution to the problem of religious plurality in education. It is favored by many religious groups because it strengthens and sustains the commitments of the young, binding them by habit and loyalty to the faith of their fathers. It helps to overcome a special and trivial attitude toward religion and to establish appreciation for the many-sided relevance of faith. In sectarian schools there are opportunities for amply demonstrating the outworking of religious concerns in the life of the mind and in the manifold social relationships within the school. The individual has the reassurance derived from day-by-day active association with those of similar convictions and standards of value. Home, church, and school are bound together in a united effort to educate the young in the light of the same ultimate objectives.

The main objection to segregation of religions is that the school fails in this respect to make its contribution to social integration. Differences between groups are accentuated and perpetuated. The student does not learn how to relate himself constructively to persons of differing faiths. He is also poorer in sympathy and understanding for not having learned in school by direct confrontation how members of other faiths think and act. There is the further practical problem that segregation by religions may be uneconomical. Where there are many different religions, the number of pupils of a particular faith in any community may be too small to justify a school. In that event other ways of meeting the problems of religious pluralism in the school must be employed.

The method of segregation still does not exempt the school from teaching those matters of public faith which underlie the entire social order. The religion of every group within an integral society must not conflict with the basic principles of public justice and procedure upon which the security of all rests. To this extent even the religious school can and must make its contribution to social cohesion.

The secular common school. Instead of operating separate schools for each religion, the problem of religious pluralism can be solved by maintaining schools which serve all members of the community but whose program avoids religious instruction. Religious conflicts within the school are eliminated by secularizing the curriculum. Sacred matters are handled by the home, by the special institutions of religion, or by separate classes in religion, as in the so-called "released-time" program, while secular or non-religious instruction remains the province of the school. Secular education is regarded as the prime binding force, teaching the culture common to all citizens, without the confusion and controversy engendered by religious questions.

The idea of a secular common school is reasonable only when religion is conceived in the "special" sense, as a particular domain of belief and act. When it is thus considered, religious subjects can be distinguished from non-religious ones and assigned to sacred and secular auspices, respectively. Such division is not possible when religion is understood as comprehensive life-orientation, for then religion is ingredient in every subject studied and is woven into the very texture of the educative process.

The establishment of secular common schools tends to confirm the popular and superficial view of religion as a separable compartment of thought and practice. If religion can be effectively removed from the school's curriculum, that stands as eloquent testimony to the irrelevance of faith to the major concerns of life. Insofar as specialized religion does have significance for the common life, the school is impoverished by the separation. By the same token, religion is robbed of such support and field of application as secular life might supply. In short, even with the special view of religion, it seems doubtful whether the complete separation of the religious from the non-religious is either possible or beneficial. Since human life is or ought to be integral, any rigid compartmentalization such as a religion-free curriculum presupposes is contrary to the proper office of education.

A *thoroughly* secular school would seem to be a *fully* satisfactory solution only to those who regard religion as superstition. Historically, the occasion for secularizing has usually been destructive religious conflict, and the legitimate goal of secularizing has been social cohesion. Many individuals and groups favorable to religion staunchly support secular schools because they fear and wish to avoid ecclesiastical domination of the schools. But they do not consider this solution wholly acceptable; it is merely the best available within a plural culture. However, some of those who fight for secular schools in the name of social unity are really motivated by the conviction that religion is an unintelligent anachronism. Their strategy is well-conceived, for there is nothing which will more surely trivialize and negate whatever real value religion has than to fence it off as a separate domain of life. Those on the other side who believe in the essential validity and permanent significance of religion in human life may well ponder whether the cost of secularizing, both to religion and to general culture, is not too high a price to pay for the absence of religious conflict in the schools.

The common school with a common faith. The third possible solution to the problem of religious pluralism is to gather up the diversities of faith within a larger common faith. As pointed out earlier, the unity of society rests upon certain convictions held in common, having primarily to do with the ways members of the community relate themselves to each other. A school operated by the community for all its members must reflect these common principles, which constitute a common faith. Such a faith is generally not a comprehensive set of beliefs and hence does not qualify as a religion in the fundamental sense. The governing values of the school may not, however, be substantially at variance with the schemes of life-orientation actually operative in the lives of the citizens. Otherwise the school program would not win public assent.

The common school with a common faith need not be secular in the sense that all religious teaching is excised from its curriculum. The function of public policy is to mediate differences and organize diversities harmoniously. The common faith of the public school, therefore, may be expected to recognize and weld into an enriching unity the diversities of religious faith represented in the society. This will be its function regardless of whether the constituent religions are considered from the special or the comprehensive point of view, though the task will be more easily accomplished in the former case than in the latter.

Society as a whole must deal constructively with the religious differences of its citizens. Segregation by religion accentuates differences and requires the schools to make no contribution to harmonizing the diversities. Secularizing education is merely a means of avoiding the problem. Only the public school which seeks to comprehend the religious faiths of the community within the unity of its curriculum and in accordance with its common faith makes a direct contribution to the creation of a society where persons of different convictions may dwell together in peace.

We turn now to a concluding section devoted to some of the problems and specific ways of including religion within the program of the common school.

Religion in Public Education

Church and state. The question of religion in education is connected with the general problem of how the religious institutions are related to the political organization of society. There are three possible types of relationship. First, church and state may be organically connected, either through a theocratic state, with church officials exercising political power, or through the establishment of a church under state authorization and control. In either case public education would include instruction in the official religion. The regulations of the state and the creeds of the church would be the presumed common faith of the society and the problem of religious diversity would be solved by imposing one official faith on all citizens by law.

At the other extreme is the complete separation of church and state. The political authority maintains complete indifference toward the religious institutions as such and the churches have no political prerogatives. The consequence of this policy for public education is the maintenance of secular schools. Religious instruction is not given in the schools, but is reserved entirely for the home and church. It should be noted that the state must set certain limits to freedom of religion in the interests of fundamental social order. For example, no religious group would ordinarily be permitted to forbid its members to pay taxes, even though conscience and religious principle might so decree. Thus complete separation of church and state is never possible. Religious diversity has restrictions defined by basic public policy.

The third type of relationship is one of varying degrees of cooperation and interaction between state and church. For example, the state may encourage religion by exempting church property from taxation or by making special allowance for alternate forms of military service on grounds of conscience. In other cases the state may limit freedom of religion by specifying which faiths are acceptable and which are not, yet without actually setting up a single official church. In the public schools the role of religion depends upon the nature of church-state interaction. Some religious teaching would be permitted, its precise nature being governed by the prevailing diversities of faith in the community and by judgment as to the best way to bring these together for mutual enrichment.

In the United States much of the discussion of religion in the public schools has centered on the problem of church and state. In the colonial period there was generally an organic connection between the two, and such public schooling as was provided included instruction in the official religion. Later, in the face of the plurality of religions in the federal republic, it was provided in the First Amendment to the Constitution that "Congress shall make no laws respecting an establishment of religion, nor prohibiting the free exercise thereof." The question as to what exactly this provision means remains in dispute, despite a number of Supreme Court decisions about it. Some hold that it requires complete and rigorous separation of church and state and hence strictly secular public education. Others are convinced that it merely forbids an organic connection between church and state through religious establishment, but that it does not prevent various forms of cooperative relationships, including non-sectarian teaching of religion in public schools.

A decision about the right relationship of church and state for religiously diversified America can hardly be reached on purely theoretical grounds but only on the basis of practical experimentation and the achievement of workable means of constructively coordinating the religious differences. Since the methods adopted to a considerable extent will depend upon the social and religious complexion of particular communities, the same solutions will not apply everywhere. The public schools provide an important and perhaps the crucial opportunity for discovering whether there are ways of using religion in all its diversity for the enhancement of the common life and learning or whether secular education is the only cure for destructive religious conflict. Five possible ways of teaching religion in the public school will now be described and evaluated.

The compromise syllabus. In some communities it has proven possible for the different religious groups to work out on a cooperative basis a compromise syllabus acceptable to all. Each denomination by itself would prefer to use a somewhat different curriculum, but in the interest of unity certain points are yielded in return for concessions by other groups. Most of the churches prefer a compromise curriculum to nothing at all by way of religious instruction, and hence they avoid the destructive conflict which insistence upon their own special formulations would invite.

A compromise solution is possible only when the religious differences are not great. Thus, such Protestant Christian groups as the Methodists, Presbyterians, and Congregationalists can generally work out cooperative syllabuses. It would be less simple for the Episcopalians to participate because of the strong emphasis on their own Book of Common Prayer. The Roman Catholics would on principle be unable to join in such an effort because of the basic conviction that their church is the sole authorized agency for teaching the Christian faith. Similarly, it would generally be impossible to work out a compromise program including both Christian and Jewish groups because of irreconcilable and fundamental disagreements over the significance of Jesus.

It may be of interest to observe a sharp contrast in the matter of compromise. Christianity, Judaism, and Islam have in general been jealously watchful of the purity of the faith and have drawn sharp lines between those who belong and those who do not, thereby making compromise difficult. Hindus and Buddhists, on the other hand, believe that there are many pathways to truth and many forms of piety. Consequently, they are normally tolerant and hospitable regarding religious differences.

Besides the problems of agreeing on a syllabus resulting from differences among the religious groups, there is a further obstacle in the objections of those who claim allegiance to no institutional religion. Obviously no compromise course of religious instruction will satisfy those who reject all the historic faiths. They would argue that to give such instruction in public schools is to violate the individual's freedom of belief and in effect constitutes a form of religious establishment, which in the United States is unconstitutional. The reply to this might be that the believers also have the right to religious instruction and that satisfying this need in public education is merely one of the ways in which the state cooperates with the churches in furthering the public welfare.

The elements common to all religions. A second proposal for teaching religion in the public schools is to sift out and teach only those beliefs which all religions have in common. Every point on which the major religions differ would be eliminated from the curriculum of religious instruction, and the remaining points of unanimity would be presented. This differs from the method of compromise, in which real differences of conviction remain but are accepted in the interest of getting working agreement. Typical of what are suggested as common elements are belief in God, life after death, and the Ten Commandments. Another example is the daily reading of a passage from the Bible (preferably from the Old Testament, common to Christians and Jews), without comment (in order to avoid differences of interpretation).

This common religious-denominator method has obvious appeal as a simple, straightforward way to solve the problem of religious plurality by eliminating all controversial materials. Critical examination, however, reveals fatal defects in this approach. For one thing, it is doubtful whether there are any elements which all the major religions have in common. Belief in God, for example, does not form part of many Buddhists' faith. Many Christians and Jews do not believe in personal immortality. Nor are the moral and religious prescriptions contained in the Ten Commandments part of the code of all religions. It would be difficult to find any article of faith to which some religion did not take exception.

Even granted that some common elements could be found, the resulting product would be but a pale reflection of a religion. The full life and vigor of the complete faith would be lost. Only the bare skeleton would remain. A religion is an organic structure. Bits and pieces cannot be taken in isolation and still retain their meaning. For a Jew the moral law is integrally related to the covenant relation between God and the people of Israel; for the Christian it gains its meaning through the believer's faith in Christ. To teach the moral principles apart from the whole faith in which they are rooted is to rob them of their true significance.

Related to the last point is the further difficulty that the interpretations of alleged common elements are almost certain to differ widely. Two groups may both claim to believe in God, but the nature of the deity may be quite different in the two faiths. For one, God may be regarded as a personal loving Father, for the other as an impersonal cosmic principle. Thus what appears to be a shared belief in reality is not. The common-element approach, like the compromise curriculum, also fails to take account of those who have no religious affiliation.

Furthermore, it may be asked whether a common-denominator method which simply avoids controversy is educationally sound. Intelligence and faith thrive best when called upon to resolve difficulties and withstand testing. Little secure religious growth can occur if all differences of belief are avoided. At least in the school, it would seem that the interplay of alternative convictions is an essential part of any sound religious instruction.

Though the widespread practice of reading the Bible without comment may conceivably have some symbolic or ritualistic value, it seems clearly unsound both educationally and religiously, because the potentially deeply significant scriptural materials readily come to be regarded by the student as beyond discussion, analysis, or interpretation, and frequently as personally meaningless.

A civic religion. A third approach to religious instruction in the public schools is to recognize explicitly the common faith by which the society's life is guided and to teach this civic faith. As pointed out earlier, no religious group (or, for that matter any other kind of group or any individual) may have a system of belief which operates in opposition to the fundamental values of the social order. These basic values constitute the foundation of a public faith which may be taught and celebrated in the public schools. For instance, the democratic way of life, as defined in such documents as the American Declaration of Independence and the federal Constitution, could be taken as a new civic religion. Respect for the rights and dignity of the individual, personal freedom, representative government, and justice through law would be articles of the common faith. Similarly, in a Communist society the Marxist principles of scientific materialism, economic determinism, the class struggle, and dictatorship of the proletariat would provide standard articles of belief. Whatever the civic religion, the teachers would be expected to expound, recommend, and exemplify it in the conduct of school life. Appropriate celebrations would also be arranged, including flag ceremonies, pledges, and special civic holiday exercises. These would correspond to the collective ritual practices of the churches.

An obvious objection to teaching a civic religion in the school is that society is not the arbiter of ultimate values and that such teaching would promote chauvinism and an intolerable conformism. It can further be observed that since any public faith contains only the barest minimum of beliefs for social coexistence, the same deficiencies apply as in the case of the common-denominator approach.

Still, it would appear that every educator inescapably operates on the basis of *some* faith—some basic criteria for guiding educational policy—and that that public faith is appropriate for the public school. This faith need not be narrowly nationalistic in nature, for the public ideal may include due concern for all peoples. It need not lead to total conformity, since one major article of faith may be individual freedom and the right to differ (within limits).

Even non-public schools are implicitly governed by the civic faith; if they were not, they could not remain within the society, for the common faith concerns the basic principles of the community's cohesion. Yet the non-public school usually teaches its own religion, which may not conflict with the public faith. In contrast, the civic religion would seem to be the only faith appropriate for teaching in the public school, and the purpose of such instruction would be to make explicit and vivid the basis upon which the whole society rests.

The problem still remains as to the place of the historic and traditional religions in the teaching of a civic religion. Extreme advocates of strictly secular public education have urged that the instruction should be free of all reference to the traditional religions. Against this it can be argued that such secularism is really simply another particular sectarian faith, usually taking the form of scientific humanism, and that it does not represent the actual common faith. The real public religion includes the various particular faiths (including scientific humanism) in a more positive and more hospitable fashion. Two ways of relating the many faiths within a common faith for public education will form the substance of the following concluding sections.

Factual study of religion. One element to be expected in a public faith is concern for truth. True knowledge is understanding of what actually exists. Now it is true that there are religious beliefs, institutions, and practices of various kinds which play a not insignificant role in human affairs. Therefore, it is appropriate that the curriculum includes the facts about religion in all studies where relevant. The study of history should do justice to the religious factor in the development of civilization. Courses in literature may not properly avoid the abundant allusions to religion in every kind of writing nor omit from consideration specifically religious books such as the Bible. Social studies falsify the picture of society unless they take account of the institutions, beliefs, and behavior patterns associated with religion.

On the surface such factual presentation seems easy to attain. On closer examination difficulties appear. There is no such thing as an isolated fact. All knowledge consists of systems of meaning, and individual facts always reflect a larger framework of ideas. To take a crucial example, it is a fact that orthodox Christians believe in the resurrected Christ. The meaning of this fact is, however, quite different within the framework of the whole Christian perspective than it is from the standpoint of natural science. To "believe in" for the Christian means to "rely wholly upon"; in the scientific view it means to "have reasonable rational certainty about." The adequate presentation of this fact about Christian faith would then require a sympathetic treatment of the entire Christian perspective within which this one element has its meaning. To present it from the standpoint of natural science might make it no longer true.

The difficulty in all this is that it takes a very wise and generous teacher and much patient explanation to deal fairly with whole systems of ideas, especially when they are alien to his own beliefs. Only a gifted and sensitive Protestant could truly represent the facts of Roman Catholicism, Judaism, or naturalistic humanism. It would take unusual insight and good will for an atheist to give a true account of theistic beliefs. There are teachers who can enter sympathetically into the meaning of faiths other than their own, but this kind of objectivity or inter-subjectivity is neither common nor easy to attain, and it poses problems for the factual study of religion (or any other subject where disputed values are involved).

The difficulties are compounded by the fact that objections are usually raised by parents and religious groups to the treatment of their religion by anyone except themselves. They especially oppose its presentation by a teacher of another faith. This is a problem in the politics of education, which can only be solved by having a strong principle of teacher independence and adequate evidence of the teacher's competence in whatever he undertakes to teach.

Religion and the human situation. Another component of a public faith ought to be concern for the deepest questions which confront every person simply because he is human. Everyone has been born and one day must die. Everyone is conscious of his selfhood, his moral responsibility, his suffering and failure, his freedom, and his creative potential. Everyone wonders on occasion about the source and destiny of his life and the meaning of his existence within the whole of things. It is with these searching and ultimate questions that the religions of mankind have been concerned. The answers given in creed and rite have been many and varied, but the concern and the predicament have been the same for all.

Thus, with all their differences of faith, men are bound together in their common confrontation of the deepest questions of life. Just as scholars who have opposing theories ought to be at one in their search for truth, so men of various faiths can be united in the common situation of being human and in asking the fundamental questions which their predicament arouses. Teaching religion in public schools in this respect means primarily helping the students to understand and to articulate the really profound questions of life, death, and destiny and to choose their own answers to them. The many faiths of mankind (including those not traditionally called religious, such as scientific naturalism) may then be presented as alternative ways which have been found for answering the ultimate problems.

Such teaching of religion may occur throughout the curriculum. It is not restricted to special courses of study. Any subject—language, health education, science—may be the occasion for raising the ultimate questions of existence. Great literature is especially appropriate for stimulating thought about the meaning of life, about the supreme ends of human striving, about the mysteries of evil. There is no field of study, however, where the religious perspective may not be considered. Natural science gives rise to basic questions about the intelligibility of the world, the birth and destination of the cosmos, man's place in nature, and the social responsibility of the scientist. The social sciences abound in searching questions about the nature of man, of freedom, and of the good society. The arts may similarly suggest possible religious meanings in the interpretation of sensible forms as symbols of the infinite. In like manner every other part of the curriculum may in some way or other provide the occasion for seriously confronting the human situation.

When a universal human question is raised, the sensitive and informed teacher can suggest some of the classic ways in which men have sought to express and answer it. Students ought to learn, for example, some of the ways in which the sense of guilt has been dealt with—through acts of penance, through faith in divine forgiveness, as well as through psychotherapy. As they face the ultimate problems of natural origin and of selfhood, they should become familiar with the religious accounts of creation and of the human soul as well as with the mechanistic accounts of nature and personality. In confronting the fact of death they should be informed about the hopes and faiths of men in personal immortality, in resurrection and judgment, and in reincarnation, as well as about the belief that man dies like a dog or that he lives on solely in the lives of those whom he influences during his mortal span.

Perhaps the diversities of religious faith can best be reconciled by recognizing the deeper unity which all men have in confronting the same final mysteries of existence. When this oneness is profoundly felt, confrontation by different faiths in the school curriculum becomes a means of confirmation and enrichment rather than of estrangement. A mature program of public education will not avoid differences of belief, but will seek for a way of using contrasts to provide a more comprehensive harmony. The treatment of religious plurality in the light of the common fundamental concerns of human life would seem to provide a signal opportunity for such maturity.

6

School Administration

The Administrator

A school ordinarily has, in addition to teachers, students, and curriculum, a number of other persons who may be designated by the general term administrators. School principals or headmasters, superintendents of schools, curriculum coordinators, college presidents, registrars and admissions officers, business managers, and the various deans, are included within this category. The purpose of this chapter is to define the several roles of these officers and to indicate some of the assumptions upon which their activities rest.

Administrators as educators. Whatever his special office may be, the school administrator is concerned eventually with the development of the student. His activities, whether in the field of public relations, in fund raising, or in selecting teachers, are in principle all dedicated to the furtherance of the teaching-learning process. Thus he is an educator. His aims ought ultimately to be the same as those of the teacher, the test of his success being the progress of the pupils.

Any educator may, of course, lose sight of this basic purpose of his work and become so engrossed in the activities of the job that these means to an end are treated as ends in themselves. Education frequently comes to be regarded as a self-justifying and self-perpetuating routine of lecturing or examining without any conscious and deliberate concern for its effect on the student's development. The administrator is perhaps especially subject to this temptation to lose sight of the educational goal. He is often not directly and intimately associated with the students and so does not have them as a living reminder of his proper objectives. In many cases also his particular function is to maintain in effective motion the machinery of education, and he feels free to leave to others the question of how this mechanism aids the learner's growth. Whenever administrative activity ceases to have any vital relation to educational objectives, the administrator ceases to be an educator. One of the fruits of reflection on the meaning of his task should be a renewal of the sense of its educational relevance.

Teaching and administration. It is not really possible to make a sharp distinction between the work of teaching and that of administration. Whatever helps to create a situation in which desirable learning effectively occurs deserves to be called teaching, regardless of how remote it may be from direct association with the student. Much of the proper work of those who are ordinarily called teachers does not involve face-to-face relationships of teacher and student. Much preparing, organizing, and arranging is necessary in order that the pupil's studies may proceed successfully. In many cases also the teacher performs functions which would ordinarily be called administrative rather than teaching. Teachers serve on school committees, help frame school policy, represent the school to the public, handle registration and admission, and plan the curriculum for the school as a whole. Thus administrators teach and teachers administer, and both are properly educators. Still, there are administrative roles which are generally distinct from the central and usual functions of the teacher. These will form a main topic of the sections to follow.

Administration and Social Organization

Social order. The existence of a class of persons called administrators—whether in education or in other fields—is a consequence of certain social necessities. The primary factor is the increasing complexity of society. With the advance of civilization the range and variety of human interests and activities increase, and measures must be taken to give some regularity and stability to these functions. In some respects society is like a living organism, the articulation and balance of whose component parts must be safeguarded if the organism is to survive and prosper. One function of the administrator is to oversee the operations of his special part of the social organism and to take thought for the relation of that part to other aspects of the social complex.

An entity is complex whenever contrasting simple elements are harmonized into some kind of mutually compatible relationship. This organization requires rules of order, assignments of place, function, and role. An administrator is a person whose particular business is the recognition and implementation of those ordering principles in the social scheme. Every cultural achievement is some kind of organization. An artist deals with the harmonizing of color, shape, movement, and sound. A scientist is concerned with ordering observational data by means of concept systems. In contrast to these, the elements which the administrator brings together are human beings, and the outcome of his efforts is not a painting or a theory, but a team, a business organization, or a school.

Institutions. The administrator further reflects the rise of social institutions. These are embodiments of the principles of social order designed to afford greater permanence than would be possible were all functions exercised purely as individual personal contributions to social well-being. In an institution one holds a position or an office which could in principle be occupied by any other qualified person. The administrator is responsible for the welfare of the institution, for maintaining it in health by keeping its positions filled by persons whose qualifications match the specifications of the job. Institutions and their administrators come into being when the organization of society moves beyond the relatively fortuitous association of individuals to the suprapersonal regulation of life through designated and continuing role assignments.

Division of labor. Complexity of social organization rests upon the development of specialized functions and a corresponding division of labor. The functions to be performed within an institution are specialized, and each institution in turn fulfills certain unique roles within the whole social scheme. The administrator is a specialist, but in a somewhat different way from any of the other specialists. His specialty is the linking together of the specialties of the others. He makes possible their relatively independent and highly differentiated activity. The larger and more complex an institution becomes, the more administrative work is required to maintain the organization. In the case of educational institutions, administrators become necessary when the number of students, teachers, and course offerings is so large that it is impractical for individual teachers both to do their specialized teaching and to take account of the multiple relationships within and outside of the school by which they and the students are governed.

Power. Every social order requires for its maintenance a power structure. Power is the ability to act to achieve desired results. Effective action is only possible in a society when there are recognized and accepted channels through which information and authority flow. Each office within an institution is defined by a specified array of powers and entails certain authority. It is by virtue of this social power that the officeholder is able to accomplish the duties assigned to him. Administration may be broadly defined as the exercise of social power. It is the performance of the duties attached to and fulfilling a particular position within the power structure of a social institution.

The Administrator's Roles

We have considered the nature of administration as a general aspect of social organization and have indicated its broad relevance to education. We now turn to a discussion of some of the types of specific roles which administrators may be called upon to play. Some administrators fit chiefly into one category, others into several categories. The nature of the roles taken by any given individual depends upon the character of the school and the requirements of the particular job.

These role descriptions can also be regarded as alternative conceptions of what administration ought to be—that is, as normative or evaluative rather than purely descriptive statements.

Judge. One method of administration is by rendering judgments in cases of dispute, infraction of rules, or uncertainty in applying rules. Possibly this is the primal source of all administrative activity. If there were a natural harmony in human affairs such that the interests of one person never clashed with those of another, or a clear law which all understood and obeyed, an administrative structure would not be necessary. Unfortunately, this condition does not prevail. Therefore, there must be some means for resolving conflicting claims, some persons designated as referees in event of doubts and disagreements. The social order is defined by custom and law; but the application of general regulations to particular cases is not always clear or acceptable to everyone. For this reason adjudication by a custodian and authorized interpreter of the regulations is sometimes essential.

As a social institution a school must have certain rules of procedure and recognized conventions by which its life is defined. On occasion, members of the school community break the regulations or disagree about their meaning and concrete application. The administrator is then called upon to decide what penalties or remedial measures shall apply to the lawbreakers or what the specific import of the rules is in the case at hand. In this role the administrator acts as guardian of the integrity of the institution.

It is especially on such occasions of testing, of conflict, and of search for clarity that the true governing principles of the institution become vividly apparent. For example, a school may claim to stand for the principle of academic freedom. If, then, participation by a teacher in certain disapproved types of activity leads to censure or dismissal by the administration, the meaning and limits of that freedom will be defined. In being required to render such a specific judgment the administrator is forced to define precisely the meaning of the principle professed.

Again, there is no educational institution where various interests do not compete with one another for a larger share of funds, building space, or time in the curriculum. Certain teachers press for more attention to science and mathematics, while others urge greater emphasis on social studies, and still other groups argue for more athletics or manual arts. The task of apportioning resources is ultimately an administrative one. When judgment has been given, the school's educational principles become clear and definite in a way that would never have been possible merely through generalized policy statements.

Very often educational objectives are never actually formulated except through administrative judgments. They are worked out step by step through the resolution of conflicts and the forced clarification of aims in concrete situations. The real principles by which the school is governed are created in the succession of decisions which must be made in the resolution of actual institutional problems.

Two contrasting ways are available to the administrator to make his judgments. The first is to refer to some precedent or explicit rule to which the members of the organization are expected literally to conform. The second way is to weigh each case in the light of a system of values. The first procedure is mechanical and is concerned only with insuring conformity to the letter of the regulation. The second method is personal and moral, since it is based on the determination of what is right. Of the two, the first approach is far the less costly in effort and concern. It deals in simple alternatives of keeping or breaking the law, while the consideration of values leads into countless ambiguities and complexities. While the legalistic method is rigid and backward-looking, the value approach is generally more adaptable to new situations. On the other hand, the reference to values does not exclude consideration of the tradition nor the use of rules, but these inheritances from the past are regarded as data which enter into the making of the judgment and not the sole criteria of judgment.

Ruler. Administration as entering judgments presupposes that there are conflicts to be resolved. It begins with problems. According to this view of administration, when there are no perplexities or disputes the administrator is not required to act. A second concept of the administrative role is concerned not with differences to be harmonized but with power to be exercised and action to be initiated. The administrator is a ruler who controls the activities of other persons and wields authority over them. Positive direction is given by superior officers to those of lower rank in the hierarchy. Since specific procedures are determined in advance and obedience is exacted, differences of approach are minimized and maximum efficiency of operation is assured.

The school administrator who rules assumes entire responsibility for the direction of growth of the students. The nature of their educative experiences is determined by the program decisions made at the top and implemented in the lower echelons. The institution is but the extension of the man who governs it. Its aims are his, and it is ultimately he alone who is the educator; his subordinates are, so to speak, his hands and voice.

The idea of administration as exercise of power over others raises at least three fundamental philosophical issues. The first involves the nature of man. Can human beings fulfill their being as persons when their lives are controlled by external agencies? This is the issue of freedom. It has been one of the deepest convictions of mankind that freedom is essential to the good life and that the subjection of one person to another violates the distinctive nature of man. From this standpoint, then, authoritarian school administration undermines a basic human principle and thus vitiates the very educational process it was created to serve. When the entire institution becomes infected with the attitude of submission and unquestioning obedience, creativity and individuality are submerged and the healthy growth of persons as unique, independent, and responsible agents is discouraged.

A second issue is concerned with the basis for maximum stability and effectiveness of social institutions. Every society must have power structures, by means of which necessary work can get done and social order can be maintained. The question is how much power should be vested in the administrator and how absolute his control ought to be. Increase of power beyond a point may actually reduce the institution's efficiency. Power often corrupts those who possess it so that they use it for foolish and vain purposes. Also those who become too dependent on authorities lose their initiative and their individual effectiveness is diminished. Furthermore, an autocratic type of organization often lacks flexibility and adaptability to new situations since such power structures tend to generate rigid and unquestioned codes of procedure.

A third philosophic issue relates to the source and grounds of the administrator's authority. How does he justify his rule? By what authority does he command obedience? One answer is that the authority is purely personal, that the only justification for his rule is that he can maintain himself in power. The will of the individual is then the source of the law. This is pure autocracy, according to which might makes right. Another answer is that authority comes from social consent so that the administrator's activity reflects the intention and interest of the community. Still another answer is that true administrative authority comes neither from the individual nor from society but from an independent moral law by which all should be governed. The administrator in this case governs in accordance with what he believes to be true and right, whether or not it conforms to his own desires or to the conventions of his society.

These approaches to the problem of authority reflect essentially different conceptions of the administrator's role and engender quite different types of response in those subject to him. In the first case the response is submission based on fear, in the second it is cooperation for the sake of social adjustment, and in the third it is dedication to the right. Students learn from the manner of organization of their schools whether the highest value, according to those in whom authority is vested, is power, social adjustment, or justice.

Servant. Instead of being a judge or ruler the administrator can be cast in the role of a servant. Every social institution has its special work to do and its experts who engage in the basic tasks of production. For example, in the manufacture of automobiles the men who operate the mills and the lathes and who plan the engineering designs are the actual producers. They cannot do their jobs easily and successfully unless provision is made for a place to work, necessary transportation, salary payments, and a constant flow of supplies. It is the function of the administrator as servant to facilitate the producers' work in such ways as these. His role is auxiliary; he is an aide or a helper of those who actually create the product. He is not a commander, but in a sense is a subordinate partner doing whatever is needed by the specialist to make the main work of production most effective.

In the school the teacher is the producing specialist. The teaching function is basic, and all other activity must subserve that function. The serving role of the administrator is then to do everything necessary to facilitate and expedite the work of teaching. Recruitment and admissions officers release the teacher from the burden of securing suitable students for the school. Registration officers are employed to keep the essential records. Some teachers may desire to have the work of examining and evaluating students taken over by an administrative agency. The handling of discipline problems and of difficulties with parents and civic authorities may be turned over to principals, deans, or professional counselors. Teachers who are called upon by students for help in choice of vocation, of further schooling, or of occupation can be relieved of much of this responsibility by school guidance and personal services. The procurement of necessary classroom equipment and supplies and the provision and maintenance of school buildings are further important administrative contributions. Finally, the school administrator is normally responsible for securing necessary financial support, providing salaries sufficient to free teachers from worry and hardship, and obtaining requisite funds for the other auxiliary operations.

In short, the administrator's role as servant is to simplify the life of the teacher so that he is free to devote all his energy to the specific task of teaching. Many things have to be done merely to provide facilities and conditions in which teaching can take place, and these often do not require the special competence of the teacher. These provisions may become the responsibility of the administrative staff.

In the larger institutions the administrative officer has associates and subordinates who work under his direction. Much of the detailed work is done by secretaries, clerks, and various kinds of craftsmen. A school is a community in itself and thus requires the help of such service personnel as carpenters, typists, and cooks. These workers are not themselves regarded as administrative personnel, but they do enable the administrator to have the service function fulfilled. When such a staff of workers is employed, the administrator has a dual role as manager and as servant. He exercises authority in relation to his staff, and together they provide services for the teaching faculty.

A strict service role for the administrator presupposes that educational policy is decided by the teachers themselves. Then it is not the administrator's function to determine what shall be taught or how but solely to facilitate the teaching process as directed by the teaching staff. Under this arrangement the administrator is an educator only in an indirect and derivative sense. (This question of educational policy-making will be developed in the next chapter.)

If too many auxiliary functions are taken over by the administration, the teacher's role may become too narrow and specialized. Sometimes the influence of the teacher is most profound when he helps the student in ways which are not immediately connected with the regular work of instruction. Academic advisement often passes over into personal counseling, and subject-matter teaching sometimes leads to vocational guidance. Routine activities, on behalf of a student, which could be done by the administrative staff are frequently occasions of more educational significance than classroom instruction. Hence the proper division of labor within the school needs careful examination in the light of actual educational consequences. A simple principle of maximum specialization of function does not suffice.

Leader. According to another conception, the administrator is a leader. His role is not primarily to resolve differences, nor to exercise authority, nor to facilitate the teacher's work, but to inspire and persuade, to plan and direct the work of the school. He is a man with vision, with ideas and enthusiasm. His role is to infuse energy into his staff, by his own example stimulating interest in and providing insight into the educational task of the institution.

A leader-administrator is in the full sense an educator. He is, in fact, an educator's educator, a teacher of teachers, since he is not only concerned with the advancement of the pupils in the school but also with the growth in understanding and in competence of those who teach them. He is not content merely to make the institution run smoothly. He seeks to develop better teachers and to make the school a concrete embodiment of his educational ideals.

The leader as here conceived differs from the ruler in that he influences by persuasion rather than by command or through the authority attached to his office. There are three different grounds for this persuasiveness, reflecting corresponding conceptions of leadership. One type of leader succeeds on the basis of personal qualities not directly related to the specific work of the institution. His educational program may be quite ordinary and uninspiring, but his personality may be so winning that his associates find great satisfaction in working with and for him. Cheerfulness, sincerity, fairness, faithfulness to the job, and genuine appreciation of other people are examples of the kind of qualities in a leader which inspire loyalty and devotion to the common effort. This type of leadership based on the appeal of a personality suffers from the following defects: when individual leaders move away, retire, or die, the institutions centered around them may suffer excessively from the resulting changes in leadership. A strong personality may encourage too much dependence on the part of his followers so that they fail to think and act responsibly for themselves. Finally, since a powerful personality can exert his influence on behalf of an inferior educational program as well as for a superior one, his very success may be a catastrophe for the school.

A second type of leader persuades through the logic, the inherent appeal, and the demonstrated power of his ideas. The members of his staff respond not because of the magnetism of his personality but by virtue of the confidence which his educational program itself inspires. Such leadership does not remain with the administrator but becomes objectified in the structure of the school and in the working practice of the teachers. It thus promotes institutional stability and personal independence and demonstrates its intrinsic worth by the conviction it generates and the success which it brings.

The strength of a third kind of leader lies in his ability to discover the deepest interests and most cherished ideals of his associates and to make these explicit and to some degree attainable. He leads not by promoting his own ideas but by implementing the convictions and aspirations of those with whom he works. Instead of telling others what they should do he listens to them and finds out what they really desire. He then tries to express these goals clearly and invents means of making them effective in action. This type of leadership is likely to bring maximum staff response and to generate the most profound loyalty to the institution. It poses the problem that since there are usually conflicts of ideals within the staff the administrator cannot satisfy everybody and must find some criterion for decision among the divergent possibilities. It is also a question whether the best leadership ought not to transcend the current ideas of the staff members, suggesting new horizons and inspiring new educational aims.

It is sometimes said that the idea of leadership is undemocratic and aristocratic. It is true that this view does lend itself to hierarchical, inequalitarian forms of social organization. However, as the preceding discussion shows, leadership can be of a type which is based on the expressed interests of those who are led, and thus it may remain democratic in character.

One further observation is that an important function of the leader is to generate and sustain *morale*. This is a feeling pervading the staff of confidence and well-being, a sense of the importance of the job to be done, and genuine zest in doing it. While many factors contribute to morale, including working hours, compensation, conditions of work, and general social and intellectual climate, the leader is frequently the real key. His enthusiasm, awareness of purpose, and concern for the success of the enterprise are contagious. The morale of teachers and students in a school is often a reflection of the spirit of those who administer it. Sometimes educational institutions are very truly the lengthening shadows of the men who lead them.

Coordinator. A role of the administrator which is implicit in all of those discussed above but which deserves separate emphasis is that of coordination. Any social institution to be effective must have a certain unity of structure and purpose. It consists of individuals performing a variety of special functions which need to be brought into a pattern of mutual reinforcement. There must be a common goal to which the activities of the constituent members all contribute. It is the special task of certain administrative officers to do this work of coordination.

Coordination in an organization may be achieved in two contrasting ways. One is through centralized control with a plan of operation in which each worker is assigned his part and need only do his specialized job faithfully. Only the administrator has to know the plan of the whole, and knowing it, he can appropriately correlate the contributions of individual workers. The school administrator works out his master plan based upon his conception of educational aims and of the curriculum best designed to fulfill them. He then assigns teachers and students to appropriate tasks within this scheme. If everyone follows the designated regulations, order and harmony will prevail and well-educated persons will presumably emerge from the process.

Quite different is the way of coordination in which every individual knows the plan of the whole and makes his special contribution in the light of this total view. The administrator's coordinating role here is to keep the members of the organization well informed about the work of the entire institution so that each will know how best to serve the common cause. This approach places far more responsibility upon every individual than does the centralized method. It may not be as immediately efficient as the way of regulation, but in the long run it may be more productive because each participant feels more important and derives satisfaction from knowing what his work means for the enterprise as a whole. Even if it were not eventually more efficient, the method of participation could be defended on the basis of the greater intrinsic job satisfaction and sense of significance which it provides.

Coordination requires communication, for it is only by this means that distinct parts of the organization can be brought into working unity. The nature of the coordinating activity can be analyzed in the light of the process of communication employed. Three types of process may be distinguished. First, there may be one-way communication from administrator to subordinates. The school principal sends memoranda to the teachers and pupils, who are expected to put the directions into effect. The unity of the educational program is thus charted in the administrative office and implemented by the compliant action of individual members of the school.

A second possibility is to have two-way communication between the administrator and other members of the institution. The officer receives requests and information as well as gives orders. He asks questions of staff and students in order to benefit from their experience and to know their feelings and expectations. His administrative decisions and regulations take account of what he learns from incoming communications, and they are continually tested and modified in the light of the effects produced. The administrator is responsible for harmonizing as far as possible the divergent interests and functions. He creates the unity of the whole, but always in the light of understanding of the parts and consultation with them.

The third way of coordinating through communication is for the administrator to act as a clearing house for information which serves to keep the members of the organization aware of what others are doing and thinking. The administrator does not use the data received to build a coordinated program, but merely facilitates its dissemination to all concerned. The actual task of coordination is then accomplished not by the administrator but by the individual members of the organization, acting with knowledge of the whole and with the consciousness that the effectiveness of the institution depends upon each doing his part for the good of all.

Representative. The last of the administrative roles to be considered is that of representative. The administrative officers of any institution are concerned not only with its internal affairs but also with its relation to individuals and groups in its social environment. There is need both for coherence among the members of the organization and for fitting the institution into the larger patterns of society. While every member of the school community is to some extent responsible for creating right relationships between school and society, a major obligation in this respect falls upon the administrative officers. They are ordinarily designated as the official representatives of the school in relation to the public. They stand for the school and speak in its name. They enter into agreements committing the school to certain programs and policies. They negotiate with other agencies concerning the division of labor as between the school and other institutions.

But it is not only the school that the administrator represents. He is also a representative of society to the school. He must to a considerable degree reflect the concerns and demands of those beyond the school who support it and expect to be served by it.

Thus the administrator functions as a link between his school and the society in which it exists. He occupies a dual representative role; he faces two ways, in toward his organization and out toward his public. He must seek to resolve in the best possible fashion the conflicts of value between the two. His is in essence a political function and as such depends for its success upon the skillful use of compromise. If he represents the interests either of the school or of society exclusively, he will fail. He must be as faithful as possible to his educational ideals within the framework of community demands. He must seek to interpret the goals of the school to the society which uses and sustains it, and he must communicate to the school the relevant concerns of its public.

The administrator in this two-way representative function is an educator in two spheres. He helps to guide the development of those within the school community. In addition, he has the task of educating the surrounding community, of persuading its citizens to enlarge their perspective so that their objectives may become a stimulus rather than an obstacle to the educational progress of the school.

Organization of the School

Thus far in this chapter we have considered some general conceptions of the nature of administrative activity, with special reference to the school. It is apparent that the notion of educational administration needs discriminating analysis. There is no single simple idea by which the subject may be comprehended. A full view requires recognition of a variety of complementary and to some degree contradictory roles.

The remainder of the chapter will be devoted to a quite different aspect of administration, namely, an approach to certain basic questions of school organization. Such problems as these concern the substance of administrative action rather than its method. They require official decision whatever the administrator's role is conceived to be. Three problems will be briefly treated. They do not by any means exhaust the field, but merely illustrate an approach to a philosophy of school organization.

Class Size

It was pointed out in Chapter 2 that one of the reasons for the existence of the school is the economy afforded by the teaching of many pupils at the same time. Consequently, one of the administrative decisions to be made is how large the classes should be. What factors must be considered in making this decision?

Economic factors. The most obvious factor is the total number of students and the available funds and teachers. Class size equals the number of students divided by the number of teachers. But class size is not necessarily the only variable. The problem may be presented in the form: What is the best class size, and how many teachers must be secured to make such classes possible? On the other hand, if the class size is regarded as fixed, for educational reasons, and if the teacher supply is not sufficient to staff all the classes needed, some of the students must be refused admittance. Thus a decision must be made by those ultimately responsible for educational policies between having fewer students taught in more favorable class-size conditions or more taught in less favorable ones, that is, the choice is between quality and spread of educational resources.

The per capita cost for small classes is obviously greater than for larger ones. Therefore, class size tends to vary with the society's economic condition. But it is chiefly a question of relative values. A wealthy society which places a low relative value on schooling may not be willing to provide for small classes, while a modestly endowed society which highly values the life of learning may make the necessary sacrifices to have the optimum class size.

Physical facilities. Physical factors also need to be considered. The size of available rooms sets definite limits. However, in the long run room size is governed by class size and not vice versa. Equipment is limited too. Places and facilities in laboratories are generally at a premium. The problem of managing a large class is another limiting factor. If there are too many in the class, the teacher has difficulty communicating effectively with all the students. However, modern amplifying systems and television equipment have greatly extended the possible range of communication.

Teaching methods. Besides these economic and physical aspects of the problem of class size, there are factors which are more directly related to the educative process itself. One fundamental consideration is the method of instruction used. If teaching consists in the verbal transmission of knowledge, class size is a matter of indifference. With proper equipment a thousand students can be instructed in this way as readily as one. There may be differences psychologically. Some lecturers are stimulated by a large audience, while others perform best in a small group where every face can be seen and reactions noted; some students prefer the social reinforcement provided by a large crowd, while others feel lost in the impersonality of the mass and respond more favorably to a more intimate type of association. Because the lecture method is feasible with large classes, when good teachers or money for education are scarce there is pressure to employ this method rather than other approaches which may be more appropriate but require smaller, more expensive classes.

At the other extreme, when teaching consists of face-to-face interchange between persons, small classes are essential. In this case it is the individuality of the student that counts. What the teacher says at any moment is not contained in a predetermined lecture but is governed in part by what individual students have done and said the moment before. Some kinds of teaching, such as guidance of individual research or counseling on deep emotional problems, can only be done properly when the class consists of one student. Still other teaching methods, such as group discussion or work and play in teams, determine by their very nature the exact or optimum class size.

Reconciling cost and quality. The task of administration is to devise ways of most effectively reconciling cost and quality of instruction. Are there schemes whereby there can be large classes yet with individual instruction? A number of plans have been used. The class may be divided into parallel subgroups or into special committees, each with responsibility for periodically reporting back to the whole class to share findings. The more able students may be assigned under the teacher's direction as monitors with duties ranging from helping to maintain order to actual tutorial instruction. More frequently, instead of student helpers the teacher may be assisted by other instructors, usually with less experience or training. The master teacher then determines the content of instruction and supervises the work of the assistants.

These systems are ways of economizing teaching talent by special forms of organization within the class itself, including division of labor and specialization of function, all comprehended within a total plan of coordination.

Subject matter. Finally, the administrator should take into consideration the differing class-size requirements of the different subjects taught in the curriculum. No standard size will ordinarily be satisfactory for all teaching purposes. Ultimately the criterion for determining optimum size is a functional one. What do teachers and students actually need to do to insure the learning of a given subject? How many students can receive instruction at the same time and still function in these essential ways? Organization into classes must therefore not be mechanical and uniform but should be based upon knowledge of and provision for the specific activities within the respective curricular offerings.

Class placement

Another consideration more fundamental than class size from the standpoint of educational process is the problem of deciding which students should be included in the same classes. This problem is, of course, closely linked with that of class size. If a community can afford to hire only one teacher for all its children, there is no question of class placement; the one-room school is the result. In general, the larger the classes must be in any school, the more limited will be the range of choice regarding class placement. Division into very specialized types of groups is possible only when small classes are economically feasible or when there is a very large student population to be subdivided.

Individual differences. The problem of class placement is, however, chiefly a qualitative rather than a quantitative one. Basically it goes back to the fact of individual differences. If every person for educational purposes were alike, placement could be on a purely quantitative basis. Actually, since persons differ considerably from each other, they require different educational provisions. Ideally each person would have his own teacher or teachers who would provide the course of study best suited to his needs. For economic reasons this tutorial system is not usually possible. In place of it students are grouped in classes with others of similar educational needs. Thus, the factor of individuation is reconciled with the demands of economy by means of a classification system.

There are two questions now to be considered: First, is this system of segregation into more or less homogeneous groups educationally desirable? Second, by what criteria should the classification be made?

Homogeneous vs. heterogeneous groups. Concerning the first question, it may be urged against homogeneous grouping that it is important for the pupil to learn to associate with others who are different from himself. If the student is always placed with those who are very much like himself, he will be poorly prepared to meet the problems of actual social life where he should be able to understand and deal with all sorts and conditions of men. Furthermore, since students learn not only from their teachers but from each other, they should not be so much alike that the stimulus of variety is lost.

In favor of homogeneity is the greater efficiency it affords in accomplishing the particular jobs for which the group was organized. It permits the use of specialized teachers with maximum skill in their areas of professional competence. The greater uniformity in student performance minimizes frustrations and conflicts in the teaching-learning process.

It seems clear that there are some values afforded through homogeneous grouping and other values gained by the heterogeneous approach. Every person needs some of both. There are parts of the curriculum in which the experience of association with different sorts of people is the very basis of the learning process and other parts where the goal is maximum concentration on a common object of study without the distraction of adjusting to personal differences. As a general rule, heterogeneous grouping provides unique opportunities for learning human relations, while homogeneous grouping is normally best for intellectual growth and mastery of specialized techniques and skills.

Age grading. Let us now turn to the second question, concerning the criteria to be used in making the division into classes. The most common criterion is age. From an administrative point of view this method has the great advantage of simplicity. Age is definite and easily ascertained and makes class assignment a mechanical and clerical procedure. It is at best, however, a very rough measure of educational needs. If the basic principle of classification is that individual differences be provided for, chronological age is not an appropriate method of grouping. A person may well differ far more in educationally significant respects from one of the same age than from another person considerably older or younger.

Grading according to age is actually a compromise between heterogeneous and homogeneous grouping. Within the very gross similarities associated with age there are wide differences in mental and emotional competence. In such a compromise situation provision may be made for individual differences by giving the more able students an opportunity for additional work which will broaden and deepen their grasp of the subject under study without actually moving ahead to advanced topics and by giving extra remedial work and special assistance to students of less than average ability. In this manner the boredom and frustration inevitable in a uniform program for persons of considerably different capacities are minimized, and the social values of diversity are to some degree achieved along with the meeting of individual needs.

Achievement-level grading. A second possible criterion for class placement is achievement level. This is the proper way of grouping to insure readiness for any given educational task. A student is not advanced in grade until he has achieved a required level of competence. The difficulty in this is that there are many kinds of achievement, and not all of them are realized at the same rate. For example, a certain child may mature intellectually with exceptional speed but be average or below average in rate of emotional growth. Then at which achievement level should he be classified—the intellectual or the emotional? By the principle of homogeneity there should be classes for all combinations of levels, e.g., grade (6,2) for intellectual level 6 and emotional level 2, grade (6,6) for intellectual and social levels 6, and so on. In practice there would seldom be enough students in a single school to permit such refinement.

Another method of handling the problem of differential achievement is to have a flexible and functional system of classification in which the student is assigned to different grades for different types of learning. For example, one student might be grade 10 for art but grade 5 for mathematics, while another student would be placed in grade 5 for art and 10 for mathematics. The difficulties in this approach are its administrative complexity, the problem of finding tests for fairly evaluating levels of achievement, and the intimate interrelationships between the areas of learning which make the separation into fields somewhat arbitrary and knowledge in one field to some degree dependent on familiarity with certain of the others. For example, the study of most subjects presupposes a certain level of prior language achievement.

A further objection to the system of assignment by achievement level is its frequent psychological ill effects. In many cases it produces anxiety and unhealthy striving for success. For those who fail there is not only loss of self-esteem and of prestige but the weakening of ties with the successful group who move on to the next grade. These losses compound the woes and increase the resentment of the less able and usually make them even less likely to achieve in the future. Achievement classification also directs the learner's attention away from the intrinsic values of his studies to the rewards of an examiner's approval, thus robbing education of its proper satisfactions and creating perhaps lifelong defective attitudes toward the purpose of study.

Assignment by vocational intention. A third basis for assignment to class is vocational intention. Those who are preparing for the trades may be placed in one group, those preparing for positions in business and the professions in another group, and those who aim to be scholars and scientists in still a third group. Such separation is obviously necessary when dealing with specialized subjects directly pertinent to the respective occupations. The issue is whether in the general education of man and citizen it is desirable to make these distinctions. For greatest efficiency in preparing specialists there may be some advantages in orienting even general education toward the job. Against the system is its tendency to create marked occupational stratification and to cause the individual to lose his sense of being first a person and a citizen and only after that a particular kind of worker. Also, since a person usually cannot early decide on his life vocation, he needs a general course of study which will fit him for any of a variety of types of work and enable him, if he desires, to change from one occupation to another.

Other criteria. The three kinds of criteria examined illustrate the problems which arise in trying to provide for individual needs by more or less homogeneous grouping. There are many other criteria which might similarly be discussed. Some others which have been employed are separation by sex, color, number of years in school, or aptitude. More will be said about some of these in Chapter 8 below in connection with the distribution of education.

Size and Scope of the School

Another administrative problem is how to constitute a school. How large should the school be and what should be its scope? Should there be many small schools or a few large ones, and should a school include all grades or should there be separate schools for certain groups of grades? In making intelligent administrative decisions in regard to such questions there are several types of factors which need to be considered.

Population density. One obvious factor is population density. In a sparsely populated area small schools as a rule will be necessary. In a thickly populated region, on the other hand, either large or small schools are feasible, and the decision must be made on other grounds.

Transportation facilities. Efficient means of transportation offset geographic separation. Thus, even in a thinly settled region good transportation facilities make possible schools of considerable size. The number of one-room schools has so sharply diminished in the United States in recent decades largely because of improved highways and automotive equipment. However, there is still a problem of how far and how long pupils may be required to travel to school without impairing their health, safety, and personal effectiveness.

Economy. School size is considerably affected by economic considerations. Two kinds of costs are involved in operating a school: those which vary directly with the number of students and those which are concerned with the operation of the institution as a whole. Food costs are proportionate to the student population. Cost of instruction is another such item; if the size of the school doubles, the number of teachers will double also, assuming class size and distribution of courses remains the same. On the other hand, certain other costs, such as administrative expenses, cost of publications, and building maintenance, are not incurred for individual students but on an institution-wide basis. Usually these general costs rise less rapidly with the increase in the number of students than do the direct costs. For this reason the cost per student is generally less for the larger school. However, a size may be reached at which the complexities of organization required are such that general costs increase faster than direct costs. At that point further enlargement becomes uneconomical.

School administrators must decide approximately what the optimum size is from the economic standpoint, but this does not mean that this is the optimum size in other respects. To determine this, other factors besides the economic one must be examined.

Program possibilities. The previous factors have all been independent of curricular considerations. There are two other aspects which do have direct educational significance. One is the fact that in a large school opportunities for learning exist which are not available in a small school. A small school cannot have a full-scale orchestra or band, as many a large school can. The small school cannot so readily organize an extensive intramural athletic program. It cannot secure prominent speakers who will take the time only to address large audiences. The large school can also provide a greater range and variety of persons with whom the individual student can become familiar.

Differentiation. The second curricular factor is the larger differentiation of subject matter which the greater size makes possible. Specialized teachers can be secured in the larger school, and a wide variety of course offerings may be made available. This differentiation also makes for a higher standard of excellence for the school as a whole. With many students from whom to select, better athletic or debate teams, for example, can be expected, on the average, than in smaller schools, other factors being equal. These particularly able people represent the school as a whole, thus raising morale, generating pride in accomplishment, and setting standards for others to emulate.

Differentiation may, however, lead to narrowness in the curriculum. In some small schools the fact that fewer courses are given saves the student from pursuing too restricted a line of study, thus preserving wholeness and balance in the educative process.

Social aspects. It is usually argued on behalf of small schools that they are more favorable from the social standpoint. Each member of the community knows the others, and lasting bonds of friendship may be developed. The individual does not feel lost in the impersonal mass, as sometimes happens in the large schools. Each feels that he counts for something. On the other hand, the impersonality of the large school can be mitigated by having small classes and appropriate arrangements for living, dining, and recreation. Doubtless, however, the sense of the whole is never as easy to achieve as in the smaller schools.

Size as a value in itself. There is a further largely irrational factor which has an influence on decisions about size. In some cultures there is a presumption about size as a value in itself. In American life, for example, bigness tends to be regarded as intrinsically preferable to smallness. This is a reflection of the general quantitative emphasis in the culture. Big business is considered better than small business, big cities as more important than small ones, big churches as preferable to small ones. Large size means success, and success is a reward for virtue. By the same token, large schools are sometimes considered preferable to small ones, on general principles. This is, of course, a prejudice rather than a reasoned conclusion. There is no merit in size—large or small—as such, but only in size as related to other demonstrable defects or benefits.

The psychology of scope. The question of scope obviously depends partly on the problem of size. Many communities cannot narrow the scope of the school beyond a certain limit without making it uneconomically small. Even more important are the psychological considerations. The needs of six-year-olds are so different from those of adolescents or of adults that it is generally desirable to teach them in separate schools. The general principle governing scope would seem to be that students should be placed in the same school only insofar as they can be satisfactorily regulated by the same basic policies and objectives. For example, one major reason for separating college and university students from those in the earlier stages is that they are presumed to be ready to take the main share of responsibility for managing their own lives. The institutional arrangements when the student is regarded as independent are quite different from those which prevail when considerable adult direction is considered necessary.

All grade groupings, such as the common American one of nursery and kindergarten, elementary, junior high, senior high, junior college, four-year college, graduate and postgraduate, are based on judgments about the generally compatible stages in educational development and about the points at which fundamentally different characteristics and needs come into such prominence that they require new institutional arrangements.

Administration as a Philosophical Problem

The reader may wish to inquire at this point what is specifically philosophical in the above analysis of school administration. How does it differ from a simple description of the administrator's functions and an elementary statement about school organization?

As pointed out in Chapter 1, any domain of human experience is an appropriate subject for philosophic inquiry. School administration is no exception. We began in this chapter by showing how two superficially different activities, teaching and administration, are fundamentally similar when considered in the light of their common educational role. Next an attempt was made to interpret administration by means of certain social concepts of wide generality, thus placing the subject directly within the province of social philosophy. The subsequent sections on the administrator's roles were designed to present a critical discussion of the range of possible administrative functions, together with certain of the basic assumptions regarding man and society upon which they rest. A philosophic consideration of administration implies serious reflection on just such a variety of possibilities. The presentation of the six types of roles above is equivalent to saying: "If you wish to think philosophically about administration, here are some factors of which you should take account." Each person must weigh the possibilities in his own way, using his own scale of values. The best that the general philosophy of education can do is to suggest some of the elements which ought to be evaluated.

The last section, on school organization, is to all appearances least philosophical, since it deals mainly with fairly obvious practical considerations. It is true that decisions about class size, for example, do not for the most part stimulate the most profound inquiries. Yet there is a difference between setting class size by sheer tradition or mere circumstances rather than by reflective deliberation on the range of relevant factors relating to economics, the values of society, methods of instruction, and the nature of knowledge. Similarly, the survey of possibilities in connection with class placement and school size and scope is what makes them potentially philosophical.

Any subject is treated philosophically when some of the pertinent concerns entering into decisions about it are indicated and appraised and when it is analyzed in the light of concepts of wide generality.

The Control and Support of Schools

Control

The school is a creation of society. It is not a product of nature, but one of culture. Like all cultural creations it has no uniform and invariable way of functioning. The nature of the school is determined by human decisions about the direction the development of the young should take. Since there are so many different courses which may be followed—some better, some worse—it is of utmost importance who controls the schools. Those who control the schools influence in significant ways the growth of individuals and the future of society.

Control of the school has two components: first, decisions about educational policy, and second, power to execute the policies. The execution of policy is the task of school administration, which was discussed in the preceding chapter. The other component—policy-making—remains to be discussed. A policy is a projected pattern, a set of working principles or guiding ideals. The detailed working out of these objectives is left to the executive agencies, subject at any point to review, to insure that the desired policies are being realized in action and to make necessary policy changes in the light of the results achieved.

Who Decides School Policy?

There are a number of different agencies within society in which the responsibility for making school policy may be vested. In practice many individuals and groups usually have some influence in deciding the pattern of education. There is generally no one agency which in isolation from all others determines the nature of the school program. The policy decided upon is thus a result of weighing and balancing the interests and demands of many persons. In the paragraphs to follow the more important of the possible centers of influence in making school policy will be discussed. These are some of the possibilities which should enter into a reflective and critical, and hence philosophical, consideration of school control.

The individual student. To some degree the school pupil himself may make educational policy. An extreme view would be that all policy-making should be in his hands. According to this position, all true education is self-education, and it is wrong to impose upon the growing person any external and alien pattern of development. Learning ought to proceed according to the dictates of the student's emerging felt needs. Since the individual can be depended upon to know better than anyone else what is good for him, all matters of educational policy should be determined solely by himself. Teachers, administrators, parents, and all others concerned with schooling are necessary to supply the student's needs, but they should serve within the framework of the policy laid down by the pupil himself and not attempt to guide him by their own lights.

Critics of this extreme position point out that it rests upon a naive and unrealistic view of human nature. There is no inner compass that unerringly points the child's true way. More often than not what an immature person thinks he needs is quite different from what he really needs. Impulses and desires must be disciplined by proper environmental conditions in order that a personality eventually capable of sound independent judgment may be developed. The child's originally unrealistic interests and expectations have to be brought into harmony with the realities of the surrounding social and physical world.

Besides this, the individual determination of policy is equivalent to having no policy at all. Educational policy for a school is a plan of operation for the institution as a whole. Individual self-determination would mean that each went his own way and hence that there would be no policy for the school. Complete disorder and confusion would result from any such system. There is no pre-established harmony, as some have supposed, bringing into natural accord the independent strivings of autonomous individuals. Working unity can only be achieved by a conscious plan of coordination, i.e., by some deliberate institutional policy.

There are, however, schools in which the deliberate policy is to give the greatest possible freedom to the individual. It is important to recognize that in such cases the educational policy is not determined by the student but by other responsible persons. In these programs also the student's freedom is subject to definite limitations. Freedom is permitted only insofar as the liberty of others is not violated. These restrictions on freedom in the interests of social harmony constitute school policy decided by persons other than the individual student.

Despite objections to the extreme form of self-determination, there are real values in a school policy which gives considerable latitude of choice to the individual. An "open" policy of this type minimizes institutional control and places the emphasis on personal self-regulation. Such a program is most feasible with older students who have had consistent and intelligent earlier direction with progressively increasing opportunity to make their own choices. It also works best when the students have had fairly comparable backgrounds and so possess generally similar values.

Organized students. Another approach is to place school policy in the hands of the student group as a whole. In this way student control is maintained without the disorder entailed in pure individualism. A number of persons may desire to receive instruction and agree together on certain objectives and rules of association. They may then secure the necessary teachers and facilities to maintain a school operated in accordance with their own interests and intentions.

There are also on-going educational institutions in which provision is made for varying degrees of genuine self-government by the students. Officers are elected and appointed to school policy-making boards. They may be given the responsibility of deciding on such matters as acceptable codes of conduct for the school community, judicial and disciplinary procedures to be used when rules are broken, and plans for school activities. Students may even be charged with determining course offerings and academic requirements and with approving faculty appointments. The extent of control placed in the students' hands is, of course, a function of the maturity they have attained, the nature of the community in which the school is situated, the past success of the student government, and the strength and stability of the tradition of responsibility which has been created.

Control of educational policy by student government usually occurs under the supervision of some superior agency, such as faculty boards, administration, or trustees. Hence, student self-determination is generally derived rather than absolute, a privilege granted by higher powers and subject to review and revocation by them. The ultimate authority, and therefore the real control, is in other than students' hands. Under these circumstances what appears as student self-government is in reality simply a means used by the ones in control to secure student cooperation in the detailed implementation of official school policy. The proof of this relationship is that when the student organization departs too radically from the intention of those ultimately responsible, countermeasures are taken to restore the officially approved program.

Control by organized students is chiefly of value as a method of teaching responsible social participation. When regarded in this light, it may quite appropriately be exercised within the framework of a more ultimate school policy. Practice in making decisions about their own education is an important part of the students' education, and for this very reason merits guidance by those to whom the control ultimately belongs. But if the decisions are to be real, meaningful, and truly instructive, the students need to be given enough freedom to make some mistakes and discover from the consequences why they were mistakes. By granting this freedom also the authorities may discover in the students new and wiser ways than their own policies had provided for and thus learn from students as well as teaching them.

Teachers. A third view is that the making of school policy should be entrusted to the teachers. Who knows better than the teachers about the needs of the students? Who is as well qualified as the teachers to recommend the most appropriate ways to serve those needs? In a sense the teacher is the key person in the educational enterprise. The policies of the school, it is argued, are but means for expediting the teaching function and should thus be decided by those who do the work of instruction.

As in the discussion of student control, a distinction must be made between control by individual teachers and by the faculty as an organized body. There is the obvious danger of confusion and conflict when too much individual policy determination, even by teachers, is permitted. Yet a considerable measure of teacher autonomy, within a larger policy framework determined by the whole faculty or some other agency, is usually practicable and is conducive to originality, initiative, and high morale.

Though ideally teachers should know and serve the interests of the students, in reality this is not always the practice. Teachers have their own interests to consider, and if school policy is fashioned by them, it may unduly reflect their own individual and group concerns. The problem of control is one of deciding whose values are to govern. It cannot be assumed uncritically that those who are vocationally committed to education will be dedicated solely to the welfare of the students. There is a tendency for any human enterprise, including teaching, to become autonomous and self-justifying. The habitual activities come to be of intrinsic value to those who are professionally responsible for them, and the larger purposes which they serve are forgotten. Thus school policy formulated by teachers is sometimes such as to perpetuate the customary institutional functions without regard to their real value to the students.

The view is also held by some that the teacher is primarily a technician, a specialist in the work of producing educated persons, but not responsible for the education of the whole person. This specialized teaching must be done within the context of a comprehensive educational plan devised by other persons whose responsibility it is to decide on school policy.

If, on the other hand, teachers are to be accounted educators in the full sense, they must be concerned with the objectives of the entire teaching process and their voice must be heard in the formulation of policy for the school. Their personal and group interests as teachers are also not without some bearing on policy decisions.

Administrators. Since certain school administrators are concerned with the institution as a whole, one can take the position that these officials are best qualified to make school policy. This would presuppose a conception of the administrator as judge, as ruler, or as leader. These roles were discussed in Chapter 6 and need no further development here.

While it is true that the school administrator ought to have the comprehensive perspective and the competence as a professional educator which will make him a valuable policy adviser, it can also be maintained that his central function is to supervise and expedite the policies decided by others such as teachers, parents, or government officials. According to this view, the administrator's job is to serve rather than to control the school establishment. Perhaps even more than the teachers it is the administrator who is subject to the temptation to make the institution and its workings ends in themselves and to utilize his position to advance his personal interests in status, power, and financial reward. From this standpoint it is essential that control not be vested in the administrator, but that he be required to execute the policies laid down by others whose interests are wider or more representative.

Yet even if the ultimate control of the school does not rest with the administrator—as evidenced, for example, by the power of others to appoint and remove these officers—it is usually necessary and desirable to give a certain degree of policy-making power to him. Control of the more specific processes and procedures of education may be placed in the administrator's hands, subject to periodic review in the light of the general policy determined by the ultimate controlling authority. Such discretionary powers appear to be necessary if the administrator is to have a sufficient sense of freedom and responsibility in the control of his work.

The school board. Most educational institutions are controlled by a specially designated board. Major policy questions are decided by these trustees and are carried out by administrative officers appointed by them. However, the ultimate control does not necessarily reside in the school board either, but in those who have the power to choose the board members. When the board is self-chosen, it does possess final authority, within the limits of its charter, which defines the general nature of the institution and states the powers vested in its governing board by society as a whole. When the board is not self-constituting, but is appointed by other agencies, its members have a representative function. The ultimate control then rests with those whom the board members represent. These may be the citizens of the local community, parents, teachers, students, or any of the other possible policy-making groups referred to above and below. Sometimes the board members all represent the same group (as in the case of public election by the citizens). In other cases the charter provides for representation of various different interests, including (for example) alumni, faculty, and state officials.

The basic idea of control by a school board is that the school is an institution which has responsibilities to and privileges in the society of which it is a part. Generally speaking, the board chiefly represents the interests beyond the school which are to be served in and by the school and which are in turn dedicated to its maintenance and defense. If control is vested in the students, the teachers, or the administrators, the school is autonomous and cannot be held continuously accountable to the society beyond the school. A case can be made for such independence, but usually the members of society have seen fit to place control in the hands of those who represent interests other than the school itself. It is this basic fact of control which generally makes it impossible for the school to depart too radically from the dominant accepted values of society or, more specifically, from the values of the groups which exercise authority over them. Because control is imposed on the school from beyond itself, it must chiefly conserve and transmit the existing culture in certain of its aspects rather than serve as a means of transforming it. A decisive prophetic role is reserved for independent persons or institutions. Of course, a school can play such a role if it is organized to represent some independent interest which itself seeks to reconstruct the existing order.

Alumni. Those who have attended a school have a special concern for its welfare which may make it desirable to give them a voice in making school policy. As products of the school, intimately acquainted with its traditions and ideals, they can insure the perpetuation of these values. More perhaps than any other group they belong both to the school and to the larger society. They know from personal experience in what ways their education has fitted them for the various offices of life and in what respects it has failed to do so. Hence, they might be expected to give valuable advice on ways of improving the school program. The loyalty of some alumni provides the motivation for dedicated service to the school, and their experience both in and beyond it sometimes gives them a basis for making policy decisions wisely.

There are other considerations which suggest the limitations of alumni control. The graduate of a school may tend to be excessively conservative in his judgments about it because he makes his appraisals in the light of conditions in his own student days rather than those prevailing currently. The school may need to have a dynamic policy rather than merely to preserve the traditions of the past. Furthermore, because alumni are sometimes unduly sentimental about their school days, their judgments about the nature and purpose of the school may be unbalanced, unrealistic, and without perspective. Others who have no such emotional attachment to the institution may on this account be better qualified to formulate the policies.

Parents. The school, at least during the years of a child's dependency, may be regarded as an extension of the family, with teachers serving in place of the parents. That which parents cannot do to educate their young, because they lack the economic or technical resources, they may delegate to the school. On these grounds it might appear that the parents ought to control the school. The inculcation of ideas and values which the parents wish their children to have would then be the primary objective of school policy.

While a strong argument can be presented for parent representation in school policy-making, the serious difficulties in their exclusive control should be recognized. The major problem is the temporary and constantly changing nature of the parents' concern for the school. The child grows rapidly and soon passes out of the school, and the parents' interest follows him on to the next stage in his education. Meanwhile the school must plan not for only one but for generation after generation of pupils. The educational perspective of the parents is thus likely to be quite different from that of the school.

Parents are also generally so concerned with the welfare and special problems of their own children that they tend to assess the entire school program in the light of their particular interests rather than to consider the good of all the students. Furthermore, many parents become so deeply involved emotionally in seeking their children's advantage that they lack the objectivity and discrimination necessary for sound policy-making.

The control of education by parents is usually achieved indirectly rather than by direct representation on school boards. When there are several different kinds of schools to which children may be sent, it will generally be possible to choose one whose policies reflect the values cherished by the parents. Thus general control of policy is exercised by the operation of supply and demand. A school with any particular program will be formed and patronized if there are enough parents whose educational objectives for their children are fulfilled by it.

The case for parental control of education (either direct or indirect) rests upon the premise that since the family is the basic social unit, in it is vested the ultimate responsibility for the nurture of the young. When parents are denied the privilege of choosing schools for their children, the family loses a considerable portion of its authority and influence. The competitor of the family for this authority is, of course, the state as the institutional embodiment of society as a whole. Society, as well as the individual family, obviously has a claim on the young, who are to be its responsible members, and hence has a stake in their education.

The problem of the primacy of family or state is a fundamental issue in social philosophy. It is to be resolved partly on the basis of actual social conditions. When, for example, economic conditions make it necessary for many mothers to work outside the home, family life is undermined and responsibility for the young proportionately shifts to society as a whole. The question is also partly one of fundamental values. If individuality and diversity are highly valued in a society, freedom of parents' choice for their children's education will generally be approved. If unity and order are considered more valuable, and if education is regarded primarily as the means of conserving the traditions of the whole society rather than of individual families, then the primacy of the state in matters of education will be affirmed.

Religious organizations. Many schools are controlled by religious organizations. The reason for this is that religion purports to be—and frequently is—a total scheme of life-orientation for its adherents, and as such it contains guiding principles for education as well as for all other human concerns. When religion is believed to express the highest ideals and to provide answers to the most important human problems, it is natural that schools should be established with policies based upon these religious convictions. Probably no other human interest besides religion so encompasses the whole nature and destiny of the person and thus in principle has so clear a right to the control of education.

The difficulty with this position is that one cannot equate the principle of religious control with that of ecclesiastical control. Religious organizations do not always in fact embody the ultimate values of life. Their claim to represent the supreme reality and to show the true path of life often seems poorly justified in actual experience. The religious group may become a self-perpetuating social institution whose actual educational purpose is to maintain its own special tradition. In that case ecclesiastical control of the school does not serve the true ultimate welfare of the young but merely the continuity of the organization.

Further light on this question may be gained from the discussion on religion in the school in Chapter 5.

Special interests. Church control of the school is usually simply one of a class of arrangements which may be designated as control by special interests. It is generally possible and often seems desirable for a subgroup within society to set up schools for its own special purposes and regulated by itself. Thus, while one may question the wisdom of having all education under ecclesiastical control, for the reasons suggested in the preceding paragraph, one would naturally expect each religious organization to found and manage schools dedicated to instruction in its special beliefs and practices, possibly for all its members but in any case for the preparation of its leaders.

In modern industrial society an increasing share of educational responsibility is being assumed by business and industry. In view of the highly specialized and technical nature of much modern enterprise and the rapidity of change which characterizes it, many organizations have found it necessary or advantageous to conduct their own schools. Some types of learning are so peculiar to the industry that no outside school could give the required instruction. Other more general subjects could be taught outside, but appear to be most conveniently or efficiently learned in company schools. In some communities (e.g., in "company towns") all schooling is controlled by the business organization.

Labor unions are another powerful special interest which may seek to control school policy. Veterans' organizations and other types of civic and patriotic associations also work to keep the school from teaching anything which they regard as objectionable. In fact, any of the numerous and varied special-interest groups which thrive in a free society may either have its own schools or seek to gain some voice in the making of school policy.

It would appear right and necessary for the special interests to run specialist schools. It is doubtful, however, that the complete program of education should be controlled by any such group. In exceptional cases and with unusually imaginative leadership a company school, for example, could consistently produce competent and well-educated persons. But, in general, school policy would be too much colored by the special values and viewpoint of the controlling interest. Education is the means by which the character of society and culture in succeeding generations is determined. Any special interest by its very nature as a limited domain of concern is unfit to serve as custodian of the general cultural heritage and as sole fashioner of the society of the future.

The local community. Another solution to the problem of control—as in the public schools in the United States—is to vest it in the citizens of the local community. The actual making of policy is usually done by the school board, chosen by the citizens and thus in theory representative of the various interests within the community, such as parents, teachers, business organizations, and churches.

When policy is made by the local community, the school reflects the dominant interests and values of citizens in the area represented. Formal education is regarded as a matter of public concern. Such a school does not exist for its own sake nor for the benefit of any special group or class within society, but exists to serve the many and varied groups and individuals that together make up the community. In this role the school constitutes a powerful instrument for social cohesion, since those who are educated in a community school have a living demonstration of the possibility and method of working together for the same civic values.

A school controlled by the citizens through the established channels of government is a public school. All others are private schools. The central issue in social philosophy raised by the question of whether education should be carried on in public or in private schools (or if in both, in what proportions) is that of unity and diversity. Public education serves the cause of social unity, of public values, of interests shared, while private education tends to accentuate the differences between groups within society. Public education fosters the development of one comprehensive community; private education is likely instead to be associated with a federation of relatively independent and culturally distinct subgroups.

It is not necessarily true, however, that a society with public education is as a whole less hospitable to differences than one with a system of private education. Social stability requires some means of insuring coordination among contrasting elements—some unifying, community-creating principle. When there are public schools, education contributes to this coordination; when the schools are private, some other means of unification must be employed such as a strong central government. If the schools do make a contribution to social unity, other instruments of cohesion are not so necessary.

Public control of the schools, then, need not result in uniformity and collectivization. In a democratic society the basic principle is the bringing together of different interests into a working unity. This does not mean the overcoming of differences, but the discovery of modes of cooperating to the maximum advantage of all. With community control of education, the distinct and contrasting claims of various local groups come to a focus in determining school policy. The program of the school is accordingly a reflection of the process of adjusting and balancing competing claims within society. The students also bring to the school their differing outlooks and values, which in general parallel those of their policy-making citizen elders.

Thus the community-controlled school has the advantage of serving as a continuing laboratory for the practice of democratic living and hence as a powerful means of propagating and strengthening the ideals and practices of democracy in the whole society.

As suggested in an earlier paragraph dealing with parents as policy-makers, the question of public or private schools is a matter of whether the family or the community should be primarily responsible for the nurture of the young. If the family is considered to have the exclusive right of education, private schools must be permitted. If the community as a whole is regarded as requiring through education the means for its own continuation and unification, the public school will be the rule. It is also possible to establish a mixed system, with some private schools and some public schools. Under such an arrangement, if parents are free to send their children to either type of school, the ideological freedom and priority of the family are affirmed and the educational influence of the community as a whole is minimized. In actuality since practical considerations, usually financial or geographical, often greatly limit the parents' choice of a private school (especially if public schools predominate numerically), the community usually remains the decisive factor in making school policy even in mixed systems.

The state or nation. Control of the school by the local community has the advantage that education can be directed to preparation for citizenship and not merely for membership in family or special-interest groups. But society is generally more than the local community, and to be a citizen usually means more than adjustment to the ways of the neighborhood. This suggests that the control of the school ought perhaps to be vested in the state or nation. Once more, the decision about the degree to which control should be centralized has to do with the extent to which education is to be employed in the service of social unity. Local control allows for maximum freedom and variation in school programs and thus tends to maintain the differences between communities. Centralized control makes for greater uniformity.

There are, of course, many possible degrees of government control and levels of centralization. Any of the political units above the local community (which itself may be variously defined) can serve as the final authority in educational matters. The highest authority may then delegate to other agencies the power to decide most questions of policy, reserving for itself only the supervision of certain basic requirements. For example, the state may establish minimum standards for the licensing of teachers and for attendance at school but leave decisions about curriculum to local school boards.

The freedom and variety made possible by local control of schools are generally regarded as high values in a democratic society. Yet even in a democracy there are fundamental values which transcend localism and which the people may believe should be ingredient in all schools. The extent and nature of these national concerns will determine the degree and kind of school control exercised by the state.

The Support of Education

In the above paragraphs some of the possible systems of control for the schools have been discussed. This question of who makes and executes school policy is of fundamental importance, for upon the answer depend to a considerable extent the values which are to be realized in the coming generations. Those who control the school are the ultimate educators. Even though they may not actually do the work of teaching, their convictions about what should be learned determine how the school will affect the development of students.

Closely linked with the question of control is that of support. Education does not take place in a realm of pure spirit. As a concrete social enterprise it requires material resources. There can be no effective control without the material supplies necessary to implement it. Educational aims are but idle hopes apart from the physical means to embody them.

How are the control and support of schools related to each other? One view is that the two functions should be kept separate and distinct. One set of agencies may be given the authority to make school policy and another to provide the material support. For example, the state may be asked to provide the money, from general taxation, to finance education, while the control of the school rests with the teachers or the parents. Or there could conceivably be a system in which the parents would pay the bills while the state made policy. The rationale for separating control from support is that the ability to make appropriate educational decisions may be independent of the ability to pay; the sources of educational wisdom are not necessarily the same as the sources of material wealth. Thus the general principle of differentiation within society would seem to indicate that for the good of all some are called upon for financial aid while others are expected to contribute their skill in making school policy.

Critical reflection on this conception of independent functions casts serious doubt on it. Financial support, in the long run, is provided only for that which is regarded as valuable. The amounts of material wealth which a society apportions to its several activities may in fact be taken as a fair measure of its scale of values. But educational policy is also a reflection of values. It would therefore be reasonable to expect that the allocation of material wealth to education would be an effective means of expressing judgments of value about school policy. Schools whose programs are regarded as valuable will receive support, while those which cannot command approval will be denied sustenance. Control and support both reflect the same real values which actual people have. It follows that ultimately the control of the school resides with those who are able to command the economic resources which it requires. Financial support is thus an indirect means of making school policy.

The actual machinery of school control may be to some extent distinct from that of school finance. A board of trustees, for example, one of whose major functions is to secure financial support, may leave curriculum planning to a relatively autonomous faculty committee. In the last analysis, however, these curriculum decisions must be made effective by continuing economic sustenance in the form of teachers' salaries, living expenses for students, and provision of buildings, equipment, and supplies. The supporting agencies in these concrete ways tacitly endorse the educational decisions made by the ostensibly autonomous faculty group.

Sources of Financial Support for Education

Especially in view of the intimate relation between control and support, it is important to consider the possible sources of financial support for the schools. It is one thing to make judgments about school policy solely in the light of educational or political considerations; it is another thing to weigh the alternatives when the economic factor is also taken into account. The question of what shall be done in the schools is, in the long run, a question of what someone is willing and able to pay for. Who, then, can and does pay for education? The major possible sources will now be critically examined.

Students. The student himself can be one important source of financial support for the school. This may take the form either of payments in cash or of services rendered. Normally the amount the student can be expected to pay for his own education increases with age. However, even fairly young children can, in appropriate situations and with competent guidance, help substantially in keeping costs down by doing simple but necessary chores.

When the student pays his own way, in whole or in part, there are several favorable consequences. He tends to appreciate and to take greater interest in his studies. He will not continue to sacrifice his labor and his capital for an enterprise which he does not take seriously. Furthermore, the paying student is in a position to influence the type and quality of instruction.

He is in effect a buyer in the market, with power to bargain for the product which he will purchase. Good instruction will be bought at a premium price; bad instruction will go begging. The student is in any event the consumer of educational goods. When he is also the buyer, he can exercise control over the quality of education received. Another favorable result of student support is the close connection it helps to maintain between the educational endeavor and the practical concerns of life. A student who engages in gainful work while in school frequently has an opportunity to apply what he learns to the job and to see in his studies relevance and meaning which might otherwise escape him.

On the debit side of financing by students are the strain, distraction, and interruption which result from being both a student and a job-holder. If too much time is taken from school in earning one's way, the continuity and concentration needed for an effective study program are impaired. Often, too, the part-time employed student is deprived of the leisure to engage in the more informal types of learning and hence tends to develop personally in a one-sided fashion.

It would be possible in principle for the student to pay his own way and still go to school full time, through a system of deferred payment. Education would then be considered as an investment, with its cost amortized over a period of years out of later earnings. Such a system would, of course, require a considerable initial capital outlay by someone other than the student.

Perhaps the most undesirable result of student support of education is the close link it tends to establish between the individual's choice of school or course and the monetary return it is expected to yield. When education is thus evaluated largely by financial criteria, other less tangible but even more important educational values may easily be lost sight of. A student may regard the love of knowledge in and for itself, the appreciation of beauty, and growth in ethical and religious insight as the highest fruits of learning and yet feel the pressure to renounce these goals in favor of ones economically more profitable and more clearly consistent with the financial sacrifices required to obtain schooling.

Finally, to require students to pay their own way is to deny the principle of general social responsibility for education. Study is one important kind of work, and the student deserves appropriate financial rewards for doing his part in the total labor of society. Whenever students must pay for their own schooling, that is evidence that the community does not value the work they do enough to support them in it, except perhaps through the promise of future financial benefits. On the average and in the long run, therefore, student-supported schooling will need to be provided only to satisfy those special interests, needs, and ambitions of individuals which extend beyond the general intention of society and the more limited concerns of its subgroups. For example, the public may pay for the child's education through high school and the parents see him through college, but circumstances may be such that if he cares enough personally to go on to graduate study, he must finance that schooling himself.

Parents. When the family is given primary responsibility for the nurture of the young, it may follow that parents are expected to assume the burden of financial support for the schools. Such direct parental support yields maximum assurance that the school's program will implement the ideals and values of the individual family and stimulates keen interest by parents in the development of their children. When the parent makes financial sacrifices for his children's education, he will normally select with great care the quality of schooling for which he pays.

The obvious shortcoming of the system of parent support is that educational opportunity becomes linked to economic status. Because those who have had more schooling can generally command higher financial rewards than those with less, family-supported schooling tends to perpetuate economic differences between families. It also seems evident that the ability of the family to pay is not an educationally relevant criterion for the choice or availability of schooling for any given child. Furthermore, the very fact that there are children to feed, clothe, and house makes a family with children that much less able to bear the further cost of their education. These considerations point to the need for a broader economic base for education than the parents alone.

Other sources of private support. In the discussion of school policy-making agencies it was pointed out that alumni, religious institutions, and other special-interest groups including business organizations can and often do participate in the control of education. Since financial support is such a powerful means of exercising control, either directly or indirectly, it is to be expected that these same types of agencies would be called upon to contribute to the cost of education. The fundamental rationale for such private support is that students and parents do not have the resources to bear the whole economic burden of education and yet that the financing should not be turned over to government either, in order that the flexibility, variety, and initiative which accompany private interest may be preserved.

Alumni may be appealed to on grounds of loyalty and gratitude to the school that helped to make them what they are. Especially when their financial success is in some measure a result of schooling, alumni contributions can be regarded as the discharge of a debt—as a voluntary payment for value received. The school is here the analogue of the family: children are supported by their parents and then when grown they repay the debt, sometimes by caring for parents who can no longer make their own way, but more often by seeing their own children through to maturity. In like manner alumni may be called upon to provide for the new generation of students as they were themselves provided for by other benefactors when they were at school.

Religious groups appeal for funds for their schools in the interests of preserving and extending the faith. Members are generally expected to contribute in proportion to their ability to pay, on the grounds that wealth is not one's own unalienable property but a portion of the divine bounty, given as a trust to be administered by wise stewards. Generous gifts to the work of the church are considered as a measure of religious zeal and sometimes also as a means of obtaining salvation. The powerful commitments and emotional appeals in religion frequently make possible a strong financial basis for schools under religious auspices. When religion is truly a matter of ultimate concern, extraordinary financial sacrifice will be made to insure that the young are well instructed in the cherished faith. When religion is nominal and conventional—merely one interest among many—substantial financial support for schools by religious institutions cannot be expected.

Business and industry support schools which they establish for their own training purposes and for the general welfare of their employees and families. They may also underwrite students and programs in other schools when these directly contribute to the supply of competent personnel available for the industry. A crucial question in the financing of education is how far business enterprises ought to support school programs which do not clearly and directly serve their special interests. Does business have a general social responsibility to prepare the young both as producers and as consumers of the products of industry? The narrower policy may provide needed specialists for the short run, but in the long run it may be that the economic commonwealth will prosper only when it is inhabited by broadly educated people.

Another source of private support for education is philanthropy. Individuals who have prospered financially often give their money either during their lifetime or in their wills to advance what they believe to be good causes. Individuals and families with considerable wealth sometimes establish foundations, non-profit corporations with boards of trustees and executive staffs, for the specific purpose of wisely managing and distributing the available funds. Much philanthropic giving has been for educational purposes. Like all forms of private support for the schools, philanthropy tends to advance by educational means the special interests of those who make the gifts. As a result, the values of the well-to-do receive proportionately greater weight in education than those of persons with ordinary means. Yet there seems to be no correspondence between economic status and priority of values; the aims and ideals of the rich are not necessarily superior to those of the poor. Hence it would not appear desirable for financial support for schools generally to be completely or largely drawn from private philanthropy. In favor of some such support is the freedom afforded for experimentation and for advancing significant types of education which do not at the time command widespread interest or assent.

The public. In contrast with the foregoing methods of private support is the financing of education by public funds. Since ultimately support means control, the issue of public versus private support is the same as that of public versus private control. The case for public schools is that education is a concern of society as a whole and not merely of individuals, families, or special interests. Parents will pay for schools to perpetuate their family ideals, corporations will finance programs which will help their enterprises to prosper, and philanthropists will endow schools to teach what they as individuals prize most. But ability to pay is no measure of educational wisdom. Hence public schools need to be established, supported by taxation and dedicated to the good of the community as a whole.

This question is also intimately connected with the problem of who shall be educated, which is the topic of the next chapter. In general (though not by logical necessity) private support is associated with exclusiveness in allocation of schooling, while public support is associated with universality of educational opportunity. If the public pays for the schools, as a rule they will be open to all citizens of the community who can profit from them.

Public support of the schools does not necessarily involve detailed control of them by governmental agencies. Normally schools supported by the public are controlled by public agencies. However, it is conceivable that though funds for education were secured through taxation, they would be distributed to independently operated schools. Or there might be a system of state scholarships which any student could use in the school of his choice, even though controlled by a church, business organization, or some other private agency. In the broadest sense there would still be public control in these cases, since the grant of public funds would constitute tacit approval of the schools supported. Schools which stood in basic opposition to the public values of a society would not continue to receive public funds. Hence there must always be some test by which the public acceptability of any school receiving tax funds is determined. This constitutes a general basis of public control, even though detailed direction might in some cases be delegated to private agencies.

The fundamental question in public support of education is precisely how the machinery of taxation should be employed to finance the schools. One position is that education should be provided for simply as one set of items in the regular budgetary appropriations of government. Thus education would compete with roads, housing, defense, social security, and other such claims for its share of funds and would be subject to the same political determinations as these others. The opposed view is that education is a very special community concern and should accordingly be financed by a special and independent taxation system. This removes education from the chances and changes of ordinary governmental manipulation and dramatizes the particular and unique obligation of the public for the perpetuation of its culture through the schools. Under this second system there would be school districts with independent taxing authority and budgets separate from those of the municipalities or states in which they were situated.

The nation. A special case of public support, so important that it deserves separate discussion, is the use of funds from the national treasury to finance the schools. The fundamental argument for federal assistance to schools is that education is a concern of the nation as at whole and hence that all the people, through their government, should provide the material means necessary to insure good educational facilities for everyone. Some communities are less able than others to support good schools. Economic levels differ widely as between localities, states, and regions. National support of education makes it possible for the relatively less privileged communities to provide better schools than they could otherwise afford. Such a redistribution of economic resources for education presupposes equality of opportunity as a fundamental social value.

The question of federal aid is also in part a technical one having to do with systems of taxation. Quite apart from the ideal of geographical equalization, national support may be desirable because the federal tax structure is more efficient, more equitable, or more reliable than that of the local communities. Some local districts are peculiarly blind to the needs of the schools and do not provide adequately for them in their own tax systems. For example, such a local tax base as assessed value of owned real property may be quite inequitable, exempting many who ought to help pay for education, placing an undue burden on a few, and having little or no logical relation to the educational function. A sound federal tax structure would ideally provide a uniform and equitable means of distributing the burden of school support among the citizens. On the other hand, since the federal tax system may also be inefficient and unfair in comparison with local systems, the taxation argument is not necessarily in favor of federal support for education.

In some nations federal funds are employed to maintain a national, centrally controlled, and uniform system of education. Schools not in the national system are then either forbidden or forced to rely on local or private sources of support. When federal aid is used in this way, the objective is the unity, efficiency, and security of the nation as a whole. To proponents of such a system it seems unwise to allow so important a concern as the nurture of the young, and consequently the future of the nation and its culture, to be subject to the vagaries of widely scattered and diverse communities.

Those who oppose the use of federal funds for education do so chiefly in the interests of local autonomy. They believe that centralization means regimentation, and that freedom is more important than national unity. Let the people be united in dedication to liberty, they say, rather than being forced into a uniform mold. A national system of education, they believe, tends to make the individual a creature of the state, instead of the state being dedicated to the well-being of the individual. Their assumption is that if local funds are used for the support of education, local autonomy in school policy will best be preserved.

It should be pointed out, however, that federal aid is not necessarily inconsistent with the preservation of a considerable degree of independence in school policy-making at the state, county, or district level. The people may decide, as a matter of national policy, to use funds from the national treasury for grants to states and local communities to be administered completely by them. In this way the strength and equity made possible by federal economic resources would be combined with freedom and local autonomy in educational policy-making. There would normally have to be certain general regulations governing the granting of national funds, to insure that the money was not grossly misused. This would entail some degree of control. But control of the schools is not necessarily in direct proportion to support. Given reasonable confidence by the nation as a whole in the wisdom and good faith of state and local educational authorities, there seems to be no reason why federal funds cannot safely be used for the support of locally controlled public schools.

As pointed out earlier, public funds, including those of the federal government, might even be used to support independently controlled schools, whose virtual autonomy could be guaranteed by law as a matter of national policy. In this case, however, certain perplexing political and social questions would arise. Should funds derived from all the people be used for purposes which are not within public determination? Would federal support make schools in fact so dependent on the government that independence of policy, though guaranteed at one time, could easily be denied at another? Would long-established and carefully articulated principles such as those governing the relations of church and state be compromised?

Of course federal control or support may be provided in all degrees from none at all to full and complete. Normally but not necessarily the greater the support, the greater the degree of control. It is possible also to designate carefully the specific purposes for which the federal funds may be used. For example, federal aid might be provided for such general welfare purposes as bus transportation or school-lunch programs, even for private schools, but probably not for textbooks or teachers' salaries, since the latter would be concerned with the more particular objectives of the educational program. On the other hand, it might be decided that building funds, either on a loan or on free grant basis, would be provided from the federal treasury and locally administered for the benefit of public but not private schools.

Thus the problem of federal support for education leads not only into technical questions of administration and taxation but inevitably also into fundamental issues of social and political philosophy. There seems to be an ever-present tension between diversity and unity, freedom and authority, individuality and society, the desirable balance between which calls for sustained reflection on the available alternatives in the light of basic personal and cultural values.

8 The Distribution of Education

ATTENDING SCHOOL is only one of the many activities in which members of a society engage. While some study or teach, others must raise food or children, build houses, run machines, or write books. Some criteria, therefore, are needed for deciding which activities belong to each person. The principles for making such decisions are the basis for the ordering of social life. The customs and laws by which social arrangements are regulated define the roles which each person is expected to play in the various circumstances and stages of his life. Attendance at school is the particular role which concerns us in the present chapter.

On what basis is it decided who is to attend school? Does everybody go, or do only some go? If only some go, how are they chosen? Are students required to attend, or is formal education only an opportunity for those who desire it? For how long a period is one required or permitted to remain in school? Questions such as these are the subject of inquiry in the paragraphs below. They all involve the distribution of education, i.e., how time and persons are to be allocated to study in schools.

The schools are part of an integral complex social order. Hence, questions about the distribution of education cannot be answered on general theoretical grounds, but only in the light of the entire material, social, and cultural situation. When material goods are scarce and human energies must be directed largely toward securing a livelihood, the human and material resources for schools will be extremely limited and a far more exclusive selection criterion must be employed than would be necessary in a wealthy society. The social situation, too, is reflected in the distribution process. Thus, a society generally segregated by class or color will assign students to schools in the light of this stratification. The distribution of education is also a reflection of a society's system of values. For example, universal education is evidence that the society places a high value on every person, while education of a scientific or religious elite manifests the special value accorded knowledge or sanctity.

Actual decisions in education must always be made in the light of concrete situations with their special conditions and circumstances. A general philosophic analysis of the problem of distribution can at most suggest some of the factors which need to be examined in deciding who shall be educated and some of the guiding ideals which may appear relevant.

Three Perspectives on the Problem of Distribution

The three points of view from which the problem of distribution can be approached yield different selection criteria and are to be justified in quite different ways. They represent three distinct meanings of the question about who shall be educated.

The obligation to attend school. Since education is a means of perpetuating a society's culture, it may be necessary to require attendance at school in order to insure the desired continuity of valued traditions. The answer to the question "Who shall be educated?" is then to be formulated on the basis of social needs and goals. In this case the individual or his family does not decide whether or not he will go to school. That decision is made as part of general social policy and is enforced by the appropriate governmental machinery.

Compulsory education is based on the principle that society suffers from the ignorance and incompetence of its members and benefits from their knowledge and skill. It is further grounded in the conviction that education may not safely be left to the inclination of individuals and the accidents of private circumstance. Unless specific means are set up for propagating the culture, its treasures may easily become dissipated through the carelessness and inattention of those who take them for granted, as if they were provided by nature.

The obligation to attend school rests upon those who are regarded by the society as the essential custodians of its culture. In an aristocratic society it is the able or privileged few upon whom rests the responsibility of creating and preserving the fundamental values, and hence it is these select few who must be required to receive an education. In a democratic society, on the contrary, all citizens are held responsible for the common good, and compulsory education for everyone is therefore appropriate.

The right to attend school. Quite different from the question of obligation is that of right. Instead of society making a claim upon the individual by requiring him to be educated, the individual (or his family) from the standpoint of rights exerts a claim on society for a share of the available educational resources.

The systems of educational rights run the same gamut as those of obligation—from the right of an elite to the right of every man to go to school. But now the basis or justification of the right becomes important. While compulsory education is simply a matter of preserving the social order, the right to education may contradict the established system. Whether or not such contradiction is possible depends upon whether rights are regarded as established by society or as independently grounded. If rights are a matter of social convention, then whatever custom and law decree as valid claims for education are by definition one's rights to schooling. If it is agreed, for instance, that only males are to attend school, then only males have a right to education. If only those who can pass a specified examination are to be permitted to go to college, then this test defines the right to higher education.

If, on the other hand, right is not determined by social convention but is regarded as given by nature or by God, then the right to education may well contradict the actual decisions of society about the distribution of education. As an illustration, it can be affirmed that every person has a natural right to the maximum development of his capacities and that this implies the right to education. This principle of universality would stand as a judgment against any system of education for the few alone. However, the argument can also be turned around and claims made for elite education on the basis of presumed natural or divine law. Some have insisted that those of superior intellect or of a designated race or nation have the right to rule over inferior breeds of men and possess the right to an education which will make this rule possible.

As this illustration shows, the idea of a source of right independent of social convention does not settle the problem of what the right is. In fact, it opens the way to continuing conflicts and controversies about the right. It is the special merit of the conventionalist view to be able to settle such differences by social compromise and adjustment. The view of natural or divine right encourages the efforts of prophets and reformers, who refuse to be convinced that social agreement makes right. The right to be educated is, for them, not to be determined by society, but society should be ordered according to the system of independent rights, including that of education.

The opportunity to attend school. The distribution of education can be considered, finally, from the standpoint of opportunity. Much education is neither an obligation imposed by society nor a right to be claimed but simply an advantage to be enjoyed and appropriated by those who have the requisite interest and ability. One may wish to study music, literature, or science after or apart from the compulsory schooling, and quite beyond any claim of right to such instruction. Or, in the interests of business or professional advancement one may take courses which are neither required by society nor part of any system of educational justice but merely an opportunity to increase vocational competence.

Education as an opportunity is a concomitant of freedom. In a society which is strictly regulated the individual's life is circumscribed by law and custom and his education is largely a matter of obligation. In a society where personal and institutional independence and variety prevail, schools are established to satisfy the special demands of the able, the curious, and the ambitious. In addition to a degree of political independence, the freedom which makes such schools possible involves sufficient material support; a very poor society cannot afford the luxury of wide educational opportunity.

Universal Education

We turn now to an analysis of the major patterns which have been employed in the allocation of schooling. An idea which is dominant in most educational thought of modern times is that of universal education. According to this principle, schooling is not for the few but for everybody. This universality may be interpreted in any or all of the three ways suggested above. It may mean compulsory education for all members of society in the interest of social efficiency and unity as well as for the benefit of the individual himself (a benefit which he sometimes does not appreciate until after he has gone through the required experience). It may mean that everyone has a right to attend school, either by social enactment or by virtue of some natural or God-given insight. Or universal education may mean that for any who desire schools and are willing to pay the necessary price in effort or money, instruction is available to satisfy their needs and interests.

Interdependence. How is the ideal of universal education defended and justified? One basis for it is the fact of human interdependence. In a complex social order the good of each is bound up with the good of all. If any person is ignorant, the consequences are usually visited not only upon him but upon many others. A person who does not know the basic principles of hygiene and sanitation may not only become diseased himself, but also spread the infection to others around him. A badly trained workman by his blunders can cause costly damage to life and property. In the intricate mechanism of industrial society a single wrong turn of a lever may spell catastrophe. If the voters in a democratic election are poorly informed and incapable of intelligent choice, everyone may have to suffer from bad government. Citizens who have not learned how to govern themselves intelligently are also fair game for tyrants who will gladly take charge of their lives.

The modern demand for universal education is in no small measure a consequence of the vast increase in the complexity of civilization. In simpler cultures the adjustment of the social mechanism was not so refined as it is today. The safety and advantage of all was not so vitally dependent on the competence of each in his own task. Contemporary civilization is an intricately articulated organism the health of which can only be assured through the health of its component parts. It is the purpose of universal education to provide for this well-being of each individual and to make him aware both of the nature and needs of the whole and of his privileges and responsibilities within it.

The nature of personality. A second ground for justifying universal education is the nature of human personality. The human being is defined by the unique powers which he possesses—such as reason, imagination, artistic creativity, freedom in moral choice, and aspirations toward the infinite. It is the function of education to bring these powers to fulfillment. If they are not well developed, the individual is deprived of his full humanity. Education is not something added to an already existing human being. It is the very making of man. To withhold from anyone the chance to learn how to speak and write correctly, to employ abstractions, to make intelligent decisions, and to create things of beauty and use is to deny him the opportunity of really becoming a person.

Then the case for universal education is that since the most basic obligation and right of every individual are to be a person, everyone ought to have the education which makes that possible. Formal schooling is, of course, not the only way of educating; much takes place in the family and in the many other associations of life. But the school as a deliberate and systematic means for the pursuit of learning constitutes the appropriate way for society to recognize its universal obligation to create persons.

Contrary views. The opponents of universal education might counter the argument from interdependence by appeal to the principle of hierarchy in social organization. According to this principle, only a few people need to know the plan of the whole. Most persons need only play their minor parts by the rules laid down by higher authorities. With proper organization their functions can be made so simple that a very minimal education suffices. Hence, it is argued, modern man, as a replaceable part in a great technical machine, actually needs less education than the common man of an earlier age, who had a much greater variety of functions to fulfill.

The fundamental issues are whether in the long run society can be efficient and productive when persons are reduced to such subordinate roles and, if this is in fact the way to efficiency, whether this constriction of human function and dignity is not too high a price to pay.

The case for universal education based on the nature of personality could be attacked on one of several grounds. One could deny the assumption that everyone has a right to become fully human. If some by unfortunate circumstance do not have the advantage of an education, so much the worse for them; there are usually not enough educational resources for everyone, so some must remain less than fully human. It might also be argued that human nature is given by birth and not by education and hence that no one has to be educated to be a person. (On this point see the full discussion in Chapter 27.) It is sometimes even claimed that education tends to corrupt rather than to create or improve human nature by making one either conceited and imperious or conventional and artificial.

Thus it is clear that whether one favors or opposes universal education, the case for or against it turns upon the basic issues concerning the nature of man and his modes of association.

Educational Equality

The concept of universal education is by itself insufficient to define the distribution of education. Even if it be granted that everyone should be educated, the question remains as to what counts as "education." If everyone had a day or a year in school, the requirement of universality would be literally met. But since education does not take place in so brief a time, there would not be any true universality under such an arrangement. If only a few were to receive substantial schooling and the many only a token period, the reality of universal education would be denied despite its literal fulfillment.

In order to strengthen and make more precise the idea of universality the concept of educational equality may be introduced. Then instead of asking merely that everyone have the obligation, right, or privilege to attend school one may affirm that everyone should be equal with respect to education. Yet even superficial reflection suffices to show that the idea of educational equality is itself too ambiguous to serve as an effective principle for the allocation of schooling. What does it mean to say that everyone is to be equal in regard to school attendance? At least five meanings can be distinguished.

Time in school. All students may be required or permitted to spend the same number of years in school. There may be a series of grades, each one representing a year of attendance completed. Or there may be specified ages during which everyone must or may attend school. The chief merit of this approach to educational equality is its administrative simplicity. It suffers from the failure to take account of the fact that some people learn much faster than others and hence do not need as long to learn the same things. As a result, equality of time in school accentuates natural human inequalities. The allocation of education on the basis of equal time in school also diverts attention from the really significant qualitative aspects of learning to a false quantitative conception of education as the completion of years in school. Finally, if everyone had the same period of schooling, some might have more than they could profitably use and others too little. Thus some would be bored and frustrated by the experience, and others would fail to fulfill their personal gifts and their usefulness to society.

Level of attainment. In order to overcome the problems occasioned by natural differences, equality can be taken to mean that everyone is to go to school until he has reached a level of attainment which is the same for all. Standard tests of achievement could be set up and each person required to stay in school until he could pass them satisfactorily. This system could only work if there were a very low level of achievement, since there are some people of very modest ability, and the standard would be set so that all could attain it. If the level were extremely low, the education would not be adequate to prepare the majority of citizens in any advanced society. If it were somewhat above the minimum, the least able would have to spend long years in school at great expense to society and at the price of personal anguish, while the most able would still easily acquire the designated competence but would find no provisions made for their further development.

Another crucial objection to the achievement level concept of equality is the difficulty of defining and measuring achievement. There are many kinds of human attainment, and no one of them is in itself a measure of personal competence. One individual may excel in manual skills, a second in abstractive powers, a third in the ability to create new forms, and a fourth in human relationships. In theory, society might require competence in several such dimensions. In practice, this would be possible only if the level of each were too low to be educationally significant. A more reasonable procedure would be to educate every person to a designated level in any one of certain specified kinds of ability. To do this, however, would be in effect to abandon the principle of equality since qualitatively different abilities are strictly not comparable.

Finally, the concept of achievement level is defective for one of the same reasons as the concept of duration in school, namely, that education may not properly be evaluated on a purely quantitative basis. The growth of a human being cannot sufficiently well be summed up in numerical indices. To date, at least, testing devices are not such that studying to pass an examination is equivalent to learning to be a person.

Common curriculum. A third possible definition of equality is that all students should pursue the same course of study. They would normally complete the work at different rates, and some would do it more competently, but all would have the same curriculum. Under this plan equality means commonality of subject matter studied. Then no one can claim superiority over another because, for example, he has had the "academic" rather than the "commercial" or "vocational" course. All students would be given instruction in what every member of society should know.

This type of educational equality does contribute to the unity of society by providing a core of knowledge and experience common to all. It creates and preserves the awareness of a common tradition and establishes community in language and idea. Its limitation lies in the fact that individual abilities, interests, and needs differ so much that the common curriculum can at best constitute only a part of an adequate school program. Hence if individual differences are to be provided for, either the demand for equality must be given up or a still different meaning be assigned to it. In addition, not only do individual educational demands vary widely, but society requires many different kinds of ability, which can be developed best through different courses of study. Thus from a social as well as from a personal standpoint it appears necessary to transcend the equality of a common course of study.

Attendance at the same schools. To overcome the foregoing problems, equality may be taken to mean that everyone attends the same schools. Within the same school individual differences can be provided for, the many sorts of competences required in a complex society can be developed with a degree of independence, and all these separate paths can be integrated into one comprehensive community of learning. This conception of equality excludes special schools for the elite, with their attendant temptations toward snobbery and false pride.

Like the common curriculum, the school meant for all fosters social unity but in a more profound way, in that it is founded on the unities which underlie and are enriched by differences. The school becomes the training ground for membership in a democratic society where contrasts of ability and function are gathered up within the fundamental equality of citizens who recognize the mutuality of need and the duty and privilege of respect for one another.

Yet this definition of equality, like the previous ones, has evident limitations. Is the presence of students in the same school buildings really a significant kind of equality? Different courses of study within the same school may generate cleavages as sharp as or sharper than those between students in separate schools. Physical proximity does not necessarily create mutual understanding and appreciation. There are also special difficulties in teaching and administration in schools which must provide for a wide range of students and curricula. Separate schools for considerably different courses of study may be much more effective and economical. Finally, any requirement that all must attend the same schools denies the freedom of individuals and families to decide how and where education shall take place and threatens to subject everyone to the domination of the social group, and ultimately to control by the state.

Equal opportunity. Is it possible, then, to define educational equality in such a way as to respect individuality and freedom? The answer would seem to lie in the concept of equal educational opportunity. This means that for those who desire and are able to profit from instruction, schools should be equally available to all. By this definition the fundamental equality is the freedom to choose what will be studied and to develop one's powers as fully as possible.

The problem is how to conceive of this freedom so that the enhancement of individual powers is at the same time for the common good. Otherwise opportunity for one means privation for some other, and this negates equality. For example, assignment to school on the basis of a system of competitive examinations, open to all, may appear to constitute equal opportunity, but it does not in fact do so if the winners gain at the expense of the losers. Equal opportunity means the distribution of schooling in such a way that the interests of each are served to the maximum, consistent with the equal claims of others. This general principle is not easy to apply in practice because different interests are not truly comparable and thus no definite meaning can be attached to their equality.

Perhaps equality of educational opportunity in the last analysis means simply that the distribution of education shall be determined through discussion and agreement within the democratic community, where each person has the same right of voice and vote and the same standing before the law.

Factors Affecting the Actual Distribution of Education

While the ideal, and to some extent the practice, of universality and equality in the distribution of education are important features of the modern scene, there are several other factors which actually enter into the determination of who goes to school. For the most part these factors reflect and perpetuate various social or personal inequalities. In the past and at present there are many people who do not believe in educational equality and who seek to justify the inequalities based on one or more of these factors. Others believe in the value of equality and are conscious that it is to be achieved only by taking due account of these individual and group disparities and welding them into some satisfactory scheme of mutual adjustment.

Privilege Factors

There are certain differences between people which profoundly affect the privileges which they enjoy in the social order. By circumstances of birth or fortune or by personal endeavor each individual has endowments which greatly affect the attitudes and actions of other people toward him and which govern the advantages he enjoys. These privilege factors may determine in large part the allocation of schooling.

When the distribution of education is governed by privilege, the effect is generally to perpetuate the existing social order and to harden and confirm the privilege arrangements. This would only fail to be true in the most exceptional event that the education received on the privilege basis was itself dedicated to the alteration of the privilege system. Almost invariably educational programs are designed to confirm the social order that creates and supports them.

Four important privilege factors affecting the distribution of education will now be discussed.

Wealth. Usually those who have ample economic resources can afford more and better education than people with modest means. Money establishes a claim on the total store of society's goods and services, including educational facilities, and the more money one has the larger the share he can claim. Education is one of the means of acquiring the ability and the prestige which underlie economic success. Therefore, those who have wealth can secure for themselves and their families educational advantages which will make possible further economic gain, while those who are poor cannot afford the education which might help them to improve their financial condition. In this way the distribution of education on the basis of wealth tends to confirm the economic stratification of society.

Those who possess wealth frequently seek to justify their favorable position on the basis of superiority of effort, ability, or importance to society, and these are sometimes valid claims. Yet there are obvious inequities in an economic system which tends to perpetuate itself and to determine its benefits so largely by accident of birth. Hence a society dedicated to equality seeks by various means to overcome these injustices. With respect to education four principal ways of economic equalization are available.

One method is by the general social control, limitation, and redistribution of wealth. Largely by means of its taxing power the government can effect more equitable economic allocation. Salaries, wages and prices can be controlled. The less privileged can exert pressure for equalization of benefits through non-governmental agencies such as labor unions. The result of these general social controls is to reduce the inequality in funds available for education.

The second method is private philanthropy, whereby the well-to-do help the less able voluntarily rather then by compulsion. The endowments of schools and colleges and the many programs of privately supported scholarships illustrate this approach. Private philanthropy has the advantage of preserving individual freedom of enterprise and of encouraging the spirit of generosity. However, it leaves the unjust and ungenerous untouched and has proven in practice too limited in scope to solve the general problem of economic redistribution.

A third alternative would be to limit the education anyone could have, regardless of how much he could afford. This would constitute a serious restriction by the state on personal freedom and would be difficult, if not impossible, to put into effect since one could almost always hire tutors to give the desired instruction.

The fourth method is to use public funds to subsidize schools which are open to all regardless of financial ability or to provide scholarships for students who would otherwise be unable to afford an education. This method presupposes also the application of the first method above, since public funds for education must be obtained by taxation. The merits of this way are that the connection between the just distribution of wealth and the equitable distribution of education is recognized and that additional or alternative educational advantages beyond the public provision may be bought by those who can still afford them, thus permitting some freedom of private initiative.

Social class. A second set of privilege factors are included in the term "social class." Class refers to the levels of prestige which the members of a society consciously or unconsciously acknowledge. There are a number of possible bases for such classification. Wealth may be one. Ancestry is another. Occupation is a third. Any specifiable difference between people can become the basis for granting or withholding prestige. It should be noted that although wealth may determine social class it does not necessarily do so. There are cultural patterns where material possessions have little bearing on prestige, or at least far less relevance than other factors.

Social class provides a possible criterion for distributing education. In general, the upper classes have the better educational opportunities. But societies differ in the nature of the classes regarded as superior. In the traditional aristocratic society it is the children of "blue bloods" or of the large property holders who have the best school privileges. In Communist society, on the contrary, it is the children of industrial workers who in principle are to have the maximum educational opportunity. Again, in the theocratic community the major educational privileges are usually granted to the priestly class.

As suggested earlier, the result of distributing education by social class is to solidify and maintain class distinctions. This might only be justified on the grounds of social stability, but such a static condition would usually suit only those who have the privileges. Equalizing educational opportunity has the effect of breaking down rigid class distinctions by enabling members in lower-class groups to improve their condition. While education does not automatically raise one's class level, universal education does serve as a powerful factor in upward social mobility. Thus, a society with widely distributed educational benefits is likely to be far more dynamic in its social arrangements than one with class-determined schools.

Race. In some societies race is an important factor in the allocation of schooling. It is not possible to state simply and accurately what "race" means as it is popularly used in making educational distinctions. The commonest criterion cited is skin color. Other physical features, such as type of hair, shape of nose, or set of eyes may also be appealed to as indices of race. Manners and customs, or even place of birth, are sometimes taken as further signs of racial type. In whatever way race is specified, it can become the basis for discriminating between one group of people and another. Those with the "right" skin color, for example, are given better educational advantages than those of the "wrong" color.

There are two principal kinds of arguments used by the proponents of distributing education by race. The first affirms the superiority of one racial group over another and the corresponding right of privilege and power over the inferior races. Thus, it is said that the favored race is intelligent, while the others are stupid, or that the one is kind, while the others are vicious. Regarding this type of argument it is chiefly necessary to point out that scientific evidence does not in any way confirm the alleged relationship between so-called racial characteristics and such qualities as basic intelligence and innate tendencies toward constructive social behavior. The supposed facts upon which claims to racial superiority and inferiority are based have been unconfirmed by controlled and critical inquiry.

Individuals do differ widely from one another in such respects as temperament, imaginative power, manual dexterity, and habitual behavior patterns. These differences result from both genetic factors and environmental influences. The basic point is that according to clear scientific evidence the racist incorrectly attributes the personality characteristics which he likes (such as good manners) or which he does not like (such as ignorance) to the "racial" factor (e.g., skin color). In fact, significant personal qualities are a consequence of certain gene combinations having no demonstrable connection with superficial "racial" features and of environmental influences. Hence, if certain groups in a society designated by skin color or other superficial indices are actually found to be inferior in character or intellectual attainments, this must be a result of unfavorable environment and not of race. To discriminate against the members of the group in educational opportunity only completes the vicious circle of indignity.

Modern knowledge of how personality develops ought to lead to improvement in the opportunities of those who as a result of racial prejudice have been thought inferior by nature rather than by want of proper nurture. To the extent that such prejudice does not yield to the fuller knowledge, it becomes clear that distinctions based on race are simply a way for the dominant group to maintain its power and privilege as over against the subject group. In the light of the known facts, such distinctions have no justification except that of sheer power to maintain the existing order of things unchanged.

Even if the racist could demonstrate the superiority he claims, it would not necessarily follow that his group should receive the greater share of educational and other advantages. Perhaps with better logic it could be argued that the need of the inferior is greater; therefore, they ought to have more schooling than the members of the superior race. The racist's reply to this would be that one of the marks of inferior races is that they respond poorly to education, while the superior ones profit greatly from it. There is, of course, no basis in fact for such a claim. It is simply another device for rationalizing the dominance of one group over others.

The second type of argument put forth by the advocates of race allocation in education is that the races should be kept separate. In reality this is a variant of the superiority argument. The races should be kept separate, it is said, because their mixture in education would lead to interbreeding and mongrelization, and this would corrupt the blood of the superior race with that of the inferior. In order that civilization may be kept on a high plane the purity of the superior race must be maintained. It is argued that this is essential even for the welfare of the lower races, who depend on the superior ones for leadership.

It is also claimed that mixing of the races tends to produce destructive differences through conflict in attitudes and natural modes of behavior. Therefore, it is better for the sake of harmony and consistency to educate members of each group with their own kind.

It has yet to be shown that having people of different race go to school together necessarily increases the rate of intermarriage. In any event that is not the crucial point. The real issue concerns the pure blood concept of the superior race. In the first place, race, defined in any of the popular ways, has no relation whatsoever to blood. The science of genetics has made it plain that inherited personality characteristics are determined by the genes. In the second place, there is no such thing as a "pure" race. Every person has genes from a wide assortment of forebears. Each person is genetically what he is by virtue of the particular and largely chance combination of genes which he has received drawn from the vast and variegated "gene pool" of all humanity. At most, certain groups may be racially classified by reference to the statistical predominance of certain physical traits. Thirdly, as pointed out earlier, there is no warrant in fact for the inherent superiority or inferiority of persons with designated "racial" characteristics.

Separation in the interests of harmony is equally difficult to justify. People with similar physical or cultural characteristics can conflict just as bitterly as those with different qualities. Differences may well be an educational asset, providing an opportunity for richer and more varied experiences than are possible in a homogeneous school. Since education is also an important means of developing common cultural values and behavior patterns, the maintenance of schools assigned by race merely serves to emphasize cultural separation and estrangement and to hinder the foundation of a true community.

Sex. A fourth privilege factor is sex. In most societies males are given an advantage over females in the distribution of education. Attempts by the favored males to justify their privilege on the basis of inherent superiority can easily be refuted on factual grounds. In some respects the female is, on the average, somewhat weaker than the male, while in other respects she is stronger. There is no warrant for any claim of male superiority which would be educationally relevant.

The only tenable basis for sex differentiation in education appears to be that of social or biological function. Society may be organized in such a way that males are expected to assume leadership in business, government, scholarship, science, and the arts, in preparation for which considerable formal education is required, while females are expected to serve in the home, in subordinate and less highly skilled positions in business and professional life, and in fewer occupations demanding long educational preparation.

But why this distinction of function? Any satisfactory answer must ultimately lie in the biological and social factors surrounding the bearing and rearing of children. Here the issue is clearly drawn. On the one side are the extreme champions of equality who point out that childbearing is not incompatible with active and practically continuous pursuit of nearly any occupation and that part or all of the care of the child, once born, can be entrusted to others, including the father. Consequently, females should receive exactly the same educational advantages as males, all occupations should be equally open to both sexes, and both sexes should take responsibility for the rearing of the young.

On the other side are those who believe that the difference between male and female is not merely one of explicit biological function in childbearing but is even more fundamental with respect to the raising of the child and the maintenance of the home. The effort to gain complete equality for the female, it is claimed, has undermined the family by luring women out of the homes where they rightfully belong into competition with males in the affairs of business and profession. Children have been made insecure by the threat or fact of losing their mothers' care. Women themselves have become unsettled by the loss of a clear and unquestioned claim on them. Those who have received advanced education and who then establish homes become restless with the routines of the home or feel guilty in not putting to better use their academic preparation.

The question of equality of the sexes, including educational opportunities, involves the very foundations of the social order. What needs to be decided —and there is at present no conclusive answer—is whether an enduring and productive social system could be devised where for all functions except that of procreation male and female would be interchangeable, or whether the development of human personality in the family is such as to require a much greater differentiation of function between the sexes. Are there distinctive functions which by nature are appropriate for females, and if so, what do they entail as to educational opportunities?

What does seem clear is that allocation of schooling by sex cannot be justified on the basis of mere privilege, but only with respect to function. Once the proper difference in function has been specified, it then is in order to ask how the nature of the schooling for females should differ from that for males.

Ability Factors

Privilege factors such as those discussed in the preceding paragraphs are alike in being extrinsic to the educative process itself. There is nothing about having money, or belonging to a certain social class, or being of specified race or sex which has any bearing on the quality or rate of learning, despite what proponents of school allocation by privilege may affirm. A second group of factors entering into the distribution of education are directly relevant to the educative process itself. These factors have to do with individual differences of ability. All persons are not created equal in respect to inherited personal endowments. The problem is to decide how different individual capacities are to affect the distribution of education.

Education in proportion to ability. One position is that educational opportunity should be made available in proportion to ability. Since each should be given the schooling needed to develop his talents, the gifted should receive greater educational opportunities than those of modest ability. This view rests upon the fundamental assumption that human life is good and that it is better to actualize potentialities than to allow them to remain only as possibilities. This reflects an essentially optimistic and affirmative attitude toward existence, according to which it is better to be than not to be and better to use powers than to neglect them.

Education to minimize differences. The opposition contend that educational advantage in proportion to ability only serves to increase the disparity between persons and that the proper system is to grant educational opportunities in inverse proportion to ability, with the aim of minimizing differences. This view presupposes the primacy of equality as a social value over the individual value of self-realization. Implicit in it also is a radical qualification of the earlier assumption that the actualizing of powers is good in itself. Goodness depends on how the powers are used in relation to other persons, and there is in this view the pessimistic presumption that those with the greater powers will tend to use them to the disadvantage of the less gifted. Hence, according to this position, it is better to suffer from educational inefficiency due to investing the most educational resources where the rate of return is least than to risk the loss of freedom and dignity for the many resulting from giving larger advantages to the most able few.

A moderate view. Between these extreme positions is the moderate view that educational opportunity should be so distributed as to assure everyone a certain minimum education and to permit persons of unusual competence to develop their abilities further than this minimum. In addition, provision should be made for systems of social control which would prevent the most able from using their superior powers to the disadvantage of the less able. This would mean that political power, including ultimate authority in education, should not be vested in an elite of especially competent people but in all the citizens. This wide distribution of political power is another reason for providing certain basic educational opportunities for all. If the able elite are given political control, including responsibility for allocating education, not only is there the danger that they will use their power for their own benefit but that selection based on ability will be transformed into selection based on privilege.

The meaning of "ability." The use of ability factors in deciding who shall be educated presents the difficult problem of defining and measuring ability. "Ability" refers to any power of accomplishment or any potentiality of becoming. What is accomplished or become needs to be specified. Abilities are of many kinds. Ability in one respect does not necessarily indicate ability in any other respect for one and the same person. The problem in distributing educational opportunity on the basis of ability is then to decide what kind of ability is to be sought and developed. The choice will depend upon the dominant values of those who are empowered to make the choice.

When education of the gifted is discussed, ability is generally understood as intellectual competence. This usually includes ability to employ abstractions, to use language correctly, to reason logically, to see relationships, and to do these things with comparative rapidity. These abilities can be determined with reasonable adequacy by a variety of psychological tests. When the intellectual elite ("academic" people) are entrusted with selecting the ones to be given further schooling, they will normally seek to reproduce their kind, by favoring those with high intellectual ability.

But there are other kinds of ability which other people may decide are more important than intellectual competence as revealed by the intelligence tests. Moral competence, the ability to choose wisely, is a second and perhaps far more valuable kind. Ability to make friends and to cooperate in undertakings with other people is a third kind, while esthetic sensitivity is a fourth. Managerial ability—leadership potential—is still another. These other abilities are not easily measured nor accurately defined, yet they may be far more relevant to the health of society than intelligence alone.

These varied meanings of ability are cited in order to underline the danger of selecting a single easily measured factor, of special interest to a group who themselves have more than average strength in this respect, and utilizing it as the chief basis for distributing educational advantages.

Pertinent in this connection is the question of what abilities the school as an institution is in a position to develop. If by its very nature the school chiefly serves intellectual purposes—as many would affirm—then allocation of schooling on the basis of intelligence would be justified. If moral, social, esthetic, and leadership capacities can also be significantly nurtured in the school, then distribution of school opportunities in the light of these other ability factors may be justified.

Functional Factors

There is a third set of factors, different both from those of privilege and of ability, which enter into the determination of who shall be educated. Privilege involves social or individual factors extrinsic to the educational process. Ability is concerned with individual factors intrinsic to the educational process. The third type, the functional, has to do with social factors intrinsic to the educational process. A complex society depends upon the contributions of many different kinds of workers, some of whom require longer and more intensive educational preparation than others. A research chemist or a lawyer, for example, must ordinarily have more school preparation for his job than a sales clerk or a housewife.

There may, of course, be a relationship between function and ability or privilege. It can be decided that persons with the highest aptitude for a given type of activity should receive the opportunity to prepare for it, or that occupations are to be assigned on the basis of wealth, class, race, or sex, and schooling provided accordingly. But such a relationship of factors is not inevitable. Frequently it is chance circumstance or individual interest rather than privilege or ability which determine the part one plays in the social scheme. The essential point, in any case, is not how persons are chosen for the various social roles but how these roles by their differing requirements impose certain inequalities in the distribution of educational resources. From the functional standpoint these inequalities are not inequitable or unjust. They are simply necessary for the effective operation of society, in the light of the organic principle of specialization and differentiation.

The idea of functional allocation throws light on one special distribution problem scarcely mentioned hitherto, namely, that of assignment to school by age. It is often taken for granted that school is for the young and that mature people, while they may continue to learn in informal ways, have put away childish things, including school. As a result, a common answer to the question, "Who shall be educated?" has been "all or certain children between the ages of x and y." From the point of view of functional needs such distribution by age can hardly be justified. There are lessons to be learned at every stage of life, and some things cannot be learned as effectively during childhood as later. Experience has shown that many young people would profit far more from having full-time or part-time jobs than from spending all their time in school and that formal education is often most meaningful to mature people who may have had children of their own, engaged in military service, and worked for some years at an occupation. Furthermore, the continued usefulness of workers in fields where rapid changes are taking place can often best be assured by periodically or continuously sending them to school for instruction in the new developments.

Thus, attention to functional factors suggests a thorough consideration of the effective relation of school to social role, and in particular indicates the need for a flexible system in which education is available at any age, on a full-time or part-time basis, to those who can make good use of it. Needless to say, this kind of program raises important issues regarding the nature of the school as a social institution, the content of the curriculum, and the manner of control and support of education.

9

Education as a Profession

ORGANIZED EDUCATION in modern industrial society is a vast and influential enterprise. Schools, colleges, and universities are prominent among the enduring institutions of society. A considerable segment of the population is engaged in study at these institutions, and a great many people serve in them as teachers and administrators. In an undertaking as extensive and socially significant as organized education, it is expedient that careful thought be given to the position and conditions of work of those who are educators by occupation, for it is they upon whom rests the main responsibility for the effectiveness of the whole educational effort. The purpose of this chapter is to examine reflectively some of the problems connected with this occupational group.

Professional Education

A class of workers who have become self-conscious about their function in society frequently aspire to become a "profession." As the educational enterprise has grown and as educators have become more aware of their social roles, the idea of professional education has grown in favor among them. Many leaders in education have fought for increasing professionalization of teachers and administrators in the belief that along that path lies not only improvement in the position of educators themselves but also in the quality of education provided by the schools.

Are or ought educators to be professionals? To answer that question it is necessary to define what a profession is and then to see if the work of the educator fits the definition. The major characteristics of a profession will now be suggested, and the applicability of these to educational workers will be analyzed.

Special Competence

A professional, first of all, is one who possesses some special competence. He knows things which most other people do not know, or he has skills which the average person does not have. A profession in this respect is an exclusive society. There is an inner circle of initiates who understand the mysteries and who are distinguished thereby from the rest of mankind, to whom this understanding does not belong. Part of the attraction of belonging to a profession is that the members have a sense of superiority, of possessing insights which are reserved for the select few. The professional resists the claims of outsiders to understand or practice his occupation, and he is generally not eager to disseminate his special knowledge so that it becomes common property. He does not wish to give outsiders grounds for making judgments about his work or a basis for dispensing with his services altogether.

Educators as non-specialists. Is the educator a professional, according to this first and most basic criterion? Does he have special, distinctive knowledge and skill which the average person does not possess? On this question convictions differ sharply. According to one view, the educator, as such, needs no special competence. Anyone can teach, it is said. The educator cannot claim any unique skills or qualifications which the average intelligent person does not have. Of course, the educator may need to be a professional in some other respect. For example, a teacher of law would ordinarily have to belong to the legal profession, and a school psychologist would normally need to be a professional in the field of psychology, but in neither case (according to the view under discussion) would these people be professional *educators;* they would merely be other kinds of professionals who happened to practice their professions in a school setting.

The assumption upon which this non-professional view of education is based is that education is a "natural" process, requiring nothing more than common sense and competence for normal human association. Reading is taught by having a person who can read associate with those who cannot. The non-readers will learn from the reader by observing him and by getting help from him where necessary. Education in the school is no different in kind from education in the home. Everybody knows that the child learns naturally from parents and siblings simply by daily association with these others who are more mature. Parents do not ordinarily claim to be professionals so why should school teachers claim to be?

Educators as specialists. The opposed position affirms that special knowledge and skill are required to be a good educator. It is pointed out that education does not take place naturally, but by deliberate design. Simple association and common sense are not sufficient for good teaching. The best conditions for learning are not matters of common knowledge, and the average person has had neither the time nor the skilled guidance necessary to master the arts of instruction. Some learning usually does occur when the beginner observes the expert, but this approach is limited in application and is generally far less efficient than other methods which the professional understands.

Consequences for the preparation of educators. These contrasting views have quite different consequences for the preparation of educators. On the basis of the first position, it is only necessary that the one who educates understand and practice well what he wants to teach others. That is, he should himself be a well-educated person, exemplifying in his own person what he expects his students to become. A teacher of history must know history, a teacher of religion should be religious, and a teacher of religious knowledge ought to know about religion. In short, each must be a master of the "subject matter" which he wishes to teach. Similarly, according to this position, the school administrator need only be an expert general administrator.

On the basis of the second, or specialist, position, the educator must not only himself be well educated in what he is expected to teach, but he also should undergo professional preparation to give him special competence in instruction. He needs technical understanding about how learning takes place, about the most efficient ways of organizing the materials of instruction, and about the processes of communicating ideas and facilitating the development of skills. Broadly speaking, this is the field of educational technique or method.

It should be noted that the conflict is not in principle between preparing teachers in subject-matter competence *or* methods competence but between the position that subject-matter preparation alone is necessary and that preparation in the methods of instruction is also needed. In practice, a conflict of subject-centered *versus* method-centered teacher-preparation does occur because the limited time available for this preparation has to be apportioned between these two emphases. Those who believe the educator is not a professional generally think that "education" courses are empty and deadening and that time spent in them to that extent deprives the prospective educator of the real understanding he needs if he is to teach his subject effectively.

Underlying the view of those who deny the need for any special educational competence is the assumption that the teaching-learning process consists simply of the duplication of the instructor's knowledge in the student. The supporter of professional education takes a much broader view of this process. He regards the student as an active, creative agent who utilizes whatever is presented in his environment as material and occasion for his personal growth, in ways which may be quite different from simple repetition of the teacher's states of being. Hence the teacher needs special knowledge of the probable effects of different kinds of school environment upon the development of students and of the variations to be expected because of the individual characteristics of different students.

If one simply teaches what he has himself learned, as the deniers of professionalism in education say, it is clear that they object to the study of "education" as a subject in teacher preparation because they do not want the teacher to teach "education" but mathematics, spelling, social studies, or stenography. Some anti-educationists think, for example, that many teachers put too much emphasis on the *manner* in which students present reports and make displays and too little on the content of learning. The explanation suggested is that in doing this the teachers are naturally but inappropriately transmitting the concern for method (rather than content) learned in their professional "education" courses. On the other hand, those who take the professional view are convinced that teachers can and do utilize their special professional knowledge to help the student learn what he needs to know, which may be and usually is something quite other than the professional knowledge itself.

Implicit in this controversy also are contrasting conceptions of knowledge. The anti-professional tends to think of knowledge as a definite self-subsistent body of intelligible material available for transmission and appropriation. The advocate of professionalism, on the other hand, tends to be concerned more with knowing as a process, and believes that the *manner* of teaching and learning is inseparable from its *matter*. Thus he is likely to reject the separation of courses for educators into "subject-matter" and "methods" types, on the premise that the content of knowledge is inseparable from the methods of acquiring it.

Validating the professional claim. The claim of educators to possess special competence can be justified in the long run only by actually developing a stable, well-tested, generally accepted body of educational knowledge and techniques. The results of professional leadership also need to be demonstrated in actual school practice as substantially superior to those achieved by persons without this special competence.

Those who take the professional position presuppose that good educators are in part made, not born, and that specific and reliable steps can be taken to prepare persons for effective educational work. They assume that teaching does not succeed solely by inspiration, but in considerable part because the teacher has acquired and deliberately uses the necessary tools for doing his job well.

Theoretical Insight

Special competence alone does not make one a professional. There are skilled craftsmen who possess specific and unusual manual abilities, yet who are not properly designated thereby as members of a profession. This is because a second mark of a profession is theoretical insight. By this is meant a rational understanding of the how and why of one's special ways of functioning. A skilled mechanic may know how to construct or repair a machine by reference to an instruction book or as a result of previous explanation of the proper procedures, and he may do the job well without having any understanding of why he takes the steps he does. The professional engineer, on the other hand, has to know not only what to do to build or service the machine but also the relevant principles of physics upon which these procedures are based. The skilled mechanic, without this theoretical insight, would not be able to invent the machine in the first place, nor to prepare the instruction book, nor even perhaps to deal with exceptional problems of maintenance and repair. His competence is routine. He functions in his trade by habit and rule of thumb. The professional transcends routine by understanding the rationale on which habitual routines and rules are based.

Similarly, medicine is a profession not simply because the physician knows what to do when confronted with specific symptoms in a patient, but because he also has a broad understanding of human biology which helps to guide him in diagnosis and therapy. The lawyer is professional not only because he knows the provisions of the law, but because he also understands such matters as the sources of law, the principles of interpretation, and the rules of evidence.

Theory in education. Applying the test of theoretical insight to education, it follows that an educator who merely knows how to teach or to administer the school but has no rationale for his procedures practices a craft rather than a profession. A teacher may know "tricks of the trade" which enable him to achieve certain desired results with great effectiveness, yet have no idea of how or why they succeed. The professional educator not only has the ability to teach, but also has a broad understanding of such matters as the nature of human personality, learning theory, educational values, conditions of effective communication, and the influence of social environment on personal growth, as well as a thorough grasp of the fundamental ideas and theoretical structure of what is being taught. A teacher is not professional simply by virtue of knowing certain methods of instruction or of curriculum construction. An administrator is not professional merel because he has learned the techniques of selecting staff, raising budget: and securing adequate buildings. The professional educator has to know the basic facts and assumptions on which the successful methods and approved rules are grounded.

Why does the professional need theoretical insight? Is it solely for the intellectual satisfaction of more comprehensive understanding? No, it is necessary also on strictly practical grounds. Routine skills are static and rigid. They do not provide any basis for improvement nor for dealing with exceptional cases and new conditions. Dynamic and flexible practice is possible only when the guiding theoretical framework is comprehensive enough to include unusual and novel circumstances and to suggest promising avenues for experimentation. The educator who has merely learned to follow the rules is lost in cases where there are no rules or where they give the wrong results. Only the professional who has sufficient theoretical understanding to modify old procedures and create new ones is in a position to turn such emergencies into opportunities rather than failures.

Consequences for the preparation of educators. It follows from what has been said that professional preparation for educators cannot be concerned merely with instruction in techniques of teaching and administration. It has to include also studies which provide fundamental theoretical grounding in the educational process. Of particular importance is knowledge of educational psychology, of the major social and cultural factors in education, and of historical, philosophical, and comparative perspectives on education. Adding these requirements to those suggested in the previous section, the essential preparation of the professional teacher will be seen to include the following three components: (1) mastery of the subject to be taught (with considerable breadth of knowledge in this field), some experience of penetrating analysis in it, and ability to relate it intelligently to other areas of thought and action; (2) development of competence in the organization of teaching materials and learning experiences, development of skill in communicating ideas, and development of ability to excite in the student the desire to learn; and (3) understanding of the fundamental theoretical and factual structure upon which educational practice is based and by which its improvement is directed.

Can education be scientific? The requirement of theoretical insight presupposes that to some degree education can be scientific. Science is concerned with the development of systematic explanations of phenomena, and a scientific understanding of any field of human endeavor means that a theoretical rationale of some precision is available to justify it. One of the grounds on which critics of professional education deny its professional status is their claim that with all the talk of research and with all the technical jargon, education still cannot boast the name of science. Its facts are too uncertain and its hypotheses too imprecise or untestable to warrant such designation. Education, these critics say, is an art, and those who practice it successfully can never give a sufficient explanation for their accomplishment.

In reply to this objection it can be said, first, that while educational theory has not reached and probably never will reach the stage of precision of the physical sciences, and while there are undoubtedly those who make premature and unwarranted claims for educational research, still there are bodies of fairly reliable knowledge and consistent theory which underlie and guide intelligent educational practice. Furthermore, education shares with the other professions and fields of inquiry concerned with human problems the special difficulties and limitations resulting from the fact of man's freedom and the extreme complexity of man and his culture. Education can be as scientific as law, politics, or even medicine in some of its aspects (e.g., psychotherapy). And certainly it has a claim to scientific status far easier to establish than has the ministry. Probably in some sense education, like medicine or the ministry, should be considered as an art. This does not exclude attention to the systematic foundations for the successful practice of the art. The good artist does not depend solely upon the inspiration of the moment. He has reasons for what he does, and he is probably a better artist for becoming aware of them.

Certification

Special competence and theoretical insight alone do not make a professional. There must also be some means of determining who is qualified to practice the profession and appropriate ways of giving social recognition to professional status. One belongs to a profession not solely because he so desires nor because he has attained the necessary technical mastery, but also because he has been certified as a member of the profession by a duly authorized agency.

Certification may be granted by either one or both of two kinds of agencies. The first kind is governmental and reflects the public interest in insuring professional competence. If anyone might at will represent himself as a professional, assuming the responsibilities and claiming the privileges of that position, it would be easy for unqualified persons to engage in practice, to the possibly serious detriment of individuals or of society. To give protection against such false representations it is usual to require anyone who practices a profession, offering his services as a qualified expert, to present evidence of his attainments satisfactory to a designated public agency and to receive authorization from that agency to practice.

The other kind of certifying body represents not the public but the organized profession itself. It is not only the public that suffers when unqualified people practice a profession, but the qualified practitioners also pay a price in loss of prestige and decline of public confidence. Hence, it is essential that admission to professional standing be subject to determination of the applicant's fitness by the professional body itself. As a matter of fact, only professionals themselves are competent to judge the attainments of any person in their field. For this reason it seems evident that governmental certification agencies should always be in the hands of professionals, and preferably in close working relationship with the certification agencies of the professional organizations.

The physician can practice medicine only when properly licenced by the state, after having satisfactorily completed a course of study in an approved medical school and having served a designated period of internship. The practitioner of law must be admitted to the bar, having passed the necessary written examinations. The clergyman may perform all the functions of the minister's office only when he has been examined by the appointed ecclesiastical agency, and he may perform a rite of concern to the state, such as marriage, only when licenced by the designated governmental agency.

Certification of educators. Similarly, the state may require anyone who wishes to teach to present evidence of competence and to be licenced to practice the profession. In the United States state certification is required only of those who teach in public schools. There is no official test of individual qualifications for those who serve in private schools. Under these conditions it is clear that certification is simply an aspect of public control of public schools and not primarily a recognition of the educator's professional status.

Even if certification is required, the problem remains of finding appropriate means of measuring educational competence. The ideal way of determining the educator's ability would seem to be to give him a probationary job in the school and to observe the results of his work. This would seldom be practicable, and it would have the further crucial defect that the results of teaching are in many ways so subtle and so slow to come to light that a fair evaluation of the teacher's work would be a matter of extreme difficulty. Certainly more economical and probably far more valid would be carefully constructed psychological tests of intelligence, aptitude, and attitude, evaluated by reference to the results obtained in giving the same tests to persons who have proved in the long run to be outstanding teachers, as indicated by testimony of colleagues and students.

A simple and widely used standard of professional achievement is the satisfactory completion of certain designated courses in education. In effect, this places the burden of evaluation on the teachers of education courses rather than on the certifying agency itself. Since these instructors are in a sense professionals among the professionals, they might perhaps well be trusted to pass judgment on prospective members of their guild. This is on the disputed assumption that the education courses do deal with matters of real and necessary special knowledge and skill. It needs still further to be demonstrated that ability to succeed in a course of study in education is reliable evidence of ability as a practicing educator. On the whole it appears doubtful that completion of courses in education should be the exclusive basis for professional certification.

Not only is certification of educators by public agencies as currently practiced in the United States incomplete and of questionable validity, but the educators themselves have failed to establish standards for defining professional status. Many other professional groups have standard procedures for determining qualifications and admitting to membership. Such professional self-determination is in general not practiced by educators.

However, there is one important indirect means of setting professional standards which should be noted. That is the practice of accreditation of educational institutions. Government education authorities establish certain minimum requirements concerning teachers, curriculum, and facilities, for all schools, public and private, to insure the safety and fundamental welfare of the students, and these requirements are enforced through periodic inspections and reports. In addition, schools and colleges form associations devoted to the cooperative exploration of common problems and the pursuit of common interests. They also determine criteria for membership in the associations. These criteria are concerned chiefly with the quality and the adequacy of preparation of the teachers, the nature of the curriculum offered, and administrative policies and practices. These matters are evaluated by special committees of the associations who visit and study evidence submitted by the institutions seeking admission. Since the standing of an institution among educators and the public alike is considerably affected by its association accreditations, such organizations serve to some extent to create and maintain minimum professional standards.

Apart from the indirect effects of institutional accreditation and the questionable procedures for certifying public school teachers, there are no generally recognized social means for determining who is a qualified teacher. This is in contrast with the situation in such occupations as medicine or law. In this respect education falls short of professional standing, assuming that definite and generally applied standards of certification are an essential mark of any profession.

It may be suggested that improvement in the professional qualifications of educators can best be achieved in three directions. First, and probably most important, is the maintenance of high standards of scholarship and teaching in the colleges and universities which prepare teachers and other school personnel. Second, there might well be an internship requirement for every certified educator and also an extensive program of continuing advanced in-service study. Third, a system of examinations for professional qualification, similar to the bar examinations in law, might be established.

Vocation

A fourth characteristic of a profession is that its members engage in it as a gainful occupation—as a life work or vocation. This is the main difference between a professional and an amateur. There are persons with great special competence in a special field who engage in its activities solely for the personal satisfactions it affords and not as a means of livelihood. The professional, on the other hand, engages in his special work expecting and claiming commensurate economic rewards. He does not consider his activity as recreation, as does the amateur, but as gainful work. The social recognition of the professional as a person with special qualifications for rendering useful services ideally entails also the allocation of economic benefits in proportion to the social value of the work done.

The professional performs his special functions regularly and continuously as his daily work, while the amateur does so only as time from other more essential occupations becomes available and as the inclinations of the moment suggest. The professional may also be considered to some degree as having an obligation to society to serve in his field of particular competence, while the amateur has no such responsibility.

As a vocation, a profession is more than merely a paying job. A vocation is a calling, a work with which one becomes personally identified and in which the purpose of his life is in large part fulfilled. A "mere job" is separable from the man who does it; it does not constitute a major source of meaning for his existence. In the vocation, on the other hand, the person and his work become one. The work is the expression of the whole person, and requirements of the task govern the development of the person. This presupposes in the professional a considerable degree of dedication to his vocation and a sense that the significance of his life is to be found in faithful fulfillment of it.

Education as a vocation. How does the educator measure up with respect to this fourth characteristic of a profession? Certainly education is a gainful occupation. Teachers do expect monetary recompense for services rendered. Though they may enjoy their work, they do not regard it as recreation. Furthermore, they have to do their work regularly and not merely as inclination dictates because they are staff members in institutions with on-going social obligations.

With regard to the educator's personal identification with education as a life work, however, the case is not so clear. Some are thus dedicated. For others, school work is merely a means of livelihood. They drift into it through accidents of college attended or of personal associations. Many teach as a temporary expedient, until some more coveted life work becomes accessible. This is especially true of the many women whose preferred career is marriage and who teach only as long as they remain single.

As long as any substantial proportion of educators regard their occupation simply as a way of earning a living or as a temporary expedient and not as their chosen means of life fulfillment, education would not seem to qualify fully as a profession. It appears that the professionalization of education can be realized only as the great majority of educators consider their work a life-long calling to which they wholeheartedly devote themselves as their way of finding and giving significance to their personal existence.

Salaries in education. How do educators fare with respect to the financial rewards of their vocation? On principle they should receive economic benefits commensurate with the services they render to society. In practice there are many factors, usually difficult to assess, which influence their financial position. One factor is professional status itself. A group which by its distinctive competence is able to establish clearly its professional position can claim the commensurate rewards. To the extent that educators are unable to demonstrate their special abilities so convincingly that their claims are generally acknowledged they will obtain less than professional compensation. If it is widely believed that anybody can teach and that so-called professional preparation in education either does no good or even does harm, educators will have little prestige and relatively low salaries.

As pointed out earlier, it is very difficult to demonstrate educational competence. A surgeon can perform an operation, a lawyer can prepare a brief, an architect can plan a house, and in each case the success or failure is plain for all to see. But in teaching, as in the ministry, the outcomes are often slow to come to light and difficult to trace. Hence the educator cannot so readily establish his special competence and make effective his claim for financial support.

Furthermore, because money is measurable and definite, it is best adapted to dealings in concrete, specifiable things. Since educational benefits are not of this character, it is difficult to assign money value to them and to the educators who are supposed to dispense them. In the economic realm, where the competition of rival claims is keen, those whose services cannot be quantitatively assessed will tend to be underpaid in comparison with workers whose products are more tangible. For this reason one way of raising salaries in certain fields of education is to show statistically the higher financial expectancy of persons who have had the benefit of instruction in these fields.

A related factor influencing salaries in education is the common assumption that teachers have to do with "higher things" and therefore are not concerned about the earthy matters of economic advantage. It is often thought improper for a teacher, a minister, or a social worker (all of whom are on the average modestly paid) to be concerned about salary. Such people are supposed to be dedicated to ideals of serving and giving and not to be selfishly interested in what they receive. This would be a tenable position if someone else would take sufficient thought for their adequate financial support. Unfortunately, those who are interested in serving rather than getting are frequently taken advantage of or are neglected by those who possess economic power. What is too easily lost sight of is that the very ability of the educator or other servant of "higher things" to give effective service is contingent on sufficient economic resources and some measure of financial security.

Possibly, however, there is something in the nature of the educator's work which might warrant a somewhat lower money return than would be indicated by the standard of social usefulness alone. Many teachers find the process of guiding personal development and of contemplating ideas so intrinsically satisfying that they are willing to remain in teaching at a lower salary than they could secure in some less appealing type of work. The non-money rewards of an occupation are usually referred to as "psychic income." Such returns are especially characteristic of the true vocation as distinguished from a mere job for pay. In a vocation one gives his life to his work and receives back from it not only certain financial rewards, but, more significantly, he regains his own life deepened and enriched. Regrettably, this fact of psychic income in education and certain allied fields is too frequently used as an excuse for paying unreasonably low salaries.

The income in any occupation is greatly affected by the place of the worker in the power structure of society. Those who possess authority of decision and command normally have a larger income than those who work under the direction of others. This is perhaps most clearly the case where the power has to do with the production and distribution of material goods, but it extends also to other types of power structures, such as military, political, ecclesiastical, and educational. In the school the higher salaries usually go to the executives—the superintendents, presidents, deans, departments heads, and supervisors, who have the greatest power within the institution. Since the individual teacher exercises authority largely in relation to his students, who generally occupy a very low position in the power hierarchy of society, his own power position is normally unfavorable. Consequently, he seldom secures substantial financial benefits.

Organization of teachers. Collective action is an effective means of enhancing the power of the teacher. Labor unions have successfully applied such action to raise wages and improve the conditions of employment. Through collective bargaining and the strike unionized teachers can exert power to secure a level of economic justice which the individual teacher could not achieve.

Is union membership for teachers consistent with the claim to be professional, and in particular with the ideal of vocation? Advocates of the teacher union see no inconsistency. They believe that every occupational group has a right to take whatever measures may be necessary to gain their fair share of material goods. Opponents maintain that while wage earners who work primarily for the pay may be justified in organizing labor unions, this is not appropriate for the professional, who should be dedicated personally to his calling and who should remain true to it even if he may have to suffer economic inconvenience. They hold that a true professional has a kind of sacred trust, which he profanes whenever he uses his office in any way for personal advantage.

Against unions it is also urged that they tend to create animosities and divisions of interest within school and community, setting teachers against administrators and parents and thereby destroying the mutual confidence and cooperation which are essential to a constructive educational program. Another alleged result is the decline in professional standards which occurs when the teacher is no longer dealt with on his own merits but only as a member of a bargaining group. Proper discrimination between the more and the less able teachers is then less feasible, and a deadly mediocrity is thought likely to prevail.

The opponents of teacher unions point out that teachers may and should still organize professionally and, consistent with their calling, should exercise their influence by education and persuasion rather than by sheer collective power.

Those who support union-type organization and practices for teachers reply to these arguments by saying that while harmony and professional dignity may be commendable, and while associations dedicated to persuasion through education may serve some useful purpose, none of the ideals of the profession can be securely advanced unless basic justice prevails in matters of salary and conditions of employment. Moreover, they contend that political realism makes it clear that only through collective strength can this justice be obtained.

Finally, in the matter of organization a distinction must be made between education and such professions as medicine and law. In the latter professions the practitioner can in most cases largely determine his own conditions of work and can come to agreement with individual clients on compensation. In education, on the other hand, since the practitioner is usually an employee in an institution, he cannot enjoy as high a degree of self-determination. Thus, while the professional association is the only feasible way of exercising the concerted influence of the medical or legal profession, in education the union type of organization, designed as it is for workers with employee status, may also be appropriate and effective.

Vocational rewards and the values of society. When one takes a broad view of the question of compensation, it seems likely that in the long run individuals in each occupation will be rewarded for their services roughly in proportion to the relative worth of what they produce, according to the scale of values prevailing in the society. If knowledge is truly valued most highly, the scholar will be most highly paid. If amusement on the average is rated higher than knowledge, the entertainer will receive the greater rewards. If executive ability or musical creativity are most prized, the manager or the composer will receive the largest compensation.

If the salaries in the vocation of education are relatively low, the basic reason for this is the correspondingly low place that formal education has in the prevailing average scale of values. When teachers on the average and over a long period receive substantially less income than doctors, this is evidence that what is acquired at school is less esteemed than being cured of one's sicknesses. Perhaps this is as it should be. Many would claim that without health all the other values disappear, and hence that of all the occupations doctors should be the best paid. But it does not seem so easy to justify the low valuation of school learning indicated by a situation in which many teachers are forced to forsake teaching to take better paying positions in almost any other type of endeavor. Under these circumstances one may well ask whether the trouble is with the schools or with society's scale of values. It may be that teachers are paid poorly because the average person is not convinced that they really contribute much to the growth of the student. On the other hand, the low salaries may indicate a basic public indifference toward learning itself. In the former case improvement in teaching or better presentation of the teacher's contribution to the public, or both, are indicated. In the latter case improvement can occur only as the dire consequences of neglecting learning are made manifest, both through the resulting actual dislocations and impoverishments of life and through the advance warnings of respected and eloquent leaders.

It should be noted that the formation of teacher unions to enforce economic demands cannot create values, but can only bring to light values already held but not yet translated into financial benefits. Hence, by collective action teachers may be able to improve their economic condition, but not beyond the point of actual value placed on schooling in comparison with other enterprises claiming support. The organizing of educators does not in itself give social value to their vocation. It merely helps to provide the means necessary for expressing the existing value of their work in economic terms.

Code of Ethics

The fifth mark of a profession is a distinctive ethical code. The professional's special knowledge and skill carry with them special moral responsibilities. The professional has unusual abilities which can be turned either to good or to evil purpose. Every person, professional or not, has his own unique powers which he can use morally or immorally, and it is the office of ethics generally to distinguish the good from the evil uses. The ethical code of a profession is a specific working out of the general ethical principles. It is designed to take cognizance of the distinctive powers which define that particular vocational group and cognizance of the distinctive moral obligations which accompany the exercise of those powers.

A physician, for example, has the knowledge which will enable him both to save and to destroy life. It is then part of his professional duty always to heal and never to kill. An attorney's knowledge of the law gives him power to secure justice or to circumvent the law for his own or his client's private advantage. The ethical code of the lawyer bids him work for justice and observance of the law. A clergyman in his pastoral functions shares many of the deepest secrets of his parishioners' lives. It is an article of his professional ethic that what has been thus confided to him he will not disclose to any other person.

Foundations of professional ethics. All professional codes of ethics rest upon two foundations. The first is the security and integrity of the profession itself. A profession will be respected and rewarded by society only if its members for the most part can be relied upon to perform faithfully that for which they have special competence. It is not here a question of avoiding mistakes or of having ability; the ethical question rather concerns the faithful employment of whatever powers one actually has. A thoroughly qualified doctor, for example, may make a mistake, or through faulty certification procedures an incompetent person may be admitted to practice, but these cases differ from the breach of professional ethics involved when a competent doctor deliberately acts so as to bring harm to one who comes to him for help. Any profession can enjoy the confidence of those whom it professes to serve only if its members pledge themselves to faithful performance of their special offices and collectively employ whatever judicial and corrective machinery may be necessary to insure a high degree of compliance. A profession with a high reputation is a favored target for unscrupulous individuals who wish to profit personally from the confidence reposed in its members. Against such impostors and charlatans, a few of whom can bring discredit on the many, the profession must for its own integrity take vigorous action.

This first foundation of professional ethics is largely prudential. It is required simply for the sake of the profession's own continued advantage. The second foundation is the ideal of disinterested service. According to this ideal, the true professional does not engage in practice solely for personal satisfactions or financial rewards, nor does he do his work faithfully merely for the honor of the profession, but he is also motivated by the pure ideal of rendering service. He finds intrinsic value and a sense of fulfillment in making available his special ability for the welfare of others. The vocation of the professional at its highest is one of service rather than of gain for individual or group. The professional is a trustee to whom has been given the stewardship of gifts which are for the good of all. It is this spirit of disinterestedness which gives to a profession such nobility, elevation, and honor as it may deserve.

The ethical code of educators. If education is to be accounted a profession, it must have its distinctive code of ethics. The nature of this code will be determined by the special nature of the educative function. There are many different ways in which the unique moral obligations of the professional educator can be expressed, and many particular elaborations of any general principles which may be enunciated. It must suffice here to suggest only three articles which seem fundamental to an ethical code for the professional educator.

Concern for the student. The first principle is that the educator ought always so to act as to give first place to the welfare of the student. Since education is the process of appropriately guiding the development of the student, no one can rightly call himself an educator unless he is first of all dedicated to that objective. For a teacher or administrator to govern his behavior chiefly so as to serve his own ends, whether of prestige, material rewards, or intellectual satisfaction, is to violate the ethics of the profession. The student is entrusted by himself or by parents or guardians to the educator. It is, therefore, the educator's duty to be faithful to that trust by always seeking in his work the pupil's advancement in knowledge, skill, and character. If he has no such intention, he has no right within the profession.

Dedication to truth. The second basic article of the educator's professional code is that he should seek and teach the truth. The growth of the student should not be merely any kind of growth, but should be toward truth. As to what "truth" is there are wide differences of conviction. Each educator will have his own conception of it. Despite the differences, each must seek his students' development in the light of truth as he sees it. It is unethical for the teacher deliberately to mislead or falsify. It is also unethical knowingly to let error and falsehood in the student go unchallenged. Nor is the teacher worthy of the profession if through sloth, personal insecurity, or rigidity he refuses to consider the claims of alternative positions and to provide, when called upon to do so, some convincing justification for the views he presents.

Implicit in this principle of devotion to truth are several components. One is sincerity. The educator should endeavor to appear as what he is. He should be true to himself, not seeking to impress the students by claiming knowledge or virtues which he does not have. Another component is reliance on intelligence. The educator must be reasonable, open to inquiry and discussion. This does not mean that he has to be narrowly intellectual, without emotion or commitment of will, or lacking a sense of mystery. It does mean that he is dedicated to the use of intelligence, broadly conceived, as the sole instrumentality for apprehending truth. The ideal of seeking for truth also suggests that truth in its fullness is not to be identified with the educator's own convictions. The virtue of sincerity—of personal identification with the truth one advocates—needs to be coupled with that of humility, by which one is aware of the greater truth waiting to be known and lived, beyond what he or any other person has comprehended.

In summary, it would be unethical for the educator to be hypocritical or pretentious, to refuse to discuss sincere questions about matters of fact or belief, or to regard himself as in full possession of ultimate and unassailable knowledge.

Loyalty to the heritage. A third fundamental principle of professional ethics for the educator is that he should be loyal to the heritage he is expected to conserve and transmit. Devotion to truth is essential for the educator, but it is not enough. There may be cases where that very devotion leads him into conflict with deeply rooted values of society. When that happens, he can no longer in justice to his profession serve as an educator. The educator is one who is entrusted by society, or by certain groups in it, to guide the less mature toward an acceptance and implementation of traditional cultural values. The teacher is not expected to create his own individual ideals and direct his students in the light of them. He is charged rather with the responsibility of helping to develop his pupils in the light of the accepted ideals of the culture.

Loyalty to the heritage does not necessarily or even usually mean that the educator must teach a fixed and well-defined set of ideas or practices, and hence that the search for truth wherever it may lead is largely precluded. Whether or not this happens depends upon the nature of the heritage. If it is one where the highest value is placed on strict adherence to certain fixed codes of conduct and thought, then only those who are able sincerely to subscribe to these codes as true can rightly serve as educators. If, on the other hand, the heritage includes as part of its ideal the exploration of new ideas and values, and if diversity of concept and conviction are welcomed for the vitality and enrichment they bring, then service as an educator need not conflict with unrestricted inquiry.

Academic freedom. These considerations of the relation between devotion to truth and loyalty to the heritage underlie the crucial issue of academic freedom. The question is how to reconcile the educator's dedication to the right and true as he sees them with the differing convictions of other individuals or groups in society. To what extent should the teacher be allowed to teach what he wishes without limitation by other persons? To what degree ought immunity from investigation and control be a prerogative of the professional educator?

It is clear that the claim of academic freedom cannot take precedence over the claim of professional competence. The teacher is not free to be incompetent. It is right and imperative that no educator should be permitted to persist in practices which fail to meet the basic standards set by the professional group to determine the qualification of its members. No teacher should be allowed to give instruction which is judged by consensus of professionally qualified persons to be false, injurious, or grossly ineffective.

But is competence the sole condition for educational freedom? Should one who knows his subject well and who can teach it effectively be subject to no restraint? There appear to be other conditions which must be imposed both in the interests of truth and of social integrity. For one thing, the educator's work must be subject to scrutiny by those whom he professes to serve. This is part of the ethic of truthfulness. It would be deceptive for one to accept appointment as a teacher and then intentionally to give instruction quite at variance with the understanding and expectation of those to whom his services were offered. This does not mean that the educator must agree at every point with the views and values of his public. That would usually be impossible in any event because of the variety of prevailing attitudes. What it does mean is that knowledge of the educator's stand must be readily accessible to those whom he offers to serve. If there is disagreement between clientele and educator, it should be open and recognized and not concealed by the teacher.

The ethical principle of devotion to truth further suggests that no educator should have the freedom to teach in such a way as to deny the freedom of the student. He should not be at liberty to close the door to the student's own insistent questionings, nor so to instruct him that the pupil's range and depth of inquiry are diminished. By the ethic of concern for the student, furthermore, the teacher is not free to employ his school position as a means for advancing his own interests rather than those of the student.

Beyond these requirements there are the strictures imposed by the principle of loyalty to the heritage. In a society where a high degree of conformity to an established tradition is expected, the educator should not expect academic freedom, and it is unethical of him, *as an educator,* to contradict the accepted order. In such a society, if he wishes to protest or reform, he is obliged to do so from some other position than that of educator. The situation is quite different in an "open" society where diversity of belief, freedom of dissent, and independence of inquiry are integral to the heritage. In that case the educator has the privilege of a high degree of academic freedom which permits him openly to teach ideas within his sphere of professional competence which may be sharply at variance with generally prevailing convictions.

Loyalty to the heritage implies that the teacher may not deliberately teach so as to subvert the social order itself. In a society based on conformity to fixed rule and obedience to recognized authorities the teaching profession is bound to respect these demands. In a free society the educator is bound to teach the way of freedom. In the latter case he is not at liberty to teach in such a way as to destroy the freedom upon which the society rests. Thus, in a free society an educator cannot ethically advocate a social system in which freedom would be extinguished. Whether or not the propagation of such ideas should be tolerated outside of the educational position is another question. The principle of loyalty to the heritage may not necessarily be a universal ethical principle. But as part of the educator's code he must refrain from teaching anything which he believes and expects would undermine the foundations of the social order which he represents.

The Profession and Professionalism

In the present chapter the chief criteria of a profession have been suggested and applied to the work of the educator. Education can qualify as a profession provided its practitioners are able to demonstrate their special competence, to develop a sound theoretical foundation for their work, to possess adequate standards of social recognition and consciousness of vocation, and to govern themselves by a high ethical code.

The temptation of a profession or of a group that aims to become professional is a spirit of exclusive professionalism. There are professionals who delight in affecting the manners of the guild and who revel in its prestige and privilege but who are concerned little with its intrinsic joys and responsibilities. There are many for whom the chief satisfaction of the profession is in being superior to others, in having attained a favored position from which others are excluded.

In contrast to these, the true professional, though he is a special person, at the same time is a representative man. By the ideal of service he belongs to humanity. The educator may become a professional, but this should not set him apart. It should rather unite him more firmly with those whom he is called to serve for the sake of the right and the true toward which all together aim.

PART II

Education in Nature and Society

10

Man and Nature

THE DISCUSSIONS of Part I were concerned largely with the development of persons through the recognized social agencies for education. In the present Part the analysis will be broadened beyond this central concern for the school to include some of the other major types of educative experiences which developing persons have in their environment, both physical and social, and within themselves.

Education as a process of directing personal growth requires a context in which individual potentialities can be actualized by interaction with surrounding entities. The nature of the realized potential depends in considerable measure upon what the environment is and upon the nature of the interactions experienced. A person's character is in part a reflection of his experience with such factors as nature, family, peer groups, and job. Hence, a consideration of such relationships is important for understanding education.

The first topic will be the relationship of man and nature, or nature as a context for the educative process. The word "nature" is admittedly ambiguous. It can be taken to mean everything that is, in which case man, society, and all cultural creations must belong to nature. Such an inclusive concept of nature is generally set in opposition to a dualistic world view which holds that there are two realms, nature and supernature, and that the supernatural is prior to and even more real than the natural. Against this, the naturalist maintains that there is but one world, one reality, called "nature," which consists of all existing entities.

In the present chapter a more limited meaning of nature is intended, namely, the non-human part of man's environment. This includes the physical world and all living things, other than man, which inhabit it.

In the modern world, so greatly transformed by human technology, in modern society, so largely composed of dwellers in cities and towns, it is easy to overlook the importance of nature in the development of persons.

This is unfortunate, for apart from his fellow men and whatever supernatural agencies there are, nature is the one great reality which surrounds man, sets conditions and problems for his life, and in general determines much of the direction his development must follow. Nature is thus one of the major influences in education, and the character of the educative process depends to no small degree upon the type of relationships established with the non-human environment.

In the paragraphs below eight conceptions of man's relationship to nature will be discussed, and the consequences of each for education will be indicated. The different positions are not necessarily mutually exclusive. In practice, attitudes toward nature usually combine several of these conceptions. The viewpoints are separately treated for clarity of analysis and to show certain major types of emphasis.

The reader is reminded that the purpose of such a presentation of alternatives in the philosophy of education is simply to suggest the range of possibilities which should be considered in comprehensive and critical reflection on the problem at hand. According to the conception of the philosophic task upon which this book is based, it is not the author's function to supply answers, but rather to provide agenda for discussion, pointing out the major positions which can be taken, some of the arguments for and against each, and some inferences which can be drawn from them. It then remains for the individual reader, on the basis of his own system of values and the intrinsic appeal of the respective arguments, to reach a position, no matter how tentative, which he can defend and which he can claim as his own.

Nature as Man's Enemy

The first conception is that nature is man's enemy. No person could long exist apart from the defenses provided by civilization against the hostility of natural forces. Without clothing and man-made shelter one could prevail against the rigors of weather only in a few unusually benign climates. Wind and rain, the scorching heat of summer, and the bite of sleet and snow forever threaten to extinguish life. Natural calamity also lies in wait for man. Floods sweep whole towns away. Tornados and hurricanes in a few brief moments exact heavy toll in life and property. Landslides and volcanoes, avalanches and earthquakes mercilessly destroy whatever of man or his works stands in their way. Despite the best efforts at prevention and control fires continue to consume whole forests, bringing death and deprivation to individuals and communities.

As if these elemental forces were not enemy enough for man, the world of living things also conspires against him. If man but rests from the battle, the jungle begins to move in. Weeds infest his gardens and what they do not choke out the insects greedily devour. Countless armies of microorganisms stand ready to invade his body, bringing disease, suffering, and death. When medicines are found to cure one disorder, another ailment comes to take its place. Larger animals, too, are arrayed against man. They only unwillingly give way to this human usurper of their rightful kingdom.

Nature is a battleground, and the strongest survive. Sentimentalists would picture it otherwise, but the facts refute them. Man is pitted against natural enemies on every side. The law of life is warfare, and it is only through struggle that the unfit are eliminated. Only because nature is man's enemy has humanity progressed so far. In the forces arrayed against him man has been given a challenge, to which his growing powers of intelligence and his magnificent cultural achievements are a fitting response. From this point of view it is good that nature is opposed to man. Were it friendly, there would be no suffering, and without suffering no attempt to alleviate it, and hence no civilization.

Civilization represents the result of human triumph over and subjugation of nature. Culture is opposed to nature, and the goal of human striving is to produce a new, anti-natural world in which every wild, untamed force and creature will be either destroyed or put in bondage to man. Progress is measured by the excess of human artifice over unimproved nature. It is man's glory—even his sacred obligation—to subdue the earth and to hold dominion over every lower creature.

Unfortunately, however, nature may have the last word. Even though man has largely succeeded in subjecting it to his will, it can afford to wait, and in the long run may prove itself the stronger. As explained further in Chapter 20, physical processes take place in such a way as to make energy less and less available for use. According to the Law of Entropy, the result of any natural happening is to increase the randomness or disorganization of total energy resources. The conclusion seems inevitable that the universe is running down, passing inexorably from a condition of highly organized systems to a dead level of random heat motion. The temporary victories of life and civilization have been won by drawing upon the rich resources of available energy, such as the sun. In due time all such resources seem destined to fail. Meanwhile, man and his culture merely accelerate the process of exhaustion. The end will be the "heat death" of the universe, when all life will be stilled and there will remain only senseless collocations of colliding atoms.

Nature thus seems to be no friend of man, but a cruel deceiver, allowing life to come into being and to rise to apparent power and security, only to fall the more ingloriously into the oblivion of entropic night.

If nature is enemy to man, a major aim of education must be to arm him for effective combat with this foe. In the case of non-industrialized peoples, the young had to be made familiar with the omnipresent hazards of the physical environment, taught skill in hunting, fishing, and trapping wild animals, and instructed in ways of escaping dangers from fire, wind, and water. In industrialized societies, though man is no longer surrounded by untamed forces, it is still necessary to teach children at an early age the dangers of certain natural powers, particularly fire and water. While an inordinate fear of them is not desirable, a realistic sense of the perils of burning and drowning must be imparted.

In advanced cultures the major emphasis shifts from teaching ways of hand-to-hand combat with nature to instruction in organized and mechanized assault upon it. The development of the vast apparatus of technology can be understood as the marshalling of scientific intelligence in a concerted attack on nature. The education of engineers provides experts in controlling rivers, building structures which can withstand winds, earthquakes, and fires, and fashioning machines which defy the forces that would bind man to earth or submerge him helpless beneath the waters. Other specialists are taught to combat the insect hordes, and still others learn ways of destroying bacteria and virus, postponing further nature's universal decree that man must die.

Technical knowledge enables man to hold his enemy in check by turning nature against itself. Human strength unaided could not avail against the overwhelming power of natural forces. By learning the ways of nature man can fight fire with fire or water, insects with poison, and bacteria with bacteria (e.g., in immunization).

Modern education is largely dominated by this conception—often only implicit—of nature as enemy. The child soon learns that he is to be ruler of earth and that the nature which threatened his forefathers is now to be in bondage to him. He generally learns neither love nor respect for nature, and considers it not only a right but a duty to subjugate it. This conviction when freely developed becomes an invitation to destroy nature. The final fruit of this is, of course, the destruction of man and his civilization, which cannot exist apart from a sustaining natural environment. Education based on the idea of opposition to nature would, therefore, appear to be fraught with the gravest dangers for the security and progress of human life itself.

Nature as Obstacle

Instead of viewing nature as an active antagonist, it may be regarded as an obstacle to human progress, an inert mass to be moved, a barrier to be surmounted or circumvented, a dead weight to be lifted. The spectacular happenings—forest fires, volcanic eruptions, and epidemics—are the exceptions rather than the rule. Nature as experienced in everyday life is simply that dumb intractable stuff which with great effort we have to manage. To call nature an enemy is to impute purpose to what can have nothing like human intention. Man alone has intelligent goals. The world he inhabits is on a decisively lower level of existence. It is largely passive and completely unreflective. Man as the active agent must make his will effective by fashioning the environment in accordance with his desires.

Nature as obstacle is exemplified by the resistant stone which defies the mason's chisel, the unwilling soil from which the farmer wrests sustenance at cost of unremitting toil, the broad rivers which man must cross by sturdy boat or bridge or deep-bored tunnel, the mountains which must be moved to allow highways to pass, the mines and wells to be blasted and bored to get at their treasures, the stupid beast so hard to teach, the unwelcome and persistent vermin or insect pest.

But even more than these natural obstacles, man may be inclined to regard his own body as part of that nature which he must endure and seek to manage. The spirit is willing but the flesh is weak, it is said. We could accomplish much were we not hindered by our heavy bodies, which require so much food and care and consume so much time in sleep. Our inertia in performing necessary tasks and our inevitable falling short of the goals we set are a consequence of the material structure we must inhabit. From this perspective, "nature" is contrasted with "spirit" or "soul." Spirit is imprisoned in matter during this life, and the efforts of the soul are directed at securing eventual freedom from this obstacle.

Another source of the view that nature is an obstacle is the difficulty experienced in solving practical and theoretical problems. It is true that great advances have been made in science and technology, but it is equally true that most of these achievements were secured at the cost of enormous effort. It is easy to take for granted the results of invention and discovery, forgetting the endless toil and tireless experimentation of whole generations of men that have made them possible. Nature does not yield its secrets easily. The structure of things is not immediately apparent to human intelligence. Anyone who has actually engaged in pioneering research knows how inscrutable, intractible, and stubborn nature is, and how slowly and after how many fruitless attempts the solutions to problems finally appear.

The experience of nature as obstacle tends to sap human energy, creates a feeling of frustration, and leads to discouragement about the value of effort. Persons overwhelmed by the inertia of things become dull and resigned to an unproductive existence. Infants are particularly aware of their impotence within an environment of things they have neither strength nor skill to manage. Unless they are sufficiently assisted by older people to cope with their surroundings, they may develop permanent attitudes of resignation and helplessness. For the very young child nature really is an obstacle; it is too big and he is too small to deal with it effectively. For the adult the balance is redressed, and though nature may interpose difficulties, they may no longer be insuperable.

The task of education, given this attitude toward nature, is obviously to prepare man to solve problems by the use of intelligence. Nature is not organized to agree with human purposes and must thus be reformed so as to serve man's interests. In solving problems man uses his mind to order the physical world according to his own plans. Civilization is maintained by educating successive generations in effective ways of using intelligence to reorganize the physical environment to suit human desire.

With this view of nature there will also be emphasis on the need for effort, patience, and persistence. Not only intelligence but *will* is required for the successful resolution of the problems presented by the environment. In the growing personality this is perhaps best developed by insuring that as far as possible the tasks set at each step be proportionate to ability, that ample opportunities for successful achievement be provided, and that success in overcoming difficulties be appropriately rewarded.

Like the concept of nature as enemy, the view of nature as obstacle is negative, and sets man in opposition to his environment. It ignores the active and supportive qualities of the surrounding world and encourages the destruction of essential resources. Doubtless there are some aspects of nature which can properly be dealt with negatively, but in many other respects this is clearly unwarranted. It seems unfortunate that the outlook of the Western world has been so largely dominated by the ambition to subject nature wholly to the will of man. This obsession has impoverished man's spiritual life and also damaged, perhaps beyond repair, the natural capital upon which all life, including man's own, ultimately depends.

Nature as Resource

Far more significant than the threatening and resisting aspects of nature are her values as a resource for human use. Ultimately all material support for human life comes from the rich storehouse of nature. First, there is food, without which man's life could continue but a few days. This comes directly from the soil, or indirectly through animals who in turn derive sustenance from vegetation. Some food grows within the sea. It is easy to mistake processing for production and to think of food as coming from factories. But even synthetic foods in their basic components are derived from the resources of "unimproved" nature. Second, there is the fundamental resource of air, without a continuous supply of which man would quickly perish. All plants and animals similarly require from the atmosphere nitrogen, oxygen, or carbon dioxide to sustain their life. Third, everything living requires water, a liquid of extraordinary physical and chemical properties singularly suited to sustain the economy of organic processes. And fourth, there is the sun, whose energy supplies the heat required for any life to exist and the light required for the essential process of photosynthesis in green plants.

Besides these minimal essentials of food, air, water, and sunlight, nature supplies every other material need of man. His clothing comes from furs or skins of animals, from the fibers of plants, or perhaps indirectly—in synthetic materials—from organic deposits such as coal or petroleum. His dwellings are constructed from materials supplied by forest or mine. Materials for tools are dug from the earth and fashioned to shape by other earth products. Books, magazines, and newspapers, in which the symbols of human culture are recorded, are made from paper derived from forest or field. So it is with the trains, planes, automobiles, and ships and with every other product of civilization: all are made possible solely through the bounty of the earth.

The essence of modern civilization is that human beings have learned how to use, to a degree hitherto unrealized, the resources so richly supplied by nature. To a considerable extent the function of contemporary education is to give instruction in the efficient exploitation of these resources. This is certainly the basic goal in all technical studies and the usual consequence of the "pure" scientific disciplines as well. The Age of Science is not merely an era of increased knowledge, but more significantly, one of maximum utilization of natural riches.

As a result of research first carried on chiefly in institutions of higher learning, the secret of the atom has been revealed and the vast resources of atomic power have been made available for human use. This development has two kinds of consequences. First, it means that the supply of power at man's disposal has been greatly increased and the scope and intensity of human activity correspondingly expanded. But second, and working in the opposite direction, it means that the rate and thoroughness of possible exploitation of nature have been multiplied many times and, hence, that the consumption of materials can proceed at a much faster speed.

The limitations of natural resources. These considerations lead to the fundamental question as to whether or not natural resources are unlimited. Man has become a major geologic factor. Human beings are today making more profound changes in the earth than floods, winds, fires, and ice. By felling great forests, by forcing the top soil to give up its long-accumulated richness in a few years of profitable crops, by piping or hauling away the subterranean stores of oil, coal, and metals, by hunting wild animals out of existence, by fishing out streams and lakes, by shooting down birds, by covering over vast areas with buildings and pavement—in all these and many more ways man has transformed the surface of the earth. The problem is: Will he in the process so deplete the earth as to make it uninhabitable, or will he always be able to find new sources of supply when old ones have been exhausted? It is at least certain that the quantity of any particular resource is always limited. Oil reserves are rapidly being depleted. Coal is probably in sufficient supply to last for several hundred years at current rates of consumption, but not indefinitely. High-grade ores of certain metals are being used up at an alarming rate, requiring a shift to other metals and the use of lower-grade ores more difficult to process.

Probably the most serious threat is in the shortage of water. So enormous is the quantity of water used in homes and factories and for irrigation that in many areas the water table has fallen below the critical level, and it seems unlikely that new sources of supply can be found to replenish existing ones, much less to provide for the increasing needs of a growing population and an expanding economy. Another cause of major concern is the deterioration of the soil as a result of too intensive cultivation, failure to rotate crops, and inadequate measures to prevent erosion.

There are four ways of answering the question about limitation of resources, and four corresponding programs of education.

New discovery. One answer is to affirm the limitlessness of nature's resources, in the faith that the discovery of new sources of supply will more than compensate for the loss of old ones, even if this requires ventures to other worlds than earth. Central in such a program must be scientific and technical education with major emphasis on research of an imaginative and daring kind far transcending earth-bound and tradition-fettered conceptions.

Slow exhaustion. According to a second view, nature's resources are limited, the discovery of new supplies will inevitably fail to keep pace with depletion, and certain exhaustible substances such as water are so essential that no substitutions will do. Under these conditions to maintain human life for as long as possible on the earth three measures are urgently called for: First, every effort must be made to utilize materials as efficiently as possible. Waste must be minimized by such measures as proper storage and transport of foods, effective use of by-products in manufacture, and careful scheduling of transportation facilities. Many kinds of studies may contribute to this efficiency—home economics, industrial management, engineering design, traffic control, and accounting, to mention but a few.

Second, not only must materials be used efficiently, but also the level of consumption must be reduced to a minimum. Only food necessary to health should be eaten. Clothing should not be subject to changing fashions requiring frequent purchase of new designs. Large houses and pleasure cars should be dispensed with. Travel should be limited to necessary business. Luxuries of all kinds must be eliminated. Education for such austerity requires strict regulation of life, emphasis on law, order, and obedience, deep convictions about the moral superiority of the rigorous life, and encouragement of activities such as reading, conversing, contemplating nature, praying, and making music, which consume relatively little material.

A third way of reducing the use of materials to a minimum is by the control of population growth. The pressure on natural resources in modern times largely results from the phenomenal increase in the numbers of people to be fed, clothed, housed, and transported. Efficiency and austerity are of no avail if the population continues to increase. The problem of how to control population growth is extremely difficult to solve. Control by legislation would doubtless be ineffective and repugnant to moral sense. Perhaps economic factors are a more effective incentive for restriction of family size. It is one of the tasks of education, in home, school, or church, to make the young aware of the population problem and to point out ways of regulating family size consistent with the highest principles of moral, religious, and social responsibility.

Rapid exhaustion. A third view of the problem of resource limitation rests upon the same premise as the view just described, namely, that material supplies are limited and are rapidly being exhausted, but moves to the quite different conclusion that it is better to have a relatively brief period of expensive and brilliant civilization than a somewhat longer period of drab asceticism. Therefore, the recommendation is that resources be used fully and freely while they last, in the conviction that the intensity and quality of culture are more to be prized than mere prolongation in time. Education for this kind of civilization would place emphasis on consumership, the refinement of taste, the imaginative consideration of new uses for materials, and the development of all possible technical means to secure maximum production. Persons would be prepared for the fullest possible enjoyment of material things in a society dedicated to the continuing increase of population and wealth.

It seems likely that the many who enthusiastically embrace this view can do so only by suppressing the thought that the recommended expansion can not go on indefinitely and that a time must come when population pressures and material shortages will occasion bitter personal distress and violent social disorders.

Balance through conservation. There is a fourth position which avoids the unqualified optimism of the first position and the fundamental pessimism of the second and third positions. It is the qualifiedly optimistic view that the resources of nature can be unlimited *if properly utilized.* Nature is not merely a storehouse of inert material piled up waiting to be hauled away. The riches of the earth are not like money in a bag, which is drawn upon until nothing is left. Nature is *alive,* and its resources are continually being regenerated. If natural resources are improperly exploited, nature will be killed, its riches will become only a heap of dead or dying matter, and the pessimism of the second and third views above will be fully justified. The problem of resource use is how to establish a stable balance between man and nature, how to adjust the character and rate of human consumption to nature's continuing powers of creation and reconstruction.

This calls for a program of *conservation.* Conservation is not mere hoarding of resources. It is the development of a constructive and cooperative relationship of man to nature whereby the productiveness of nature is preserved. Of chief importance is the proper use of water and soil so as not to interfere with the replenishment which the normal cyclic processes assure.

The education of man to live in permanent balance with nature has several components. As in the first position discussed above, the search should constantly be continued for new materials. Nature's resources are greater than we know, and there is every reason to discover as fully as possible what and where they are. As in the second position, man must learn how to use materials most efficiently, eliminating waste and getting maximum benefit from every natural product. He must also be taught to restrict or abstain from use of certain materials which once used can never be replaced. Of central importance also is knowledge of the population problem and acquisition of the understanding and motivation necessary to control it. Finally, education for conservation should teach ways of actually increasing the regenerative powers of nature. Man need not only deplete nature, he can also by technical means enhance her powers of creation and recuperation beyond their unimproved levels.

Nature as Esthetic Object

Thus far we have considered approaches to nature which presuppose actual physical transformations, through destruction of natural enemies, removal of obstacles, or utilization of resources. But nature may also be considered as an esthetic object, not to be used or abused, but contemplated for its intrinsic perfections. Men have always viewed with admiration and delight the majesty of mountain peaks, the stateliness of great trees, the quiet mystery of the desert, the restfulness and restlessness of the sea. An inexhaustible source of wonder are the myriad designs of natural objects: the endless varieties of snowflake patterns, the shapes and colors of leaves and flowers, the curious forms of insect life, the parade of animals small and great, each with hair or skin, wing or fin, tooth and claw, characteristic of its kind and fit to the task that each must perform.

The sights and sounds of nature may bring to mind man's esthetic creations. An evening sky suggests a vivid painting. The sounds of wind and water may be music to the ear. Clouds and rocks form statues. Rain and leaves engage in dance. To the receptive beholder nature is a work of consummate artistry.

Unfortunately, man in his eagerness to employ nature for his own benefit has disfigured her, exchanging beauty for ugliness. He has chopped down her forests, leveled or cut gashes in her hills, befouled her waters, polluted her winds, extinguished many of her animal kinds, and encrusted her surface with pavemented towns and cities. Every advance in urbanization and industrialization removes man further from unspoiled nature and from the esthetic delights which she affords.

This is a matter of crucial importance for the well-being of persons. Man's spiritual nature requires adequate nourishment, and one of the sources of this sustenance is the contemplation of natural beauty. A person tends to take on the likeness of that with which he constantly associates. An environment of ugliness may tend to produce in persons ugliness and insensitivity to beauty; surroundings of lovely things may enhance appreciation for beautiful things. Life amidst scenes of natural beauty can contribute to spiritual health and esthetic enrichment. Dwellers in drab cities and countrysides laid waste must pay a heavy price in loss of those simple delights which may be the daily mental diet of those who inhabit unspoiled nature.

It is possible, however, to become unwisely sentimental about the effects of nature on the soul. Not all who live in beautiful surroundings have learned to understand and enjoy them. Nature merely provides a ready resource for spiritual education for those who by native endowment, personal encounter, and the example of others have become sensitive to beauty.

Teaching the esthetic enjoyment of nature is largely a matter of communicating enthusiasm and of taking care in pointing out and describing things of beauty which might otherwise escape the learner's notice. Such education further requires rejection of the spirit of ruthless exploitation of nature and the affirmation of a value system where beauty is not wholly subordinated to use. Finally, the esthetic attitude toward nature is encouraged by a culture in which the intrinsic beauty of nature's goods is used to enhance the appeal of man-made things. For example, handsome wood products, brilliant metals, shining crystals, well-tended parks and forests, and well-cared-for animals are all objects of esthetic delight which do justice to the beauty of the natural objects from which they have been derived.

Nature as Source of Knowledge

The inquiring person tends to regard nature not as something to be fought, moved, used, or enjoyed, but primarily as an object of knowledge. For him nature is a wonderful book lying open before him waiting to be read. As he recounts the benefits received from nature's hand, he remembers foremost the lessons taught, the insights imparted, the guidance provided.

It is from nature that the young child in part learns what it is to be a person. The physical world which surrounds him becomes a testing ground for the discovery of reality. By actual encounter with things which more or less resist him he comes to realize an "out-there" which is at the same time a "not-me." The growing awareness of this "not-me" is coupled with a developing consciousness of the "me" which perceives the external world. Thus the genesis of "self-hood" is based upon the experience of environment as "not-self."

Furthermore, nature teaches the child that reality has its own ways and cannot be wholly accommodated to his intentions and inclinations. The environment appears as qualitative, as structured, as definite. This is the beginning of knowledge—the recognition of reasonably stable, predictable characteristics in the world of things. Through actual experience the child discovers the qualities of hard and soft, hot and cold, bright and dull, distant and near, and he becomes aware that these are realities of which he must take account and by which his activity must to some degree be regulated.

This elemental, universal, everyday knowledge of the real world is not essentially different from the knowledge elaborated and accumulated in the natural sciences. A scientist in his laboratory is merely studying in a more systematic and sophisticated way the lesson the child must early learn from nature's pages. Thus the whole development of science exemplifies the view of nature as a source of knowledge. The scientist as such (as contrasted with the engineer) is not concerned with controlling nature for human purposes but solely with understanding the lesson it has to teach. He does not seek to impose his will upon it, but patiently asks questions to which in experiment and observation he hopes to receive answers. This attitude of waiting, watching, and seeking in humility and expectancy is at the opposite pole from the largely dominant modern notion of human mastery and exploitation of nature. This contrast underlies the usual tension between the claims of pure and of applied science, respectively, and between the ideals of scientific education corresponding to each. Those who are motivated by the desire for power and control approach the study of science from a practical perspective, while those who love knowledge for its own sake have a predominantly theoretical interest.

But nature not only provides instruction in science, it also teaches the knowledge of beauty. As pointed out in the preceding section, nature can be an object of esthetic delight, having served as a major source of inspiration for the esthetic creations of man. Painters, sculptors, architects and composers have before them in nature consummate examples of artistry. Though the artist's task is not simply to imitate nature, but rather to transform its designs in the light of his own creative perception, he still receives impetus and suggestions from the contemplation of natural beauty.

Nature is also sometimes regarded as a source of moral knowledge. Those who take this position believe that the *right* way is the *natural* way, that human conduct should as far as possible be conformed to nature's processes, and that artificiality is the evil to be avoided. Such qualities as orderliness and patience in nature are taken as worthy of human emulation. The trouble with this view is that there are ugly and brutal aspects of nature which can hardly be considered morally valuable. Hence nature may at most be a basis for moral suggestion, and man must choose by an act of independent judgment those qualities which seem right to him. In view of this, nature is at best the context for moral education rather than its guide and ground.

One more word should be added concerning the educational role of living things. Much understanding can be gained of the processes of life and growth —of the patient cumulative activity of organic development—from such activities as planting and cultivating gardens, caring for trees, and raising animals. Children's pets are valuable both for the pleasure they afford and as means of teaching responsibility for other living things. Animals may also play a significant role in the child's socialization process. Sometimes pets are better teachers of social behavior than persons are because they are largely free of the frequently critical, ambivalent, and hypocritical attitudes of human beings.

Nature as Parent

Another concept of nature is embodied in the phrase "mother nature." Of all the views considered, this one most emphasizes the unity of man and nature. The world is not something alien to man, something apart from him which he knows, contemplates, consumes, or subjugates. It is his own very being. From nature he came and to nature's family he must always belong.

The concept of nature as parent is not merely romantic fancy. The theory of evolution supports it. Apparently the human species is the highest product of a process which began with the simplest forms of life, which in turn were derived from complex inorganic compounds. Therefore, man is directly linked to the non-human world by right of ancestry. According to this genetic analysis, he cannot pride himself on superior spiritual or divine origins. He is equal to, part of, and essentially no different from the world of animals, plants, and non-living things.

Along with this recognition of ancestry, the parent concept is acknowledged in the fact of man's complete dependence on nature. This has already been commented on in the discussion of nature as resource. The continuance of human life depends upon the maintenance of favorable material conditions. Air, water, food and shelter are absolute essentials, as necessary as the provision a mother makes for an infant.

The appropriate human responses to nature as parent would seem to be filial respect, love, gratitude, and reciprocal concern for nature's welfare. As in the case of human parent-child relationships, the right response is often not forthcoming. The species man has generally treated his parent nature with arrogance and disrespect. Instead of love he has shown indifference or hostility. In place of gratitude he has complained at the meagerness of the benefits supplied and has sought by every means to extract more. But especially has he been remiss in concern for nature's welfare. Plundering and wasting its substance, he has forgotten that, dependent as he is, in destroying nature he destroys himself.

The conditions of modern civilization make it difficult to remain vividly aware of nature as parent. "Nature study" has become largely a pastime or hobby. Material goods are made by man in factories. "Nature," like art, is a luxury, a decoration, something one can venture into on week-ends when the serious work has been done in the man-made shops and offices. Industrial civilization obscures the vital connection between human life and its sources in nature, giving man a false sense of autonomy.

This situation requires in education a special concern for the study of the many aspects of man's dependence on nature. It calls particularly for a renewed emphasis on geography, defined broadly as the study of nature as man's home. It seems clear that economic, political, social, ethical, and religious problems—to name only some of them—must all take account of fundamental geographic factors. That nature is indeed parent to man is an important presupposition in the whole program of education and not merely in marginal nature-study activities. Awareness of this is most essential in urban areas and in industrial and commercial programs, where the facts of natural dependence are most easily overlooked.

Nature as Object of Religious Devotion

Among some peoples nature is regarded with religious devotion. This is at the opposite pole from the view, with which the present chapter began, that nature is man's enemy. Nature worship probably has its basis in the sense of kinship and of filial relationship through which natural powers are invested with living and personal qualities, in the spectacular or mysterious character of certain natural occurrences, and in the awareness of man's direct dependence on nature for the material essentials of life. Whatever is of supreme importance, whatever man regards as determining his life and destiny, becomes his god. The deification of nature—of the heavenly bodies, of the sources of wind and rain, of the earth itself—is an expression of the conviction that in some incomprehensible way human weal and woe are decided by these powers.

It is customary for educated moderns to congratulate themselves on their emancipation from the allegedly primitive notion that the natural world is peopled with spirits. They think that such animism was long ago replaced by true scientific ways of thinking. Enlightened man knows that nature is inferior to him and is to be subjected to his will. Yet perhaps something of value has been lost in becoming so modern and scientific. Even today's children often have a kind of awe and fascination in the presence of nature which is only gradually dispelled in the light of growing knowledge. Maybe the nature-worshipper recognized meanings which are different from the metrical truths of natural science but perhaps just as true and even more important. Possibly it is more tragedy than triumph that modern education replaces the child's sense of wonder and delight in nature by the adult's technical mastery of it.

One of the dominant motifs in the religions of the East is the belief that all life is sacred. This belief engenders an attitude of "reverence for life," which issues in compassion, tenderness, and considerateness in relation to all sentient creatures. The human being does not consider himself as lord of creation but as one member of a great and diverse brotherhood of living things. Does the East in this reverence for life have an insight needed by the West in its preoccupation with "power over" rather than "compassion for"? Does education exclusively for control of nature tend to produce qualities of insensitivity and callousness in personality?

Does modern technical man need to reconsider his relationship to his natural environment, and if he does not bow down should he not at least take thought for spiritual values he may have lost sight of in nature? Does he need to consider the honor and respect due to nature but not accorded to it?

Nature as Symbol of the Divine

It can be charged against nature worship that it obscures the special dignity of man and subordinates him to actually inferior levels of being. Non-human nature does not possess the unique human powers of thought, imagination, and freedom. Why, then, should man revere what is beneath him in excellence? Devotion to nature—to what *is*—also means renunciation of moral choice and rational discrimination, which are concerned with what *ought to be*. Cultures in which nature is deified accordingly tend to suffer ethically and spiritually.

In advanced religions, therefore, the worship of nature has given way to worship of a transcendent deity, Creator and Lord of Creation, the ground of being for both man and non-human nature. Man is not set in opposition to nature, nor identified with it, nor made subordinate to it. Each order of creation—human and non-human—is regarded as a product of the divine craftsman, and each through its special excellences manifests something of the divine nature and intention. According to this view, nature is not divine, but is symbolic of the divine. That is to say, in and through nature the eye of faith discerns the hand of God the Creator. Nature takes on a sacramental aspect. To the faithful, food, clothing, and shelter bespeak God's love and care. Even the pains and disasters caused by nature's forces may be seen as means used by God to execute judgment and to detach man from reliance on earthly security.

With this sacramental view man develops a respectful and responsible relationship toward nature. He does not reverence it in its own right, but neither does he arbitrarily subject it to his will. He regards himself as trustee of an estate which he is privileged and obliged to administer in accordance with the will of the God who made both himself and nature. In the light of such a faith, the primary objective of education must be to teach the will of God insofar as it has been revealed by intelligence or by supernatural illumination, and in particular to teach the right use of nature's gifts in the light of the universal divine plan. In such an essentially religious education the natural world—whether viewed in its intellectual, esthetic or practical aspects—may in turn be used to strengthen and vivify religious conviction; as by the light of faith man is guided in the right employment of nature, so may nature be a text from which man reads of nature's God.

11

Interpersonal Relationships

IN ADDITION to non-human nature, the environment of the growing personality includes other persons, and these persons are of profound importance for education. In this chapter we shall consider those members of the human environment with whom the developing personality establishes informal face-to-face relationships. The total human context for education is much larger than this, including formal and impersonal types of relationships in the wider community and in political and economic organizations. For the present we shall be concerned with family life and friendship as the main focuses of informal interpersonal relationships, leaving other aspects of the human environment to subsequent chapters.

The Social Factor in Personal Development

Human personality can develop only through association with other persons; there can be no personal growth in isolation. It is not merely that other human beings constitute a favorable environment, giving protection, enjoyment, and instruction. They play a more fundamental role than that. Other people are essential because the relationships the growing person has with them are actually constitutive of the self. A person is not a self-contained entity which happens to be related to other persons. The relationships enter into the very being and essence of the personality. A self is not a thing-in-itself but always and necessarily a person-in-relationship. This does not mean that when no overt interaction is occurring between persons, selfhood disappears. Solitude is a possible and often a desirable state. The constitutive role of the interpersonal simply means that the self, whether alone or in company, is what it is largely by virtue of the encounters experienced with other persons. There would be no self had solitude been the only experience. The very purpose and value of solitude lie in the opportunity to consolidate and coordinate prior experiences of association. Such reflective activity is itself an internalized form of social activity possible only because of earlier interpersonal encounters.

Of the person's entire human environment, that part which enters into face-to-face relationships is incomparably the most important to his development. Those who are direct associates not only exert the most profound influence, but they are the only links through which association with other persons beyond the immediate circle can have any effect. For example, the far-away official who governs a state can influence the development of a personality in a local community only by virtue of the attitudes toward authority engendered in face-to-face encounters with family or neighbors. Again, one who is inspired by the example of a great scientist, artist, or saint whom he has never seen in person is actually reflecting sensitivities and values developed through his immediate associations.

Interpersonal relationships are not only necessary for the growth of any sort of personality at all and for making effective any influence from the wider circles of society, but they also go far to determine the character and quality of the personality that does develop. There is scarcely any characteristic of a person which cannot be traced to some experience with other people. Ways of speaking, of eating, and even of walking generally reflect the customs of the people with whom one grew up. Standards of value, aims, ideals, and conceptions of right and wrong have their roots in the culture in which one has been nurtured, most particularly as it has been mediated through the members of one's immediate circle.

It follows that when the explanation for a given person's behavior is sought, the first place to look is in the pattern of interpersonal relationships which he has experienced. The quality of the person is in large part measured by the quality of those relationships. Family and peer groups are not merely neutral surroundings in which one happens to grow up. They are active formative agencies in relation to which the nature of the self is fashioned.

Education and the social context. Recognition of these facts is necessary for any true perspective on the nature and effectiveness of education. It is often assumed that education chiefly takes place in schools and by the verbal communication of ideas. The study of human development has made it increasingly clear that these formal and rational factors are but a part of the process of guiding growth, and in general they are not the primary and most important part. It is the relationships to significant persons, particularly in the early years of life, that in large part determine the direction and set the dominant emotional tone and style of the personality. It is upon these foundations that the entire learning process rests, including those developments of intellectual capacities and technical skills which are often regarded as the main objectives of education. When a child successfully masters knowledge and techniques, he not only reflects credit upon the educational agencies in which this manifest learning took place, but upon the less obvious resources for personal maturity in his early interpersonal associations. By the same token, failures scholastically may rest upon deeper failures in the face-to-face relationships through which the quality of the personality was created.

Good schools alone do not suffice to produce well-educated persons. Desirable personal qualities are mainly a result of growth within a healthful society. It is quite unfair to place the full load of responsibility for character development on the schools when it properly belongs to the whole complex of social arrangements.

Self-direction in interpersonal association. From the fundamentally social nature of the educative process it does not follow that the nature of the personal environment is the entire basis for personality. No human being merely reflects the quality of life of his close associates. To affirm this would be to deny human freedom, which is as essential to man's nature as the social context is to his growth. No person is simply a replica of other persons, nor even a compound of social influences. A person is what he is by virtue of what he as a free unique individual makes of the environment in which he grows. There is a "choice of the soul," a directing by the self of what the self shall be, within the limits imposed by environmental factors. Furthermore, as pointed out in the last chapter, there are non-human surroundings which also have an effect upon the quality of the person resulting from interaction with them.

Thus, the self in part determines itself, even in interpersonal relationships. An interpersonal relationship has two poles: the person himself and the person to whom he is related, and the quality of experience in that relationship is a function of both parties to it. Thus, what happens to person A through association with person B is not simply A modified in the direction of B, but A modified by his own response to B. If A's response is affirmative to some aspect of B, then A will tend to change in the direction of the B quality, but if A's response is to reject this aspect, A will be confirmed in the opposite direction. Speaking generally, the social nature of education does not mean that the development of personality occurs by conforming the individual to the social environment. Rather, it means that only through interactive associations with other persons does the growing person have the means of creating the self he wills to become.

Knowledge and Interpersonal Relationships

The use of psychology. Since the growth of persons is so closely linked to their relationships with other people and since these associations are so fundamental to the educative process, it may be useful to inquire about the role of knowledge in the improvement of these relationships. Can man by taking thought modify the patterns of personal interaction in desirable directions? Are there established bodies of knowledge which can be brought to bear on questions of human relations? The answer given to these questions largely depends upon one's judgment of the science of psychology. Admittedly, the investigation of human development is enormously complex, and many findings are but rough approximations. Nevertheless, there is a considerable body of fact and theory which can be used in the adjustment of human relationships. This knowledge takes the form of statements about the probable consequences for personality development of certain types of interpersonal relationship. Examples of such statements are: Extremely rigid and strict child-training practices will tend to produce an anxious personality. Early persistent rejection and insecurity will tend to produce anti-social and hostile reactions. Consistency of act and attitude toward the growing child will favor the development of a well-integrated personality. Appreciation and affection will make for a self-confident and loving personality.

These generalizations are statistical in nature. They are not determinate principles which state what must surely result from given types of personal relationship, but they do provide valuable suggestions concerning probable optimum conditions for personality development in desired general directions.

The question of values. The problem still remains as to what constitutes desirable personality. Psychological knowledge may show how to encourage the development of certain personal qualities, but it is not clear that we possess reliable knowledge about which qualities are desirable. This is a question of values and of educational aims, upon which there is no unanimity even among the experts on such matters. The most we can say is this: Knowledge of human development is useful in realizing specified personality goals. If it could be assumed that those goals are also known (whether by scientific ethics, by rational intuition, or by divine revelation), then we would possess a basis in knowledge for the choice of the best types of interpersonal relationships and hence for the determination of this perhaps most important single aspect of educational policy and program.

Association and cognition. Not only may knowledge thus contribute to the optimum conditions of human association, but the nature of interpersonal relationships also has its effect on the cognitive processes. Intellectual inquiry is not an activity wholly detached from the emotions and vital interests of the personality. Every act of reason has its roots in the entire nature of the thinker. Hence the methods and results of a person's rational efforts are conditioned by the quality of interpersonal relationships as they have entered into the formation of his personality.

This is not to say that all reason is rationalization, that one thinks only what he wants to think or emotionally needs to think. There is a certain autonomy and objectivity in reason. But the ideal of complete objective detachment and impartiality is never attained, and it is even doubtful if it should be, for knowledge is a human concern, and hence cannot exclude subjective components. In the determination of this subjective element the character of personal associations plays a major role.

A child who does not learn well in school—for example, one who has difficulties with reading or with arithmetic—is not for that reason alone to be judged unintelligent. More often than not such problems have an emotional basis. In that event the solution lies not in further rational explanation but in discovering and as far as possible correcting the personal relationships which have contributed to the emotional disturbances.

True knowledge is communicable, and the goal of knowing is to establish community. The psychotic is one who inhabits a private world; his "knowledge" is uncommunicable. He is unable to relate himself satisfactorily to other persons through conceptual symbols. Sanity—the healthy mind—on the other hand, consists in the ability to use ideas so as to establish wide and deep understandings with other persons. The sage, the truly wise man, is he whose knowledge springs from human insights and sympathies embracing all mankind, that is to say, whose knowledge is a key to the universal human community.

Particular fields of knowledge, such as the special sciences, history, the arts, religion, and philosophy, are defined by symbolic systems understood and accepted within the respective communities of discourse (see Chapter 17). Thus the content of a person's knowledge depends upon the kinds of communities of discourse in which he can participate, i.e., upon the possibility of certain kinds of interpersonal relationships. Really to know mathematics, chemistry, sociology, surrealist art, or Buddhist religion is possible only for those who can agree to the criteria of meaning which form the bond of association among mathematicians, chemists, etc., respectively. Hence, there would appear to be an intimate connection between the quality of a person's relationships with others and his intellectual competence.

The Nature and Functions of the Family

Of the many agencies of education probably none is more important than the family. It is in the family chiefly that the most significant face-to-face relationships are experienced and the essential characteristics of personality are formed. There are five aspects of family life which will now be considered.

Biological. The primary reason for the existence of the family is the biological preservation of the species. Human beings are in part distinguished from the lower animals by their long period of early dependency. The family is a social institution designed to fix responsibility for the protection of the young during these years of dependency and for training the young eventually to assume independence. There is no reason in theory why this protective function needs to be performed by families. There could be state nurseries, for example. However, the family system appears to be the most effective way of getting the job done. The intimate bonds of mutual interest and affection normally prevailing between parents and children make for a quality and persistence of concern which could scarcely be duplicated by any other type of social arrangement. The protective and supportive functions of the family are, of course, more than physiological in character. Parents are not merely responsible for feeding their children and guarding them from physical injury. The biological role of the family relates to the entire personality of the developing child. Protection and support are educative functions, and the manner of their performance may have profound effects on the character of the child. Excessive zeal in shielding a child from danger, usually stemming from the parent's own fearfulness, is itself a danger to the child's personality, producing anxiety, frustration, and inability to cope with the physical environment. On the other extreme, carelessness in the matter of protection may lead to actual physical injury and to anxiety about being neglected. Similarly, a policy of immediate gratification of all the child's demands is at least as harmful as insufficient material support.

The parents are also responsible for providing an environment in which the child may best develop basic physical skills such as walking, running, and manual competence. These are learned largely by imitation of older persons, with much trial and error. The physical setting should be safe but not without variety and moderate challenge. Parental interest in the child's achievements is helpful, but anxiety to accelerate the learning process is harmful. Parents should know that physical skills can be acquired only after requisite physical and neural maturation, and they should know both the major stages which the child's development may be expected to follow and something of the range of individual differences in the growth patterns.

Psychological. The family also serves basic psychological functions. This was clear even in discussing the biological functions, the performance of which, as indicated above, has important psychological aspects. The connection between the biological and the psychological consists primarily in this: that the qualities of a child's personality—e.g., motivation, emotional tone, intellectual development, and goals—are greatly influenced by the manner in which parents, or parent-substitutes, minister to the child's basic physical needs—e.g., for food, warmth, safety, and cleanliness. This empirically established fact refutes any view of human nature which too sharply separates mental from physical or soul from body. The nature of "mind" or "soul," however these may be defined, is clearly influenced in large measure by the way in which bodily needs are met in the early years of life.

This organic, unified conception of human nature to which developmental studies point leads to a repudiation of the concept of education as concerned only with the "higher" sphere of the "mind" and to a new appreciation for the educative role of the family. Possibly the most important single factor in determining the direction of a person's growth is the way in which his bodily needs in infancy and early childhood are met. Thus the parents through the most simple, humble, and earth-bound activities on behalf of the child lay the foundation for the entire educative process, including the highest intellectual or spiritual achievements of later years.

Psychologists differ in their judgments about the decisiveness of the early years. Some believe that by the age of six, (say), the essential characteristics of the personality are set. Others hold that the first year is the crucial one. Some believe in the possibility of fundamental personality changes as a result of experiences in later childhood (e.g., in adolescence) or even as an adult. Whatever the age level of effective influence, the interpersonal relationships within the family are of major significance. Brothers and sisters, as well as parents, play their role, helping to develop mature relationships with peers as well as with elders.

There is abundant evidence that the basis for confident, responsible, co-operative adult personality lies in interpersonal relationships within the family characterized by consistent and genuine concern for the well-being of others, sensitivity to their needs, and generosity in fulfilling those needs, within the framework of an intelligent and realistic appraisal of competing claims on time, energy, and material resources. Psychological damage of the most various sorts results, on the other hand, from family relationships involving arbitrariness, neglect or rejection, insensitivity, injustice, and thoughtlessness.

Economic. The family also performs fundamental economic functions. It is largely as family units that claims are made upon society for a just share of the available store of goods and services. Parents must secure and administer resources which the dependent young could not obtain for themselves. It is also chiefly in the family that basic attitudes toward property are developed. In one family the child learns by observation of parental behavior and perception of parental attitudes that property is something to be possessed, accumulated, and protected from the grasp of others. The resulting personality tends to be fearful of loss, anxious about the precariousness of life, and hostile toward other people. Another family considers that property is meant for consumption, and that material goods are valuable only as they provide immediate enjoyment. The corresponding personalities tend to be sense-oriented, governed by pleasure rather than by rational or moral principles. In a third kind of family property is considered as a means for attaining intellectual, moral, or social goals. It is not for security, nor for consumption, but for use. Material goods are instruments or tools for achieving more ultimate values. In such families economic life becomes the means of teaching practical idealism, responsible stewardship, and renunciation of immediate satisfactions for the sake of long-range values.

Once again, as in the question of meeting simple biological needs, the educative impact of the parents' attitudes toward property is profound. Education is not simply a matter of the mind, of books and ideas, independent of gross material concerns. It is in the family's concrete dealings with economic goods—whether through heaping up for prestige and security, consuming for pleasure, or administering for ideal ends—that decisive traits of personality are determined in the child. To a considerable extent it rests with the family whether the growing child will prefer to hoard or to share, to compete destructively or to cooperate.

Cultural. The family is an institution through which much of the cultural capital of society is transmitted from generation to generation. The child's way of speaking is largely a reflection of what he hears at home. His attitudes toward books and music are greatly influenced by the values his parents place on them. Ideas of right and wrong and standards of what are worthwhile vocational goals are learned primarily within the family. In general, the profound cultural significance of the family lies principally in its influence on the growing child's system of values. The values learned in the home—usually not explicitly or verbally, but through subtly communicated feelings and by the implications of overt behavior—are a major factor in the motivation of learning in school, on the job, and in every other activity of life.

Parents are also normally at some pains to teach their children manners. On first consideration this seems a relatively superficial part of education. Ways of greeting friends or strangers, habits of extending courtesy, respectful behavior in relation to older people, etiquette in dining and dating—these and other customary behavior patterns vary widely between cultures and between subgroups (e.g., social classes) within the same society. There is nothing fundamental or universally human about manner systems. Yet some parents believe that "manners make the man," and hence place great emphasis on learning the social proprieties. Such education tends to produce persons more concerned with conformity and with appearing acceptable to other people than with "being one's self," or with having inner integrity, originality, creativity, and initiative.

On the positive side it must be granted that, superficial though they may be, manners do fulfill an important social function. They help to keep the social mechanism running smoothly by providing certain definite rules of expected conduct which can easily become habitual. They dramatize and thus help to maintain a host of useful social distinctions. They may also serve as outward signs of deeply significant ideals, such as the sacredness of human personality. In any case, there is no avoiding education in manners; there can be no social order without them. The aim should be to teach them as useful social instruments so that they may become facilities and resources for free and creative personalities rather than chains which bind men to arbitrary convention and condemn them to the hypocrisy of external conformity.

Spiritual. Finally, it may be urged that the family is not ultimately an institution of human contrivance but that its foundation is in the divine ordinance. "God has set the solitary in families." On this view the family exercises essential spiritual functions. The spiritual nature of the family is symbolized by the consummation of marriage as a religious rite, indicating thereby that the establishment of the new family is in accordance with God's intention and plan. The arrival of children is further celebrated in rites such as baptism, circumcision, and naming ceremonies, in which parents are reminded of their spiritual obligations to the young.

To the believer, the relationship of parent to child is but a dim reflection of the divine paternity; as God the Father creates and provides for all his children, so the human father begets and cares for his young. Similarly, the love of mother for her child is a partial manifestation at the human level of the love which God has for his whole creation. According to this view, the most important educational contribution of the family is to impart to the child some knowledge of God, not primarily through doctrinal instruction but through that loving concern which is the mark of the divine nature.

Looked at from the human side, it is also quite evident that the nature of religious beliefs is deeply influenced by parent-child relationships. A child whose parents have provided him with tenderness and security will be inclined to look upon life and destiny and the powers that govern them with confidence and trust. On the other hand, one who has grown up in an atmosphere of hostility and deprivation can easily believe in a world managed by devils, by blind impersonal forces, or by a tyrannical God of wrath. In fact, from the nature of a person's real religious convictions it is often possible to infer the quality of interpersonal relationships within his early family life. The family, then, plays a central role in the spiritual nurture of the child, in forming his basic outlook and attitudes toward the meaning and worth of his life, of the universe and his place in it.

The School of Friendship

Face-to-face relationships do not, of course, occur only within the family. We propose now, therefore, to consider the significance of friendship generally, both within and outside of the family circle, in the development of persons. "Friendship" is a vague and ambiguous word, and the relationship called by that name has many facets. In the paragraphs that follow a number of types and motives in friendship will be discussed.

Dependency. On one extreme, friendship means a relationship of dependency. A "friend" is someone who will supply what one wants or needs. If that person asks something in return, he is no longer a friend. Such friends are valued not for what they are in themselves but solely for the gifts they bestow. The relationship in these cases is not truly interpersonal since concern is with the self and with the goods to be received rather than with the other person.

Friendship of this kind is usually unstable and short-lived because there are few people who are willing to continue giving without return. Hence, the dependent ones are forced to seek out a constant supply of new friends to replace those who have become tired of being used. As this goes on, the favor-seeker often becomes disillusioned and cynical about other people, and even more confirmed in his self-centeredness. There is the hope and the possibility, however, that the repeated experience of loss and the real emptiness of the purely dependent relationship will drive him to more productive and truly satisfying types of friendship.

Friendship dominated by the acquisitive motive is obviously unfavorable to the development of personality since it tends to enclose the person within the boundaries of his own present interests and to minimize his opportunities for the genuine interpersonal associations which are essential to personal growth.

Companionship. Another basis for friendship is the desire for companionship. Man is a social animal. He does not like to dwell alone. He has the deeply grounded insight that his very existence depends upon relatedness to other persons and that his own nature has been fashioned through encounters with them. Hence isolation means not only loss of others but, what is more painful, threatened loss of self. In companionship human beings seek to confirm and advance that interpersonal mutuality in which man's social nature is grounded.

Friendship is one of the ways in which the growing child comes to know himself as a self. In the gang, club, or play group he identifies himself with his peers, and in the behavior of the friends with whom he has identified he sees his own selfhood objectified. Furthermore, through the conscious effort to belong he incorporates characteristics of the social milieu into his own personality. Habits of speech, manners, interests, and values are taken over from companions, each assisting the other to achieve a sense of belonging, of being accepted, and above all of being somebody definite. The exclusiveness of many childhood associations, the fierce loyalties, the secrecy and closedness of the cliques are to a considerable extent merely devices for dramatizing the definiteness of selfhood by persons who are still very unsure of who they really are.

Clearly the friendship of companions is one of the essential factors in education. It is through these interpersonal associations that the developing person benefits from and learns to participate in the wider social existence beyond the confines of the immediate family.

While companionship is essential to the formation and discovery of the self, there may also be important values in solitude. As mentioned earlier, solitude is necessary for the consolidation and assimilation of experience in association. It is an unhealthy sign when a person feels a constant need for companionship, when he can never be comfortable alone. Association for such a person may actually be a way of escaping rather than of finding the self. Thus companionship does not, in itself, guarantee personal growth. Identification with others may be either a means of realizing the self through social experiment or a means of avoiding the challenge of becoming a self in one's own right. The ideal condition for personal development would appear to be constructive companionship and solitude in mutually enhancing alternation.

Cooperation. A third basis for friendship is the mutual advantage that results from cooperative endeavor. By working and playing together greater achievements are possible than could be attained by solitary action. In friendships of cooperation each person depends upon the other for certain benefits and in return makes his own contribution to the common good. By virtue of this reciprocity, cooperation is likely to be a more stable and productive basis for friendship than sheer dependency. However, neither type of friendship rests upon genuine concern for other persons, but solely upon satisfaction of wants. When persons or circumstances change in such a way that advantages no longer accrue from cooperation, the friendship may dissolve. Such essentially expedient and prudential relationships are not in the truest sense interpersonal, since each implicitly regards the other as a commodity or facility to be used rather than as a person to be accepted and respected in his own right.

The experience of cooperative endeavor teaches the crucial lesson that man can gain his ends effectively only by joint effort. Man's social nature rests on this practical basis as well as on metaphysical and psychological grounds. Without mutual effort the greater part of the benefits of civilization would not be available. It is therefore a necessary task of education to introduce the young to the arts of cooperation.

Competition. "Friendly rivalry" also has a place in friendship. There is competition wherein each seeks to out-do the other in some work of wit, skill, or endurance. The competitive spirit is destructive when the defeat of another person becomes a source of satisfaction in itself or when precedence over others becomes the criterion for success and the measure of personal worth. But competition need not be of this sort. It can be a useful means of stimulating constructive effort, wherein each person serves as an example and a challenge to others and each is honored for the sincerity and dedication with which he uses the powers available to him.

Therefore, it is not a question, as frequently suggested in educational discussions, of cooperation *versus* competition. One need not decide for one or the other. It is rather a question of the attitude, method, and objectives of both cooperation and competition. Some forms of cooperation are as cynical in spirit and unworthy in aim as the worst forms of competition. And competition rightly conceived may actually be a high form of cooperation, a person-enhancing interpersonal stimulus to the fulfillment of individual potentials.

Shared values. The preceding analysis of good competition touched upon a further conception of friendship as dedication to shared values. A friend is one who has the same ideals, interests, and enthusiasms, who is dedicated to the same causes and motivated by the same concerns. The friend is prized because he embodies and illustrates what one considers of worth, and not for any efficiency which association would promote. Such friendship is less subject to alteration by changing circumstances than the prudential type. It is as enduring as personal value systems and character structures. It is also more truly personal than friendships for advantage since one's pattern of values is a better measure of personality than the objective tasks he feels obliged to accomplish.

Against this basis for friendship should be mentioned the injustice of judging the worth of another person by one's own standards of value. A person is a unique self who cannot be understood rightly if constrained within the appraisal system of any other person.

Even with this defect, the friendship of shared values is an important educative influence. It is difficult to develop and maintain ideals without the support of other like-minded people. Sharing one's interests and concerns with friends is the surest way to keep motivation high.

Devotion. A final basis for friendship is devotion to another person for his own sake. Such friendship is not founded on receiving but on giving, not on overcoming one's own sense of isolation but on contributing to the fullness of life for another, not on mutual advantage through cooperative endeavor but on advantage to the friend through effort on his behalf, not on values shared but on benefits contributed. All the earlier types of friendship are entirely reasonable by some standard. The friendship of devotion, in contrast, essentially defies explanation. One is not devoted to another for any reason of gain or even of ideal. The question of why one should care for the friend is regarded as an impertinence. There is no reason but the friend himself.

Devotion is the practice of self-surrender on behalf of another. It is consummated in the life of sacrifice. Beyond all calculation, efficiency and gain, beyond all idealism, the devoted friend gives of himself, if necessary even sacrificing life itself, for the sake of the other.

Devotion to others is regarded by many as the finest flower of human life. It is not easily taught, if it can be taught at all. Some have considered it as an infusion of divine grace, a supernatural virtue, rather than as a product of human nurture. Perhaps it is best fostered by example. One who has been the recipient of devotion which asks no return, makes no judgments, seeks no advantage, and advances no interests, may from sheer thankfulness for the privilege of such friendship seek to relate himself to others in the same way. In whatever manner it is learned, such friendship is a high achievement, showing evidence of an unusual degree of maturity. It is only possible in persons who are so free and secure that they do not need constantly to protect themselves from loss nor to receive from others confirmation of their own worth and power.

Love

In the preceding paragraphs some of the varieties of friendship have been indicated, beginning with the purely acquisitive and concluding with the utterly sacrificial type. The latter extreme would certainly merit the name love. Indeed, friendship of several kinds is associated with the idea of love. At the same time, love would commonly be regarded as a more intense and a more intimate type of relationship than friendship. One may have a friend for purely practical reasons, without the deep attachment suggested by love.

On closer examination it turns out that the concept "love" is as ambiguous as that of friendship. In what follows some of the meanings will be suggested, and the connection among these and with education will be explored.

The meanings of love. In a metaphorical sense love can refer to a relationship of persons to things, as in the exclamation "I love my new automobile!" Such love is simply desire for or attachment to things. Not very different is the love which merely expresses sexual desire. Such love is not truly interpersonal, since its goal is only the gratification of a physiological hunger and the other person is treated as an object to be used. The most common meaning of love is the feeling of approbation and of emotional satisfaction in the presence of a person whose outlook and interests are similar to one's own or different in such a way as to complement and enlarge one's own experience. This kind of love, built upon a many-sided mutuality—physical, social, moral, intellectual, and esthetic—is the foundation of many a happy marriage and other forms of affectionate association.

A child's love for its parents is somewhat different. It is a response of gratitude for benefits received and a recognition of the blood kinship wherein the child sees the parents as the source of his whole being. Still more generalized is love of family, group, or country, expressed in loyalty to them and willingness to make sacrifices for them in the face of external threats. An even more inclusive kind of love is the spirit of benevolence for all mankind, the attitude of concern for the welfare of the whole human race. More abstract yet is the love of the ideal, dedication to the good, the true, and the beautiful, as experienced by the prophet, the scholar, and the artist.

It is even said that there should be love of enemies. From the standpoint of liking, of approbation, or of mutuality enemies cannot be loved. Love of enemies must have a different basis, namely, a will-to-good for the enemy, an intention to heal a broken relationship by acts and attitudes of reconciliation. Such love brings us again to the relationship of sacrificial devotion, of love for others based solely upon active concern for their welfare and not upon the pleasure or profit to be derived by oneself from the relationship. Finally, the theist speaks of the love of God as the highest, wholly perfect form of love, purely outgiving, forgiving, and sacrificial in character, a love manifest in the creation of the world, in its preservation and continuous replenishment, but particularly in the provision made for the enrichment, elevation, and healing of the life of man.

The unity of love. In the face of these many meanings of the term love, is there any justification for using the same word for them all? Is there some quality in which all the varieties share? Is there some unity amid the diversity of meanings? It would appear that there are two qualities which all types of love have in common. First, there is no love without depth of feeling. Whether it be a biological craving or a longing for the ideal, love stirs the emotions. Even love of the enemy, while not based on a feeling of pleasure in his presence, presupposes a deeply felt conviction which overrides the also deeply felt natural antipathy.

Secondly, every form of love is a seeking for completeness, an effort to complement one's being by establishing a relationship with another being. It arises from a sense of want, of insufficiency, of need. The differences in types of love are due to the variety of wants and the corresponding variety of modes for their satisfaction.

Are the different kinds of love united only in a formal way, standing to one another in an analogical relationship, or is there a more organic connection between them? One answer emphasizes the distinctness of types. Sexual love is regarded as related to love of truth only metaphorically. The former is physiological, the latter intellectual. The two kinds of love are functionally independent of each other. Against this view is the conception that there is an intrinsic relationship, an actual functional correspondence between types, as for example, between the love of a child for his parents and general benevolence. This view is based on belief in the essential unity of human nature, which means that man *as a whole* seeks to grow by establishing complementary relationships, and the particular manner of this one seeking will depend on personal and temporal circumstances. Thus, the infant's love for the mother who gives the milk, the love which seeks fulfillment in sexual union, and the mystic's love for God can be seen as different ways of responding to the basic human urge for enlarging life by becoming linked to other beings.

Assuming the essential unity of love, there are two opposite conceptions of the relative priority of the different types. The first position is that the intellectual and spiritual types of love are simply an outgrowth and manifestation of the biological types. Thus, devotion to a moral ideal may be interpreted as the sublimation of the sex drive, and the celibate saint's dedication to God may be seen as a diversion into different channels of erotic energies that would normally go into conjugal and parental relationships. The second position is that physical craving and the other "lower" forms of love are manifestations of a pervasive spiritual principle which is more purely revealed in intellectual, moral, and esthetic aspirations. On this view, for example, sexual attraction might be regarded as an embodiment, on the physical plane, of the love of God in and for his creation.

Love in man and in cosmos. Consideration of the types of love and their possible unity prompts speculation about the place of love in human nature and in the whole scheme of things. Is love, in all its kinds, a fundamental human need? The drive to become related to other beings, to overcome isolation and estrangement, is pervasive and persistent in human life. The craving for satisfaction of bodily wants, the social impulse, the intellectual quest for cognitive relatedness, the yearning of the soul for God—may not all these be different manifestations of a basic striving for togetherness? Furthermore, may not the same drive be at work in the entire cosmic process? Elementary particles uniting to form atoms, atoms combining into molecules and molecules into manifold material substances, the further combinings to produce living substances, cells, plants, and animals—may these not be so many examples of a cosmic tendency toward coordination, a tendency manifest at the human level as love? And in this universality of love, which furnishes a key to the interpretation of human and cosmic evolution, may there not possibly be found a basis for designating love as the ultimate *good,* as that tendency to which the whole scheme of things appears to be dedicated?

Education and love. To the extent that love is of the essence in human nature and crucial in human development, and particularly if love also has cosmic sanction, it constitutes a basic criterion for the educative process. It provides a standard of educational aim and context (all growth to be directed toward enlarging and deepening feelingful relationships) and of educational method (all teaching to be an expression of loving concern of teacher for pupil). Education is seen in this light as the means by which man consciously participates in the furtherance of the whole evolutionary process.

The question of the unity of love also has important consequences for education. If sexual love and love of truth, for example, are organically related, then intellectual education cannot successfully proceed in disregard of the sexual factor or in repudiation of it. By the same token, sex education cannot be satisfactorily conducted without reference to intellectual factors. Again, religious education cannot be effective in the absence of concern about the affectional quality of interpersonal relationships within the family. Similarly, it can be urged that family relationships will prosper most when the relevance of religious factors is clearly recognized.

If man is an organic whole, education in love and for love must be based upon an awareness of the many-sidedness and interpenetration of the human being's strivings for relatedness. From this standpoint there can be no education of the mind alone (nor, for that matter, of the body or the emotions alone). It is the whole person who learns. Love of goodness, of beauty, and of God have roots deep in love of parents, friends, and teachers, and the love of persons is in turn enlarged and deepened when transfused with the love of truth and holiness.

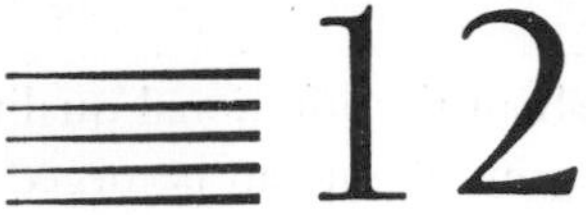

12 Citizenship

THE DEVELOPMENT of persons is influenced not only by direct personal encounters in family life and friendship, but also by membership and participation in more inclusive social groupings. These larger spheres of social belonging may be included under the general designation "citizenship." In contrast with the face-to-face relationships of the more intimate associations, citizenship is concerned with *public* relationships. Public matters concern not the individual person in his particularity and uniqueness but the person as a member of the social organization. The relationships are based upon social function and upon the nature of the social structure rather than upon specific personal qualities. Life as a citizen is in this sense impersonal. The primary consideration is the body politic, in which the individual must find his place.

Direct interpersonal relationships have a direct impact on the formation of personality. The educative effect of citizenship is important also, but operates indirectly. The larger social structure determines the nature of the general human environment in which the person grows. It sets conditions and limits with which the developing individual must come to terms and provides resources which enlarge enormously the scope of his possible activities. The general structure of society also gets reflected in interpersonal relationships; families and peer groups operate differently under different types of political arrangements, which thus indirectly influence the direction of human development.

Human Nature and the Social Order

Man as a political animal. The social nature of man is not fulfilled through participation in face-to-face groupings alone. There is a dynamism which drives human beings on to more inclusive forms of social relatedness. Above all, man wants and needs his immediate associates, but by themselves they cannot satisfy his social needs. He aspires to build towns and cities, to establish states and empires, even to envision a world community. Man is a political animal in that he manifests as a species an intrinsic drive to establish ever wider and more complex social structures. His imagination forever transcends the narrow bounds of custom and necessity to invent new forms of corporate existence. The lower forms of living things know only how to live within the environment set by physical nature and by instinctual patterns of social coordination. Man, by contrast, not only transforms the physical environment to suit his purposes but also creates his own social patterns. To say that man is a political animal means that human beings construct their own forms of social organization, that community-making is the very essence of being human. Of all the creatures, only man has such an endless variety of social arrangements; he alone is not restricted to some standardized, built-in type of association. It is as characteristic of human nature to build communities as it is to use language, and the kinds of social relationship established are as diverse as the languages of mankind.

The purposes of community. Why do human beings organize themselves into communities? What purposes do the many forms of association serve? The most elementary answer is that mere coexistence requires some kind of social structure. Each person has his own interests and needs, which will frequently conflict with those of other persons. Two different people cannot occupy exactly the same space at the same time nor eat the identical piece of food. Hence principles of assignment and distribution must be set up. There is no inherent harmony in the nature of things which will automatically regulate the affairs of men. This is a task which man himself must assume. The many different kinds of social arrangement are simply the various ways discovered by man for rendering coexistence possible.

But the political life of man serves more than this minimal purpose. It enables human beings to fulfill their goals more efficiently than would be possible individually and to accomplish tasks which could never be done separately. The effectiveness of a community is not merely the sum of the powers of the individuals who compose it. With the right kind of organization the efficiency of the whole may far exceed the sum of individual powers. A community is not, like a mechanical structure, only as strong as the weakest member. On the contrary, the strength of a good community exceeds the power of its strongest members. This multiplication of efficacy is accomplished through the coordination of parts into a mutually reinforcing whole.

The basis for the existence of social organization is specialization of function. All persons do not perform identical tasks; each concentrates his effort along certain directions in which he can become particularly proficient.

He then supplies many others with the fruit of his special skill and expects in return a share of the products from many other specialists. The character of a society consists essentially in the nature and distribution of specialized functions and in the provisions made for exchange of available goods and services.

Doubtless the purposes of association are grounded in more than these practical considerations. It is not only that men must coexist and that without social organization there could be no cities, no orchestras, no universities, no abundant food, no science, literature, or engineering. Society also satisfies man's basic urge to create. Communities are like works of art and scientific theories. They are products of the human constructive capacity, of the imagination and spirituality which are man's unique qualities. It would be to miss the most interesting aspect of social existence to ascribe it solely to practical motives. The rich diversity of human organization is evidence of man's delight in creating meaningful forms of existence. And the materials for these forms are the most fascinating of all entities—other persons. Hence the unremitting concern human beings have for the communities they have made.

Personality and the social order. If man is by nature a political animal and if the purposes of association have to do in part with intrinsic features of human nature, it would seem to follow that there should be some correspondence between the form of the state and the personality characteristics of its citizens. It is not uncommon to refer to the personality of the typical Frenchman, Englishman, Chinese, Russian, American, or Irishman. Granted that no stereotype does justice to the characteristics of a people, much less to the character of its individual members, the persistence of such group typing is evidence of the belief in a correlation between personality and the social order. The social structure developed by any people through many generations of corporate life is designed to express certain dominant personality traits, and these social arrangements in turn tend to perpetuate and confirm the corresponding qualities of personality. In fact, it is not possible to assign priority in time to either the personality type or the nature of the social order. The United States is a political entity whose democratic social and political structure was created by men personally dedicated to ideals of freedom and equality. Yet these democratic personalities were nurtured in societies—English, French, Dutch, and the like—which had previously embodied important democratic ideas in their systems of organization. The quality of personality and of the social order are indissolubly bound together. It is as true to say that the state is the citizen writ large as that the citizen is the state in miniature. Social organizations and their constituent members grow and evolve simultaneously and in qualitative correspondence.

It is chiefly in relation to systems of value that the relationship between personality and social structure is evident. The institutional arrangements of a society are the concrete embodiments of shared personal values. For example, a society with a strong centralized governing authority reflects the high value placed on order and security. Again, a society whose teachers and artists are economically and socially neglected reflects a low general valuation of intellectual and esthetic experience. The quality of one's personality is defined by his system of values. It is only necessary to study the nature of the social arrangements—the status system, the political structure, the character of the various non-governmental associations—to discover what on the average counts for most with the individual citizens, and it is likewise easy to predict, on the basis of the dominant social institutions, the ideals to which life in the society will predispose the young.

Education and Social Organization

Society as educator. The connection between personality and the social order noted above makes clear the educative significance of society. The structure of social institutions is a major means for directing the development of the young. The patterns which growth should follow are not primarily in the form of abstract principles within the teacher's mind; they are concretely embodied in the actual institutions of society. There are laws to obey, and penalties for their infraction. There are political, professional, cultural, social, religious, and philanthropic agencies, participation in which provides the only practicable way of making one's will effective in shaping social policy. There are channels of governmental authority through which the conduct of public life is determined. The growth of human personality takes place within this complex web of institutional arrangements in such a way that the habit patterns and value systems developed will enable one to live successfully in his particular society.

Individuals come and go, while institutions remain. Laws and customs generally change slowly, in comparison with the change which occurs in individual development. Hence the social order can be the relatively constant standard by which the growth process may be guided. Any educational program which is not built upon the solid foundation of actual social institutions must certainly fail to produce persons who can live useful and satisfying lives. The educative efficacy of society is not realized primarily through formal instruction (e.g., by the reading of textbooks in civics or sociology) but by actual participation as a citizen in the life of the community. Respect for law, recognition of public authority, and knowledge of how to exercise power through organization are also early learned by the young through observation of their elders' activities as citizens and through perception of their attitudes toward the various agencies of social life.

Education and social conservation. Society as educator seeks to propagate itself from generation to generation. The fundamental purpose of education is to transmit to the young the social gains embodied in the culture. Civilization is not self-perpetuating, not naturally immortal. It can be maintained only as it is continually re-created in each new generation. If for only one generation children were left without instruction in the cultural heritage, all the gains of civilization accumulated through centuries of human effort would be lost, and the long, slow upward climb would have to begin all over again. Knowledge is not transmitted by genetic inheritance but only through education. Education is the means of social conservation. It is the life-line of civilization.

There are many types of social organization, many ways which human beings have discovered for relating themselves to each other in communities. But this does not mean that just any system will do, that every kind of institutions and laws will be satisfactory. Enduring cultures are long-tested and hard-won attainments, resulting from much costly social experimentation. These achievements are not easily regained when lost. Hence, it is important to conserve them and to transmit them intact to each succeeding generation as a precious legacy.

It is natural for those who have been nurtured in a given culture to take it for granted, oblivious of the price that had to be paid to construct it and of the completeness of their dependence upon the accomplishments of their predecessors. One of the tasks of education is to instruct the children in the achievements of the fathers who created the commonwealth. This is the purpose of giving a prominent place to courses in American history in American schools, English history in English schools, Russian history in Russian schools, and so on. Similarly, there is every reason to acquaint young people with the history of their state and city and of particular organizations to which they belong, such as religious groups, business associations, and political parties. The function of such education is simply to heighten the awareness of values in the social order of which one is a part so that it may be understood, appreciated, and protected by those who have inherited it. Perhaps even more effective than formal instruction is the celebration of social values in various rites such as parades, initiations, and pageants and by the use of appropriate symbols such as flags, uniforms, and emblems of office. In any case, whether by history or by rite and symbol, the significance of the social achievement needs to be made evident so that the debt of the present generation to the past may in part be paid by conserving the tradition intact for the future.

Education and social reconstruction. Social conservation is certainly one legitimate aim of education. But another possible objective is social reconstruction. Is the new generation merely to learn of past achievements and seek to preserve them unimpaired to their descendants? Is the role of education to be exclusively the transmission of a tradition? It seems clear that even faithfulness to the creative past would indicate the duty of further creation in the present so that not merely a tradition but an improved inheritance may be handed on to future generations. Specifically, the American heritage did not become fixed and final for all time with the framing of the Constitution. The American tradition is as truly revolutionary as it is conservative. Or better, the true American conservative is one who transmits not an unchanging social system but a revolutionary tradition.

It would seem that both conservation and reconstruction are necessary aspects of education in relation to the social order. Exclusive attention to conservation leads to stagnation and rigidity. Children need to learn not only the story of their own society but the history of other peoples and cultures, whose ways of life may provide valuable suggestions for the improvement of understanding and conduct. It is possible, however, to be so concerned with change and with alternative schemes that the important values of the established tradition are neglected or even despised. The new generation perhaps needs first of all to be made vividly aware of the social system which nurtured them and gives meaning and structure to their existence, and only then to learn how loyalty to the best they know and true devotion to their own heritage require the search for means of social betterment.

The Levels of Citizenship

There are several levels of citizenship, characterized by the inclusiveness or scope of the communities to which the citizen belongs. Each level presents its own peculiar educational problems and opportunities.

Local community. Every citizen is first of all a member of a local community, contained within a relatively small geographic area such as a borough, village, or town. It is small enough to permit immediate personal knowledge, by any member, of events and situations pertinent to the life of the community. The relationships are not primarily or necessarily face-to-face, as in the family and among friends. Much organized activity even at the local level takes place impersonally, in the sense that the institution and the function rather than the individual person are the primary consideration. Taxes, police protection, provision for schooling, and property regulation are public rather than personal and individual concerns. But the distinguishing feature of the local community is that these impersonal functions can easily become personalized by the establishment of face-to-face relationships among those who perform them. The tax assessors, the policemen, the teachers, and the school board or zoning committee members may each be known and treated as individual personal friends and associates. Public duties are not performed by distant people known at most by name and reputation, but by neighbors whom anyone can know personally if he so desires. It follows that the local community provides a transition from impersonal to interpersonal relationships, establishing a means of making the essentially impersonal civic functions personally relevant.

The local community also makes possible forms of community organization specifically designed to serve the particular needs and interests of its constituent members. Geographic, historical, and other factors create groups with special characteristics and unique traditions. These distinctive values can be preserved only if there is provision for variation in social and cultural patterns from community to community at the local level.

The state. Beyond the local community the citizen holds membership in one or more larger associations, which can be designated as the state (a term meant to include the nation as a whole and its political subdivisions down to but not including the local level). The operation of the state is largely impersonal since centralized controls and services for large numbers of people cannot possibly be provided on a face-to-face basis. The state links local communities together in such a way as to enable the larger commonwealth to accomplish what the separate communities could not achieve. The diversity of endowments is utilized for mutual advantage, with rural communities, for example, supplying food for cities and cities in turn providing manufactured goods and commercial facilities. The exchange is, of course, not always equal. Depending on the nature of the state, the rich and strong may be called upon to make sacrifices on behalf of the poor and weak, or the former may be even further favored at the expense of the latter.

The state also acts to set limits to local prerogatives and to establish certain national traditions and standards. For example, in a nation dedicated to the ideal of freedom no local community can decide that it will permit the owning of slaves. Again, in a monogamous state the people of a particular town may not practice polygamy. Nor can segregation of the races in the use of public facilities be a local option within a nation which has an established policy of equal civil rights for all citizens.

Thus the state provides the educational setting within which appreciation can be gained both of the value of group differences and of the necessity for the renunciation of special claims in the interests of the common good.

The world community. The most inclusive of all communities would be that of all mankind. Is world citizenship possible, or is membership in the state the highest practicable level? Is the world community the dream of Utopia-makers, or is it in some sense an actuality? Until the twentieth century a case could possibly be made for national isolation. But with the rapid development of the means of travel and communication and the expansion of trade and commerce the lines of interconnection and interdependence have become so many and so deeply woven into the whole fabric of modern civilization that some conception of world community appears essential. Whether one likes it or nor, what the people of one nation do has some effect upon the people of every other nation. In the modern world no nation can live wholly unto itself. In war and in peace the destinies of all people are indissolubly linked.

Actually world community is both a fact and an ideal. Men are by force of modern circumstance citizens of one world. But the task of organizing that world for maximum peace and progress is still far from accomplished. World community is related to individual nations in somewhat the same way as the nation is related to local communities. In a world commonwealth of nations the family of man can achieve heights of civilization impossible to individual states. Each nation has its special resources and skills which it can trade with others for mutual advantage. Ideally also the strong can aid the weak, and the rich help to supply the poor.

One price of world community is the surrender of absolute and complete national autonomy and sovereignty. The peoples of the world cannot at one and the same time be fully independent and interdependent. The actions of nations cannot always be unilateral. There must be some willing renunciation of immediate national prerogatives in the interest of the family of nations. This calls for devotion to the good of all mankind which may at times call into question the traditional standards of national interest.

The actuality of world community, made effective largely through mass communication, exerts a powerful influence in education. It is scarcely possible any longer to grow up in total ignorance of the customs, achievements, ideals, and privileges of other peoples. The momentous consequence of this fact is the growing awareness that conditions and ways of life handed on by traditional educational systems and long accepted unquestioningly are not the only conceivable ones and are neither inevitable nor beyond the possibility of change. The reality of one world is making evident to all the enormous disparity in material and cultural attainments among different peoples. The world-wide revolutionary movements of the twentieth century, resulting directly from this awareness, are attempts, often perhaps inappropriate in method, to redress the balance and to create economic and social conditions more conducive to the realization of human potentialities for all people.

It is something of a paradox that the actuality of one world should cause revolutionary movements which emphasize nationalism and independence and thus pluralism and separateness rather than unity. The contradiction is only apparent. The struggle for autonomy is both a fight against an outmoded form of unity, in colonialism, and a fight for the creation of national and cultural identity, quite analogous to the struggle of the growing child to become a person in his own right and not merely an appendage of the parents. Only when a people has realized its selfhood can it enter into a new and maturely responsible relationship with other peoples in the world community of nations.

Education for world citizenship calls for opportunities through such media as books, pictures, and travel to learn about the ways and works of other nations and to understand sympathetically the alternative systems of life and thought open to mankind. It does not, however, call for any diminution of loyalty to the best traditions of one's own people. The special characteristics of different national cultures may be sources of enrichment for the life of all nations. World community does not rest upon the uniformity of all but upon compatible diversity. Hence there need be no conflict between education for citizenship in the state and in the world. In the long run it would appear that the highest loyalty to country must presuppose devotion to the world community as well.

Voluntary Associations

Life within the social order comprises two kinds of associations, voluntary and involuntary. On the face-to-face level, family membership is involuntary: the child does not choose his parents. Friendships, on the other hand, are voluntary associations. Among the more impersonal types of association considered in this chapter those based upon residence in a particular town or nation are essentially involuntary. To be sure, one can usually choose the town where he will live, but generally nationality is decided by circumstance of birth. The rules of life for the state are then applicable to all who live within its borders. Thus citizenship in the usual sense is for the most part a matter of involuntary association.

But the citizen also establishes relationships based upon the sharing of special interests with certain other citizens. These associations are analogues and extensions of the friendship associations at the face-to-face level. These voluntary associations are of great variety. They are as multiform as the desires and concerns of man. Veterans of military service organize and support an American Legion, Veterans of Foreign Wars, or a Grand Army of the Republic. Doctors join forces in medical associations and lawyers gain professional standing through bar associations. Businessmen have common concerns in trade associations and chambers of commerce. Employees seek to advance their common interests through local, national, and international labor unions. People of similar political persuasion combine in political parties, operating at every level from the local precinct to the national scene. Social interests are shared in clubs and fraternal orders. Scientists and scholars belong to societies dedicated to the advancement of their special disciplines. Students join student associations and the more or less able get elected to honor societies. Artists by professional association seek mutual stimulation and solace in the face of an often indifferent or hostile world. People of similar religious convictions join together to form sects or denominations, and persons with zeal for the same ideals lend their names and support to organizations designed to advance their special causes, whether these be conservation of wildlife, promotion of an international language, or the advancement of cancer research.

Implementing values. It is chiefly through such voluntary associations that particular ideals and values may become socially effective. No idea can be implemented apart from some actual institutional channel. Values held individually, without social embodiment, can have only individual and private significance. To influence the community at large interests must be dramatized and reinforced through social organization. One of the imperative lessons each generation needs to learn is how to implement goals by associated effort. It is not enough to teach high ideals in the abstract. Without an understanding of the practical social means of effecting these ideals, frustration, disillusionment, and cynicism are likely to ensue. Not only should children be made increasingly aware of the activities of adults in voluntary associations but they should also be encouraged to participate in their own joint efforts, such as Boy and Girl Scouts, Junior Red Cross, or organizations of future farmers or future teachers.

Diversification. Voluntary associations also make possible a diversified society. Each person may ally himself with those groups which represent and advance his own interests. In this way his individuality is confirmed. His right and privilege to differ from others are given concrete social expression through the special interest groups to which he belongs. He may join the Republicans, the Democrats, or even the Prohibition party. He can be a Protestant, a Jew, a Catholic, or a Freethinker, and proudly declare himself such by membership in the group of his choice.

The free society. Obviously voluntary associations can flourish only in a free society. Where there are rigid social controls, association is limited to prescribed forms, there is great pressure for uniformity, and deviation from the standard is regarded as evidence of disloyalty, the penalty for which is social disapproval or punishment. In a free society, in contrast, diversity is welcomed, and voluntary associations as its institutional expressions are encouraged. Of course, in every society there must be limits to the freedom of association. Vice rings, crime syndicates, and political parties dedicated to the suppression of freedom for all except themselves, as forms of voluntary association which impoverish and threaten rather than enrich and strengthen society, are not welcomed.

Apart from these vicious and subversive types of association, voluntary organizations are educational agencies of great importance. They bear witness to the possibility and practicability of freedom and individuality and provide the tangible means for making these personal goals effective.

Flexibility. Finally, voluntary associations serve to maintain flexibility in the social order. Every society is in danger of losing its vitality by having its institutions harden into fixed forms. Voluntary associations provide for the rise of new organizations appropriate to the needs of the time and for the decline of institutions which no longer serve useful purposes. Being voluntary, they prosper only as long as the interests which they reflect remain alive. The relative vigor of the various free associations of any society is one of the best measures of its real values, and the changes in what its citizens regard as important are indicated by the rise and fall of these organizations. With respect to the individual citizen voluntary associations provide the principal means for him to contribute to the process of social change. Hence, education for a dynamic social order, responsive to changing conditions in a rapidly evolving civilization, needs particularly to take account of the role of these organizations.

Government

Every social system requires some principle of authority by which its order is maintained. The institutional embodiment of that principle is its government. Normally government is thought of in connection with political organization, but it applies also in voluntary associations and even to some extent within the family. Government is a necessary aspect of all institutional organization. There can be neither stability nor efficiency in any social institution which lacks a set of regulations setting forth the respective rights and obligations of its members.

The educational relevance of government is twofold. First, the young citizen needs to be prepared to live usefully within the framework of the governing system of his society. In a democracy the child will be taught how to discuss issues and to vote, while in an autocratic state education will be dedicated to insuring unquestioning obedience. Second, the system of government is itself a powerful influence in the development of persons. Those who grow up in a society where the rich rule the poor will differ in outlook and behavior from those whose society grants authority to the most able, regardless of economic status.

The Function of Government

The attitude of the citizen toward government depends upon the view he holds regarding its essential function in the regulation of human affairs.

Enabling. According to the first and optimistic view, the function of government is to facilitate the completion of projects which could not be carried out as well if at all by unregulated individual or private effort. Thus, the immensely costly system of public highways could be constructed only by governmental agencies financed by public taxation. A nation-wide system of social security similarly depends upon federal legislation and administration, and an adequate system of military defense is only possible through the exercise of considerable governmental authority over life and property.

This view generally presupposes the goodness of human nature and in particular the beneficence of the governing authorities. Government is regarded as a useful instrument for increasing social efficiency, an invention for augmenting through coordinated effort the effectiveness of individual activity.

Restraining. The opposite position stems from the premise that human nature is infected with evil impulses. The essential function of government is then conceived as that of restraining these impulses. Man is regarded as fundamentally self-centered, motivated by the desire for power over others, predatory and belligerent in seeking to extend his own claims and anxiously defensive about what he already possesses. Under these circumstances the role of government is to curb aggression, maintain the peace, and protect rights of life and property. Government, then, is necessary for maintaining social order. Unfortunately, however, those who govern are not exempt from the desire to gain power and wealth at the expense of others. Hence, government is not only necessary, but it is also itself a source of evil, requiring within its structure safeguards against the abuse of power by those who govern. In short, government is an evil necessity, and the less government required to keep order the better.

A moderate view. It is quite possible to combine the optimistic and the pessimistic views, recognizing the usefulness of government in achieving valuable positive social goals as well as in providing police protection. Perhaps human nature is neither basically good nor evil but ambiguous, manifesting at times or in some persons generous social tendencies and at other times or in other persons behavior based on hate and fear. If this is the case, government needs to serve both enabling and restraining functions. It is neither an unquestioned good nor an inescapable source of evil but as ambiguous as the human nature which it reflects.

Where an optimistic view of government prevails, children grow up to expect benefits from collective enterprises, to have confidence in the good will of duly selected leaders, and to recognize the limitations of private initiative. Where pessimism about government prevails, the young learn to distrust bigness and centralization and to hold political leaders in low esteem, surrounding them with many checks on their power. They learn that the source of strength is in individual effort and that one must engage in a competitive struggle for power and prestige. Between the two extremes are those who come to understand the complexity of the human situation and who accordingly judge government not by a fixed rule or prejudice but with full awareness of both the merits and the dangers of organized social endeavor.

Political Authority

All government rests on some view of political authority, of which there are three general conceptions.

Anarchy. The first is anarchy, the essence of which is the denial of any authority. A purely anarchic society is really impossible since all society depends upon coordination of persons with different interests and capabilities, and this requires at least some limitation of individual prerogatives. The anarchist seeks to have all the benefits of social existence (which he wrongly attributes to nature or to his own efforts) without making any personal sacrifices (the need for which he denies). Not only would a completely anarchic society be self-defeating through internal conflict and failure of coordination, but the personalities developed within it would tend to be correspondingly disintegrated. Anarchy stands in contradiction to every ideal of education, since all education is dedicated to the development of persons with definite principles of inner organization and control.

Rule of men. The second conception of political authority is the rule of men. According to this view, the social order is determined by the will and desire of individual persons who by chance or by superior force or wit have gained power over others. There are definite principles of organization and control, lodged in particular people and reflecting their special personality orientation. But the rule of men, as such, is by definition arbitrary. That is to say, whatever the one in authority decrees becomes the rule for the society. Such societies suffer from the limitations of their rulers and from the disorders associated with the inevitable changes in governing authority. Life in societies under the rule of men tends to produce persons with attitudes of dominance and submission in relation to other people. Successful social existence depends upon knowing the authorities and understanding the demands made on the people subject to them.

Rule of right. The third conception is that of the rule of right. According to this view, the authority is not that of individual human beings but of moral principles. These principles are generally embodied in codes of law. Law, of course, is also necessary under rule of men. In that case the laws simply contain the command of the ruling authorities. Under the rule of right the laws are regarded as in some sense suprapersonal so that all persons, including the rulers, are subject to them. Men still exercise authority, but under law rather than merely by virtue of their position of dominance. The rule of right arises from the attempt to overcome the arbitrariness of personal authority, replacing it by more stable and long-standing principles. The social order is then no longer subject to the will and caprice of powerful individuals but rests upon a well-established and well-tested tradition which governing authorities are bound to respect.

The source of law. A conception of right does not necessarily imply a superhuman source of law. The right may be determined by men as, for example, by some system of social agreement. On the other hand, right may be conceived as given in nature or by divine ordinance, on the theory that values have a status independent of actual human desire. The concept of the rule of right is not intended to settle the question of the source of law one way or the other, but simply to point out a view of political authority which transcends the arbitrary rule of individual power figures.

A society under the rule of right educates its citizens to respond not primarily to the personal demands of authority figures but to certain social ideals which have become the accepted guiding principles of the community. Understanding of moral principles is a relatively high achievement, depending upon the intellectual capacity for abstraction. In order to stimulate personal enthusiasm for such abstract principles, ways must be found for dramatizing them and for fashioning concrete symbols to represent them more vividly. This task of making social ideals impressive and memorable is fundamental to citizenship education. It is accomplished by such means as recounting the life stories of men who have sacrificed personal gain for the sake of the right, engaging in appropriate celebration of commemorative festivals, and providing specific opportunities for implementing ideals of right in concrete social action.

Who should rule? Assuming the rule of right, the question must still be answered: Who has the right to rule? Laws by themselves cannot govern; only persons can exercise leadership, by making necessary decisions in the light of the accepted principles of right. Furthermore, who is to decide what the principles of right are? The answers to this question provide the clue to some of the classic varieties of political organization. One answer is that might makes right and, therefore, that the strong should rule. This principle in effect equates the rule of right with the rule of men. A second answer is that the rich should rule, and a third would favor the "well-born" by virtue of family, social class, or race. In still other societies rule is vested in an intellectual elite, in men of virtue, or in holy men. Finally, political authority may reside in the people as a whole.

Each of these types of social organization reflects a different set of social values. In the first kind power is the highest good, in the second wealth is supreme, in the third social or racial status, in the others knowledge, virtue, holiness, and equality, respectively, are the highest values. Persons growing up in these societies will tend to adopt the value standards written into the institutional structure. Where the powerful rule, the young will learn to seek above all for power and dominance; where the intelligent rule, intellectual achievement will be most prized; similarly for the other kinds of rule. By the same token, an educational system dedicated to values other than those implicit in the political institutions of the society will act as a reconstructive agency within that society. For example, persons educated to the value of equality will attempt to transform a society based on the rule of the strong or the wealthy into one in which all the people rule.

Democracy

Democracy is that form of social organization in which the governing authority resides in the people governed. The accepted principles of right by which rule is to be exercised are decided by all the people and not by any special segment such as the intelligent or the "well-born."

Equality. Thus, the fundamental principle of democracy is equality. This means that in the determination of social policy every person has the same right of consideration. No person is to count for more than any other person; each person is to count for one in political decision. This is the democratic ideal. In reality the strong or the rich usually do count for more than the weak or the poor. When this happens, the less favored have the right and duty to seek to restore the balance.

Diversity. Equally fundamental to democracy is the principle of diversity. Equality does not mean uniformity. The principle of diversity assures to the individual and to groups the right to be different. It is sometimes said that democracy is based upon majority rule. This is not to be understood as the elimination of minorities in favor of a majority way of life. Minorities and majorities are to have equal rights to be different. The ideal of equality does, of course, set limits to the allowable diversity. Those who would imperil the security or infringe the rights of others cannot be permitted to be different in these ways. But within these limits democracy is a means of encouraging diversity within unity, of creating a society in which the maximum individuality prevails consistent with equal rights for all.

Representation. The mechanism for democratic rule is government by freely elected representatives. In small groups each can count for one by his personal presence. In the larger community the individual generally cannot make known his will in person and must entrust to his chosen representatives the decision and execution of social policies. By the ballot he still counts for one, though he must act by proxy.

The constitution. The fundamental principles of democratic government, specifying the rights guaranteed and the institutions through which they are to be secured, are contained in written constitutions. The constitution makes explicit the nature and means of exercising political authority and expresses that law to which all are equally subject.

Education and democracy. Education and democracy are intimately related in that both presuppose that the individual matters. Education in and for democracy is education for everyone. The ideal of equality means that all should receive the opportunity to develop their personal resources to the full. The ideal of diversity means that the program of education should not be the same for all but that subject to the limitations of practice each should receive that type of education which will advance his own special interests and abilities. Democratic education is education for individuality-in-community, for being different from others in ways which will enhance the good of all, or at least not interfere with the self-determination of others. The citizen in a democracy must also be taught to think intelligently about social policy and to choose wisely those who must represent him. He should also be taught respect for law and an understanding of its basic principles as formulated in the written constitution of his commonwealth.

13

Work

A LARGE PART of the life of every human being is spent in work. The nature of the social and material environment also is greatly affected by the occupations in which persons engage. It follows that education is inevitably concerned with work. By education one may be prepared to do the chosen or required job, and the work process itself may be the means and occasion for education. Therefore, it is essential in a philosophic study of education to reflect upon the significance of work in the development of persons.

General Attitudes toward Work

Three negative conceptions. The effect of work upon personality is in part a function of the view held about the value of work in general. One attitude is that work is punishment for transgression. In the biblical Garden of Eden story, before the act of disobedience by which man fell from the state of innocence into sin, the earthly paradise provided by God yielded its fruits freely and without effort on man's part. With the fall of man nature also fell from its condition of original harmony, and man was thenceforth required to earn his bread by the sweat of his brow. That is, he was required to work for his living. Whether or not one interprets this story literally or symbolically, it can be seen to reflect a widespread outlook toward work. The argument in brief is this: Work is evil; God is good; God made the world and man good; in all creation man alone has freedom to misuse the good; therefore, work must be a consequence of man's misdeeds. Man must labor because he is a sinner. He is condemned to this servitude as a result of his guilt. This attitude is implicit in the feeling that by hard work one can atone for the follies committed in the pursuit of pleasure. Work is a form of penance exacted as the result of man's waywardness.

A less personalistic view is that work is simply a necessary evil. Life and the world are far from perfect, not primarily through human wrong-doing, but by the very nature of things. Conflict and disharmony are to be expected in a world of contrary and competing powers. Work is man's way of exerting his power against the forces that oppose his will. The world is imperfect as judged from the standpoint of human desires, and work is necessary to bring the environment more nearly into conformity with those desires.

A third attitude is that work is an unpleasant good. It is neither a consequence of sin nor evidence of the natural disharmony of things but a creative and constructive activity. However, man is by nature lazy and hence finds this good activity unsatisfying. He is inclined to ease rather than to effort, and must constantly be prodded to perform the labor which is appointed for him. The work itself is not sufficient stimulus to insure activity; hence external incentives such as material rewards, social approval, and threats of loss must be provided.

The above three attitudes toward work are all negative, leading to distaste for labor and to the greatest possible avoidance of it. Since education is necessarily so largely concerned with preparation for lifework, and since the actual performance of work is the principal method of preparing for the job, negative attitudes toward work are accompanied by aversion to education also. There are children for whom school is a prison to which they are daily sentenced and for whom release from this penal servitude is the most cherished goal. There are parents and teachers who consider it their proper function to impose tasks upon the unwilling young so that they may learn the hard truth that to live man must labor. When this negative outlook prevails, education includes a large element of compulsion. Students are driven to learn by threats of disciplinary action and by systems of rewards, prominent among which is exemption from additional work.

Persons educated to aversion for work develop a cleavage in life outlook and behavior. One compartment of life consists of the inescapable work. The other and completely separate part consists of those desired pursuits which are made possible by performance of the disagreeable duties of labor. When this attitude prevails, personality fails to achieve that integrity in which every act is the expression of the whole self.

An affirmative view. In contrast to the negative attitudes toward work is the affirmative view that work is a satisfying opportunity for personal fulfillment. It is not a punishment, but a privilege. It is a necessity, but a good rather than an evil one. It is at one and the same time constructive and pleasing. Far from being repugnant, the right kind of work is the most attractive and enjoyable of pursuits. Such work provides its own rewards and needs no external incentives nor penalties for failure to do it.

With this positive outlook, education is also seen as a source of satisfaction.

Educational opportunities are prized as good in their own right and as preparation for the enjoyment of more responsible work activities in the future. The motive for learning is not fear of loss or penalty but the promise of fulfillment in the work itself. Teaching is not the exercise of compulsion but the invitation to satisfying achievement. Furthermore, the person educated in this way can develop a unified perspective on life, in which all of his activities, but especially his work, truly reflect his integral personality.

Grounds for the negative outlook. It is obvious that it makes a very great difference in education whether work is regarded negatively or positively. A negative outlook on work corresponds to a highly distasteful view of education, while an affirmative attitude toward labor leads to an attractive conception of education. It is therefore of interest to consider the cause of an unfavorable general outlook toward work. One possible answer is that the negative view is actually justified by the facts, that work really is a punishment for sinful man, that the world really is disharmonious, and that man really is naturally lazy. If this is the case, then hope of human fulfillment through work is illusory (and would be further demonstrated through the nullification of all personal fulfillments at death), and education is doomed forever to be an irksome chore.

On the other hand, the negative outlook may result not from any inescapable predicament but simply from the failure to match the work required with the special interests and abilities of the individual person. Certainly not all work is desirable for all people. Each person has tasks which are appropriate to him, in which he finds maximum use for his powers. If he is assigned to work demanding different kinds of capacities, negative attitudes toward work in general are likely to develop. The promotion of a constructive outlook on work and education therefore rests upon the use of appropriate guidance techniques and upon an educational program in which work is assigned on the basis of levels and types of personal competence and not by a uniform and rigid schedule.

Work and Man's Place in Nature

Meeting biological needs. Work is, in part, simply a biological necessity. All living things participate in characteristic life cycles involving functions which facilitate nutrition, growth, and reproduction. These activities which sustain and expand the life of the species are the work proper to it. The honey bee's proper work is to build the comb and to gather the nectar which will enable a new generation of bees to live and grow to maturity. The bird's work is to build the nest for laying and hatching eggs, to bring food to feed the young, and to make such journeys as seasonal changes make necessary.

The work of man arises in part from these basic biological necessities. Human occupations revolve to a considerable degree about problems of housing, feeding, and reproducing the species. Competing with other living things, man seeks to secure and extend his domain in the world of nature. Nature is the context within which all human activity must occur. It provides both problems to be solved and resources to fulfill human wants. Thus the foundation upon which all understanding of work must be built is the recognition of man's participation with all other living things in the elementary life processes and of his interdependence with both living and non-living things in the total economy of nature.

Creating culture. But man's work differs in one decisive respect from the work of all other living things. Man is not merely a creature of nature. He does not only seek for food and shelter to perpetuate his species. He also undertakes to transform nature according to his own imagination and design. Hence, it is not possible to speak of any specific functions which are the proper work of man as a species. There is no set of fixed operations, calculated to advance human biological claims, which can be designated as the characteristic sphere of man's activity. The work of man is distinguished by the enormous and in principle limitless multiplication of activities in which he decides to engage. A relatively small proportion of human energy goes into work which is dedicated solely to biological survival. Most of man's occupations contain a considerable element of cultural elaboration.

The extent to which humanity transcends basic biological needs is somewhat obscured by the fact that the habitual practice of culture-produced functions creates psychological needs which seem just as real and urgent as the elementary needs for food, shelter, and the like. The desire to read, to make music, to travel, or to engage in religious rites may be for persons whose lives have been fashioned by these practices as commanding as the drive of hunger. For this reason the many occupations directed to the satisfaction of culturally generated needs are just as essential for the well-being of the human community and are true and serious work just as clearly as those occupations which serve man's natural needs.

The twofold task of education. The fact that man both belongs to and transcends nature determines the character of education as related to the development of occupational competence. Each new generation must learn what the basic human needs are, what resources nature has provided to meet these needs, and the procedures to be followed to make these resources available to man. Such basic occupations as farming, forestry, and mining, through which man in pre-industrial society directly supplied his wants, and for which the young had chiefly to be prepared, have in industrial society become linked to and transformed by vast new undertakings in manufacture, distribution, finance, and advertizing. For all of these newer occupations appropriate educational provision must be made. And beyond these, preparation is necessary for the many who labor to satisfy cultural needs not directly related to material supply.

Thus the education of civilized man is an immensely complex undertaking. There can be no standard, uniform procedure for training persons for their proper human functions. Man's proper work is as various as his culture is diversified, and his educational needs are as many sided as the interests his creative imagination has generated.

Work and Society

The division of labor. The multiplicity of occupations is not simply the result of man's cultural ingenuity. It is also a consequence of social organization. The obvious value of social existence is that more can be done by working cooperatively than by each making his way alone. The fundamental principle of all social order is the division of labor. The work is divided in such a way that each person becomes proficient in one set of activities, the fruit of which he contributes to others in exchange for a share of their production. By specializing in one line of work which he does expertly the individual is more efficient than he would be if required to scatter his energies in many directions. The more advanced the civilization, the greater the variety of occupations and the more intricate the network of interdependencies.

The division of labor necessarily requires a diversified system of education. In a simple society where everyone has substantially the same tasks, a uniform program of education suffices. As the complex arrangements of a more advanced social order generate new occupations, the need for different kinds of preparation becomes apparent and new means of instruction are devised to meet this need. Whether through individual training on the job as an apprentice or by the establishment of special schools and courses, experts in each field of endeavor train new generations of specialists after their own kind.

The problem of unity. A complex civilization is not, however, merely an aggregate of specialists. The division of labor has meaning only in the light of an effective system of coordination and exchange. The specialized individual cannot subsist by his own efforts, but requires the products of a host of other workers in different occupations. Hence, it is not enough that experts be trained to do their particular jobs. Education must also teach the members of society how to relate themselves to one another in mutual helpfulness. The advance of civilization thus imposes a twofold burden upon education: to prepare specialized workers and to promote social coordination. The greater a society's occupational diversification the greater must be the emphasis on social unity.

There are two principal ways in which this twofold task can be accomplished, and these alternatives reflect two fundamentally different conceptions of social organization. One way is to produce a class of specialists in coordination whose function is to regulate the social order so as to insure the maximum harmony and efficiency of exchange. The other way is to educate everybody so as both to make him competent in his particular line of work and to prepare him for responsible membership in the community. According to the first method, the organization of the common life may properly be left to a few well-trained people. According to the second method, the maintenance of social unity despite diverse interests and abilities is everybody's business. One approach is that of a governing aristocracy or elite, the other is that of democracy, or rule by the people. In actual practice both ways must to some extent prevail. There must always be experts in social management to whom is entrusted a larger than average share of responsibility for coordinating human affairs. Except in the most highly centralized organizations there will also always be some responsibility of each individual as a member of the community for promoting the good of the whole.

One of the key problems of education in a democratic society results from the tension between the requirements of specialized competence and of good citizenship. Limited educational resources must be most wisely divided between these two objectives. Neglect of specialized education reduces the productive capacity of society. Neglect of common general education threatens the cohesiveness of the community. Perhaps the greatest danger to a free society is the temptation to hand over its management to professional coordinators. Such surrender may in the short run make for increased efficiency, but in the end it usually means subjugation and tyranny. The best guarantee of freedom would seem to be in the maintenance of a vigorous program of common education, in which everyone becomes familiar with certain fundamental ideals and traditions of his society and culture, and from which each learns the meaning and method of taking responsibility for the life of all.

The nature of society and the distribution of labor. The kinds of work called for in a given society are a reflection of the nature of that society. Or more precisely, the nature of a society is to a large extent defined by the occupations of its members. For example, an agrarian society is one which centers about the occupation of farming. A commercial society is one in which merchants play a dominant role. An industrial society is one in which a considerable portion of its members are employed in the production of manufactured goods. Actually, of course, there are many different kinds of occupations in any diversified social order, and the particular nature of a society depends upon how the labor force is distributed among the various types of work.

The distribution of labor is important educationally in two ways. First, it determines to a considerable degree the kinds of instruction which must be provided to prepare workers for their jobs. A modern industrial society can prosper only if provided with an ample supply of well-trained scientists, engineers, and technicians. A religious community, on the other hand, would above all need to prepare competent ministers and teachers for positions of leadership. Hence the relative demand for various kinds of workers is reflected in the relative predominance of different kinds of education.

Second, the distribution of labor is in part an expression of the values prevailing in the society, and these values also govern the aims of education. People in the long run expend effort only on what they consider important. They are also willing to pay high prices for the goods and services they most prize, and their society will attract many able workers, with good pay, into occupations which will provide what they most want. Jobs which are poorly paid and which attract few workers are an indication of kinds of activities and products which the society on the whole does not value. The relative standing of various occupations is a good measure of the real values of a society and hence of the true educational aims of that society. A nation unwilling to pay the salaries and to accord the prestige needed to attract enough of the most able people into teaching manifests thereby a relatively low esteem for the intellectual life. On the other hand, substantial amounts spent for the production and distribution of luxury items indicate a high value placed on sense pleasures.

Values and educational aims are, however, ultimately individual rather than corporate, and in the long run personal goals have their effect on how society uses its human resources. Educational aims in any given instance need not reflect the average values of society. It would seem incumbent on the educator to guide and be guided by higher values than those which commonly prevail and thereby to exert an influence toward a more ideal distribution of labor.

Specialism and personal development. The division of labor, by requiring the production of specialists, sometimes creates a conflict between the ideal of maximum occupational efficiency and the ideal of total personal development. A complete person is more than a competent mechanism, and the one-sided training of the human organism to perform certain specific functions with great skill is not conducive to the optimum growth of personality. A highly specialized system of social organization tends to replace the wholeness of the person by the completeness of the society, so that the individual loses his sense of autonomous selfhood and seeks to regain it by participation in the group. The result of excessive specialization is the dehumanizing and depersonalizing of man. The individual becomes a replaceable part in an essentially impersonal social mechanism. Training for mere technical proficiency is not truly education since it is concerned with the development of human tools rather than of persons.

The enthusiast for collectivism might argue that membership in the social group, wherein the specialized individual can find wholeness of life, is really a higher stage in attainment than being an independent individual. Against this it can be urged that a society made up of dehumanized individuals is itself nothing more than a machine and that collective or group personality, if it has any meaning at all, is only possible in a society of complete persons. The reality of personality must be manifested in individuals; it is not a quality which can be imputed to the social body apart from the integral persons who constitute it.

Furthermore, it is quite clear that even the requirements of technical proficiency in a specialized occupation call for some attention to the development of the whole person. The human organism is not an interchangeable part in a mechanism and if treated as such will not function efficiently. Human beings are most efficient, as specialists, when they are treated as persons and not as things. Several empirical studies have demonstrated conclusively the importance of "the human factor" in occupational proficiency. The best specialists must at the same time be well-developed as human beings in respects other than their particular technical competences.

It is also true that specialization does not necessarily have a depersonalizing effect. Properly utilized, it may actually have a profoundly humanizing influence. Specialized achievements give one a sense of individual worth and a unifying focus for personal energies. There is justifiable pride of accomplishment in work well done. A good doctor, carpenter, teacher, or salesman may find in the exercise of his special skills the best means of expressing his complete nature and of fulfilling his truly personal objectives. Specialization also makes possible a depth and concentration of experience which are not possible with more superficial undertakings. There are unique satisfactions in becoming master of some art, craft, or science, for which no breadth of general acquaintance can serve as substitute.

Thus it is not necessary to choose between narrow specialized training and education of the whole person. It is possible to produce well-educated whole persons with special competences. The outcome depends upon whether specialties are taught humanistically or mechanically. Humanistic specialized education is person-centered rather than job-centered or society-centered. It takes account of feeling and motivation as well as overt occupational performance. The individual is made aware of the significance of his work in the social order of which he is a part. Through his own integral understanding of the unifying reciprocities of society he contributes to the wholeness of society rather than deriving his sense of wholeness solely from participation in the group.

Education and machine civilization. The problem of dehumanization is not due mainly to the requirements of specialization itself but to the mechanical character of most modern industrial processes. Economy in production depends upon large-scale establishments in which the work is subdivided into many distinct elementary operations. The assembly-line worker has no opportunity to take pride in a finished product wholly of his own creation. He lacks the satisfactions afforded the specialized craftsman—the watchmaker, the cobbler, the carpenter—who makes a complete article from start to finish. The industrial worker has become a new kind of specialist assigned to the endless repetition of a few simple operations. This kind of occupation does not require an educated person for its performance, and its effect upon those who engage in it is to inhibit that optimum development of personality to which education is dedicated.

Fortunately, it now appears that the very impersonality of machine mass production contains the key to the solution of the depersonalizing problem. Any function which is mechanical in character can be done by machines instead of men. In fact, all of the specialized repetitive elementary operations can be performed much more efficiently by mechanical devices than by human beings. With advances in electronics it is now clear that even very complex processes can be handled by machines. Not only the work of human hands, feet, and eyes but also many of the coordinating and discriminating functions of the brain can be assigned to the new automatic machinery.

The effects of this new industrial revolution are certain to be profound. Occupationally, it means the possible end of routine and mechanical jobs and establishes the need for many highly skilled technicians who can develop, construct, repair, and manage the automatic devices. This will call for the discovery and fullest development of persons of high intelligence and for the careful planning of ways to utilize the highest intellectual competences of persons at every level of ability. Thus, while the first effect of machine civilization was to force many workers into jobs which were below their intellectual capacity, the age of automation will do precisely the opposite:

it will put a premium on intelligence. Herein, of course, lies a great opportunity for education. The new machine civilization requires maximum educational provision, not only for general development of citizens and of persons with well-informed outlook, but also for specialized competence in work calling for a high degree of skill, resourcefulness, and imagination.

Industrialism and changing needs. One of the marked features of industrial society in comparison with simpler societies is the rapidity of change, particularly in occupational requirements. A constant stream of new inventions and the continuous improvements of production methods tend to render established work procedures rapidly obsolete. The old-fashioned craftsman spent a lifetime perfecting his skill in the performance of his particular occupation, using for the most part techniques established by many generations of earlier practitioners. No such continuity and stability characterize most modern occupations. Not only are the methods of this generation of workers likely to differ radically from those of the preceding one, but the required competences during the working life of one person in most fields of endeavor are subject to drastic modification. The profound changes in communications techniques introduced within a relatively short time by the advent of television, the shifts in methods of power production with the coming of atomic energy, and the transformations in medical practice brought about by new drugs are instances of the changing occupational needs characteristic of an age of continuing discovery and persistent technical development.

At least three major consequences emerge for education in a rapidly changing industrial society. First and most important, the quality of education must be such as to develop flexibility and openness to new ways of working rather than fixation on one set of ideas and practices. This ability is best engendered by encouraging a scientific and experimental outlook, by constantly emphasizing alternative possibilities, by rewarding originality, imagination, independence, and resourcefulness rather than conformity to established ideas, and by welcoming an attitude of critical inquiry rather than of unquestioning acceptance. Workers educated in this way do not resist, resent, and fear the inevitable changes in ways of doing things, but welcome them as opportunities for further personal growth and for contributing to the advancement of civilization. They even seek to put their ingenuity to work in bringing about desirable changes.

Second, the content appropriate for education in a dynamic civilization necessarily differs from that of a static society. It no longer suffices to transmit a fixed tradition. The student must learn the basic ideas and key principles of his discipline and not merely specific conclusions. A grasp of the general rationale of the subject, together with methods of inquiry with broad relevance, are more necessary than knowledge of particular facts and special techniques.

In the third place, in a rapidly changing civilization education can no longer be considered as a definite and limited period of preparation for life and work, usually terminating somewhere between ages sixteen and twenty-five. If workers are not to become obsolete, they must keep abreast of new developments in their occupations. They cannot depend on a fixed store of knowledge and skill acquired before going to work as a life-long basis for success on the job. Education must continue indefinitely and become an integral part of the occupation itself.

Work and Human Nature

Occupation and the formation of personality. A substantial portion of most people's lives is spent at work. Of all one does, the work activities also tend to be taken the most seriously. Consequently, the nature of a person's work has much to do with the shaping of his personality. One cannot year in and year out expend the major part of his energies in certain occupational functions without having them become "second nature." To the question "What is individual human nature?" a good answer would seem to be "A person *is* what he *does*." How can a human being be described if not by his ways of behaving? If then, an important segment of one's behavior is determined by the requirements of his occupation, it follows that to a considerable degree work makes the man.

While it is unwise to adopt occupational stereotypes for individuals, and to assume that if a person is a doctor, teacher, or salesman, for example, he will invariably have certain attitudes characteristic of those respective occupations, it is nevertheless true that the type of work does leave its mark on personality. A physician is not simply an ordinary person who happens to practice medicine. The healing arts have entered into the very being of the person. He is not a self who incidentally serves as a doctor. Doctor-hood is constitutive of the self itself. Similarly, with every kind of work the job in which a person invests his life defines in important ways the nature of the self.

Making a living and making a life. Unfortunately these facts are too often lost sight of in the mistaken assumption that work is merely a way of making a living, and that the occupation has no bearing on the true nature of the self. Work is a way—usually the most important way—of making a life. The manner of working is the manner of living. What a person makes of his life is not so much defined by how he uses what he earns from his job as what he does on the job. It is in the daily work that the question of what an individual's life will count for is principally decided. Many a person drifts into a lifework, accepting it as an economic necessity and regarding it as something of which as a person he can remain independent, only to find, often too late, that the choice of the job was the choice of a life.

Work and meaning. To a large extent work contributes to a person's sense of the meaning of life. A meaningful life is one whose activities contribute to the fulfillment of what one regards as worth-while goals. A sense of meaninglessness arises from a failure to discern any connection between what one does and what he believes is important. Disillusionment with life is not infrequently the result of the divorce of work from dominant life-goals, while meaningful existence is due in large part to having found a lifework in which one's cherished values are fulfilled.

For occupational activity to form part of a meaningful life-experience there must be a right correspondence between the job and the nature of personality. Granted that a person is what he does and that work has much to do with the formation of character, there are limitations to the modifications which occupation can produce. It is, after all, a human being with his own inborn potentialities who does the work, and whatever he does and can do best must have some correlation with these native capacities.

Work and individuality. This correspondence between work and human nature has two aspects. First, there are the special characteristics of the individual as a particular person different from all other persons. Here there may well arise a conflict between individual and social needs. Society may require a person to serve as a soldier or an engineer when by basic disposition he would best do the work of an artist or a farmer. It is not always possible to educate individuals to do effectively the particular jobs the community wants done. Hence in any social order dedicated to the optimum fulfillment of the individual person, provision must be made, as far as practicable, for taking account of individual aptitudes and preferences in job allocation and preparation. For this purpose psychological testing is of great value in providing some objective measure of individual differences. Willingness to make allowances for unique competences also presupposes that human nature is not completely plastic, and as a consequence, cannot be modified arbitrarily in any desired direction and for any purpose, but that each individual has particular personal rights and prerogatives as a free subject with his own inner integrity.

Work and essential human nature. In the second place, work to be meaningful must correspond not only with individual human nature but with what may be called essential or general human nature, i.e., with those qualities and functions which characterize persons as such. It is at this point that the aforementioned distinction between humanizing and dehumanizing occupations is relevant. Some kinds of work are destructive of fundamental human characteristics, while other kinds confirm and enhance essential humanity. Dull, purely repetitive, mechanical work which makes no use of the functions proper to man, such as reason, imagination, memory, and free choice, or which tends to deaden these capacities, is destructive of human nature, while occupations which make use of these abilities and stimulate them are favorable to real personal growth.

The use of tools. It is perhaps in work that man can most fully make good his essential humanity. One of the unique characteristics of the human species is the ability to use tools, and human work, in contrast to that of the other animals, requires the use of tools. Now a tool is in essence an extension of the personality. It is a means of enlarging human power beyond the limits imposed by man's own body. All tools, from the simple lever and wheel all the way to the mighty engines of the machine age, are products of human intelligence applied to the problem of multiplying the power of the unaided human body. The invention of tools, in fact, is one of the clearest evidences of man's capacity for self-transcendence. By the imaginative envisagement of more ideal conditions of life he is no longer restricted to an adjustment to existing surroundings but is able to reconstruct his environment according to his own purposes.

Work is humanizing or dehumanizing depending upon whether man in his occupation is a tool-user or is himself merely a tool. Work which enables a person to multiply his own most cherished powers by the use of implements of the appropriate sort—whether artist's brush and pigments, machinist's lathe, scientist's telescope, or scholar's book—can be person-enhancing. Work in which the human being is himself an unwilling instrument in the hands of other persons, serving only to augment their powers but not his own, is dehumanizing in its effect. The most noble work of all is service wherein not only one's own strength but also that of others is enhanced, a work the very secret of whose meaning and appeal lies in the union of individual and social gains effected by it.

Intelligence in Work

Habit. The special quality and effectiveness of human work derives from man's intelligence. This does not mean that all work should be accomplished through conscious rational deliberation and that the preparation of the good worker requires primarily the development of reasoning powers. A competent practitioner of any occupation is one who has acquired a large number of appropriate habitual activities which can be performed without deliberate reasoning. A musician, for example, performs well only if through long practice he has developed a great store of automatic responses appropriate to his art. Similarly, a skilled surgeon is one who largely without taking detailed thought performs the series of acts proper to a given operation. Even the writer or teacher, directly concerned with reasoning processes, must develop a fund of habitual actions establishing good writing and teaching techniques.

Good human habit is simply funded intelligence. It is patterns of rational activity built into the human organism, available for instant and effortless use when called for. Not all habits are good. Bad habits are modes of activity which are not based on intelligence and hence are not appropriate to the situations which bring them into operation. The task of occupational education is to encourage the development of good work habits and to eliminate bad habits.

We are now in a position to understand one role of intelligence in man's work. Primarily its function is to make possible the acquisition of good habits of work. Conscious deliberation about procedures is required in the learning stages, and each new appropriate habit is gained only at the cost of careful and discriminating thoughtful effort. The worker with true understanding of his craft has not merely learned his skills by rote, but at each stage has mastered the rationale of his activity so that he knows not only what to do but why he should do it. Only under those conditions is his store of habit really funded intelligence.

Improvement of procedures. But there is a second role of intelligence in human work, and this relates not to the learning of an established set of occupational activities but to the improvement of job procedures. No occupation has reached perfection, and no work is beyond the possibility of enhancement by further invention. Intelligence is called upon to guide the creative reorganization of work functions. A good worker is one who not only does the job well in the accustomed way, but who is also constantly alert to new possibilities for improving the customary ways. Education for work ought accordingly to stress not only intelligent understanding of standard processes, but should also make the learner aware of existing alternative procedures and encourage experimentation with entirely new ideas. Likewise, the job itself can be a valuable context for further personal growth only if the worker is invited to exercise his ingenuity in improving work processes. In that way also he can be made to feel his own personal stake in the job, seeing it as an extension and expression of his own personality and eliciting from him a sense of dedication.

Perspective. There is one further function which intelligence serves in connection with the occupations of man, and this is to make possible a sense of meaning and perspective in the job. As mentioned earlier, the consciousness of meaning comes from seeing the work as contributing to the attainment of cherished values. This awareness is possible only if one is able to trace the consequences and connections which relate his special work to the total production process or even to the more generalized ideals of life. For example, a highly specialized worker on an automobile assembly line would not see meaning in his job apart from his intelligent understanding of its essential contribution to the production of a finished automobile, and his perspective would be even further broadened if he also had a sense of the role of the automobile in the entire modern economy, in creating new ways of life, opening up new possibilities for satisfaction, and serving as a democratizing influence. Again, it is easy for a teacher, busy with the necessary routines of the classroom, to lose sight of the larger objectives to which these procedures contribute, such as the awakening of youthful curiosities and enthusiasm, the fostering of a mature emotional life in the students, and the participation in a work dedicated to the right, the true, and the excellent. The restoration of insight into these larger dimensions of the task at hand is the work of intelligence. Every worker, in whatever field, is in need of this wider view. Only a broad education can supply the knowledge necessary for it. Workers prepared only to do a particular special job are not equipped to see the meaning of their work in the industrial, social, or cosmic scheme and hence are deprived of that sense of meaning which is every person's due and which properly instructed intelligence is equipped to discern.

Vocation

The meaning of vocation. Much of what has been said in the foregoing paragraphs may be summarized in a discussion of the concept of work as *vocation*. This word is now commonly used as a synonym for job or occupation. In such phrases as "vocational school" it has come to signify chiefly the work of the artisan or tradesman. It is important, then, to remember the primary and proper meaning of the term. A vocation is a calling, and one's vocation is the work that he is called to do. Now a calling implies a caller. To religious faith the one who calls is God. Thus, from a religious standpoint a person's vocation is that work which he is bidden by God to do. This does not mean that an occupation is a vocation only if connected with organized religion, as in a so-called religious vocation. The religious concept of vocation refers to any and all work, including farming, teaching, house cleaning, or scientific research, which one believes God appoints him to do.

The idea of vocation need not, however, be restricted to a particular theological connotation. More generally, it may refer to any work which is done with dedication and wholeheartedness, with some conviction about its rightful place in the total scheme of life, and with a persuasion that it is in some sense the particular appointed task for the individual who does it. A vocation is that which one devotes himself to as his special and personal obligation and opportunity for service and for self-fulfillment.

Kinds of vocation. Different kinds of people have different callings. There are some whose proper appointment is to exercise manual skills, in working with material things, whether as carpenters, cooks, watchmakers, or laboratory technicians. Others are called to use their abilities in social organization and human relationships. In this group would fall such people as salesmen, foremen, executives, and government officials. A third group have their vocation primarily in the realm of ideas. Artists and writers, scholars, scientists, and engineers are of this type. This threefold classification into those who work with things, with people, and with ideas is, of course, only a rough indication of major focuses of activity. Every job has something to do with objects, with persons, and with concepts, and many vocations combine two or all three of these concerns in substantial proportions. For example, most teachers need ability both in human relations and in the intellectual sphere, and some kinds of engineers must have a high degree of manual, personal, and conceptual competence.

Vocational guidance. Every society rates the vocations according to a prestige scale. In one society certain manual skills are most highly prized, in another competence in human relationships, and in still another intellectual abilities. The idea of vocation, however, is intended to counteract such notions of prestige and to emphasize the worth of each type of work in its own place and for the appropriate persons. The task of fitting the right occupation to the right person is the function of vocational guidance. Few aspects of education are more crucial than this. Since the major part of any person's life is devoted to his chosen work, it is of the utmost importance that the choice be made wisely. The problem of vocational guidance is that of helping a person hear his call. Now with what voice does the one who calls speak? There are at least three messages to which attention should be given, i.e., three criteria for choice of occupation. The first is objective appraisal of aptitude through the best available testing devices. Other things being equal, each person will find maximum satisfaction and fulfillment in the kind of work which he does with greatest success. The second criterion is interest or sense of value. Though one might have great skill in some work which he despised, that work would not be his vocation. Again, if one had great interest in an occupation where his competence was only moderate, that might or might not be his vocation. Fortunately, ability and interest tend to reinforce each other so that conflict between these two criteria is the exception rather than the rule. The third factor in choice of vocation is social need. One's duty to society has a legitimate role in his decision about occupation. In time of total war all are called in one way or another to the defense of country. In any period persons may feel duty bound to become teachers, nurses, engineers, or doctors in response to social need, even though solely by aptitude and interest they would have chosen some other work.

Vocational guidance consists in helping others to weigh the three factors of aptitude, interest, and social need. The work which best satisfies the demands of all three criteria is one's vocation. It should be added that no vocation ought to be considered final and irrevocable. Although for practical reasons radical changes in occupation become less feasible as the person grows older, the best interests of personal development would seem to be served by keeping the question of vocation always alive and responsive to fresh needs, new values, and developing competences.

Vocational education. All guidance in preparation for work is vocational education. The conception of such education should not be limited (as it has been in common parlance) to training in the manual arts and to the strictly utilitarian studies such as typing and home economics. Whatever contributes to occupational competence, whether it be higher mathematics for the professional physicist, history for the prospective lawyer, or fine arts for the homemaker, is vocational education.

In the widest sense, perhaps, all education is vocational education since every person's calling is to be most truly and most completely human. All efforts to direct wisely the development of persons thus contribute to education for the universal vocation to become men.

14

Recreation

IN DIRECTING the development of persons it is not enough to take thought and to make provision for occupational activities, through which the necessary business of civilization is carried on. Life is more than labor for daily bread, and the process of education is affected by that something more and in turn affects it. This other side of life, this complement to the experience of work, may be designated generally as recreation.

One might take the position that recreation is exactly that domain of life with which education is not concerned. Control, direction, guidance are appropriate in preparing people for the job, but the essence of recreation is precisely freedom from all confines and restrictions imposed by the necessities of the work-a-day world. Recreation is release from all control, emancipation into a world of liberty and individual self-determination.

This position appears to be untenable. Recreation is no vacation from life. What one does in recreation has its inevitable effect on the kind of person he will become. There are many ways of using the time available away from the job, and a choice must be made among the alternatives. Every decision about the activities to be engaged in is an educational choice because it gives direction to the course of human development.

A considerable segment of most people's time is spent in recreation. Furthermore, unlike work, there is an almost universal presumption in its favor. It is neither punishment nor an evil or unpleasant necessity. It is usually regarded as a reward and an undeniable good. Being freely chosen, it is also a reliable reflection of personal interests and goals. For these reasons recreation is certain to exert a marked influence on the development of character. It is therefore not appropriate that recreation should be considered a subsidiary educational concern. Personal growth through recreation cannot safely be left to haphazard arrangement, accidental circumstance, and the vagaries of momentary inclination. Provision for recreation needs as careful deliberate consideration as preparation for the job. In some respects the educational opportunities in the former are even greater than in the latter. It is clear in any event that a philosophy of education must include an analysis of the function of recreation in the growth of persons.

Conceptions of Recreation

We begin by pointing out some of the different ways in which recreation may be conceived, together with their significance for personal development. These conceptions may also be regarded as components in a comprehensive view of recreation, each of which in its own time and manner may have a significant role.

Rest and relaxation. One form of recreation is cessation of activity, temporary withdrawal from effortful striving. The most common mode of such recreation is sleep, which is an essential part of every person's existence. This is in part a physiological necessity, to allow the proper conditions for energy replenishment and tissue repair. But even more clearly, sleep fills a psychological need for relaxation of tensions and recuperation from emotional stress. More precisely, it is a psychophysical function, a lowering of the activity level of the entire organism. In sleep, of course, all activity does not cease, but only consciously directed behavior. There are all levels and degrees of efficiency in sleep. Anxiety and tension may persist, resulting in little if any refreshment. The best sleep comes from a wholehearted surrender of purposeful striving. The effectiveness of rest seems, in fact, to be a function of the unity or integrity of the personality, whereby inner conflicts are minimized. Good rest also requires a basic sense of security which allows the person to lay aside his daily concerns without fear of loss while detached from them.

Sleep is merely one type of rest, ideally producing the greatest lowering of activity level. There are also ways of wakeful resting. But whether sleeping or awake, the secret of restfulness appears to be in the ability to relax. Without relaxation there can at best be the appearance of rest. Being able to relax is in part a result of neurological factors and of endocrine balance; in some cases restlessness may perhaps best be overcome surgically or by drugs. There is also a long tradition, particularly in the Far Eastern civilizations, in which it is affirmed that relaxation can be learned. By deliberate application of empirically developed techniques of mental concentration, it is held, remarkable mastery of bodily functions—even of the apparently involuntary ones—can be achieved. In particular, it is believed possible by this means to attain at will a high degree of relaxation and consequently to increase greatly the available resources of personal energy.

The problem of relaxation is closely linked to the concerns of religion. One of the main religious ideas is that of faith, as confident trust in a higher power or powers. To have faith in this sense means not to be anxious about one's life but to live in the quiet assurance of being cared for and provided for. Such faith clearly contributes to the capacity for relaxation. A person who is genuinely convinced that the issues of life do not ultimately depend on him can set aside his tasks at the close of the day without anxiety. It is, therefore, frequently urged that the recovery of religious faith is a prerequisite to release from the pervasive restlessness and tension of modern living and the basis for the successful practice of the art of relaxation.

There is evidence to indicate a positive correlation between the ability to relax and efficiency in learning. The tense person is not as receptive nor as appropriately responsive to new stimuli as the relaxed person. It follows that relaxation is an important factor in education and that those who direct the development of persons should consider the sources and resources for the restful attitude. It is likely that the application of pressure and compulsion to the learner may retard rather than advance him, by causing feelings of anxiety and resentment. There is no opposition between relaxation and activity or aliveness. It is tension which impedes and deadens. The most vital personal growth may therefore take place under conditions which invite relaxation.

Failure to recognize the positive significance of restfulness is often associated with overemphasis on purely rational and deliberate processes in the conduct of life. It is frequently assumed that a person need only decide by reason what he is to do and then proceed by a simple effort of the will to do it. The trouble with this assumption is that there are even more important factors of habit and emotion which enter into the determination of behavior, and these may not agree with what has been decided by reason and ordered by will. The efficacy of relaxation results in part from renunciation of the simple reason-and-will approach to the control of behavior, in favor of an attitude of total openness and watchful receptivity to what appears in accord with one's whole personal capacity and intention.

Pleasurable activity. In recreation as rest or relaxation the emphasis is on negation of effortful endeavor. A somewhat different conception results from emphasis on deliberate pleasure-producing activity. For some people a holiday is an occasion for rest, while for others it is a time of exhilarating activity. Examples of the latter sort of recreation would be climbing mountains, sailing, fishing, dancing, making music, playing games, traveling for pleasure, and even reading books. Every sort of hobby from stamp collecting to beekeeping would further illustrate this conception of recreation. Characteristic of these pursuits is their great variety and the intensity of interest and application which they evoke.

The appeal of this type of recreation rests upon the fact that human beings are living, active organisms who find satisfaction in the exercise of the powers with which they are endowed. Pleasure is the subjective feeling resulting from the functioning of the human organism in accordance with its proper abilities. It is the emotional interest returned from the investment of personal talents. There is no pleasure in mere inactivity and in unused capacities. Recreation as pleasurable activity is enjoyment through employment of personal abilities.

Individual taste for one kind of recreation rather than another is largely acquired. Activity which is satisfying to one person may have no appeal to someone else with a different background of experience. Undoubtedly inherited characteristics have some effect in predisposing one to this or that type of recreation, but the major factor is certainly prior learning. Hence education is of first importance in determining what kinds of activity a person will enjoy pursuing. A person does not automatically and by nature enjoy reading good books, playing baseball skillfully, or making good music. These abilities are slowly and often painfully learned. During the learning process it is important that sufficient supplemental satisfaction be given by way of appreciation, encouragement, and promise of future competence to offset the immediate discomforts of undertaking new functions. Eventually the exercise of the familiar functions yields its own satisfaction, but in the process of educating to desirable forms of activity it is generally necessary to provide extrinsic rewards.

The educator must also make a choice between desirable and undesirable forms of recreational activity. A person can develop a passion for roulette as well as for scouting, for hot-rod racing as well as for sailing. How is the decision to be made for one form of pleasurable activity as against another? It can only be done by reference to a system of values and of educational aims. Three criteria for judging between activities, which would probably command wide assent, are as follows: First, no form of recreation is desirable if it detracts in any way from the well-being of other people. By this test pursuits which are flagrantly wasteful of material resources, or which endanger life and property, as in the unrestricted use of firearms and intoxicants, would be excluded. Second, recreations are undesirable if they interfere with the successful performance of other necessary and desirable personal functions. Games requiring exertion which leave insufficient energy for performance of job duties and for maintaining satisfactory personal relationships would be ruled out on this count. Third, types of recreation which make use of the specifically human capacities such as reason and language occupy a higher place, other things being equal, than do activities which utilize only the animal powers. In this sense writing stories or poems and engaging in dramatic productions are higher forms of recreation than rolling dice or eating.

It would be easy to cite any number of other standards by which to judge between pleasures. It is pertinent here only to point out that personal enjoyments are largely acquired rather than inborn and that those who seek to direct wisely the growth of others need standards of value by which to distinguish the more from the less desirable forms of recreation.

Entertainment. Instead of conceiving of recreation as pleasurable activity it may be regarded as pleasurable passivity, or entertainment. Instead of doing something himself the one being entertained watches other people perform. He is a spectator rather than a full participant in the activity. This mode of recreation has always had an important place, as in athletic contests, dramatic presentations, and religious festivals. It has become especially dominant in modern mass society, both because of the general collectivist, anti-individualist tendencies of the times and more especially as a result of motion pictures, radio, and television.

In the twentieth century entertainment has become big business, and its influence on the formation of attitudes and character is considerable. It has even been asserted that the educative effect of the mass media of communication now considerably exceeds that of the schools. In view of this it is evident that the quality of public entertainment provided is a matter of broad social policy which ought to be decided in the light of the best available educational wisdom. To leave the decisions about what shall be publicly presented solely to the entertainers, their managers, and the special interests which give them financial support is to surrender a large educational province to those who in general are neither primarily concerned with human development nor competent to guide it.

The appeal of entertainment consists in the experience of vicarious participation. By watching the performers the observer in imagination and intention enters into their activity. He becomes emotionally involved through identification with the entertainers. The spectator's apparent passivity is then in reality an implicit, internal responsive activity.

From an educational standpoint, the defect of entertainment is that the watching of others may become a substitute for personal participation, which seems to be the most effective way of learning anything. No amount of listening to concerts will give one competence in playing music. No watching of baseball games will in itself produce good players. It seems evident that substantial expenditure of time on entertainment is educationally wasteful. It is therefore important that in the present age of widespread entertainment facilities educators be prepared to offer attractive alternative recreation programs calling for direct personal participation.

On behalf of good entertainment, however, it should be said that in three respects it can serve to enrich and enlarge the spectator's experience. First, it makes possible a greater range of appreciation than could be achieved by personal activity. Few can themselves become musicians, dancers, reporters, and sportsmen, yet they may with profit vicariously share in what these performers do. Second, entertainment can afford a greater intensity of feeling than might otherwise be possible. Great acting and moving oratory may release emotional springs which would normally remain untouched. Finally, the entertainer can uphold a standard of performance which the layman on his own could seldom achieve. Gifted comedians, experienced lecturers, and champion athletes usher the observer into a world of excellence which he could not or would not enter without their aid. However, it can be insisted that the most constructive response to this familiarity with expert performance is not to be satisfied with the vicarious experience alone, but to use it as stimulus for improving the quality of the spectator's own activities.

Escape. Many people regard recreation as a means of escape from the unpleasant realities of ordinary life. Finding little satisfaction in the customary pursuits, they look to recreation for excitement and forgetfulness. For such people, the world of recreation must be as different as possible from the world of everyday. The bizarre, the grotesque, the unconventional are welcomed as relief from boredom and monotony. The rule of reason is for the time being suspended, and blind impulse is given sway. Tiresome restrictions of social custom are thrown off during the interval of respite from the tyranny of civilized conformity.

The particular means devised for escape are of great variety. The use of alcohol and other drugs is a common method, probably second only to the various types of sexual stimulation. Frenzied, seductive, and sentimental music is another means. Tales of mystery, intrigue, adventure, and romance, as well as scientific and poetic fantasy, also carry one away into a new and unreal world. Doubtless much religion serves the same purpose, by providing promise of escape from the present dark and painful existence to a heaven of light and happiness. Riots, mob violence, gang fights, and wars are further occasions when the rules of civilized life give way before uncontrolled passion. To a lesser extent the same is true of some folk festivals and of certain patriotic, political, and religious celebrations.

The widespread employment of escape techniques suggests that they satisfy certain basic human desires. It demonstrates at the very least that man is a creature of passion as well as of reason and that human nature cannot be presumed always to prefer the most civilized ways. It shows that there are powerful destructive impulses in man, and that there may be in outwardly conventional people deep longings to break the bonds of routine and tradition.

Though it would appear that escape recreation as such is undesirable, it may be a necessary reaction to oppressive and excessively restrictive conditions of life. Periodic eruptions of irrationality may be required in a too highly rationalized existence. Excursions into fantasy may help to make bearable an otherwise intolerable routine. But preferable to this movement from drab or grim reality to an artificial world of excitement and illusion would be the development of such a rich and satisfying life that there would be no need or desire to escape from it. The yearning for escape seems to be a symptom of social and personal inadequacy rather than a necessary human condition. Education should therefore aim to develop in persons appropriate interests and skills which will insure an affirmative attitude toward the whole of life so that no need will be felt for oblivion, retreat, or destruction.

Play. A particularly important general conception of recreation is contained in the idea of play. The typical instance of play activity is participation in games. The essence of a game is the set of rules which define the choices open to players and the rewards or penalties resulting from various developing circumstances. Implicit in this are three characteristics of play which are worthy of special emphasis. First, play is associated with human freedom. The person chooses to play, he may decide what the rules will be, and generally he must make further decisions between alternative courses during the progress of the game. Play can never be compulsory. It is essentially a manifestation and an exercise of personal freedom. Second, this freedom operates within the context of agreed-upon principles. The good player obeys the rules of the game. Play is no arbitrary and haphazard activity but is carefully planned and definitely structured. Thus law and order are of the essence in play. Third, this freely chosen pattern is in effect a new miniature world created by human artifice. The world of play is one of make-believe. The player constructs situations which may or may not resemble actual life conditions but which have the special distinction of constituting a world of his own making rather than one forced upon him by nature or society.

Conceived in this manner, play is clearly of the highest significance educationally. It provides opportunities for the growing person to experiment with different types of occupation. The child who plays doctor, teacher, or fireman constructs a make-believe world in which he performs the activities proper to these occupations, and in this way he gets some genuine sense of his personal reaction to them. Through play the child also best learns the true meaning of the laws and customs of society. He becomes keenly aware that anyone who breaks the rules spoils the game, and he may readily learn from this that the seemingly arbitrary regulations imposed by his elders are designed to fit him for satisfying participation in the game of responsible adult life. Finally, through play one may develop an awareness of the wealth of alternative possibilities open to man. There are many games and correspondingly many ways of life. There is room for variety, invention, imagination, and novelty in existence. Man has it within his power to construct new worlds, and the proof of this is in the creative activity of play.

Renewal. The desirable features of each of the preceding conceptions can be found in the root conception of recreation as renewal. Taken literally, recreation is the process of creating again. It is the making over of persons so that they are like new. It is an act of refreshment and rejuvenation in which all staleness, frustration, and deterioration are overcome. From such recreation the person should emerge free from the burdens and disappointments of the past, eager for the future, and hopeful of its outcomes. The re-created person feels that he is making a new beginning, that life is full of promise and opportunity rather than burden and boredom.

Renewal would seem to be a useful criterion for judging the worth of any kind of recreation, whether it be rest, pleasurable activity, entertainment, escape, or play. There are conditions of rest which produce merely weakness and atrophy of powers, activities which only exhaust energies, entertainments which impair initiative and discourage endeavor, escapes which degrade instead of giving respite, and play which is wasteful and trivial. On the other hand, in any of these categories the outcome may be a sense of restored vigor, fresh outlook, and heightened expectancy. By the criterion of renewal, only these latter constitute authentic recreation.

In the ideal of renewal the fundamental contribution of recreation to education becomes evident. The basic intention of the educator is to participate constructively in the creation of persons. This purpose is defeated when the educative process becomes burdensome, repetitive, or coercive. It is the function of recreation in education to provide appropriate means of refreshment whereby the creative objective may be fulfilled.

Work and Recreation

Recreation is commonly considered simply as the antithesis of work. Critical examination forces the revision of this view. There are interesting relationships between these two domains which illuminate the significance of each. Four main ways of viewing these relationships will now be discussed.

Work as recreation. According to the first view, work is looked upon as a form of recreation. Of course, no one would claim that any and all work is recreation, but there are people who believe that all work should be renewing and refreshing and who feel that they themselves or certain other persons have found types of work which are satisfying and rewarding. Some jobs are so interesting and absorbing that the worker actually feels rested as a result of doing them. Some occupations offer more pleasure and genuine entertainment than any possible leisure-time pursuit. Some people find in labor a far more effective means of escape than in recreation. Furthermore many occupations are in effect adult games. It takes little imagination to see the busy executive with his telephones, conferences, social engagements, and trips as a big boy at play with other grown-up boys and girls, or to picture the scientist, artist, teacher, or craftsman as seriously engaged in their own special games of playing with apparatus, pigments or sounds, words, and tools.

Work which renews the worker is, of course, not only incomparably more satisfying than tasks done with a sense of unpleasant necessity but is also likely to be far more productive. If the occupation contains within itself both stimulus and reward, wholehearted efforts are consistently encouraged without the application of external incentives. A prime objective of vocational guidance should be to help students discover kinds of work which they find keen pleasure in doing. Frequently a consideration of the hobbies in which the individual engages may provide clues to the lifework for which he is best fitted. Recreational interests may thus be the best indication of the types of activity which call forth one's maximum enthusiasm. Fortunate is the person who can direct those interests into vocational channels.

Recreation as work. The identity of recreation and work may also be seen from the other side. Not only may work have a recreative quality, but recreation may take on the aspect of work. There are people who look upon recreation as a job to be done. They make a business out of play and enter into leisure-time activities with the same methodical seriousness that characterizes their work. When the business day is over, an executive may take on the next job of playing a round of golf or working his garden. Though he may say and even believe that these are refreshing activities, it is possible to do them in such a way that they are simply further obligations to be dutifully accomplished. He may worry more about his low score or his weeds than about his business affairs, and he may struggle competitively up the success ladder as much in his recreation as on the job.

It is natural to expect a person to approach his work and his recreation in much the same way. After all, it is the same person who does both. Just as it is possible to do the job in the spirit of recreation, so it is not surprising to find a vocationalized outlook in some people's play. Importing a negative attitude toward work into recreation is certainly undesirable. On the other hand, if one's work is creative and genuinely interesting, the carry-over into play is desirable.

Essential in education is the recognition that the young child's play is his proper work. Manipulation of objects, construction projects, games, caring for animals—the many childhood activities that are usually regarded by adults as "mere play"—are to the child significant and serious business. They constitute his childhood vocation, the work that he is called to do. The successful accomplishment of these playtime pursuits forms the basis for the development of adult social and occupational competences.

It would thus seem important for the educator not to make a sharp distinction between work and recreation, but to see play for the young as a basic kind of work and recreational activities as essential parts of the curriculum. Both work and play can be purposeful, serious, and productive experiences of doing and learning. The main difference between them is that work has to do with long-term purposes and with contribution to social demands, while play serves more temporary and purely individual purposes. But functionally, in promoting desirable personal growth, both types of activity occupy similar and in many respects indistinguishable roles.

Work for recreation. According to a third view, work and recreation are quite distinct modes of activity, and the main purpose of work is to provide financial resources for engaging in recreation. Many a worker considers his job as an inescapable chore which he does solely to earn the money which he spends for leisure pursuits with friends and family, in sports and hobbies. He does not find true satisfaction in the work itself but only in his free-time activities. Frequently people will labor and save for fifty weeks in the year for the sake of two glorious vacation weeks at a resort or in travel to exotic places. Most workers who are covered under pension plans or who are otherwise able to provide financially for the later years look ahead longingly to the time of their retirement, finding in the anticipation of carefree days a major justification for the efforts of the working years.

As pointed out in the previous chapter, the worker is frequently unaware of the extent to which the nature of his character and the meaning of his life are bound up with the job. Hence, the hours after work, the vacation periods, and the years in retirement frequently do not measure up to expectation. Recreation which must compensate for boredom in work is also likely to become an escape rather than an experience of renewal. The full life needs to be based upon intrinsic satisfaction in both work and recreation.

Recreation for work. A fourth view also assumes a clear distinction between recreation and work, but makes the former instrumental to the latter. The purpose of recreation is to enable one to do the job more efficiently. One takes just enough rest to be fresh for work, and he engages only in those leisure activities which will restore the energies necessary to do his job most effectively. This attitude is typical of business and professional people who are so deeply interested in their work that they would keep at it continuously if the human organism did not demand some respite. These people often tend to judge the recreational needs of others by their own standards. Thus, an employer, thoroughly absorbed in his business, may take an utterly different view of the optimum hours of work and vacation periods for his employers than they do themselves, concerned as they may well be with working for pay to be used in play rather than with the job itself.

To judge recreation solely by its contribution to the occupation is really to make it a part of the job and to rob it of that spontaneity and autonomy which are its peculiar merits. Though in some sense the best work is recreative, and though play often has the seriousness and constructiveness of work, work and recreation are not identical, and it is an impoverishment of life to demand that recreation be justified only by its service to the job. Education may therefore be asked to provide for the development of personal competences both at work and in play, recognizing in both types of pursuits opportunities for the actualization of human potentialities and assigning to each a distinctive role in the realization of the good life.

Recreation and Human Fulfillment

The whole man. The above discussion of the relationships between work and recreation has emphasized the place of both in achieving the most complete development of human powers. In this fulfillment of human life the experiences of recreation are of special importance. Each person by choice, by circumstance, and by social necessity engages in some occupation and is required to participate in certain activities of family, community, and nation. These more or less permanent and obligatory tasks and relationships have a profound influence on the quality of life and character. It is largely by virtue of recreation that the possibility is provided of supplementing these influences by kinds of activity needed to produce a well-rounded, balanced personality. The conditions of job and the circumstances of environment by themselves often promote a narrow, one-sided kind of life. Through recreation the person can develop the complementary modes of behavior needed to produce a higher degree of wholeness.

The ideal of completeness suggests that recreation usually serves its purpose best when there is some contrast between the activities of occupation and those of leisure. Consequently, the best kind of recreation for a given person will depend not only upon his individual interests and abilities but also upon the nature of his work. One who works at a sedentary job frequently needs contrasting activity out-of-doors. A person whose occupation requires solitary effort may particularly require social recreation. The scientist may with profit complement his professional critical, logical, analytical activity by the production and enjoyment of music, painting, or poetry.

Human life illustrates what may well be a universal principle of living things, namely, a "principle of alternation." Life has a rhythmic or cyclic character. Effort and rest alternate with each other, expenditure and replenishment follow one another in succession. There is always a tendency toward balance, a return from the extreme, a completion of the circle. Thus, the education of whole persons ought to take account of the rhythm of life and should teach the wisdom and way of achieving variety and balance. In the face of vocational and social necessities, it seems evident that recreation provides the opportunity for free exploration and creative participation in activities which will tend toward this fullness of life.

Individuality. The same considerations make it clear why recreation contributes significantly to the production of human individuality. A person's recreation can, or ought to be, freely chosen. No one is required to pursue one hobby rather than another or to enjoy one kind of entertainment rather than another. The choice of recreation ought always to be a free expression of individual personality. One may be forced into certain conformities in job and community, but in principle he is free to be himself in his recreation. Unfortunately society often exercises domination over the person in his recreational pursuits and thereby robs these activities of their genuinely creative and renewing power. It is of great importance that as far as possible the freedom and variety of recreation be preserved, and that in the program of education emphasis be placed not upon compulsory mass recreation, but upon the discovery by each person of those special, freely chosen interests through which his own uniqueness can best be expressed.

Meaning and perspective. A deep and persistent human need is for a sense of meaning in life. The consciousness of vocation in work is one important source of meaning. Yet this awareness is scarcely possible apart from periodic withdrawal from labor for the sake of restoration and renewal. In these times of recreation there is opportunity to reflect upon the plan and purposes of life and to consider whether or not they are good. It is through such occasions of withdrawal from the pressures of daily affairs that one can rise above preoccupation with particular events and see them in their relationships to each other and to some more or less consistent life-pattern.

Recreation thus makes possible the regaining of perspective, which tends to get lost through one's immersion in immediate concerns. Perspective requires detachment, and this should be one fruit of freely chosen, work-complementing recreation. Steady application to occupational and communal concerns can rob a person of his sense of proportion. He may come to regard these concerns as being really the most important in all the world, and he can best be delivered from so distorted a viewpoint by regular disengagement from these affairs in the complementary pursuits of recreation. Human fulfillment includes the ability to play, in which one demonstrates this capacity for detachment. For the world of play is one which the participant enters and leaves at will. Anyone who is a slave to what he regards as the serious duties of life cannot play because he cannot even for an hour be free of his cares. Learning to play is thus an indispensable component in the education of free man.

Humor. A sense of humor is one manifestation of the spirit of detachment. It is found only in those who do not take themselves and their world with deadly seriousness. Humor has two components: first, an awareness of disproportion or incongruity; and second, a capacity to take surprised delight in this eccentricity without demanding that it be adjusted to the "right" or judged "wrong" by reference to the customary state of affairs. Both components are based upon the play outlook, that is, the ability to enjoy a "make-believe" world which is accepted as significant in its own right.

Recreation as religious. In a profound sense also recreation is related to religious worship. It is no accident that the holy day is also a holiday, that the day of rest is also a day of worship. The act of worship, like the experience of humor, is based upon the delighted envisagement of alternative worlds. There can be no true worship as long as one is absorbed in the routines of daily life. There must be a withdrawal, a periodic relinquishment of striving, an occasion for deliberate consideration of the whole scheme of things, for the re-establishment of proportion and perspective. In the biblical story of creation it is related that God worked six days and rested from his work on the seventh, and the command is given that man, made in the likeness of the Creator, do likewise. Thus according to the religious tradition of the West, "re-creation" has divine sanction and both cosmic and primordial significance.

Self-transcendence. Much of what has been said in the foregoing about the contribution of recreation to human fulfillment may be summarized in the idea of self-transcendence. To be a person is to possess the power through intelligence and through creative imagination to enlarge the domain of perception indefinitely beyond the limits of the immediate setting in space and time. Free, rational, self-transcending man does not merely inherit an environment and adjust to it; he envisions a new world and sets about to create it. This he can do in all aspects of cultural activity, including his occupation. However, it is especially in recreation that the spontaneity and infinitude of the human spirit may be manifested. The exigencies of life often make men prisoners in work and in obligations to family and state. Recreation then becomes the principal area of existence where in creative detachment the person can transcend those confines and affirm his own unique being.

The art of living. Recreation also helps to realize the ideal of living as an art. A work of art is a human creation in which the materials of nature are transformed so as to express some deeply felt intelligible form. The life of each individual ought to be such a work of art. It ought not to be a chance product of physical or social circumstances but a deliberate self-fashioning in which a unique personal pattern is day by day sketched on the canvas of the years. It is particularly through recreational pursuits that this consciousness of the artistry of life may be kept alive because especially in these activities the person can see himself, be himself, and decide what self he will become.

Recreation in Industrial Civilization

The economics of recreation. The nature and extent of recreational opportunity in any society are to a large degree influenced by prevailing economic conditions. When the struggle for physical survival forces men to devote all available energy to making a living, there is no question of how to use leisure time. Recreation under these conditions must largely be such as to enable workers to continue working, often including means of temporary escape from the dreariness and drudgery of daily routines. Recreation becomes both an opportunity and a problem only when there is sufficient material wealth to free man from the incessant fight to remain alive. True relaxation of effort, enjoyment of entertainment, and participation in play activity are possible only when there are more than enough material goods to sustain physical life.

In some social systems of the past the necessary surplus of wealth was produced by the use of slaves to do the work so that their owners might engage in "genteel" activities of their own choosing. Even when slavery was abandoned, it was still necessary to have a large proportion of the people assigned on a family, class, or caste basis to the major tasks of production so as to permit the smaller privileged group to enjoy leisure pursuits. With the coming of modern industrialism the contrast of privilege as between working people and owners or managers persisted and in some cases became even more acute, but eventually the working people won a larger share of the benefits. The use of machine power in place of manpower can have two effects: it can increase output and it can reduce the amount of labor required per unit of production. It is in the interest of the owners and managers to increase output, while the workers are interested also in shorter hours of work. The growing power of labor organizations has assured an increasing proportion of the income from industrial output to working people (in the form of higher wages) and has also gained for them substantial reductions in the work week.

When there are marked contrasts of economic class there are corresponding contrasts in types of recreation. The lower classes have less time for play and less range of possible activities than the privileged groups. There also tend to be qualitative differences, the poor engaging in activities requiring less refinement of taste, less sensitivity and cultivation of perception, and of course less material outlay than the recreation of the well-to-do. The spectacular improvement in the lot of working people in advanced industrial society has tended to reduce the economic contrast and to alter greatly these disparities in recreational opportunity. In fact, many an industrial worker has more leisure than the executives who run the business in which he is employed.

With the coming of the automatic factory the virtually complete emancipation of the human being from all forms of routine labor, both physical and intellectual, is being achieved. At the same time the development of vast new resources of power is making possible an abundant supply of material goods for all people. Under these conditions man can turn over to the machine nearly all of the functions which have traditionally constituted his labor and can be free to devote himself to the pursuits of leisure. Thus, in the world of tomorrow recreation may become the central concern of life rather than a set of peripheral and marginal activities, and the sense of meaning and value in existence may be derived from recreation rather than primarily from the job.

Education in an age of abundance. If man is no longer to be bound by the exigencies of labor to a circumscribed pattern of life, it follows that a major task of education in the world of automation will be to prepare the young to utilize their freedom most advantageously. There must, of course, be education for technical competence (to make and run the machines) and for social competence (to insure satisfactory human relationships and a just and stable social order). But in addition to these requirements there must be ample provision for developing competence in the optimum use of the hours of leisure. In every age there have been a few favored persons who were sufficiently well endowed materially and who were politically and socially secure enough that they could devote themselves freely to the pursuit of what they saw as the ideal life. Now for the first time in human history the way is open to give this opportunity to everyone. The life-plan for the majority of mankind need no longer be determined largely by the economic struggle. The new vocation of man is to realize his full humanity. This has always been his calling, but the conditions of existence made it an ideal few could approximate. Today the sharp reduction in working hours which machine power makes possible provides the opportunity for anyone, in recreation, to choose and to proceed toward the goals of life which seem good to him. The choice and the process may be wise or foolish, significant or trivial, and it is by education that the habits of decision are influenced the former way or the latter. The personal fulfillment of modern man will be determined largely by how well he has learned to employ his time in recreation.

In the age of abundance, for the first time, the highest aims of education have become intensely relevant. To ask what a human being ought to be and how he can be helped to become that ideal is no longer merely a theoretical question for philosophers and theologians but the practical question for every educator. The greatest potential benefit of machine power is not material wealth in itself but the *gift of time* in which the truly educated man can freely fashion a life and fulfill a chosen destiny.

15

Freedom

IN THE PAST five chapters of this part consideration has been given to the process of education within the context of nature and of society, including family and friends, the state and voluntary associations, job and recreation. In this and the following chapter we shall deal with two problems, of freedom and of moral values respectively, which are directly concerned with the nature of the developing self rather than primarily with the environmental conditions in which personal growth takes place. Freedom and morality are two especially important qualities of the mature person. It is to an inquiry into the meaning of these characteristics and the conditions for developing them that these two chapters are devoted.

Freedom and Human Nature

Freedom is one of the distinguishing marks of man's nature. To be a person is to be able to choose what one will be and do, and not merely to follow the bidding of instinctual or mechanical necessity. Inorganic matter moves in the manner described by the laws of physics, and the behavior of living things is defined by biological principles. It is possible that man's behavior is nothing more than an extremely complicated case of physical and biological activity and that there is nothing really distinctive in quality about human nature. But it seems more likely that what every person understands inwardly as his freedom is a power qualitatively different from the working of ordinary biophysical mechanisms. It may be that this freedom also prevails to a lesser degree in the lower organisms, only in man becoming a decisive factor in his nature. Regardless of this larger problem, it does appear that freedom to choose is a dominant factor in a human being's commonsense awareness of what he is.

Furthermore, freedom has come to be widely regarded as the birthright of every man so that a person is somehow less than human without it. The struggle for freedom is probably the major objective in revolutionary movements of all ages, and particularly of the twentieth century. Freedom is not always completely realized in the life of man, but can be suppressed and denied in unfavorable social circumstances. Thus, freedom is a goal to be attained rather than a possession guaranteed by nature. If freedom is part of the essence of being a man, then there are individuals who are less than fully human, and the struggle to become free is at the same time a striving for complete humanity.

Freedom and Education

Since education is the process of directing the development of persons, and since freedom is inherent in the realization of true selfhood, one of the aims of education must be the growth of freedom. The outcome of education should be the free person. But what does it mean to be free? Does it mean that the individual is to be completely unpredictable, without any law or principle? Does it mean that he is to be subject to no restrictions and independent of every other agency? How does the person become free? What methods of education best insure his emancipation?

Like truth and justice, freedom is one of the values in which nearly everybody believes. It is a thoroughly respectable goal of education. The problem is to know just what the term means and precisely how any particular advocate of freedom would propose to advance it. Hence a major task in a philosophical discussion of freedom is to analyze the concept to show its different intended meanings and in this way to remove its ambiguity as an educational objective. Three principal distinctive meanings will be discussed in this chapter, and the relevance of each to education will be explored.

Freedom as Indeterminacy

Determinism. In some ways the most fundamental meaning of freedom is defined by contrasting it with determinism. According to determinism, any state of affairs at a given moment is in principle completely explainable by the appropriate set of antecedent causes. The condition of things at one instant in time is a consequence solely of the conditions prevailing at the immediately prior instant. Similarly, the nature of things which are to happen in the future is wholly determined by what now prevails. Just as the present is wholly explicable by past factors, so the future is without remainder contained in what presently is. The whole world process is governed by inflexible laws. Nothing happens by accident or arbitrarily but always and entirely by necessity, according to determinate principles.

This determinist world view has been implicit in the faith and practice of science. The goal of scientific research is the discovery of the general laws which the processes of nature exemplify. To explain any phenomenon scientifically means to analyze the causal factors which determine it. Even more important than explanation, and deriving from it, is prediction. Knowing the laws of causal sequence, it is possible, on the basis of known present circumstances, to predict what will happen in the future, to reconfirm the explanatory laws when the predictions come true, and to improve them when the forecasts are not fulfilled.

The determinist assumption has been amply justified by its fruits. There can be no doubt about the spectacular success of modern science. Laws have been discovered which permit predictions of great accuracy far in the future. The application of this knowledge has led to a wealth of inventions for the control and use of nature's powers. This triumph of modern technology is a direct confirmation of the determinist principle.

Indeterminacy in physical science. Only in relatively recent decades have some physical scientists found reason to doubt the universal applicability of the determinist assumption. In the sub-microscopic world of the atom it appears that exact simultaneous predictions of the position and momentum of a particle are not possible, and that the best obtainable measure of these quantities is a probability formula describing the range and relative frequencies of position and momentum for large numbers of similar particles. Thus precise determinism of individual particles has been replaced by a statistical determinism. These discoveries have introduced into physical science a principle of indeterminacy which sets limits to the absolute and rigid determinism of classical science.

Some philosophers and scientists have sought to apply the principles of physical indeterminacy to explain the creative features of life and mind, and in particular to account for human freedom. In the delicate balance of the complex organic structures they believe that the undetermined behavior of the whole may be a result of the indeterminacy of certain key elementary particles, whose extremely minute effect is multiplied in much the same fashion as a sensitive electrical relay can produce a large-scale response to a weak signal. Other careful thinkers believe that there is no connection between physical indeterminacy in the realm of the very small and the alleged freedom of human beings, whose behavior occurs at the macroscopic level, where the classical principle of determinism is still believed fully applicable.

The two realms of being. Most critics of absolute determinism in human life do not rest their case on the recent developments in atomic physics. Instead, they argue that there are two distinct realms of being, one physical or material, in which deterministic principles apply, and the other mental or spiritual, in which determinism is replaced by freedom. This distinction also sets a limit to the applicability of science. Scientific knowledge is concerned with determinate causal sequences. On these premises the realm of spirit, which is the realm of freedom rather than determinism, is beyond the reach of scientific analysis. This is no derogation of science. It is merely a direct consequence of *defining* scientific procedures deterministically.

According to this view, the scientific study of man can at best yield knowledge of the human being as a complex physical system and not as the free being he truly, inwardly, and essentially is. The significance of freedom is known only from the subjective experience of spiritual awareness, from the inward consciousness of being able to choose, never from applying to man the freedom-denying methods and assumptions underlying the study of the behavior of material things. Hence it is claimed that the study of man as a free being requires radically different methods from those which have been utilized so successfully in natural science. Little wonder, say the proponents of this position, that the prediction and control of human affairs have been so unsuccessful in comparison with the subjugation of nature through the physical sciences.

In reply to this the upholder of determinism would say that the sciences of man are so relatively young and their subject matter is so extremely complex that the analysis of the mechanism of human behavior has not yet been as complete and successful as in the physical sciences. Nevertheless there have been important accomplishments in modern psychology, making possible fairly accurate prediction of human conduct. Man is not indeterminate in behavior. He is no less subject to determinate laws than are the stars in their courses, though the laws are more complicated and more difficult to discover in the case of human behavior. We must not give up the basic determinist premise of science in the most important of all areas of research—the human—just because the problems presented are more challenging.

Time and creation. The fundamental point at issue between the determinist and the indeterminist is whether or not the complete explanation for the present state of things lies in the past, and similarly whether or not from present conditions only a single series of future conditions can possibly develop. In other words, is the present wholly accounted for by reference to the past, and is the entire story of the future contained in the present? The indeterminist believes that there are different possible pathways from past through present to future, and that the world process involves the continual coming into being of entirely new and different entities and configurations. With the passage of time real change and genuine novelty occur. The world of the future is not hidden and fixed in the world of the present, like a motion picture reel, waiting merely to be unrolled by the passing of the years.

To affirm indeterminacy is to hold that creation is not something which merely happened once in the past and that the universe is not now what it always was and forever will be, but that creation continues. Human freedom is part of this scheme. Man is a true creator. He freely chooses to bring into being something that never existed before the act of choice and that could not have been predicted solely by reference to antecedent circumstances. Human life is not the mere reading of a script which is already written. Free man is at once playwright and actor. The world is not finished, ready made. Man's freedom consists in his ability to participate in the making of his world.

Indeterminacy and education. The indeterminist view has important bearings on education. If a person is really convinced that his behavior is entirely determined by prior conditions, he cannot take seriously the notion that one course of action is "better" than another. Whatever happens is bound in advance to occur; facts simply *are,* they are not better or worse. Education is merely part of the process of living out the determinate sequence. It is not a means of "improving" human life or of fulfilling ideals; these are but ways of speaking about emotional attitudes toward the inevitable course of events. The indeterminist, on the other hand, sees the future as open, and he regards education as a way of presenting real alternatives and of recommending the better ones in preference to the worse. The purpose of recommendation is to help determine the decision one way rather than another, but the final outcome is in the hands of the one who makes the choice. He may choose the worse rather than the better, no matter how strong the persuasion for the latter.

An indeterminist outlook presents to each person as he faces the future a challenge to make something of his life. There can be no genuine challenge if the future is already decided by what now is. Determinism destroys incentive for creative adventure, inducing a spirit of resignation to an inescapable fate. This outlook undermines the motives which stimulate educational effort.

On the other hand, indeterminism also places limitations on the influence of education. It is usual to think of education as determining behavior, and the conduct of life as governed by educational factors. If freedom means indeterminacy, then education in freedom will not determine a life, but can only present alternatives from which the person may make his choices. Hence the educator who respects human freedom will not regard himself as a fashioner of persons, but as one with the far more limited responsibility of presenting for consideration certain ways of life which he believes particularly worthy of being chosen. With such an outlook, the educator recognizes that his effort cannot wholly determine the lives of those whom he seeks to guide but that there is an inevitable creative novelty, a fundamental contingency and unpredictability, through which the future will always upset his best-laid and most carefully executed plans.

Freedom as Independence and Self-determination

Indeterminacy and chance. There is one serious difficulty with the idea of indeterminacy which suggests the need for other more adequate concepts of freedom. The problem is that the doctrine of indeterminacy denies the possibility of complete explanation for any event. Whenever anything happens it becomes a definite fact. If we take indeterminism literally, it is necessary to say that to some extent this happening is uncaused, that there are no antecedent circumstances which fully explain it. Indeterminacy thus reflects the defeat of reason. It introduces the notion of "chance," not in the sense of the unknown causes of unpredicted events but as the *causelessness* of unpredictable events. Such a strong concept of chance is hard for rational man to accept. He resists the thought that on principle no reason can be assigned for certain events. This idea is especially unpalatable to the educator, whose interest is to cause appropriate effects in the persons under his direction. If freedom means that what a person does is without cause or reason, but purely by chance, then the educator will not advocate freedom. He regards his job as the encouragement of behavior based on good causes and right reasons, and as the elimination of the accidental and irrational in life.

Self as cause. It is possible to avoid this difficulty with freedom as indeterminism by using instead the concepts of independence and self-determination. According to this view, every event has a cause, but the free entity differs from one that is not free in that the cause of its behavior lies within the entity itself and not in any external agency. That is, freedom is defined as self-determination. By this definition freedom is not in contrast with determinism. On the contrary, freedom is a special type of determination. A material body is said to move freely if it is not constrained by any forces acting upon it to deviate from its straight path and uniform speed. An animal is free if it is not fenced, harnessed, or otherwise governed by powers beyond itself.

Independence and self-determination are complementary components of the same idea of freedom. Independence is the negative side, meaning absence of external influence in the determination of behavior. Self-determination is the positive side, meaning that the explanation for the behavior lies within the entity in question. Independence means that there is no external cause; self-determination means that there is an inner cause.

Three types of dependence. There are three different types of dependence which need to be noted, absence of which constitutes corresponding types of freedom. One type simply sets the limits within which activity may take place but does not control the activity within those limits. For example, a prisoner may be free to move about in his cell but not beyond it; he is free, but within certain strict limits. A traveler abroad is free to visit only those countries for which he has proper passport authorization. Independence may be limited in this way by certain barriers beyond which the self cannot determine its behavior. A second type of dependence is external control of activity. In this case freedom as independence is wholly lacking. The citizen of a totalitarian state who is forced against his will to do a certain type of work, to live in a specified place, and to affirm designated ideas is wholly dependent upon the governing powers. His conduct is not his own; he is simply an instrument for the execution of state policy. A third type of dependence is the partial rather than complete determination of behavior by external factors. The causes of activity lie both without and within the self. There are external influences which modify but do not completely control what is done. For example, a person's determination of what clothing to wear is compounded of both personal preferences and social expectations. Similarly, what a child does is usually something of a compromise between what he would do if left to himself and what his parents or teachers require him to do.

In contrast to these types of dependence, independence means absence of limiting restraints and full determination from within rather than from without. It is doubtful if complete and absolute independence is possible. Everything exists in a complex network of interrelationships with other things, which set limits and exert influence on behavior. Yet there are degrees of independence; some things are relatively self-explanatory and self-regulating in comparison with other things and are in that sense more free.

Education and independence. Earlier it was pointed out that education is fundamentally at odds with freedom as indeterminacy. It now appears that the same contradiction exists between education and freedom as independence. When one person directs the development of another, he sets limits to the activities of the other and exerts influence on his behavior. What point could there be in education if not to cause modifications in conduct? In its very essence the interconnection and mutual influence of persons are presupposed. Each of the three types of dependence has its place in education. Sometimes, particularly in the case of the very immature, activity must be completely controlled by the parent or teacher. For example, a child may have to be removed bodily from the street or required entirely against his will to go to bed rather than stay up with the adults. With the more mature it is possible to grant more independence, but there is still education by others only to the degree that limits are set and behavior is at least partially determined externally.

Self-education. However, we should not too hastily conclude from this analysis that freedom and education are opposed. For education is not only the guidance of one person by another, and freedom as here discussed is not only absence of external agency. Education includes self-guidance, and freedom includes self-determination. Self-education and freedom as self-determination are obviously entirely compatible. Perhaps the ideal of all education is self-education. In such education external factors are taken account of, but they do not directly determine behavior; they simply supply data to be included in the self's determination. Any external element may be accepted or rejected, modified or incorporated unchanged, as the self decides. When there is self-determination, teachers, parents, and associates simply provide the materials from which the person constructs his own self-designed world.

Dependence and independence in the development of the self. But self-determination presupposes a self which can make the determinations. Is that self purely self-made, or does it have causes beyond itself? It is evident that the nature of the self is at least in part necessarily determined by environmental factors. The very young child cannot be allowed in every respect to govern himself. Some limitations and controls must be imposed upon him in order that he may become a determinate self with a sufficiently definite functional pattern to be able to make decisions leading to consistent growth and to adequate harmony with the social and physical environment. It seems clear, therefore, that not all education can be self-education. At least in the early stages of development, there must be a considerable amount of determination from beyond the self. Upon the nature of this determination greatly depends the quality of selfhood from which further self-determinations may be made.

The conclusion appears to be that education must include both dependence and independence and that the right proportion of each is a function of the learner's level of maturity. To give a child independence before his own selfhood is definitely formed tends to produce a sense of inadequacy and may result in a life-long struggle for security. On the other hand, withholding the right of self-determination too long may destroy initiative and creativity and engender feelings of frustration and rage leading to destructive forms of behavior. The goal of education, then, is freedom—in the autonomous, self-directing person—and the ideal of education is that continuing self-tuition which the mature person has learned how to conduct. But one pillar upon which these achievements rest is the good dependency, in the years of immaturity, which makes an adequate self possible.

Determination by the future. Let us return to the contrast between freedom and determinism discussed in an earlier paragraph. It was observed that a determinist scheme, where the past completely explains the present and future, makes nonsense of the idea that there are real options and undermines the urgency of moral decision. Does this hold for the concept of freedom as self-determination? It appears not. For self-determination introduces a new element into determinism. There is a mechanical type of determinism in which each event is wholly explained by its past. But what if there were also determination by the future? This is exactly what self-determination by human beings reveals. Human behavior is not the outcome only of prior conditions but of expectations and intentions. The motion of physical bodies can be sufficiently well explained by reference to antecedent external conditions. The conduct of an intelligent organism cannot be fully understood in this fashion. It requires for its explanation some concept of purposes or goals. According to this view, human actions are not indeterminate, but their principle of determination must include the future as well as the past. A person is free when his purposes for the future determine his conduct.

If the future enters into human determination, then one need not resign himself to a fate already decreed from the past. The educator's recommendation of improved courses of action may become part of the learner's envisagement of future possibilities. Education is necessarily oriented toward the future; it is concerned with what persons may become. If there is determination solely by the past, education is but the acting out of a drama already written. If aims can determine the path of life, then education becomes a genuine process of realizing what was before only an ideal possibility.

Efficient and final causes. The meaning of freedom as self-determination is further emphasized in the distinction between efficient causes and final causes. The efficient causes of an event are the past events considered necessary to explain it. Final causes are goals or intentions for the future considered necessary to explain the event. Freedom as self-determination means that human behavior is not to be fully accounted for on the basis of efficient causes, i.e., influences from the past, but that the idea of final causes, or purposes, must also be introduced. Education which presupposes only efficient causation leads to the view that the educator fashions persons as a sculptor produces a statue, by working on the material to force it into the desired shape. On the other hand, education which includes the idea of final causes makes a place for persuasion and for the presentation of alternative possibilities, with the opportunity for the learner to respond to those goals which seem to him most worthy of future realization.

Freedom and the nature of the self. The quality of freedom as self-determination depends upon the nature of the self which effects the determinations. A material body unconstrained by external forces is free in the sense of being independent, but it is not self-determined in any very significant sense. An unconfined animal is independent and self-moving; the determination of behavior lies within the organism. But in human beings selfhood reaches a new level and freedom takes on a new dimension. For in man there is the ability to entertain alternative future possibilities in imagination and to reflect on which of them is most compatible with the existing organization of the personality. The unique feature of human freedom is this capacity of the self to envisage not only the unactualized future but an entire range of possible futures.

Freedom and the realm of possibility. The essence of freedom as self-determination is found in this singular property of human personality to construct new worlds in imagination, using materials from the past, but adding entirely new elements and reorganizing all into new patterns. Then does this creativity in the human self lead us back to indeterminacy? If the envisaged future patterns are in some respects really new, are they undetermined? No, not necessarily. It can be argued that intelligence is able to grasp certain real and unchanging alternative structures of possibility and apply them to the special materials at hand. To take a simple example, a person may wish to decide in which direction to move from a given location. He makes the decision in part by a preliminary imaginative envisagement of alternative possible paths. The range of possibilities is given in the geometric idea of directionality. It is then merely necessary for the person to adapt this general rational structure to the particular situation, including perceived obstacles, objects of interest in various directions, and so on. According to this account, new creations arise from the bringing to light of erstwhile hidden or unperceived possibilities. The problem of where these possibilities reside or how they subsist apart from human perception and concrete embodiment is of major concern in metaphysics and theology, into which we cannot inquire further here.

To summarize, the meaning of freedom as self-determination is bound up with the meaning of selfhood, and the realization of personal freedom depends upon becoming a mature human being, with intelligence for reflective consideration of future possibilities.

Freedom as Power to Achieve Goals

Positive and negative conceptions of freedom. The concepts of freedom as indeterminacy, as independence, and even perhaps as self-determination put the emphasis on negation. They deny the relevance of external agencies in the explanation of free behavior. They stress autonomy and disconnection. We now consider another way of looking at freedom which places the emphasis on the affirmation of power to become. It is important to complement the negative meanings by this positive approach. A beginning of such an analysis was made in the discussion of self-determination, but a still wider affirmation is desirable.

Two preliminary examples will illustrate the meaning of a positive conception of freedom. Suppose there were a railroad running between place A and place B. What does it mean to say that the train runs freely from A to B? Negatively, it means that there are neither barriers in the way nor compulsion from an outside force. Positively, it means that there is a good roadbed and track, a competent engineer at the controls, and an adequate supply of fuel. For the train to run freely certain supportive and directing conditions must exist. Though the track appears to be a limiting agency, it is also a condition of freedom, since the train cannot reach its destination without that restriction. Again, what does it mean to say that a young person is free to become a great scientist or political leader? Negatively, it means that there are no factors such as racial or caste regulations which would rule out such a career in advance and that the individual will not be forced against his will into the position of eminence. Positively, it means that the cultural and personal factors are such as to lend support to a seriously entertained scientific or political ambition.

Thus, in the positive sense freedom means power to achieve goals, and this power depends upon the right kind of connections rather than upon isolation. It is a conception of freedom which emphasizes the need for interdependence if human potential is to be fully realized. It also provides a further development of the idea of self-determination through a recognition of the personality factors making for goal-fulfilling power. Hence we may conveniently distinguish between the outer and inner conditions of freedom and in turn analyze each into several component factors.

Outer conditions for freedom. A person is not free to realize his goals unless there are sufficiently favorable circumstances of physical and social environment. These conditions may be divided into material, social, and cultural factors.

Material. No human being can be free in the absence of essential material resources. While there is a sense in which the poor man can be as free or even freer than the rich man, the person who suffers material privation does not have the range of possibilities open to him that are available to the well-supplied person. There is little virtue in being free to starve. It is for this reason that people who live at a bare subsistence level are usually more responsive to a promise of economic improvement than to more intangible types of freedom, such as the right to vote or to choose their occupation. Only when there are material goods more than sufficient to meet minimal survival needs does man have an opportunity to realize a variety of objectives. The great potential freedom of modern man consists in his mastery of the physical environment, which has brought vast material resources under human control. This is by far the most important contribution of modern technical civilization to the ideal of freedom. For the first time in history it is possible for all men to possess the material resources necessary for a high degree of goal-achievement. The world-wide revolutionary convulsions of the twentieth century are a direct expression of this dawning recognition. Unfortunately, the material advances have not been accompanied by equally impressive improvements in the other conditions for freedom, both outer and inner. This imbalance imperils the freedom which the control of nature has made possible.

A plentiful supply of material goods is one requisite of education for freedom. Growing persons are not free to fulfill high potentials unless they have the appropriate physical facilities, such as houses, school buildings, books, and laboratory equipment and supplies. Not only does material sufficiency make possible education for freedom, but education is in turn the chief means of insuring material welfare. Modern scientific and technical education is the basis for the control of the physical environment, and social, political, and economic education helps to make possible the equitable distribution and proper human use of those material benefits.

Social. Just as a person cannot realize his goals without the necessary material facilities, neither can he be free in the positive sense without social reinforcement. This is not to say that the prophets and martyrs who stand against the accepted ideas and practices of society are without freedom. They are, however, less free to achieve their ideals than they would be if they had cooperation instead of opposition. Even one who seeks to reform an established social order is indebted to that society for giving him a platform from which to make his protest and a community which he cares enough about to want to improve it. In contrast to these people who exercise their freedom through criticism, most members of a society find personal fulfillment in activities which have general social assent and active cooperation from the community.

The family is the earliest and most important channel for social reinforcement in the life of every person. The consistent interest, encouragement, and assistance of parents for a child are major factors in giving him power for achievement. Friends and teachers also make it possible to realize aims which could not be reached without their aid. The freedom to succeed in business, in research, or in the arts is based upon the indispensable support of colleagues and of a receptive public. Power for achievement does not reside solely within the individual. No person is free, purely on his own, to rise to eminence in science, in the entertainment world, or in political life. Freedom of enterprise is by grace of a social order which provides the necessary human resources and supports. This holds not only for so-called leaders but for every person, whatever his calling and status in the social scheme. The power to fulfill personal objectives is to a considerable degree dependent on a correspondence between those goals and the aims of other people, particularly as these are embodied in the institutions of society.

An important feature of social support is the legal system. It is commonly thought that laws limit freedom. Yet even more significant is the sense in which they undergird it. Laws represent the accepted principles of social order. Without them the individual could not plan his activities with any assurance of success. Through laws some degree of regularity and stability is provided, making it practicable for persons to have aims and to attain them. Even the lawbreaker is to some extent free through the law because he can predict, for his own subversive ends, how the law-abiding majority will behave. Of course, the maximum freedom belongs to those whose personal aims are consistent with the laws. In that case the power of the law becomes available as power for self-realization.

It follows that education for freedom should include instruction in the nature of the social order of which one is a part, in the customs governing accepted behavior, in the institutions in which social arrangements are crystallized, and in the values which are socially approved. It is not always necessary, of course, that a person conform to the accepted pattern, but he is not fully free to achieve his goals if he fails to take account of the social milieu and as far as possible to draw strength and inspiration from it.

Cultural. The power to realize goals further depends upon the availability of cultural resources. This is actually an extension of the foregoing idea of social support, since culture includes such phenomena as customs, laws, and social institutions. Cultural, as distinguished from social, reinforcement is here meant to emphasize the support provided from the accumulated products of human creativity rather than directly from other persons as such. A successful scientist needs not only the encouragement of colleagues, the use of material resources, and protection of the laws, but even more especially does he depend upon the whole body of accumulated knowledge in his field of research. An artist builds to a large extent upon the foundation laid by previous generations of artists and upon inspiration from the products of his contemporaries. The same holds for every other department of human activity.

Culture can, of course, be a burden as well as a liberator. Recognizing this, some educators have protested against the imposition of the culture of the past on the young and have advocated a system in which each child is expected to discover and create his own world afresh. The result of such a plan is actually to enslave the child by rendering him impotent. Each generation cannot possibly start anew and recapitulate the toilsome history of the race. Such positive freedom as man has he owes in no small measure to the accomplishments of his forebears. Hence education that liberates must make use of the hard-won and well-tested knowledge and funded experience of mankind. This does not mean that education should be devoted simply to mastering a body of dead tradition. It means that the cultural treasure needs to be made available as a living resource for use by the individual in fulfilling his own life-goals. A liberal education—one that makes persons free—thus necessarily includes wide and varied instruction in the cultural heritage.

Inner conditions for freedom. In addition to the above three outer conditions for freedom, there are several inner factors which contribute to the power for goal-realization. These inner conditions are in effect criteria for the maturity of personality. They define qualities of the self required for the freedom of self-determination.

Physiological. Corresponding to the outer condition of material support is the inner factor of physiological well-being. A person with a weak or disabled body is less free to accomplish most objectives than he would be if endowed with physical strength. The ability to fulfill aims is often to a considerable extent due to sheer abundance of energy. One who operates at a low energy level, perhaps through gland deficiency, cannot truly be called free. Every improvement in health is a contribution to freedom. Hence education for freedom needs to include instruction in the care and culture of the human body.

Emotional. Similarly, positive freedom requires emotional health. Any person who is beset with fears, distracted by inner conflicts, or driven by compulsions cannot effectively realize his goals. An unrelieved sense of guilt, constant anxiety, or chronic indecisiveness interfere drastically with personal productivity. Individuals in such emotional bondage cannot fully utilize their powers. Oftentimes ordinary growth and further experience bring restoration. Sometimes medical treatment or psychological counseling are required. In every case, love and understanding by other people, especially by parents, other kinsfolk, friends, and teachers are of major importance in fostering emotional well-being. Whatever in education contributes to healthy emotional life helps to make persons free.

Habit. Power of accomplishment necessarily rests upon a solid foundation of appropriate habits. Most human actions are to a large extent automatic. Walking, eating, speaking, and other such common activities are usually performed without taking deliberate thought, at least in the details of execution. As a matter of fact, the attempt to give step-by-step conscious direction to routine behavior usually causes confusion and failure, as many have discovered to their discomfort in trying to descend a stairway by thoughtful planning of each step. Freedom of action is based upon habitual reaction patterns, perhaps originally developed through conscious effort but eventually built into the nerve structure. The ability of the skilled mechanic, pianist, lecturer, or ball player to achieve his goals depends upon an intricate web of habits patiently acquired through years of learning. Not only do these extraordinary accomplishments require a well-stocked armory of habits, but everyday life also absolutely depends upon previously acquired automatic responses. Without habit human life would cease to exist. The whole fabric of civilization is in large part a vast network of habitual modes of behavior.

A major function of education is to emancipate human beings from the burdens and uncertainties of the completely novel and unfamiliar, through the development of appropriate routine behavior patterns. These habitual modes of conduct release the person from concern with problems he has successfully dealt with before, making it unnecessary to solve them afresh each time they are met. He can then turn his attention to new difficulties and opportunities. The capacity to learn from experience is thus one foundation for human freedom. The nurture of persons with power to realize their goals requires the fostering of habit patterns consonant with those objectives.

Intelligence. Intelligence is an inner condition of freedom in two respects. First, it is solely by means of man's intellectual powers that he is able to envision future goals. Through his memory he can recall past experiences and through imagination he can refashion them as future possibilities. There can be no freedom as power to achieve goals unless there is a vivid apprehension of possible objectives. Other things being equal, that person is most free who has the most facility in projecting a variety of possible goals for successive imaginative consideration.

This self-transcending activity of entertaining alternative aims needs to be complemented by a second aspect of intelligence, namely, the ability to formulate effective means for realizing the ends projected. The person who has ideals which he does not know how to attain is a prisoner to his dreams. No one is made free merely by imagining what might be, but only through insight into the means of actualizing future possibilities. There is no true freedom in the visionary's undisciplined play of ideas, but only in the practical idealism of one who has the intelligence to relate ends to appropriate means for realizing them. A liberating education, then, must be concerned with the development of intelligence, by encouraging imaginative exploration and experimentation—the habitual envisagement of alternative possibilities—by giving guidance and practice in carrying projects to completion, and by equipping the student with a sufficient supply of well-tested knowledge.

Integrity. A person may have physical health, emotional and intellectual strength, and good habits and yet not be free, if these powers work at cross purposes to each other. The free person has integrity, or wholeness. His component inner powers are in harmonious balance with each other. His bodily strength is employed to fulfill the goals to which he is emotionally committed, for which his habit patterns are appropriate, and to which his intelligence gives assent. In one sense every person is necessarily integral: intelligence, habit, emotion, and body are all aspects of a single organism. Nevertheless, these component functions can be either mutually enhancing or antagonistic. Bodily impulses may agree with conscious intentions or be at war with them. Emotion may deny or support reason. There may also be either discord or concord among functions of one type: conflicting or mutually confirming goals, ambiguous or harmonious feelings, inconsistent or consistent habits or bodily functions. Freedom for goal achievement is greatest when all of the functions exercised by the human organism operate so as to reinforce one another.

The gift of true freedom is reserved for the integral personality. And how is integrity developed? It is the fruit of an educational process in which the whole human being is cared for, a program the aim of which is the harmonious development of all the component functions of the personality. Any educational program which concentrates on intelligence, emotion, habit, or physical culture to the neglect of the other factors comes under condemnation by the ideal of freedom.

Relation of outer and inner conditions. There is, of course, an intimate relationship between the outer and the inner conditions for personal freedom. It is through growth in an environment which gives material, social, and cultural support that inner resources of physical, emotional, habitual, and intellectual strength are acquired. Furthermore, the integral personality is most likely to develop in a reasonably unified social context, as for example in a family where the parents are consistent in their attitudes and reflect a system of values not too sharply at variance with those of teachers and friends. If major social influences operate in opposite directions, inner tensions may be developed which will impede the integration of the personality.

Even after the main characteristics of the personality have been formed, the full freedom to realize aims continues to depend on consonance between the outer and inner conditions. For education, the interaction of outer and inner factors during the most decisive period of growth is of chief importance, but if the fruits of a liberating education are to be well enjoyed, there must remain an adequacy and a wholeness in the environment to support and enhance the resources and the integrity within.

Perfect freedom. In analyzing freedom from the standpoint of power to achieve goals nothing has been said about the nature of the goals. A thief or a murderer is free, according to this definition, to the extent that he has the power to fulfill his objectives of stealing or killing. Yet this freedom is in a moral sense inferior to the freedom of the physician and the teacher to achieve their respective goals. That person is most truly and fully free who has the power to realize the best objectives. One's conception of best objectives depends upon his basic value system. For example, if freedom for all is taken as the highest value, then the freedom of the individual is to be construed as the power to participate with others in a harmonious community of persons each dedicated to using his own capacities for enriching the life of the whole and for advancing the interests of others. This is the ideal of integral persons bound together in an integral cooperative commonwealth.

It is sometimes said that the consummation of freedom, *perfect* freedom, is realized only in relationship to God, who is the Ultimate Reality, creating and sustaining nature, society, and individuals, whose will for the universe is the cosmic goal, and whose support is required for any aim to be realized. The highest freedom is then believed to consist in making the universal divine goals one's own and in drawing strength from the infinite divine resources to fulfill them, either directly or mediately through ordinary material or social agencies. Perfect freedom is thus not human independence but trustful reliance upon God and willing obedience to His will.

Whether or not the religious interpretation of freedom be accepted, it seems evident that the educator needs to be concerned about the quality of freedom and not merely the fact of it. The goals envisaged are inevitably influenced by the dominant values embodied in the process of education.

16

Moral Values

The Nature of the Moral

The discussion of freedom in the preceding chapter could not avoid some consideration of the problem of moral values. Indeed, there is no area of educational concern where the moral question is not pertinent. Our first task is to explore the meaning of the term "moral." What aspects of human experience are subject to moral judgments? What does it mean to say that behavior is moral, immoral, or non-moral? Or is the moral concerned with behavior at all?

Three conceptions of morality. In popular conception the idea of morality is a highly specific and restricted concept. It is customarily used principally in connection with sexual behavior. A person who abides by certain approved codes governing sex is called moral, and one who acts contrary to these codes is called immoral. By this narrow definition most of human experience would be non-moral since it would not be concerned with sexual matters.

A somewhat more sophisticated conception of the moral associates the term with compliance with a code of conduct covering a broader field than sex. A moral person is one who does what is right, according to the approved standard. Or more frequently, he is identified as one who does not do wrong. To be moral, for example, a person must not be dishonest, must not steal, and must not hurt other people. By some codes he must not gamble, nor drink intoxicating beverages, nor perhaps even smoke. This broader conception still leaves the largest part of human experience beyond the scope of morality. Most of the concerns of occupation, recreation, and education would be considered non-moral, since they would not ordinarily be covered by the moral code.

In the philosophic tradition the conception of morality has been far more comprehensive than these popular conceptions. While the everyday idea of the moral is based on conformity to a specified and limited code of conduct, the comprehensive definition extends the concept to include every area of human experience. According to the broad view, moral judgments are not limited to such particular concerns as sexual relations, gambling, drinking, and murder, but are relevant also to such matters as choice of friends, selection of occupation and manner of pursuing it, participation in civic affairs, and decisions about recreation.

Two criteria for the moral. If morality in this broader sense is not defined in relation to specified modes of behavior in certain areas of experience, what are the defining characteristics of the moral? There are two such characteristics. The first is that the moral is in the realm of decision. There is no morality without a choice among alternatives. Thus morality is a concomitant of freedom; there would be no moral problems if man's behavior were completely determined by external agencies. The moral problem is how to decide between different possible courses of action. Animal behavior, governed by instinctual mechanisms or by automatic learned responses, is not moral because there is no choice between alternatives; the structure of the organism and the nature of the environment completely determine action. Human beings have moral concerns only because they are endowed with self-transcending intelligence, by means of which alternatives for the future may be envisaged.

The second defining characteristic of the moral is that it concerns values. The moral problem is to decide between alternative possibilities on the basis of their respective values. A moral choice is a decision for the better alternative; an immoral choice is a decision for the inferior alternative; the choice between equally valuable possibilities is morally neutral.

Can evil choice be deliberate? Reflection on the conception of morality as decision on matters of value suggests the following questions: Does a person ever make an immoral decision? Does he ever deliberately choose the worse rather than the better alternative? There are three main answers to these questions, each reflecting a distinct characteristic conception of the nature of values and of human personality.

One answer is that values are strictly individual, subjective, and private and that a person makes his decisions in accordance with what seems best to him, i.e., on the basis of what he prefers. The fact that one chooses the profession of medicine rather than business, for example, is *prima facie* evidence about his personal scale of values. On this view all decisions are moral; there is no immorality. The immoral can appear only when the choices are measured against some standard exterior to and different from one's own value system.

The second answer is that a person always chooses what appears best to him, but that what he values may not always be truly valuable. There are objective, suprapersonal criteria of value, which may differ considerably from the apparent values. A decision is moral only if the truly good is chosen. Immorality is due solely to ignorance of the true good, the apparent good being chosen instead. No one deliberately and intentionally decides for the evil way. He always elects the alternative that he believes to be best, so that his moral failure results entirely from lack of knowledge of the good.

The third answer is that immorality may be due either to ignorance of true values or to deliberate and intentional choice of evil. A person may know that a certain course of action is undesirable and still decide to pursue it. According to this view, there may be demonic tendencies in human nature, evil wills which in full knowledge lead men to choose darkness rather than light, defeat rather than victory, death rather than life, destruction rather than creation.

These three answers suggest three corresponding conceptions of education for the moral life. According to the first view, education should foster free individual decision guided solely by personal preferences and not by any more general or external standard of value. An example of this would be a curriculum in which the student is given complete freedom to choose his courses. From the second standpoint, education should aim at extending knowledge of what is good through description of alternative possibilities together with analysis of their respective merits. Thus, criteria of what constitute really good music or literature would be used in deciding on materials in such studies, regardless of whether or not the student initially enjoyed them, and a careful justification of these standards would be presented, so that the pupil could understand their validity for himself. The third view calls for measures which not only make available knowledge of the good but also restrain and convert the evil and rebellious will. This may be done in various ways: by punishment or threat, by promise of rewards, by persuasion, but perhaps best of all by love.

Is morality in the act or in the person? It is commonly assumed that morality pertains to particular acts. Thus, sexual offences, stealing, and murder are accounted immoral deeds, and sobriety, honesty, faithfulness, and gentleness are regarded as moral. The definition of morality by reference to deliberate decision among alternative values locates the moral in the person rather than in the act itself. There may well be a close correspondence between the choices a person makes and his overt behavior, but the two are by no means identical. The values which govern a decision are frequently quite different from those which announce themselves in the act. A person may be courteous to someone not because he respects the other (as the behavior itself would seem to indicate) but because he wants to win some favor which the other can bestow. In that case the decision to be courteous may be regarded as immoral (selfish) rather than moral (generous), as it appears to be. There are other acts, such as killing, which in themselves can be judged evil but which are committed in the service of worthy ends, such as the security of the community.

The point is that overt behavior is often highly ambiguous in its moral import. A given act may stem from any number of different and quite contradictory values. It is not strictly true, at least in the short run, that a person is known by his fruits. One of the most significant discoveries in modern psychology has been the untrustworthiness of a face-value interpretation of human behavior and the complexity of attitudes and motives which underlie the observable act. The broad conception of morality presented above is consistent with this psychological insight. Morality refers to free decision and the values upon which it is based and not to the resulting act in itself. The moral life has to do with the very core of personal existence and not with the externals and observables of existence.

Conscious and hidden motives. But the matter goes even deeper than the contrast between inner motive and external behavior. So complex is human nature that the actual values which govern a decision are often not apparent even to the person himself. Most people are at many points as unaware of their real motives and of the actual personal significance of their behavior as are casual observers. Under such conditions of self-ignorance or self-deception the quality of the decision derives from the real values and not from the conscious, apparent ones. To illustrate: A young man decides to become a teacher instead of entering business. His actual interest in teaching is to exercise authority over other people, as he could not so readily do in the competitive struggle of the business world. He is not aware of this real motive, and makes his decision on the basis that teaching is a noble service while business is a selfish enterprise. In this case the morality of the decision should be judged in relation to the interest in power rather than by reference to the professed idealism. In general, the moral has to do neither with the overt act in itself nor even necessarily with values consciously subscribed to in making decisions, but with the actual, often deeply hidden, motives which determine choice.

Moral education, then, must evidently be concerned with the actual values which govern free conduct and not merely with the production of certain approved modes of behavior. It is not enough to teach a person how he should act, by instructing him in conformity to a so-called moral code of conduct, or by providing him with a set of ideals to which he may pay lip-service and by which he may conveniently justify himself to himself or others. The proper work of education is to foster the development of moral personalities, who prize and are inwardly determined by what is good.

It should be added that external moral codes and rational ideals may be of great value in supplementing and reinforcing the actual governing values. The optimum condition is for the person to have real motives which agree with his conscious and professed ideals and with an approved standard of overt behavior. One main goal of education can well be to develop habits of intelligent scrutiny of values, ideals, and moral codes in the interest of uncovering discrepancies, and of adjusting to make them consistent. For example, the well-educated citizen should be able to frame social ideals which take account of the complexities of political reality. He should see through the slogans of opposing parties that regard one side as wholly wrong, the other as wholly right. He should also understand how his own special concerns influence his political judgments and should learn to accept himself as an interested party rather than posing as an impartial spokesman for the ultimate truth.

Education as a Moral Enterprise

When morality is defined broadly by reference to decision among values, it is evident that the enterprise of education itself inescapably involves moral choice. Education is the process of deliberately guiding the development of persons—either the self or others. So long as there are alternative directions in which growth may take place—different possibilities for future development—decisions as to the better or the worse paths must be made. All educative activity is therefore based on moral considerations. It is not merely a question of helping individuals to become moral. The educator himself is engaged in moral activity, and the nature of his choices determines the character and quality of the educational experience provided.

It is not merely in one area of educational activity—in so-called moral instruction—that the moral nature of education is manifest. To restrict it thus would presuppose the narrow conception of morality as specified rules of conduct within a limited domain of experience. Education is not to be regarded as a moral enterprise solely or primarily to the extent that the program of study includes lessons in the approved moral code. It is in every area of education where decisions must be made—about what shall be taught, how and when it shall be taught, who is to teach it, and who is to learn it—that the morality of education becomes pertinent. The teaching of English, the work of the school superintendent, the nurture of children by parents, vocational guidance, a person's choice of recreation—all these varied types of educational endeavor as well as every other imaginable type—presuppose deliberation about alternative values and hence fall within the scope of moral concern.

The meaning of a pervasive moral conception of education may be made clearer by contrasting it with a number of other views where the moral dimension is absent or minimized.

Neutralism. It is the belief of some that the educator should not be concerned with values, that he should refrain from taking sides in any disputed issue (e.g., concerning what kind of social or economic system is best), and that he must remain as far as possible neutral in all matters where alternatives exist. His function is to be aware of the variety of positions one might take but not to take any position himself. He should always be objective and impartial, having no preference for one possibility rather than another, not becoming emotionally involved or even intellectually committed to any one view lest some personal bias detract from his fairness to the opposite position. The ideal in education is complete neutrality and utter detachment. Facts alone are worthy of consideration; values are subjective and introduce an undesirable sentimentality into the work of the educator.

This neutralist view of education is associated with the ideal of objectivity in science. It reflects the attempt to introduce into the conduct of human affairs the same impartial concern for fact apart from personal preference that has proven so fruitful in scientific inquiry. In science it has been a source of pride to be free of values, and especially to be unhampered by the judgment-blinding, alternative-destroying prejudices of traditional religious and ethical systems, as well as of common sense.

The critical question to be raised about neutralism is whether it is really possible, and whether it does not in fact contradict itself. Can the educator—or the scientist for that matter—actually be detached and impartial in all respects? Can he avoid judgments of value and decisions based upon them? No person can live as a free, rational human being without making choices. The regular practice of examining alternative positions is itself a chosen procedure. The determination to remain uncommitted to either side in a dispute is itself a commitment to a certain way of life and thought. Hence, the neutralist is not really neutral. He cannot escape from the responsibility of decision for one value rather than another. The person who insists he has no bias makes clear by his behavior a predisposition in favor of rational reflection on a variety of possibilities instead of active and whole-hearted participation in one particular possibility.

It follows from this analysis that neutralism does not actually contradict the moral nature of education. The one who claims neutrality must still decide what, when, how, and whom to teach. He ought to be aware that he really is making moral judgments and not to think that he has discovered an approach which exempts him from the responsibility of decision.

"The noble savage." According to a second apparently non-moral view of education, any interference with the simple natural life of man corrupts him; hence, the ideal human condition is that of the noble savage, whose virtue results from his not having been tainted by civilization. From this perspective the best education is provided by nature; human agencies only interfere with the perfection of unspoiled nature.

This romantic notion of the noble savage cannot, of course, be maintained by anyone familiar with the most elementary facts of anthropology and of psychology. Personality necessarily develops within a social context, and the "savage" is no less influenced by his social relationships than is a member of an advanced industrial society. In spite of this, there are educators who in effect still advocate a noble savage approach. They believe that the developing person should be allowed to do what comes naturally and that any attempt to alter the natural tendencies will cause frustration and damage to the personality. Therefore, the educator ought to pursue a hands-off policy, making no judgments, offering no structure, leaving the situation entirely fluid so that the person may grow freely, naturally, and creatively, unsullied by artificial and external demands.

Carried to the extreme, this position amounts to a denial of education. If the person should be left alone to grow according to nature, then education as the process of deliberately directing the development of others ought to be abandoned. There would still be self-education. But, once again, the basic facts of psychology make it clear that not all education can be self-education. There must be some association with others in order for a self to develop at all. Insofar as there is education for and by others, moral judgments are necessary. The decision to provide an "unstructured" environment, to gratify a child's every wish, never to deny but only to confirm, is one choice among alternative teaching possibilities. A hands-off permissive policy requires a judgment about values; it is chosen because it seems better than any other policy. Thus, even a noble savage approach to education does not in reality relieve the educator of moral responsibility.

Unfolding. According to a third position, human beings develop by the unfolding of latent abilities. In this case growth takes place in its own way and time, and the most that education can do is to provide a favorable environment. There is no moral dimension because the nature of the person is fixed from the start in the hereditary equipment. There are no genuine alternatives: blood will tell; a person simply *is;* he is not made nor does he make himself. The educator need make no decisions about direction of development, since that has already been foreordained in the cell structure. For example, a teacher may consider a child as "poor material," believing that he will turn out bad regardless of what is done for him. Or an instructor may be so confident about a student's "innate ability" that he becomes careless about the learning environment provided for him.

This position can be dismissed on two counts. First, it negates the very conception of education as guiding growth; there is then no point in discussing the question of morality in a non-existent process. Second, there is abundant empirical evidence that human development does not take place by simple unfolding, but that factors of environment and of personal decision are of major significance. The only relevance of the doctrine of unfolding is in the recognition of certain hereditary potentialities which set limits to developmental possibilities. The educator cannot decide on just any course of growth; he needs to take account of the available personal potentialities. This does not make the decisions any less moral, since all decision is among *possible* alternatives.

Determinism. As pointed out more fully in the preceding chapter, a system of mechanical determinism, where the future is wholly contained in the past and present and completely predictable by them, is contrary to freedom of choice and to moral decision. If the one who is educated and the one who educates are alike simply acting out the parts already written for them in the determinate nature of things, it is but a figure of speech to talk of the better or the worse paths of human development. There is only one possible path, which must inexorably be trodden. Education is no moral enterprise because there is no morality, only inescapable fact.

The moral dimension can be affirmed only when there is freedom, and freedom is compatible with determinism only when the future as well as the past enters into the determination of events. When freedom is understood as self-determination by self-transcending rational persons who are drawn into the future by their purposes as well as conditioned by their past, the morality of education consists in deciding how this freedom is to be employed in the determination of goals for personal development.

Routine. Another educational attitude which seems to negate morality is that of pure routine. Here the educator does his work by rote and ingrained habit. He has developed certain techniques and used certain materials in the past, and these constitute his pattern for the future also. No decisions are necessary because a completely satisfactory system has been worked out and is in hand. Why disturb the even flow of an established routine by constant criticism and evaluation? Perhaps someone, sometime, had to make a choice of materials or methods, but once that was done no further decisions are required.

It is true that much of what people do, in education or in any other field of activity, is necessarily done by habit. One cannot always and in every aspect of behavior be making choices among alternatives. The well-learned routines are the basis for consistency and efficiency in conduct, while deliberate decisions only gradually modify the main pattern of organization. The conception of education as a moral enterprise does not deny these facts, but is based on the recognition that even habitual practices presuppose a tacit decision in their favor. To continue in an established routine is a choice to be made, and in many cases it may be the best choice. Education only escapes from morality when routine completely displaces deliberate consideration of the values espoused and wholly excludes reflection on alternative procedures.

Absolutism. Finally, moral concern is minimized whenever education is conducted in accordance with an absolute, unquestionable tradition received from an unchallengeable authority. When one derives his conceptions and values from uncritical obedience to another person or institution, he is not truly free and hence his acts are not genuinely moral. If submission to political, religious, or other authority is the basis for conduct, the only possible moral question is whether or not to remain subject to the system, and in many if not most instances even this choice is not open. Much of mankind's education is carried on within such a context. Human beings are frequently reluctant or unable to claim their freedom and to assume full responsibility for what they shall do, in education or in any other field. It is easier or safer to accept without question the prescription of another, who wields more power or enjoys more prestige.

Yet absolutist education is not really exempt from moral judgment. Though the absolutist educator himself may not act with moral responsibility, one standing outside the system can evaluate it in relation to alternative systems. The most rigid program of education handed down by a state, by a reigning intellectual elite, or by ecclesiastical authorities can be adjudged by an independent critic as better or worse than some other program. In this sense education is still a moral enterprise. But the full moral dimension of education is not realized until the educators themselves exercise their freedom to decide among alternative aims and methods for directing the development of personality.

Ethical Theory and Education

In the preceding section an attempt was made to show that education is a moral enterprise, in the sense that deliberate decisions must be made about the manner and content of what is to be taught. The fundamental question is how the decisions are to be reached. On what basis is one moral conviction to be preferred over another? How are moral beliefs to be justified? By what method are decisions to be defended or criticized?

The consideration of these questions is the task of the branch of philosophy called ethics. A moral judgment is an assertion about what is right. It is then the business of ethics to exhibit the grounds upon which such assertions rest. In particular the function of ethical theory in education is to show what criteria are available for reaching and supporting claims made on behalf of various educational goals and procedures. Ethical issues arise because there seem to be no unambiguous, self-evident, and universally agreed-upon moral values. There are conflicts between claims for man's interest and allegiance, which ethical analysis is called upon to help resolve.

It is doubtful how much effect theoretical ethics has upon the actual solution of human problems. The real logic of behavior is usually far from the logic of pure reason. In making moral choices a person rarely adopts the results of a strictly rational ethical inquiry. Nevertheless, ethical reflection does carry some weight in decision-making, and in the long run it seems likely that consistently well-grounded moral beliefs will prevail over those for which no persuasive justification can be provided. Thus ethical theory in education probably has more to do with the formulation and criticism of generally influential philosophies of education than with the day-by-day solution of practical problems by individual educators.

More especially, ethical analysis of educational problems serves to show how the choice of particular procedures is related to the most general aims of education. These general aims are basic values to which appeal is made in justifying less ultimate values. For example, a decision to spend more time in the study of mathematics might be justified by reference to a primary aim of developing intellectual potential, while a choice of increased emphasis on social dancing might be defended on the grounds of emotional health as a fundamental value.

Justification of moral beliefs usually occurs in this manner by showing how these beliefs are connected with other more general value convictions. Proximate values are shown as contributing to more ultimate values, or as being special cases of them. Moral choices should be based on facts, but these facts must have significance as values in order to be ethically persuasive. The realm of the moral is the realm of what *ought to be* and not merely of what *is*. Hence, ethical analysis has a further dimension beyond scientific demonstration, which is concerned solely with what actually exists. The value dimension adds to intellectual recognition the affirmation of the whole person that whatever is valued ought to continue in existence, or if it is only an ideal, that it ought to become actual.

Moral Sanctions

The principles used for justifying moral beliefs are called moral sanctions. It is frequently asserted that moral behavior does not validate itself but needs to be supported from some source of authority beyond itself. That is, morality is supposed not to be self-authenticating; right conduct is not engaged in because of its intrinsic appeal but because of extrinsic factors.

Critics of this view hold that true morality is self-justifying and that any system which does not have intrinsic appeal cannot in the long run endure. Persistent values are those which validate themselves in human experience and do not need external support to recommend them.

There would seem to be merit in both views, which need not be mutually exclusive. Sanctions may be both intrinsic and extrinsic. Moral behavior may prove itself in direct experience and at the same time receive further support from other sources. For example, one may believe that respect for the rights of every individual is an immediately perceived value which needs no justification beyond itself. Yet this belief can be strengthened by appeal to the social benefits of peace and cooperation which result from it or to the authority of the religious teaching that every man is created in the image of God.

Moral sanctions are especially important in education because they are one of the principal means both of persuading others to adopt a recommended rule of conduct and of sustaining one's own moral convictions. Furthermore, they help to fulfill the educational ideal of intelligence in behavior since reference to sanctions to some degree replaces blind, unthinking activity by rationally justified conduct. This does not mean that all sanctions are equally admissible. Many if not most of them arrest rather than stimulate further thought. One objective of a philosophically concerned educator is to analyze the sanctions commonly invoked, to distinguish the valid from the invalid ones, and to suggest both new moral possibilities and more effective sanctions for beliefs.

Method of sanction. There are several types of moral sanctions to which appeal can be made. These may be classified first as to method of validation. In this group are the sanctions which are based respectively on authority, insight, and consequences.

Authority. The first approach to moral sanction is the appeal to the promulgator of the moral idea in question. This is the method of traditional authority. If it is asked why one should be honest, the answer might be: because the ideal of honesty has been taught by the wisest and best men of all times; or by parents, whom one trusts and respects; or by the church, which is the channel for God's will; or by the state, which incorporates this moral principle in its laws.

The appeal to authority is widely used and may be extremely effective. It places the power and prestige of important individuals and institutions behind the moral effort. Its shortcoming lies in the fact that it really does not justify the moral idea at all since the question must still be raised: On what grounds does the authority base the recommendation of this belief? By what right is one a moral authority? Do power and prestige make him the arbiter of right? If so, then, moral ideals will change as authorities come and go. Also there will be no way of resolving conflicts among men of eminence.

Insight. A moral belief may, in the second place, be validated by direct insight. This immediate apprehension of moral truth is sometimes called conscience. It does not exclude the exercise of intelligence in surveying the possible alternative beliefs. But the final basis of judgment is an inner persuasion of rightness which one cannot deny and still remain true to himself.

It seems clear that direct insight must be the basis for any truly personal conviction about what is right. Even if the method of authority is used, the selection of the authority and the response to it, if free and wholehearted, depend upon some insight about the trustworthiness of certain persons and institutions and the value of what they endorse. On the other hand, it appears that conscience is to a considerable extent internalized authority: what parents or other authorities required or recommended when one was a child greatly influences the adult conscience. From this point of view sanction by insight reduces to sanction by authority. Yet this does not tell the whole story either, for conscience is no mere reflection of values held by others but always the person's own reaction to and recasting of those values. This unique and highly personal determination of what is to be prized is the essence of human freedom. To the extent that man is free, direct insight—the personal and inner persuasion about the good—would seem to be the final sanction for moral belief.

Consequences. The third main method of sanctioning moral ideas is by reference to consequences. To illustrate such sanctions: Honesty is desirable because it leads to social harmony and consistency of personality. Fidelity in marriage is right because it is conducive to family stability and enduring mutual confidence. The private property system is good because it results in maximum incentives for productive effort. Or, the social control of property is good because it makes possible a more equitable distribution of wealth. In each case a moral belief is supported by exhibiting its consequences.

The method of consequences is based on the recognition that no human act can be fairly appraised in isolation, but should always be considered in the light of the effects produced by it. No decision is merely a choice for the moment but is in a sense a choice for all eternity, since from it spring an infinity of future consequences. No moral judgment can be made intelligently without knowledge of its effects. When they are known, the content of the moral judgment is greatly enlarged and enriched. When they are not known, there is no true choice of the right but only of the apparent right. This superficial perception of right may well prove to be illusory and deceptive.

Still, the method of consequences does not in itself provide a basis for moral sanction since a judgment must still be made about the value of the consequences. For example, in sanctioning honesty on the grounds of the resulting social harmony and personal consistency it is presupposed either that these consequences need no justification or that they are validated by some other method, such as direct insight. All that the analysis of consequences can do is to give a more comprehensive picture of what any given moral belief really involves; it cannot by itself actually provide any sanction. In this respect it is like the method of authority under which the reliability of the authority is presupposed. It would seem, then, that both the method of authority and the method of consequences are only preliminary and provisional ways of grounding moral belief and that the ultimate court of appeal must be to direct moral insight—the inner personal persuasion of the right.

Location of sanction. Having now discussed the three main methods of sanction, we next consider the three types of sanction according to location, which include reference to the individual, to society, and to the transcendent, respectively.

The individual. The simplest form of individual sanction is expressed in such a statement as: "This action is right because it pleases me." A moral philosophy of this type is called hedonism. Instead of pleasure, the standard might be inspiration, illumination, or peace of mind. In any event the sanction is based on a sense of rightness for the individual, without any assumption of wider applicability. The most comprehensive form of individual sanction is in the ethic of "self-realization." Here the test of moral conduct is whether or not it will contribute to the fulfillment of the self. Unfortunately, this is not a satisfactory test since the moral question is still implicit in the problem of what constitutes "fulfillment." The self can be many things, and the basic moral problem is not whether the self will be realized or not but *what kind* of self will be developed.

Individualist sanctions recognize the uniqueness of each person and the special circumstances surrounding moral decisions. They presuppose that no useful moral rules can be devised so as to be applicable to everybody in all circumstances. Free moral judgments are made by the solitary individual in the depths of his own soul, and he alone can be the arbiter of what is right for him in any given situation. Against such individualism it can be urged that moral conduct takes place within a social and material context and that unless judgments of right refer to the larger scene there can be no basis for harmonious coexistence. If the right is grounded solely in the individual, how can the chaos of anarchic relativism be avoided except by the rule of the strong over the weaker? Then life would be governed by fear and force rather than by truth and justice.

Society. To overcome these difficulties the sanction for morality may be located in society rather than in the individual. The right is then what is good for society. By "society" may be meant either all mankind or a particular social group, such as a family, class, caste, party, race, or nation. Merely to base morality on the social good does not, however, solve the problem of the quality of the desirable social life. The good society may be conceived on the one extreme as the dominance of one group over others or on the other extreme as a system of equality under law. Some would regard economic efficiency as the highest good, while others would prefer that society which best stimulates creative work in science and art. One social philosophy would put the greatest emphasis on order, control, and security, while another would stress individual freedom, variety, and adventure.

Social sanctions have the advantage of taking account of the social relevance of the moral life. Although free decision is an individual act, every decision inevitably concerns the self in relation to others. No person lives wholly unto himself; everyone is part of a network of interdependent selves. Therefore the rightness of any moral belief must rest upon a conception of the good society. But if the sanction is actually found in society itself, then conflicts arise because of the differences in social systems and in the values associated with them. At crucial points there are disagreements between systems and between individuals and systems. Again, it would seem that fear and force will rule unless there is some sanction for morality to which both the individual and society are subordinate.

The transcendent. From such considerations arises the idea of a transcendent moral sanction. This means a basis for right which is prior to the actual interests or desires of persons and in some sense independent of them. The usual form of such a sanction is in the conception of a moral law by which all human decisions are judged. Usually this law is thought of as absolute and unchanging, though there is no reason why it could not be regarded as varying in time. Some believe that the moral law is humanly knowable (as in the Ten Commandments); others believe that the ultimate right can never be known by man and that his best moral efforts are but approximations to an unknown yet dimly apprehended ideal. According to one view, the moral law is an abstract principle of right which can be discovered by intelligence, somewhat as the laws of the natural world can be found through scientific inquiry. According to another view, the right is an expression of the will of a sovereign God and can be known only as he chooses to disclose it by revelation.

The conception of sanctions which transcend the individual and society confirms the moral insight that the right is not right because people approve of it but that what is right *ought* to be approved of, whether or not persons actually do so. A transcendent sanction is required if actual human preferences are to be considered as always subject to a higher judgment. In practice, individual or social sanctions are frequently absolutized as if they had transcendent status. This engenders fanaticism and destructive conflict and discourages moral inquiry and reconstruction. It seems evident that a better use of the idea of transcendent sanctions would be as a perennial reminder that every moral conviction should be held firmly but provisionally and in all humility, in the confidence that while some illumination on the path of life has been received, doubtless more light will yet shine forth.

Moral Education

The two moralities. A review of the analysis to this point will show that there are two moralities in education. One is the morality of the educator in choosing among alternative teaching procedures. The other is the morality of the person being educated. The moral educator must freely decide about subjects and methods in the light of optimum objectives, and the moral person must have learned through his education to make decisions intelligently on the basis of his own highest life-goals. The important point to note is that these two moralities are not independent and unrelated but are intimately connected. There are not two separate realms, one of educator-morality (concerned with such matters as educational aims, teaching methods, and curriculum) and the other of personal morality (referring to the patterns of right conduct one has learned). Personal behavior patterns are based on the values implicit in the educational process. The moral standards of the developing person are fashioned in the context of the educator's moral choices.

Thus "educational" decisions about what, how, when, and to whom instruction will be given inevitably have their effect upon the moral nature of the persons taught. For this reason the basis for choice of educational procedures should not be simply technical considerations of the educational specialist but should be the general ideals of human excellence which the procedures ought to subserve. That is, the morality of education should be one with the morality of civilization. The point seems obvious, yet in practice it is easily lost sight of in the face of immediate concern for educational results. The rightness of every decision by the educator is to be judged by the standard of the ideal, complete, and mature human being.

The teaching of morality. It follows from the foregoing that moral instruction is imparted through the entire process of education. It is the values implicit in the choice of materials and methods of teaching that influence the learner's moral development. It is not mainly through explicit moral precepts that values are learned. Enunciation of general moral principles may have some use in suggesting desirable types of behavior, but such verbal tuition is insignificant in comparison with the effect of values tacitly recommended through the actual conduct of education. Thus, the love of truth is better taught by the teacher's eagerness to accept new and perhaps uncomfortable insights than by any amount of exhortation on behalf of truth. The value of democracy is far more effectively taught by using democratic procedures in teaching than by merely preaching democracy.

This is not to deny the worth of an explicit reflective analysis of values, along the lines indicated in the earlier discussion of ethical theory and moral sanctions. The ideal moral education is one in which the values implicit in the system of education are explicitly recognized, critically analyzed, and rationally defended.

Character. The outcome of successful moral education is good character. The term "character" means those patterns of behavior which have become habitual. Character is "second nature," consisting of the individual's learned (rather than instinctive) persistent modes of conduct. These conduct patterns have become integral to the personality of the individual; they are definitive of his selfhood, of his nature as a unique person. Character is the name for what the individual can be reliably expected to do. He may, of course, occasionally as a free agent act "out of character," but by definition he usually behaves in character. Good character is moral conduct built into habit. It results from making good choices so consistently and persistently that they become second nature. Character education requires the vivid presentation of high values, continued exposure to the attractions of goodness, truth, and beauty until they are woven into the very fabric of personality.

In a sense character supercedes morality since behavior which has become automatic requires no deliberate decision among alternatives. But it also confirms and fulfills morality because the structure of good habits based on earlier right choices becomes the basis for new choices on a higher plane of achievement. For example, a person who has learned always and as a matter of course to render a true report has laid the foundation for accepting responsibilities entrusted to him by others who know that his word can be relied upon. He then has the opportunity to choose among these responsibilities and decide how best to fulfill them. This is a phase of morality which goes beyond the earlier decisions to be trustworthy.

Thus not only is character built on morality, but morality rests upon character. The relationship between the two is further indicated by the observation that intelligent choice among values is itself a desirable habit. The regular practice of deliberate decision is one aspect of character. One can learn to make thoughtful choices naturally, consistently, and habitually. Many would affirm that a principal goal of education should be the development of such free intelligence as a firmly established trait of character.

Spiritual values. The term "spiritual" is frequently linked with the word moral in discussions of "moral and spiritual values" in education. The meaning of this concept is seldom clearly defined. It usually covers the whole range of "higher" human functions. Sometimes it refers specifically to the religious aspects of experience. Frequently it includes esthetic activity. Even the use of reason in science and philosophy may be considered spiritual in nature. Moral concerns are also usually taken to belong to the spiritual realm. In general, spirituality is contrasted with materiality, gross practicality, and whatever is believed of inferior value. In most cases it presupposes a dualistic scheme of things, such as matter *versus* mind, work *versus* contemplation, or nature *versus* supernature, the spiritual referring to the second term in each of these pairs.

Perhaps the most useful conception of the spiritual dimension is obtained by reference to man's freedom and to his perception of values. According to this view, spirituality is freedom to know and to serve ideal ends. But this is precisely the definition of morality in the broad sense described early in the present chapter. Hence, our discussion of the moral aspects of education may properly be viewed also as an analysis of spiritual values in education.

What is the good life? In this treatment of moral values in education, one might have expected a presentation of the qualities of personality which ought to be developed. Instead, we have dealt largely with the nature and justification of morality and its place in the educative process. This is because questions about the good life and the nature of the ideal personality arise in every topic in our study of educational philosophy. All aspects of the process of directing the development of persons presuppose some conception of what a person ought to become. The varieties of individual styles of life, political and economic systems, social arrangements, and religious faiths are reflections of the many different moral beliefs of mankind. The chapters in this book on education as related to nature, family, state, job, recreation, and freedom, the discussions of the fields of knowledge, and the treatment of school problems all necessarily deal with various aspects of the good life. The most explicit analysis of certain major alternative views of ideal ends is contained in Chapter 30, on the Aims of Education, which may profitably be studied in relation to the present chapter.

The problem of moral values, broadly conceived, is the fundamental problem of education. It is not possible in a single discussion of limited scope to state and to give a philosophic critique of the principal human value systems. The chief point of this chapter has been to show why moral values cannot properly be presented as codes of conduct or as self-contained descriptions of human virtue. *All* philosophizing about education contributes to the exhibition and defense of educational values.

PART III

Education and the Field of Knowledge

17

Knowledge

Knowledge and human nature. Intelligence is one of the chief distinguishing marks of being human. The powers of reason and reflection, memory, and imagination are the special glory of man whereby his prodigious cultural achievements are made possible. One product of this human intellectual activity is knowledge. In a sense to know is to be human; man does not attain his proper stature apart from knowledge. He may eat, grow, reproduce, and move about, but these useful and indeed necessary activities do not show him to be a man. He shares such functions with birds, beasts, fish, and insects, who may perform them with even greater zeal and efficiency. He is not truly a man apart from knowing, and he does justice to his manhood only if he develops his intellectual capacities.

It follows that one of the chief objectives of education must be the acquisition of knowledge. Though this would seem indisputable to most people concerned with education, there are some who in principle or in act deny the importance of knowledge. For example, if the accepted goal of education is to produce persons who will conform blindly and uncritically to a standard pattern of behavior, knowledge (except of the most restricted kind) will be regarded as a threat rather than as a valued resource. Again, if it is believed that man is so intrinsically evil that he will misuse whatever knowledge he acquires, it will be better to keep him ignorant. Once more, if one believes that emotional development is primary and that knowledge contributes mainly to the construction of defense mechanisms and rationalizations, intellectual development will be given a subordinate place in the educational scheme.

Theory of knowledge and philosophy of education. The conviction underlying this chapter and the rest of Part III is that knowledge has a fundamental role in education. It is the aim of these chapters to examine the meaning of knowledge and to study its special characteristics in some of the major fields of intellectual activity. One of the important aspects of philosophic inquiry is *theory of knowledge* or *epistemology*. Since knowledge is basic in human development, it follows that the theory of knowledge must become a part of any satisfactory philosophy of education.

Before entering upon our discussion let us pause for a moment to ask what purpose is served by such philosophical analysis and what use the reader may expect to make of the material which appears in this and the following eight chapters. The main goal is simply to increase understanding of what knowledge is, in itself and in its various branches, and to give insight into some of its complexities, ramifications, and connections, thus providing a critical and comprehensive view rather than a limited conventional outlook. This understanding in turn ought to provide a basis for appraising more fairly the claims made for knowledge, showing *in what sense* we know something and by what criteria the claims for knowledge can be made good.

Such philosophical inquiry should also suggest some new concepts and distinctions which may be employed with profit in approaching the practical and theoretical problems of education. If knowledge is to be taught, it is important to know what knowledge is. The ways and content of teaching and learning depend very much on what one understands knowledge to be.

In particular, it is hoped that a philosophy of the fields of knowledge may help to porvide an understanding of their *essential* features, and thus enable the teacher to place emphasis on central and definitive matters rather than on a host of subordinate details, the relevance of which may not be clear to the student. That is, a philosophical analysis of the *key ideas* in the respective fields of study may help to maintain proportion and perspective in the teaching-learning process.

Contrasting Aspects of Knowledge

"Knowing" and "having knowledge." It may be useful first to distinguish between "knowing" and "having knowledge." Knowing is a process or a function. A person who knows has certain skills and behavioral capacities in the realm of intellect. Having knowledge, on the other hand, suggests a storehouse conception. Knowledge is something which one can possess and put away for use when needed. This is a substantive rather than a functional or process concept of knowledge.

Both of these ways of thinking about knowledge have their place, and it is unfortunate when one is completely lost sight of in favor of the other. A "knower" is a person who has learned how to function intelligently. He "has knowledge" by virtue of individual or social memory through which personal and social experiences are preserved in readiness for use. Hence the process of knowing is dependent on having knowledge. A person cannot behave intelligently unless he has available a large amount of accumulated experience either as personal recollection or as recorded in books, institutions, or other cultural artifacts. But having knowledge can avail nothing unless there are knowers who can employ the accumulation intelligently.

There are educators who are so concerned with developing the processes of knowing, through instruction in "problem solving," in "research," or in "critical thinking," that they neglect or repudiate the hard-won knowledge which has become the accumulated intellectual treasure of mankind. By this rejection they unwittingly undermine and impoverish the very process which they so single-mindedly seek to promote. On the other extreme are the educators who are so concerned to preserve the knowledge which has been handed down by the wise men of the past that they fail to develop in the learner any adequate competence in judging, applying, and creating knowledge. In this failure of relevance lies the greatest threat to the security of the very cultural heritage which they seek to conserve. Knowing can only be well grounded if the knower also has knowledge and having knowledge can only be significant if the possessor is a knower. The process of education requires both a healthy respect—even reverence—for the gathered intellectual capital of civilization and an ever-present concern for the active exercise of intellectual powers in the discovery and application of knowledge.

"Knowledge of" and "knowledge about." Another useful distinction is between direct, immediate knowledge *of* something and indirect, mediate knowledge *about* something. The former has been called "knowledge by acquaintance" and the latter "knowledge by description." A person may have knowledge through direct experience, or he may have knowledge about things which he has never directly encountered but which have come to him by the word of others. By the study of geography books one may come to know much about faraway lands, but this knowledge is not the same as that of the world traveler who has actually seen these places. This is not to say that there is no relation between the knowledge by acquaintance and knowledge by description. There ought to be a close correspondence between the two, so that, for example, the geography student on traveling abroad would recognize as familiar the places he had read about earlier. Neither is it to be inferred that knowledge by acquaintance is intrinsically better or worse than knowledge by description. There are cases where knowledge of something is far richer than knowledge about it would be, and there are other cases where knowledge about something is far more useful and penetrating than knowledge of it would be. For example, in making friends, acquaintance knowledge is better than descriptive knowledge, while for the theoretical physicist descriptive knowledge takes precedence over direct experience of physical events.

There is a certain tension between a plan of education in which "knowledge of" is emphasized and one in which "knowledge about" is stressed. In the former, care is taken that the student have firsthand experiences rather than secondhand reports. Knowledge by description is minimized in favor of knowledge by acquaintance. Field trips, experiments, and projects are provided to give the rich, immediate experience desired. The other plan tends to be more verbal and book-centered, and while those who follow it do not deny the worth of direct knowledge, they do not consider descriptive knowledge as invalid or meaningless without personal testing in concrete activity. They are convinced of the efficiency and economy of learning through the experiences of others in comparison with a system in which everything has to come through direct personal experience. Any actual program of education, of course, includes both types of knowledge. Knowledge about is as far as practicable verified by personal test, and knowledge of is consolidated and confirmed by descriptive accounts.

Different persons, subject matters, and social conditions may require different emphases. Some people are adept at the use of verbal symbols and others are not. For the former, knowledge by description is better suited than for the latter. Some kinds of experiences (e.g. scientific) lend themselves well to descriptive statement, while other kinds (e.g. artistic) require immediate awareness. In some cases material and personal resources are such as to make the most rapid and economical communication of descriptive knowledge imperative, while in other situations more personal exploration is feasible. Because of these differences no one rule about the type of knowledge appropriate in education can be laid down.

Perceptual and conceptual knowledge. Closely related to the distinction between knowledge of and knowledge about is the distinction frequently made between perceptual and conceptual knowledge. Traditionally, perception has referred to the immediate awareness of things, especially as observed through the senses, while conception has meant the products of thought and imagination based upon the perceptions. Perceptual knowledge is thus primary and basic, while conceptual knowledge is secondary and derived. By direct visual observation one perceives a tree, and from many such perceptions one forms the abstract or general idea of "tree" as a concept representing the whole class of objects that go by that name. Experiences of rhythm in music or poetry are perceptual, and from these may be formed the concept of "rhythm" whereby the common rhythmic quality of the entire class of such experiences is designated. Similar remarks apply for experiences other than sensory. For example, it would seem proper to speak of moral perception as a direct awareness of the right (e.g., in situations calling for honesty), and from such experiences to derive class concepts of "right" and of "honesty."

In the process of personal development both perceptual and conceptual knowledge are necessary. Percepts without concepts would provide no real meaning or understanding. Knowledge would consist of accumulated fragments of experience without any inner relationship or coherence. Concepts without percepts would be empty ideas, words with no concrete significance. Growth in understanding requires both direct perceptual experience and conceptual elaboration of that experience. A good educational program provides a wide range of opportunities to gain the primary data of sense, feeling, and conviction and also for cognitive reflection on these data. Which of the two aspects of knowledge will be more emphasized depends upon individual differences between learners, upon the subject matter to be learned, and upon differing basic convictions about the respective values of the two sorts of knowledge.

Propositional and non-propositional knowledge. A fourth variation of the same basic distinction discussed in the three foregoing sections is the contrast between knowledge contained in propositions and knowledge not so expressed. A proposition is a sentence which asserts something. Thus, "The earth moves in an elliptical orbit around the sun," is a proposition which asserts an item of knowledge. In addition to such knowledge, there are kinds of understanding or insight which either have not been put into propositional form or could not be expressed in that way. For example, a child before he can talk cannot formulate propositions, yet it would be difficult to deny that he knows *something*. Even with mature persons, it often seems that what is known best is not contained in propositions, e.g., the knowledge of a mother's love or of a scholar's devotion to truth. Many would say that the deepest and most intimate knowledge can never be stated as verbal assertions and that the expression of insights as propositions inevitably robs them of some of their significance.

The distinction appears in contrasting views of what it means to become wise or intelligent. Some would hold that the intellectual goal is reached through learning propositions. A wise person is then one who can assert many true propositions. Others would say that important though propositions may be, they are not the chief glory of the wise, but that true wisdom consists in apprehensions and awarenesses which in their fullness cannot be expressed as verbal assertions. There is a tendency, especially in an age of science, to exalt propositional knowledge to a position of exclusive validity and honor and to make of education an enterprise of mastering bodies of factual information. The restoration of balance requires the recognition of non-propositional knowledge also, and the use of teaching resources which will give due weight to intellectual life beyond the limitations of verbal assertion. It is perhaps chiefly in the areas of moral, religious, and artistic achievement—regarded as contributing genuinely cognitive insights—that the requisite breadth of knowledge may be gained.

Knowledge as Subjective and Objective

To know means to have a certain kind of relationship (usually called cognitive) between the knower (the "subject") and the known (the "object"). It then seems reasonable to suppose that the character of knowledge will reflect both the nature of the subject and that of the object, or in other words that knowledge will have both subjective and objective components. This view is not universally accepted. If a person says, holding an object in his hand, "This is a small grey stone," is he saying something about the object or about himself or about both? Four different answers to this question are possible, consideration of which will clarify the meaning of the subjective and objective aspects of knowledge.

Pure objectivism. It may be affirmed that the proposition asserts something about the object and nothing about the perceiving subject. This would be the view of those who hold that knowledge is or can be completely objective. In the example it would be assumed that stones are a real class of objects existing as a class independently of any human decision to classify them as such and that the size and color of the stone are real properties inhering in the object. The person viewing the object is regarded as a passive recipient of the sense data, faithfully registering and then verbally reporting the nature of the object.

Pure subjectivism. The opposite extreme is a complete subjectivism according to which the proposition is regarded as reporting a state of being of the perceiver and nothing at all about the object. In this view there are no objects except as projections of subjective experience. The fact that several people may perceive the same "object" simply means that each for some reason has the same inner experience. The external world is thus a construction of human imagination and nothing real in itself.

Separable subjective and objective components. One mediating view is that the proposition says something about the object and something about the subject and that it is possible to separate the respective components. First, it is obvious that the language used in the proposition belongs to the subject. The fact that it is expressed in English suggests that the subject speaks English. In no sense is the English a quality of the stone. The verbal form of the knowledge is another subjective contribution; to speak is human and not pertinent to the stone. On the other hand, to the stone belong its existence and its stoneness; it is not by the perceiving subject's decision that the object exists nor that it belong to the stone class. But when it comes to the size and color of the stone it may not be so clear whether they are objective or subjective. Some would hold that both color and size are properties of the object. Others would distinguish between the "primary" quality of size, which belongs to the object, and the "secondary" quality of color which is a subjective component. Still others would consider both size and color as subjective, as ways the human mind organizes the raw data of sense.

The relational view. A fourth position is that the proposition states something about both subject and object but that the respective components cannot be separated. This position in effect rejects the independence of subjective and objective components and affirms the *relational* character of knowledge. To call an object a stone is to relate a physical order with a conceptual-linguistic order. The use of conceptual classes to designate objects is not an arbitrary subjective act but evidence of a correlation between the structure of objects and the structure of thought and language. Similarly, the qualities of smallness and greyness of the stone are neither properties solely of the perceiver nor of the perceived. The stone really is small but only in terms of human standards of measurement. The stone really is grey, but only with respect to human color perception. Both qualities express aspects of the relationship between stone and observer.

Application to other areas of knowledge. The example of the stone would generally be considered a particularly objective kind of knowledge. Yet the variety of interpretations even in this simple case indicates the general possibility of alternative viewpoints about the objective-subjective aspects of knowledge. In other areas of knowledge or with knowledge differently expressed the relative weight of subjective and objective components might differ considerably. For example, if one should claim that the perception of beauty is a kind of knowledge, that knowledge would usually be regarded as heavily weighted on the subjective side, in the sense that the imagination and esthetic sensitivity of the beholder would necessarily enter largely into his judgments of beauty. Similarly with moral judgments. Granted these differences in areas of knowledge (about which much more will be said in the following chapters of this Part), it is still possible in every case to apply each of the four types of interpretations. These four modes of considering the subjective and objective aspects of knowledge are therefore meant to be quite general and are not restricted to the illustration cited.

Relation to learning. The view one takes of the subjective-objective aspects of knowledge has significant bearing on the learning process. If knowledge is completely objective, learning consists in becoming conformed to what is outwardly true. The mind must then be repeatedly impressed with the nature of external things. Drill, memorization of well-established information, careful observation, and constant checking of facts would be some of the means of molding the understanding to agree with what is objectively so. If knowledge is completely subjective, teaching is really not possible at all. Development must occur from within by the implicit laws of one's own being. If knowledge is regarded as having certain subjective and certain objective components, whether separable or inseparable, the guidance of learning will take place with due concern both for the given nature of the external world and for the inner factors—feelings, purposes, and perspectives —which condition knowledge. Perception and understanding will not be forced into the standardized molds of allegedly incontrovertible fact nor will they be allowed the unchallenged freedom of private preference. Rather they will be derived from and checked by rigorous exploration of the world, yet in such a way as to do justice to the specifically human elements—both individual and corporate—implicit in all humanly relevant and meaningful knowledge.

The Sources of Knowledge

Of primary importance for education is the problem of the *sources* of knowledge. What does one do to gain knowledge? Where does one seek for understanding? There are many possible answers to these questions. Each answer suggests a different kind of educational activity, and the relative emphasis placed on the various answers determines major differences among educational programs.

The senses. Bodily sensation is an obvious source of knowledge. Sights, sounds, tastes, smells, and sensations of touch are ingredient in much if not in everything a person knows. The organs of sense are the primary channels through which the human being becomes related to the world about him. Receptor nerve cells are stimulated by some form of energy, such as light, heat, or sound, and a nerve impulse is transmitted to the appropriate brain center. Such signals enable the person to act so as to take account of actual physical conditions. It would appear that no learning can occur without such sense information. An infant without sensory equipment could never develop. It is through the senses that the structure of the surrounding world, in which the human being must live and to which he must to a degree adjust, is made known to the person. The senses are thus a primary guide to reality.

But what sort of knowledge do the senses provide? Is it simply a flood of sight and sound impressions? Perhaps in early infancy it is something like this. But generally sense perception is much more than such a disorganized stream. It has definite structure and pattern. Things appear as colored, extended, shaped, enduring in time, and so on. For this to happen certain physiological equipment is necessary. There are color-blind or tone-deaf people whose sensory facilities do not permit normal vision or hearing. An inanimate object can be bombarded with light or sound but lacking organs of sense it sees or hears nothing. The character of sense perception is thus in part a function of human physiology. Lower organisms with simpler perceptual apparatus have correspondingly limited sense knowledge.

Sense perception also depends to a considerable extent upon the entire condition of the percipient organism. What one sees, hears, or feels may be greatly influenced by hopes and fears, expectations, memories, and desires. A hungry person may perceive his surroundings quite differently from a well-fed person, and one who is under drug stimulation may perceive the world in an abnormal way.

The knowledge gained in sense perception thus appears to have its source both in the physical world which provides the energy stimuli and in the nature and condition of the human organism. For this reason, those who guide the learning process need not only to select appropriate stimuli but also to take into consideration the physical, mental, and emotional states of the learner. Sense knowledge is not imparted simply by presenting the relevant stimuli. What will actually be learned is a function of the way the perceiver reacts to the stimuli presented, and different persons or the same person at different times will react in different ways.

Reason. A second source of knowledge is the process of reflection or reasoning. This source is closely linked to sense perception in that, as just pointed out, the content of perception is conditioned by expectations, memories, and other mental states. There is thus a rational component in all sense perception. It is by reason that abstract concepts are formed out of concrete perceptions. For example, the abstraction "dog" is a concept based upon the concrete perception of particular dogs. But it is not only true that percepts underlie concepts; it is also true that concepts influence perception. What one observes with his senses is conditioned by the entire conceptual scheme which reason has elaborated. To a considerable degree what one sees depends upon what he is looking for, and this in turn is based upon the pattern of concepts used to organize experience. A skilled appraiser of horses—a person who "knows horses"—will perceive a particular horse in a far more complete and sensitive fashion than the average person would. A musician hears a piece of music in a more profound way than the untutored because he has a scheme of musical conception which directs him to listen for certain things which the layman would fail to notice.

Knowledge through reason is thus inextricably related to knowledge through the senses. Two corollaries for the learning process should be noted. One is that reason is of great value in guiding sense perception. One of the main values of theory is to guide observation into fruitful channels. A rational scheme in this way increases the efficiency of the senses and reduces the waste of random, disorganized observation. It directs attention into paths which past experience has shown likely to be profitable.

The other corollary is that reason may by virtue of this very directing function harmfully limit perception. A child learning to draw or paint may be hindered in his development of creative and original artistic perception by a teacher who explains what one should look for when depicting an object or scene or who too readily suggests standards for judging good or bad artistic style. A student of science may miss important observational material because he is guided too strictly by a theoretical system into which he expects his observations to fit. In relation to sense perception, therefore, reason may be both a useful guide and a hindrance to adequate observation.

Up to this point we have spoken of reason only in its function in the organization of sense perception. It has frequently been asserted that this is not reason's true and unique office, which is to create or discover knowledge independently of the senses. Knowledge resulting from particular sense perceptions is called *a posteriori* (following after experience). Knowledge gained by pure reason is called *a priori* (prior to experience). Such "pure" knowledge rests upon the conception of *innate ideas,* which are regarded as springing naturally and directly from reason as a source of self-evident truth. In modern philosophy and science this doctrine of *a priori* innate ideas and of self-evident truth has been rather completely discredited. Ideas which were once held unquestioningly have in many cases been questioned and found wanting. Concepts once regarded as innate have been conclusively shown to be derived from culture. Modes of thought which were believed universal have been proved relative to time and situation. Despite these criticisms, there still remains a place in informed modern thought for some conception of reason as a relatively independent source of knowledge. While human experiences may never be fully free of sense elements, because man has a body and lives in a material world, there is, nevertheless a degree of autonomy in rational processes and of independence in intellectual creation which are important in the production of knowledge. The formation of hypotheses in science, the elaboration of conceptual frameworks in philosophy, and the formulation of symbolic systems in the arts are examples of human activity which illustrate how reason is one primary source of knowledge. In education ample provision must accordingly be made not only for wide-ranging sense experience and for the guidance and coordination of sense perceptions through rational understanding, but also for the development of originative and constructive thinking.

Intuition. It is often claimed that there is another source of knowledge called *intuition* which is not a kind of sense perception nor a cognitive process in the ordinary sense. Such knowledge is characterized by its directness and immediacy. It does not come as a result of systematic reflection, nor does it consist of the ordinary data delivered by the senses. A good example would be the knowledge of right and wrong which many would consider intuitive. The ethical sense, according to this view, is a natural endowment; the moral law is "written on the heart." Esthetic judgments are also often regarded as intuitive. Some people believe that by intuition they can read the thoughts and discern the motives of other people. Similarly, persons who are skillful at quickly appraising what needs to be done in situations calling for decisive action are sometimes thought to have intuitive powers. It may also be reasonable to place within the category of intuition the phenomenon usually called "extra-sensory perception." A number of experimenters in this field are convinced that information may to some extent be communicated between objects and persons or between persons without the use of any known sensory facilities. Related to this are the alleged instances of "pre-cognition," in which events are said to be known prior to their actual occurrence.

The idea of intuition as a separate source of knowledge has been vigorously challenged but has by no means been decisively or universally discredited. Opponents object to the vagueness and elusiveness of the concept. They believe that every case of alleged intuition can be interpreted as sense perception or as an aspect of ordinary cognitive processes. They think that the concept of intuition invites obscurity and encourages intellectual anarchy because there are no adequate canons by which the authenticity of intuitive insights may be tested.

The educator's view of intuition as a source of knowledge has a bearing on his approach to teaching. Intuition is a form of self-instruction, in that such learning takes place without mediation, directly and inwardly. The question is whether or not one can trust such intuitions or whether or not it is necessary to correct and refine them by the discipline of the senses and of reason. If one is convinced that intuition is a true source of knowledge, he will encourage the development of such powers in the individual and will be slow to subject the insights claimed to continual rational and empirical scrutiny. On the other hand, if one believes that there is no independent intuitive source of knowledge, he will see as one important educational task the progressive elimination, through careful thought and observation, of the vague and confusing modes of thought which are called intuition.

Existence. There are beliefs about knowledge which are based upon the conviction that neither sense perception, conceptual thinking, nor intuitive insight are the sources of knowledge at its personally most significant levels, but that such knowledge is gained solely by *existence.* One *knows* most profoundly only what one *is.* On this view, knowledge is not *about* existence; it *is* existence. True knowledge is a state of being. This is not to deny that ordinary sense knowledge and the results of reflection and of intuitive perception have their place. But these sources of relatively objective knowledge do not have the personal power and relevance of knowledge by existence. Ordinary knowledge permits a degree of detachment of knower from the known. In contrast, knowledge by existence presupposes active involvement to the point of identification between knower and known. In fact, one criterion for this "existential" knowledge is that the distinction and separation of knower and known are overcome.

Two examples will help to clarify the meaning of existence as a source of knowledge. A person learns from books and conversations about the meaning of being poor, hungry, or fearful. He can even become an expert on the underprivileged. He can learn to feel their suffering and to predict in detail their attitudes and actions. But this knowledge is not the same as the knowledge of one who is actually himself in want and distress. To be poor is to know poverty in a far more profound way than the objective conception of poverty would permit. Again, one can claim to understand the rightness of personal integrity, but this knowledge is superficial until one wills and acts with honesty and sincerity and thus becomes an integral person. His knowledge of integrity as a moral virtue is then rooted in his very action and being.

It may be objected that this existential idea is too individualistic and subjective. If the most profound knowledge is only had through being, there must inevitably be severe limitations on what one can know because a person can only be himself and not any of the multitude of other different actual or possible selves. Does one have to be a criminal really to understand criminality? Is it not the unique power of mind that it can through imagination achieve cognitive identity with, and hence true understanding of, that which the knower has not embodied fully in his own existence? Reason or intuition may enable one to know poverty without being poor even more truly than the poor can know it, just as one can often understand what happens in a game better as a spectator than as a participating player.

When knowledge is identified with being, growth in knowledge becomes identical with personal becoming. Knowledge is conceived of as personal maturity or wisdom. The educational process from this standpoint requires the greatest patience and devotion, since there are no short cuts to knowledge by means of purely rational pursuits. True knowledge cannot be gained merely by observation, by the study of books, or by sustained reflection, but only by active participation in, personal identification with, and real embodiment of, that which is known. Learning is by doing, and nothing is considered learned until it becomes an expression of what the whole person is. Avoided are the spectator attitude, the development of an appearance of knowledge, sheer verbal cleverness, routine memorization of facts, and all other attainments which make of knowledge a veneer rather than a revelation of the depths of personal being.

Tradition. The source of knowledge is *tradition* when what one knows is simply received ready-made from others. Such handed-on knowledge is, of course, received through the senses and requires a degree of rational activity to comprehend it, but in essence its source is neither sense perception nor reason. Even more clearly is it neither intuitive nor existential in character. Traditional knowledge is usually given in the form of words, though it may also be presented in demonstrated act or by a variety of non-verbal symbols.

Most of what a person regards as his knowledge has its source in tradition. Originally the knowledge may have come from sense, reason, intuition, or existence, but in one's own life most of what he knows is secondhand. He knows the approximate population of the nation from statistics quoted in a report which in turn was derived from the Census Bureau, agents of which originally determined the figure by a combination of sense observations and rational calculation. He knows that heredity is controlled by entities called genes, though he has never seen a gene and probably would be hard put to it to say just what it is or how it governs heredity.

Tradition is particularly the source for knowledge of manners and morals. One knows the courteous thing to do, how to eat, and how to dress by observing and being informed by others, chiefly parents. Knowledge of right and wrong is similarly handed down from generation to generation. One knows it is wrong to murder, not because of the sense perception of murder, nor primarily by rational reflection on it, nor intuitively, nor by having committed the act, but simply by tradition.

The trouble with traditional knowledge is that it tends to become routine, repetitive, meaningless, and stale. One knows mechanically and habitually rather than vitally, inwardly, and meaningfully. Such knowledge may inhibit fresh sense perceptions, critical reflection, creative intuitions, and existential commitments. Yet so vast is the accumulated store of cultural treasure that tradition is absolutely essential to the requisite transmission of knowledge. There is much more to be learned than can possibly be derived from the other sources alone. Hence, tradition must remain a basic source of knowledge in science, morality, art, religion, and in every other field of human endeavor.

The distinction between tradition and the other sources of knowledge is that the latter are original, while tradition is derivative. One of the truly fundamental issues in education concerns the relative weight given to these two kinds of knowledge sources. On one extreme are those who emphasize the transmission of the cultural tradition as the chief task of education and regard the personal discovery of knowledge as unnecessary and inefficient. On the other extreme are those who reject the traditional and believe the only worth-while knowledge is that gained firsthand from original sources. It is difficult to defend either extreme as a complete basis for the educational program. It would seem that the educator's goal should be to develop an effective coordination of the original and derivative, utilizing the original to confirm and vivify the traditional and using tradition as foundation, support, and enrichment of the necessarily more limited original knowledge.

Revelation. A final source of knowledge, called *revelation,* is historically of chief importance in the field of religion. While the term is frequently employed in many areas of knowledge virtually as a synonym for insight or intuition, it most properly applies to communication from the deity to man. God is believed to reveal his will, purpose, and judgments, usually to specially selected persons—prophets, seers, saints, or mystics—through inspired thoughts, visions, or deeply rooted moral convictions. The other sources of knowledge may be used in the process of revelation, as when a prophet observes and reasons about an historic event which he then understands in its deeper significance as a message from God. In such cases the content of the revelation is regarded as more than the contributions from the other sources such as sense perception and reason. In other cases revelation is thought to come directly from God without mediation or assistance from any of the other sources, as for example in a seer's interior vision. Strictly speaking, revelation, like all the other sources except tradition, is original rather than derivative, though the tradition derived from this source, usually recorded in a Sacred Book, is often also called revelation. Revelation differs from all the other sources in presupposing some sort of supernatural or transcendent reality which breaks through into the natural order, while the other sources require no such metaphysical belief.

Critics of revelation deny the need for any such transcendent reality. They believe the natural sources of knowledge are sufficient to account for the content of alleged revelations. Furthermore, they consider many if not most revelations as illusion rather than knowledge, and they regard the claim of revelation as merely a device to secure prestige and authority for the claimants.

Revelation is usually considered to be the special gift of God so that the knowledge which comes from that source cannot be gained by systematic education. There are many who hold, however, that it is possible by special discipline, both physical and mental, to prepare oneself for the reception of revelation. The best way to learn these disciplines is to imitate a master who has himself had communications from the divine. But there are very few who are able and willing to prepare themselves in this way. Hence the education of the great majority of persons in revealed knowledge necessarily comes through sacred tradition, to which the learner is expected to be reverently receptive and unquestioningly obedient.

The Validation of Knowledge

Knowledge not only needs to be discovered; it also needs to be validated or tested. There must be ways of assessing the reliability, truth or falsity, adequacy or inadequacy of what is considered known. This takes us back at once to the sources of knowledge, for the ways of gaining knowledge can also be the only means of validating it. However, the sources of knowledge in the validation process are sometimes not the same as those used in discovering it in the first place. The following examples will help to make clear the meaning of validation.

Let the item of knowledge be "I see green." This is a simple case of knowledge coming from the senses. How could this be tested to be sure that it is correct? The most obvious way would be to go back to the original visual source and take another look. This repetition of the original observation would either confirm or refute the statement. However, note that the statement could be validated in this way only on the assumption that the passage of time between the two observations makes no difference in the situation or nature of perceiver and perceived. Another way of testing the observation would be to photograph the light through a spectrograph and then find the color by measuring the positions and relative intensities of the darkening produced on the photographic plate. This method of validation assumes certain principles of optics which relate color to wavelength and wavelength to spectrographic positions. It also assumes in this case that the person saw green because of an actual light source, when in fact the image might have been produced internally by chemical or electrical changes. In such circumstances the spectrographic test would be of no use.

Again, suppose a person claims to know that all bad people die young. How could this be tested? There are many different sources from which this knowledge may have come. It might have come in a flash of direct insight, from direct experience of bad people early falling dead about one, as a revelation, as a saying accepted on the authority of a revered teacher, or it might have had its source in reason, such as in the argument that all bad people are punished, punishment is to die young, hence all bad people die young. To validate the knowledge one would either return to the original source or check it against another source. Thus, it might be reasoned that if one aged bad person can be found, the proposition must be false, and one could then seek such a person. If such an individual were found, the so-called knowledge would be shown to be false. If none such were found, the issue would still remain undecided. The present example is complicated by the fact that the world "bad" is ambiguous. Its meaning would have to be specified before the proposition could be intelligently discussed.

As a third example consider the statement, "That picture is beautiful." The knowledge claimed could have had any of several sources. The normal source would be esthetic intuition, an immediate awareness of pleasing quality. Instead, it might be derived from a tradition in which everybody takes it for granted that that picture is beautiful. Or it could come by using a rational definition of beauty such as balance or proportion and observing the quality of the picture in relation to that standard. The proposition could be validated only by reference to one or another of the sources of esthetic knowledge. In the present example one might test it by having many people view the picture, then setting down their reactions as either negative or affirmative, and taking the measure of beauty as the preponderance of affirmative over negative votes.

Meaning. Knowledge can be validated only if the testing procedures are definitely specified. These procedures refer to ways of getting knowledge which can then be matched with the knowledge to be tested. It is by such procedures that *meaning* is indicated. Obviously knowledge cannot be validated unless the meaning is definite. A statement which is not understood can be neither confirmed nor denied. The required understanding can be provided by indicating what would have to be done to test the statement. Thus the meaning of the proposition "That light is green" may be given by saying that one must look at the light and see if it produces a visual sensation comparable with earlier sensations associated with the word "green." The meaning of the proposition "All unicorns have only one horn" would be indicated quite differently. Here it would not be appropriate to go out in search of unicorns in order to check their horns since the meaning is linguistic and conventional rather than empirical. Accordingly, one would be directed to a dictionary of mythology in which the accepted usage of the word "unicorn" would be found, including information about the number of horns appropriate to this imaginary animal.

The important point is that meaning is defined by the method of validation. If knowledge is claimed but no way of testing it can be indicated, it is meaningless. Any knowledge is meaningful only to the extent that procedures to confirm or disconfirm it are provided.

On the above point there would seem to be little room for disagreement. The diversity of viewpoints comes rather on the question of what procedures for validation are admissible, and this takes us back once more to the sources of knowledge. Everyone would agree that sense experience and reason are at least sometimes appropriate approaches for testing knowledge. Some would hold that *all* testing must ultimately be by reason and sense and that other alleged sources of knowledge such as intuition and revelation do not provide a suitable basis for validation but must themselves be checked by rational and empirical means. Others would maintain that reason and sense perception do not exhaust the realm of meaning and that knowledge which cannot be validated by such means is not necessarily meaningless but may be defined by reference to one or more of the other sources of knowledge. For example, some might deny that the statement "Stealing is wrong" has any intrinsic meaning because moral intuition is not admissible as a basis of validation. They might add that the proposition would have meaning only if consequences observable by the senses, such as social disorder or economic loss, were introduced as validation tests. Again, lacking empirical tests, some would deny any meaning to statements about a life after death, since they would not admit revelation, tradition, or mystical intuition as appropriate criteria. On the other hand, there are those who believe that rational and sense criteria are not by themselves inclusive enough to serve as ultimate standards of validation and that moral, esthetic, and theological knowledge may be meaningful on the basis of criteria particularly appropriate to these fields of inquiry.

Truth. Knowledge which is confirmed by validation procedures is called true. Hence it is possible to speak of truth only within the context of the validation tests through which meaning has been defined. That is to say, truth presupposes some criterion or standard by which it is measured. Each of the sources of knowledge has been called upon to supply such criteria. One common test of truth is rational coherence. An item of knowledge is accounted true by this standard if it agrees with the system of concepts and relations already accepted as true. If, for example, someone should say, "This pencil suddenly came into existence out of nothing," it would at once be denied as untrue because it does not agree with the generally accepted system of ideas about cause and effect in material processes. Another example would be a theorem in Euclidean plane geometry, the truth or falsity of which could be demonstrated by examination of its consistency with the axioms of the Euclidean system.

Sense perception is another common criterion of truth. The truth of a theory is usually tested by using it to predict consequences and then making a sense observation to see if the prediction is confirmed. It should be noted that this method requires reason (for making the prediction) as well as sense perception.

In addition to rational coherence and sense verification, truth may be defined by reference to intuition, existence, tradition, or revelation. Many a dispute over truth could be avoided if it were always made clear what criterion is being employed. By the standard of revelation one might affirm something which would be either meaningless or false by the standard of rational coherence. It is fruitless to argue such matters without agreement on a criterion for defining meaning and measuring truth.

Error is belief which by the appropriate criterion could be shown false. An error in arithmetic can be shown as such by reference to the rules of calculation. Erroneous sense perception can frequently be checked by tests which combine reason and other sense perceptions. Mirages and other illusions are cases in point. Where authoritative tradition is taken as the criterion, error consists of deviation from the accepted belief.

Ignorance is not the same as error; it is lack of knowledge rather than false belief. It is therefore always measured in relation to knowledge either actual or potential. There is no ignorance in general, but only ignorance of such and such knowledge.

But it must not be supposed that the concepts of truth, error, and ignorance sufficiently account for knowledge or its absence. There is a kind of knowledge which is, as it were, a compound of truth, error, and ignorance. This may be called *probable* knowledge. Some knowledge is certain, in that the tests by which it is validated are complete and definitive. This is largely the case in mathematics. But much knowledge is such that its validation can never be final and unquestionable. Thus the proposition "All men die" is not contradicted by any available tests, but these cannot in the nature of the case be absolutely conclusive, as some future man might conceivably live forever. Hence, the knowledge contained in the proposition is only probable.

Education and the validation of knowledge. One of the major tasks of education is to teach standards for evaluating knowledge claims. It is not enough for a student to acquire knowledge. He must also be equipped to test what he knows or what others think they know. Such testing is necessary to reduce error to a minimum and to provide a basis for consistent rather than haphazard personal growth. The optimum development of personality requires a reasonably stable pattern of judgment, and this can be provided in the sphere of knowledge only by definite criteria of meaning and truth. Perhaps even more important than the specific knowledge imparted in education is the development of habitual patterns of thought or action by which the validity of knowledge may be effectively judged.

It is not enough only to point out the significance of such standards.

There are many different criteria which can be adopted—as many as there are sources of knowledge—and each kind of test will in the long run tend to produce a different kind of person and reflect a corresponding kind of educational program. When sense perception is taken as the final test of knowledge, life will develop around the senses as primary sources of meaning and truth. When reason is the criterion, a reflective, logical orientation will result. Intuitive standards will emphasize the importance of feeling and inwardness in personal growth, and existential tests will put greatest stress on action, will, and decision. Tradition as a standard will tend to produce obedient, conservative personalities, while revelation as an ultimate court of appeal will engender reverence and devotion.

The social nature of knowledge. These differences in standards for validating knowledge—which also reflect varying educational aims—are essentially social in nature. It is a social group which accepts a particular criterion of meaning and truth. To be sure, there is a sense in which knowledge is inescapably private, particularly knowledge by acquaintance and knowledge in its subjective components. But knowledge is primarily for use in the human community, and this requires that it be communicable. Communication cannot occur unless there is a common standard of meaning; there must be rules agreed to by all who wish to understand each other, regarding the methods by which knowledge is to be judged. There can be no communication—no mutuality of understanding—if one person defines his meanings by the methods of empirical science and another person uses intuition as his final court of appeal. Communication can take place only within a community of consent about the methods of establishing truth. Such a social group may be called a "community of discourse." Knowledge in its social dimension is always relative to a given community of discourse. There is no truth-in-general, but only truth within the definitions agreed to by a particular communicating group.

Effective education takes place only within such communities of discourse. Knowledge cannot be meaningful nor truth powerful in the absence of clarity about the standards by which these communities are defined. Much teaching is ineffective because of confusion about the criteria of meaning. If knowledge is to be tested by reference to tradition, that should be made clear so that the student is not frustrated by attempting to validate it by reason or sense perception. If the procedures of natural science are to be employed as the standard, the student cannot be expected to understand or to accept purely traditional knowledge.

It is possible, of course, to employ different sets of criteria in different domains of experience. Thus, it is frequently said that the standard of revelation is appropriate for religious knowledge but not for knowledge of the physical world. This view leads to difficulties because the areas of knowledge inevitably overlap, as, for example, in such matters as the creation of the physical world, and then the question arises as to what standards are applicable to resolve disagreements between ways of knowing where the subject matter is the same.

The point here is not that a single method of validation should be adopted, but that for any given area or item of knowledge meanings must be clearly defined by stating precisely what must be done to test the knowledge claimed. That is to say, there must be definite communities of discourse for all meaningful knowledge. It is only within such social contexts that growth in understanding can reliably take place.

The Organization of Knowledge

The fields of knowledge. It is customary to divide the realm of knowledge into more limited areas, each with its special characteristics. The succeeding chapters of this Part represent one way of making this classification, generally along the lines of the traditional academic disciplines. There are, however, other ways of organizing knowledge which for various purposes may be preferable. Five principal ways of defining the fields of knowledge will now be described. (In this connection the somewhat parallel analysis of curriculum organization in Chapter 3 may be referred to.)

Classes of objects. The fields of knowledge may be characterized by the types of objects which are studied. Metallurgy concerns knowledge of metals, biology consists of the study of living things, theology is concerned with God or the gods. This way of classifying knowledge has the advantage of concreteness, simplicity, and apparent exhaustiveness. However, there may be differences in knowledge within any one field so defined which are more important than the similarities, and this suggests the need for alternative modes of organization. For example, the difference between knowledge of the thought processes of man and his weight (both within the field of study of man) is far more important than the difference between knowledge of the weight of a man and of a stone.

Aspects of experience. Knowledge may be organized according to aspects of experience instead of by entities known. For example, a tree may be known in its physical aspects—size, shape, weight, age; in its economic aspects—cost of growing it, market value, types of use to which it can be put; or in its esthetic aspects—symmetry, massiveness, proportion. This method of organizing knowledge is a valuable complement to the first way because it takes account of important qualitative distinctions in types of knowledge and provides a means of establishing intelligible relationships between entities in different object classes. It also has the merit of permitting a rich, many-sided, and comprehensive basis for understanding, through the use of several different perspectives in the study of any given entity. The main defect charged against this approach is a certain vagueness of definition, whereby any impression may be designated as knowledge on the ground that it is simply another aspect of human experience.

Methods. In order to overcome the difficulty just mentioned and to render the basis for knowledge more precise, the principle of organization adopted may be the methods used to gain or to validate knowledge. From this viewpoint each of the sources of knowledge described earlier in this chapter may be used to define a field of knowledge. There are sense knowledge, rational knowledge, intuitive knowledge, existential knowledge, traditional knowledge, and revealed knowledge. In addition to these basic subdivisions, there may be methods which are based on a combination of sources, as, for example, scientific method which is supposed to combine reason and sense perception, or theological method which may unite revelation, reason, and tradition. The special value of the methodological approach to the classification of knowledge is that it provides definite procedures for inquiry, for solving problems, and for settling disagreements and misunderstandings. In practice it has the disadvantage that it invites exclusiveness and narrowness of approach by those who regard their methods as the only admissible ones.

Theories. A fourth approach is to organize knowledge according to theories. The area of knowledge called "organic evolution" comprises the phenomena associated with the theory that living things undergo a process of development from simple to complex forms. "Cybernetics" is the field of knowledge which grows out of theories about the possible application of electronic communication technology to the analysis of human thought and language. "Psychoanalysis" refers to a field of knowledge associated with a group of theories concerning the cause and cure of mental illness. This method of organizing knowledge has the merit of adaptability and flexibility. If knowledge is organized by kind of object, by aspects, or by methods it may not be possible so readily to make the adjustments required by enlarged experience. In education, centering attention on theories makes the student aware of the framework within which research is necessarily carried on. It also facilitates the development of insight into relationships and provides deeper understanding than does the mere accumulation of facts.

Communities of discourse. Finally, the organization of knowledge may be understood from the standpoint of communities of discourse. In discussing the social context of knowledge, it was pointed out that meaning and truth are established within communities of discourse in which the rules for gaining and validating knowledge are explicitly or implicitly agreed upon. A field of knowledge may be defined on the same basis. The field of knowledge called "physics" can be defined as the content of the special technical communication that occurs among physicists. By means of certain accepted definitions of objects to be studied, of aspects to be investigated, and of methods and theories to be employed, a special community is created. Though the language used and the rules of investigation may change, altering correspondingly the character of the community of discourse, the process of agreement assures continuity of membership and definiteness of definition for the fields of knowledge.

This approach is really not so much an addition to the four already discussed as a standpoint from which all of the earlier ones can be interpreted and in which they can be to some degree united. Metallurgy is not merely knowledge of metals. It is the field of the metallurgists, who have established a community of discourse about certain aspects of metals, using particular methods and theoretical systems. Esthetic knowledge is not only a dimension of experience. It is also the property of a community of appreciation in which certain objects, methods, and conceptual constructs are agreed upon. Similarly, science and theology are not solely methods, nor are organic evolution and psychoanalysis merely theories. In each case a particular kind of community of consent and understanding has been created, and it is this which in the last analysis constitutes the field of knowledge.

This leads to the suggestion that in the realm of knowledge education has to do with the creation and maintenance of effective communities of discourse. The organization of knowledge to be learned should be such as to take account of these communities where mutually intelligible discourse actually occurs. It is not enough merely to learn subjects, facts, methods, or theories; these all need to become means of establishing understanding within living human associations.

Pure and applied knowledge. The traditional divisions of knowledge treated in the following chapters of this Part, as well as the five other ways of defining fields of knowledge just discussed, all presuppose interest in knowing for its own sake. However, much human knowledge reflects more immediately practical interests, and a large part of man's study and teaching is concerned with such applied knowledge. Therefore it would seem insufficient in a philosophy of education merely to consider such comparatively "pure" theoretical disciplines as mathematics, history, and philosophy. Do we not need also to treat such more directly practical fields as home economics, agriculture, engineering, and accountancy? There is a wealth of useful knowledge in these technical fields which would appear worthy of philosophical analysis.

The decision to devote the space available for a discussion of knowledge in a book of this kind only to the "academic" fields is based on the fact that the technical knowledge in the last analysis rests on these more purely theoretical disciplines. Home economics has its foundations in such fields as psychology, chemistry, sociology, and economics. Agriculture rests on both biology and chemistry. Engineering and accountancy have roots in mathematics as well as in the physical and social sciences. Any of the practical fields may also draw on the other disciplines such as history, language, philosophy, and even the arts and religion. Thus, a philosophical consideration of these practical fields of knowledge inevitably leads back to the basic issues in the academic fields. This is the reason for concentrating our attention on the latter in this book. Knowledge in the practical studies is no less real and important than in the more purely theoretical ones. It is simply that the latter constitute the foundation for all the rest and hence provide the best approach to a basic philosophy of knowledge in education.

The unity of knowledge. Our discussion of the organization of knowledge naturally suggests a last question about the unity of knowledge. Is there any sense in which all knowledge is one, or is knowledge an aggregate of many essentially different kinds of ideas and experiences? The answer is important in education since the formulation of a unified perspective for knowledge would greatly simplify the guidance of learning.

Those who affirm the essential unity of knowledge usually do so by one or both of two means. First, they may deny the validity of certain alleged kinds or sources of knowledge. For example, it is frequently asserted that revelation is not a valid basis for knowledge and that claims made for it must simply be ruled out as erroneous. Similarly, intuition and existence are often excluded as unsuitable sources of knowledge. This process of exclusion reduces the number and variety of knowledge types to be correlated. The second means of unification is to show that the apparently different kinds of knowledge are not really independent but are merely special forms of one single type. This is clearly the case with respect to knowledge derived from tradition, which may always be traced back to its source in firsthand experience. One might similarly try to explain revelation as a kind of intuition or vice versa and reason as sensation or vice versa.

In modern times the most sustained efforts have been made to establish the unity of knowledge on the basis of a combination of sense perception and reason, usually under the designation of "science." Much of what is called knowledge, according to this view, has no genuine cognitive significance; it may have emotive or expressive value but does not count as knowledge because it cannot be validated by logic and the senses. The opponents of this view believe that the sphere of knowledge should not be restricted in this manner. They think that there are other means of access to valid knowledge which this exclusive and reductive procedure refuses to admit. They consider such narrowness too high a price to pay for securing the unity of knowledge. It seems to them that the result of such a position is an enforced and artificial unity which does not do justice to the true richness and variety of man's cognitive life.

Perhaps the goal of unified knowledge—of that Truth which unites all partial truths—is not to be reached by restrictive definitions and reductive procedures but by the progressive enlargement and interweaving of the various communities of intelligible discourse. The ultimate unity would then consist not in a single set of facts, nor in one source or method, nor in one tradition or revelation, but in one community of persons who in all the manifoldness of their experience would be able to understand one another. It is one of the primary offices of philosophy and of the philosophy of education to assist in the creation of such a community.

18

Science

THE MODERN AGE has often been called the Age of Science. And so it is, if the effects which science, both pure and applied, has had on modern ways of life and thought be the measure. Similarly indicative is the great prestige which scientists and things scientific have acquired. Such an influential and dominant motif in modern culture must clearly be an important factor in education. What a person learns, the goals toward which his development is directed, and the methods by which he makes progress are matters to which science is relevant. Therefore, in the study of education it is necessary to consider what science is and how it contributes to human growth. In this chapter we shall examine science in general and in several following chapters the special areas of scientific inquiry.

Science and Knowledge

The place of science in education has much to do with the relationship between science and knowledge. Taking for granted that the acquisition of knowledge is an important goal of education, the role of science then depends upon the view taken concerning the place of science within the realm of knowledge. On this question a variety of positions may be distinguished. The differences are in part due to real contrasts of conviction about what is significant and in part to different conceptions of the meaning and scope of the terms "science" and "knowledge."

All knowledge scientific. At one extreme there is the position that all significant knowledge is scientific, that nothing except science provides real or valid knowledge. Whatever else is called knowledge is either meaningless nonsense or an accidental approximation to scientific truth. According to this view, education must above all be scientific. Pre-scientific ways of thinking must be eliminated, traditional assumptions and customary modes of thought subjected to critical scientific scrutiny, and inherited ideas reconstructed to conform to scientific criteria. The goal of education is to develop individuals and a society in which the scientific outlook prevails.

A variation on this position is that there are levels or degrees of knowledge and that science is the highest. Common sense, intuitive insight, and ordinary practical understanding may contain elements of truth, but they do not have the reliability or the effectiveness that scientific knowledge has. Accordingly, the function of education is to tighten up loose thinking and to rise from the low levels on which thought in the past has rested to the truth now available in science.

Scientific knowledge inferior. On the opposite extreme is the position that science does not yield real or true knowledge because it is not concerned with actual things in their concreteness and individuality but only with abstractions and generalizations which enable man to exploit and control rather than really to understand. Science thus conceived is artificial and technical, obscuring instead of revealing the most significant truth. Insight into reality is better gained by the intuitive approach, by emotional attachment or ethical commitment, or even by the ordinary methods of common sense. From this standpoint there is a place for science in education, provided its subordinate role is recognized. Technicians are needed in an industrial society, but it should never be supposed that the scientific study which they require makes them truly or liberally educated. Since scientific knowledge contributes little toward the goal of personal fulfillment, it should occupy a minimal portion of the learner's time.

Mediating views. Relatively few thoughtful people would accept this view of science as an inferior sort of knowledge. More, but still perhaps not the majority, believe that science yields the only true and reliable knowledge. It would probably be most generally held that there are many different kinds of knowledge, each valid and significant in its own way and by its own standards, and that science is only one of these kinds. Or, it may be said that there are various areas of knowledge, some of which are scientific and others of which are not, that each area is a legitimate province of human understanding, and that science is not to be regarded as superior or inferior nor as challenging the right of other areas to their own independent truths. Another variation of the moderate view would be to say that there are many methods of knowing and that science is only one method, legitimate but not omnicompetent. In brief, the mediating view is that cognition has more than one mode—the scientific—and that science has an important but by no means exclusive place in the realm of knowledge.

For education, the intermediate view suggests the need for breadth and variety of approaches to knowledge. Knowledge of the unique should be considered as significant as knowledge of the general. Personal sensitivity and appreciation should be cultivated along with critical analysis. Understanding of the good, the beautiful, and the holy should have their place along with knowledge of material facts. The role of other than strict rational-empirical procedures for the discovery and justification of knowledge ought to be explored. Knowledge should be regarded as a mansion with many rooms, and the well-educated person should be considered as one who is at home in more than one of them and not only in the scientific one. The fulfillment of personality, from this standpoint, demands the mastery of scientific knowledge but without neglect of the other important ways in which man gains understanding.

What is Science?

It is impossible to resolve such questions as the relation of science to knowledge and the role of science in education unless we know what science is. There is considerable vagueness and misunderstanding among laymen about the meaning of science, and even scientists and philosophers of science are frequently unable to give complete and consistent accounts of the nature of the scientific enterprise. It is not the purpose of the present discussion to offer a definitive answer to this difficult question, but to indicate something of the complexity of science and to suggest some considerations relevant to a more adequate understanding of this important human activity.

Five somewhat different responses to the question "What is science?" will now be outlined. Each of them contributes something to a well-rounded conception of science, and each has its special educational values.

A historical movement. Human beings have always sought to understand their world and to put that understanding to use in the harnessing of nature's powers. But these efforts at explanation and control have not at all times been equally successful. One of the most remarkable phenomena of man's history has been the relatively rapid rise, from about the fifteenth century on in the Western world, of the movement called modern science. There had been centuries of preparation for it. The ancient Greeks had made notable contributions to the interpretation of experience. The Babylonians and Egyptians had acquired considerable knowledge in mathematics, astronomy, and engineering. There may have been aspects of the Jewish and Christian religions which provided essential ingredients for the new movement. But whatever the background in ancient and medieval times may have been, the fact remains that only in the modern period has there been an extraordinary and rapid advance in man's understanding of the natural world.

Perhaps civilization does not show quiet orderly growth, but advances instead by creative bursts. Thus, in the eighth century B.C. there occurred the great movement of Hebrew prophetism. Athens in the fourth and fifth centuries B.C. was the center of a brilliant and unprecedented philosophic development. Sculpture and architecture were also crowning glories of ancient Greece. The Romans developed within a relatively brief period systems of law and political administration of unparalleled ingenuity and scope. Christianity ushered in an Age of Faith, an insignificant Jewish sect becoming within a few centuries the dominant spiritual force of Western civilization. The Renaissance brought the Age of Discovery and Rediscovery, with the flowering of the arts and the vast extension of geographic knowledge, and the Reformation and Counter Reformation brought new religious insights and the revival of old ones. Such cultural epochs have continued to occur to the present time. But while earlier ages were characterized by creative advances in the arts, in religion, or in philosophy, the modern period has been dominated by the scientific movement. This is not to say that other phases of human concern have ceased to be of interest, but that by far the most striking and influential factor in modern life has been the growth of science.

Science as a historical movement is, then, a set of ideas and practices which have become the chief distinguishing feature of modern civilization. Modern man is modern because he possesses science. Men have long had language, art, religion, morals; modern man does not differ from his precursors primarily in respect to these. He does differ—or his culture differs—essentially in his having science. Thus, one way of answering the question "What is science?" is to say that it is that movement in human history the full development of which qualitatively distinguishes modern industrial civilizations from all previous ones; it is that factor which in the course of a few generations has changed the face of the earth and transformed man's position from one of conscious dependence on nature to one of considerable mastery.

It should be evident that a historic movement so influential ought to receive careful attention in education. If modern culture is virtually by definition scientific culture, a modern person can understand his age and himself only if he knows the essential features of the scientific movement as it developed historically. The student should be introduced to some of the classic scientific discoveries and be helped to share imaginatively in the unfolding of the new world view which he might otherwise take for granted.

A body of knowledge. The objective of scientific research is to obtain factual knowledge. In the age of science there has been an enormous accumulation of such information. Knowledge qualifies as scientific if it is reliable, well tested, and open to further checking at any time by any qualified observer. The scientific goal is to replace guesswork and vague impressions by authentic fact. Science thus aims to provide a basis for man to build his civilization in a solid and reliable fashion rather than blindly and haphazardly. The facts which science accumulates are the structural elements of which this secure civilization is constructed.

The vast increase in modern scientific knowledge imposes a heavy responsibility upon education. To be well informed a contemporary person must know a great many facts in a great many different fields of knowledge. Some understanding of geography, nutrition, the weather, electricity, heredity, and dozens of other subjects is necessary for minimal competence in everyday living. To engage successfully in almost any occupation requires the mastery of a considerable body of facts in one or more special fields of knowledge. So great is the accumulation of knowledge through science that one of the basic problems of education is the choice of what must be learned and what can be omitted. Much more must be left out than can possibly be included; hence the principles of selection are of great importance. The point here is simply that science as a body of knowledge is responsible for this embarrassment of riches and thus creates the critical problem of curriculum selection.

Another educational difficulty which may result when science is considered as a body of knowledge is that learning tends to become a process of memorizing facts. The truth lies ready at hand as reliable information, which need only be committed to memory or stored in reference books and brought out for use when needed. Knowledge conceived in this way is largely dead, inert material, and learning becomes a dismal chore rather than an exciting discovery. Accumulated facts tend to become independent entities without living relation to genuine human interests.

A network of theories. A conception which overcomes some of the difficulties of the previous view is that science is a network of theories. Science is more than a collection of isolated items of information. The facts of science are as far as possible connected with one another by means of theoretical principles or general laws. Individual facts are particular cases of general principles, and when one understands the general law, a considerable number of particular instances are accounted for. It is the aim of scientific inquiry to reduce the disconnectedness and multiplicity of things to relatedness and unity.

The body of scientific knowledge must find expression in special conceptual schemes, which constitute the languages of science. There are no "bare facts" which speak for themselves. Words like "mass," "energy," "chromosome," and "ego" are part of the vocabulary of science, and the theories in which such concepts are employed are constructed in accordance with the appropriate grammar of science.

From this standpoint, scientific learning consists not primarily in accumulating factual information but in becoming familiar with the interpretive schemes and conceptual systems through which perceptual experience may be meaningfully organized. Instead of adding to the burdens of memory, the theoretical structure relieves memory of the necessity of holding isolated items of experience in storage. Theories can become powerful sources of insight and effective understanding. The theory of organic evolution, for example, makes logical sense out of what would otherwise be a bewildering array of apparently arbitrary and unrelated plant and animal species.

Education in scientific theory may be regarded as the teaching of a new language. To be literate in the modern age a person must master the vocabulary and grammar of science. It is not enough merely to enjoy the fruits of scientific advance. There are basic concepts and fundamental modes of thought by which citizens of the scientific age may understand one another, and it is the duty of modern man in the interests of the human community to gain some familiarity with that language.

A method. The three previous answers to the question "What is science?" have all been concerned with science as a product—as historic movement, as a body of reliable knowledge, and as a set of theories. These answers do not indicate the process by which the product comes into being. The first view does not suggest precisely what it was that made the modern age unique. The second and third do not state the procedures by which the facts and theories were discovered and authenticated. Thus a fourth answer is needed, to the effect that science is a *method*. According to this view, the historic movement called science was based on a new method of gaining knowledge. Reliable facts and useful theories also exist outside of science; hence the essence of science is apparently not knowledge or theories but a special process by which they can be discovered and validated.

Science and common sense. Later in this chapter we shall consider a number of aspects of typical scientific procedure. These will include observation and experiment, hypothesis formation, and verification, which are frequently taken to be the essentials of the scientific method. But it should be noted that these activities are also features of common-sense thinking which would not ordinarily be called scientific. Suppose, for example, that when I get up in the morning I find that my electric clock is one hour behind my spring-powered watch. How can the discrepancy be explained? I can form a number of hypotheses: that my watch has run fast, that the electricity went off for an hour during the night, or that someone has set clock or watch back or forward. I can then check these hypotheses by getting a radio or telephone time signal, by calling the power company, or by inquiring among members of the household who might have set the timepieces. By one or more such checks I can discover which explanation is most probably true. This is just one instance of common-sense procedure which in extended and elaborated form is found in scientific methodology.

To assume identity between scientific method and common-sense thinking leads to one of the following three conclusions: (1) There is no such thing as a distinctive scientific method; (2) anyone who observes and thinks carefully in everyday life is being scientific; or (3) the conception of scientific method suggested is oversimplified and inadequate. If the first conclusion is accepted, the distinctive character of science does not lie in any special method but in some other factor such as subject matter or theoretical structure. If the second conclusion is adopted, it becomes difficult to explain the obvious and far-reaching differences between the achievements of science and of common sense. The third and mediating conclusion permits the recognition of certain similarities between everyday thinking and scientific methods but also recognizes that there are other respects in which scientific processes are unique.

The variety of methods. Observation of what scientists actually do reveals that they utilize a great variety of methods, some routine, some extremely ingenious or even spectacular, some akin to common sense and others directly opposed to common sense. From this it is clear that there is no such thing as *a* scientific method in the sense of a single clear-cut procedure which one must follow to be scientific. What the scientist does in relation to any particular problem depends on the special nature of the subject matter with which he is concerned. The psychoanalyst goes about his business in an utterly different way from the physicist or astronomer, and a physicist may attack two different problems in his science in two completely different ways.

Hence it does not seem possible to describe *the* scientific method, but only to indicate the great variety of methods which are used in actual scientific work. It needs especially to be emphasized that there is no such thing as a *technique* by the mechanical application of which one can automatically produce scientific results. Scientific method is not a special formula which can be used to bring forth scientific knowledge.

Method in discovery and in justification. The problem of method in science is further complicated by the fact that the process of discovery may be entirely different from the procedure used to justify and confirm what has been discovered. Many an important discovery has been made accidentally. The most significant results of research are frequently by-products rather than direct objects of inquiry. Scientific ideas are also in many cases formulated as shrewd guesses rather than by any systematic process. Some investigators seem to have a kind of intuitive grasp which leads them to a fruitful theory without having gone through the usual labor of an established methodology. Such persons appear to function more in the way of creative artists than that expected of hard-headed scientists. However, once the discoveries have been made, it is necessary to develop procedures for establishing them firmly within the framework of scientific knowledge, and this calls for a kind of logical rigor and experimental adequacy which might have been lacking in the process of discovery. Though the methods of discovery are probably of greater variety than the methods of justification, the latter must still be framed in each case to fit the problem under investigation; hence for neither type of method is it possible to describe any generally applicable or standardized process which could be called *the* scientific method.

Education and method. The consequences of these considerations for science education are clear. To the extent that scientific method is an application and elaboration of common-sense procedures, the study of science has its foundation in and intimate connection with any thoughtful inquiry in everyday affairs. Careful observation and logical thinking in general become the best preparation for the specific study of science, and such study in turn should help one to develop habits of responsible analysis, criticism, and interpretation. To the extent that scientific method is something more than elaborated common sense, the study of science will yield insights and skills of a distinctive character. However, it is necessary to guard against the assumption that the distinctive fruit of such study will be the acquisition of a particular technique which can generally be applied to the solution of problems. Recognition that scientific methods are multiple and specific rather than single and general should lead to a due respect for the complexity of scientific study and an awareness of the rigorous discipline necessary for the attainment of scientific competence. The fact that there is no single method also underlies the requirement that science be studied by discipline, by areas, or by problems, and not simply in general.

An attitude. A final answer to the question "What is science?" is that it is an attitude. Perhaps the greatest value and most profound influence of science is not in either its products or in its methods but in the creation of a scientific outlook. The spirit of science may be more significant than facts, theories, or techniques. Possibly the most pervasive effect of science has been the new perspective or world view engendered in modern man, layman as well as scientist.

Curiosity. The scientific outlook has many components. One is a high order of curiosity. Science feeds upon the thirst for knowledge. The primary motivation for research is the lure of discovery. There are problems which invite solution, obscurities which call for clarification, contradictions which need to be resolved. The scientific mind can never rest content with the inadequacies of present understanding. It must always push out into the unexplored regions beyond the established conquests of knowledge. The scientific spirit is that of the explorer and pioneer, whose life is dominated by the desire to open up fresh domains to human habitation.

Belief in progress. It follows directly from the pioneering quality that science is wedded to the idea of progress. The expectation of discovery rests upon the belief in progress. In the age of science men do not look to the past nor remain content with the present but have their eyes on the future, assured that something larger and better awaits those who seek it. The advances are not expected to come automatically, inevitably, and without human effort, but only as a reward for the faithful pursuit of empirical inquiry. The scientific outlook is basically optimistic. It is opposed to any notion that the future has nothing new to promise, that the frontiers are gone, or that the resources of life are limited.

Confidence in intelligence. A corollary to this optimism is the attitude of confidence in the power of human intelligence. Science rests squarely upon the conviction that human reason is fundamentally trustworthy and that by intelligence man can solve his problems. The scientific spirit is generally unfavorable to the view that human nature is corrupt, that man is impotent, and that superhuman agencies must be relied upon to extricate man from his difficulties. Intelligence may, of course, be used for evil purposes, but this does not necessarily require resort to irrational or suprarational resources since intelligence must itself recognize the evil and devise ways of combating it.

Faith in the orderliness of nature. The scientific spirit also rests upon a faith in the reliability and orderliness of the natural world. The forces of the universe are not in the last analysis arbitrary, unpredictable, and uncontrollable. The world is, by and large, law-abiding. If not absolutely unchanging, its principles are so for all practical purposes. Man can feel relatively secure in a world whose patterns of operation are to a degree both comprehensible and stable. Gone, for the scientific mind, are the vagaries of an existence subject to the inscrutable will of capricious deities or the devious designs of demonic powers.

Modesty. Though the scientific attitude is one of confidence in human powers and in the reliability of the natural order, there is in it no claim to omniscience. In fact, one of the important components of the scientific outlook is a spirit of humility or modesty. The scientist characteristically disclaims completeness and finality for his theories. He is convinced that the progress of knowledge can best be served by attacking limited problems one by one. He refuses to claim ultimate knowledge and does not venture to answer questions about the whole of things. Though confident that intelligence can provide solutions, he is duly aware of the complexity of the problems which are posed by nature and is patient in his search for answers, which when found are held tentatively, subject to improvement and correction.

Respect for evidence. One more ingredient of the scientific attitude is respect for evidence. The scientist is not a respecter of persons nor of traditions as such. To the scientific mind personal prestige and long-accepted usage are not in themselves grounds for acceptance of ideas. Knowledge can be authenticated only by evidence which is relevant to the knowledge itself. This characteristic of the scientific spirit has a profound effect on the conception of authority. For the scientific mind the authority—the one to be believed—is not the one with the greatest emotional appeal, personal eloquence, popular acclaim, long-standing reputation, or wealth and power. He alone speaks with authority who can present the evidence for what he asserts in such a way that the evidence speaks for itself. He then becomes not the source of the truth but merely the bearer or demonstrator of it.

Education and the scientific spirit. If science is an attitude, a basic outlook, a spirit, such as suggested above, then scientific education will engender these personal and intellectual qualities of curiosity, expectation of progress, confidence in human intelligence, a sense of the reliability and orderliness of the natural world, intellectual humility, and respect for evidence. In so far as these qualities are considered desirable aims of personal development, the study of science will be an appropriate means for realizing them. But it is especially important to recognize that the conception of science as an attitude or spirit implies a profound and personally transforming view of science education—making it something far different from the mere mastery of bodies of knowledge, of theoretical systems, or of techniques of inquiry. Education for the scientific attitude precludes the view that science is simply one area of study to be included in the curriculum. The scientific attitude is a pervasive personal outlook, which cannot be made to operate only in a restricted field. To become scientific-minded is to become a special kind of person with attitudes which will be apparent in all of one's thought and behavior.

Some Crucial Aspects of Science

We have now indicated five views concerning what science is. In the course of this analysis some of the major features of science were suggested. In the present section several of the same and certain additional aspects of science which appear to be of crucial importance in understanding it will be considered in more detail. In fact, the features treated below constitute one attempt to state the quintessence of science, whether regarded as historical movement, body of knowledge, theoretical system, method, or spirit.

Observation and experiment. The lifeblood of science is a continuing supply of fresh perceptual experience. The basic data of science are provided by observation, which presupposes a receptivity to new experience. It is a common tendency of man to establish routines of life which are repeated and sustained in such a way as to insulate him effectively from influences that would modify the established pattern. This tendency helps to maintain individual and social stability and continuity in what is at best a precarious existence. But it also has the effect of inhibiting growth and hindering progressive development. The first rule of science is to renounce this insulation of life from modifying experiences and to remain open to new data, whatever they may be. Observation is in its essence the constant subjecting of the existing modes of understanding the world to testing and retesting by further experience. It requires the refusal to be satisfied with the familiar and habitual and the willingness to have existing securities of knowledge and practice judged in hitherto untried circumstances. In fact, the primary function of observation in science is to reveal the deficiencies of existing knowledge. The first step in discovery is to demonstrate some contradiction between expectation and actuality. The next step is to modify the knowledge structure so as to make the expected and the actual agree.

The practice of observation thus requires the courage to accept challenge by new facts. From such acceptance comes intellectual growth with its attendant pains as well as satisfactions. The scientific person is never content with his existing understanding of the world. He makes it his business to look about for new ways of putting his knowledge to the test, and he particularly rejoices when he finds it deficient, for he believes that from this failure a new success can come, in the form of more comprehensive knowledge. This in turn he subjects to the test of further observations.

Experiment is a process of observation under controlled conditions. So eager is the scientist to open himself to new experiences that he is not content merely to observe what takes place in the natural course of events. To supplement these natural observations he creates artificial situations in which he can vary certain factors and keep others constant and can accentuate, accelerate, and combine conditions in such a way as to make his testing of existing knowledge far more rigorous and precise than would be possible with natural observations alone.

The primary article in the discipline of science is thus faithfulness and perseverance in observing and experimenting. The cardinal scientific sin is complacency. The scientifically educated man will, as a matter of course, prefer the surprises and perplexities of a world which may at any turn contradict expectations to the comfortable certainty of a world which remains the same because one's eyes are shut.

Theory in observation and experiment. The aim of scientific activity is not simply to make observations. The ultimate goal is knowledge, which requires theoretical interpretation of what is observed. Observation cannot be general and indiscriminate; its success depends upon the directing of attention toward certain entities. To observe is to focus perception selectively. To a degree one can observe only what he seeks. To be sure, observation may yield surprising results, but the possibility of any results at all rests upon having been attentive to certain things. Similarly, experiments can be conducted only by selecting particular aspects of the world for special inquiry and by creating particular test conditions. Now the basis for selection in observation and experiment is an idea or theory. An astronomer does not simply observe the starry sky. He looks at the light pattern in a special way, guided by a well-developed theory of the nature, positions, and movements of astronomical bodies. The experimental psychologist who builds a maze for rats to run in is not simply interested in watching rats run; he has a definite theory which he wishes to test, and the maze structure and the use to which he puts it are both determined by that theory. Nature and perception are such that the variety of possible observations and experimental arrangements is infinite. Hence some way must be found to avoid wasteful dissipation of effort in random exploration. Perceptual activities must be conserved and channeled. This is precisely the role of theory in science, and indeed to a considerable degree in everyday life.

In teaching science and scientific ways of thinking it is important to stress this regulative function of theory. The erroneous idea is often entertained that one makes observations and then constructs a theory from this raw data. There is no such thing as completely raw data. *Some* theory underlies the gathering of any and all information. The student of science needs to learn how to observe and experiment effectively by approaching his material with useful preconceptions. One does not become scientifically competent merely by persistent observation and experimentation but by learning how to organize and economize perceptual inquiry most effectively. It is the quality of the observations, the ingenuity of the observer, and the depth of insight into what to look for rather than sheer bulk of data that constitutes good scientific procedure.

Levels of theoretical interpretation. There are at least three levels of theory in science, each reflecting a somewhat different mode of organizing perceptual experience.

Classification. The first level is classification. This activity is based upon the recognition of certain similarities among the objects of experience. Of course classification is not peculiar to science; ordinary language presupposes it. Common nouns like "dog," "tree," and "person" have meaning only because there are entities with certain identical qualities which define these classes. In science this process of classification is greatly extended and is made as precise as possible. Classification is really the process of *naming* in such a way that things which for certain purposes and in certain respects are interchangeable have the same names. One mark of scientific shrewdness is to be able to discern similarities and to frame corresponding concepts which show hitherto unrecognized relationships between things. In geology, for example, the recognition of rock types by means of certain structural characteristics lies at the basis of the whole science. Similarly, classification of plants and animals in the life sciences rests upon the identification of significant structural factors by which species, genus, family, order, class, phylum, and their various subgroupings are defined. Similarly, classification in the other special sciences permits the relatively precise and complete description of the world of nature.

Explanation. The second level of interpretation in science is explanation. This requires a prior development of descriptive categories. Explanation is the discovery of causal relationships between events. Suppose one should seek to explain why water boils. First it would be necessary to understand the concepts "water" and "boil," which are classes of things and processes. Then these concepts would need to be set in causal relation to other concepts such as "heat" or "atmospheric pressure" in such explanatory propositions as these: "Sufficient heat made the water boil" or "Reducing atmospheric pressure low enough caused the water to boil." Propositions like these mean that the event to be explained would not have occurred as it did except for the prior occurrence of the event designated as cause. From the entire array of events taking place immediately prior to the event to be explained, the cause or causes are singled out for their special relevance. Thus, in our example, the boiling of the water was specifically dependent upon the prior happening of heat addition (or alternatively, of air pressure reduction) but not upon any of the myriad other prior events such as the death of a famous man, a rise in the price of bread, or a downpour of rain. Scientific acumen requires a sharp eye for relevance. Good explanations are those in which effects are shown to be related to truly relevant causes. Weak explanations are marred because they claim linkage between events which are in fact relatively independent of each other.

Formulation of general laws. The third level of theoretical interpretation is the formulation of general laws. An explanation shows a causal linkage between particular sequential events. A general law is an extension of the process of explanation by the formulation of widely inclusive principles. These general laws are the highest goal of scientific inquiry. To return to the example of boiling water, it is possible to develop a much more general interpretation than the simple causal explanation, say, of adding heat. A general theory of liquids and gases founded upon the idea of molecular organization can be formulated, and on this basis the process of boiling for *any* liquid, not only water, can be understood. Also heat can be interpreted by this theory as a form of molecular energy, thus demonstrating, in a fashion that the earlier explanation could not achieve, the real basis for the causal relationship between heating and boiling. The addition of heat causes boiling because heat and boiling are both fundamentally manifestations of molecular energy. Similarly, because atmospheric pressure can also be shown to be a manifestation of the energy of motion of air molecules, the reduction of air pressure can also be understood as a cause of boiling.

The process of scientific inquiry is aimed ultimately at the framing of laws of the greatest possible generality. These laws constitute interpretations which provide a more comprehensive kind of knowledge than do descriptive classifications or the causal connections of ordinary explanation. Examples of such laws are the Newtonian laws of motion and of gravitation, Einstein's revisions of these laws, the quantum theory, theories of stellar and of organic evolution, and Freud's psychoanalytic theories. These and other important theories provide fundamental principles for the understanding of a great range of particular phenomena. It is this feature which most sharply distinguishes science from the concerns of ordinary practical intelligence. In everyday life the role of intelligence is to find solutions to particular problems; the goal is not, as in science, the formulation of fundamental theory. Possibly the one unique and distinctive aspect of scientific activity is the drive toward theoretical generality. No student has appreciated the full spirit and motive of the scientific mind until he has understood the lure of this highest level of theoretic abstraction based on empirical data.

Simplification. The function of theoretical interpretation in science, whether as classification, causal analysis, or generalization, is to simplify experience. The world directly appears as a maelstrom of unconnected impressions. The effort of reason is to organize this complicated disarray into some sort of manageable order. The possibility of classification shows that things are not absolutely and irreducibly individual but that for some purposes and in some respects distinct things are interchangeable. The possibility of causal explanation shows that successive events in time may be related to each other, and the possibility of general laws proves that many particular explanations may be special cases of a single comprehensive principle.

To say that simplification is the function of theory is not to claim that scientific understanding is easy to attain or that scientific theory is itself simple. The study of science at advanced levels is full of complexity and difficulty. The point is that any good theory, regardless of how complex it may be, is incomparably less complex than the mass of uninterpreted experience to which it seeks to bring order and sense. But more than this, there is a scientific bias in favor of the simpler theory. In fact, the principle of simplicity is one of the basic rules of theory construction. For any given set of data there may be many possible interpretations. The preferred theory is the simplest one which faithfully represents the data. A famous case in point is the contrast between the Ptolemaic and the Copernican astronomy. Under the Ptolemaic theory the observed motions of the heavenly bodies were fairly well explained by means of a complicated system of interdependent celestial spheres rotating at various speeds. The great work of Copernicus was to show that by taking the standpoint of a stationary central sun instead of a stationary central earth a far simpler description of stellar and planetary motions could be achieved, without resort to the cycles and epicycles of the Ptolemaic system. Ptolemy was not really *wrong;* his system was merely *inconvenient* in comparison with that of Copernicus. The Copernican theory is scientifically preferred because it more simply coordinates the plethora of data which observation of the heavens produces.

The principle of parsimony. A corollary of the principle of simplification in science can be called the "principle of parsimony." This is to the effect that concepts, explanations and theories should not be introduced beyond what is necessary to account for the data of observation. Complication of theoretical interpretation is to be kept to a minimum; elaborations and embellishments which are not really required are to be avoided. For example, it was assumed in the nineteenth century that a "luminiferous ether" was required as a medium for the propagation of light. Just as sound waves are vibrations of the material substances which transmit the sound, so, it was said, light waves must be vibrations of a subtle substance called ether. In recent decades this concept has been discarded, not so much because it is wrong but because it is now considered unnecessary. There is no way to test for the presence or absence of the ether or to determine its properties; to assume it or to deny it makes no observational difference. Hence, by the principle of parsimony, the concept should be discarded. By the same principle some psychologists would reject such concepts as "soul," "instinct," "intuition," or even "the unconscious" as adding nothing to our understanding of human behavior. It is also in the interests of parsimony that theological concepts such as Divine Creation and Providence have been so largely eliminated from the *scientific* description of nature.

The study of science should give the student an appreciation of the quality of simplicity. He may gain thereby a feeling for rigor and directness in thought. He can acquire economy of exposition, care in the selection of the most effective ways of communicating ideas, and skill in detecting the superfluous, the redundant, and the ostentatious. Scientific simplicity is actually a kind of esthetic or even a moral quality. It is a matter of *style*. There is no reason to suppose in advance that nature itself is simple. But there is something in human mentality that seems to respond affirmatively to the achievement of simplicity of interpretation. It is to the development of this style of thought that scientific education is in part directed.

Hypothetical formulation. No theory in science is regarded as final or absolute but always as hypothetical. It is always subject to revision in the light of new evidence. In modern times science has gained great prestige, and the pronouncements of the scientists are often taken as ultimate and unquestionable truths. The "laws of nature" discovered by scientists are frequently considered to be eternal principles with undeniable validity. Such attitudes as these are contrary to the proper scientific outlook, according to which every concept, explanation, and law is hypothetical or tentative. Scientific principles are attempts to coordinate past experience, and there is no guarantee that future experience will always conform to these formulations. In fact, the history of science is a story of the successive revisions of theory. When new evidence reveals the inadequacy of old hypotheses, new theories must be formulated to accommodate this evidence.

It is commonly believed that scientific laws are "proved," in contrast to the unproved assumptions of unscientific thought. This is true only if proof is understood as "test"; it is not true if proof means final, unchallengeable demonstration. The laws of nature are constantly being tested by observing whether or not predictions made on the basis of these laws are verified. But the laws are not proved beyond any doubt as a result of such verification since some time in the future an observation may fail to verify a prediction based upon the law. Though for practical purposes a well-tested law can generally be relied on, the warrant for this reliance is not a logical demonstration; it is faith in the uniformity of nature, a belief or working assumption that nature's rules of operation remain constant with the passage of time.

Understanding the hypothetical character of scientific knowledge engenders a special kind of intellectual temper: an openness to new evidence, a willingness to consider alternative proposals, a capacity for change, a due sense of the complexity and richness of the world, and a corresponding modesty about human knowledge. In this respect scientific education should help to develop persons who regard the life of reason as a continuing adventure rather than as a finished attainment and who are neither skeptical about the possibility of rational understanding nor ever satisfied with having reached the final truth.

Induction and deduction. Theoretical interpretation in science has both inductive and deductive aspects. By induction is meant the use of observational data to suggest concepts, explanations, or laws. For example, the study of many different societies may suggest to the anthropologist the utility of a general concept such as "culture" and may further provide the basis for designating certain kinds of characteristic cultural patterns. By the further study of these societies he may formulate causal explanations for such facts as the observed geographical distribution of certain customs. He may finally draw from his data some general laws of human behavior such as that certain kinds of culture tend to resist change more persistently than other kinds.

By deduction is meant the logical manipulation of theories to produce further theoretical consequences which may then be subjected to empirical test. For example, from a theory that matter is composed of molecules which in turn are combinations of atoms, the chemists may infer the possibility of producing a great number of new artificial compounds. This theoretical possibility has been abundantly verified in the laboratory. Again, the possibility of artificial disintegration of atoms and the means for effecting such results were deduced from the theories of atomic structure and subsequently verified in the atomic energy program.

Induction starts from concrete data and produces abstractions and generalizations. Deduction starts with the general and leads to the prediction of particular consequences. Scientific theory requires both forms of activity. Without induction, science would lose its intimate connection with and rootage in observation. Without deduction, theory would be merely an economical way of summarizing the results of observation, would fail in its major function of furnishing predictions, and as a result would cease to have any practical application.

From an educational perspective it is important to note the special human capacities which are called into play in the processes of induction and deduction respectively. With regard to induction, there is no simple, direct, or mechanical way whereby scientific generalizations can be abstracted from the raw data of observation. It is the failure to understand this that underlies the erroneous assumption that there exists a scientific method which anyone with sufficient interest and intelligence can apply with assurance of success. Scientific theories are not produced merely by following a standard rule of procedure. Induction requires the use of *scientific imagination*. It is only by a kind of intuitive penetration that useful abstractive concepts, causal connections, and general laws may be discerned within the data of observation. The search for a principle which will coordinate the material of direct experience succeeds only when the mind is alive to novel possibilities and active in imaginatively exploring in succession the fitness of a series of alternative interpretive schemes. Scientific imagination in the process of induction is thus a kind of mental trial-and-error operation. The best scientific thinking is that which is most original in setting up imaginative trial hypotheses, most alert to the fitness or lack of it in the successive trials, most flexible in shifting readily to new theories, and most gifted with that intuitive grasp which leads with fewest trials to a fitting concept or hypothesis.

Deduction exercises a somewhat different competence than induction, namely, that of logical reasoning. The consequences of a theory are derived by logical inference. Hence in deduction the important qualities are rational clarity, rigor, and accuracy. As will be shown in the next chapter, the discipline of logical precision in deductive processes is most highly developed in mathematics. It is for this reason that one of the ideals of the scientist is to express his theories in mathematical form. The most exact and most advanced sciences are mathematical because by this means the deductive process can be most efficiently and explicitly performed.

In summary, the development of scientific knowledge has both inductive and deductive components, the former depending upon lively conceptual imagination and theoretical insight and the latter requiring that logical competence which is best exemplified in the mathematical formulation of scientific theory.

Fruitfulness. One of the marks of the scientific movement is the high value placed on the fruitfulness of knowledge. By this is meant that the test of valuable knowledge in science is the degree to which the knowledge in question opens the way to further discoveries based upon it. An important theory in science is not primarily one which solves a difficult problem or has great practical utility but one which becomes the foundation for further research and additional theoretical elaboration. If there is any one distinguishing feature of the modern scientific movement in contrast with earlier science and with the critical and empirical but not specifically scientific thought of any period, it is this concern for fruitfulness. The unique genius of modern science has been the persistent search for concepts, techniques, and principles which would open up new doors for inquiry. The methods by which these ideas are discovered are of the greatest variety. The ideas themselves are often unorthodox and even seemingly unreasonable. They are nonetheless taken seriously if they promise to extend the field of inquiry. Thus, certain aspects of relativity and quantum theory seem utterly paradoxical yet they are welcomed because they have proven so enormously productive of new insights and suggestive of new problems. The same is the case with some of the rather bizarre conceptions of modern depth psychology. In contrast, such theories as that of the ether, of the indivisible atom, of "vital force," or of mental "faculties" have been largely abandoned because they do not lead anywhere.

Fruitfulness in science is possible only because scientific knowledge is *cumulative*. Facts and theories are not isolated items independently discovered. They are, rather, like links in a continuous chain or stones in a building, each new idea being linked to or resting on those which precede it. These metaphors are not wholly appropriate because the reconstruction of scientific conceptions often takes place by a complete redesigning of the theoretical edifice, but they do, nevertheless, point to the constructive, interconnected character of scientific knowledge.

The study of science should result in sensitivity to the vitality of ideas. The student ought to learn to recognize the difference between concepts and theories which, though interesting and useful in themselves, are essentially sterile and those which are truly seminal. He should come to appreciate the progressive, dynamic character of the scientific enterprise and understand it as a major achievement in the cooperative fashioning of a growing edifice of truth, wherein each generation of researchers builds upon the foundations laid by those who have gone before and in turn prepares the way for those who are to follow.

Science as "public." Scientific knowledge is further characterized by its *public* nature. It is not the property or prerogative of any particular individual or group. It is open to test and verification by anyone. But the public nature of scientific knowledge does not mean that it is *common* knowledge in the sense that everyone has it or could have it without cost or conditions. Scientific knowledge is public only in the sense that anyone who is willing and capable of submitting to the discipline agreed upon within the scientific community can confirm the truth of what is asserted. The disciplines of science are frequently so rigorous and the techniques of research so highly specialized that relatively few persons can qualify for membership in the community of scientists. Hence, scientific knowledge is public only in a qualified sense. It means that the conclusions of science are not private, individual, or arbitrarily personal but subject to investigation, challenge, or confirmation by anyone who has the requisite competence.

Objectivity. This public character of science explains the meaning in the statement that science is objective. The objectivity of science is sometimes taken to mean that the nature of the perceiving subject (the observer) is irrelevant. This view is not justified. It has become increasingly apparent in many branches of science that the observer's frame of reference and human decisions about the procedures of inquiry are presupposed in scientific statements. In this sense there is a subjective component in all scientific knowledge. The objectivity of science means that individual subjectivity is eliminated and replaced by the disciplined or controlled subjectivity of the scientific community. The role of the observer is carefully defined by the precise statement of procedures which are to be used in verification. Thus, to affirm the objective truth of a proposition in science is to assert that anyone who follows faithfully the set of testing procedures by which the meaning of the proposition is defined will be able to confirm it.

The scientific community. Science as public and objective depends upon the creation of associations of persons who have a common scientific vocabulary. These communities are made up in the first instance of professional researchers and teachers in the several fields of scientific inquiry—the physicists, zoologists, anthropologists, and so on—but secondarily also of the informed lay people who understand the language of a science and accept the canons of meaning whereby in principle they could, like the experts, test the validity of what they accept as scientific truth.

One of the contributions of science education is, of course, to prepare scientists—those highly equipped specialists who alone can advance the frontiers of scientific knowledge and effectively apply what is known to the solution of human problems. But of equal if not greater importance is the development in non-professionals of an understanding of what science is, in all of its aspects, but especially as a public and objective enterprise. From this can come a new vision of the democratic community—not as a collection of persons living on the level of the lowest common denominator—but as a society containing communities of inquiry and understanding each of which is open to any and all who have the intelligence and the dedication to accept the discipline by which its knowledge is defined. Herein lies one contribution of science education to the achievement of a free and open society of equal men without sacrifice of intellectual excellence or of specialized competence.

19

Mathematics

AMONG the special sciences mathematics occupies a unique position. It is the most exact and certain, the most general and self-sufficient, the most purely intellectual of the group. It has been called the "queen of the sciences," perhaps because it establishes the ideal form toward which all scientific knowledge ought to tend or perhaps because the concepts formulated in it are so essential to the full development of the other branches of science. Mathematics is the "language of science" par excellence: the perfection of scientific theory is to achieve expression in mathematical form.

Unfortunately, many people have never learned to appreciate the true beauty and power of mathematics. They came early in their education to regard it merely as a technical discipline, a minimum study of which may be necessary for everyday arithmetical computation, larger acquaintance being required only for engineers and scientists. They failed to see in it anything more than a tool, a process of manipulation of numbers, letters, and diagrams to get answers to problems. Common attitudes such as these result from faulty mathematical education, above all from uncritical acceptance of widespread misconceptions of the nature of mathematics, from a superficial view of its function, and from unconcern for the fundamental human values which study of it promotes. No educated person ought to be unaware of mathematics as one of the loftiest achievements of the human spirit, and none should miss the joys of understanding in an authentic and fundamental way what the mathematical enterprise is really about.

One of the special tasks of educational philosophy is to indicate something of the meaning of fundamental mathematical understanding by suggesting what lies behind the rules and routines of computation. Many who are skilled in the use of these techniques do not appreciate the full meaning of their activity. The unskilled are likely to have still less insight into the true significance of mathematics. The present chapter is an attempt to point to some of the ingredients in a view of mathematics as a basic educational resource.

The Foundations of Mathematics

It is common knowledge that mathematical knowledge includes statements about numbers, such as $3+5=8$, or about geometric figures, such as $a^2+b^2=c^2$ for plane right triangles. Not so common is reflection on what this knowledge refers to, where it comes from, and how it can be justified. Three major positions can be taken on these questions, each of which has implications for the human significance of mathematics and for the nature of mathematics education.

Empiricism. According to one conception, mathematics is an empirical science. The proposition $3+5=8$ is looked upon as a hypothesis that can be tested, say, by counting three oranges, then five more oranges, putting the two together, and finally counting the whole collection of oranges and finding that there are eight. Similarly, the proposition $a^2+b^2=c^2$ for plane right triangles can be empirically tested by carefully drawing many such triangles, measuring the lengths of their sides, squaring and adding as indicated and checking the degree of approximation to equality.

The two examples differ in that the counting procedure yields exact results while the measurement procedure yields only an approximation, due to the inevitable margin of error in physical instruments like rulers, protractors, and pencils. The second hypothesis can therefore never be tested with complete accuracy, and one might be led to reformulate it as a proposition not about actual physical triangles but about imaginary perfect triangles measured by instruments of absolute accuracy. To make this modification at once removes the proposition from the strictly empirical realm since one cannot devise any physical experiment which could confirm it.

A similar conclusion holds for the proposition $3+5=8$, for a different reason. Here there is no question of error of measurement. Precise confirmation is possible in each counting operation. The remarkable thing in this instance is that it makes no difference at all whether one counts oranges, apples, clouds, imaginary sheep, or fences. The proposition holds whatever the counting operation applies to. It is especially noteworthy that it applies just as well to imaginary objects as to existing physical ones. Now the hypotheses of empirical science do not ordinarily have this property. They apply to specific kinds of concrete entities, and different things give rise to different hypotheses. In any case, they are not customarily used with respect to imaginary things. The suggestion to be drawn from these observations is, once again, that mathematical propositions can be regarded as independent of the world of physical things and as possessing an ideal quality.

Can experience disconfirm mathematical propositions? If mathematical propositions were empirical generalizations, it would follow that actual experience might some time produce a contrary instance. In the process of counting up oranges, some time the total of 3 and 5 might turn out to be 7. This would come as a great surprise, but on empirical grounds the possibility cannot be dismissed, since all generalizations in natural science must be considered subject to revision in the light of further experience. Similarly, the triangle-measuring process might show a disparity between $a^2 + b^2$ and c^2 which would exceed any possible error of measurement, and this would require revision of the hypothesis in question. In point of fact, to mathematicians such disconfirming evidence would not merely be surprising; it would be incredible. The empirical scientist welcomes negative instances as indications of needed revisions in his theories. It is a prime article of his creed that no hypothesis can be expected to stand eternally unchallenged in the light of more ample evidence. The mathematician takes no such position. He does not believe that negative instances of his firmly established propositions can ever occur, and he does not think that any fresh empirical evidence can ever require revision of what has once been proved. These convictions are not the result of a closed-minded, narrowly dogmatic attitude nor of a stubborn disposition. They reflect the view that there is an essential difference between the theorems of mathematics and the theories of empirical science. According to this, mathematical knowledge is not empirical in character. It is not in essence a description of the properties of the world perceived by the senses.

The proper role of the empirical in mathematics. This line of argument leads to the conclusion that mathematics is not based upon the data of observation and experiment, but that mathematical knowledge has to do in some sense with ideal entities. The nature of these entities will be discussed further below. Before doing that it is well to emphasize that from the essentially non-empirical character of mathematics one cannot infer the irrelevance of empirical facts and methods to mathematics, and vice versa. In point of fact the connection is very close. The world of sense objects can be of great assistance in the initial formulation and in the vivid expression of mathematical ideas. Diagrams and measurements may suggest approaches to problems and may also supply approximate solutions to them. The right triangle theorem $a^2 + b^2 = c^2$ cannot be considered *proved* in the mathematical sense by showing that it holds true, within the limits of measurement, for real triangles drawn on a piece of paper. Yet such a visual and manual testing of the equation can provide a tangible kind of confirmation which may be psychologically satisfying. Furthermore, many an important mathematical discovery has doubtless been made by the study of pencil-and-paper diagrams. In this sense the inductive process of experimental science has a role to play in mathematics, as a part of its logic of discovery. But the logic of verification in mathematics is not that of experimental science, in that the truth of mathematical propositions does not depend upon confirmation by sense observations.

Mathematics in scientific theory. The mutual relevance of mathematics and natural science is further corroborated by the fact that mathematics is so useful in the construction of scientific theories. Even if one grants that mathematical propositions may not be treated as empirical hypotheses, the remarkable and consequential fact still remains that these propositions do apply to the world of things. The truth of $3+5=8$ does not depend upon verification by counting objects, but it is nonetheless true that the proposition will surely hold when actual things are counted. Similarly, for all practical purposes $a^2+b^2=c^2$ will hold for all physical right triangles. Thus, the propositions of mathematics are such as to be serviceable in the description of the natural world. The case could be put even more strongly by asserting that the very structure of the real world is mathematical in character.

Intuitionism. A second conception of mathematics, toward which the analysis of the empirical view persistently pointed, is that mathematical knowledge refers not primarily to the world of things but to a world of ideas or essences. Mathematical truth is certified, according to this view, not by sense observations but solely by rational intuition. Valid mathematical conceptions must be capable of direct inner presentation "to the mind's eye," and there is no court of appeal beyond this immediate rational illumination. Since truth in mathematics must rest upon self-evident insight, the only help for one who does not understand a concept or idea is to look and listen again or to break down the item in doubt into simpler components each of which can be grasped. The mathematician also has confidence that all who understand what is being proposed will agree unanimously in its truth or falsity.

What is the nature of the ideal world to which mathematical intuition gives entrance? There are three principal answers which can be given to this question.

Immanent forms. One is that there is a world of ideas—of number, form, and relationship—which are not "laws of nature" as the generalizations of natural science are, but which nonetheless are resident only in actual things. Thus, the form of a circle is a structure to which entities of sense may very nearly approximate. Measurements of length reveal relationships of greater or less which belong to the physical things compared. According to this view, then, mathematics deals with certain immanent principles of form in real things. These principles are conceived to be unchanging and perfectly general, in that they apply to all possible things.

Supersensible ideas. A second answer is that the ideas with which mathematics deals are not inherent in the sense world but have an independent supersensible existence. If we are restricted to the material world, there can be no circles or triangles, since no material thing can perfectly embody these ideal concepts. There *can* be numbers since actual entities are perfectly numerable, but the generality of number which has no regard to the nature of the things numbered makes it natural to assign an independence to the number system. It seems not unreasonable to consider the world of things as being patterned after the image of the supersensible world, the mathematical forms being the perfect types to which material things in varying degrees approximate. This mathematical world is the most real because it alone is perfect, and as eternal it is prior to the actual world which is fashioned in its image. Access to this ideal-real world is through pure thought, unhindered by things of sense. It is especially by the power of imagination, whereby thought may range freely through the realm of ideas, that mathematical truth is perceived.

Patterns of cognition. The third answer to the question about the nature of the world of mathematical ideas is that they reside not in the things of sense nor in an independent supersensible world but in the structure of the human mind. Number and spatial configuration are ways in which the mind organizes the raw data of sense perception. This is not a decision of the will but an inescapable consequence of the nature of the thinking person. If this is so, it is not surprising that mathematics applies with complete generality to all actual entities. If by its very nature mind arranges things numerically and geometrically, it is evident that mathematical propositions will turn out to be invariably and absolutely true and not dependent upon experimental verification.

Formalism. The third major conception of mathematics is that it is neither an empirical science nor a revelation of universal structure, whether of material things, or of a supersensible world, or of the human mind, but that it is the science of rational symbolic systems. In this view the truth of mathematics is not material (derived from the world of physical things) nor ideal (derived from an ideal world) but *formal*. Mathematical propositions have reference to formal relations between symbols—hence, the term "formalism." Furthermore, there is no one mathematical system which is dictated by the material world, by an ideal realm, or by the structure of human mentality. One of the most striking facts in the development of modern mathematics is the discovery that there are many different possible systems of mathematics and that these systems can in fact be defined and elaborated indefinitely. Many such formal systems have been thoroughly investigated in modern mathematical research.

Geometric systems. A particularly significant instance of alternate systems is found in the study of geometry. It was long thought that the geometry of Euclid was the only and the true geometry. Some believed that this geometry could be authenticated by sense perception of a world which spatially agreed with the Euclidean theorems. Others thought this was the revelation of the structure of an ideal world of triangles, circles, and other figures. Still others thought that the mechanism of human perception was inherently Euclidean. Then the astonishing discovery was made that it is possible to construct geometric systems in which some or all of the propositions differ from those of Euclidean geometry. For example, a standard Euclidean proposition is that through a point outside a line one and only one line can be drawn parallel to the given line. This proposition was long taken as self-evident irrefutable truth. Then alternative non-Euclidean geometries were developed, according to which either an infinite number of parallels or no parallels could be drawn through the given point outside the given line. These systems led to no paradoxes or contradictions and also proved to be of great practical value in physical science. Thus a death blow was administered to the belief in the uniqueness and self-evidence of Euclidean geometry. The proliferation of other geometric systems confirmed this result.

Multiple symbolic systems. The same kind of development has taken place in other fields of mathematics. For example, if the letters a and b represent ordinary numbers, then $a + b = b + a$ and $a \times b = b \times a$. One might think these propositions self-evident. *Naturally,* if we add b to a we will get the same sum as if we add a to b, and *obviously,* if we multiply b by a we will get the same product as if we multiply a by b. What mathematicians have discovered is that it is possible to define symbolic systems for which these equations do not hold. Then a and b will not be numbers as we ordinarily understand them, nor will addition and multiplication mean just what they do in standard arithmetic. But a perfectly good system of symbols and of symbolic operations can be set up in which some of the accepted rules of arithmetical calculation do not hold. Some of these alternative systems of calculation have also proved essential in the working out of certain scientific theories.

Postulates. What, now, is the lesson of these discoveries of multiple mathematical systems? The result is to make emphatic and explicit the formal character of mathematics. A mathematical system is founded ultimately on a set of *postulates* or *axioms* which define the relationships and rules of operation connecting the entities which enter into the system. For example, the proposition that between any two points one and only one straight line can be drawn may be regarded as an axiom connecting the entities called "points" and "straight lines" in a geometric system. The proposition that things equal to the same thing are equal to each other may be taken as an axiom defining a rule of operation called "substitution." The various *theorems* within any system are obtained by carrying out the operations expressed in the axioms, combining and recombining in a variety of ways the elements of the system so as to exhibit new relationships.

Different mathematical systems are possible because the axioms are *chosen* rather than *given* in nature or mind. It cannot be too emphatically stated that mathematical axioms are not self-evident truths; they are chosen assumptions or primary postulates which define a particular symbolic system. The axioms chosen are not wholly arbitrary since they must be consistent, complete, and independent. Inconsistent axioms would lead to contradictory conclusions and conflicting rules of operation. An incomplete set of axioms would leave certain relationships and rules of combination undefined, thus making the progressive development of a system of propositions impossible. Dependence of one axiom on others is objectionable only when one wishes to state without redundancy the basic assumptions upon which a system rests. In the formalistic view it is recognized that there are many possible consistent, complete, and independent sets of axioms, and that the mathematical systems defined thereby are equally true—though from the standpoint of practical application or intellectual attractiveness one system may be preferred to another. Truth in mathematics is not "material," "natural," or "spiritual," but purely *formal*—i.e., it pertains to the relationships within a formal symbolic system.

Mathematics as a game. One striking way to understand the formal conception of mathematics is to regard it as essentially a *game.* A game has certain elements—players, goals, balls, cards, boundaries, etc.—and certain rules defining permissible relationships and procedures—order of play, what is to be done by the player, scoring, etc. The elements and the rules are chosen so as to permit definite decisions in all cases of possible dispute and to ensure interesting and varied play. A great many different kinds of games may be invented, and each is as "true" as any other. The nature of each game, like the nature of a mathematical system, is defined by the basic rules of play, and these rules are chosen rather than given in nature or mind. According to formalism, mathematics is basically gamelike. Frequently, mathematical ability is associated with skill in games such as chess or bridge. This is due to the formal identity of the two activities.

Proof. It is now possible to state the nature of *proof* in mathematics. Proof is not, as in empirical science, observational verification of predicted consequences, nor is it, as in intuitionism, direct rational insight. A mathematical proposition is proved by demonstrating that it can be derived by application of the axioms which define the mathematical system. That is, a theorem is proved by showing that it falls within a given system of propositions related to one another by strict logical implication. To use the figure of the game, proof consists in indicating how the proposition in question is an outcome of playing the mathematical game according to the rules. It follows that mathematical propositions are not true or false in general but only within the context of a particular axiomatic system; it is fruitless to ask whether any proposition in mathematics is true or false unless this context is specified.

Reconciliation of these views. Three positions on the nature of mathematics have now been presented. Extreme proponents of each would tend to regard the differences as irreconcilable. It would seem possible and preferable, however, to find a way of reconciling them so as to produce a synthetic conception that will do justice to essential features of each position. Although it appears that mathematics is, strictly speaking, not a natural science depending on observation and experiment, it is possible to employ mathematical concepts fruitfully in the description and control of the natural world. Hence, in some degree mathematics belongs to and pertains to actual material things and is to that extent empirical. But mathematics is also inescapably ideal. Its material embodiments are only approximations to the perfect forms with which pure mathematics deals. There are many systems of such forms, but these systems are not entirely arbitrary. Formalism may be regarded not as refuting intuitionism but as deepening and broadening it. The existence of many possible symbolic systems invalidates the theory of a single true mathematics, fixed in an ideal realm or in the structure of the human mind, but it is not inconsistent with a more profound intuitionism which would recognize an infinite world of ideal systems or of human minds constrained by the structure of thought to consistent logical inference, out of which an endless variety of mathematical systems may be built. Such a union of intuitionism and formalism avoids the conclusion that mathematics is *merely* a game, in the sense of a trivial pastime. It is game-like in its formal structure, but it is not trivial since the various systems represent the possible architectures of logical thought, and these may be regarded as a major revelation of the nature of ideal reality.

According to this synthetic view, then, mathematics is the study of the possible forms of systematic logical thought based on complete sets of consistent independent axioms. These forms not only reveal the nature of the world of ideas but also by their applicability in natural science are rooted in the nature of the world of concrete entities studied in the empirical sciences.

The Teaching of Mathematics

The preceding analysis of the nature of mathematics is relevant to the problems of teaching mathematics. All three conceptions—empiricism, intuitionism, and formalism—need to be considered in the teaching process. But the problems of teaching and learning mathematics are psychological as well as logical in nature. In teaching it is not enough to ascertain the nature of the material to be learned; it is also necessary to know how that material can most efficiently be appropriated by the learner. From a psychological standpoint it is not expedient to try to teach mathematics from the very beginning as a deductive symbolic system based upon a set of axioms. To the beginner such an abstract logical conception would be meaningless.

Empirical beginnings. Learning takes place most effectively when it starts from the concrete and particular. It is of the essence of mathematics to be abstract rather than concrete, general rather than particular. Hence the paradox that good teaching in mathematics depends upon procedures in the early stages which seem to contradict its very essence. In the beginning mathematics should be treated empirically—as being drawn from the qualities and relations of real physical objects. Number is learned by successive touching and seeing of blocks, beads, pencils, oranges, coins, and so on. Triangles, squares, and circles are comprehended by observation of actual things of these shapes or by diagrams.

Emergence of intuition. Out of these sense experiences gradually emerges some notion of mathematical concepts as in some degree independent of particular things. Numbers and geometrical figures begin to appear as entities real in their own right and not only as attached to the objects of sense. The student gains facility in the manipulation of symbols, and may come to enjoy the processes of dealing with these abstract entities as much as with physical things. At this stage he has moved beyond empiricism to intuitionism. Mathematical truth comes to have an intuitive certainty and self-evident quality which clearly distinguishes it from the particular facts of sense observation.

Formalism as the goal. Some people never advance beyond the empirical stage in their understanding of mathematics. They do not conceive of numbers, for example, except as designating quantities of things. But probably most people do eventually acquire some intuitive grasp of mathematics. They have at least an elementary idea of logical relationships and of an independent domain of symbolic calculations. Unfortunately, however, only a relatively few advanced students learn to appreciate the formal axiomatic nature of mathematics. Without this understanding the most unique and profoundly significant intellectual quality of the subject is missed. To teach arithmetic as a way of counting objects, or algebra as a technique of symbol manipulation, or geometry as deduction from self-evident truths is to leave untouched the basic formal and systematic character of these disciplines and thereby to ignore some of their most fundamental human values. Only when the formal aspect of mathematical systems is recognized can the empirical and intuitive aspects be understood in proper perspective. The power and freedom of human reason as manifest in mathematics can be appreciated only when systems are seen in their variety and not as unique and absolute. Thus, the full richness of the world of symbolic forms is comprehended solely within the context of formalism.

While the full understanding of the nature of mathematics is much to be desired, it needs to be emphasized again that this cannot be taught all at once. In general, the student must work through the empirical stage before he can feel at home in the intuitive stage, and he will not readily grasp the formal view until he has some mastery of symbols in the intuitive sense. However, it is true here as in all areas of human development that proficiency and satisfaction at one level may deter as well as assist in progressing to the next higher level. To ensure advancement in mathematical understanding the teacher must at the empirical and intuitive stages give the student some intimation that there lies ahead a freer and more exciting way of understanding the subject. This requires of the mathematics teacher a keen sensitivity to the student's degree of progress in abstract reasoning, patience in working through required disciplines of increasing difficulty, and especially, imagination in devising ways of suggesting the larger significance of the mathematical enterprise as a whole.

Combining the levels. Understanding mathematics on the most sophisticated level as formal systems does not mean that intuition and empiricism are then abandoned. Indeed, the teaching of systematic mathematics always needs to be made vivid and relevant by concrete illustrations and applications and by appeal to intuition. Thus the cycle of levels ought to go full circle, empirical and intuitive understanding leading to formal insight and this, in turn, opening new areas of practical relevance and immediate intellectual satisfaction.

The levels and the branches of mathematics. It must be clearly understood that the movement from an empirical to a formal conception of mathematics does not correspond to progression from elementary to higher mathematics. It is *not* true, for example, that arithmetic is empirical, plane geometry intuitive, and calculus or tensor analysis formal. The three conceptions of mathematics and the corresponding ways of teaching apply in all branches of the subject, whether elementary or advanced (in the usual sense). The simplest counting operations can be understood from the sophisticated standpoint of formalism, and the most complicated non-Euclidean geometries can be interpreted empirically. The point is, therefore, that an adequate understanding of the nature of mathematics does not depend upon studying the so-called advanced branches of the subject, as only the specialist will be able to do, but upon getting a grasp of *some* mathematical disciplines, especially the elementary ones, from such a three-fold perspective as has been outlined above. This calls for *general* as well as specialized mathematical education. Such general education cannot dispense with technical discipline—with the laborious learning of skills in manipulation of symbols and with development of an inner and outer eye for mathematical fitness. It cannot consist merely of generalizations *about* mathematics, including its formal properties. It requires participation in mathematical processes, but always with the aim of seeing these processes fully in the light of their empirical, intuitive, and formal dimensions.

Educational Values of Mathematics

It remains to point out more explicitly than has been done some special values gained from the study of mathematics.

Abstraction. Mathematics is the most abstract of the sciences, and the study of mathematics is the study of abstraction par excellence. This statement may appear confusing in the light of some popular usage of the word "abstract." Some might say that mathematics is not abstract but is thoroughly concrete, in the sense of being definite and precise. Such an assertion would be based on an incorrect use of terms. Abstract as contrasted with concrete refers to designation of selected features or aspects of things rather than to things in their wholeness. An abstraction is a *form* or a *type* which may be applicable to the description of particular things. Mathematics does not have to involve things in their complex unity but certain formal aspects of things. It is concerned with ways in which experience may be analyzed and organized according to certain formal patterns. Length, for example, is an abstraction which singles out one aspect of a given entity for consideration. When possible lengths are considered as numbers rather than only as geometric segments, it becomes necessary to define what the mathematicians call the "real number continuum." This includes not only all the integers (1, 2, 3, etc.) and all the rational fractions (numbers of the form $\frac{m}{n}$ where m and n are both integers) but also the "irrational numbers" (of which

$\sqrt{2}$ is one example) for which no *m* and no *n* can be found whose quotient is these numbers. The system of real numbers is a formal scheme whereby all possible lengths can be defined and put in order.

The power of abstraction is one measure of the maturity, power, and independence of human intelligence. Without abstraction reason must remain tied to individual perceptions. Generalization is only possible when by abstraction some formal aspect is discriminated which may apply also to other particular cases. The study of mathematics is especially useful to demonstrate the beauty and power of thinking which can transcend particular instances and move on to the creation and use of concepts of wide generality.

Logic. Mathematicians and philosophers are not agreed on precisely what is the relation between mathematics and logic. But all are agreed that mathematical reasoning is thoroughly logical in character and that mastery of mathematics is impossible without a mastery of basic logical tools. Logic has to do with the principles of correct reasoning. If one starts with certain premises and from them arrives at certain conclusions, it is necessary to establish canons for judging the validity of the deductions. Such canons are provided by logic. Since mathematics is based upon postulates from which theorems are derived deductively, it follows that the validity of mathematical reasoning rests upon adherence to the rules of logic, and that valid mathematics is necessarily logical in structure. Both logic and mathematics involve necessary inference, i.e., propositions of the type "If *x* is the case, then *y* necessarily holds true." This "If, then" relationship shows that logic and mathematics are both formal in character. In neither case is there any assertion of facts about the world of things, but only of the ways in which one idea follows from another. The theorems (*y*) necessarily hold true *if* other theorems (*x*) are true, and these in turn must be derived eventually from the basic postulates of the system.

Ordinarily one thinks of logic as broader in scope than mathematics. Logical reasoning is required to some degree in almost all areas of intellectual endeavor, many of which seem remote from mathematics. Yet the character of logical inference is essentially the same wherever applied. One of the unique values of studying mathematics is that probably in no other study except logic itself is there such ample opportunity to learn how to reason logically. In most areas of thought ideas are presented without any explicit statement about the grounds on which they rest and the steps by which they were derived. In contrast, the main purpose of mathematics is to make postulates explicit and to show what follows deductively from them. Unfortunately, the study of mathematics does not of itself guarantee logical competence in all the other areas of thought. The learning process appears to operate in a largely specific fashion so that a skilled mathematician may be grossly illogical in matters outside of his field. Yet the example of mathematics is available for one who has studied it as a vivid demonstration of logical process, and it is possible to use this example as a resource for improving the formal adequacy of reasoning in any field.

Formal interdependence. A third educational value of mathematics follows directly from the second, and though actually one aspect of the logical character of this discipline, it is worthy of separate mention. The entities which enter into human experience cannot be regarded as wholly isolated from each other but need to be considered in their mutual interrelationships. The essence of *meaning* in experience is in the connectedness of events. One of the contributions of mathematics is to deal systematically with the possible forms of interdependence. A relationship is defined by some rule whereby one or more entities are associated with a corresponding set of other entities. Mathematics deals with the formal structure of such rules of association.

Functions. A good way to illustrate the meaning of formal interdependence in mathematics is by use of the basic concept of a *function.* In the equation written $y = f(x)$, the symbol $f(x)$ is read "function of x." The letter x is called the "independent variable" and the letter y the "dependent variable." x and y are called variables because they stand for any of a number of different possible quantities. The equation states that to a selected quantity x corresponds a quantity y, and that y depends on x in the way specified by the function f. For example, if $f(x)$ is x^2, the equation is $y = x^2$. This means that each y number is obtained from an x number by multiplying the latter number by itself. The set of numbers y is associated with the set of numbers x by a rule of correspondence given in this equation, which states the form of interdependence between the two sets.

The example given applies to number sets, but the functional principle is quite general. The human mind in its search for meaning discovers that events do not always occur haphazardly and without connection with one another but that certain regularities of relationship exist. The mathematics of functions is the theory of possible modes of correlation between things. The study of this subject has the value of making vivid the basic nature of rational meaning.

Transformations. To show further the power of the functional concept, another interpretation may be mentioned. Formal interdependence may refer not only to relations between existing sets of entities but also to the changes produced when given entities are subjected to transformation according to a specified rule of operation. Thus, x's are changed into y's by subjecting the former to the operation designated as f. By this interpretation, $y = f(x) = x^2$ means that the numbers y are the result of performing the squaring operation on the numbers x. An important part of mathematics is concerned with the study of such transformations. The objective is to analyze the effect produced by changes made according to any given functional rule. The intelligent conduct of life requires the understanding of how change takes place and the effects produced by specified actions. Since mathematics provides the clearest and most systematic treatment of the formal properties of possible transformations, an important contribution is made by mathematical study to the deeper understanding of intelligence in human affairs.

Certainty. Mathematics is the one branch of knowledge in which the established results are certain rather than probable, final rather than tentative. As pointed out in the previous chapter, natural scientific knowledge is always hypothetical in that a future event may upset the best-attested theory. Mathematical knowledge differs essentially from the theories of natural science in this regard. A demonstrated proposition in mathematics is considered certain and indisputable for all time. The basic postulates of a mathematical system are not like the hypotheses of natural science. They are not facts to be tested; they are definitions and rules which specify the system. From the postulated definitions and axioms various propositions are derived. Within the specified system these propositions are completely final and not subject to subsequent revision or correction.

The certainty afforded by mathematics is a source of considerable intellectual satisfaction. In a world forever changing one may find special delight in affirmations which remain unaltered. These rational truths that are beyond dispute and contrary evidence satisfy in some degree the perennial human longing for the absolute and the eternal. It is this quality which partly underlies the quasi-religious devotion mathematics has sometimes inspired.

The characteristic certainty of mathematics does not, of course, eliminate the possibility of error. There are miscalculations and lapses in logical reasoning in this field of inquiry as in any other. Mathematical certainty consists in the finality of what has been thoroughly checked so as to eliminate such mistakes. Whatever has been correctly demonstrated stands firm for all time. Of course there still remain many unsolved problems in mathematics. From the certainty of demonstrated conclusions it does not follow that all possible conclusions have been successfully demonstrated. In fact, there is unlimited scope for further exploration. By continued combinations and recombinations of ideas and by setting up new definitions and axioms, further elaborations of propositions can be carried out indefinitely. Hence the finality of mathematical truth does not mean that it is a domain closed to exploration beyond what is already known. It is a special attraction of mathematics not only that it supplies boundless opportunities for new discovery but that what has already been established remains forever secure.

Rigor. The study of mathematics is an exercise in intellectual rigor. Most ordinary thought is to some degree vague and imprecise. Even in science, where exactness is aimed at, the goal of complete rigor is seldom attained. In mathematics alone is the demand for precision and strict logical purity pushed to the limits. Of course, not all mathematics is actually rigorous; particularly at the elementary levels much must be done on a common-sense intuitive basis. But the ideal of rigor is an abiding one and is largely fulfilled by the more mature students of the subject. A mathematician does not consider a proposition demonstrated if he merely feels intuitively satisfied and psychologically at ease about it. He demands nothing less than complete logical rigor.

In what does this rigor consist? It is in the full exhibition of the grounds upon which every statement rests. Nothing is to be taken for granted. Whatever is affirmed must be shown to follow necessarily from some previously established proposition. Axioms must be clearly designated as such and used as the primary defining propositions of the system rather than as self-evident assumptions which need no justification. A rigorous proof is one in which the basis for each step in the deductive process is clearly and explicitly indicated.

By insistence on rigor mathematics comes closer than any other discipline to the ideal of rational perfection. It is unfortunate that mathematics is frequently presented merely as a set of tools and techniques for solving practical, scientific, and engineering problems. These applications are of great importance, but if in the concern for solutions the student ignores the demand for rigor in reaching them, he will fail to understand mathematics truly and deeply. The purity, clarity, and precision of rigorous mathematics are major triumphs of man's reason. Mathematical education which gives due attention to questions of rigor thus makes a significant contribution to the understanding and development of the power and dignity of the human intellect.

The language of mathematics. The most obvious distinctive characteristic of mathematics is its extensive use of a special language. As far as possible the mathematician seeks to substitute for ordinary words a new notation designed especially for his purposes. This is possible largely because of the abstract and general character of mathematics. An equation $y = f(x)$ is concerned with formal relationships between x's and y's which are not specific individual things but any entities whatsoever for which this functional correlation holds good. The use of a special notation thus releases one from the limitations of the world of particular things and permits freedom of operation in a world of abstractions.

The language of mathematics is extraordinarily efficient. The required complex computations and demonstrations could never be carried out if everyday language were employed. By the use of shorthand signs like $+$, $\times$, and $\int$, but particularly by substituting letters for whole sets of entities, attention can be concentrated exclusively on formal properties and relationships. Manipulations of these symbols can be performed with maximum facility and minimum chance of error.

The efficiency of the artificial language of mathematics does not render it superior to natural language for all purposes but only for the special purposes of mathematics. Ordinary language communicates kinds and shades of meaning quite foreign to mathematics. It is precisely the elimination of these humanly important but mathematically irrelevant meanings that makes the abstract language of mathematics so successful in its own field.

A fundamental educational value in mathematics is the insight provided into the nature and function of symbolic systems. The student of mathematics comes to see that there are ways of communicating which are different from ordinary language and that it is within man's competence to fashion new languages which for certain purposes are far superior to natural languages. Since the power to use symbols is one of the unique gifts of man, one of the main objectives of education ought to be the full development of symbolic facility and adequate understanding of the variety and flexibility of possible symbolic systems. A study of the language of mathematics can make an unusually significant contribution toward this objective.

The Sciences of Nature

The meaning of "nature." This chapter deals with the scientific study of the material world in its non-human aspects. For convenience this world is called "nature" and the sciences which explore it are called "natural sciences" or "the sciences of nature." Examples are astronomy, physics, chemistry, geology, zoology, botany, and animal psychology. These are distinguished from the sciences of man, including such disciplines as human psychology, sociology, and economics, which are the subject of the next chapter. This distinction should not be understood as necessarily implying that man, society, and culture do not belong to nature, and thus that the sciences of man are not natural. It is simply that the methods and problems of what we here call the natural sciences are sufficiently different from those of the human sciences that the two deserve separate treatment, and it leaves open the question whether the distinctively human may not include dimensions essentially beyond the purview of natural science analysis.

Natural science and the modern world view. The natural sciences have been in large part responsible for creating the world outlook of modern man. The astronomers, physicists, chemists, and biologists are considered the seers and sages of our times. Their ways of looking at the world—their basic concepts and explanatory schemes—are regarded as authoritative and are eventually woven into the fabric of common thought. Hence natural science plays a key role in the education of modern man—a role far beyond the direct influence of formal science courses in educational institutions. Natural science ideas are a potent factor in setting the general tone and temper of all thinking and in providing fundamental intellectual orientation for contemporary man.

It is a mistake to think of the natural scientist as primarily a technical expert in a narrow field of study. His concerns are often extremely profound and the implications of his discoveries may be wide. Some of the best philosophy today—especially in the theory of knowledge—is being produced not by professional philosophers but by physicists, astronomers, and biologists. Natural scientists are asking fundamental questions, about the nature of truth, about life and mind, about what is ultimately real. And these inquiries are not incidental speculations; they are implicit in the very analysis of the material world, profoundly conceived. Hence, out of natural science have come not merely detailed knowledge of nature but exciting and revolutionary conceptions of the world which have been of decisive importance in the making of the modern mind.

In the following paragraphs an attempt will be made to describe briefly some of the major concepts of natural science which have pervasive human significance. In this way some sense may be gained of the basic contribution which natural science makes to the development of personality and thus to the process of education.

Measurement

At the root of all natural science lies the concept of *measurement.* Natural science is the systematic investigation of the measureable or metric aspects of things. But what is measurement? It has two essential elements.

Standards. The first is a standard. Length is measured by such instruments as yardsticks or meter sticks, and these are more or less accurate copies of a standard measuring stick, such as the famous platinum meter bar in Paris. Similarly, time is measured by reference to a standard clock, such as the one at Greenwich, which in turn is regulated by astronomical observations so that the ultimate standard for time is the orbital motion of the earth. The most important qualification for a standard of measurement is that it remain the same through the course of time. It is for this reason that durable platinum is used for the standard meter, and this bar is also assumed to be at a constant standard temperature to avoid the variation in length due to thermal expansion. In modern physics some new standards for length and time based on the wavelength of light and on the frequency of oscillations within the atom have been developed because they promise a degree of constancy and accuracy unattainable with the best meter sticks or clocks.

Coincidence. The other essential element of measurement is summed up in the concept of coincidence. Measurement is the exhibition of coincidence between what is measured and the standard of measurement. An object is one yard long if its two extremities coincide with the ends of the yardstick.

An event occurs at a specified time if the event and the clock's arrival at the specified point on its scale are temporally coincidental, or simultaneous.

From these two defining characteristics of measurement two important conclusions about the function of measurement follow.

Regularities. The first is that one aim of measurement is to discover constancies or regularities in the natural process. Since standards are chosen for their constancy and since measurement demonstrates coincidence between objects and standards, measurement must reveal constancies in the nature of things. Natural laws, which are the ultimate objective of science, are statements about regularities within the flux of events. The possibility of such laws is dependent upon the basic character of the measurement process.

Relationships. A second conclusion is that measurement permits the discovery of relationships. If each of two objects coincides metrically with the same standard, it can be assumed that the two objects coincide metrically with each other. The standard of measurement is thus a link between different objects. Entities which are identical in any given metrical aspect can then be considered as a class, with resulting economy of intellectual and practical effort. Classification is a basic principle of science which alone makes possible generalization. Thus, again, the possibility of formulating general laws depends upon the nature of measurement.

Abstraction. The natural sciences are *abstract* in that they are concerned only with the metric aspects of things. The precision and power of these sciences are due to the fact that certain definite features have been selected for study and that other aspects have been declared irrelevant for the purposes at hand. Natural science, then, does not aim to state the whole truth about the nature of things, but only that part of the truth which falls within the domain of measurement.

Precision. The exactness and reliability of natural science depend upon care in defining the measurement procedures to be used. The standard must be very carefully selected and the precise method of determining coincidences must be stated. A number of discoveries of great importance in modern science (e.g., in the relativity and quantum theories) have been made as a result of determined effort to specify clearly the measurement procedures applicable to certain concepts.

Instrumental design. The advance of modern science has also depended to a considerable degree upon the development of instrumental design. It is only by measurements of great accuracy that some of nature's most significant secrets have been revealed. It is wrong to suppose that the natural world has become intelligible and controllable primarily by the exercise of either pure thought or of sheer power. Man's knowledge has grown in large part because he has skillfully and patiently developed precision instruments—microscopes, telescopes, spectrographs, etc.—and used them in carefully defined measurement operations.

Mathematics and measurement. A final point about measurement is that in this defining characteristic of natural science lies the clue to the importance of mathematics to science. Measurement is most conveniently expressed in numerical form. Coincidences of measured objects with the standard are translated into numbers by the use of graduated *scales* or numerically ordered subdivisions of the standard. This is in effect the same as creating a whole array of standards of various magnitudes (one for each division point on the scale) and then arranging them in order of increasing size. Each such standard is designated by the appropriate number. When measurements are thus expressed numerically, the entire apparatus of mathematical analysis becomes available for formulating the general laws which are the ultimate goal of science.

Space and Time

The relativity of motion. Of all our concepts about the nature of the world none seem so simple and self-evident as those about space and time. Yet modern physics has disclosed the confusion and inadequacy of these common-sense concepts and has created new ideas to take their place. It all came about by an analysis of *motion*. It seems perfectly reasonable to say that object *A* is at rest while object *B* is moving, until one reflects that if *A* and *B* are both on the earth, they are both moving with the earth, and hence *A* is not really at rest but is so only with respect to the earth. Then one might say that the earth is moving but that we know (since Copernicus) that the sun does not move. But this too is doubtful, since probably the whole solar system is moving. Considerations like these make it clear that there is no definable sense to such statements as "this object moves through space," as if "space" were a fixed something to which motion could be referred. It only makes sense to speak of the motion of one object with respect to another. That is, motion is a measurable quantity and must be defined in relation to a standard. Non-accelerated straight-line motion, according to the theory of relativity, can be actually specified only with respect to some "frame of reference" which for purposes of measurement is considered at rest. Thus uniform rectilinear motion is entirely relative to the selected frame of reference and has no independent, absolute reality. The recognition of this destroys the common-sense notion of a fixed space in which things move.

The speed of light and the principle of invariance. But the absolute comes back in another way. In an attempt to establish the existence of an all-pervasive "ether" through which light is propagated and to which motion could be referred, Michelson and Morley, in a classic crucial experiment, measured the speed of light in a direction parallel to the earth's orbital motion and in the perpendicular direction. By common-sense notions the measured speeds should have been different. Surprisingly, they turned out to be the same. This experiment erased the idea of a stationary light-carrying ether and established the remarkable fact that the speed of light (in a vacuum) is the same whatever the state of motion of the observer who measures it. Light velocity thus turns out to be a new absolute, independent of the frame of reference. This is one instance of what came to be a basic theoretical principle of the theory of relativity, namely, that the laws of nature should be so stated as to be independent of the observer's frame of reference. In other words, a true law of nature is some property (such as the speed of light) which is *invariant* as one passes from one observer's perspective to another. Thus, relativity theory established in a new and fruitful way both the idea of the relative and of the absolute in the world of physical events.

Simultaneity. Just as the old idea of absolute space had to be abandoned, so did absolute time. This came about by a consideration of the notion of *simultaneity*. One can perhaps imagine what it means to say that all events happening at the same moment throughout the universe are simultaneous. But how is the meaning to be made physically evident by actual measurement? The only way is to use signals such as beams of light or electrical impulses. Two events at a distance from each other would then be simultaneous if at a point half way between them their respective time signals coincided. Difficulties arise when the time signals are received by an observer at the halfway point who is moving relative to the two end-points. He would know that because of his motion he was not at the mid-point when the time signals started and hence (since according to the Michelson-Morley experiment light travels at the same speed regardless of the state of uniform motion of the observer) would find that the time signals did not coincide as they did for the stationary observer. The conclusion is that time, like space, is relative to the motion of the observer and cannot be defined in measurement as an absolute quantity.

Space-time. Accordingly, in the modern world view, the common-sense ideas of independent and absolute space and time must be abandoned. These have been replaced by a concept of four-dimensional space-time. That space and time are inextricably interrelated is evident from the fact that actual measurements of distance and of time require the use of signals which travel at a finite speed, and speed has both space and time dimensions in it (e.g., *miles* per *hour*). If signals could be transmitted instantaneously, i.e., if their speed were infinite, then space and time would be separate and absolute. Everyday ideas of space and time refer, as a matter of fact, to an imaginary world where communications are made, as it were, by instantaneous thought signals. Space-time has to be accepted by the sober and realistic scientist who has to make actual measurements by means of signals which plod along at a mere 186,000 miles per second! In fact every educated person has the obligation and privilege of understanding how an operational metric analysis of the physical world leads to the concept of space-time.

Events. In space-time it is customary to speak of *events*. An event is an occurrence specified by one temporal and three spatial dimensions. Events are separated by a space-time interval and not, as in the old world view, by simple distances and times. This space-time interval has the fundamental property of remaining the same for all observers whatever their state of relative uniform motion. That is, space-time intervals are invariants and hence fundamental to the formulation of physical laws. Ordinary length and time intervals are not invariant so that moving rods become shorter and moving clocks run slower, the contraction of the space dimension and the increase in the time interval being such as exactly to balance one another so as to maintain a constant space-time interval. For ordinary speeds these surprising phenomena are not noticeable, but for motion comparable with the speed of light (as in the case of the high-speed particles of atomic physics) the spatial contractions and time retardations become of great practical and theoretical importance.

Accelerated motion. Thus far we have considered the alterations necessary in the fundamental concepts of space and time arising from the special problem of relative uniform motion. What about the laws of nature as seen by observers moving relatively to one another in a non-uniform or accelerated fashion? The daring and far-reaching hypothesis is made by the modern physicist that nature's laws can be so expressed as to be the same for all observers whatever their state of motion. This leads directly to a consideration of force, gravity, and mass. Force is measured by the acceleration produced on a given mass, and gravity is one kind of force which produces the acceleration of falling bodies. Now suppose an observer were in a box freely falling under the force of gravity. Events in the box would occur just as they would were he located out in interstellar space, entirely removed from any appreciable gravity pull. Hence the force of gravity is non-existent from the point of view of an observer undergoing acceleration with respect to the earth's gravitational field. From this standpoint the "force of gravity" has no real existence but is introduced entirely by the state of motion of the observer. A freely falling body is not constrained by contact with any other object to move as it does; this is its "natural" state of motion. How, then, can the laws of motion be so expressed that they do not need to invoke any gravity force? This can be done by assuming that the existence of matter produces a *curvature in the space-time structure* so that a body freely moving in the vicinity of a large mass such as the earth will naturally move along a curved path, in the same way as the body in empty space would move in a straight line.

It is at this point that the non-Euclidean geometries mentioned in the previous chapter enter. Freely moving bodies travel along the shortest path between two points. In the space of Euclid's geometry this path is a straight line. In curved space it is not a straight line but a "geodesic" (like the "great circle" course of the navigator on the approximately spherical earth surface). The geometry of curved space is non-Euclidean, and what the physicist has found is that for simplicity in stating the laws of motion he must employ a non-Euclidean system. Thus, the natural geometry of space-time is not the familiar Euclidean one, but a system in which, among other things, the parallel postulate does not hold.

From the fact that space-time is curved, some have concluded that the universe is finite rather than infinite. Since the curvature is caused by the presence of matter, the size and shape of the universe depend on the amount and distribution of matter—the more matter the greater the curvature and the smaller the size. From astronomical measurements it is possible to estimate the total mass of the stars and hence to calculate approximately the radius of the universe.

Implications from the new world picture. There are two points of major importance to be drawn from the preceding sketch of modern developments in the study of space, time, and gravitation. The first is that results of the greatest importance followed from determined and consistent attention to the problem of measurement. Knowledge increased not when inquiry was made to answer the question, "What are space, time, and gravity force?" but when the problem was in the form, "To what concepts do our actual measurement procedures lead us?" With the latter question, the common-sense edifice of absolute space, absolute time, and imponderable gravity attraction forces came tumbling down and a magnificent new world view of curved space-time was brought into being—a world view which is becoming part of the cultural capital of educated modern man.

The other main point is that these developments well illustrate the scientific drive toward interrelatedness and unity of thought. Space, time, electromagnetic waves (e.g., radio or light signals), matter, and gravity have all been brought into a meaningful conceptual unity, and their hitherto unsuspected intimate interconnections have been clearly demonstrated. It is part of the continuing but as yet not completely successful effort of the physicists to bring into this unity other seemingly unrelated factors such as electrostatic and quantum phenomena. However, the elegance, generality, and interpretive power of the unified theory thus far achieved are most impressive accomplishments.

The Quantum World

Careful definition of the operations by which space and time could be measured, and the development of precision techniques (as in the light speed determinations of Michelson and Morley) led to the radical revision of the basic ways of thinking about the nature of the physical world discussed above. The same kind of care and precision in measurement lies at the basis of a further set of fundamental ideas of equally great significance in fashioning the world view of contemporary man. The analysis of space and time affected chiefly the picture of the world in the large, culminating in the theory of curved space-time. The developments now to be discussed concern the world of the very small.

Continuity in nature. A perennially useful concept for thinking about the nature of things is the idea of *continuity*. We call something continuous if there are no breaks, gaps, or interruptions in it. We can in imagination subdivide a continuous entity into smaller and smaller parts indefinitely. Between any two portions of continuous substance, no matter how close together, there is intervening substance. In measuring entities which form a continuous series one would in principle need an infinite number of divisions on the measuring scale, since between any two division points there must by definition be other points to each of which some entity might correspond.

An important question is whether or not and to what extent the material world is continuous. It is obvious in the first place that the world is not completely continuous, since there are separate and distinct objects with gaps between them. Nor can the continuity of apparently homogeneous material substances be maintained. From many lines of evidence in physics and chemistry it is clear that material substances are composed of molecules, atoms, and even smaller constituents which appear to be indivisible. It appears, then, that discreteness and discontinuity are the rule in nature.

The same is true of energy. Suppose one were to measure the amount of light energy emitted from a source. One would think that this quantity could be of any size, varying continuously from virtual darkness to brilliant intensity. Actual measurements, using instruments of great precision and ingenious design, show that this assumption is not tenable. Energy does not vary continuously, but comes in very small but discrete units. These energy units are called *quanta*. Thus not only material substances but energy in whatever form—e.g., as light, heat, or motion—are by nature discontinuous.

Mathematically the principle of discontinuity can be expressed by saying that the integers have a fundamental role in the description of nature. There cannot be fractional quanta of energy but only whole numbers of them, just as there cannot be a piece of an electron but only whole electrons.

The Uncertainty Principle. The fact that energy comes in quanta has a remarkable consequence when applied to the measurement of position and speed of motion. In describing a physical entity one needs to determine both its position or location and its speed. It seems reasonable to suppose that both quantities have definite values. According to fundamental natural science principles, these quantities have physical meaning only provided the relevant measurement procedures are specified. The measurement of position and speed requires the use of light, electricity, or other means of communicating information between whatever is measured and the observer. But since the agency of communication necessarily possesses energy, the interaction of this agency with the object to be measured will modify the energy state of that object. Hence, what the observer perceives in his measurement is not the state of the object itself but that state as modified by the measurement process. For all ordinary large-scale measurements the disturbing effect of the measurement can be made negligible. This is not so in the case of the extremely small particles—electrons, neutrons, etc.—which are the elementary constituents of the physical world. If one seeks to measure the position and speed of such particles, say by the use of light, a difficulty arises because the energy of the light used for this purpose comes only in whole numbers of quanta. The very least energy that could be used for making the measurement would be one quantum. Thus what one observes is not the energy state of the particle but only an approximation to that state, the minimum error being a function of the quantum of energy. This irreducible minimum of error is distributed between position and speed. It develops that if the measurement procedure is set up so as to determine position very accurately, the speed can be known only inaccurately, and vice versa. The product of the minimum errors in position and in speed is a constant amount, proportionate to the quantum of energy.

These discoveries have made it clear that there is a limit to the accuracy which physical measurement can attain. In the world of the extremely small these limits are of great importance because the minimum errors of measurement are of the same order of magnitude as the entities to be measured, and thus the whole character of the possible knowledge structure is changed. Since in natural science knowledge always means measurement information, limits on the possibility of measurement mean limitations on knowledge.

Measurement and finitude. It is significant that the fundamental ideas about space, time, and motion in both relativity theory and quantum theory have the same twofold basis: first, an insistence on the exact definition of measurement procedures using light signals or their equivalent, and second, the discovery of special properties of such signals—in the former instance a very large but still finite speed of propagation, the same for all observers, in the latter instance a very small but not infinitesimal minimum energy unit. If measurements could be made by means of instantaneous signals which could vary continuously in intensity rather than in discrete energy units, the new metric world of space-time and of indeterminable position and speed would not have had to displace the older accepted ideas. In broadest terms the lesson of the modern world view is that in natural science thought must be related to action. By the power of imagination man's thoughts can run off to infinity. There are no bounds to his mental explorations, including concepts of infinite space, infinite time, universal simultaneity, infinitesimal energy, and ideal measurements. But man's power for action is limited, and he cannot in act make good on his infinite thoughts. Spiritually infinite, human beings are physically finite, and they inhabit a world of finite material realities. In natural science the thought must be linked to the finite realities and must renounce its infinite prerogatives. The world of relativity and of quanta is simply the world as perceived by men who in scientific humility have submitted to the discipline of measuring the world by means of the finite tools which nature supplies. The understanding of this basic principle ought to be a major objective of natural science education.

Uncertainty and the principle of causality. The discovery that knowledge of the physical world is inevitably infected with a degree of uncertainty has the further effect of calling into question a principle which has undergirded all of man's attempts to construct a rational picture of the natural world, namely, the principle of causality. According to this principle, every event is explicable by the causal factors which determine it. Furthermore, if we know the laws determining the events, it should be possible to predict future occurrences. But the uncertainty necessarily involved in measurement places a limit on the power of prediction—a limit which becomes of decisive importance in dealing with the world of the very small. For example, it is not possible to predict the precise physical state (e.g., the position and speed) of an electron, but only the approximate values of these quantities. Gone, then, is the hope of exact and definite predictability. In effect, as far as knowledge is concerned, gone also is the principle of exact causal determination. It could still be argued (as some eminent scientists have done) that it is only our *knowledge* which is uncertain and that the law of causality still holds exactly in the "real" world of events which our instruments cannot fully represent. This is a minority position. Most scientists believe that it is not useful for scientific purposes to talk about a real world behind the world as known through physical measurements. They are convinced that the measured world is the only real world it makes sense to discuss. From this standpoint, in the new world of quanta the time-honored principle of precise causal determination must be abandoned. The physical world is thus no longer conceivable as a precisely articulated mechanism but as having, as it were, loose joints with some freedom of variation in the connection of its events.

The statistical nature of physical laws. It must not be thought, however, that the abandonment of strict causality implies the renunciation of the search for physical laws, for causal relationships, and for the means of prediction. These are still major objectives of inquiry in natural science. It is simply that a new conception of the natural order has become necessary. This new conception may best be designated as *statistical.* Physical law is now regarded not as a fixed rule to which physical processes in every case exactly conform, but as a statement of average behavior in a large number of cases. For events in the world of ordinary-sized objects the uncertainty of measurement is relatively so small that the statistical character of physical laws does not become apparent, and it is legitimate to retain the customary notion of law as a fixed rule. In the world of the very small, however, the statistical perspective is imperative. For example, it is not correct to describe the motion of an electron around the nucleus of an atom in the same way as one can describe the motion of a planet around the sun. Because of the Uncertainty Principle it is impossible to attach any precise meaning to both the position and speed of the electron at each moment, as could be done in the case of the planet. But from this it does not follow that there is no possible scientific description of the electron's motion. Such a description is possible in the form of a statement of "probability distribution," that is, of the statistical averages of position and speed of large numbers of identical orbital electrons.

It is a great and illuminating idea that the world of natural science is only known statistically. This is connected with the primary fact that natural science is the study of the metric aspects of things. Measurement is necessarily statistical. Since it is never absolutely exact, our assurance about what we know can only be increased by making many independent measurements and obtaining statistical distributions. Consider the nature of life insurance as a parallel case. The companies do not know when any one person will die, but by statistical methods applied to the actual experience of large populations the probabilities of death at any age can be determined with considerable accuracy, thus permitting the business to operate with a high degree of predictability and security. All statistical laws follow this basic principle.

It needs to be emphasized that from the point of view of quantum theory statistical analysis in natural law is not merely a device to avoid the trouble of dealing with individual cases. In the past it has been assumed that there were exact laws governing individual behavior, that with sufficient knowledge of the laws this behavior could be predicted exactly, and that a statistical description is employed only when the more detailed individual analysis is not required. The Uncertainty Principle implies that the statistical formulation is basic rather than merely convenient and that the alleged exact laws of individual behavior do not in reality exist. The study of natural sciences ought, then, to make clear this general principle, that the metrical order of the world is fundamentally statistical in nature and that the intelligibility of nature rests upon statistical measurements.

Matter and Energy

Waves and particles. By numerous experiments it can be shown that light has a wave-like character, with definite wavelengths and frequencies of oscillation. It can also be demonstrated that light exerts a mechanical pressure on whatever it strikes. According to quantum theory, light also comes in units of energy rather than continuously. The latter two facts seem more consistent with the view that light consists of a stream of particles. The conclusion adopted by contemporary scientists is that light has characteristics of *both* waves and particles. Even more surprising are the experiments which show conclusively that matter (e.g., a stream of electrons) has wave-like properties as well as the usual particle character. These waves are connected directly with the Uncertainty Principle discussed above and reflect the statistical distribution of position and speed. Light energy and matter thus both have properties of waves *and* of particles.

Equivalence of mass and energy. It develops further, according to the relativity theory, that just as objects in motion decrease in length and clocks go slower, the mass increases with velocity. The difference in energy between a body at rest and in motion is called the kinetic energy or energy of motion. It thus appears that energy of motion produces increase in mass.

From both lines of analysis comes the suggestion that matter and energy are similar in nature. Actually the bold conclusion is drawn that they are identical. Upon the equivalence of mass and energy rest the revolutionary developments in atomic energy, whereby through the artificial transmutation of one element into another of lower mass great quantities of energy, equivalent to the loss of mass, are released. But even more important for the fashioning of a fundamental view of the world is the discovery that in the concept of energy has been found a great unifying idea. Even apart from the equivalence of matter and energy, the concept of energy covers a great variety of phenomena. Light, x-rays, and radio waves are all forms of electromagnetic energy. Heat and sound are energies of vibration of material substances. When, now, matter is also shown to be a form of energy, we have arrived at an idea which makes possible a unification of knowledge on a grand scale. This idea permits the realization, to a degree, of the age-long search for a single key to the nature of things.

The description of nature. The fact that energy, whether as matter or as electromagnetic waves, has both wave and particle properties leads to another conclusion of major importance for the general world view. It is not possible to *picture* the nature of something which is both wave and particle at the same time. Waves alone, particles alone, or a mixture of the two can be imagined, but not one entity with both properties. A particle is by definition concentrated within a limited volume; a wave is spread out in space. How, then, can anything be both wave and particle at the same time? Mechanical models to make the duality clear are not possible. Common sense and intuition are contradicted, yet measurement procedures which define waves and others which define particles are both applicable. The conclusion is that the modern mind must in certain respects renounce its dependence upon pictures and models to represent the nature of things and rely instead upon the defining measurement operations, preferably expressed in the appropriate mathematical symbolism.

Conservation of energy. Another principle which reflects the fundamental role of energy in the nature of things is the law of the conservation of energy. According to this principle, energy may change from one form to another, as from light to heat or from matter to gamma radiation, but the total amount of energy in an isolated system remains unchanged. The law may be expressed by saying that energy is neither created nor destroyed in the course of any known natural processes. Here again energy appears as an answer to man's search for a primal stuff of which all things consist.

Entropy. Although the total amount of energy is conserved, in passing from one form of energy to another the usefulness or availability of the energy always decreases. Thus, when coal is burned, energy in a highly concentrated form is converted into heat which is eventually dissipated widely through the atmosphere and can never be captured again. Energy always changes from an organized to a less organized form. In all natural processes it is transformed to increasingly random or disorganized forms. This is known as the *law of entropy,* where entropy is defined as a measure of the randomness of energy. This law is of great general interest in two respects. First it provides a basis for measuring the direction of time. Everyone takes it for granted that time goes from past to future. But suppose someone made a clock which ran backwards. How would one know, except by intuition, that this clock was wrong as compared with forward-running clocks? What *measurement procedure* would reveal this? A motion picture can be run backwards, and the results are amusing, but how can we know by measurement that time cannot *really* go in reverse? The answer is found in the law of entropy. The forward direction of time is the direction of increasing entropy. The past condition of things cannot be re-entered because energy cannot be restored to its earlier state of organization.

A second general consequence of the law of entropy is the pessimistic cast which it imparts to the view of cosmic natural history. The universe appears to be running down. The universal store of energy, though constant in amount, becomes progressively less useful, tending toward an ultimate state of maximum disorganization as uniformly diffused heat. This prospect raises the question as to how the original condition of high energy organization was produced and whether there may not be factors still operating to create and restore order in the cosmos.

Life

Analysis of living things. One of the most powerful tools of science is analysis, that is, the division of a problem into simpler constituent parts. The analysis of matter and energy in physical science has had enormous success. By this process the key to the nature of material things has been found in the identification of elementary particles and energy units organized in a vast variety of possible ways. The same type of analytical procedure has borne fruit in the study of living things. Constituent parts called cells, roughly analogous to the atoms of physical science, have been identified, and these cells have been further analyzed into smaller constituents. Of particular importance are the chromosomes and genes which determine the characteristics of each living thing. The genes appear to be extremely complex protein molecules. Thus the analysis of living things is linked to the general physical and chemical analysis of matter. This is another example of the essential and growing unity of natural science. The same analytical process has proven applicable both to living and to non-living things, and though the secret of life has not yet been revealed, the relevance of further knowledge of atomic and molecular structure to the explanation of life seems increasingly evident.

Organisms. To analysis must be added synthesis. It is not enough to discover elementary constituents, whether electrons or genes. Full understanding includes also the principles whereby the parts are united into wholes. This is particularly important in the study of life. A fundamental property of living things is that they are organized and operate as wholes. An organism is more than the sum of its parts. This is true of the non-living too; an atom is more than a heap of electrons, protons, and neutrons. But the special contribution of life science is to emphasize the organic wholeness. The point becomes clear if the gene is compared with the electron. Both are units discovered by analysis. But the gene contains within itself the power to direct the growth and development of a whole organism. It thus embodies the principle of the whole. The electron, by contrast, is a much more elementary unit, in that it cannot determine any whole but must be determined by other organizing agencies.

Organic wholes are further characterized by a principle of conservation or persistence. Analogues are found in the physical science concepts of stability and equilibrium, but in life science this principle becomes of central importance. A living being is organized in such a way that through mechanisms of growth, assimilation, repair, and reproduction the dynamic structure of the whole is as far as possible preserved. This is a principle of permanence amid change, of basic striving for immortality within the chances and changes of material existence, a law of conservation of form and function.

Evolution. The concept of organism and of persisting wholes is a special contribution to the world view of modern man from the study of the life sciences. Another contribution of equal or even greater significance is the idea of evolution. This idea is of general applicability. It is not relevant only to organisms, but to the processes of inorganic development and to the development of cultures. In the biological sciences, however, the concept has been most clearly and influentially expressed. The essence of the idea of evolution is that the many varieties of things are what they are by virtue of past events in which antecedent generations participated. Implied in this are four basic attitudes of the modern mind.

Emphasis on change. The first is that everything changes, that the kinds of entities familiar to us were not always in existence and that future entities will be different from today's. The world is dynamic; existence is not static being but vital process. Thus nature herself does not support the status quo, and man must learn to adapt to and participate in a forever-changing world.

Responsibility for the future. Second, whatever happens now will tend to make a difference in the future, since each generation is an essential link in the evolutionary chain. However, changes in the present generation are not necessarily passed on directly. What is handed down depends on the mode of intergeneration communication. In biological inheritance the germ cells are the carriers, and evolution probably occurs indirectly as a result of natural selection, the procreation of certain individuals with special inheritable characteristics being favored in comparison with others. In cultural evolution, on the other hand, the changes are more likely to be handed on directly through education.

Belief in progress. Third, evolution tends to favor the idea of progress. The present is better than the past, and the future will be still better. The world process moves not only onward but upward forever. The long path which nature has trod from the most elementary forms to the present highly organized structures warrants the expectation of a bright future.

Genetic explanation. Finally, the evolutionary principle encourages the explanation of the present solely by reference to the past. According to this genetic view, we can understand what things are by asking where they have come from. This is the basis for a natural history conception of scientific explanation. It is inhospitable to the idea of purpose, which seeks for explanations of the natural process in an immanent factor of expectation or intention. There has been a determined effort in natural science to avoid reading human motives into the processes of nature, using instead mechanisms which can be objectively defined and measured.

Probably no idea coming out of natural science has been so profoundly and widely influential as evolution. Its very persuasiveness may, however, have led to unwarranted generalizations of the principle. Without denying the value of evolutionary explanations within the proper limits, one may question the exclusive emphasis on change, the tenability of the idea of inevitable progress, and the denial of immanent purpose.

Classification in the Natural Sciences

One of the necessary aspects of natural science is the process of classification, the definition and careful description of entities grouped according to certain common features. To each class a name is given. By this process a technical vocabulary is created, permitting precise communication within the respective scientific disciplines. Classification is of particular importance in such natural sciences as botany, zoology, and geology, within which a major task is the identification and description of the many types and subtypes of organisms and physical structures. This is one kind of measurement procedure, the standard being the designated class characteristics, with which the characteristics of certain individual entities must be shown to coincide.

Necessary though it is for the provision of scientific language, classification is only a preliminary phase of scientific endeavor. It is important that the student of natural science not be submerged in a sea of technical terminology which hides from view the more essential objectives of fundamental causal explanation and general theory formulation. Failure of concern for basic theory also tends to crystallize the natural sciences into unrelated fixed fields of inquiry, each with its own special concepts, and to obscure the underlying relationships and unities. Fundamental research in the natural sciences is breaking down boundaries between the disciplines. Chemists and physicists not many decades ago had considerably different languages and theoretical schemes. Now both are united with respect to basic atomic and molecular theory. The rapid development of "bridge" sciences like astrophysics and biochemistry is further evidence of the growing unity of natural science on the basis of fundamental ideas.

Education and the Sciences of Nature

One aim of the present chapter has been to point out the definitive character of natural science as based on the process of measurement and to indicate how some of the most fundamental ideas illustrate this process. These ideas are important in education because they have become essential elements in the total world view of modern man. They provide clues to the most illuminating ways of looking at the nature of things. They are ideas which, though new and revolutionary, are on the way to becoming the established perspective of contemporary man.

From the educational standpoint it is also important to teach science not merely as a vast accumulation of facts to be absorbed and of technical apparatus to be mastered. The facts and the techniques should be regarded as illustrations of truly fundamental and pervasive conceptions and processes. From the most elementary to the most advanced levels, for generalist and specialist alike, the prime objective in the study of natural science is to gain true appreciation of the meaning of measurement and an understanding of great concepts like space-time, quanta, statistical law, energy, organism, and evolution, by which the multitude of special facts are brought into meaningful unified perspective.

It would seem that only by understanding natural science in this way can the inherent beauty, power, and interest of the subject be preserved and the student be rescued from the drudgery of a discipline of "cold" facts. The employment of key ideas is also the secret of economy in education. One need not master the whole vast accumulation of knowledge in order to understand science truly. True understanding comes through appreciating the defining procedures and basic conceptual schemes which specific facts serve to exemplify.

21

The Sciences of Man

The Study of Man

The needs. Significant though the sciences of non-human nature are, it would appear that they cannot equal in ultimate practical importance the scientific exploration of personality and society. The natural sciences have gone far in unraveling the mysteries of the material world and in making possible prediction and control of the forces of nature. The same degree of success has not been achieved in the study of man. Yet here is where the need is most urgent. Problems of personal and social malaise abound. Wars and rumors of war, prevalent mental illness, delinquency, social injustice, poverty amid plenty, world revolution, race prejudice, and intergroup tensions bear eloquent witness to the persistent and deepening crisis in human affairs. They cry out for solutions, especially for ones based upon the secure foundation of scientific method. Man has well cultivated the garden of non-human nature, while the weeds have largely grown unchecked in the garden of his own soul. If indeed the proper study of mankind is man himself, then the sciences of man are an eminently appropriate employment for human intelligence.

The accomplishments. Despite the urgency of the task and the size of the stakes, the success of the human sciences has up to the present fallen far short of needs, hopes, or expectations. In comparison with the breath-taking achievements of the physical sciences, the assured results of the sciences of man have been meager. Large amounts of data about man and society have been assembled, but from this accumulation few fruitful hypotheses of wide generality have been obtained. Many say that the sciences of man are in their infancy, that they have not had the opportunity to come of age, that they are growing normally and rapidly, and that before long they will begin to show in abundance the fruits of maturity. And always this is said with one eye on the physical sciences, which have become models of precision, predictive power, and theoretical elegance.

The methods. So impressive are the attainments of the physical sciences that the methods, concepts, and symbols employed in those fields have tended to be copied in the sciences of man. Ideas of measurement, statistics, mathematical formulation, and mechanical causation which have proved their value in physics and chemistry have been taken over directly into psychology and economics. This has been done in part on the assumption that science is a method and that when the method has worked well in one field of inquiry it will probably work well in other fields. Unfortunately this somewhat uncritical and unimaginative imitation of the physical sciences has not yielded the expected harvest in scientific results. It has consequently been in order to ask whether there are not different and unique methods of inquiry appropriate to the social sciences and whether the effort to carry over natural science methodology may not be a mistake.

One mark of a mature science is the development of a consistent and widely agreed-upon set of concepts and theories. This goal has been to a large extent realized in the physical sciences. Even the revolutionary concepts of relativity and quantum theories are now fully accepted by nearly everyone acquainted with them. In the case of the sciences of man this general unanimity does not prevail. The same terms are used in different ways by different workers. Methods and basic assumptions vary widely. There are numerous conflicing "schools" of anthropology or economics. The student of these subjects has the task not only of mastering a difficult discipline but of taking account of the conflicting viewpoints of the partisans. In short, in the sciences of man there has been only limited success in creating stable, representative, and productive communities of scientific discourse with the attendant well developed schemes of categories and working assumptions.

Education and the Sciences of Man

In seeking an explanation for the special problems which beset the human sciences one is led to probe more deeply into the special character of these sciences. Before doing that, however, something should be said about the general relation between education and the sciences of man. It is evident that the relationship is more direct and intimate than in the case of the natural sciences. The sciences of nature are influential in the development of persons chiefly because they suggest basic ways of looking at the natural world—general concepts such as space-time, energy, and evolution. Such ideas do much to set the tone and determine the character of human experience. They are not, however, nearly so deep and so personal in their effect as are the ideas held about man, society, and culture. One's views about the non-human world exert essentially secondary effects upon the development of persons. The effects of knowledge about man and his works are primary, for this knowledge has reference to the very self which is undergoing development. In a sense the processes of learning and teaching are the main concern of the sciences of man; to a large extent the social sciences are an inquiry into education. Clearly, the first order of business for all who guide the growth of human beings is to know what persons are and the conditions which influence what they become. It is evident, then, that an understanding of the sciences of man is of central importance in education, both for those who learn and for those who teach.

Special Problems in the Study of Man

It was indicated that the study of man in some ways has not succeeded so well as the study of non-human nature. May there not be special characteristics of human sciences which help to explain why this is so? Perhaps the difficulties result from the mistaken attempt to introduce natural science ideas too directly into the human sphere.

One's view of the nature of the sciences of man will reflect his view of man's relation to non-human nature. If man is regarded as in essence continuous with the non-human world, the sciences of man will be regarded as essentially identical with the natural sciences. If, on the other hand, the uniqueness of man is stressed, the special character of the human sciences will be emphasized, and the ways in which these sciences differ from the natural sciences will follow from the distinctive features of man. In the study of man five problems need particular attention.

The problem of complexity. Man is unquestionably the highest of the creatures as measured by the complexity of his functions and structures. A great deal is known about the human organism and about society, but because of the many factors which need to be accounted for, this knowledge does not have the same degree of precision, elegance, and completeness as knowledge of the physical world. The biologist has not yet uncovered the secret of life in a single cell. How much less, then, has the investigator of the human being discovered adequate explanations for the conjoint activity of the myriads of cells that constitute the human organism. Complex almost beyond imagining are the structures of the human nervous system, with its amazing networks of interconnecting fibers from which by some remarkable principle of synthesis comes the coordinated activity of the whole person.

Still more difficult are the problems when one seeks to understand the behavior not just of individual persons but of social groups, in which the complexities of the single organism are compounded many-fold by the interactions between persons.

It is believed by many that the chief difference between the more exact physical sciences and the sciences of man is in degree of complexity, that there is no real difference in kind but only in multiplicity of factors. By this view, the same type of analysis applies to man as to atoms or stars, and it should be possible, in principle, to work out theories of personality and of society on the basis of the fundamental laws of physics and chemistry. It is foolish to introduce special concepts such as mind or consciousness, which are simply names for functions too complicated for currently available explanations. It would be well, proponents of this position say, to regard the sciences of man in the same light as one of the complex physical sciences such as meteorology, where the need to account for the influence of many interacting forces has thus far prevented the development of consistently successful weather prediction. This inadequacy does not prompt one to invoke mysterious weather-forces as special explanations. So it is with the sciences of man, some say; their difficulty and inexactness result solely from their complexity.

The problem of abstraction. It has been emphasized that the natural sciences are defined by the process of measurement, which in turn makes possible classification, causal explanation, and theoretical generalization. Hence, knowledge in natural science is necessarily abstract. It deals only with the metrical aspects of things. When we come to the sciences of man, it is necessary to ask whether or not they also deal in metrical abstractions. To a large extent they clearly do. Social scientists count and name groups of things. Psychologists and economists gather statistics. As far as possible mathematical concepts, which are the ultimate in abstraction, are applied to the formulation of psychological and social laws.

The problem of abstraction in the sciences of man is whether the metrical aspects yield true knowledge of man in his uniqueness. Are persons and societies of persons truly known only in a concrete way? Does the particular organization of functions and powers in the unrepeatable person constitute his essential nature? Does man essentially defy classification and generalization? Those who would answer these questions in the affirmative would usually contend that man can only be known truly in the successive acts of decision in which his own continuing selfhood is fashioned and in the immediate encounter of self with other persons. Human beings can then be truly understood only in a way analogous to the appreciation of a work of art and not by scientific measurement.

It may be granted that there are ways of knowing persons by other than abstractive means. But this is true of everything, and not merely of persons. Every tree is also unique and thus requires appreciative as well as abstractive modes of understanding. Thus the problem of abstraction is one for all knowledge and not only for knowledge of man, although because of the freedom and creativity of human beings the problem in this area may be particularly serious. One may then acknowledge the validity and usefulness of the sciences of man within their proper scope and for their special purposes and admit also the need for other non-scientific approaches to the full understanding of human life.

The problem of bias. The goal of science is to gain knowledge which is free of personal bias. Scientific truth is what the evidence compels one to believe, not what one personally and subjectively wants to believe. One may wish to believe that a certain disease is the direct consequence of evil conduct, but this belief must be abandoned in the face of experimental evidence about its bacterial causes. One may prefer to believe that people with one skin color are more intelligent than those with another, but scientifically the belief cannot be maintained in the face of statistical evidence to the contrary. In the sciences of man the problem of bias arises from the fact that where the object of inquiry is man himself his own interests and prejudices actually influence the evidence by which he seeks to overcome these subjective factors. Evidence is always selected, and to a considerable degree it is possible to cite evidence in support of contrary theories. It is surprisingly easy to find justification, convincing to one's self, for doing what one wants to do. To other people the alleged "reasons" may appear to be only "rationalizations." Again, in analyzing an economic problem two reasearchers favorable to and supported by labor and by management respectively will almost surely emerge with different conclusions, each favoring the interests of the group represented. It is not that there is conscious and deliberate falsification. There are actual differences in perception and in judgment about what constitutes suitable or significant evidence.

Objectivity. It was pointed out in Chapter 18 that the objective and public nature of science consists of the creation of communities of discourse defined by specified sets of verification procedures to which the members of the communities agree. These procedural rules are a matter of human decision and are based upon specific human interests. When the object of inquiry is not man, it is generally possible to find procedural rules upon which all investigators will agree. When man, society, and culture are being studied, such unanimity about verification procedure—about what constitutes relevant evidence—is not readily attained because in such studies individual and group interests are frequently at stake and influence the choice of verification criteria. Hence, in the sciences of man there tend to be a number of schools of thought, each regarding itself as objective and impartial but each in actuality reflecting certain special group or personal biases.

It might be supposed that these biases when recognized could be removed and a fully impartial science established. To a degree this is the case. The operation of special interests can be recognized and corrected for by establishing a modified set of rules of inquiry. The disagreement arises over the question of how far this impartiality can go. On one extreme are those who believe complete objectivity can be attained. On the other extreme are those who believe that human nature has a deeply ingrained self-centeredness which will inevitably color convictions about the procedures of inquiry. Whatever the position held on this point, one thing should be clear—in *all* science the methods of inquiry are influenced by certain human interests and not simply by the nature of the external data. The problem of bias is concerned with the extent to which it is possible to organize inclusive communities of scientific discourse in which the *same* human interests will govern the choice of procedures. It has been suggested here that the difficulty of creating such communities is greater in the study of man than in the study of non-human nature.

The problem of freedom. The most critical problem of the human sciences arises from the fact of human freedom. The worth of scientific knowledge is measured by the accuracy of the predictions which it affords and the completeness of the control which it makes possible. Such prediction and control presuppose invariable causal sequences in which results are strictly determined by antecedent conditions. The question is whether the behavior of human beings is included within this kind of strict causal scheme. Can future human conduct be predicted on the basis of present conditions, or is there a factor of origination which makes complete prediction impossible? Can persons be harnessed and controlled like the forces of non-human nature?

There is no doubt that human beings are to some extent predictable and controllable. Intelligence tests are a reasonably good measure of what can be expected of a student academically. Thorough acquaintance with a person enables one to predict his conduct in various situations with considerable accuracy. The study of cultural patterns is an excellent clue to the probable reactions of groups to specified influences. The question is whether the negative cases, where results fail to confirm predictions, may not be more characteristically human than the cases where expectations are confirmed.

It can be argued that because man is free he is not determined by the past alone but also by the future, and hence that the ordinary scientific analysis of causation, which always looks to the past for explanations, is inapplicable to man. Not only this, but because man alone has true memory, even his use of the past is of a different sort than ordinary causal determination. Thus, conditions and events surrounding a person do not determine his behavior; they merely provide the context within which and the materials out of which he determines his own behavior. Man is not the product of his past; he is the producer of his own future. It is then a contradiction in terms to speak of the "laws" of free human behavior because free action is *sui generis* and not obedient to any generalized rule.

Considerations such as these are taken by some as casting doubt upon the possibility of a true science of man—i.e., a science of classification, causal explanation, and general laws as applied to the uniquely human capacities of freedom, self-transcendence, imagination, etc. The specifically human dimensions of man's behavior are believed to elude the scientific net and to require for their understanding a different set of categories and ways of knowing, as developed chiefly in the realms of history, art, philosophy, and religion. In short, according to this view, the most authentic knowledge of man comes not from the sciences but from the humanistic studies.

The problem of value. It is widely held that the business of science is to describe, not to prescribe, that science deals with facts, not with values—with what is, not with what ought to be. In the study of the non-human world this creates no problem because values and prescriptions, arising from the sense of obligation, are specifically human phenomena. Values first become a problem in the attempt to construct a science of man. Since values are an extremely important factor in human life, can a science which fails to consider them give a true picture of man? There are three types of answers to this question and three corresponding conceptions of the sciences of man. The first and probably most commonly held view is that values occupy a different realm from facts and that values are not the concern of the scientists but of the moralists, philosophers, and theologians. The second answer is that values are completely reducible to physiological hungers and established stimulus-response patterns which can be adequately treated within the framework of ordinary scientific fact. The third answer is that there is a realm of values not wholly reducible to physiological and neural factors and that the sciences of man must deal with these values.

The problem of values is a crucial one in the conduct of human affairs because on it depends the question of how far the resources of scientific inquiry are to be available for directing and coordinating man's choices. The really critical issues of education, indeed, of civilization generally, are questions of values, aims, and goals, on which the light of scientific knowledge is desperately needed. There are indications that scientific investigators of man and society are becoming increasingly concerned with questions of value and that not all of them are inclined to explain away values or to relegate them to other disciplines. The debate on this point still continues. Our intention is merely to call attention to this further problem which is peculiar to the sciences of man, suggesting thereby something of the unique difficulties and opportunities of this area of inquiry. Now we shall consider particular branches of the sciences of man.

Individual Psychology

What is psychology? What sort of knowledge does the science of individual human psychology seek to provide? Originally this study was a branch of philosophy concerned with the first principles of self-moving things. The principle of self-motion was called the "psyche" or soul, and psychology described the nature of the psyche. Scientific human psychology has the same basic aim, namely, to discover the nature of the animating principles of human beings. In short, it is the science of individual human behavior. It seeks to explain why people act as they do, to predict how they will act in the future, and to discover ways of modifying their patterns of conduct. It is evident from this last point that of all the sciences psychology is the most immediately relevant to education, the function of which is to direct the modification of behavior in the light of the best available goals.

In a sense psychology is the one indispensable science. For what is the purpose of human endeavor if not to utilize as completely as possible one's capacities for growth and fulfillment, and what is psychology but the study of how this personal development takes place? Psychology seeks to provide understanding of who a person is, how he came to be what he is, and how he may develop further in the future. There are no questions of more central and universal interest and importance than these. Consequently, there is no subject which in principle is more essential in the study of education.

Subject and object. In modern psychology a sustained effort has been made to be objective. It is for this reason that the very definition of the science has been based upon the concept of behavior. What a person *does* can be objectively described; the mystery of subjective animating principles is avoided. On the same grounds the once-popular method of introspection as a means of internal observation has fallen into disfavor. To be scientific, knowledge must be public, and this is possible only when verification can be made by any competent observer. This requires evidence of an outward and objective kind.

Yet a person is not in essence an object. He is a subject. There is a difference between a *person* and a *thing*. Hence, it is a question whether a scientific procedure which insists on objective observation can yield true knowledge of personality. A person is in certain respects and for given purposes an object. But these objective qualities are shared with things and do not reflect the unique quality of being a person. It would seem to follow that the psychologist must admit as evidence something more than externally observable behavior. He must consult his own immediate and inner experience of himself, constructing therefrom conceptions of personality which by analogy can be employed in the description of the states of being of other persons. Externally observed behavior may serve as a clue to the inner states, indicating which are appropriate to any given situation, but such behavior in itself is not a sufficient basis for the description of the person. An adequate description of a person must rest upon an immediate qualitative understanding of uniquely personal experiences such as hope, fear, love, hate, joy, and anxiety. This requirement imposes conditions which define the competence of the observer in psychological investigation. Verification within the scientific community can be made only by competent observers who are willing and able to employ the procedures and to understand the concepts by which the knowledge to be tested is defined. In psychological inquiry any given fact about a person can only be verified by those who in imagination or in actuality have personally experienced that fact in themselves. For example, only those who in their own being know love or shame can verify psychological hypotheses based upon such concepts.

The preceding reflections illustrate an important conclusion about knowledge in general, namely, that the conditions for competence as an observer become more exacting as one passes from the study of the physical world up through the study of living things, to the study of man. *Every* man can, in principle, undertake the measurement operations of the natural sciences since these reflect qualities only of a subhuman order. In the human realm, on the other hand, the requisite verifications can be made only by those who have themselves attained such a level of personal fulfillment as in some sense to embody the personal qualities to be verified. Since there may be many who have no such attainments, the communities of discourse about man may be considerably more limited than in the natural sciences. This may also provide an explanation for the existence of many different schools of thought in psychology in contrast to the considerable unity of the natural sciences.

Individual and statistic. Akin to the problem of subject and object in psychology is the question whether scientific knowledge of man can and should be of the individual in all his particularity or merely of a statistical nature. Is the psychologist supposed to study the general laws of human behavior or the behavior of particular individuals? In practice psychologists answer the question both ways. Some studies are directed to the development of general theories of human behavior. Others are concerned with predicting individual behavior. For instance, the individual has been of central interest in clinical psychology, where the case study is used and where the primary objective is to render practical assistance in meeting individual problems. In rendering such assistance the psychologist does, of course, make use of the general principles of his science, but his focus is the unique person rather than the formulation of general laws. The point of special philosophic interest is that in the insistence on the scientific validity of a truly individual psychology a new dimension is introduced into scientific methodology and a bridge is built between natural science and the humanistic disciplines such as history and the arts, which are necessarily and essentially particularistic. To admit the study of the unique personality and the explanation and prediction of his unique behavior patterns to the realm of scientific psychology is to lend support to a concrete conception of truth and reality which has always been affirmed in art, religion, and letters but which has in modern times been threatened by the exclusively abstract, mathematical ideals of natural science.

Learning. One of the central concerns of psychology is the study of learning. This is the process whereby the living organism is able to conserve and make later use of its experiences. Because of learning, past events participated in by a person have continuing and cumulative relevance in influencing his present and future patterns of behavior. There are many different psychological theories of learning which provide alternative conceptual schemes and causal relationships to describe the process. Underlying every theory is one fundamental idea—namely, that learning cannot be understood as acquisition, but only as *becoming*. To learn is not to acquire skill or knowledge, as a truck takes on a load of coal. To learn is to undergo changes in one's whole being: skill and knowledge are manifestations of the nature of the person, who has become competent in certain ways through earlier activities.

Thus learning is a process of modifying personality; one has only truly learned something if it has become part of his very being. Furthermore, behavior is a function of the whole organism. A person does not play the piano merely with his fingers; such a skill is a coordinated activity of the whole person. Now learning takes place by virtue of the coordinating mechanisms (chiefly nervous systems) which make the living entity an organic whole. As pointed out in the last chapter, organisms also manifest a principle of conservation of form, or of persistence of functional capacities. But learning requires just such functional persistence or conservation.

One additional factor needs to be noted. There can be no learning for which the organism is not by maturation structurally prepared. For example, there can be no coordinated movement without the development of the requisite nerve structure. Summing up, then, learning may be broadly understood as modification, by experience, of the whole organism in ways for which there is adequate structural foundation, with resulting persistence of functional capacity so that the behavior produced in the original learning situation may by appropriate cues be reproduced at later times.

Motivation. Another basic concern in psychology is the problem of motivation, or the dynamic of human behavior. If one takes a process view of the nature of things rather than a substance view, change is regarded as inherent in existence and motivation is interpreted as the subjective aspect of the ceaseless tendency-to-become. Motivation may also be considered as the counterpart, in the human realm, of the concept of energy in physical science. Motivation is the manifestation of the special energy forms of living systems.

But what determines the direction of motivation? A motive is not merely a general impulse. It is, in developed forms, a selective or directed striving. In the human sphere this leads at once to the problem of values. A human value-scheme is revealed in the system of operative motives. One most highly values behavior for which he has maximum motivation. Thus the psychology of motivation involves also a study in human values. Because of this, psychology cannot avoid the problem of values, as many psychologists have sought to do. Furthermore, philosophical questions about the status of values need to be raised in connection with motivation. Are motives solely an expression of physiological need? Do they indicate the existence of an immanent principle of preference within organic processes? Are they a reflection of a realm of values independent of and prior to but effective in the material embodiment of things? Do they have any relation to the will and purpose of a deity? Such questions illustrate the way in which psychological inquiry leads inescapably to basic problems in metaphysics and value theory as well as in the theory of knowledge. These questions are discussed at some length in Part IV.

Conscious and unconscious. The development of a distinction between the conscious and unconscious or subconscious aspects of the psyche is another good example of the creation, from within a special science, of a fundamental concept of considerable importance for the general outlook of modern man. Prior to the rise of depth psychology mental processes were assumed to consist entirely of perceptions, feeling states, and rational functions. The discovery of the unconscious vastly expanded the realm of mind to include hidden impulses, invisible mechanisms, and irrational processes.

At an earlier time human behavior which could not be explained by conscious mind was attributed to various extra-human occult powers—demons, spirits, angels, and the like. The concept of the unconscious brought these mysterious phenomena within the scope of human life, thus establishing the focus of responsibility within man and greatly deepening and widening the view of human nature. According to the new conception, there is a great reservoir of unconscious activity of which conscious mentality gives only partial, ambiguous, and paradoxical indications. But in modern psychology this realm of the unconscious is not merely pointed out and named. Methods have also been devised to chart the unconscious by a careful reading of the signs sent up into consciousness. By these means phenomena formerly considered mysterious and beyond human scrutiny and control have been brought within the purview of scientific understanding. The significance of these developments for the general outlook of modern man on the nature of mind and spirit is enormous.

Normal and abnormal. A final illustration of the special character of psychological knowledge is the distinction between normal and abnormal behavior. In the physical sciences such a distinction would not be useful. Events occur as they do, and it is the task of the scientist to describe them. In human affairs, on the other hand, some kinds of behavior are considered normal and other kinds abnormal. Everything depends, of course, on what is meant by normality. Some standard of reference is presupposed. This standard may, for example, be an average, in which case abnormality means deviation from the average. Again, the standard may be one of law or tradition, which may be far from average behavior. Normality in this case is adherence to the tradition. Or finally, the standard may be an ideal, with normality measured by approximation to this goal.

The distinction of normal and abnormal once more introduces the problem of values into the sciences of man. Can psychology remain a purely descriptive science, or should it have also a *normative* function? Is it within the psychologist's province to make judgments about the standards chosen to measure normality? Can he, as a scientist, say "This behavior pattern is good; that pattern is bad. This is what persons ought to become; that aim should be avoided?" These are crucial questions for the educator. They are questions of the moral and ethical relevance of the sciences of man. Upon the answers depends the significance of psychology and the other human sciences for the guidance of personal development.

The Sciences of Society

The study of psychology leads inevitably to the study of society. Personality and society are correlative realities. There can be no persons apart from a social context, and society is nothing apart from its constituent members. "The individual" and "society" are both abstractions from the concrete reality "persons-in-association." Associations are an aspect of what a person is, and the quality of individuals determines the character of their associations. Indissoluble though the connection of person and society may be, it is still possible and useful to distinguish between the study of the individual person (in psychology) and the scientific study of society. Society is more than the sum of its member persons. The purpose of the sciences of society, including such fields as anthropology, sociology, social psychology, political science, and economics, is to make inquiry into the behavior of groups of persons and into their modes of association.

Social organization. One important task of the social sciences is to describe the actual forms of social organization. It is characteristic of the human species that these forms are extremely varied. Man is not restricted, as lower creatures are, to a few standard, largely instinctive modes of association. The structure of human society is determined by human interest and choice, which, because man has freedom and imagination, have extraordinary range and scope. The study of the social sciences is of great value in delivering the student from a constricted outlook on the social order. He comes to see that his own familiar forms of social relatedness are not the only possible ones, and that there are innumerable other interesting and viable modes of association.

Institutions. An extremely important part of the description of social organization is the analysis of institutions. A social institution is a relatively permanent, established, formal pattern of social organization. Some forms of association are temporary and informal, depending upon the special interests and circumstances of particular persons. By contrast, institutions—such as the family, church, state, and school—are abiding forms of association which persist though persons come and go. The study of social institutions gives insight into the elements of stability within the social order. One objective of all scientific inquiry is to discover uniformities and regularities within the flux of things. The careful identification of social institutions helps to fulfill this objective in the sciences of society.

Social disorganization. Inquiry into social organization leads also to the study of social disorganization. Crime, poverty, war, class strife, and the like are evidences of the failure of social relationships and institutions. Each concept of disorganization always implies a corresponding concept of social organization.

Values and social organization. The problem of values inevitably arises in connection with the study of social organization. The first lesson of social science is that one's own social order is not the only possible one. But does this mean that all societies are equally good? Can the social scientist give any help with the crucial problem of deciding between alternative systems of social organization? He certainly can assist by predicting the consequences of each system, and this will provide a basis for decision if the values of the respective consequences are agreed upon. But can social science appraise the intrinsic value of systems, and not merely their consequences? Most social scientists would reply in the negative. Some investigators, however, believe they can relate social organization to fundamental and universal human characteristics and derive therefrom certain reliable standards of judgment about the relative values of different forms of association. For example, if man is in his essential nature free, any social arrangement which negates freedom is evil. Again, if man has an intrinsic need to give and receive love, associations which promote love are good and those which lead to personal isolation and estrangement are evil.

The study of the social sciences leads to a better understanding of the complexity and variety of man's social arrangements and to a corresponding appreciation of ways of life different from one's own. But it would seem unsatisfactory to rest content with these gains. One can argue that the well-educated person should be able to evaluate his own and other societies and to promote improvements on the basis of such intelligent evaluations. From this viewpoint it is to be hoped that social scientists will seek even more diligently to explore their disciplines from the standpoint of basic human values.

Social change. If knowledge of social organization is to be effective in social reconstruction, it is necessary to understand how change takes place in the social order. Though the modes of human organization are determined by man himself and are not given by nature, it does not follow that changes in social arrangements can be effected at will. The main function of social organization is to give permanence, continuity, and stability to group life, and it is just these virtues which make institutions, customs, and laws resistant to modification. Knowledge of social change suggests ways of achieving the desired alterations. On the other hand, there may be kinds of change which are not desired and need to be checked. Factors such as population growth or movement, technical advances, and discovery or exhaustion of natural resources can produce serious social dislocations. Scientific analysis of the casual basis for such changes can help to prevent or to modify the undesired effects.

A particularly significant factor in social change is education itself. One type of educational program will favor conformity to the existing order. Another type will encourage new forms of association. Social science ought accordingly to be an important guide to educational policy. Given certain social goals and the principles of social change, it should be possible to fashion the educational system most conducive to those goals.

Culture. One of the central ideas of the sciences of society—particularly anthropology—is the concept of *culture*. This term refers to all the material things, institutional structures, and symbolic devices which have been contrived by man rather than given directly by nature. Culture represents what man has made from the material, social, and mental resources provided. Tools, dwellings, clothing, business organizations, political parties, languages, art, religions—all of these belong to culture. They are results of man's efforts to "improve" nature. It is by their cultures that societies are characterized and distinguished from one another. Though cultural patterns may change, they do so more slowly than individuals and hence provide a basis for a degree of continuity and permanence. This cultural continuity is made possible through education.

The idea of culture is of primary importance because it emphasizes the easily forgotten truth that the achievements of man are not provided by nature, like air and water, digestive systems and brains. The products of culture are human creations, results of generations of patient effort; they are society's accumulated store of costly experience. New generations readily accept the cultural treasure, unmindful of the price exacted in winning it and of the continued exertions required to maintain and improve it. A due appreciation of the fact that culture is an improvement on nature is essential to the development of a sense of responsibility for the preservation and enhancement of civilization. The educated person will not take culture for granted, as a natural and unalienable right. He will consider it as a precious heritage, a legacy from his forebears, of which he is to be a wise trustee and executor.

Politics. It has been said that man is a political animal. As such he organizes cities, states, and nations for the conjoint pursuit of common ends. Three basic ideas emerge from the study of political organization.

The suprapersonal. The first is that the political community is suprapersonal. It is not limited to personal face-to-face associations, and it is defined by functions and offices which are not attached to or the prerogative of any particular individuals. A recognition of this reality of political life is a useful corrective to excessive subjectivism or individualism in conceiving of human affairs.

Law. The second basic idea is that of law. Laws are the tacit or explicit rules whereby the suprapersonal or public functions and offices are defined. One of the crucial disputed issues of political science concerns the source and justification of law. Is it arbitrary social convention, dictated solely by considerations of convenience and expediency, or is there a natural law, discoverable by reason as basic rules of right and obligation, or does law ultimately derive from the will of a supernatural being? A profound inquiry into the problems of political life thus leads inevitably to the ultimate philosophic problems of the nature and status of value—of the good, the right, the ideal, of the normative as well as the descriptive aspects of human society.

Power. A third basic problem in the science of politics is that of power. No study yields so clear a sense of realism as politics. Human arrangements are not brought into being merely by taking thought, but only by the exercise of power. Politics is thus the science of the possible in human association. Idealists may construct utopian schemes, but these blueprints do not enter the sphere of politics until the actual power structures which make the ideals possible are demonstrated. Significant political theories always result from strict and thorough consideration of the sources and application of power.

Economics. Another concern of the sciences of society is economic organization. What special contribution does this study make to the development of an educated person? An obvious answer would be that economic knowledge can help one to gain and use wisely material things. But such a reply does not fully reveal the essential nature of economics, the subject matter of which can be analyzed into three components.

Goods. First, economics involves goods, i.e., entities regarded as valuable and desirable. Usually only material goods are considered, but there is no reason why the economy of non-material goods such as time, thought, and affection cannot also be studied. Since economics deals with goods, it is obvious that the question of values must be raised. What *is* the good? What is desirable? What is truly valuable? Economists generally avoid these questions by restricting their inquiries to what people actually do want, but it is apparent that even such purely empirical inquiries point to the deeper questions about values.

Scarcity. The second feature of economics is that it is concerned with goods which are *limited in availability*. There is no economic problem connected with goods such as air so long as the supply is relatively limitless in comparison with the demand. The economic problem arises only when there is a tension between available resources of a good and the demand for it. The study of economics leads to an understanding of the domain of finite goods. The problems are particularly acute because of the fact that human desires are essentially boundless. Man's imagination and self-transcendence make him dissatisfied with finite goods. In this sense the basis for economic problems is man's spirituality—his intimation of and inclination for the infinite. The study of economics should serve to give educated persons a vivid sense of the finite bounds within which their infinite longings must find partial satisfaction.

Distribution. The third characteristic of economics follows from the first two. Economics is the science of allocation or distribution of goods which are scarce or limited relative to the demand. It is the problem of distribution which makes economics a *social* science. The system of social organization becomes of crucial importance for allocating goods. The relevance of politics to distribution is also evident since laws and power structures are necessary for effecting the necessary allocations.

Thus the study of economics yields basic insights into such problems as the nature of values, the correlation of finite and infinite in human life, and the principles of social organization. The sciences of society are, in fact, closely interrelated. The problems of one branch or discipline lead ultimately to the problems of all the others. The above paragraphs illustrate something of the diversity of concerns and concepts in the sciences of man and the common themes which emerge from a philosophic consideration of the several disciplines.

History

UNLIKE MANY of the newer sciences, history has long occupied an important place in the realms of man's knowledge and inquiry. Yet it cannot be said that the content and methods of historical study are established beyond question. Like philosophy, history has been a parent discipline from which many special fields of study have sprung. The very comprehensiveness and richness of history make its nature a problem.

The Scope of History

Four views of what history includes can be distinguished.

Past events. History is concerned with everything that has happened. Clearly the domain of history is the past. Whatever has occurred belongs to history. It is commonly said of anything which is settled, concluded, finished, "That is history now." The "present" is a dividing line between the two great domains of being, the past and the future. Of the two, only the past is secure and definite. The future is but a phantom, a question mark. History, then, is the realm of determinate reality, of unchanging and unchangeable truth. History is pure, incontrovertible fact. No future can upset history, for what has taken place is fixed, final, and irretrievably so.

It should be noted that according to this view, history is simply all past events, and not knowledge about those past events. Thus history is considered as an object of knowledge, as the stars would be for astronomy, and not as that knowledge itself. The extreme inclusiveness and comprehensiveness of this view of history should also be noted. There is nothing in heaven or earth, nothing in all time past, which does not fall within the province of history thus defined. It is just this comprehensiveness which needs to be called into question if history as a subject of study is to have any clear meaning, for by this broad definition all knowledge except knowledge of the future (and can one really have that?) is knowledge of history.

Past human events. One way of limiting the scope of history is to restrict it to past *human* events. According to this definition, not everything that has happened is history; only those events which pertain to man are within its province. It would then not be appropriate to speak of the "history of nature." To be sure, there have been important past developments in non-human nature: stars and planets have come into being by a well-defined sequence of events. Life has arisen on earth and the vast complexes of animal and plant forms have emerged. But history proper does not begin until man arrives on the scene. History is by definition the sum of past human happenings.

Record of the past. Both of the preceding conceptions suffer from the difficulty that there is no possible way of knowing everything that has happened, either in general or, more particularly, to man. History defined as past events is to a considerable degree a realm of the unknowable. To avoid this problem history may be defined as the *record* of what happened in the past (or, alternatively, of what happened to man). A record is the means whereby the past is brought forward into the present. It represents the knowable part of past events. Obviously without this link between past and present the past would remain forever obscure.

The records of the past may be of many sorts. They may be written accounts of what happened or they may consist only of the memories of persons who witnessed them. Deposits of tools, ornaments, and clothing unearthed by an archaeologist constitute important records of a bygone age. The sedimentary layers studied by geologists, together with fossil remains, bear witness to the events of earth's history and the story of living things.

It could, of course, be argued that the present state of the whole universe is a complete and perfect record of the past and that in principle it is possible to calculate backward from the present condition of things to the state of things at any previous time. This presupposes a rigid determinism, together with knowledge of the invariable laws of determination. This assumption is not necessarily valid. It may well be that for any given state of things any of a number of antecedent conditions could be the cause. Furthermore, if really new things appear in the course of time, they cannot be considered as records of the past but rather as intimations of the structure of creativity (in whatever manner it may be conceived, whether human or divine, immanent or transcendent).

But quite apart from these metaphysical problems, there is the question of the quality of a record. A record is good insofar as it fully and faithfully preserves a past event in its original form. A poor record gives a partial and distorted representation. Thus, a clever criminal seeks to leave a poor record of his crime, and the reading of his record requires an expert and imaginative reconstruction of the event from the merest scraps of evidence. Skillful criminals aim to produce bad history. By way of contrast, modern techniques of sound and motion picture reproduction afford excellent historical records, superior in completeness and accuracy to the more familiar written record.

Considerations of record quality make it clear why history cannot be considered merely as the persistence of the past as cause into the present as effect. A true historical record is a *direct* representation of the past, and not merely a set of data from which, by a complicated process of inference, one might reconstruct the past.

Human records of the past. Instead of including in the definition of history all records of the past, the scope of history may be restricted to include only those records which man himself has made to insure the memory of the past. According to this definition, neither the artifacts found by the archaeologist nor the geologist's layers and fossils would ordinarily constitute history. A deposit of artifacts would, of course, be history by this definition if they were deliberately placed as a record of the civilization, as in so-called "time capsules." So also an exhibit of rocks or of plant forms, intended to memorialize the natural setting of a period, would be history in the present sense. Included also would be written and pictorial histories. History as a deliberate record of life and times is unique to the human species and reflects the rise of self-consciousness and a sense of the meaning of life beyond the mere sequence of events. From this standpoint also it becomes possible to speak of the "prehistoric" as the time from which no deliberate human records are now available.

History as Interpretation

The four views about the scope of history are successively more restricted, moving from the all-inclusive conception of "what happened" to the much more limited conception of "man's record of what happened." It is especially important to note that in passing from all events to a *record* of events a process of selection occurs. It is clearly impossible to make a complete record of all that has happened. The history-maker must select for his record those events and aspects of events which he regards as significant. All recorded history is thus an *interpretation* of past events, the nature of the interpretation being guided by the historian's evaluation of what is important. Furthermore, much history is not an original record but a re-telling of the story recorded by others. An ordinary history textbook, for example, is usually not a firsthand account of what the author has witnessed in his time, but a selection, arrangement, and interpretation of what others have recorded.

That is to say, it is a secondary, tertiary, or even more remote source rather than a primary one. But whether a rocord is firsthand or secondhand, it is necessarily colored by the historian's conception of significance, by his general view of the world, and by the categories he uses to organize his experience. In the following paragraphs some of the more important alternative interpretive schemes employed by historians will be noted.

Spectator's chronicle. The historian observes and records what actually occurs, as observable to a spectator. No event is to be preferred to any other; all happenings are on one level. History is a chronicle of events. Though a complete history is unattainable, an effort should be made to collect as much such neutral data as possible.

Psychology. Events have their meaning in psychological terms. Feelings, attitudes, and motives are the clue to history. One understands the past by explaining why people behaved in certain ways rather than by merely reporting their activities. The historian's narrative ought then to include a sympathetic portrayal of the inner life of man as it can be inferred from observed behavior or known by direct personal witness.

Great men. History is the story of great men and the ideas and acts for which they were responsible. Changes take place only because there are leaders, and history is concerned with changing times. There will be different estimates about which men are to be accounted great; mere popularity should not be the test. Perhaps the most satisfactory measure of historical greatness would be the extent of influence exercised, i.e., the amount and permanence of changes traceable to a given man.

The common man. The center of the historian's interest should be the common man. Great men are only great by courtesy of the common man. It is through a portrayal of average people that the true nature of human life can best be depicted. The historian's task is to bring to light those typical lives and everyday events which but for him would be lost to human memory.

Culture. The clue to history is culture. The truly significant facts about people and times are the languages, institutions, customs, and belief systems which constitute their culture. In these human creations are reflected the real character of life, the interests and capacities of the people, the motives and achievements of both the famous and the obscure.

Economics. The story of man is intelligible only in the light of the laws of production and distribution of material goods. Economic laws determine human behavior. The economic system governs social organization and culture patterns. The function of history is simply to illustrate the laws of economic life.

Politics. History is primarily an account of the balance and imbalance of political power. Significant events are those which reveal most clearly the interplay of opposing and cooperating forces in society. Parties, elections, laws, diplomacy—such categories as these are the most fruitful for an intelligent view of the past.

War. The truly decisive events of history have been the wars. In these life-and-death struggles the ultimate issues are at stake. War is the means of actually proving which ways of life are able to survive and which are doomed to oblivion. If one knows about wars and the opposing convictions which underlay them, he has a key to the most crucial factors in human life.

Morals. Man is essentially a moral creature, in that he makes judgments of right and wrong. Hence the test of significance in history is a moral one. Man's life is a ceaseless struggle between the forces of good and evil. The historian's task is to present that drama as clearly as possible, using his own moral insights to assess the good and evil in each factor and event.

Theology. A final set of categories for interpreting the past is the theological or spiritual one. History is an account of man's spiritual pilgrimage. It is the record of the perennial search of man for God or of God for man. Human events can be comprehended only within the context of the divine plan for creation and from the standpoint of the eternal.

The Nature of History

Objectivity and subjectivity. The previous discussions of scope and interpretation supply a basis for answering the question about objectivity and subjectivity in historical knowledge. If history means what happened, then it is pure objective fact and not knowledge at all. Historical knowledge requires records and interpretations, and these reflect the standards of value and schemes of orientation by which the historian decides what is significant and what is not. Since values and orientations vary from person to person, historical knowledge will vary correspondingly. The historian's account is, therefore, never wholly objective. It reveals not only something about what happened, but also something about the outlook of the historian himself. The latter aspect is the inescapable factor of subjectivity in historical knowledge.

But equally inescapable is the objective factor. There can be no such thing as purely subjective history. Though the historian must interpret the past, it is not his function to construct it. He is not called upon to create out of his imagination events that never occurred. It is his task merely to select from what actually occurred those events and aspects of events which he believes are significant. He is not a writer of fiction but an interpreter of fact. Myths, fairy tales, and legends are largely subjective and are not to be accounted as history. Historical novels are imaginative creations which make use of historical events to lend concreteness and credibility, but they are not history, properly speaking.

Is all history equally subjective or objective, or are some modes of interpretation more subjective or objective than others? There is a sense in which for all true history (as distinguished from fiction) equality prevails in this respect. Every selection of facts or aspects is a choice, and this act of choice—whatever its character—introduces subjectivity into history to the same degree for all interpretations. On the other hand, there are some types of interpretive schemes which are in a different sense more objective than others. One measure of objectivity would be the degree of acceptance of a given interpretive orientation. For example, a spectator's chronicle would win the assent of virtually everyone; all could agree that the reported events did occur, though they might not consider such an account *good* history. Economic, political, or psychological interpretations would be less universally acceptable, and moral or theological orientations would be still more limited in number of adherents. In this sense subjectivity can be taken to mean the degree of privacy or of specialization of the chosen scheme of interpretation. So defined, some kinds of historical knowledge are more subjective or objective than others.

Is history a science? There is a long-standing and continuing debate over the question of whether or not history is a science. The answer depends upon one's view of history and of science respectively. If all well-established factual knowledge is regarded as scientific, then objective history (as defined immediately above) is scientific. The facts of history are actually more settled than the theories of science. What has happened is fixed and unalterable forever, while theories may be contradicted by future evidence. History thus has a certitude that even the exact sciences do not claim. By the same token, however, it can be said that history is not science, since science is concerned with prediction, while history deals only with the settled past.

The major point of difference between history and science as ordinarily understood is that the former is concerned with concrete events in their singularity, while the goal of the latter is abstraction and generalization. Even on this point there are differences of opinion. Some who call themselves historians use the record of the past as data for making sweeping generalizations about the course of human affairs—about the rise and decline of civilizations, the influence of geography and climate, the effects of population growth, and the like. In this way they seek to make history a theoretical social science. It would seem that in so doing they really depart from history, for the particular happenings that constitute the past are lost from view and replaced by laws or principles which presumably hold for events in general. The natural scientist in the last analysis is not concerned with the particular happenings which suggested his generalizations but only with the principles of which the individual events are illustrations. History which loses the particular event in the generalization is no longer history. It is of the essence of history to record and interpret the unrepeatable. Science deals with repetition. The laws of science call for verification, i.e., testing by new instances. There can be no such verification in history. What happened happened, and no future event can confirm or disconfirm the past.

Science as history. As pointed out in Chapter 18, one way of understanding science is as a historical movement. The student of science can gain insight into the problems and methods of the scientist by acquainting himself with some of the classic experiments and with earlier attempts at theoretical formulation. By reliving in imagination the crucial events of scientific history, the student can secure a vivid and concrete picture of the struggle for scientific truth such as could never result from learning the established principles and theories.

In a second sense also science is history. One speaks of "natural history" as a description of natural processes in their temporal sequences. For example, geology may be regarded as the history of the earth, an account of how this planet was born and developed, and of the path by which its present structures came into being. Anthropology as the natural history of human beings contains a description of the successive stages in the development of man and his culture. Yet it can be argued that such scientific natural history is no true history but only quasi-historical, because its objective is causal explanation and understanding of general processes rather than interpretation of any particular sequence of past events.

A third aspect of science as history is found in clinical studies. Here the center of interest is presumably the individual. The analysis is made by constructing a "personal history," which becomes the basis for a case study. The person and his problems are to be understood in the light of the particular factors which have operated in his past. But once more it needs to be asked whether this is not really quasi-history, since the purpose is not to understand past events in themselves but solely to explain present conditions and to give guidance for the future.

History as an art. In Chapter 24 the nature of the arts will be treated. To anticipate what will be more fully discussed there, it can be stated that art, in contrast with science, is a realm of the particular rather than the general, of the concrete rather than the abstract, of the unique rather than the repeatable. With respect to these contrasts it is clear from what has been said above that history is more like art than like science. The historian has an interest in individuals and in specific events of the past that is similar to the artist's concern for the esthetic object.

Furthermore, both the artist and the historian are interpreters. Both must select from the boundless wealth of available materials those which they regard as most significant. The scientist, too, is an interpreter, but his rules and categories are more limited and more strictly defined than those of the artist or historian. Good history is a vivid and compelling *picture* of selected past events. The effectiveness of the account is in proportion to the clarity and aptness of the interpretive scheme employed, by which significant aspects are highlighted and less significant ones are relegated to the background.

Yet history is not identical with art. The artist has a freedom of imaginative construction which is not the historian's right. The historian tells a story, and he should relate it with imagination and interpretive skill, but he still must produce fact rather than fiction. In his evaluation of what is significant he will necessarily and properly introduce subjective factors, but the objective structure of the events which he describes imposes strict limitations on his subjectivity. The artist's materials also somewhat limit his subjectivity but far less than in the case of the historian. In fact, history clearly lies between natural science and art in respect to the balance of objective and subjective factors.

In one other major respect history differs from art. It is of the essence of history to represent the past. There is no such concern in art. Art is essentially timeless. There are, of course, temporal elements in the arts, as in music, dance, drama, and poetry. But these elements are matters of formal structure and are not tied to any particular moments in the historical sequence. History, on the other hand, is not an expression of formal time relationships but of occurrences in a real stream of time, each of whose moments only once and irrevocably, in a flash of presentness, passes from the womb of the future to the everlasting rest of the past.

Historical method. How does the historian proceed? What methods are employed in historical study? The first essential of historical method is the collection of records of the past. This might appear at first sight as a straightforward task, but such is not so. Many types of records are available. Some provide direct and relatively complete evidence. Others are mere traces of past events from which inferences at best tenuous and speculative can be made. Actually everything that now exists is a record of the past, but it is difficult or impossible to read cause-effect sequences backward accurately and thus reconstruct the past from the present. The able historian must sift the evidence so as to distinguish the useful and relevant from the relatively insignificant. The most relevant material will not always announce itself as such. On the face of things, for example, the fall of Rome was the result of barbarian invasions, but a perceptive historian would not be satisfied only with an account of such obvious factors. He would probably be even more concerned with certain basic economic, social, and religious conditions in the ancient world which underlay the decay of the empire.

But how does the historian decide what is significant? The answer to this question brings in the second essential of historical method, namely, the need for a point of view, value system, or interpretive scheme. History will be an incoherent, haphazard heap of data apart from the application of a well-developed total world view. The historian cannot even begin his work of assembling the records of the past—much less of rendering an interesting and persuasive account of it—unless he brings to bear a fundamental value orientation. And how does he arrive at the right scheme? That question is hard to answer. It may well be that there is no one right system, or that if there is, no one has yet fully discovered it. The total outlook one does adopt is derived from the whole complex of influences—social, intellectual, religious, biological—which have helped to make one the person he is. It is the view of things which most convincingly coordinates and makes sense out of the manifold experiences of his own life.

A third essential of good historical method is that the historian be aware of his scheme of values and that he recognize and take account of the corresponding presuppositions of others. Only by so doing can he rise above sheer subjectivity and attain a kind of objectivity. True objectivity does not mean the absence of a system of interpretive values. Any historian who thinks he has achieved an objectivity which avoids all presuppositions thereby illustrates his own subjectivity. True objectivity comes from understanding the basic value premises of oneself and of others. Another way of stating this is to insist that good historical method requires a *critical* outlook, an explicit awareness and statement of the criteria used in selecting and evaluating the records of the past.

The critical approach also governs the historian's use of sources. Primary sources are original records. Secondary sources are interpretations of primary sources and cannot safely be used without a critical awareness of the interpreter's orientation. But it must be recognized that primary sources are also selective and interpretive in character and must accordingly be critically scrutinized. The difference in historical value between primary and secondary sources is simply that in using the latter the subjective element is compounded and the task of criticism becomes more complex.

The historical outlook. History is not just for historians nor is it only the formal study called by that name. There is a historical outlook which is deeply ingrained in the consciousness of modern man and which exerts a profound influence on his feeling and conduct. The essence of this outlook is the conviction that the explanation of any situation or event is to be found by tracing the temporal sequence leading up to it. When farmers' incomes drop sharply in a given year, modern man does not explain the fact by reference to fate, or bad luck, or the operation of demons. Rather, he seeks for a sequence of prior relevant events such as bad weather, industrial unemployment, or the loss of government subsidies. For contemporary man the historical has become the basic mode of explanation, both in everyday affairs and in the sciences. The question "Why?" is considered the same as the question "How?" An account of the origin and development of anything is then the only satisfactory explanation of it.

Some would wish to transcend the historical outlook by arguing that description is not a true explanation. Valuable though such descriptions may be, it is said, they are themselves in need of explanation by invariant or eternal principles. The formulation of scientific generalizations moves one step in this direction beyond the mere relating of particular temporal sequences. The use of metaphysical or theological explanations, whereby an Ultimate Reality or Creative Mind is offered as the final ground of all events, reflects the full absorption of the historical into the supra-historical.

Meaning in history. Is it possible to see any meaning in history? If history were a succession of absolutely unrelated, singular, unique events, then the answer would be no. History has meaning only to the extent that what happens can be seen as some kind of order or pattern. Meaning is connectedness, lawfulness, regularity, structure. When a war breaks out, the event has meaning because it is related to certain prior events, such as political rivalries, cultural conflicts, or economic dislocations, but not to most other events such as a recent eclipse of the sun or the publication of a new encyclopedia.

The meaning which the historian perceives in history is implicit in his principles of interpretation. The historian who presents merely a chronicle denies meaning because he fails to discern any connection between events. A psychological interpretation is based on the belief that events are related to each other by the laws of psychology, e.g. that Nazism was in part a result of Hitler's earlier repressed aggressions. A great-man theory holds that the meaning of a series of events can be found in their connection with a dominant historical personality. According to a common-man interpretation, a delineation of the character of the average person of an age is the best key to the connection between the events of that age. Similarly, the meaning of history may be discovered in cultural, economic, political, military, moral, theological, or other terms. In each case the meaning is defined by the principles which bring order out of the otherwise confused and disconnected series of happenings.

It is not being suggested that history has only one kind of meaning. Several interpretive schemes may be simultaneously applicable. The outcome of an election can be understood in psychological, cultural, and moral as well as in political terms. Historical meaning is complex because there are many kinds of order which events may be seen to exemplify. But though there are many meanings, all may not be equally adequate or significant. For understanding the meaning of the scientific movement military and political categories would not be as useful as cultural and economic ones. Church history would obviously require moral and theological concepts. Despite the multiplicity of meaning systems, many historians tend to choose one scheme as more basic than the rest and to read all events in the light of that system. The economic determinist sees all events fundamentally as illustrating the laws of material production and use, and moral, psychological, and other factors as derivative from the economic meanings. The Christian regards all history as the drama of salvation, economic and cultural movements being the relatively superficial aspects of a basically theological plot.

History and human nature. The making of history may be regarded as one of the marks of man's essential nature and uniqueness. Human beings do not merely exist in time; they also have the spiritual capacity to stand above time and record their passage through it. History is possible only because man has the power to remember the past as past and the imagination to project himself into a past that was never his own. Human beings only realize their selfhood through history, for the very essence of the self is the power to transcend the self in time. Human existence also has meaning only through the historical consciousness, for by definition meaning is the perception of order and connection of events. Furthermore, history is the clue to human freedom. Man is free in that he is capable of determining his own behavior, and this is possible only because the person can transcend himself in time, i.e., reflect on the past sources and future consequences of his acts and this reflection is the essence of historical understanding, of seeing events as personally significant.

History and truth. Does historical knowledge give insight into the true nature of things? Is it as reliable as knowledge in the sciences? Perhaps the best answer is that historical knowledge does yield truth, but of a somewhat different kind from that of the natural sciences. Historical knowledge embraces the particular and unique as well as the generalized and abstract qualities of things. By its interpretive schemes it also integrates value factors into knowledge. History thus provides true insights into the nature of things as perceived within the context of human significance. Truth in history is thus broader in scope and more personal in reference than the abstract metrical truth of natural science. The communities of historical discourse are likely to be correspondingly smaller and more varied than those that give assent to natural science propositions. Each community of historical discourse represents a dominant system of interpretation which is convincing to its members. Such truth, as persuasive meaning of the course of events, would seem to provide important clues to the real nature of things.

The Study of History

We turn now to a discussion of the question, "Why study history?" What part should historical knowledge play in the process of education?

A negative view. The study of history is a waste of time and should accordingly be avoided. Much of man's backwardness has come from looking backward instead of forward. The past is dead and gone. Only the idle and the curious will have any interest in seeking to resurrect it. A person ought to live in the present and plan for the future. If the past has been evil, it cannot be mended by taking further notice of it; the mistakes are irrevocable, and dwelling upon them is morbid. If the past has been good, recollection of it breeds a nostalgic conservatism and robs the present and future of the attention they alone deserve.

This is an age of science, and scientific knowledge is cumulative. Hence what we now know contains the distillation of the past experience of the race, summarized, organized, and criticized so as to eliminate former errors and confusions. The study of history transports one back into the times of relative ignorance and superstition. What possible value is there in reliving in imagination the gropings and false turnings of an earlier time? Why not rather keep attention focused on what we now securely know, and dedicate ourselves to the task of using this hard-won knowledge in the creation of a still better future?

Largely because of science, man now possesses the key to progress. The world today is better than the world of yesterday or the day before. To study history, therefore, is to reflect on what is inferior. This is foolish when one has the better present as an available subject for study. The student should be exposed only to the very best that is known, and in a world of progress this means that the study of the past should be abolished.

Furthermore, it is idle to think that the past can really be understood. The feeling and flavor of bygone times cannot be recaptured by us, who only succeed in reading our own biases into the record of the past. Consequently, the study of history is a venture into illusion and a cultivation of falsehood. It is far better, then, to remain within the context of our own experience and not become confused in what can never be our proper affairs.

Understanding the present. The purpose of the study of history is to understand the present. The current state of things has been produced by the events of former times. Unless the background out of which the present situation arose is understood, the contemporary scene will be a baffling mystery. To make anything intelligible is to trace its causes. But to show the causes of the present it is necessary to describe the past events which produced existing conditions. There is no such thing as purely present knowledge. All knowledge whatsoever is a reporting and an interpretation of past experience. To live absolutely in the present is to know absolutely nothing.

How can the peculiarities of rock formations be explained apart from the history of the earth? How can the many present varieties of plants and animals be understood without a story of evolution or of creation? How can the languages, customs, and institutions of man be made intelligible except through a study of the temporal growth and development of cultures? How can the conflicts and tensions between nations be interpreted except in the light of political, economic, and social history?

Perhaps of chief importance in the study of the past is the achievement of self-understanding. The person who does not understand himself has not become fully human, for self-awareness is one distinctive mark of being a person. To know who one is requires historical perspective. The special interests and habits that mark a given person are an outcome of his past interaction with a particular environment. Everyone has a heritage which is uniquely his—a combination of racial, national, family, and individual traditions which are woven into his very being. Without inquiry into these historical factors man must remain a stranger to himself. Similarly, in the absence of historical study, groups of persons will fail to comprehend their own identity. Without history, Americans will not know what it means to be Americans; Republicans and Democrats will not truly be aware of what they stand for as parties; Presbyterians, Roman Catholics, and Jews will not really understand their respective faiths. Only in the light of past events does the present character of individual and group life become evident.

Lessons for the conduct of life. The value of studying history lies in the lessons it teaches about the conduct of life. The past experience of the race is a vast source of suggestions about what kinds of action are successful and what kinds are not. By looking to the past it is possible to repeat fine achievements and to avoid mistakes. The history of mankind is the record of innumerable human experiments, each of which yields some insights of warning or encouragement. The study of the past ought, therefore, to be a useful guide to present activity. It should be an important factor in making decisions. Though conditions in the present are never exactly the same as in the past, there is sufficient similarity to *some* past situation to enable one to derive from the earlier instance wisdom for the present.

In the conduct of affairs between the nations there is abundant evidence about courses of action which make for peace and prosperity and others which lead to war and depression. The record is clear as to the policies of government which lead to security, contentment, and social progress and as to the decisions which stir up resentment and rebellion. The testimony of the past is also eloquent regarding successful and unsuccessful kinds of interpersonal behavior. One's own personal history is a particularly valuable resource for the guidance of conduct. The wise person, remembering his mistakes, does not repeat them, and recalling his successes, he seeks to reproduce them.

From this standpoint history is a study of great practical value. The justification for giving attention to it is not any purely theoretical appeal nor esthetic interest but its immediate usefulness in suggesting wise courses of action.

Predicting the future. Unfortunately human beings do not always behave as rationally as the immediately preceding view presupposes. Instead of learning well the lessons of history, mankind often repeats its past errors again and again and fails to take full advantage of the favorable opportunities presented. In this fact lies the partial truth of the statement "History repeats itself." If man really took to heart and head what history teaches, history would not repeat itself. The lessons of the past would be applied to the creation of a new and better future. To the extent that the past is repeated, the study of history provides a basis for predicting the future. Although scientific knowledge is cumulative, practical wisdom must apparently be acquired afresh by each generation. In the process of acquisition the trials and errors follow a familiar pattern which is clear in the historical record. This pattern provides the basis for prediction of things to come.

But of what use is prediction? It affords the wise observer the satisfaction of seeing his analyses of the human situation verified in the course of events. It has the additional practical value of suggesting ways to prepare for the future. It also saves one from frustration and disillusionment in expecting more progress in human affairs than sober reflection on past achievements would warrant. It seems incredible that man should continue to destroy himself and his civilization in military conflict. It is unbelievable that crime—which manifestly does not lead to happiness—should continue to plague mankind. There seems no reason why material goods cannot be fairly distributed to all. Furthermore, it is easy to formulate programs for the elimination of these and other evils. But the study of history makes it evident that men have in the past made plans and in imagination built utopias, only to have their hopes bitterly disappointed. A lesson of history is that the factors which govern the course of human affairs are beyond simple calculation and control and that the actual course of past events may be a more accurate measure of what is possible than are the best-laid schemes of reformers.

Understanding the past. The primary value in the study of history, it can be urged, is not to explain the present (Why be so self-centered?) or to learn lessons (Must one always draw a moral?) or to predict the future (Is not history the realm of the unique and of the free?) but simply to understand what did happen in the past. The world of our own experience is all too narrow. How can one better widen horizons than by becoming acquainted with the significant persons and events of the past? To be only and always concerned with the past as relevant to the present and to the guidance of contemporary affairs is the height of provincialism. Why study history? Simply for the enlargement and enrichment of experience, for greater breadth of view, for deeper appreciation, for more adequate insight into the nature of persons and things. History then becomes a source of inspiration, of spiritual satisfaction. Is history only for understanding the present and the future? Why not rather for understanding the past itself?

From this standpoint the aim of historical study is not primarily practical or theoretical (in providing the basis for generalizations) but esthetic and contemplative. Events and persons are appreciated in and for themselves and not because of their usefulness for present purposes. The past has a dignity and sovereignty of its own; it should be no tool or servant of those who now happen to be alive. One who has due respect for the truth of history asks only to be permitted to see and to comprehend. He willingly submits himself—the yet incomplete and undecided—to the discipline of the complete and decided past. It is not for him to speak to and direct the past but only to listen and seek to understand.

The historian who respects the past in and for itself seeks not to sit in judgment upon it. He tries to tell as objectively and dispassionately as possible what actually took place, without moralizing or generalizing. Individual happenings are not taken as illustrations of *a priori* principles but as suggesting their own patterns of meaning. While in the last analysis the necessity of selecting materials introduces an element of evaluation, historians of the type described in this paragraph resist the idea that they are interpreters. They prefer to regard themselves as channels through which past events can speak for themselves.

Providing insight into time and freedom. The study of history is of value because it enables one to understand the meaning of time and of freedom. The natural sciences are not required to take time seriously. They are concerned with classes, regularities, and generalizations rather than with singular events. Time is one factor in the scientific analysis of processes, but this time is not the series of unrepeatable moments which are the stuff of history. The study of history makes one vividly aware that each moment comes but once into the focus of the present and then passes into the irrevocable past. In history it is not statistical averages that count, but each solitary event in its unique decisiveness. For natural science, apart from the law of entropy, the past and the future are essentially alike. For history, the past and the future are profoundly different. The future is the realm of possibility, open and still indeterminate. The past is closed and determinate. The historical event is an occasion of passage from possibility to actuality, a unique and irreversible creation of concrete reality out of what were before only potential ingredients.

This view of historical study especially serves to make vivid the significance of human freedom. One's own life is still unfinished. Many possibilities lie on ahead. Which of these will be realized? Decisions once made cannot be revoked. One can only make further decisions to strengthen or weaken the effect of earlier ones. History is the drama of decisions made once-and-for-all and of the consequences growing out of those decisions. The study of history serves to remind one of his own part in the drama and of the fact that he has only one life to live. Within this one life he must find the clue to the meaning of his existence.

Developing a philosophy of life. A final view of the purpose for studying history is that it provides valuable insights into various possible schemes of life-interpretation. Each historian, as pointed out, has certain standards by which he judges what is significant in the past. For this reason a history not only portrays the nature of the past but also something of the historian's philosophy of life or system of values. Histories are ways which historians have found to make sense out of existence.

An economic interpretation of history demonstrates how the operation of economic factors provides a clue to the otherwise puzzling and apparently irrational course of events. A cultural conception of history shows how tools, institutions, and symbolic systems may be taken as a key to the meaning of human affairs. A theological approach to history considers each event as an incident in the drama of redemption.

From this standpoint the student of history should be in an improved position to make an intelligent choice of his own philosophy of life. By considering the ways in which others have sought to discover meaning and order in events he can choose those perspectives which in the light of his own experience seem most adequate. Every person needs a reasonably coherent schemes of values and consistent principles of life-orientation. The study of history may be a basic source of suggestions for the development of these fundamental attitudes.

23

Language

ONE OF THE IMPORTANT competences which education should foster is the ability to use language. What kind of knowledge does the study of language yield? How does this field of knowledge compare with the other fields analyzed in this Part?

Language as a cultural product. It will be useful to begin by considering the nature of what becomes known through the study of language. In natural science the object of knowledge is the world of material things—stars, atoms, plants, chromosomes. In the sciences of man the entities studied are persons individually and in association. Included in the human sciences are the manifold products of cultural creation, including sciences, histories, languages, arts, and religions. Hence the analysis of language falls within the province of the sciences of man. But to know about language as an anthropologist would is not the same as to "know language" as a young child would. What entities are known in this latter sense?

It is clear that the entities known in language are products of culture and not of unimproved nature. Language is part of the cultural treasure of mankind, preserved and transmitted from generation to generation by means of education. It does not spring up simply by the maturation of the human organism. Language is not determined by the distribution of genes, nor are particular linguistic characteristics built into the germ cells. Americans speak English because they are members of an English-speaking society and not because of any inherited characteristics. A person will learn whatever language prevails in the culture in which he is reared. Many generations of one linguistic tradition have no effect of predisposing descendants of that line to that tradition. A Chinese baby, born of an unbroken line of Chinese-speaking people stretching back for thousands of years, would, if educated in an English-speaking community, acquire English with as much facility as a person with English-speaking ancestry and would have equal difficulty at a later time in learning the Chinese language.

Language, then, is a cultural achievement rather than a natural growth, and as such it is subject to all the variations and peculiarities which characterize the products of human creation. It is also influenced by the special historical circumstances surrounding the culture in which it has grown.

Linguistic symbols. But what is the nature of the linguistic entities thus produced and transmitted culturally? At first thought the answer seems simple: The objects of language knowledge are words. And what are words? They are sounds articulated by the tongue and other speaking apparatus. Or they are certain discernible marks made on a contrasting background, such as the present page. Yet this does not really answer the question, for not all orally articulated sounds are speech nor are all written marks true language. Only a small proportion of the variety of possible sounds and marks count as words. Hence, though it is true that language entities are sounds and marks, this specification does not reveal their essential nature. The constituent elements of language are of a very special sort, and to this distinctive quality we must turn for an answer to our question.

Marks, sounds, or other sense materials are linguistic when they have a *symbolic* character. By this is meant that they stand for something else, that they point beyond themselves to that which they symbolize. Now what is it to which language symbols point? To this question two answers suggest themselves. One reply would be that language symbols refer to specified real things. For example, the two words "John Smith" may be regarded as proper names for a certain person. Again, the noun "ink" can be considered as a symbol for the particular kind of substance used for writing.

This answer is insufficient in at least two respects. In the first place, the noun "ink" in the example does not actually refer to a specified real thing. Ink-in-general is not a specific entity, as a particular bottle of writing fluid would be, nor does the noun refer to all existing writing fluid. It does not directly refer to specified real things at all, but to a *kind* of substance, i.e., to qualities in which any of a number of real things participate. In the second place, the statement that language symbols refer to specific things is insufficient because many words are not nouns. Verbs may refer to a process or activity, while other parts of speech such as conjunctions, prepositions, and articles may appear to have no objective referent at all but only to play some role within the system of language itself.

These objections lead to the second suggested answer to the question about the nature of that to which the symbols of language point. According to this answer, they refer not primarily to actual things but to *ideas* or *meanings*. These ideas are intellectual or rational realities. They are mental in character. They presuppose the fundamental human functions called intelligence or reason. The word "ink," from this standpoint, refers not primarily to a material substance but to the idea or concept of such substance. The verb "run" refers to the idea of rapid movement along a surface. The conjunction "and" points to the idea of joining together other ideas.

Of course, actual things are not irrelevant to the ideas. The meanings are gained in relationships of persons as rational creatures to real things. The word "ink" stands for the idea of a real substance encountered in a variety of actual situations. The idea summarizes certain features of rational man's relationship to his environment. The particular meaning of the word "ink" is defined by the form of intelligent commerce with certain things, in the process of using, manufacturing, or testing the writing substance. Similarly, the meaning of "run" is defined by reference to certain actual activities or processes. But the fact remains that the ideas themselves through the operation of human rationality become detached from particular things and become the entities to which the language symbols refer.

Language and Meaning

Four components in language. The nature of language as a meaningful symbolic system may be clarified by reference to four components in the language complex. First, there is a world of real entities such as trees, stars, and persons. Second, there are human beings who are endowed with the power to relate themselves in many ways to that real world. Third, there are symbols—sounds and marks which are the outward garment of language. The fourth component is the set of ideas which constitute the meaning of the language symbols. Though all of these components are necessary to the existence of language, the fourth is the most crucial and central. The world of objects has other business besides language. Persons also do other things besides speaking. The symbols are solely for language purposes, but they do not explain themselves. The ideas which constitute the meanings are the truly central factor which links the other three together. The idea or meaning is the common denominator in the two relationships: person/entity and person/symbol.

Persistence of association. The ultimate secret of language lies in the fact of persistence of association. In the moment of becoming intelligibly related to some entity (e.g., a book) a person becomes also related to a particular symbol (the word "book") which is designated as the name of the object or class of objects. The simultaneous occurrence of the two relationships modifies the intelligent organism in such a way that the subsequent presentation of a book brings to mind the word "book" and the perception of the word "book" brings to mind the idea of the object book. Thus the symbol "book" can serve as a substitute for the object which goes by that name for purposes of calling to mind the idea or meaning common to both. The persistence of association which makes such substitution possible is evidence of a principle of conservation of form within the sensitive organism.

Plurality of symbols. The primacy of meanings rather than of symbols becomes evident from the fact that the choice of particular symbols to be associated with given meanings is largely arbitrary. There is no necessity that the concept book be represented by the particular sounds or marks which make up the word "book." Any other sounds or marks could be used, provided only that they had not already been employed in another representative capacity. In this connection it should be noted that much of the vagueness, confusion, and ambiguity of human discourse results from the use of the same symbol for more than one representative function. Many words seek thus to serve more than one master and for that reason can be truly faithful to none.

The main point now, however, is not this confusion of tongues but the primacy of meaning made evident in the essentially arbitrary nature of particular language symbols. People the world over have substantially the same concept of "sky," for example, but the symbols used to represent the concept—*ciel* for the French or *Himmel* for the German—are quite different. The designations in Hebrew, Sanskrit, or Chinese would depart still more from the English word.

It is not entirely true that the symbols of language are arbitrary since there are languages and instances where the form of the symbol corresponds in some way to the form of the idea for which it stands. Ideographic language, as exemplified in the traditional Chinese characters, is pictorial in form, characters being selected so as to suggest in outline form the represented ideas. In this case the best symbols would be those which most faithfully or vividly pictured the corresponding ideas. Even in non-pictorial languages there are instances of symbol-idea similarity. Thus, the word "hiss" when spoken has the general character of the idea it represents. In sound and in mouth formation the word "round" partakes of roundness, and the words "clip" and "chop" sound like the activities they symbolize.

Though for convenience in remembering and vividness of effect these symbol-idea relationships have frequently been established, the principle of arbitrariness is not overturned. Symbols *may* correspond to ideas but they do not need to. It is in no way of the essence of language that there be any similarity of form. The possibility of many different languages referring to substantially the same world of ideas and the possibility of translating from one language to another make it evident that the symbols used are really arbitrary and that the heart of language is the ideas or meanings represented and not the symbols themselves.

It may, in fact, be urged that one indication of superiority in a language is that its symbols are not required to embody the form of the idea. Such a requirement immeasurably complicates and multiplies the symbols, thus sacrificing the manageability and economy of the language as a whole for the sake of immediate vividness. Culture is a transformation of nature rather than a copying of it. It would seem, then, that one mark of high linguistic culture is the use of symbols which are not merely copies of ideas. If this is the case, the arbitrariness of symbols underlies the development of maturity and sophistication in language.

Education and the primacy of meaning. The primacy of meaning in language has the consequence for the teaching of language that not mere words but meaningful symbols are to be learned. Rote memorization is relatively inefficient and useless because the symbols learned are not significant. To know words and to be able to speak or write them is not necessarily to know a language. Everything depends on meaning. The teacher of language will succeed only as the student has meanings—ideas, concepts—which he genuinely seeks to express. Only then is the occasion prepared for that union of inner substance with physical expression which is the consummation of language.

The Senses—Space and Time

Language is based upon the employment of sense materials to represent ideas or meanings. Since the specific symbols are arbitrary, any of the senses may be used for these representations. By far the most important language senses are sight and hearing, corresponding to written and spoken language respectively. Sign language, used by those who can neither hear nor speak, is another visual type of symbol system. The sense of touch is the basis of the symbol system for the blind. Braille, for example, is such a system of tactile representation of ideas.

An important distinction in symbolic types is between the *spatial* and the *temporal* modes of representation. An ideograph, in which, for example, the idea of a house might be represented by the symbol ⌂, is entirely spatial in type since the form of the idea is presented all at once as a spatial image. On the other hand, any spoken word is a temporal symbol since its form is presented as a series of sounds following one another in time. Written language in general has both spatial and temporal dimensions. Individual symbol units (such as ideograms or letters) are spatial, and these are further arranged in spatial order with a rule of succession (such as "read horizontally from left to right") which defines a temporal sequence.

Phonetic languages are designed in such a way that a fairly direct correspondence exists between the audile and the visual symbols. This is done by assigning a visual symbol to each sound and then arranging the spatial sequence of these symbols to correspond with the proper temporal sequence of sounds. For example, the symbols "b," "u," "g" each stand for a definite sound and the usual rule of succession requires that the spoken word "bug" be written *bug* and not *ubg, gub,* or $\overset{b}{ug}$. Ideographic language would not have such correspondence. The spoken word "bug" might be represented by the ideogram , and one would have no clue from the sound as to how the word should be written, and vice versa.

The advantage of phonetic systems over ideographic ones is that in the former it is easy to pass from written to spoken forms and from spoken to written. This greatly facilitates the learning of writing and reading. Under an ideographic system the written and the spoken words are completely independent of one another. Thus the phonetic system is a human invention of the greatest importance in facilitating the mastery of the different forms of symbolic systems. Of course, the correspondence of sound and sight is by no means perfect. The rules of translation are in many cases ambiguous. The sounds of the English words "rough," "plough," "dough," and "trough" are by no means as similar as the spelling suggests, nor can one be sure from the sound of the word "air" that it should not be spelled "heir" or "ere." Such ambiguities merely diminish somewhat the effectiveness of the sound-sight correspondence without invalidating the basic principle of educational economy implicit in it.

The linkage of sight and sound symbols is not in all respects economical. Visual perception is in general more efficient than audile perception simply because the former may be instantaneous while the latter is necessarily extended in time. One can grasp the meaning of a visual form at a glance; the same form translated into spoken symbols would require sufficient time for the series of sounds to be completed. The use of phonetic language systems thus tends to reduce visual perception to the relatively slow pace of audile perception. This is one cause of slow reading; each visual symbol is treated as though it were a sound and silently or vocally uttered in proper temporal sequence. The improvement of reading—both in speed and comprehension—requires the breaking of the link between sight and sound and the establishment as far as possible of purely visual modes of perception. Efficient reading also depends upon the predominance of perception in the spatial rather than the temporal mode. That is, the reader learns to grasp whole words at a glance rather than syllables in order. He further learns to understand whole phrases, sentences, or even paragraphs by regarding written words as spatial symbolic forms instead of as a series of sounds in time.

As pointed out earlier, the link between visual-spatial and audile-temporal symbolic modes is an important aid to the learning of reading, writing, and speaking. For purposes of analyzing the written word and for helping the child to learn how to read by bringing to bear his earlier acquired understanding of the spoken word, some use of phonetic methods in reading is surely desirable. But if this learning device is made part of the regular reading habits, inefficiency results. The mature reader is one who has established independent perception in the visual mode. He is capable of analyzing the visual symbols into their component parts and of translating them into spoken syllables, but he normally perceives synthetically, in wholes rather than in parts.

Rules of Combination

It was stated above that language consists of ideas represented by symbols. There are two essentially different ways in which this can be done. One way is to assign to each idea a definite symbol, with each symbol different from and unrelated to every other one. Thus, the idea "It will rain tomorrow" might be represented by the symbol , and the idea "It rained yesterday" might be symbolized by , with corresponding sound symbols in each instance. This is the simplest and most obvious approach to symbolization. Its main defect is that symbols become multiplied beyond measure, and the difficulty of mastering the symbol system becomes enormous. It suffices only in cultures where the range and variety of experiences are quite limited and where communication is restricted to certain standard essentials. This one-to-one approach also has the defect of not recognizing the relationship of ideas to each other. In the example mentioned above, the symbols and do not show in any way that their corresponding ideas both concern the same type of event, rain.

For purposes of symbolic economy and to show relationships, a second approach to symbolization must be used. Instead of inventing a different simple symbol for each idea, a set of elementary symbols is adopted and these elements are combined in various ways according to definite rules to form compound symbols representing the ideas. An example of this is the adoption of an alphabet, from which words are formed by various combinations of the letters. Another example is the set of basic elementary sounds which are compounded to form spoken words. This method of combination makes possible the easy production of an enormous variety of symbols.

But the compounding of elements goes far beyond the production of single word symbols. Words are combined into phrases, sentences, and paragraphs to form meaningful discourse. The mode of composition is governed by certain rules of combination which are called grammatical principles. The rules of grammar may differ from language to language. Different languages may have different parts of speech and the ways of organizing these into sentences may also vary. The essential point is that language expresses meanings only as words are employed in accordance with the conventional rules of combination. Thus, meanings are not only expressed in individual symbols but in compound symbolic forms such as sentences. Words which are not organized according to the rules of combination do not convey meaning. The combination of words "new has hat a She" is not a meaningful statement because its constituent words are not arranged in the conventional grammatical order, as they are in the sentence "She has a new hat."

Again, the combination of words "Hats are hungry" follows the rules of word order but it violates another rule, namely, that adjectives must be appropriate to the nouns they modify. The word "hungry" is relevant only to the class of organisms and not to inorganic entities. This is implicit in the meaning of the words "hats" and "hungry." Hence, the combination is meaningless. On the other hand, the sentence "This cat is hungry" follows correct word usage and is meaningful, though the proposition may in fact not be true (e.g., if the cat has just eaten his meal).

From the fact that language is composite in character three important consequences follow.

Formal knowledge. First, knowledge expressed through language is frequently *formal* in nature, communicating information about agreed-upon rules for combining words. Consider the sentence, "A day has twenty-four hours." This proposition does not express any fact about the nature of time or of the physical world. It merely expresses something about how the symbols "day," "twenty-four," and "hours" are to be used in relation to each other. An "hour" may be *defined* as one twenty-fourth of a "day" or a "day" as twenty-four "hours." The sentence "Spring commences with the vernal equinox" similarly expresses merely a relationship between the component words and not anything about objective nature. To understand language correctly it is necessary to be aware of the purely formal nature of such sentences.

Variety of meanings. Usually language expresses something more than information about how words are used. In this expression the formal arrangement of language elements (e.g., letters and words) is the decisive factor. Therefore, the variety and scope of what can be said depend upon the adequacy of the rules of combination adopted. There are many different kinds of meaning, and these can be represented in language by certain conventional arrangements of symbols. Thus, the imperative sentence "Shut the door" conveys a different sort of meaning from the declarative sentence "He shut the door," or from the interrogation "Is the door shut?" There are conventions which make possible metaphorical use of language. The sentence "The wind sang a soothing lullaby" is not strictly and literally meaningful because singing is defined as an activity of living beings such as birds and persons. But by literary convention such a sentence is admissible for the purpose of expressing a metaphorical meaning, the incompatible aspects of wind and lullaby-singing being tacitly ignored in favor of their compatibilities.

The variety of meaning types is such, however, that language usage is not always without ambiguity. What meaning is expressed by the sentence "This is a free country"? It could be intended as an imperative "Stop interfering with me!" or as an expression of an ideal of national life which is far from being fully actualized, or as a simple statement of fact (e.g., that the nation is a sovereign state). Particularly difficult are sentences such as "That painting is beautiful" or "Socialism is evil" because they have the form of simple factual assertions, while many would argue that they really convey quite different kinds of meanings (e.g., emotive, imperative, etc.).

One of the major tasks of language education is to develop skill in analyzing the formal structure of sentences so as to express and interpret meanings as clearly and unambiguously as possible. Such clarification of language is a particularly important part of the philosophic enterprise. But this is not only the duty of the professional philosopher using the disciplines of logical analysis and semantics. Every student and every teacher, at every learning level, should strive for precision in the ordering of language symbols.

The limitations of language. Finally, the composite nature of language necessarily imposes certain limitations on what can be expressed. The compound symbols produced by combining certain letters or sounds according to specified rules are a very special set of symbols, constituting only the merest fraction of all possible symbolic forms. In fact, there is no limit to the variety of symbols which can be conceived. It should not be surprising, then, if any language system should not only express ideas but also circumscribe them within its own limitations. Thus, language is confining as well as liberating. It cannot symbolize all meanings nor express all truth. The realm of meaning is wider and richer than any language can encompass. Great is the power of language, but it is not sole lord in the kingdom of meanings.

It follows that a degree of modesty is in order in making claims for language. Since there are other than linguistic modes of symbolizing meaning, fullness of understanding requires something more than verbal education. Powerful as words are, they need to be supplemented by such symbolic forms as music, the dance, painting, sculpture, and religious ritual. Whatever is known by language is inevitably infected with the limitations imposed by the chosen rules of combination of the language elements.

Language and Human Nature

The ability to use language is a distinctive mark of human nature. Animals other than man use a variety of sight and sound signals, but they do not possess, except possibly in the most rudimentary sense, the symbolic facility that man displays in language. Language differs essentially from animal signals in its symbolic character, for the essence of language is in *meaning* and not simply in a cue to action or in a response to an organic condition. A bird may utter a cry at the approach of danger to its nest, and this cry may alert other birds to the danger. But the cry is not truly language unless it stands for an idea, and this is probably not present in birds, for whom the cry is simply a direct response to the situation or a stimulus to action without any conceptual intermediation. For human beings the cry of "Fire!" is a danger signal, but it is also more than that since the word evokes a concept of fire and not simply automatic action to escape it.

Language depends on the power or reason. From the immediate data of perception certain aspects are abstracted and these form the basis of concepts or meanings to which word symbols are assigned. Language is thus the external evidence of the reflective activity of the human intellect. A human being does not achieve the fullness of his manhood as a rational being apart from the development of language. For this reason the mastery of language is an absolutely crucial aspect of education. Furthermore, verbal competence is a good measure of intellectual maturity and aptitude. One who speaks, reads, and writes well, or learns to do so readily, is generally shown thereby to be intelligent since the essence of intelligence is the ability to use symbols.

Language and Society

But why should man seek an outward symbolic expression for the meanings he entertains? Why not keep his own counsel and remain silent? Why does he read and write books and give and listen to speeches? Human beings do these things because they are by nature not merely individuals but also members of society. Man is not by accident or by choice social; he is naturally and inescapably social. He would not be human apart from the human associations that alone enable him to develop. Society is the necessary matrix for the actualization of any human potentiality.

Language is one of the primary means for effecting this socialization. Words are interpersonal currency whereby meanings may be objectified and made common property. Without language ideas would remain private; by means of language they become social. To be sure, community of life is possible through means other than words. All forms of activity involving more than one person—in work, in play, in caring for each other's needs—are socializing in effect. The social importance of language lies in its extraordinary efficiency in establishing meaningful relationships between persons. Socialization without language would be like trade without money. If all exchange of goods had to be on a barter basis, the efficiency of economic transactions would be low. By the use of money as symbolic of economic value, commerce is greatly simplified, the efficiency of exchange is increased, and material growth is stimulated. So it is that language provides readily exchangeable symbols of meaning which make possible community of experience other than through immediate joint activity. Thus an experience verbally related to another person becomes common property without any necessity for the other person actually to go through the same experience. Of course it is necessary that the one to whom the experience is related understand through personal experience the meanings of the constituent words and accept the principles of grammar. Given these requirements, the verbal account stands as a substitute for the experience itself.

By the use of language the scope of man's social relatedness can also be immeasurably increased. It is possible through books to participate in the lives of persons dwelling in distant places. The child may, by reading or hearing accounts of life in India or Palestine, Russia or England, actually establish community of understanding with those peoples without physical presence among them. Also by means of language, social participation can be extended into the past. A student today may, through reading about Abraham Lincoln or Julius Caesar, experience the influence of their lives on his. Language and history are, in fact, intimately interwoven since language is the chief form in which the human records of the past are preserved for later use.

Language thus provides an important basis for social continuity. Thoughts and events are evanescent unless they are embodied in substantial form. Written language is an efficient means for such physical embodiment. Language symbols conserve for posterity meanings which might otherwise be irretrievably lost.

Communication. The social nature of language is summed up in the assertion that its basic function is communication. Communication means the making of a community or the enjoyment of experiences in common. It is the act of sharing life with others. To learn language is thus to acquire a means of participating in social existence. Language is both a product and producer of society. The symbols used in linguistic communication are the result of social agreement or convention, and once established they become powerful means of creating a new generation in the image of the one which adopted them.

But social continuity and creation—"preserving the heritage" and "building the future"—are generally regarded as the main business of education. It then follows that the mastery of language must be a principal objective of education. To acquire the means of communication is to gain access to the life of the community. Whoever does not know the language must remain a stranger and whoever speaks the common tongue in an important sense belongs to the community. Language is a fundamental instrument of social cohesion. Effective cooperation, the conduct of business, the resolution of conflicts, the mutual enjoyment of interests and pleasures, and the pursuit of common goals all require adequate means of communication, the chief source of which is in language.

Language and culture. A distinguishing feature of man is that by cultural creation he seeks to transform and improve nature. Language is one of the products of this cultural creativity. As pointed out earlier, the ability to write and speak is not given through biological inheritance but only through education within a particular cultural tradition. Evidence for this is the variety of existing language systems and the fact that, whatever his genetic constitution, each person invariably learns to speak in the manner of his own culture.

Culture includes much more than language. Customs, institutions, laws, religions, occupations, and skills—everything man-made—belong to the realm of culture. Yet among all these aspects language occupies a unique place, for it is a mirror of the whole culture. Whatever man makes has its name. His laws, institutions, and religions have their verbal expressions. Things that are in nature also appear within language, but always from the perspective of a particular culture.

Thus the language of a people is probably the best single source of knowledge about their culture. Through language the character and outlook of civilizations may be appraised. An agrarian culture will develop a language rich in terms applicable to crops, soil, weather, and domesticated animals. A people living by hunting will speak a huntsman's language. Desert peoples express their dominant concerns in languages well elaborated around items such as tents, sun, water, and camels. With the rise of urban cultures a whole new vocabulary is developed, reflecting the growth of specialized occupations, complex social institutions, and the intricacies of commercial life. The coming of the machine has made necessary the invention of a vast technical language to express the nature of modern industrial civilization.

It must be emphasized, however, that language does not change with culture simply by the addition or subtraction of words corresponding to things introduced or abandoned. Language is more than a catalogue of names for things. It is a system of meaningful symbols, expressing the whole organization of life and thought of a civilization. The language of modern man is not distinguished simply by the presence in it of many technical words, but by a whole system of meanings—a fundamental way of thinking—which reflects the dominant concerns and outlooks of the age. The importance of science, for example, has imparted to all modern thinking a literalistic, factual cast. Declarative sentences, indicative of factual statements, are considered the most reliable mode of speech. Metaphorical usage is suspect. Impersonal terms are regarded as more trustworthy than personal ones, confused as the latter are with private emotions and individual bias.

Utterly different is the language of a religious, as contrasted with a mechanical, civilization. The difference is not only that the former contains many words about the sacred rather than about machines, but that the whole network of meanings is oriented around the divine. Personal categories are preferred to impersonal ones. Even inanimate things are invested with spiritual significance. Myth and metaphor are given an honored place. Events are explained in the purposive mode rather than by mechanical necessity.

The illustrations could be multiplied at will. The main features of every culture are mirrored in its language. It follows that language has a twofold dependence on culture. First, there are the different ways of expressing common meanings as, for example, the variety of words in different languages for such universal meanings as mother, water, or eat. Second, there are the different meanings which need to be expressed, as indicated in the preceding paragraphs. In both respects the dependence of language on culture is evident, though much more profoundly in the second respect than in the first.

The Study of Foreign Languages

The distinction between the above two kinds of dependence is relevant to the question of studying foreign languages. The question is frequently asked: "Why should one learn a language other than his own?" It might be argued that as long as one plans to remain within his own culture—as most people do throughout their lives—no good purpose is served by learning a foreign language. This argument is strengthened by the assumption that languages differ only in the words assigned to the same basic meanings so that it is possible to pass from one language to another by appropriate translation. A few language specialists can do the necessary translations, and the average person can then read everything in his native tongue.

Foreign language for travel. A preliminary case for studying foreign languages can be made by pointing out the extent of travel in modern times and the advantages of being able to use another tongue when one goes abroad. The weakness of this argument is that several different languages will usually be encountered in such travel (one could hardly master them all), and it is doubtful that the brief use one might make of another language would be worth the trouble of learning it. Furthermore, the English-speaking person can usually find people wherever he goes who speak English and who would prefer to use that language rather than to try to understand the traveler's attempts to speak a foreign tongue. Exceptions to these observations would be people in such fields as business, diplomacy, or missions, who would need to attain fluency in the use of one or more foreign languages. But such people do not establish any general claim for foreign language study.

Understanding origins. Another reason given for learning other languages is that insights are gained into the origins of one's own language. Since many English words come from Latin, French, and German words, a study of these other languages in an aid to the mastery of English. Though there is some force to this argument, it may be asked whether the same amount of time spent in the critical analysis of English itself would not yield more insight than learning foreign languages.

Awareness of language structure. A stronger case for the study of other languages is based on the understanding gained of the nature and structure of all language, including one's own. Because the native tongue is learned in a largely automatic and unconscious fashion, one cannot ordinarily justify rationally his word meanings and grammatical constructions. Study of a strange language tends to make one self-conscious and analytical about language in general. The varieties of meaning and of combination rules become evident, and the kinds of questions asked about the new language are in turn applied to the native tongue.

Understanding other cultures. None of the preceding reasons for studying foreign languages touches the really basic argument, which rests upon the fundamental relationship of language and culture. As pointed out earlier, languages differ not only in the words assigned to common meanings but even more fundamentally in the different modes of thought or networks of meaning which are expressed through language. Each culture has its own special conceptions of life and the world, and these are reflected in the character of its language.

It is through language, then, that one can participate in the life meanings of a culture. The basic reason for learning foreign languages is to be able to understand truly and inwardly the culture which those languages represent. The study of Latin is not to exercise the mind nor merely to help one understand English better, nor clearly is it of any contemporary commercial value. The primary value of such study is rather to introduce one to the meaning of Roman civilization—that entire amazing complex of custom, law, and concept which for centuries provided some basis of unity and security for so many disparate peoples. The study of classical Greek brings one into intimate relationship with a civilization of profound philosophic speculation, of perceptive drama and history, of self-conscious political democracy, and of magnificent artistic creativity. The study of Hebrew is the key to the world outlook of a people with high moral consciousness, an ineradicable sense of destiny and purpose in history, and a conviction that the hand of God can be seen in every event.

The same principle holds, though in some instances with less force, for modern languages. The true feeling and perspective of French, German, Russian, or Chinese civilization can best be grasped by a knowledge of the language, and one who has not mastered the tongue cannot claim to know the culture with any degree of thoroughness.

This argument affirms in effect that ultimately one language cannot be faithfully translated into another. Japanese literature translated into English becomes Anglicized; it takes on tones and meanings which belong to English rather than to Japanese civilization. To understand another culture truly the language of that culture must be learned. Thus, the study of foreign languages is a means of widening horizons, deepening appreciations, and creating new perspectives through opening doors to the real meanings of other cultures.

Language and Reality

Perhaps the most fundamental question in the philosophy of language concerns the metaphysical status of language. Is language in some sense a clue to what is real, or is it simply a convenient way of designating things? This is a classic philosophic problem, and the differing answers generate two schools of thought: *realism* and *nominalism*. The realists hold that language does reveal the structure of reality. The nominalists believe that words are merely conventional instruments constructed by man for convenience in communication. The realist regards language as in some sense prior to man and independent of him, not invented but discovered. The nominalist considers language as subordinate to and dependent upon man, a result of his decision and contrivance. The realist accords to language far more dignity than does the nominalist. For the realist, words have inherent power to create or destroy. For the nominalist, words are created or destroyed by man.

The contrast between realist and nominalist philosophies of language is perennially a potent factor in educational thought and practice. Whether or not they know and acknowledge the position, those who place a high value on language in education—those who honor and respect the word—are realists. Those who regard words as mere tools, who greatly prefer action to talking, who are impressed with the vagueness and ambiguity of language, are in effect nominalists. In general the bookish, classical, traditional, rationalistic type of education has been realistic in orientation, while the activist, problem-solving, child-centered, experimental type has been largely nominalistic in character.

What is to be said in behalf of these two philosophies of language, respectively? In favor of nominalism is the obvious fact that there are many different languages. The realists clearly cannot hold that actual language symbols are given in the nature of things. It is evident that man does invent symbolic systems and that the particular marks or sounds used are arbitrary.

On the other hand, the symbol systems are not completely arbitrary. Every workable language has to have rational and consistent rules. Without such rules there can be no order, regularity, or reliability in communication. The realist maintains that the requirement of rationality in the structure of symbolic systems is evidence of a prior structure of being so that language is not really invented, but is discovered. Man does not actually create language; he is rather the means whereby the inherent intention of reality becomes embodied in physical form. There is a limitless number of ways in which the structure of being can be expressed, corresponding to the infinite number of possible languages. But each language system is serviceable in communication only as it obeys the laws of reason, and it is these laws rather than the particular symbols used, says the realist, which are evidence of the real nature of things.

The crux of the argument between realist and nominalist does not revolve around the question of words themselves (on this point the nominalist is surely right) but around the problem of meaning. The essence of language is not the mode of expression but the meanings or ideas expressed. The heart of the controversy over language is whether or not the concepts and ideas to which language refers are prior and powerful entities or simply human constructs. In philosophy this is the famous "problem of universals." Is the universal (class concept) "dog" an aspect of the structure of animate reality itself or is it simply a name which man arbitrarily applies to a certain group of animals for his convenience in dealing with them? The extreme realist believes that the idea or universal has a reality prior to and independent of actual things. Moderate realists regard the universals as real but inherent in actual things. Nominalists consider the universals as matters of linguistic convention.

It is instructive to consider the problem of language and reality in the light of the discussion of mathematics in Chapter 19. Mathematical intuitionism corresponds to extreme realism and mathematical conventionalism to nominalism. The view that mathematics is an empirical science corresponds to moderate realism. Mathematics is, in fact, basically linguistic in character. Symbols are devised and rules of combination are agreed upon, and from them any number of propositions may be derived, corresponding to the sentences of ordinary language. There is no one "right" system of mathematics; new systems may be organized at will. But all of these systems must conform to basic logical principals and hence may be regarded as reflecting the necessary structure of thought, in all its richness and variety of manifestations.

The problem of realism versus nominalism, then, whether in mathematics or in ordinary language, reduces to the problem of the relation between thinking and being. The realist holds that thought—idea, concept, form—is in some sense the primal reality, the creative agency, the immanent law or structure of things. The nominalist holds that thought is an instrument or tool of organic beings in their striving for adjustment to the environment. The degree of respect for and concern with language in the educational process is an indication of which of these metaphysical positions one implicitly favors, and, conversely, each of the two general orientations with respect to the nature of thought will tend to influence one's attitude toward the importance of language in the development of persons.

24

The Arts

IT IS QUITE EVIDENT that mathematics, the natural sciences, the sciences of man, and history are significant areas of knowledge and that language also is both an object and instrument of reason. But what about the arts? Do they belong within the province of knowledge? Is esthetic experience in any meaningful way cognitive? Is the study of the arts of any value in developing the powers of human intelligence? Do the arts yield any insights into the truth about the world?

Undeniably the arts have perennially performed worthy functions in human life. The persistence of interest in artistic creation and appreciation is evidence of that. But it would be said or felt by many that esthetic experience has little or nothing to do with knowledge and that art is interesting but unnecessary in the conduct of life. The serious business of men can be managed without benefit of the arts. Science is the way of knowledge and progress. Art is a luxury which can be enjoyed after the real problems have been faced and solved. Others would affirm that esthetic experience is a necessary ingredient in human life, that the arts yield genuine knowledge, and that the study of art is an essential factor in the development of the mature and rational personality.

Esthetic Experience

To understand the place of art in the realms of knowledge and to assess its role in the process of education it is necessary first to define the nature of esthetic experience. A number of components of such experience may be distinguished.

Sense. Art is concerned with the world of the senses and not with "pure ideas," as is, for example, mathematics. The art object—the object of esthetic creation and enjoyment—is a material thing. Art is not concerned with disembodied spirit but with definite kinds of material entities. Furthermore, any and all of the senses can come into play. Music is embodied in a certain organization of sounds, which are carried by vibrations of material substances. Painting is based on sight and the use of a variety of pigments. Sculpture and architecture are also visual and have their foundation in any of a number of solid materials such as metal or stone. Dance utilizes the human body as its material base and employs the kinesthetic senses as well as sight. The arts of cookery utilize edibles and depend on the senses of taste and smell. Cosmetic arts employ fragrant substances and pigments to appeal to olfactory and visual senses.

Esthetic experience thus includes the full range of sense perception and the whole gamut of material substances with which the senses can be stimulated. Because of this variety, the arts provide many different qualities of experience. Many kinds of material things can serve as substance for the esthetic object, and every organ of sense perception can be called into activity in the act of appreciation. Hence, esthetic experience is not narrowly confined to one mode of perception, but rests upon all components of human sensitivity.

The fact that art is founded in sense experience suggests that one of the main functions of the arts in education is to develop and refine sense perception. Education is more than learning how to think and how to act. The mature person also enjoys the discriminating use of his sensory equipment. He knows how to see, hear, touch, smell, and taste with sensitivity. His responses to sense stimuli are subtle rather than gross.

The arts should also give one a deeper respect and appreciation for material things and for the human body, since the art object is necessarily material and since the sense organs of the body are the means by which awareness of the object is made possible. Esthetic experience is, so to speak, the mediator between the mental and physical. It preserves a balance between pure thought —ideas apart from real things—and overt activity—ideas in working clothes. In esthetic appreciation and creation the spiritual and the material are in immediate and perfect union. Accordingly, the esthetic emphasis in education helps to preserve a unitary quality in human experience.

Individuation. The object of esthetic experience is always individual or particular rather than general. In this respect art differs essentially from science, which begins with observation of individual things but always moves on to the formulation of descriptive classifications, principles, or laws, in which the particular is swallowed up in the general. Science is based on concepts; art is based on percepts. Science deals with *kinds* of things, while art is concerned with particular things in their singularity and uniqueness. Concepts refer to ways in which entities can be grouped according to certain similarities. They represent properties common to a class of objects.

Esthetic perception is not directed to such grouping of things. The esthetic object stands by and for itself and does not invite comparison with any other object.

It is possible, of course, to use concepts and to frame theories in speaking about esthetic objects. Music may be classified as "symphonic," "jazz," "instrumental," and so on; architecture may be analyzed by styles such as "Gothic," "Byzantine," or "Georgian." But such classifications are not part of art itself; they belong rather to art criticism, which is scientific and philosophical rather than esthetic in approach. Theories which purport to explain the character, distribution, and changes in particular art forms similarly belong to such disciplines as history and anthropology rather than to art itself.

Independence. The meaning of individuation in art can be elaborated in two ways. First, it means that the esthetic significance of the art object is not dependent upon relationship to any other entity. In science a fact derives its significance from the entire theoretical framework into which it fits. A falling apple is scientifically interesting because it illustrates the principle of gravitation or the process of maturation of the fruit. A painter might observe the same apple fall and produce a picture "Falling Apple" portraying that individual occurrence. The esthetic meaning of the picture would be in its color and arrangement and not in any relationship to other apples or trees or to other instances of falling bodies or of maturation processes. Strictly speaking, every work of art is incomparable. People do in fact make comparisons, but in doing so they depart from the activity of esthetic perception and become critics.

Concreteness. The second aspect of individuation is concreteness. Not only does the art object stand alone; it also stands as a whole. The esthetic experience is a perception of things in their completeness, in their unity. It has no relation to pieces or fragments of things. Thus art is synthetic rather than analytic. It creates and preserves the integral quality. The artist does not dissect; he makes and accepts things in their undivided one-ness.

Science is abstract; art is concrete. This means that science is concerned with classes of things, based upon the identification of some common aspect of the individual things drawn from their particularity and uniqueness, while art deals with specific individual wholes. It is true that historically science studies were added to the curriculum to give concreteness and to avoid abstraction. The tangibility of the objects in science provided relief from sheer verbalism. "Nature study," however, is only the first step in science, and insofar as it is concerned with observation and appreciation of individual natural objects it is more nearly esthetic than scientific. The essence of science is generalization, hence abstraction.

There is, to be sure, a type of art called "abstract," which consists of formal patterns not obviously representative of any actual things such as people, buildings, or nature scenes. Such "abstract" patterns are no exception to the rule of concreteness in art, since the esthetic objects in these creations are the formal patterns conceived as unique complete wholes and not as mere aspects of some concrete thing. The word "abstract" in reference to such art is used in a metaphorical sense and not in its literal and primary meaning.

The principle of individuation is a major contribution of art to education. Study limited to the abstract and general leads to a distorted view of the nature of things and to one-sided personal development. The world is as truly, or perhaps even more truly, composed of concrete entities as it is of abstractions and classes of things. Appreciation for the unique and unrepeatable, for the specific and individual—the fruit of esthetic experience—is an important ingredient in the making of persons. Exclusive attention to abstraction leads to an impersonal outlook and to an interest in similarities and conformities rather than to differences.

It may be that the prevalent de-personalization and collectivization of the modern world are not unrelated to the dominance of abstractive science and technology and to the pre-eminence of conceptual modes of thought. Perhaps one cure for these ills is the revival of interest in the esthetic. The arts are a powerful support for individualism and a stout defense against submersion in the mass. Art education is accordingly essential to the development of free personalities and the preservation of a free society.

Timelessness. Another characteristic of art becomes evident when it is compared with history. Like art, history is concerned with particular entities rather than with classes of things. But historical particulars differ from esthetic particulars. Art is concerned with certain individual material forms, while history, including the history of art, deals with particular events. An event is located in time, while the time setting of an art object is *esthetically* irrelevant. A statuette from ancient Greece, a Renaissance painting, a contemporary building are each unique embodiments of form for all time. While their dates and circumstances of origin may be of interest to the art historian, these facts are irrelevant esthetically. Intrinsically art is timeless.

There is a sense, of course, in which time may enter art. In music, dance, drama, and poetry, for example, temporal succession is implicit in the formal structure. Rhythm is the regularity with which successive notes, words, or movements follow one another in time. In a play the proper timing of the scenes and acts is essential to the dramatic effect. These time relations, however, have no connection with historical time but solely with the internal structure of the work of art. It is not a question of the year, day, or second when a certain musical note is played, but solely of whether it is played before or after other notes. In art, calendar time is irrelevant.

On closer examination it appears that even internal temporality is to a degree overcome in the esthetic experience. Consider a melodic theme, for example. It can be enjoyed as a melody only because the listener does not merely hear notes in succession but remembers each note and thus progressively builds up an impression of tone structure, of sounds-in-relationship. Memory is the means whereby the past can be made present, thus converting temporal succession into relationships within the present. Esthetic experience has the quality of immediacy, of all-at-once-ness. Each moment of time may bring a new experience, but the esthetic quality is appreciated in the mode of "presentness" rather than that of succession. Sufficient unto the moment is the beauty thereof.

The sense of timelessness is an important ingredient in the educational process. When existence is deeply stirred by change, as it is in modern times, people may become uncertain and insecure. They tend to look with hope or anxiety to the future and with regret or longing to the past, all the while undervaluing the present, which they know must also pass away. Art counteracts this restlessness, this continual looking before and behind, and emphasizes the worth of present vividness and immediate satisfaction. Thus, in its timelessness art provides a kind of education for the eternal.

Intrinsic value. The esthetic experience is further distinguished as one of intrinsic value. The esthetic object is enjoyed in and of itself and not because it leads to some other value. Eating food in order to gain strength for daily work or merely to satisfy hunger is not esthetic activity. On the other hand, the immediate enjoyment of the color, smell, touch, and taste of well-prepared food is esthetic in character. This is not to say that esthetic objects are necessarily useless; they may be of great instrumental value. But the criterion for judging their esthetic worth is not their relations to things outside themselves but solely their own qualitative character. Nor does the assertion of intrinsic value settle the question of how art is related to practical life and the problem of the distinction between "pure" and "useful" arts, both of which issues will be discussed below. The point of emphasis now is only that the quality of the esthetic experience itself is such as to center upon the esthetic object itself without reference to any other objects or experiences.

As intrinsically valuable, the esthetic experience is essentially contemplative in character. Its satisfaction consists in the sheer beholding of the object. This contemplative mode of perception has two aspects. First, it seeks to prolong itself; the beautiful is that which one desires to continue beholding. In the appreciation of a work of art one implicitly affirms, "It is good to be here, now, in the presence of this beautiful thing. May this relationship endure!" Second, in the act of contemplation the observer respects as sovereign the thing which he beholds. He comes not to use, to move, or to teach the beautiful thing but to submit himself to its influence, to be moved, directed, and taught. Appreciation of art is not the same as art criticism. In the esthetic experience itself the observer responds to the lure of the beautiful thing; he does not come to judge, correct, or destroy.

The urgent need for the esthetic dimension in education should be evident from the above comments. Human beings require the ability to enjoy what *is* as well as the power to effect change. They need the serenity, sense of present satisfaction, and experience of consummation which are the special fruits of contemplation. The good things of nature and culture are not always to be improved, transformed, and reconstructed. They are also to be enjoyed for what they now are. Modern man has become obsessed with the idea of control; everything must be brought into subjection to man's will. The lesson of the arts is that subjection and control do not have the only or the last word, that man needs also to come in humility to be taught, to become sensitive, to watch, listen, and savor, to gain awareness of manifold excellences and perfections beyond his own narrow and willful orderings of things.

Art is thus for freedom and against tyranny. It proclaims the importance of letting particular things be themselves, to be valued for themselves and not for their relevance to some ulterior value. Art reminds man of the richness and variety of the possible forms of things, and protests against every attempt to bring all existence under an arbitrary dominating will-to-power. In short, the study of art should impart the grace of appreciation and of acceptance.

Creativity. The contemplative enjoyment of beauty must not be understood as mere passivity. On the contrary, the esthetic experience is one of creative activity. Art is an act of making something. This is obvious in the case of the artist, whose task is to put materials together in esthetically satisfying forms. This constructive act is evidence of the creative power of human personality. But it is also true that esthetic appreciation is a creative act. One who responds to an esthetic object must undergo something similar to the experience of the artist who makes things of beauty. The person who appreciates the object may find in it a meaning quite different from that of its creator, but it is nonetheless true that appreciation is a creative act, a work of imaginative construction under the stimulus of the beautiful thing. Thus there is a creative component in esthetic experience, whether it be the primary type of the artist or the derivative type of the beholder.

The creativity of esthetic experience marks it as a fruit of the uniquely human qualities of spirituality and freedom. In the making and enjoyment of the beautiful, human beings escape mechanization and routinization, the dull persistence in repetitive, purely habitual types of activity. Art opens the door to novelty, inventiveness, and experimentation. Its possible constructions are not forever constrained within the limits of practical interests or the canons of literal rationality. Whatever moving or satisfying forms imagination can bring forth may become embodied in the esthetic object. It is a primary function of esthetic education to encourage the development of the freedom and spirituality which such creative imagination exemplifies.

Meaning and Truth in the Arts

Several aspects of the esthetic experience have now been discussed. But these characteristics still do not go to the heart of the matter. Creative, timeless, intrinsically valuable sense individuation must also be viewed in relation to the questions of meaning and truth.

Feeling. One component of esthetic meaning is feeling or emotion. An object which fails to excite, soothe, inspire, or otherwise move the beholder's feelings is for him not an esthetic object. Effective art must bring about a heightening or an intensification of life. It should evoke a warmth of response, an affirmation of worth in the act of beholding the object. Its reward should be a sense of immediate satisfaction or enjoyment.

Form. Yet feeling alone does not define esthetic meaning. The experience of beauty is not merely an inchoate rush of emotion, a confused, formless surge of life energy. Meaning in the arts involves light as well as heat, form as well as feeling. The sense of beauty is a judgment of quality, and quality involves definite forms with clear distinctions between them. Esthetic meaning is the felt form of the beautiful.

Excessive emphasis on feeling in esthetic experience has undermined the standing of the arts in culture generally and in education particularly. Art has all too often been regarded as the province of the vague, indefinite, and purely subjective. It has been contrasted unfavorably with such substantial fields of study as mathematics, science, and history, as well as with the practical skills of vocation and profession. The cure for such mistaken estimates of art is a renewed emphasis on the role of form in esthetic experience.

The discipline of form. Forms in art need be no less definite and precise than those of any other field of study, including mathematics. The discipline of artistic achievement can, in fact, be extremely exacting. The execution of a complex dance step or the fashioning of a sonnet place high demands upon the artist and require educated sensibilities to appreciate them. It would be hard to equal in any field of endeavor the rigor exacted of the musical performer such as a violin virtuoso, the conductor of an orchestra, or one who must coordinate hands, feet, sight, and hearing to play a pipe organ.

Components of form. There are two basic aspects of form. The first is unity and the second is balanced contrast. Something is called "formless" if is lacks integrity (unity), if it is purely homogeneous, without distinction of parts, or if its contrasting elements are mutually antagonistic rather than complementary. Esthetic form is balanced wholeness. Satisfaction in contemplating an art object derives from this quality of proportioned unity.

Logic in the arts. Esthetic form is not lacking in logical structure, but the logic is not necessarily the same as that of scientific discourse. A musical form, for example, may have an introduction, a statement of theme, an elaboration of theme, and a conclusion. Harmonic "problems" may be presented, requiring harmonic "resolution." Similarly, a tragedy and a comedy both have characteristic types of dramatic structure, and any given play has its particular "premises," "argument," and "conclusion." But in music, in drama, and in every other art the mode of "reasoning" used in unfolding the complete pattern is generally quite different from that of literal factual argument.

The range of meanings. The lesson of this is that the arts open up wider realms of meaning—larger possibilities of form or pattern—than are accessible through the ordinary logic of literal discourse. Exclusive adherence to scientific meanings greatly narrows the scope of meaningful experience. It is not necessary to choose between a world of scientific fact on the one hand and a world of amorphous feeling on the other. A due recognition of the logic of the arts makes available a whole new world of esthetic meaning. One office of art education is, then, to broaden the range of meanings by introducing the learner to the wider rationality and the less rigid logic implicit in the structure of esthetic experience.

The communities of esthetic discourse. Meanings, as pointed out in Chapter 17, are based upon certain rules of testing procedure accepted by a specified community of discourse. Thus, mathematical meanings are defined by reference to the definitions and axioms of a given system of mathematical symbols. Scientific meanings are specified by certain rules of observation for verification of factual propositions. Meanings in history presuppose certain agreed-upon standards of interpretation whereby significance can be evaluated. Language meanings are determined by social agreement on symbols and rules of grammar.

Similarly, the enterprise of art creates communities of discourse wherein meanings are defined by reference to specified standards. Because the art object is particular, unique, and intrinsically valuable, the standard of meaning must ultimately be the individual object itself and not any general rule or principle. The meaning of a beautiful thing is then comprehended solely by beholding it, and the communities of shared meaning in the arts include the devotees of individual art objects. Hence, they may be very small (having perhaps only one member), often lacking the avowedly universal, public character of scientific communities, and requiring for entrance the development of very particular sensibilities. It is not that art is necessarily esoteric; there may be works of art which have wide appeal. The point is that artistic import rests upon the form of the individual object and upon the developed taste of the beholder, and these may be such as to create either relatively inclusive or exclusive communities of appreciation, with every variation from near-universality to singularity.

To be sure, there are types of style in art—such as the romantic, impressionistic, and baroque—which modify somewhat the assertion that the standard of meaning in art is in the individual object. These types have approximately the same role as the classifications and generalizations of the sciences. Some creative artists no doubt consciously use a particular stylistic idiom, and some people behold art according to rule, but it would seem that the essence of esthetic meaning still lies in the particular form rather than in the type and that stylistic classifications belong rather to the realm of criticism—a kind of science of art—than to art itself.

Is art symbolic? The problem of meaning in the arts raises the question whether or not art is symbolic. A symbol is a sense object which points to a meaning beyond itself. For example, words are symbols because they refer to ideas; the meaning is not in the word itself but in the idea which it represents. Similarly the national flag is a symbol of country and of the loyalty and devotion due from its citizens. What about the art object? Does its meaning lie beyond itself, or is art non-symbolic?

On this question views differ sharply. One position is that art is symbolic. The meaning of a poem, a musical composition, or a building is not simply in its form but is in the message which it conveys. The *Rubaiyat,* for example, may be seen as symbolic of fatalism, pessimism, and hedonism in life outlook, Beethoven's Sixth Symphony may be taken as symbolizing the joys of pastoral life, and Gothic architecture may be regarded as symbolic of divine transcendence. Sacred music is symbolic of the various attitudes of the worshipper, martial music stands for bravery, and love songs represent the lover's yearning. Manifestly art does arouse images and stimulate ideas which go far beyond the form of the art object itself, and hence may serve a symbolic function.

On the other side it can be urged that while art may be put to symbolic use, it is not in its essence symbolic. Artistic meaning resides in the union of feeling with form, and the essential structure of that meaning is in the form of the art object itself and not in any thought associations it may happen to set in motion. The philosophic attitudes stimulated by the *Rubaiyat,* the joys of nature remembered during the Pastoral Symphony, the sense of God's transcendence in the cathedral—these and other effects of art are simply by-products or concomitants of the esthetic experience and no part of its essence. The work of art stands for itself and not for anything else. Beethoven does not need the countryside to lend meaning to his symphony; it has its own unique and self-sufficient form and meaning.

To hold that art is in essence non-symbolic is to say that it does not primarily serve a representative function. The meaning resides in the thing of beauty itself. This is simply another way of affirming the essentially intrinsic worth of the esthetic object without in any way denying its possible usefulness for other than esthetic purposes.

Truth in the arts. Here and there during the preceding discussions reference has been made to the beautiful, to the worth of the art object, and to esthetic value. What are the criteria for formulating judgments of beauty or esthetic value? There are many unique objects which would not be considered worthy of the name of art and many sense experiences of particular things which would not be called esthetic. Is there any way of distinguishing the *truly* beautiful from the ugly or the esthetically neutral? Are esthetic judgments true or false, or are they merely statements of individual preference? Does it make any sense to say that everyone *ought* to regard a certain object as beautiful, regardless of differing actual reactions to it?

Esthetic judgments and the status of values. These questions bring us back to a problem already mentioned several times, namely, the status of values. Are qualitative judgments merely expressions of personal taste or is there a value structure prior to and independent of private preferences? The answer given reflects one's basic metaphysical position, and no final and compelling proof can be offered for either stand. In favor of the individual taste view are the undeniable facts of endless variety in esthetic preferences and of widespread disagreements about what is beautiful. In favor of the other view is the insistent conviction many have that what they have beheld as beautiful can be so for others, the evidence that persons can grow in powers of appreciation, and the belief that since there appear to be levels or grades of beauty there should be some basic standard of beauty.

Esthetics and cosmology. The problem of truth in the arts ultimately drives one to the question of cosmology (see Chapter 29). Is there in the nature of things some tendency, some cosmic principle or purpose, which constitutes a basis for preferring certain forms or directions of sense organization to others, or is there cosmic neutrality in such matters? Is the criterion of beauty, for example, the coordination of contrasting sense elements into a harmonious whole, and is this criterion rooted in the cosmic process itself? Is the test of beauty some striving for intensity and fullness of sense experience which is grounded in the nature of universal creativity, or in the divine will?

Whatever one's metaphysical position, it is beyond dispute that esthetic experience does reveal one important kind of truth, namely, that there are objects of sense perception which are so structured that persons formed in corresponding ways respond to them affirmatively, as manifest in the activity of contemplation, in the feeling of increased subjective intensity, and in the welcome recognition of meaningful form. These correspondences and behavior patterns of persons in relation to things are important facts about the nature of man and of the world he inhabits, exhibiting dramatically the richness of possibility in forms of experience and the varieties of affectional ties that relate man to concrete things.

The perception of beauty in this sense yields true knowledge about the nature of things. This knowledge is defined somewhat differently from that in other fields such as the sciences, language, and history. There is more variability in the significant forms, in the size of the pertinent communities of discourse, and in the corresponding personal qualities necessary for membership in them.

It is important that the program of education be fashioned with full recognition of the truth accessible through esthetic experience. The easy assumption that art is merely pleasing but neither truly significant nor a genuine source of knowledge needs to be seriously questioned. The discipline of esthetic experience not only delivers the student from narrow abstractive and generalizing conceptions of meaning and truth, but may reveal to him some value structure rooted in the very nature of things, whether conceived as rational principle, immanent cosmic tendency, or divine intention.

The Functions of Art

Art and morals. In a consideration of the relationship of art to certain other areas of human experience, let us examine first the question of art and morals. There are three main positions which can be taken concerning this issue.

Independence. Art in one sense must be independent of morals. Moralistic constraint stifles the artist's creativity. Esthetic significance is revealed in the form of the art object and not by reference to any external principle, such as conformity to a moral principle. Furthermore, the attitude of one who is absorbed in contemplation of a beautiful thing is far different from the moral concern with duty and decision. The esthetic has to do with perception, the moral with action.

Some of the criticisms of art in education have been leveled at those who claim that art is independent of morals. It is widely agreed that the role of education is to produce good persons. When autonomy is claimed for art, the suspicion arises that esthetic experience may encourage license and moral carelessness. From this premise arises the demand for censorship, to insure that no morally objectionable teaching materials shall be introduced under the guise of artistic freedom and creativity.

Identity. Those who believe in the identity of beauty and goodness hold that what is right is also really the most esthetically satisfying and that evil enjoyments in the long run bring disillusionment. According to this view, there are definite standards of beauty, measuring what one *ought* to enjoy esthetically and what will at the same time enhance moral character. The arts in education are thus regarded as instruments of moral improvement.

Mutual relevance. A mediating position recognizes differences in kind between esthetic and moral experience without denying a certain moral relevance of the esthetic and vice versa. Art does influence conduct, and hence can be morally judged. But there is also a specifically esthetic judgment which involves immediate perceptive significance. Art education should then be conducted so as to develop the specific esthetic sensibilities, at the same time harmonizing them as far as possible with the best ideals of character and conduct.

Art and personality development. Akin to the problem of art and morals is the question of the relation between art and psychological development. Modern theories of art education are frequently grounded in the conclusions of developmental psychology. The role assigned to esthetic education is then to foster personality growth. Of particular importance is the opportunity to engage in creative and constructive activity and to put to use the powers of imagination. Art is also considered a valuable therapeutic activity. Through such means as painting, music, dance, drama, and clay modeling, a child can give expression to feelings which he would be unable to objectify in other ways, thus releasing tension, relieving hostility, and overcoming frustration.

The value of linking art education to developmental psychology is that the esthetic experience can be made relevant to the actual needs and capacities of the growing personality at each stage of development. A three-year-old does not have the same logic of sense perception as a child of six, whose outlook in turn differs greatly from the adolescent's. The art which a person creates and appreciates depends in no small measure upon the nature of his personality, which changes in important respects in the growth process. For art education the lesson of this is that art is not to be imposed from without, as something to be learned, enjoyed, and imitated, without reference to individual needs or stages of growth, but is to be used in ways appropriate to each person for the release of his own developing powers.

This psychologizing of art can, however, be carried too far. If it becomes a total esthetic theory it may undermine and contradict the basic principles of the artistic enterprise. Are the scribblings of a young child really artistic creations? Are the dance steps of children in the nursery esthetically comparable with those of the accomplished ballerina? Is the youngster's backyard shack an architectural achievement? An esthetic theory which makes the sense of beauty entirely a matter of private satisfaction can make no distinctions between tastes and thus cannot transcend purely psychological judgments.

On the other hand, if there are objective standards of esthetic excellence, judgments of better or worse art can be made. It would seem that only in this way can there be any real significance to art *education*. Education is a process of directing growth. Direction implies choice between ways and this in turn implies a standard in some degree independent of the particular person. Granted the difficulty of defining such a standard, at least some guidance is available in the great works of art which have proven their power to satisfy and inspire those who have devotedly contemplated them.

In conclusion, it would appear that though art may be relevant to personality development, psychological standards cannot be the only test of beauty. In art education a tension needs to be maintained between the personality needs of the learner and the esthetic standards to which as an ideal he may progressively become conformed. Beauty is not determined by personality; rather, beauty is an ideal by which the development of personality ought always to be inspired and guided.

Art as expression. The same contrast of esthetic conceptions arises in connection with the question of the expressive function in art. It is frequently asserted that the essence of art is the expression of psychological states. The art object is the material embodiment of the artist's subjective condition. But is this all there is to art? Is it *merely* the objectification of inner states? That art has an expressive function no one can deny. But what does it express? Those who consider esthetic experience as more than feeling and who think there are valid criteria of esthetic judgment will answer that the function of art is to express the form of the beautiful and that the feeling of subjective satisfaction is merely a by-product of this participation in significant form.

From this contrast of views arise two opposed conceptions of art education.

If the function of art is to express personality, then the student will be encouraged to draw, model, dance, or compose in accordance with his feelings, and his work will not be judged by comparison with anyone else's creations nor by any standard except faithfulness to his own subjectivity. The opposing position would be that while self-expression may be psychologically helpful, it does not necessarily produce art, the sole business of which is to express not the self but beauty. Only if the self happens to be beautiful will self-expression be art. The task of art education according to this second view is not to encourage self-expression for its own sake but to guide persons, through habitual association with things of beauty, into the development of refined and exalted tastes. Self-expression is not neglected, nor are external standards applied in such a way as to discourage initiative, curb individuality, or destroy artistic inventiveness. The creative impulses are welcomed as channels for the expression of significant form in its richness and variety.

Art and realism. The work of art is a product of culture rather than of nature. It is man-made, *artificial,* contrived. An interesting problem is whether or not the excellence of art is measured by its faithfulness in representing actual things. Is the best portrait the one that looks most like the person portrayed? Is the best landscape the one most like a perfect color photograph? For art in general, it would appear that "realism"—correspondence with real objects—is not essential. (See the section on the symbolic in art, pages 432–33.) Art is frequently a transformation, an idealization of actual things. Even more often is it an independent creation, with no intended relation to any other actual thing.

The degree of realism possible or desirable varies with the different arts. In portraiture it is to some extent inevitable, if the subject of the painting is to be recognized. In music, on the other hand, independence is the rule. Because poetry is composed of words with non-poetic associations, it is usually partially realistic, though precisely because of the poetic form it also tends to transcend literal truth.

It seems that the special function of art is to give access to a new world, fashioned from the creative imagination, and not merely to imitate the world of actual things. Even when a work of art is intended to represent something else, it should provide a special perspective, an interpretation, an objectification of the artist's own vivid perception. Thus art should be not a mere reproduction of things as they are, but the projected vision of a world transformed. Similarly, the purpose of the arts in education is not to produce accurate reporters of what literally is, but to develop powers of creativity and imagination in constructing and reconstructing the world.

Art and communication. In the preceding chapter it was pointed out that the main function of language is communication. It is possible to think of art as an extension and elaboration of language as an agency of communication. Art forms can convey meanings which cannot be expressed in language. A melody communicates a form of experience which could not possibly be translated into words. Drama and poetry utilize words, but their meanings are inseparable from the particular dramatic and poetic structures used. The formative principles of the verbal arts can, in fact, be regarded as extensions of ordinary grammar, as rules of combination designed to convey wider kinds of meaning. By analogy, the various forms in dance and in music may be regarded as grammatical rules for the motions and sounds of which they are composed.

Communication in the arts differs from language in respect to generality. Words stand for concepts, which are always abstractions. Art is necessarily concrete. The art object accordingly is not meant to communicate some general truth or concept but its own immediately perceptible individual form. There is the further difference that linguistic forms are highly conventionalized; standardization of meaning is essential if language is to be effective in communication. Art forms, on the other hand, can be varied much more widely and freely. When they become too standardized, they may cease to be esthetically interesting.

Granted that through the arts communication of meanings is possible, it may be questioned whether communication is an essential function of art. Does the artist necessarily have a *message* to convey? Must he always have other people in mind when he creates his works? May he not primarily be moved by the lure of the beautiful itself to embody it in material form? May his creative work not be in essence a solitary act of devotion to the ideal of beauty rather than a means of establishing social relationships?

Regardless of how these questions are answered, it is clear that education in the arts does greatly widen the scope of communication, opening up worlds of meaning inaccessible to ordinary language and ever keeping alive the invitation to create new ways of embodying the forms of experience.

Art and the common life. How is art related to the ordinary concerns of men and to their everyday activities? There are two contrasting emphases with respect to this question. One view stresses the separateness of art from the common life and the difference between the esthetic and other types of experience. The artist is one who is set apart, and the world of art is a higher world in which one becomes free from the vulgarities and restrictions of ordinary existence. Art stands in judgment upon the gross and unrefined common life. On the other hand, if one has a preference for everyday life, he may charge art with unreality and irrelevance and regard the artist as an escapist and his productions as insignificant frills or decadent luxuries.

The opposite view on art and the common life is that they are continuous with each other and mutually relevant. Art is an enhancement, a lifting up, a transfiguration of everyday things. It is a celebration of their meaning, an attempt to express more vividly the joys and sorrows of ordinary existence. The artist is a spokesman for everyman, putting in concrete form the feelings which others cannot articulate. Similarly a work of art in turn has an ennobling and intensifying influence on the common life.

A mediating view would be that art and the common life are related but that a certain tension exists between them, that art is not only a heightening of the ordinary but also a judgment on it, and that ordinary experience is not only a motive and source of esthetic activity but also a ground of criticism for the irrelevant and corrupt in art.

Art and society. The problem of art and the common life is akin to the question of art and society. Is art a predominantly individual activity, expressing feelings and meanings for particular persons, or is it fundamentally social, reflecting the concerns of the social order? This question cannot be answered without reservation either way. Some artists are highly original and unique, while others are responsive to dominant currents in the social milieu. There are also contrasting views about what art *ought* to be. Some would hold that the artist should attend only to beauty as he sees it, ignoring all questions of social influence. Others would maintain that the artist should be concerned with social good, and that esthetic value is to be judged by service to society. A view combining elements of both these positions would be that the artist can best serve society in the long run by concentrating on the creation of beautiful things as he sees them rather than by trying to reflect current social preoccupations.

Fine and useful arts. A final related problem is that of the contrast between the so-called "fine" arts and the "useful" arts. In the former category are the seven classic arts: music, poetry, dance, drama, painting, sculpture, and architecture. To these might be added many others such as ornamental metalwork, the making of stained glass, and ceramics. In the category of the "useful" would fall such activities as cookery, weaving, carpentry, and clothing design. Actually it is impossible to draw the line at all sharply between pure and practical arts. For example, architecture, traditionally a "fine" art, is of great practical significance. Practitioners of the so-called "functional" architecture have found beauty in the usefulness of materials for certain purposes and have at the same time discovered the utility of the beautiful. Again, a "practical" art such as clothing design has in it many elements of creative imagination which bear little practical utility.

The separation between fine and useful arts would be favored by those who regard the esthetic as a realm apart and beauty as the province of a coterie of esthetes. The abolition of such a distinction would be favored by those who consider art as an outgrowth and enhancement of common life. Those who adopt this view believe that all human activity has an esthetic dimension, that the good life as a whole is a work of art, and that every endeavor should be transfused with beauty.

The answers given to these problems of art and the common life, of art and society, and of pure and applied arts obviously have much to do with the way in which art will be employed in education. If art is a thing apart, it will be treated as an independent discipline and it will be used to produce coteries of sensitive men of taste. If art belongs to all of life, the sense of beauty will be an important ingredient of education in all its phases, lifting, judging, and transforming common existence by the more vivid perception of significant forms in all their boundless variety.

Philosophy and Religion

HAVING CONSIDERED from a philosophic standpoint the nature of knowledge generally and more specifically the major areas of study ranging from mathematics to the arts, we proceed finally to an analysis of philosophy and religion, which are both characterized by a comprehensiveness and depth of concern not found in any other field of knowledge. A preliminary discussion of philosophy was undertaken in Chapter 1 for purposes of defining the enterprise of educational philosophy, and some aspects of religion were considered in Chapter 5. The reader may wish to refer again to those chapters to supplement the present treatment.

The Nature of Philosophy

Five conceptions of the nature of philosophy will be discussed. They are not exhaustive of all possible views of the subject, nor are they mutually exclusive. There are philosophers and movements of thought which emphasize one or more of these conceptions, neglecting or rejecting the others. But the field of philosophy as a whole certainly includes all five.

Analysis of language. One task of philosophy is to make a critical inquiry into language. Words come into being in many ways and generally enjoy long careers of varied use and misuse by generations of persons. As a result, language may become confused, vague, and ambiguous. Almost any word will do for an illustration. Recall the analysis of knowledge in Chapter 17. What does it mean to "know"? Does it mean "to have an immediate experience," "to be," or "to be able to give a rational demonstration"? Again, what is meant by "matter"? Is is something solid and visible? Then would water and air not be matter? Is it whatever possesses the property of inertia? Then does my reluctance to do an irksome task show that I am matter? What is the meaning of "matter" as used in the sentence "I don't know what is the matter with him" or in the phrase "subject matter" in educational discourse?

Language embodies meanings not only in individual words but also in the forms of combining them into sentences. Hence linguistic analysis is also concerned with types of sentence structure and with the distinctions of meaning which different grammatical rules make possible. On this point the reader should refer once again to the discussion of language in Chapter 23.

There are two different goals which language analysis may have. One is to set forth the precise meanings of language as actually used. Any particular meaning would thus be indicated simply by exhibiting circumstances under which the word or sentence would be appropriate. This can be done both for common-sense language and for the more exact technical language of the special disciplines. A more ambitious goal of analytic philosophy is to devise ways of reconstructing language to make it more precise. For example, the proposition "This rock has weight" could be more precisely stated by some such sentence as "If this rock were hung from a spring, then the spring would be stretched." All statements of fact could be expressed in this "if . . . then" form in order to show what must be done to test their truth. Again, sentences which appear to state empirical facts but only express feelings can be modified so as to make the intention explicit. Similarly, sentences which merely state how words are to be used can be explicitly formulated to show this. Thus, the ostensibly empirical proposition "He is human" may be reconstructed as an explicit expression of emotional concern: "He ought not to be treated like a beast!" or as a statement about word usage: "The pronoun 'he' may be used to refer to any male human being." Some analysts go even further and for technical purposes seek to reconstruct the entire language system, substituting mathematical-type symbolic systems for ordinary language.

Clarification and criticism of assumptions. Another concern of philosophy is the critical examination of the assumptions or presuppositions underlying words and sentences. The statement, "To get ahead a student needs will power" has several assumptions implicit in it. It presupposes a competitive society, in which achievement or success is measured by the degree to which one person surpasses another person. It presupposes a conception of personality in which "will" is a constituent, and it is assumed that this can be turned on like a valve or a switch, delivering power for activity. The philosophic approach to this statement is to point out such assumptions as these, indicating that what may be regarded as a self-evident truth rests upon views of society and of human nature which need to be reflectively and empirically examined in the light of the whole range of other possible views.

No word can be uttered, no proposition affirmed, without making some assumptions. One cannot say "It is nine o'clock" without implying several ideas about number, time, and measuring instruments, growing out of one's whole outlook on the world. The simple statement "I see green" presupposes ideas of color, processes of sense perception, and the existence of persons. Furthermore, there are alternatives to all such assumptions. It is the philosopher's role to point out the assumptions and their alternatives in order that the deeper implications of language may be made clear and choices may be intelligently made among the different possibilities.

Study of method. According to another conception, the primary function of philosophy is the study of method. A philosophic approach to mathematics calls for careful definition of what the mathematician does or ought to do. Philosophy of science is concerned with a perceptive study of scientific method in all its phases. Philosophy of art deals with the processes of artistic creation, appreciation, and criticism. The preceding chapters in this Part, dealing with the several major fields of knowledge, contain illustrations of this philosophic approach. In each field an attempt was made to define the unique characteristics of the area of study.

Justification of beliefs. Language analysis, clarification and criticism of assumptions, and the study of method are all employed in what is sometimes taken as the central task of philosophy, namely, the justification of beliefs. Of any affirmation it is the philosopher's business to inquire: "On what grounds does it rest?" "How can it be justified?" "What evidence can be introduced in its favor?" Metaphysical philosophy deals in this way with beliefs about the real or ultimate nature of things. The theory of knowledge and logic are concerned with analyzing beliefs about knowledge and rational inference. Ethics and esthetics cover beliefs about the good and the beautiful, respectively. To these might be added such other branches of philosophic inquiry as axiology (the general theory of value), cosomology (beliefs about the universe as a whole), philosophical anthropology (inquiry into human nature), social philosophy (general analysis of social and political organizations), and the philosophic study of special areas like history, religion, and the various sciences. In each case beliefs are tested by analyzing the meaning of the language used, by exhibiting the assumptions upon which they rest, and by making clear the methods employed in establishing the beliefs in question.

Coordination of knowledge. All four conceptions of philosophy thus far considered are particular in their focus, in that they are concerned with individual propositions and special areas of knowledge. In contrast to these, a fifth view considers the function of philosophy as the coordination of knowledge from the various separate fields as far as possible into a coherent whole. The philosopher must become familiar with all of the major fields of knowledge and then seek to relate them to one another in some comprehensive fashion. He must be a generalist rather than a specialist in one field. His task is to cross the lines which have been erected between fields of study, to see connections between diverse subjects, and to perceive ways of applying concepts and methods from one department of knowledge to others.

From this standpoint, the fruit of philosophic reflection should be the establishment and continuous reconstruction of a general world view or life outlook. New items of experience need to be tested to see how they fit into the total picture already established. The main pattern may be confirmed by new data, or fresh experiences may result in minor or substantial reformulations of outlook.

In a time of highly specialized knowledge in many diverse fields and a vast increase in accumulated wisdom it may well be that the goal of satisfactory coordination is impossible to attain. One person cannot begin to master with any adequacy the knowledge in more than a very few fields, much less in all the major ones. Yet the task of organizing knowledge into some kind of meaningful whole is so urgent, in the interests of intellectual and social integrity, that many philosophically minded persons consider it important to undertake this work. *Every* person inevitably tries to make some unified sense out of his experience; but the philosopher undertakes this common human task more explicitly, self-consciously, thoroughly, and systematically than usual.

Expression of vision. Finally, philosophy may be regarded as expressing certain deep convictions about the significance of life. Not all aspects of human experience are on a par; some are regarded as more important than others. Every person has certain persuasions about what is most truly significant. These insights provide a kind of *vision* of the meaning of life. For one thinker the central fact of existence may be the orderliness of the world. Everywhere he looks he sees structures and forms. His efforts are directed toward increasing the permanence of patterns, his intellectual powers are devoted to discovering them, and his happiness consists in contemplating them. Another thinker may be struck by the infinite variety of entities, by the looseness of their connections, and by the value of freedom for each to be itself. He seeks to promote individualism, he welcomes knowledge of particulars rather than of things in patterns, and he finds his fulfillment in "living and letting live."

Every philosophy may be regarded as some such vision of life, based upon a scheme of values which commends itself to the thinker. There is great variety in what persons consider most important, and philosophies differ accordingly. Furthermore, this conception of philosophy concerns more than the detached, objective intellect. It reflects vital interests, deep commitments, and basic involvements of the whole person.

Philosophy and Knowledge

Philosophic knowledge. Does philosophy yield knowledge, and if it does, what sort of knowledge? The answer to this question depends upon which of the above conceptions of the philosophic enterprise one has in mind. Philosophy as analysis of language aims to facilitate understanding of words and sentences and of the social conventions relating word symbols to their appropriate meanings. Such understanding of words, meanings, and societies would seem to be a legitimate kind of knowledge. Philosophy thus conceived is a compound with elements drawn from philology, psychology, and anthropology.

Philosophy as clarification and criticism of assumptions is concerned with the connections between ideas. It deals with the larger networks of meaning in which particular meanings are embedded. Such knowledge, like that of language analysis, does not provide a direct report of concrete things, but is a second-order kind of knowledge, describing the family relationships of meanings. Philosophy of this type makes it known that ideas are never independent or isolated but that they have their being in systems or structures of thought.

Philosophy as the study of method also depends upon the prior existence of primary knowledge areas. The philosophy of science is an attempt to define clearly the nature of scientific inquiry, while philosophy of history and philosophy of the arts clarify procedures in these respective disciplines. Philosophy as the study of method or as justification of belief may describe what people actually do, in which case it is psychological and anthropological in character, or it may prescribe investigation or validation procedures, in which case it is knowledge as technique and practical principle rather than as fact.

Philosophy as the coordination of knowledge certainly yields knowledge, in fact the most complete knowledge possible. But, as in the previous instances, this knowledge rests upon the prior gaining of knowledge in the various special fields. A comprehensive view of things is only possible because there are particular insights to coordinate with each other. The distinctively philosophic contribution to comprehensive knowledge is the discrimination of common features and illuminating relationships between disparate fields.

Philosophy as vision presupposes the union of cognition with the intuition of value. The philosopher's deep persuasion about what is most important is at the same time a conviction about what is most true. Here knowledge is not a matter of disinterested assent but of passionate awareness of truth value. For example, a pluralistic view of the world is held by one for whom many-ness and individuality are the most inescapable and irreducible realities. For him these categories are more illuminating and in some sense more fundamental than the ideas of unity and relatedness which would be central to a monistic view. The knowledge value of the philosophic vision consists in its use as an organizing principle which the thinker believes can render the experienced world most intelligible.

The reliability of philosophy. Granted that philosophy may yield knowledge, though perhaps of a derivative kind, is the knowledge thus afforded reliable? Is philosophy as a method of inquiry trustworthy? Opinions differ on these questions. Some critics distrust most philosophizing, especially when it yields visions and comprehensive schemes. They claim that so-called philosophic world views are nothing but subjective fancies and personal biases. They believe that the study of methodology is somewhat more reliable, since this is really a scientific approach, and that the analysis of language and of assumptions can also be carried out with some degree of precision.

On the other side are those who believe that while no philosophical method is perfect, philosophic knowledge of all the types discussed is important and worth while. Everyone necessarily has philosophical views, including ways of coordinating knowledge and of expressing convictions about values. No one can avoid reliance upon *some* philosophy. How much better, say these advocates, to pursue the philosophic task explicitly and in the light of the accumulated philosophic experience of mankind, than individually and haphazardly. For this reason they consider all of the main approaches to philosophy essentially trustworthy.

Philosophic agreement. Similar to the question of reliability is that of agreement among philosophers. Do philosophic reflection and discussion lead to progressively better mutual understanding? Is there growing consensus among philosophers? It is characteristic of philosophy that all of its major issues continue to be debated generation after generation, and that substantially the same positions on these issues are taken by each generation of contenders. Naturalism and supernaturalism, idealism and materialism, realism and nominalism, rationalism and empiricism—all of the classic viewpoints, with variations appropriate to the times—have their respective champions in every age. Is no resolution of those issues possible?

This apparent lack of progress in solving philosophic problems may be interpreted in any of a number of ways.

Philosophy is intrinsically futile. First, there are some who see in the perennial disagreement good warrant for abandoning the whole enterprise of philosophy. To every seemingly reasonable position one can adopt there is an opposite position which others sincerely regard as even more reasonable. Philosophic inquiry appears to lead only to frustration and confusion and had better be given up in favor of methods of investigation, such as the scientific, which do lead to agreement.

A scientific philosophy is the solution. A second type of reaction is not to give up philosophy but to try to reform and refine it in such a way that agreement does become possible. It is chiefly the conceptions of philosophy as vision and as coordination of knowledge that lead to disagreements. Analysis of language, of presuppositions, and of methodology are less pretentious, more restricted, and more precisely defined conceptions of philosophy which hold promise of producing concensus. Modern thinkers have developed a genuinely scientific philosophy, largely if not exclusively concerned with logic, the propositions of which can be made as rigorous as those in the most exact sciences. Though such a scientific philosophy has actually been created, there are still philosophers of more traditional stripe who persist in their vague and empty speculations. They should either be ignored or convinced of the futility of their antiquated methods.

Philosophies reflect personal differences. A third response to the fact of disagreement is to give up the idea that the function of philosophy is to state objective truth and to regard it rather as an expression of personal and subjective attitudes and preferences. A philosophic system is then considered as a type of dramatic representation of the universe, as one of an indefinite number of possible personal perspectives on the nature of things. According to this position, disagreements are to be welcomed rather than deplored because they enrich the supply of insights which people have about life and the world. A single philosophy would be as undesirable as a single style of painting or only one dramatic plot.

One philosophy is right, the others wrong. A fourth response is to affirm the truth of one particular position and to maintain that those who disagree are simply wrong. The source of their error may be merely ignorance, which can only be overcome by persuasion and demonstration, or the error may result from the use of what masquerades as philosophy to advance personal or group interests. In the latter case, the objective is not to know the truth but to gain advantage over opponents. The appropriate response here is to unmask the pretenders and meet their power plays with political rather than intellectual weapons. The failure to admit the truth may also be because of sheer perversity, hardness of heart, or sinful pride. The only cure for this condition may be a conversion, in which the truth is inwardly revealed and received.

Philosophies are partial views of infinite truth. A fifth attitude toward the fact of philosophic disagreement is to affirm that philosophy is properly concerned with truth but that because truth is infinite and man and his language are finite every human formulation of the truth must be partial. Every serious philosophy is to some degree true, but none is the whole truth. This position agrees with the third one above, in which the variety of possible perspectives was emphasized, but it differs in holding that each perspective may be a partial revelation of truth.

Philosophy and communication. In the preceding chapters each area of knowledge has been examined in relation to the idea of communication. In each case it has been indicated that there are communities of discourse within which the conceptual schemes of the particular field are understood. The various communities of scientific discourse have their accepted rules of validation, the historians have their schemes of interpretation, and the lovers of beauty their esthetic objects. What communities of discourse do philosophers create?

Each total view of the world and each system of analysis defines a community of discourse, within which the major concepts and rules have currency and acceptance. Many would go further and hold that the ultimate goal of philosophy is to fashion an inclusive community of discourse, by erecting ways of speaking about the world that can be understood by everyone. All of the conceptions of philosophy discussed early in this chapter exemplify this goal. The purpose of language analysis is to overcome failures in communication. The purpose of criticism and clarification of assumptions is to make universally evident the conceptual schemes which underlie assertions. Study of method reveals the defining principles of the communities of discourse in the special fields of knowledge and thus helps to make them intelligible to those who are not specialists in those fields. Philosophy as justification of beliefs helps to convince the doubtful and enlarge understanding. Finally, philosophy both as coordination of knowledge and expression of vision explicitly aims at comprehensiveness of view.

Hence, it may be affirmed that the fundamental objective of all types of philosophy is to extend, enhance, and facilitate communication. It follows from this that philosophy has a major *social* role. The human community is created, preserved, and transformed to a considerable degree through the processes of communication. By contributing to the more effective use of language symbols philosophy can help to preserve and to vitalize significant social relationships.

The Study of Philosophy

There are two approaches to the study of philosophy, first as an ingredient in all other studies and second as a special discipline. Of the two ways the former would seem by far the more important. As a technical study few participate in the philosophic enterprise. But no one can entirely avoid philosophic questions, and anyone who engages in more than the most routine and superficial discussion or reflection necessarily becomes philosophical. Every attempt to define the meanings of words with care or to explain the significance of an obscure or ambiguous sentence is an application of philosophic analysis. Every systematic exploration of basic principles in any field of knowledge or practice is philosophic criticism. Any study of how knowledge is secured or validated is philosophy as methodology or as justification of beliefs. Any relating of one field to another by more fundamental concepts is philosophy as coordination, and every judgment about what kinds of things are really important is philosophy as vision.

Hence it is not a question of whether one is to be philosophical or not, but of the depth, precision, and inclusiveness of the philosophy practiced. Ideally all education should be philosophic. Nothing should be taught illogically, ambiguously, or without awareness of assumptions. Every activity is better learned when the methods of procedure are clearly delineated. No fact, theory, or skill should be taught without some attempt to relate it to other experiences and to a scheme of values. Thus all parents and all teachers of reading, of history, of arithmetic, of home economics, and of every other subject at every level, as well as guidance counselors and administrators, ought to teach philosophically. It is chiefly through such people that philosophic outlook and concern can be mediated to the young.

There is need also for the study of philosophy as a formal discipline. Such study helps to systematize and make explicit the philosophic practices which are ingredient in every area of reflective concern. Particularly helpful is some acquaintance with the history of philosophy, in which the perennial problems and the classic attempts at solution may be studied. Through such knowledge it is possible to see contemporary problems in better perspective, to avoid classic blunders, and to secure resources for constructing one's own philosophic viewpoint. Useful also is the systematic consideration of problems in the several fields of philosophy such as logic, metaphysics, theory of knowledge, ethics, esthetics, and social and political philosophy. This study of philosophy as a department of knowledge is a valuable complement, for the relatively mature student, to the informal philosophizing which should be a part of all intellectual life.

The Nature of Religion

Religion is similar to synthetic philosophy in its concern for the whole and for the highest values. It is less closely related to the analytical types of philosophy. Philosophy is intellectual in character, furnishing some rationale for beliefs. Religion, on the other hand, *may* be primarily emotional or practical, with little concern for intellectual justification of belief. In philosophy the primary goal is understanding; in religion the goal is *faith*. Religion and faith, however, have many different meanings.

Substitute for knowledge. One conception is that religion is a substitute for knowledge. It is said that some things are established by the application of intelligence, while other things are to be taken "on faith," these latter beliefs constituting the special province of religion. For example, though it is possible by the scientific study of the earth's crust to explain the process of geologic formation, one may choose to accept on faith, at face value, the account of the world's creation given in the Bible. The religious revelation thus takes the place of scientific knowledge. Again, there are medical ways of dealing with physiological and emotional illnesses. The healing arts depend upon painstaking search for reliable knowledge of bodily and mental processes. Some believers in religion would consider these researches unnecessary and would rely instead upon the healing power of faith. A third example would be the time-honored resort to religion for the production of rain or for the promotion of good crops, instead of considering meteorological data, water supply, soil enrichment, and pest control. In these cases religion is used as a short cut to results which would otherwise require the disciplined pursuit and application of knowledge. Faith here means *belief,* in the sense of accepting as true what is not known but could be investigated.

This kind of religion runs contrary to the entire rational and scientific concern in education. It discourages the pursuit of knowledge and nurtures attitudes and methods quite opposed to those of intelligence. Such religion also tends to create a barrier between those who live by faith and those who live by reason and between religion and science. Growth in knowledge reduces the province of religion, and each time a believer extends his understanding about matters of faith his faith diminishes to that extent. A view of religion as a substitute for knowledge therefore not only appears unfavorable to rational education but also to the permanence and security of faith itself.

A kind of knowledge. Another conception of religion is that it is a kind of knowledge, though of a different and higher order. The mark of the religious person is that he possesses insight into truth which is not open to the unbeliever. Like the first view, this idea of religion makes faith a matter of belief. The faithful are those who believe certain fundamental truths about man or the universe. It is sometimes said that the province of ordinary knowledge is "nature," while religious knowledge is concerned with "supernature." For example, beliefs about God, the immortal soul, and miracles may be said to refer to the supernatural. The faithful believe that God exists, that there is life after death, and that certain events not explicable by any natural law have occurred.

This religious knowledge may or may not be regarded as gained through reason. Some hold that reason is competent to demonstrate beliefs like the existence of God and the immortality of the soul but not beliefs like the Christian doctrine of the Trinity, the source of which is not reason but revelation. Others consider that all religious knowledge must come through revelation and that reason is competent only in the natural sphere. On the other extreme are those who consider that all truth is accessible to reason, including matters of religious belief. Such persons are generally inclined at the same time to naturalize the supernatural, considering that the realm of the religious is not essentially different from ordinary things nor discontinuous with them.

This view of religion sometimes generates difficult problems in relating religious and non-religious knowledge. How, for instance, are the religious doctrines about the soul to be harmonized with the findings of scientific psychology? How can religious ideas about the beginning and end of the world be squared with the theories of physical cosmology? There are four ways of working out this relationship, each resulting in a significantly different conception of the role of religion in education.

Difference in subject matter. First, religious knowledge may be taken as different in subject matter from non-religious knowledge. Ideas about God and the soul are then religious, while problems of matter, life, social structure and the like are secular. This places religious and secular knowledge and education in two separate departments. It would seem that such a division cannot well be maintained. The areas interpenetrate. Secular psychologists insist on studying the soul, secular philosophers discuss God, and theologians persistently claim concern for so-called secular subjects and insights into them. In actual practice, therefore, a sacred-secular subject-matter distinction seems bound to break down.

Difference in perspective. Second, religious knowledge can be regarded as concerned with the same entities as non-religious knowledge but as exhibiting a different "dimension" or "perspective." The anthropologist and the believer both know man, but the former knows him from the standpoint of physical characteristics and culture patterns, while the latter knows him as child of God or as sinner in need of forgiveness. These are said to be different "dimensions" because they represent different components of human experience. One provides objective descriptions, classifications, and generalizations about man, while the other suggests interpretations of the personal meaning of existence. Religious knowledge aims to give answers to questions about the ultimate significance of life—questions which do not occur within the framework of scientific inquiry. Religion so conceived may become a means of enriching and deepening knowledge by adding new dimensions to understanding.

Difference in mode of expression. Third, religious knowledge may differ from non-religious in its mode of expressing truth. Scientific and practical language is literal. Religious language is symbolic. The classical Christian doctrine of "original sin," for example, is unacceptable to many as a literal statement about a biologically inherited taint resulting from one man's transgression. But as a symbolic expression of the native human tendency to be self-centered it may prove illuminating. "Heaven" and "Hell" are frequently rejected as literal cosmological designations, but they may be acceptable as appropriate symbols of the moral factors which determine the meaning and destiny of each human life. Considered in this manner, religious knowledge is more akin to that expressed in drama and poetry than to the literal truth of science. According to this view, the function of religion in education is to provide ways of communication which yield insights not accessible through other kinds of language. The symbolic language of faith involves communities of discourse different from those of the sciences, history, the arts, or philosophy, but no less authentic than they.

Continuity of knowledge. A fourth view is that all knowledge is essentially one and that religious knowledge is continuous with other forms, including the scientific. Traditionally, religious faith has been mainly concerned with such questions as how the world came to be, whether any purpose can be discerned in the world process, what happens to people when they die, and how to know and do what is right in this life. All branches of inquiry—scientific, historic, esthetic, and philosophic—can contribute to the solution of these problems. It can be argued that they are not by virtue of subject matter, method, or mode of symbolization uniquely "religious" in character; that they are universal and human. The psychological study of motivation, the anthropology of values, and the physics of creation may then be important ingredients in the formation of a religious outlook. Truth is one, and knowledge of the truth is one. If education aims at teaching this whole truth, it follows that the interests and claims of religion will thereby be satisfied, for the deepest questions of life will have been dealt with by every means available to human intelligence.

Concern for the unknown. Another general conception of religion is that it has to do with the unknown rather than with knowledge. It is neither a substitute for knowledge nor a kind of knowledge but a venture into mystery. Faith is not belief but an attitude of expectancy or awe or an activity of the will. Faith has no cognitive function but serves rather to determine feeling and conduct. No matter how seriously intelligence is applied, there still remain decisions to be made for which reason provides no sufficient guidance. All life involves some risk. Free man is never given a plain pattern to follow. The future lies open, and he must create it. What man is to be and do cannot be predicted; it can only be *made*. The life of faith requires an adventure into this unknown future. The nature of a person's religion is indicated by the kind of future he creates, and the religious statements he makes are not to be construed as knowledge but as the outlines of the future he intends to affirm. Thus, when faith is conceived as adventure rather than knowledge, the theological proposition "God is love" means that as one faces the impenetrable mystery of the future he determines to construct it, insofar as it lies within his power, according to the ideal of cooperation and mutual concern.

This conception of religion is called an "existential" one because existence —what one *is*—is considered as prior to conceptual knowledge. One cannot derive the content or direction of his existence from ideas; ideas are themselves products of prior existence. Knowledge-in-possession is evidence of an adventure of faith already taken; faith is always prior to knowledge and is the condition for its very possibility, since knowledge requires a free, choosing subject as knower.

Religion as adventure into the unknown clearly lies at the very foundation of education, if one grants the existential premise that knowledge is never a sufficient guide to human decision. The character of the educative process is determined by the underlying faith, and knowledge itself is an outcome of that faith. The opponents of this view complain that it leaves man in the dark, since there is no rational basis for deciding on a faith. They say such a conception of religion and of education is irrational, that reason must be prior to faith, and that existence projects itself into the future by the sufficient light of intelligence. To this the existentialist answers that reliance on intelligence is itself an act of prior faith, not demonstrable by reason, and that life will prove such reliance unjustified.

Relation to the ultimate. The next general view of religion centers about the idea of relation to the ultimate. Religion is a matter of devotion or commitment to whatever one considers ultimate. Faith is not primarily belief or adventure—though both may be involved—but is a matter of value and concern. One's religion is what concerns him ultimately. The object of ultimate concern may be conceived in a number of different ways.

Supreme value. The ultimate can be taken to mean whatever is of supreme or highest value. Religion is relationship to this supreme value, and this value is in effect one's God. When one's deepest commitment is to intelligence, reason is God. Complete and unquestioning devotion to country amounts to deification of the state. All-consuming interest in the accumulation of wealth manifests a religion of money. Utter loyalty to Jesus defines the faith of the orthodox Christian, for whom Jesus is God. Similarly, the Buddhist finds in the Buddha the supreme embodiment of value.

According to this definition, the religious question is relevant to every person's existence since everybody necessarily has a dominant system of values by which his life is governed. There is no distinction between "religious" and "non-religious" people but only between people with different kinds of religion. Furthermore, religion becomes of fundamental importance for education since the question of aim or direction is largely settled by reference to the supreme values. Whatever is really regarded as of highest worth finds expression in the methods and the goals of the teaching-learning process. In this sense all education is inevitably religious; the only question is, what kind of religion governs the process.

The comprehensive. A second way of defining the object of ultimate concern is as that which is comprehensive. Religion is then conceived as man's relationship to the totality of things—his response to the whole of life or to the universe. There are optimistic religions, such as Judaism and much of Christianity, which reflect positive, affirmative attitudes toward the universe, and there are pessimistic ones, such as Hinduism in some of its aspects in which the totality of created things is regarded as a source of suffering and illusion. In the former, belief and practice are dedicated to the celebration, enhancement, and prolongation of existence. In the latter, the goal is renunciation and escape. Still other religious outlooks, such as Stoicism, are concerned with understanding and accepting the comprehensive rather than embracing or rejecting it.

Religion as relationship to the comprehensive is akin to philosophy defined as the coordination of knowledge. The difference is that philosophy is concerned with conceptual formulation, while religion represents man's response as a whole person—including feelings, ideas, and volitions—to the totality of things.

Obviously the relationship to the whole is of great importance in education, not so much in determining its detailed course as in setting the temper and tone of the entire process. The sense of the importance of learning is in no small measure a reflection of one's convictions about the meaningfulness and worth of existence as a whole. Perhaps the basic problem in all education is that of motivation. To this question religious concern for the comprehensive is of central relevance.

The absolute. A third conception of the object of ultimate concern is the perfect or absolute. This differs from the first and second conceptions in that neither the highest value nor the whole of things are necessarily perfect. Money may, in effect, be one's god, but it is not for that reason perfect or absolute. Perfection and absoluteness are not easily defined; they perhaps generally signify such qualities as completeness and self-sufficiency. No addition or alteration can effect any improvement in what is perfect. Religion, then, is commitment to a reality which is regarded as complete and self-sufficient.

In actual experience, of course, man is confronted with a world which in many ways needs improvement. It is also constantly changing, and hence never complete. Thus the world of ordinary experience is not perfect or absolute. It follows that the absolute object of religion must in some way transcend the actual world. For this reason conceptions of religion as ultimate concern for a perfect reality require a supernatural realm standing over against the actual or natural world. This supernature is not irrelevant to nature, but is regarded as its source and sustaining ground. Also man, though living in nature, is endowed with spiritual powers which link him to the supernatural and enable him to see in imperfect things the perfection from which they came and to which they are destined to return.

It is agreed by all who are committed to a transcendent Absolute that this perfect being, God, cannot be "known" in the ordinary sense. Strictly speaking, knowledge is only of the actual, changing, imperfect world. Perfection can only be hoped for, imaginatively conceived, and perhaps described by analogy. Beyond these affirmations the agreement ends. There are sharp differences of conviction between those who think knowledge of the actual world provides a good clue to the nature of God and those who think natural knowledge is religiously either useless or deceptive. In practice the difference is between those who feel justified in importing the Absolute into the sphere of the finite—into laws, institutions, and human concepts—and those who believe that no absolute claims can be made for any finite actual entity such as a book, a church, a person, or an idea.

Commitment to the Absolute has the effect of providing an ultimate purpose and goal for all educational effort. The aim of the learning process is to actualize as far as possible the ideal of perfection. But given this general incentive, the question remains: What is perfection? And here the religiously oriented educators divide into opposing camps. On the one hand there are those who are quite sure that they know what perfection is —who think that God has revealed himself unambiguously—and who proceed confidently to educate persons by this clear truth. On the other hand there are those who are committed to God and who recognize the necessity of implementing the divine will in actual life but who also see that every human effort is infected with finitude and self-interest. Hence they do not absolutize or claim ultimate truth for anything they know, and they seek to educate for openness to truth beyond what they have comprehended, for humility about all human pretensions, and for forgiveness in the light of premature certitude.

Participation in a tradition. A final conception of religion is that it is participation in a tradition. From this standpoint religion is largely a matter of convention and "faith" is adherence to certain customary modes of behavior. Such nominal religion is not really concerned with knowledge or its substitutes, nor does it require adventuresomeness or serious commitment. One acknowledges such beliefs as that God exists, that there is some kind of life after death, and that there is a moral law, but there need be no very clear idea about the meaning of these beliefs nor about the kind of evidence that might be introduced in their support. They are simply taken for granted as part of the tradition in which one has been reared.

Conventional religion also has its rites—going to church, singing hymns, reading the Bible, saying prayers—which are engaged in as part of the culture pattern of one's group. These activities can give a sense of comfort and of solidarity with others, just as may any other customary acts not designated as religious. The pattern of customary religious beliefs and rites is further consolidated and objectified in particular social institutions—churches, synagogues, and the like.

From the standpoint of the sophisticated exponents of religion a purely conventional type of belief and practice is not truly religious but is only the outward form of it. Be that as it may, common usage does identify religion by its externals, and for many, if not most, people it is the customary doctrines, rites, and institutions that are the sum and substance of religion. They would neither understand nor see the relevance of a more sophisticated conception such as "ultimate concern."

Religion as participation in a tradition is educationally significant in providing a social milieu in which learning takes place and in supplying certain traditional standards of behavior. It has little to do with the claims of knowledge. Such religion also concerns certain very special types of activity and has none of the pervasiveness and comprehensiveness characteristic of religion as relation to the ultimate or as a kind of knowledge.

The Study of Religion

As shown in the above paragraphs, there are several different possible conceptions of the nature of religion. Only by clearly designating the intended meaning can a discussion of religious problems proceed profitably. For example, the question of how religion is related to knowledge is answered differently for each of the conceptions of religion outlined in the preceding section. The question of how and why religion should be studied must also be answered in ways dependent on the conception of religion entertained.

Generally speaking, as in the case of philosophy, religion can be studied either as a separate discipline, in courses designated as "religion," or as an ingredient and perspective in other studies. In the latter case the religious ingredient may be either explicit or implicit. Courses in Bible, philosophy of religion, religious ethics, and history of religions are examples of religion studied as a separate discipline. Examples of religion as an explicit ingredient in other disciplines would be the historical study of religious movements, the study of religious art, and the sociological study of religious institutions. Examples of implicit religious perspective would be the consideration of plays or novels in the light of the ultimate human concerns expressed in them, the study of certain works of art as interpretations of the meaning of life, and the use of psychological materials as clues to the essential nature and predicament of man.

As in the case of philosophy, perhaps the major part of religious learning should be carried on through other studies. But the formal study of religion also has an important role to play in providing a more self-conscious, critical, and comprehensive religious outlook.

PART IV

Ultimate Questions in Education

26

Human Nature

SINCE EDUCATION is a process of directing the development of persons, it follows that the nature of persons is a matter of central importance for the philosophy of education.

On first thought it might seem that of all things our knowledge of human nature should be the most reliable and certain, for it has to do with ourselves, whom we constantly, directly, and most intimately experience, and with others of our kind, whom we also regularly encounter in our common life in a great variety of ways. In reality, this anticipated assurance about the nature of man is not warranted. Actually nothing is more puzzling, nothing prompts such difficult questions as man himself. This perplexity partly reflects the extraordinary complexity of human beings. Man is, indeed, "fearfully and wonderfully made." But perhaps the more important reason is precisely the fact that man is himself so deeply and vitally involved in *being* human that he cannot clearly and surely *know* what he is. Our understanding is often the least reliable about things in which we are most intimately engaged.

This perplexity about human nature is a stimulus to philosophic reflection. It is precisely about such concerns that critical analysis and disciplined speculation may be most fruitful. Such thinking may not remove the perplexity; it may even deepen the mystery. But to recognize the profundity of a problem is closer to wisdom than to be ignorant of both the problem and its solution.

Whatever the difficulties in thinking about human nature, one fact is clear: that nothing is so interesting. At once magnificent and petty, exalted and debased, free yet in chains, boundless but circumscribed, man contains within himself a world of contrasts which invite inquiry, stimulate action, and stir imagination. In a sense, to understand man is to understand the whole world, for "the world" means *man's* world.

The philosophy of education therefore requires reflection about human nature, not only because education is concerned with the development of persons but also because the understanding of man is the key to every experience about which man—as mirror of the world—may reflect.

The Uniqueness of Man

It has been presupposed in a number of places in earlier chapters that a significant conception of education depends upon some sense of the special nature of the human being. We turn now to examine this question more closely. Is man unique? Is there anything which sets him clearly apart from the other animals? Are human beings fully and without remainder part of nature? There are three general types of answers which may be given to these questions. Each type forms the basis for a whole series of attitudes and decisions about the meaning and methods of education.

Reductive analysis. The first view is that such uniqueness as man has derives wholly from his greater complexity. In essence human beings are merely highly complex animals. There is no difference in *kind* between the lower animals and man but only a difference in degree of complexity. It follows that in seeking to understand human beings nothing essential is lost in studying the simpler lower forms. This is standard scientific procedure; analyze the complex by considering first the simpler analogues. Hence the best clues to human behavior should be found in research on the lower animals.

But this principle of explaining the higher by the lower—the principle of "reduction"—can be carried still further. It is usually assumed that the lower living forms can themselves be regarded as very complicated mechanisms which can be wholly understood by the ordinary laws of physics and chemistry. Thus in the last analysis man is nothing but a highly complex physico-chemical system and the lower animals are of the same kind but not quite so complicated.

This view appeals because it promises the resources of the enormously successful natural sciences for the solution of the problems of man. There is a reliability and certainty in those sciences which gives them unparalleled authority. The principle of reduction also provides an attractive method of approaching baffling problems by a process of systematic simplification.

This view invites the question as to whether it really does justice to the uniqueness of men. May it not, in the very process of reduction, explain away rather than explain the essential features of human life? Granted also that the explanation of the complex by the simple is a method of study which should be pressed as far as possible, it may be doubted that by this method alone a full and satisfying understanding of human nature can be obtained. The hope and promise of explaining man by the laws of physics and chemistry have not been fulfilled to any significant degree and may in the long run prove to be in vain.

In the field of education the view that man is only a complicated animal would tend to direct major attention to the discovery and satisfaction of biological needs rather than to the so-called "higher" functions, since the latter would be regarded entirely as an outgrowth and expression of the former. The source of learning difficulties would be sought in physiological causes, and optimum education would be regarded as that which provides the maximum organic adjustment.

Essential discontinuity. A second view, diametrically opposed to the reductive standpoint, is that man is essentially discontinuous with nature, that he has a kind of uniqueness which is not of degree but of kind, and that he has special characteristics not shared at all with the lower animals. By this theory the study of man requires the use of concepts and techniques peculiar to its unique subject matter. Analysis into simpler components destroys the very essence of the human being. The laws of physics and chemistry, while applicable to the physico-chemical aspects of the human organism, do not have any relevance to the order of reality peculiar to man. By the same token, the principles applicable to the essence of man have no relevance to the lower levels of creation.

The merit of this view is that it seems to do full justice to the obviously superior capacities of human beings. It accepts them at face value without attempting to claim in the interests of simplicity that they are at bottom something else. It also accords with man's high opinion of his species and his absorbing interest in himself and his kind, giving theoretical sanction to his inveterate conviction of being something very special. It also tends to confirm his right to master and use for his own purposes the lower creatures. Finally, while the reductive approach gains support from the success of natural science, the theory of discontinuous uniqueness agrees more fully with the deepest ethical and religious insights of mankind, in which men's special place in creation has been affirmed and celebrated.

Against this view is the difficulty it poses for understanding the relation between man and the natural world he inhabits. This will be explored in some detail later in this chapter under the "mind-body problem." Any radical discontinuity is a challenge to reason, which seeks explanatory relationships that bridge differences. A belief in man's essential uniqueness may thus discourage inquiry into the roots of human nature and lead to the acceptance of unanalyzed concepts about it. This view also may inhibit concern for the physical and biological factors which undoubtedly condition human life, however unique man may be in his essential nature.

Educationally, the present position leads to central concern for those aspects of man which distinguish him from the animals—his mental, ideational, symbolic, moral, and spiritual functions. The success of education is then measured by the degree to which man transcends the animal level and subdues and controls the beast within himself. Biological adjustment is considered only as the condition and context for the development of the unique qualities.

Non-reductive continuity. A third position is intermediate between the reductive and the discontinuous. It may be designated "non-reductive continuity" because on the one hand it affirms the continuity of man with the rest of nature and on the other hand it does not claim that the characteristics of man can be wholly explained by purely physiological or physical principles. According to this position, there is no point along the ascending scale of entities, beginning with the inorganic and concluding with man, where radically new qualities come into being. Even the apparently most unique powers of human beings, such as thought, are regarded as present in the lower orders of living things and even in ostensibly dead matter, though in latent and undeveloped form. Man is thus considered unique with respect to the development and dominance of certain qualities but not because he alone possesses them.

In this view, human nature and lower forms alike can be understood only in the light of principles and laws which include both and which operate at all levels. A study of "dead" matter and of simpler living things may help to understand human beings, but it also follows that knowledge of man, in whom certain powers are most clearly and abundantly manifest, may throw light on the nature of the lower forms.

This mediating position is intended to embody all of the advantages of the two extreme views and to overcome their disadvantages. It incorporates our knowledge of the physico-chemical processes without making them into a total explanation. In a way it does even greater honor than the discontinuity theory to the "higher" qualities, and thus to ethical and religious intuitions, by giving them a place at all levels and not only in man. By requiring a single universally applicable system of explanation it seeks to do away with the problem of relating two utterly disparate realms of being to each other. Furthermore, not only does it do justice to the dependence of the higher qualities (e.g., of mind) upon their physical and biological basis, but affirms a reciprocal dependence of the lower upon the higher.

The convinced reductionist would regard the intermediate position as an unsatisfactory compromise, taking the edge off of clean-cut scientific analysis by introducing romantic notions about the presence of mind in lower forms without sufficient evidence. The convinced believer in discontinuity would have a somewhat similar objection, but with added concern lest the dignity of the human essence be compromised by admitting any participation by lower creatures.

With respect to education, this position would direct major attention to the full development of the powers dominant in man yet without neglect of the intimate tie between the human and non-human. It would foster concern for the whole creation and encourage a sense of kinship between man and all other creatures.

The "Mind-Body Problem"

Growing directly out of such considerations as the above regarding man's uniqueness is the question which has customarily been called the "mind-body problem." It is perfectly clear to common sense that human beings think, feel, remember, imagine, and speak, that these abilities reflect something vaguely called "mind," that human beings also have weight, occupy space, move, eat, breathe, and reproduce, and that these phenomena are evidence of what is called man's "body." It also appears that these two sets of things are quite different from each other. The problem of mind and body is to ascertain more precisely what is the nature of each, what the differences are, and how the two are related to each other in the complex being called man. Human nature has both bodily and mental characteristics or qualities. Hence every view of man's nature implies some standpoint on the mind-body problem. Some of the different approaches to this problem will now be considered.

Mind as bodily behavior. One view is that there are not two separate and distinct aspects of man—mind and body—but that human nature is solely and simply bodily in character. What is called mental is, then, merely one kind of behavior of the body. This position is associated with the reductive type of analysis discussed above, and the discussion of that approach applies here also. It is a position which accords to mind an entirely derivative character. It preserves the unity of man's nature, avoiding any problems of relating two disparate elements within the human being. It renders mind readily subject to scientific observation and, even more important, to manipulation and control. Mind is no longer regarded as inward, intangible, and inaccessible but as an overt and tangible, though somewhat subtle, physical activity. This includes such things as electrical impulses and chemical modifications, which may not appear as gross, large-scale bodily movement but are still purely physical in character. Mind has traditionally been regarded as something different from body because of its more intricate and less obvious nature and because of the different kinds of physical forces involved. This is analogous to the fact that radio waves and magnetic fields are physical realities, though not so obvious nor so soon recognized as falling stones or heat from fire. Those who regard mind as bodily behavior believe that further systematic study of the physical structure of man will progressively reveal the true nature of mental processes, though physical forces and laws not yet discovered may possibly be involved.

Body as mental phenomenon. At the other extreme from the position just described is the view that bodily existence has no separate and independent reality but is merely a product of mind. Instead of mind being derivative from body, body is regarded as derivative from mind. This is a position which flies in the face of common sense, yet throughout the history of thought it has had its able defenders. It rests upon the general observation that all reality comes to us in the form of experience and all our experience is essentially mental—inward and subjective—in character. From this it is argued that the body is only a kind of mental phenomenon.

It should be noted that this view is an inverted form of reductionism. Just as the ordinary reductionist explains mind wholly in terms of body, the present position reduces body wholly to mind. It eliminates discontinuity by making everything continuous with mind. It affirms the unity of the person by making him all mind. There is no repudiation of science and the scientific understanding of bodily activity, but science is now regarded as one mode of organization of mental life, giving even further weight to the view that mind is the sole reality.

This solution of the mind-body problem appeals to those who consider it important to affirm the independence and primacy of the life of thought, feeling, and will, who regard these experiences as the most promising clue to the ultimate nature of things. From this standpoint the exploration and explanation of human nature depend upon the understanding and appreciation of the mental or spiritual life of men.

Parallelism. Another solution to the mind-body problem is to affirm the distinctness and separateness of mind and body but to postulate some third reality of which each is an aspect. This means that changes in body would be accompanied by corresponding or parallel changes in mind, and conversely that mental modifications would have bodily parallels. There would always of necessity be a perfect harmony between the two orders of being, since by hypothesis each is an aspect of one common reality.

This theory preserves the unity of the personality and explains how mental and physical states are correlated. It achieves this without sacrificing either body or mind to the other, as happens in the two previous reductive theories. On the other hand, it creates certain difficulties. What is this third something of which mind and body are aspects? Since we know things only as mind or body or both we cannot get behind them to the underlying reality. Does it then satisfactorily explain anything or does it merely amount to a restatement of the problem? Furthermore, does our experience suggest such a close parallel of mind and body? Are there not manifestly physical states without corresponding mental states, and does it not seem that many mental activities lack any clear physical parallels? In short, do not mind and body have a relative autonomy or independence which parallelism denies?

Duality. To meet the difficulties presented by parallelism it may be held that mind and body are truly separate, distinct, and independent but that they can and do interact with one another. This sets up a *duality* of mind and body. Mind and body both have their own special qualities and powers, and each may modify, limit, enhance, and condition the other. This view is an expression of the common-sense attitude. We feel, for example, that by a simple act of will (mental) we can initiate motion of our bodies. We also know that our sensory equipment in its various forms translates physical energy into mental images. Mind thus acts upon body and body influences mind. But there need be no perfect correlation. Indeed, the directives of mind often fail to be fulfilled by the body and the state of the body is often poorly represented to the mind.

While duality may satisfy common sense and preserve a degree of independence for both body and mind, it poses one major difficulty, and that concerns the nature of the interaction between the two. If there is thoroughgoing duality, so that mind and body are really separate and distinct, then how can either have any effect on the other? If mind can actually move a body, must it not share with body some of its physical qualities? Similarly, if body can create mental images, must it not participate in some manner in a non-corporeal kind of being? But if body has mental qualities and mind has some bodily characteristics, then duality has been abandoned in favor of some sort of parallelism or reductionism. In summary, while the previous theories preserved the unity of human nature by sacrificing either mind or body, by introducing a mysterious third entity, or by blurring distinctions, the present theory preserves distinctions and satisfies common sense at the expense of unity in human nature.

Critique of the problem. The mind-body problem thus seems to lead to a dilemma. Each suggested type of solution has its advantages but each also has serious flaws. In such a situation the philosopher might well ask whether the difficulty may not lie elsewhere than in the contradictory solutions, namely, in the very way in which the problem is formulated. Perhaps the contradictions arise not because there is some disharmony in the nature of man but simply because the terms used in stating the problem make these difficulties inevitable. In such a case the right procedure is to reformulate the problem so as to avoid built-in dilemmas.

The old story of the man who was asked whether he had stopped beating his wife illustrates the point. There are cruel men to whom it would be entirely appropriate to direct this question, and from whom a yes or no reply might be expected. But for the ordinary peaceable husband the question as stated poses a dilemma. If he should answer "Yes," the implication would be that he had been beating his wife and stopped—which would be untrue. If he should answer "No," this would mean he was still beating his wife—which would also be untrue. Hence, no direct answer of affirmation or denial can truly be given. The trouble is not in the man, in his wife, or in their relationship. It is in the question. The formulation of the problem is such as to make contradictions inevitable. The solution of the difficulty then consists in reformulating the question in an appropriate fashion. For example, it would be legitimate to ask *any* husband the question, "Have you ever beaten your wife?" or "Are you treating your wife gently these days?"

To return to the mind-body problem, may it not be that the dilemma posed by it comes from faulty formulation? Note that the problem has to do with the relationship of two distinct things called, respectively, "mind" and "body." Now if they are distinct in a mutually exclusive sense, it is impossible to relate them, and yet they are both necessary components of the one thing called a person, and thus must be related. Does the trouble lie in making "things" out of "mind" and "body," as if they were substances like oil and water which one might try to mix? Does it make sense to speak of mind and body as separate substances and of the person as some kind of mixture or compound of these ingredients? If one reflects about it, he does not usually think of mind apart from its embodiment in a whole person, nor of body apart from its expression of the living, thinking reality of the whole person. Thus "mind" and "body" would seem in themselves not to be concrete entities whose relationships can be meaningfully discussed. Each may be regarded as an abstraction from or as an aspect of the concrete entity which we call a person. We must then begin with the whole person and inquire what "mind" and "body" mean as aspects of that whole.

A functional interpretation. Instead of assuming that mind and body are things, we may regard them as functions. By a function is meant any characteristic mode of being or acting. The thing or entity is the whole human person, and this person has bodily functions and mental functions, i.e., characteristic patterns of operation which are designated respectively as body and mind. Thus it is not useful to say that the body has weight or occupies space and that the mind thinks or remembers, since this implies that body and mind are themselves entities. Rather it is the person who weighs so much or is this tall and it is the person who thinks or remembers, and these two aspects of his being reflect respectively his bodily and his mental nature.

How are body and mind related to one another? We can answer this by observing the correlation of bodily and mental functions in the whole person. Recent advances in medicine have emphasized the extent of this correlation. We now know that bodily conditions—gland secretions, digestive and circulatory functions, and a host of other physiological factors—may profoundly influence mental outlook, and we also know now that mental conditions—emotional experience, attitudes toward self and others, confidence or fear, and innumerable other psychological factors—may markedly affect bodily health. The field called "psychosomatic medicine" is concerned with this variety of body-mind correlations, with a view to preserving and restoring the health of the whole person in his unity of bodily and mental functions. In other words, it is now recognized that health of body cannot be assured without taking account of mental factors nor psychological health without the right physiological support.

Despite these important correlations, the functional interpretation does not require any complete correspondence between the bodily and mental processes. It is not assumed that to every physiological process there corresponds a precise psychological parallel nor that every mental function has an exact bodily correlate. One cannot understand a person's mental life purely from the study of his bodily functions nor are his mental functions the key to comprehending fully the bodily ones. Bodily and mental functions, though related in significant ways, still both have a kind of autonomy or independence. There are bodily functions for which the mental concomitants are relatively insignificant, and vice versa.

In this respect the functional approach differs from parallelism. It also differs in not postulating a third substance of which mind and body are two equivalent alternative representations. Instead of that there is the concrete complex human being with his many more or less interrelated functions.

The functional interpretation emphasizes the interdependence of mental and bodily functions in the unity of the person. A human being is regarded as a psycho-physical organism in which both mental and bodily aspects are essential. It is assumed that mental processes need a physiological base and that bodily processes require mental coordination and direction. It would follow from this assumption that bodily life and mental life begin and end together. A corpse would no longer be a person, and there could be no disembodied minds.

The latter conclusion appears to contradict certain widely held and deeply cherished beliefs, which deny that the fate of the mind is inextricably tied to that of the physical body. Suffice it to say that a functional conception of mind and body does not necessarily exclude this theological conviction. Everything depends upon the nature of the bodily functions postulated. There might be nothing impossible, in principle, in conceiving of a complete person with a new kind of body, no longer subject to the ordinary laws of physical behavior.

The mind-body problem and education. The question of psychological and physiological factors in human nature is of paramount importance in education. It is not only in psychosomatic medicine that the intimate interdependence of mind and body has been increasingly recognized. In education also it has become clear that learning cannot be effectively directed without taking care of organic needs and physical conditions, and similarly that the mental and emotional well-being of the learner tends to foster physical well-being. The emphasis on educating "the whole child" is evidence of this principle. On the other hand, many educators would insist that despite these interdependences, there are some relatively independent mental disciplines which cannot be mastered merely by good physiological coordination and similarly that there are relatively autonomous bodily functions which reflect mental dispositions very little. In short, the problem of unity and variety in the components of human nature is a fundamental one in education, for which the several philosophic orientations may provide some useful suggestions.

Distinctive Features of Human Nature

At the beginning of the chapter we were concerned with the uniqueness of man. There we considered the relation between man and the lower orders. In the next section we dealt with a similar problem, of the relation between the two natures or types of functions within the one human person. Now we return to the original theme of the uniqueness of man, in an attempt to suggest some of the main distinctive features of human nature.

Man has, of course, many things in common with other kinds of beings. He has physical properties in common with everything material. He shares with all living things in processes of nutrition, growth, and reproduction. He is like the animals in powers of self-initiated movement and in responsiveness to sensory stimulation. He is one of the mammals as concerns the bearing and feeding of offspring. Any full description of human nature would need to take account of all these facts. That is not our purpose at this point. It is rather our intention now merely to state some of the ways in which human nature differs from the natures of other kinds of beings, to discuss some of the characteristics which man does not have in common with rocks or plants or lower animals. In Chapter 29 the aim will be to see the whole picture and to show how human beings fit into the pattern of the entire world order.

Brain capacity. The physiological basis of man's remarkable development is in large part his brain. Of all animals, he alone is equipped with so extensive a complex of interconnected brain cells as to make possible the range and quality of human behavior. The human brain is actually not the largest in absolute size; those of the elephant and the whale, for example, weigh considerably more. But these largest mammals have many times the body weight of man. Taking account of normal trends of brain in relation to body weight, the brain size of human beings is phenomenal. In the new-born human baby the brain contains about one seventh of the total weight. This is a higher proportion than in any warm-blooded animal regardless of size. This is the physiological foundation for the enormous feats of learning which the infant must accomplish to become an adult human being.

Nor is the uniqueness of the human brain only a matter of size. In the character and organization of the component parts it is without parallel. Most significant is the preponderance, in relation to the other parts, of the cerebrum, which controls conscious thought and action. The outer cerebral layer, the cortex, is also characterized by deep folds or convolutions which further increase the number of brain cells within the given volume. The association centers in the cortex are complexly interconnected with each other and with other parts of the brain to permit the amazing variety of coordinated bodily and mental functions of the human organism.

Relatively few instinctive patterns. Human behavior is for the most part not instinctive. That is to say, man does not act according to certain fixed automatic and built-in behavior patterns. The new-born infant has only certain minimal automatic reflexes, such as those of grasping and sucking, which enable him to seek the food necessary to sustain life. He is not, like some of his counterparts in the "lower" species, provided with neural patterns which make him immediately competent to deal with the varied demands of his new environment. This is directly reflected in the difference between the nervous systems of man and the lower animals, particularly in the presence of the large cerebrum, which is virtually absent in such lower forms as fishes, birds, and reptiles. It is also reflected in man's much higher ratio of brain weight to weight of spinal cord (which chiefly handles the automatic types of behavior as contrasted with the learned behavior co-ordinated by the cerebral centers).

Since human beings are not mainly controlled by instinct, their behavior is largely learned. Hence the great importance of education. No education would exist or could be effective if human beings were governed wholly by instinctive mechanisms.

Human nature is plastic. It does not come in fixed molds or standard patterns. A person possesses an endless range of potentialities; the ones to be realized depend upon the influences brought to bear. He is not inexorably determined in advance by given neural structures. Man is modifiable and adaptable; he can adjust to changing circumstances. He can even, to a degree, create his own future.

Long dependency. An immediate consequence of man's lack of instinct and his need to learn is the long period of dependency which characterizes his species. Some animals are able immediately at birth to fend for themselves. Others mature quickly and after brief periods of parental protection and nourishment can carry on without further assistance. For human beings this is not the case. The human infant is utterly dependent upon its mother or mother-substitute. Left to itself it would soon die. Food, warmth, love, and protection must all be supplied if the helpless newcomer is to survive. Nor is this utter dependency soon ended. Only very gradually does the child develop his own powers for dealing effectively with his environment. In advanced civilizations the child may depend upon the parent in varying ways and degree for as long as twenty to twenty-five years. The minimum period within which competence for independent existence can normally be achieved is six to eight years. By contrast, an ape can become independent within twelve to eighteen months.

This long dependency is the price man must pay for his plasticity. Having no built-in behavior patterns, he must learn them, and learning takes time. It also takes means of instruction, and this is why the home, the school, and other educative agencies come into being. For it is only from the older individuals in whom certain human potentials have been made actual that the child's process of learning can be directed.

Culture. The special learnings which the human being must master are carried from generation to generation not in the body cells but in the social body in the form of *culture*. Culture consists of those distinctive modes of learned behavior which distinguish particular social groups. It is comprised of that whole complex of manners, customs, laws, languages, tools, rites, and the like which represent the "way of life" of the social group. Each society has its own culture—its peculiar style of life, outlook, organization, attitudes and practices, its particular kinds of housing, eating, love-making, family structure, and religious beliefs.

Without doubt it is his cultural life that is the most striking aspect of man's uniqueness. It is as the possessor and creator of culture that human beings are most signally distinguished from all other creatures. Some of the lower animals are organized into societies. Some, like the ants and bees, have complex behavior patterns which are analogous to those based upon human culture. But for the most part these are products of instinct and not of learning. They are transmitted genetically and not socially. In any case, no animal society can begin to approach human beings in the richness and variety of learned behavior systems. In this sense it can be said that man alone has culture—that it is by his culture-activity that man's uniqueness is established.

The possibility of man's culture is directly correlated with his mental structure, his absence of instinct, and his long dependency. It is the size and organization of the human brain which is the neurological basis for the conscious thought and action underlying cultural creation. It is the plasticity of human nature which makes possible the development of different patterns of thought and conduct and the endless elaboration of new modes of behavior. It is the learning which goes on in the dependent child that constitutes his incorporation of the cultural tradition of his society.

Man needs education only because he has culture. Education may be regarded as a process of developing cultural competence in persons. The content of educational learning is culture, and education is the main means for the preservation and transmission of culture. To say that man alone has culture is to imply also that education is a uniquely human activity.

Language. One of the most important aspects of culture, and one so outstanding that by itself it may be considered a distinctive mark of human nature, is language. Man is the "talking animal." Other animals can communicate with one another by means of sound signals. They may even have the rudiments of what we call speech. But without question no creature other than man has the power of full and varied communication by means of language. The essence of language is not the stimulation of a special kind of behavior in another by sound signals but the communication of *meaning,* and this is a function of rationality (which will be discussed presently) and not merely of overt behavior.

Symbols. The ability to speak and to write is only part of a more general human capacity, namely, the ability to use symbols. A symbol is any sound, visible object, or act which is intended to communicate a meaning beyond itself. Thus, a nation's flag is a symbol because it is not merely a conventional design, but because it stands for that complex of realities which the nation means to the observer of the flag. Likewise the act of saluting the flag is not to be understood literally, as the raising of the hand to a certain position, but as a symbol of one's attitudes of patriotic loyalty, respect, and aspiration. In the same way the phrase "American flag" is not simply a pair of words that looks or sounds the way it does; it is a symbol, to anyone who understands its meaning, for a material surface with a particular star and stripe design. The same thing may sometimes be taken either symbolically or non-symbolically. For example, a piece of bread eaten solely to satisfy hunger is not used symbolically. The same piece of bread eaten as part of a ritual act (e.g., in a Christian communion service) would be used symbolically.

The point to be emphasized here is that human beings alone use symbols. If some animals do engage in symbolic activity, it is of an extremely elementary nature and to a very limited extent. For human beings there is a great multiplication and compounding of symbolic forms. Symbols are the heart and soul of man's existence. By definition, the whole meaning of human life is bound up in its symbols. To speak, to paint pictures, to worship—in short, to live a rich symbolic life—is the unique power and glory of human kind. It is in the creation, modification, and communication of symbols that man perhaps most significantly fulfills his nature.

It was said above that man is characteristically a creature with culture. Much, but not all, of culture is symbolic. Furthermore there is always a tendency for non-symbolic culture to become invested with wider meanings and hence to become symbolic. A house may simply be a place of shelter, but it may easily become a symbol of economic or of social standing. Many customs which began as utilitarian and literal acts have become charged with symbolic meaning (e.g., hand shaking, the custom of the gentleman walking on the street side of a lady).

Just as culture is preserved and transmitted by education, so also the centrality of symbolic activity in human life suggests an important place for the symbolic in education. In earlier chapters, especially in Part III, we have discussed in detail some of the important varieties of symbolic learning and their place in the program of education.

Reason. It has frequently been said that the really unique characteristic of man is his power of reasoning or of rationality. "Reason" is a somewhat broad and vague concept which may be less useful than some of the more specific designations of human uniqueness. It always includes, however, the power of abstraction, i.e., of specifying classes to which particular things belong. Thus, it is by the abstractive power of reason that a human being can understand the class of objects called "chair" and can designate certain objects as belonging to that class. Another way of stating this is to say that reason involves the power of forming concepts and of making and understanding definitions. Furthermore, reason includes the ability to think, that is, to relate concepts to each other and to engage in logical processes whereby conclusions are drawn from premises.

Reason at the minimum includes logical conceptual thinking. But many students of the subject would wish to use the term in a still broader sense. There may be kinds of reason which are not strictly logical and not even clearly conceptual—flashes of insight only vaguely formulated, or intuitions persuasively felt but without logical justification. In fact, the whole gamut of emotional and intellectual activities, insofar as they are consciously recognized and ordered according to some coherent pattern, may be designated as the province of reason. Not only the logic of the scientist but also the quite different logic of music or of love or of religious faith may be regarded as belonging to the life of reason.

Used in this broad sense, reason is a comprehensive term which includes all of the cultural, linguistic, and symbolic activities hitherto discussed, as well as the five characteristics to be discussed hereafter. The first three on the list—brain capacity, lack of instincts, and long dependency—may also be regarded as necessary biological and social concomitants of the life of reason. With reason thus broadly conceived, it is appropriate to declare that man is the rational animal. Education then might be defined as the process of cultivating and directing the life of reason.

Imagination. One of the more specific powers of reason which characterizes man is imagination, that is, the ability to create an inner world to some degree independent of the immediately presented outer world known through the senses. The ingredients of the inner world thus constructed may be derived from earlier sense experience, but they are rearranged and transformed to make a new world within. Even in respect to the world directly apprehended through the senses, imagination colors, reforms, and proportions the picture so as to re-create the world within. This is only to say that man is not like a camera or a recording machine, passively and obediently reproducing energy patterns from without. He imaginatively reconstructs and transforms the world of sense data. And even when the senses are relatively unstimulated, the human mind can by the power of imagination create inner stimuli which make possible vivid and meaningful continuing experiences.

It is imagination which is the foundation of human creativity. In this power resides man's dignity as an originator. He is no mere product and mirror of the world about him. He is the maker of his own world and as such the remaker of the world about him. It is by imagination that in man a decisive reversal of the world process occurs: in all lower orders the creatures are products of the process, in man the process itself becomes subject to man's creative direction.

In common usage "imagination" is often associated with the "imaginary," and this is regarded as something less than real, solid, and significant. The life of imagination has accordingly been identified with the realm of pure fancy, fiction, and fable. Granting that these latter are products of imagination (and often valuable and important in human life), imagination itself has a much broader scope and should be understood to refer to the creative-constructive powers of mind which not only produce the imaginary but also underlie all of man's effective scientific and practical life. Thus, imagination, far from being an insubstantial frill, is at the very heart of human nature. By the same token, a central task of education is the discipline of imagination.

Memory. The ability of the human being to remember introduces a new dimension into our discussion of the uniqueness of man. Thus far we have not dealt explicitly with man's relation to time. The nature of memory is concerned with that relation. As persons ourselves it is easy to take the fact of memory for granted, to see nothing unusual, remarkable, or puzzling about it. Actually the phenomenon of memory has opened up some of the most profound questions of science and philosophy, and it cannot be said with any assurance that these have all been satisfactorily answered.

Memory has to do with the persistence or reappearance of past experiences in the present. Time moves on, sweeping away with it the events of the past. Memory halts or reverses that movement and restores the past to the present. How can that be? How can the past which is gone still remain in the present? There would seem to be two possible answers.

Organic memory. First, past experience obviously produces actual changes in the person, and these changes represent the continuing influence of the past in the present. The nature of a person is a consequence of what has happened in the past. Therefore, what has gone before inevitably influences present experience. In particular, it seems likely that physical and chemical changes take place in the human nervous system as a result of every experience, and these changes are persisting structural and functional factors which literally embody the past and make possible its effectiveness in the present.

Memory-as-such. Second, it may be asked whether the persisting causal influence of the past is really memory itself or only the physiological basis for memory, which in its essence is something quite different. For if memory is only a present structure, then the past is not really in the present *as such,* but only in the form of its effects. But the essence of memory is the consciousness of the past *as past,* i.e., the sense of being in the present yet also in some real sense in the past. Memory in this second meaning implies that man has the power really to reverse the movement of time—to stand above its seemingly inexorable onflow, as on the fixed shore of a passing stream, and comprehend the past and the present together.

The uniqueness of man would seem to lie in this second aspect of memory. The lower animals have memory of the first kind. They behave in the present in ways that bear the marks of past experience because that past has produced persisting structual or functional changes in them. But it seems unlikely that any animal except man has to any significant degree the ability to recognize the past as past, to be vividly conscious not only of a present-influenced-by-past but of the past-in-itself.

Man has this power by virtue of his imagination. The arresting or reversal of time is a work of the imagination. Memory is imagination of the past—the re-creation of the past in the present.

Conscious and unconscious. It has often been pointed out that man's memory is both conscious and unconscious. This distinction parallels the one made above. The memory built into the organism by persisting effects of past experience is to a large extent unconscious. There are vast accumulations of past experience "stored up," as it were, in the personality. Of these only an infinitesimal fraction may at any one time be brought to the focus of consciousness and thus become memories in the full and proper sense. Probably many unconscious memories never become conscious. According to our present analysis the lower animals have only unconscious memory. Though we must recognize the great influence of unconscious memory on human life, it is our contention that the uniqueness of man lies in his power of conscious remembering.

The distinction between conscious and unconscious has been emphasized chiefly by the psychoanalysts and the psychologists influenced by them. It has been clearly demonstrated that much human behavior is governed by the subconscious and that conscious, rational direction of conduct plays a much smaller part than we ordinarily think. One of the criteria for a mature personality is the ability to bring the unconscious under conscious scrutiny and control.

Memory and history. There is one further aspect of human memory which may be mentioned here, and has already been elaborated in Chapter 22. Man's unique ability to withstand complete immersion in the time-stream is reflected in his characteristic interest in *making history.* Man is the only creature that keeps records of his doings, compiles chronicles of events he has witnessed, and establishes memorials of his activity. Only man deliberately sets up markers—whether in books or stone or in founded institutions—to keep alive the remembrance of things past. The making of history, in this broad sense, is the embodiment of memory in culture. It is the creation of a kind of social and vicarious memory which is independent of the actual rememberings of individuals. Thus, the celebration of the fourth of July reminds Americans of the War of Independence, into the experience of which one living today can by the power of imagination to some extent enter, even though he can never experience it as a full contemporary. History as objectified memory enables one to be a contemporary in imagination. This power man alone possesses. Man is, in short, the historical animal.

Man's unique power of memory, both individual and historical, suggests the importance of the past in the process of education. This is not to say that education should be largely memory work. It does mean that memory, broadly conceived, is an essential aspect of being human, and that the process of directing personal development must have much to do with the recognition, appreciation, and employment of the past.

Anticipation. This is memory in reverse, the bringing of the future into the present—the leaping ahead of the time-stream to take a stand in the not-yet. Just as memory makes the past influential in the present, so anticipation makes the future a factor in the present.

In a sense anticipation is even more astonishing than memory. The past is settled, complete. It indubitably *has been*. But the future has not yet come into being. How can something that is not and has never been yet exert power? Still, we know that the future does greatly affect the present.

Purpose. The future acting upon the present in human life is called purpose. Man is unique in having purposes. An alternative way of putting it is to say that man is governed by intentions, ideals, or ends-in-view. He is moved not only by the pressure of the past but also by the lure of the future.

This is not to say that man can fully foretell the future. An intention is not the same as a prediction. The reason for this is that the future is greatly conditioned by the settled reality of the past and present. Purposes may be unrealistic in not taking account of this given reality and hence may go unfulfilled. For this reason anticipation has a somewhat more uncertain and indefinite status than memory. Nonetheless, there does appear in anticipation a real relevance of the future to the present, a genuine effectiveness of the "might be" in making the "will be" out of the "is."

Conscious and unconscious intention. Anticipation, like memory, may be either conscious or unconscious. Many intentions are a result of functional conditions which propel the human organism in a particular direction quite apart from conscious decision. For example, a person may have the unconscious aim of securing the love and protection he was denied when a small child, while his dominant conscious purpose is to make money. While the unconscious purposes may actually be far more important in determining human behavior than the conscious ones, it seems right to say, as in the case of memory, that anticipation in the true and complete sense of appropriating the future *as such* is a function of man's conscious life only, and that one of the ways in which persons make good their humanity is by transforming their unconscious purposes into conscious anticipations.

Like memory, anticipation is a work of imagination. It is by the power of imagination that the future as such is comprehended in the present. The same quality by which imagination can in a sense annul the passage of time from the past enables it to reach also into the future, lending to the present the aspect and flavor of futurity.

Will. This human capacity for anticipation is closely related to a quality of personality which has traditionally been given a prominent place, namely, the "will." This "will" is simply the active purpose or intention of the person. It is effective anticipation. It is the power of an intended future to operate in the present so as to bring itself to realization. In brief, and somewhat metaphorically, will is the future seeking to become present through persons.

Anticipation is, of course, absolutely fundamental in education. The very definition of education as directing the development of persons is founded upon futurity and its conscious use. Man is nothing apart from his *becoming* and that depends upon goals, aims, purposes, intentions, hopes, and ideals—all of which are based upon the uniquely human power of anticipation.

Self-transcendence. Many of the unique aspects of human nature already discussed have their roots in what may be called *self-transcendence*. This means the ability (paradoxical though it may sound) of the self to go beyond or rise above itself. Self-consciousness as a quality of selfhood means that the self can (as it were) stand apart and look at itself. The power of reflection implies a self at once observer and observed. Persons can engage in an inner dialogue; they can talk to themselves. A person is in his essence not a solitary unit but a bipolar unity. But self-transcendence means not only the bipolarity of self-consciousness. It also means a creative drive to become more than one is. It is a leaping beyond the confines and boundaries of the actual self to a larger possible self. The human self never simply *is*. It is part of its essence to be continually immersed in an indefinitely expansible world of wider possibility.

This can perhaps best be understood by reference once more to imagination, memory, and anticipation, all of which illustrate the meaning of self-transcendence. Imagination permits man to experience a larger world than that immediately given by his senses. Furthermore, the world of imagination has no limits; there are in principle no bounds to the realms to be imaginatively created and explored. By memory man is able to transcend his present position in time, to relive events he has experienced in the past, and to participate through the historical record in events of the distant past. By a similar power of self-transcendence man can reach beyond the confines of past and present and participate by anticipation in the life of the future. Thus human beings are not, like other creatures, wholly chained to their own particular stations in space and in time, but while still subject to space and time, they can through the power of mind transcend these limitations and lay claim to a world without limits.

Freedom. The quality of self-transcendence is probably best understood by reference to man's *freedom,* which has been further elaborated in Chapter 15. To be free means the power to rise above the limitations of one's space-time condition, not to be bound by the strict necessity of antecedent causes, but to constitute to some degree the cause of one's self. As free, then, man is to a certain extent his own maker. But a person can make himself only if he possesses that bipolarity and creative drive which are the essence of self-transcendence. Thus man is uniquely endowed with freedom—the freedom of self-transcendence.

It is the task of education to encourage growth in this power of self-transcendence. Without it man is no man at all but an automaton. There must be in education a considerable amount of routine, but only as the foundation for a higher freedom. Routinization by itself makes unreflective, uncreative mechanisms rather than persons. Training in habitual behavior has its place if it frees man for higher tasks. By itself it makes of man a domesticated animal. Education in the full sense thus requires the development of self-transcendence.

Spirituality. The last of the twelve unique characteristics of man to be considered may be called *spirituality.* This is an admittedly vague term, used to mean a great many different things. Generally it involves religious sensitivities, but the meanings of religion are also so varied that this association does not sharpen the concept much. It is proposed here that spirituality be understood as a corollary and consequence of what has been described above as self-transcendence. Let us define spirituality as the essential boundlessness of man's power of self-transcendence. It is in this sense that man can be said to partake of the infinite. Human life has certain definite limits; it is in these respects essentially finite. But this is not the whole story. There are other respects—such as in his capacity for creative elaboration and for high aspiration—to which no limits may be assigned. It is in these participations in the infinite that human spirituality may be said to consist. The connection with religion thus becomes clear, if we regard religion as man's relation to the ultimate or infinite. In the Western religious tradition it has been said that man is created "in the image of God." This phrase expresses symbolically man's spirituality. It says that human life has the unique privilege of sharing in that boundless wealth of life and being in which all finite things have their ground and goal.

If man is in essence spiritual, it follows that education must take account of spirituality and encourage its development in persons. This implies that education ought not to be concerned merely with immediate and practical finite interests, but should consider the infinite horizons of life and stimulate those apprehensions and ideals whereby the bounds of the customary and familiar are exceeded and doors are opened into a mysterious and wonderful beyond.

The soul. As a footnote to this section, perhaps a word needs to be said about the concept of the *soul.* Many in the religious tradition would say that the uniqueness of man is that he has a soul. In modern times scientific thinkers have tended to avoid this term because they feel it has led to certain obscurities and confusions. They think that the soul has been regarded as a kind of spiritual organ—an entity or thing in its own right—and this has led to some of the difficulties already dealt with in connection with the mind-body problem.

Actually there would seem to be no good reason why the concept "soul" cannot be rescued from careless or superstitious use and restored to an honored place in thoughtful communication. The word has a richness of connotation and a dignity of historical usage which makes it worthy of consideration. There is much traditional warrant for defining soul as that whole complex of qualities or functions which reflect the organized character of a living entity. By this definition even lower living things have souls. The human soul would be that set of organization patterns which human beings exhibit, and the uniqueness of man would reside in those particular soul attributes which he alone has. This would lead us back to a description of just such qualities or powers of reason, memory, and spirituality as we have already discussed. In short, there would seem to be good warrant for understanding the term "human soul" as synonymous with what the philosopher-psychologist would call "personality" or "the self."

27
Human Development

IN THE previous chapter some of the problems and concepts connected with human nature and its uniqueness were considered. We now turn to examine the question of human development. Granted that man has certain characteristics, how does he get them? By what means and from what source or sources does his nature derive? Such questions as these are obviously vital for education. They have been central to all of the discussions in this book. The following paragraphs may then be regarded as a general and comprehensive synopsis of this fundamental theme.

Static and Dynamic Conceptions of Personality

There are two essentially different ways of looking at human personality, and they imply quite different approaches to the problem of development. One view is that a person is a definite thing—a composite of many parts, a network of interrelated organs—and that as a result of various forces and influences this entity may be changed into a different one, with somewhat altered constituents and modified internal relationships. Development is the exchange of one thing for another, or the modification of one entity into another. An appropriate analogy for this might be clay modelling of a statue. In each stage materials are added or removed and new shapes imparted. Change takes place by the rearrangement of essentially inert stuff.

Although changes are admitted by this view, it is based in one sense upon a *static* conception of personality. A person at any given time is a compound of such and such structures and powers, and development is something that *happens to* this compound. The development is not considered an inherent aspect of the person's very being.

In contrast to this position is one which holds that personality is in its essence dynamic, that change is built into the innermost nature of the human organism, and that the developmental process is inherent in being a person.

The constituents of personality are regarded as ceaselessly on-moving energy systems. The relatively stable and abiding characteristics of personality reflect a condition of equilibrium among these energy systems. An analogy might be a wave of water, in which there is a rapid exchange of substance as the wave moves forward. The development of the wave—its change in form—would be due to a shifting in the balance of moving forces. So also the living organism is seen as a maelstrom of activity, endlessly changing, and development is the shift in the balance of these constituent activities. The study of living beings is different from the study of inert stuff (if indeed there really is any such thing). Aliveness means that change is of the essence.

The point of this discussion is that there is an important difference in emphasis between a view of man in which change is something secondary and derivative and a view in which it is of the essence. In the previous chapter we considered human nature in the light of its major characteristic features largely from a static point of view. It was as though we had taken snapshots of a moving scene and then tried to represent the full reality by these momentary glimpses. The question to be raised now is whether we do not need a moving picture to represent the nature of man. Do we not need to adopt a standpoint in which human personality is understood in the light of its never-ending process of development?

These two views engender quite different attitudes toward education. The static view suggests that education is itself the source of personality change, while the dynamic view recognizes much more the resources within the person upon which education depends. The static view tends to encourage standardized and traditional types of education, while the dynamic view leads one to make provision for variety and individuality and prepares one for endless surprises in what growing persons can do and become.

Growth

We shall examine some of the concepts which may be employed in understanding the development of persons—concepts which accordingly have an important role in thinking about education.

One of the most frequently used concepts in the study of personality development is *growth*. Education is often regarded as a means to help persons grow, and the value and success of education are commonly measured by growth achieved. It is therefore important to understand precisely what the concept "growth" means. There are at least four meanings. Or more exactly, there are four kinds of growth which may be distinguished.

Enlargement. The first is growth as enlargement or expansion. This involves no change in kind but only in size or extent. This is the most unsophisticated of the meanings. The child tends to think in these terms. To grow up is to become larger. Now, of course, growth may involve enlargement. Children do become taller and heavier. But this tells very little about growth itself and does almost no justice to what growth of personality means. Growing of persons is not like inflating a balloon. An adult is obviously not merely a large child (just as a child is not a miniature adult)—or, to the extent that the adult *is* a large child it can be said that he has not really grown up. The growing person may expand in various ways—in body, in intelligence, in memory—and no growth can take place without some such expansion. Hence enlargement is one necessary aspect of growth, but other concepts are required for an adequate description of its meaning.

Accretion. A second meaning of growth is accretion. This is not quite the same as enlargement, which is meant to signify only increase in size. Accretion means the addition and incorporation of new and possibly different elements. Thus, a family grows by the addition of children to it, each child bringing his own individuality to the group. By the acquisition of new components the collective entity may be changed in character. It is not a mere change in dimensions but in constituent substance. Undoubtedly the growth of persons involves such accretion. Much must be added to a child in order that he may attain maturity. Yet this concept of growth also seems to omit something. An adult is not merely a child *plus* something else. The idea of adding to or heaping on does not do full justice to what growth really is.

There is a rather prevalent view of education which derives from the concept of growth as accretion. According to it education means accumulation. The nature of what is accumulated may be variously conceived. It may be time (years of attendance at school), diplomas, course credits, facts, skills, or experience. By this standard the well-educated person is the one who has amassed a sufficient number of such items. This view of education is defective in the same way and for the same reasons as the concept of growth as accretion.

Patterned coordination. A third concept of growth is the patterned coordination of materials and functions. This may be called an organic conception. Enlargement and accretion both lack the factor of coordination or of organization. Growth is not merely expansion and accumulation; at least in the realm of living things it also involves the ways in which the component elements are related to one another to form a working whole. Organic growth generally includes enlargement of one kind or another and the addition of new components, but the most important factor is the bringing together of these increments into a unified organism.

Growth of persons can be adequately understood only if it rests at least upon this third meaning, for human beings are, at the very minimum, complex organisms. Education also needs to rest upon this organic concept of growth, taking account not only of materials to be embodied in the maturing personality but first and foremost of the orders and processes whereby the components become a living personality. The detailed scientific study of human development has been of such great value to educators precisely because it has supplied important clues to the organization of personality and the ways in which such orderly growth can best be facilitated.

For example, it would generally be agreed that every person should grow in the capacity to take responsibility and initiative, to become independent and autonomous. Now one of the clearest conclusions emerging from the study of human development is that before a person can develop independence he must have achieved a sense of secure dependence. Unless he has in his earliest experiences felt his world to be reasonably safe and dependable, he will not be able to risk the dangers of independence. Autonomy is possible only for those who have previously enjoyed the satisfactions of a good dependency. Clearly it is not enough, then, to teach independence as an item of personality to be affixed or as an incipient tendency to be stretched. One can be educated into growing independence only as this is understood in its dynamic and ordered interconnection with other aspects of the organism, particularly the factor of security.

Qualitative improvement. The fourth and last meaning of growth rests upon the distinction between the quantitative and the qualitative. All three meanings thus far have been essentially quantitative. They are expressed in terms of extension, intensity, accumulation, sequence, and connection. They do not involve any measure of value, of better or worse. It is, however, possible to employ the term growth in a qualitative sense. When we exclaim about a person, "How he has grown!" we frequently do not mean increase in size, added abilities, or the coordination of these in the living whole, but some richer fulfillment of the best ideals of human personality, the attainment of some higher level of personal excellence.

Of course, qualitative growth is not independent of the quantitative kinds. The person who advances to a higher stage of excellence does so through expansion and addition of powers and through particular kinds of interrelating of components. Every good quality in persons also reflects a characteristic mode of personality organization. This does not alter the fact that quality or value is a distinct and essentially different concept of growth.

The full understanding of growth of persons requires all four meanings—the three quantitative aspects and the qualitative one. The latter is especially imperative for education. There has been a tendency in some educational circles to neglect the question of quality in growth. It has sometimes been assumed that growth as increase in powers—as self-expression, creative expansion—is good in itself. But growth properly understood, in its full wealth of meaning, is not simply indiscriminate increase, but a sensitive, highly discriminating process of value realization. It is for this reason that education has to do with *directing* human growth. Direction implies value—better or worse. Not all possible increments and coordinations are equally good. Some directions lead to higher levels of personality, others lead to lower ones. In education, as in growth adequately conceived, quality is of the essence.

Decline and Decay

The human career is not wholly a process of growth. There also inevitably occur decline and decay which destroy what has been built up through growth. These negative processes parallel in kind the constructive processes of growth. Corresponding to growth as enlargement or expansion there is the process of shrinkage or contraction. Parallel to growth as accretion is decline through loss of substance or powers. Coordinate with organic growth is the process of disorganization. Finally, as there is growth in value, so there may be processes of value loss.

The development of persons is not a matter of simple growth. It is a complex interplay and alternation of various kinds of growth and decline. The conduct of life is ordinarily governed by the principle that growth shall be promoted and decay as far as possible prevented. The question as to how this may be achieved is the central problem of education: How can the development of persons be so directed as to maximize growth and minimize decay?

Obviously the answer to this fundamental question depends upon the standard adopted for the measurement of growth, and chiefly upon the distinction between the quantitative and qualitative meanings. For example, if one were only to maximize growth as accumulation, it would not matter greatly if integration or coordination of powers should decline or ideals be compromised. On the other hand an exclusively qualitative standard of growth might lead to disregard of length of life or strength of body if by sacrificing these some supreme value (e.g., loyalty to a person or a cause) might be realized. Again, there are some aspects of personality which grow slowly and decline little or not at all during one's life span, and there are others which blossom soon and as soon again decay. Powers of understanding, insight, and appreciation are frequently harder to come by but more durable than physical strength and beauty. One of the main tasks of education is to foster the more enduring kinds of growth so that when the more ephemeral powers begin to decline the integrity and worth of the whole personality will not be unduly threatened.

Of course, decline and decay are always present in some degree in the human organism, but at some stages they are masked by the more predominant growth. In later years decline may overshadow growth, and at death physiological growth entirely ceases. This invites the question whether or not there are kinds of growth which are permanently immune to decay. The belief in personal immortality rests upon the conviction that such immunity is possible, that there are qualities and powers of personal existence which do not decay when the body does. On such a view education would above all seek to guide the personality toward the realization of these capacities in which unlimited growth is possible. Perhaps the most distinctive mark of education in the religious tradition has been central concern for this problem of the interplay of growth and decay and the belief that the means exist for permanently frustrating the threat of dissolution. There is the interesting paradox that non-religious education has tended to think much of life and growth while believing in the ultimacy of death, while religious education has put much stress on death while believing in the ultimacy of life and growth.

Actual and Potential

Two concepts which are particularly useful in the philosophic consideration of development are the concepts of the "actual" and the "potential." The actual nature of any entity is simply what it is. The potential nature of that entity is what it might become. For example, an actual bar of iron is a potential magnet. Its magnetic potentiality consists in the possibility of magnetizing it. On the other hand, a piece of wood does not have the potentiality of becoming a magnet, since the nature of wood is such as not to be magnetizable. An actual acorn is potentially an oak tree and an actual tadpole is potentially a frog, but no acorn can become a frog nor any tadpole an oak.

The process of development consists in the actualizing of potential. An entity exchanges one actuality for another which was hitherto only a potentiality. From this it is clear that the concepts "actual" and "potential" are relative to one another since what is now actual was earlier in development only potential and what is now potential may in the future become actual.

The development of persons fits into this general conceptual scheme. The process of growth is the actualizing of personal potentialities. A person becomes what he formerly only had the possibility of becoming; a person now actually is what he potentially was.

Six observations need to be made in elaboration and clarification of this process of actualizing potentiality.

Conditions for actualization. It is to be noted that the actualizing of potentiality depends on certain conditions. Potentiality is always hypothetical; it becomes actual only if certain conditions prevail. An acorn will become an oak tree only if the requisite soil, water, air, and sunlight are provided. A human infant will develop into a mature person only if the necessary food, protection, and human association are provided.

This conditional character of actualization provides a clue to the nature of potentiality. It suggests that potential is not something which belongs to the entity itself but is a property of the entity plus the other entities required to actualize the potential. For instance, the potentiality of mature personhood does not inhere in the infant himself but in the infant plus the whole complex of physical and social conditions which alone permit him to develop to maturity.

Range of potentialities. The second observation is that there is never a single narrow sequence of potentialities to be actualized. Of no entity whatsoever can it be said that one and only one path of development is possible, that there is only one series of potentials to become actual. There is always a range of potentialities. The world of the possible is more ample than the single-track view would admit. This is especially true of human beings. Of no person can it truly be said that he could become only a slave, a scholar, a prince, or a warrior, or have only such and such traits of character. There is no fixed, irrevocable path of life to which any person by the very nature of things is assigned. The realm of human potentiality has more than one dimension. For this reason it is a mistake to speak in the singular of a person's "potential." There is no single condition or level which a person may attain and which is peculiarly and appropriately his.

Relation to nature of entity. It should be further noted that the range of potentialities available to any entity varies considerably with the nature of the entity. The seed of a plant has a rather strictly limited range of potentials. It may grow into a healthy, full-size, mature plant, given the optimum conditions, or it may become malformed and stunted as a result of less favorable conditions. But in most respects the plant functions in the same general way under any circumstance. With human beings it is different. The variety of potentialities is very great. One person may develop into a cringing, ineffectual creature capable of only the simplest human functions while another may become a confident, productive personality accomplishing prodigious feats of skill or of scientific, artistic, or practical ingenuity. It is, of course, because man depends so largely on learning that his range of potentials is so wide. In the lower forms, where the mechanisms of development are so largely built in, the variety of outcomes is minimized. Man's dependence on learning maximizes variability.

But even within the human species there are considerable differences from individual to individual in the range of potentialities. There are some persons who seem to have a far richer store of possibilities than others. Some individuals have it within their power to become expert in music or painting, while others seem to lack any ear for tone or eye for perspective and proportion. Some persons develop easily and naturally in social competence, while others seem by nature ill-adapted to life in the human family.

Influence of context. Recognizing, then, these varieties in range of potential, our fourth point is the obvious one that the particular potentials actualized in the course of development depend in part on the nature of the circumstances under which development takes place. In the case of human development, the nature of the personality is greatly influenced by cultural context, by family circumstances, and by the kinds of learning opportunities presented. A child reared in a stable home and provided with excellent schooling will actualize different potentialities than he would if he were a neglected orphan put to work at an early age.

It was said above that the conditions only determine *in part* the course of development. The other determinant is the free choice of the individual himself. The power to select among potentials to be actualized is the very essence of human freedom, and it is man's special dignity that he is not determined wholly and without remainder by the external conditions of his life.

New opportunities and closed paths. The fifth observation is that each actualizing of potential opens the door to a further line of realizations and closes the door to others. For example, the act of marriage opens the way to actualizing potentials of parenthood but makes impossible a lifelong career in a celibate religious order and the different fulfillments which such a vocation would provide. The process of development is in some degree irreversible. Each determination of one's being lays the foundation for some new accomplishment and at the same time removes one a step further (and perhaps irrevocably) from the realization of alternative potentialities. This is what makes the determination of direction in human development so important. In the early years everything seems possible; the whole world of occupations and achievements lies open to one. Each successive choice strengthens one possibility and weakens others, until at length most of the earlier options are no longer open and in compensation one has the satisfaction of deeper concentration and fuller realization in the special path of life that has become his.

Which potentials? Sixth, it follows from these observations that human development cannot be regarded simply as the actualizing of potential. Everything depends upon *which* potentials are actualized. Human development inevitably involves the question of direction, of choice, of decision between alternatives. This is the task of education, to guide and direct the development of persons, to make appropriate decisions about what potentialities are to be actualized, and to help the individual arrive at such decisions himself.

Consequences for education. On the basis of this analysis it would seem that there are four requirements for a program of education. First, there must be knowledge about the potentialities of the persons to be educated. This is very difficult to obtain, and in the absence of sufficient data it seems better to overestimate rather than to underestimate potentials. While it is clearly a waste of time and a source of frustration and disappointment to seek to actualize potentials which a person does not have, on the other hand it is wasteful not to put to use abilities which do exist. An effective educational program therefore needs the best possible testing instruments to estimate the capacities and aptitudes of the learners.

Second, assuming the potentialities are known, some basis of choice is required. Education is dependent upon the selection from the infinite variety of certain potentialities to be actualized. The standard used for this selection will be based in part on the personality of the one who directs the education, in part on the needs, customs, and prejudices of the society in which the education occurs, and in part on the individual circumstances and decisions of the learner. For instance, an infant may have it in him to become an aggressive, competitive personality or a sensitive cooperator. The parents may on the basis of their own dispositions favor the development of the latter type of personality in their child. On the other hand, the society may be organized on a competitive basis with emphasis on success, and this standard may modify the parental choice. Finally, the child himself may more and more choose for himself which of these alternative personality types he wishes to develop.

The third educational requirement is the establishment of conditions appropriate for actualizing the chosen potentials. It is not enough to decide on a direction for human development. To this must be added knowledge for making that direction effective. It is necessary to know under what circumstances each kind of potential can best be actualized, e.g., what kinds of infant care, home atmosphere, school and job situations will tend to produce peaceable or belligerent, creative or routine, reflective or irrational kinds of persons. Included in these conditions are those necessary for the encouragement of the individual's own free choices, since, human personality being what it is, no fixing of conditions by others can completely determine which potentials will become actual.

Finally, educators must take account of the resources available for the actualizing of the chosen potentials. One may have high ideals about what persons should become, and know what the conditions are that will tend to produce these results, and still lack the necessary means to make them effective. The resources required include time, materials, favorable economic and political conditions and social institutions, and skilled personnel. All such resources are in limited supply. A practicable educational program, therefore, must seek to use available resources to establish as far as possible optimum conditions for the actualizing of chosen personality potentials.

Developmental Phases

It is useful in the study of personality development to identify certain phases, periods, or stages in the process. Thus, one commonly speaks of infancy, childhood, adolescence, adulthood, and old age. Other ways of designating the stages may be devised. Psychologists especially are interested in a careful technical discrimination of developmental phases, particularly in the years prior to maturity.

The concept of periods in development rests on the observation that growth and decline do not occur in a uniform fashion but are such that during certain years the process has dominant features which differ from those in certain other years. For instance, infancy is a period chiefly characterized by dependency. In adolescence one of the dominant features is the struggle of the person to establish a sense of individual selfhood. Old age is characterized by a decline in physical powers and, in many cases, a return to a status of dependency upon others.

The existence of stages is evidence that personal development is the outcome of many component processes. Each phase reflects the dominance of one or more of these factors. Some of the periods, especially in early life, are ones of rapid change, where new factors quickly displace old ones in prominence. Other periods, particularly in middle life, are relatively stable, reflecting a slowly shifting equilibrium of factors.

Analysis of personality development by periods has the value of any abstraction. It enables a whole series of objects or events to be considered together. It simplifies the study of a very complex process by pointing out general features. At the same time there is always the danger of over-simplification. All infants or old people are not alike, nor is there really and concretely such a thing as infancy or old age with certain definite and invariable characteristics. Personal individuality and the dynamic character of development preclude any sure and simple classification into periods. One can never say with complete confidence: "He is an adolescent; *therefore. . . .*" The most that can be expected of a stage analysis is the formulation of rough general principles whereby useful hypotheses and suggestions for the better understanding of individuals may be obtained.

It is important in education to make use of the life stages without overlooking their limitations. One of the most useful fruits of modern developmental psychology has been the discovery of the differing needs and capacities of persons in various periods of development. This has led to the abandonment of childhood educational programs predicated on the adult point of view and to the creation of learning opportunities appropriate to each phase of development. While such provision is of great value, it is necessary to go even further in recognizing that developmental periods do not describe actual persons but only certain broad tendencies, and hence that the educator must as far as practicable be alert to the special problems and opportunities of each individual.

The Problem of Personal Identity

It is clearly evident that persons undergo development—growth and decay—that they actualize potentials, that they pass through stages in life. Human personality is inescapably involved in change; a person is never the same from one moment to the next. Furthermore, it is the function of education to supply direction to this development and thus to enter intimately into the process of personal transformation.

If this is the case, does it make sense to speak of an enduring, continuing, and permanent self? If a person inevitably changes from one moment to the next, is there any justification for regarding him as the same person from moment to moment? Consider the utter unlikeness of the newborn infant and the mature adult into which the infant later develops. By what right can they be called the same person? How can one who is constantly undergoing transformation in time reasonably use the pronoun "I" about his past self or about his expected future self?

Questions such as these constitute "the problem of personal identity." The problem is to state what the identity is between the person at different periods of his development. What common element unites the self in successive phases of its career?

The common-sense view. Common sense sees no problem in this. Nothing seems so obvious as continuing selfhood. The last thing that a human being could deny would be his own enduring personality. The very use of language presupposes it; one could not meaningfully utter a sentence like "I see the sun" unless the "I" were assumed to remain unchanged at least through the completion of the words "see the sun." The customs of mankind—the giving of names, the keeping of personal records, the assignment of persons to particular functions in the social organization—presuppose personal identity.

This self-assurance of common sense finds expression in the philosophic conception of "the substantial self"—of self as a kind of enduring substance that undergoes change. It is also supported by the concept of the soul, as that inner core of personal being which persists through all outward and apparent changes in personality, that fundamental entity which is the essence of the self from the moment of conception (or even before) until death (or even after).

The critical view. The *problem* of personal identity arises when the idea of the substantial self and of the soul are subjected to reflective criticism. It may be said that one looks in vain for any self-substance or soul, that one can find only a human organism with various functions which change more or less slowly in the course of development. Thus there is no real personal *identity,* but only a certain continuity of function, a relative stability of behavior-patterns, a reasonably gradual modification of personality organization during the process of development. To ascribe identity to the self over a lifetime is then merely a useful fiction, a practical device to reflect the continuity of successive functional patterns.

The condition known as multiple personality would appear to support this critical view of personal identity. In this condition there are two or more relatively independent functional patterns which the person can assume in succession. At one time he is Dr. Jekyll, at another he is Mr. Hyde. It might then seem that there is really no self-substance or soul which pertains to the several persons but simply a series of personalities defined by typical modes of behavior.

Suggested solutions. One way to solve the problem would be to say that personal identity rests on the continuity of body structure. A person may change radically in personality yet he still has the same body. This solution is not satisfactory either because the body is constantly changing. Old cells die and are replaced by new ones. The material constituents of the organism are in constant flux. Nor is the form into which the materials are organized identical from one stage to the next. The body changes just as surely and inexorably as do the behavior patterns called personality.

It appears, then, that from the standpoint of strict behavioral description there is no such thing as personal identity. It merely represents a convenient way of grouping a succession of entities or events which are intimately connected in causal relationships. The "I" at this moment is the same as the "I" of a moment before only in that the organism in its present state is predominantly dependent on the organism of a moment ago as its chief cause.

Is this the best that can be done to save personal identity? Is the deep-seated intuition of common sense to be swept away? Is there no sense in the older idea of a soul? The basis for an answer may lie in the concepts of memory, anticipation, and self-transcendence discussed in Chapter 26. There it was suggested that man has the unique power, through imagination, to transcend the limitations of time by remembering the past as past and anticipating the future as future. That is to say, man has the power to assume a perspective above the time flux; he can to a degree free himself from immersion in the ever-flowing stream of temporal process. But this could only be possible if there were some property of the self which was not subject to change, i.e. if there were in some sense personal identity. Memory of the past presupposes the same "I" in the past as in the present. Anticipation of the future presupposes the identity of self now and in time to come.

We have already suggested that the power of self-transcendence might provide a fitting basis for affirming the classic concept of the soul. On these grounds it might be said that man's ability to remember and anticipate constitute at once the definition of personal identity and of the concept of soul which expresses it.

This position raises further difficult questions. What about the person who forgets? Does he thereby lose his identity? What happens to the soul in sleep? What about historical memory; does it mean that a person's identity may in some sense extend back to a time before his biological conception? What of anticipations which project one into the distant future; do they presuppose some kind of permanence of the soul, even beyond biological death?

Relevance to education. But what difference does it make in educational practice how one answers the problem of personal identity, or indeed whether one ever considers the question? Is this simply an idle speculative puzzle invented by philosophers to amuse themselves? Some would regard it as such. To others the problem seems of the greatest importance both theoretically and practically. Their grounds for holding this would be that a conviction of personal identity is a necessary basis for human dignity and worth and that it arises from the deepest and most universal intuitions about the nature of the self. Education has been defined as the process of directing the development of persons. If there is no personal identity, then there is really no education, for the very idea of "development of a person" presupposes identity—that it is the *same* person enduring through a process of change. That a person should be nothing more than a continuous series of causally connected events or entities would seem to undermine the worth of the self by destroying its basic integrity, i.e., its unity in time. The greatest joy of parent or teacher is to assist in the development of an enduring person; it is what the ancients called "the care of the soul." The main point of education would disappear if the job of the educator were only to introduce new factors into certain designated event-sequences (called "persons" for convenience) so as to alter the course of such sequences. That sort of process could rightly be called impersonal, since identity in time is of the essence of the personal. And education loses much of its motive and meaning when it becomes impersonal. The warmth, vitality, and interest of teaching consist precisely in its relevance to the integral whole-life careers of abiding personalities. Hence the importance for education of the problem of personal identity.

Heredity and Environment

One of the perennial topics of discussion about the development of personality concerns the respective parts played by hereditary and environmental factors. A human being starts life as a fertilized egg cell—a single cell formed by the fusion of a sperm and an ovum. This cell has a definite complex structure including, among other things, its own characteristic pattern of chromosomes and genes. This single cell contains *all* the biological inheritance of the person who will eventually develop out of that cell. Everything which is added to the one cell as the person matures comes from the environment. Eventually the adult organism will contain millions upon millions of cells. Purely from the standpoint of quantitative contribution, therefore, it would appear that the one cell contributed by "heredity" was negligible. But the nature of personality cannot be understood in such quantitative terms. Everything depends on the particular ways in which the materials from the environment are organized in the growing organism. The significance of the hereditary resources in the original cell lies in the extraordinary fact that the structural pattern of that cell goes far in determining the way in which environmental resources are progressively incorporated into the living unity which is the person.

Nonetheless, environment is not merely the source of quantitative accretions to the growing body. The environment, too, is structured and influences the ways in which the organism develops. A person is not simply a single cell which has grown by successive division into an adult organism—the environment playing the passive role of supplying raw materials. A person comes into being as a result of the constant interplay of organism with an environment which is also active and which includes other living creatures. The growth of persons occurs by virtue of a process of interaction between organism and environment.

The opposing views. These two facts—the directing function of hereditary factors and the modifying function of environmental influences—have given rise to a debate of long standing over the relative importance of heredity and environment in the development of personality. There are extremists on both sides of the question. On the one extreme are the exponents of heredity who say that environment is solely the medium within which the hereditary determinants direct the drama of growth. It provides the necessary conditions but none of the peculiar and specific human traits. The differences between persons, according to this view, are due in all essential points to differences in genetic constitution and not to environment. Obviously cultural acquisitions such as language, skills, and manners are the result of the special training provided and are not inherited. But, say the hereditists, in basic matters such as intelligence and temperament the pattern is set by heredity and is not learned.

On the other extreme are those who claim that heredity provides merely the basic organic foundation and that the real determinant of personality is the environment. According to this view, the nature of a personality is a result of the processes of "conditioning" which have taken place in the encounters of the organism with its environment. Individual differences are thus due to differences in the influences which have operated on the growing person from his surroundings. This view, of course, does not extend so far as to deny all hereditary factors, but it does tend to restrict these factors to the provision of the physiological foundation of personality—the basic impulses and drives operating within an organism with the requisite skeletal structure, functioning organs, and nervous system. No environmentalist would claim that conditioning could produce a man from a stone or even from an embryo ape. But given human inheritance, the differences among human beings can be traced, say the environmentalists, to the nature of the environment in which growth occurs.

There have been competent and eloquent defenders on both sides of this debate. There have been numerous ingenious experiments designed to settle the question. Of particular importance have been the studies of pairs of identical twins. Yet no final or universally conclusive solution has thus far been achieved. There was a time when the hereditists were dominant

—this was, in effect, the classical view. Then, particularly under the influence of behavioristic and stimulus-response psychology, the balance turned in favor of the environmentalists. In recent years more vigorous proponents of the heredity position have been coming into their own once more. As in most such disputes between extremists, there clearly are important insights on both sides. In this controversy it is not really a question of either-or, but of both-and. The person develops as a result of the intimate interconnection of hereditary and environmental factors. We shall attempt below to show what the nature of that interconnection is.

Implications for education. For the educator it makes considerable difference where the emphasis is placed. If one is a strict hereditist, it follows that the business of the educator is simply to provide the proper general conditions within which the person may mature according to his own inherent hereditary principles. The nature of the educational process will be dictated by the structure of man's inherited nature and there will be little that can be done to effect any important modification in character. The scope and the function of the educational enterprise are then considerably limited, and a conservative estimate of the power of education in the amelioration of human affairs is called for. If, on the other hand, one is an extreme environmentalist, he will tend to have a high regard for the power of education in effecting improvement in man and in the social order. He will believe that a human being is in the most important respects what education makes of him and that the future of the human race is therefore largely in the hands of the educator. The ideals of human personality must then be generated and transmitted within human culture without benefit of the conserving and stabilizing influence of an assumed hereditary embodiment and linkage. The environmentalist then sees for the educator greater scope and responsibility than does the hereditist.

The heredity-environment complex. Now how are heredity and environment related to one another within the process of personality development? As mentioned earlier, the beginning of the person is the fertilized egg cell. At the single-cell stage the organism contains no environmental influence; it is solely a result of the respective hereditary contributions from the mother and father, combined according to the principles by which male and female germ cells unite to form a single complete cell. From this time forth the organism is subject to a variety of environmental influences. Before birth the relevant environment is for the most part the mother's body. After birth the environment is far more varied and extended. The important point to note is that the individual at any given stage of development is not simply the *sum* of "heredity" and "environment." It is never possible to point to some feature of personality and say simply "That is from heredity" or "This is due to environment." A person is not a *mixture,* in various proportions, of "heredity" and "environment." He is a heredity-environment complex.

Perhaps an analogy will be helpful at this point. Common salt may be produced by uniting the element sodium with the element chlorine in certain proportions according to well-established principles of chemical reaction. The salt is not a *mixture* of sodium and chlorine; it is a *compound.* A chemical compound differs from a mixture in that in the compound the characteristics of each constituent element are not preserved, but a completely new complex substance with new characteristic properties is produced. The salt, sodium chloride, is a compound whose physical properties are different from those of either the metal, sodium, or the gas, chlorine, of which it is composed.

This analogy serves to show that a compound is characterized by something more than the elements that compose it. What more, besides sodium and chlorine, is there in sodium chloride? The important additional factor is the principle of organization or composition of the compound. It is the structural interrelationships of the constituent elements which help to determine the nature of the resulting compound.

Let us now return to the problem of personality development. At each moment during the growth process it is as though an activity of chemical compounding were taking place, in which the organism is one of the elements and the various environmental factors are other elements. The single-cell organism at the time of conception, interacting with womb-environment for (say) one day, produces a new total organism at the end of the first day. This new organism interacting with a somewhat different environment produces a still different organism by the end of the second day, and so on. The organism at any given time is the resultant of the interaction of the organism at a previous time with the effective environment since that time. But this is no process of *adding together* the successive environmental contributions. It is a *compounding* process, in which a decisive factor is the principles of composition which operate. It is a matter of common experience that identical influences may produce different effects upon different types of persons. For example, the same adversity which makes one man bitter may make another more patient. The material advantages which enervate one person may stimulate another to high achievement. What a person is can never be explained solely or chiefly in terms of his genes or of his environmental encounters. He can only be understood in the light of the principles by which the particular complex which is the organism receives and incorporates the influences from these interrelationships. It is relatively easy to identify hereditary factors and environmental influences in a personality, but it is far more difficult, if not impossible—at least at our present stage of knowledge—to discern the immensely complicated laws by which these factors and influences are combined, stage by stage, into the organic unity of the growing person. A person is no more to be understood simply by pointing to the character of forebears and the nature of modifying environmental factors than the characteristics of salt are comprehended as the modification of the qualities of sodium by those of chlorine.

But in one important respect the sodium chloride analogy is quite inadequate. A living organism—especially one with powers of mind—utilizes its resources of heredity and environment in a far more active and originative way than inorganic substances ever could. In human beings the power of imagination enables projected future states to enter as a factor into the determination of the present. This means that the human being is not bound purely by influences from the past and from outside, but that the principles of organization of hereditary and environmental conditions include some genuinely originative and autonomous factors.

It is futile to argue the primacy of either heredity or environment in the production of personality. There can be no person without a definite initial organism of such a nature that it can engage in productive interrelations with the special environment provided. Nor can there be any person without the environment by means of which alone the development may proceed. Some aspects of personality may for convenience be traced more directly to hereditary sources and others may be regarded as more largely environmental. But this is merely a way of speaking. For the person is a whole organism whose nature can only be understood as the culmination of countless compounding encounters, in which *at every stage* the identity of so-called "hereditary" or "environmental" aspects is lost in the emerging unity of the complex personality.

Education and the heredity-environment complex. Education is part of the process of progressive realization of hereditary potential through interaction with environment. Education is not, as the pure hereditist might insist, merely the unfolding of the latent powers within a passive environment. Nor is education, as the pure environmentalist might claim, merely the progressive embodiment within the individual of the environmental influences brought to bear on him. It is the making good, through active correlation between the individual and his environment, of potentialities which the organism possessed at the time of conception. The importance of environment consists not only in its role as context for this actualizing process, but also—and perhaps even more strikingly—in its function as one determiner of *which* potentialities will be developed and in what manner. For it is clear that a human personality has an endless variety of potentialities—limited, to be sure, within definite ranges—and that the determination of which of these shall be actualized lies in part with the environment. No person can by education become anything for which he had no hereditary potential. But neither can the infinite variety of potentialities give any clue to what the mature personality will actually turn out to be as a result of education. Heredity and environment therefore both operate both as limitation and as resource in education. The educator requires the resources of hereditary potential but must also take account of the limits imposed by the range of potentiality within a given person. Likewise the educator needs to make use of environmental resources but also recognize that they can be effective only in the development of persons with potentialities for the actualizing of which such resources are appropriate.

Main Viewpoints on Human Development

In concluding this analysis of human development, five main viewpoints will be discussed and their relation to the process of education indicated. The first four have been mentioned earlier in this chapter; the fifth introduces a new element. In practice these views are seldom if ever found in pure form, nor are they mutually exclusive. Actual beliefs about human development usually include elements from several of the views to be discussed. The value of the analysis that follows is not to state complete theoretical standpoints but simply to clarify the several possible dominant trends in thinking about the development of personality.

Unfolding. According to this view, the development of personality is a process of bringing to light what was already present and complete but not yet in evidence. It is as though one had a tightly folded piece of paper on which were written words or designs. As the paper is unfolded step by step, more and more of the message appears until at last the whole previously hidden scheme is revealed. Or it is like the flower with petals closed at night which in the morning sun unfolds to view, bringing to light the flower's full form and beauty. Similarly, a person may be regarded as a bundle of definite potentialities which are really merely hidden actualities. They do not need to be produced, but only to be made evident. A child is a small adult, and his development into adulthood requires that what he already is be brought out and put into operation.

Development as unfolding is obviously not development at all in any serious sense. The person is at all times in essence complete. The differences from point to point in his life career are incidental and apparent rather than substantial and real. Growth is rearrangement and perhaps enlargement, but is certainly not qualitative. Personal identity is ensured since there is never really any significant change in the personality. Heredity contributes everything of importance; environment provides only the context within which the hereditary essence will be more or less adequately revealed.

When development is considered as unfolding, it is clear that education loses much of its importance. There is no *directing* the development of persons since they are what they are and there is nothing one can do to influence the real quality and content of another's life. The task of the educator is reduced to providing proper situations for the unfolding to take place. This chiefly means giving opportunities to exercise the powers which the child has but has not used, just as a young bird unused to flying is prodded to stretch its wings and bring to full strength its latent ability. It also means providing an environment as free as possible from obstacles to the natural expression of the child's inner being.

Although the unfolding view is rarely held explicitly by educators, it would seem that some of the ideas of extreme permissiveness and naturalism in child nurture presuppose it. If it is assumed that one need not or ought not direct the child, but should let him find his own way, does this not imply a view that everything essential to the child's being is within him already and only needs to be encouraged to come to light?

There is a kind of educational attitude directly opposed to the permissive which may also grow out of the unfolding view. Since the child is considered a small adult, the business of the educator is to hasten the process of revealing the full personality. This leads to emphasis on adult goals and a judging of childhood activities as mere approximations to the performances of the mature person. This discourages the appreciation of the life of the child in and for itself and stimulates a constant concern for the future rather than for the present.

Molding. Opponents of the doctrine of unfolding would say that it fails to do justice to the important influence of the environment on the development of persons. Ways of speaking, thinking, and acting are learned and reflect the social milieus in which persons mature. Even physical characteristics depend in some measure upon surrounding conditions during growth. On this view, then, development is primarily a process of molding or shaping by external agencies. If one wants to understand why any person is as he is, it is necessary only to discover the influences that have been brought to bear on him. Personalities are made by the successive impressions of exterior factors.

Under the molding theory the person is regarded as passive. Learning is something that *happens to* the organism. At the beginning personality is like a mass of clay, and development is like the process of making a statue out of it. Heredity counts for nothing; environment is everything. Personality constantly changes as new influences are experienced, and such unity as it has is due to the consistency of these influences.

From this standpoint education is of the utmost importance. Personality is infinitely plastic; there is no limit to what teaching can accomplish. It is only necessary to set up the right influences and any desired kind of person may be produced. Unless the development of persons is constantly and carefully directed, they will reflect the haphazard nature of their accidental environments. Hence the crucial importance of a careful and consistent educational program.

This view encourages the educator to take complete responsibility for guiding the immature. Autonomy and freedom of the individual have no meaning since he is only a passive recipient of outer influences. The educational process thus requires that the educator assume authority and control over the lives of the learners. Like the unfolding view, but for an entirely different reason, it emphasizes the adult world and undervalues the life of the child, which is regarded as imperfectly shaped. It also tends to encourage the use of coercive measures to mold properly the obstinate and intractable material of raw human nature. The refined techniques of the scientific "conditioners" are only somewhat more subtle instruments of coercion.

Self-creation. According to the first view personality does not really develop at all, since it is in essence complete from the start, and according to the second view development is owed wholly to outside factors. According to a third view, development is real and progressive but takes place from within. The person creates himself. He is neither initially complete nor passively shaped. He completes and molds himself. To be sure, he uses the materials provided in his hereditary structure and in environmental resources, but he compounds and fashions these in an entirely original and uniquely individual way. There is in principle no limit to what a person can become; development is limited in practice only by restricted resources. The key to human development is imagination and freedom. By imagination new directions are charted and by free decision they are chosen. Each person is responsible for what he becomes; his path is not ultimately controlled either from outside or from his own past but from within.

This view considers education self-directed. It is of paramount importance that the process of development be carefully guided, the most important guides being not other persons but a person's own self. The most that other persons can do is to provide conditions in which free decision may be exercised—removing restrictions and frustrations and supplying the requisite means for carrying out the decisions made. There should be a minimum of prescription and coercion. The autonomy and individuality of each person should as far as possible be respected. Children's lives should not be judged by adult standards, but the authenticity of personal life at every stage of growth must be recognized. The main emphasis in education would fall upon originality rather than conformity, and every means for stimulating individual creativity would be favored.

Interaction. The fourth standpoint attempts to unite the second and the third. Personal development is neither the molding of a passive subject by the active environment (number 2) nor the active utilization by the self-creating person of a passive environment (number 3). It is a process of *interaction,* whereby both the person and his environment act and react on one another. The self which emerges from this interaction then bears the image neither of an environment nor of an autonomous self, but it is a new entity compounded of these ingredients, both of them having been transformed in the process. Under the molding view the initiative in development is in the environment, while under the self-creation view it is in the self. Under the interaction view initiative is in both environment and in self, and the resulting product conforms to neither the one nor the other but is a new reality whose nature depends upon the relevant principles of interaction.

Education viewed from this standpoint does not depend on latent predetermined abilities (as in the unfolding view), nor is the full power of directing development exercised through influences brought to bear upon the growing person (as in the molding view), nor is the full responsibility for personal becoming vested in the developing self (as in the self-creating view). Education is a continuing process of interactivity wherein both the self and other persons bear responsibility for the directing of personal development. Influences brought to bear have their effect, but its nature will depend on the unique and individual response of the self. The decisions of the self have an influence, but its nature will depend on the environment (including other persons) in which the decisions are to be implemented. The educator gives due recognition to the autonomy and freedom of the growing child but also takes account of the positive control and guidance needed from others, especially at the early stages of development. There is no automatic imposition of adult standards, yet the relevance of the adult world to the personal and social needs of the developing personality are taken into account. Creativity is given an important place, yet the need for some conformity to the demands of nature and society is recognized. Finally, this view of development emphasizes the need for an educational program in which the learner is an active participant rather than a mere observer or recipient. He should be given opportunity, in a variety of appropriate experiences, to enter into relationship with other persons and things, by interaction with which his own development is advanced.

Divine creation. A final interpretation of human development is to regard it as a process of divine creation. The changes in the person are considered not as emanating from within (as in either the unfolding or the self-creation theories) nor from the environment (as in the molding theory), nor yet from interaction of self and not-self, but from a divine creator. What a person becomes he then owes not to himself or to others but to God, the source of all life and being.

This leads to the difficulty that the deity becomes responsible for undesirable as well as desirable personality developments. To avoid this conclusion it is held by some that God creates the good while the self (and other human beings) are responsible for the evil. This involves a combining of the present view with one of the previous ones.

The four earlier views discussed all regard development as a natural process, while this fifth view seems to imply influences from outside the natural order. Actually, however, the contrast is not so absolute as this might indicate since the natural agencies (including the self and its environment) may be considered as important if not the sole means or channels for the divine creative power. That is to say, God need not be regarded as acting apart from persons, things, and their natural interactions but through them as instrumentalities of the divine intention. With this understanding, the divine creation view need be neither inconsistent with nor independent of the four previous views, but may be regarded as an elaboration and further explanation of them.

The educational implications of the divine creation view depend on how one regards the creation taking place. Insofar as the various actual processes discussed above are God's means, the comments made in connection with each of the "natural" views apply here also. To the extent that divine creation is regarded as a genuine intervention, discontinuous with and independent of the natural order, education in the ordinary human sense would be nullified. The course of personal development would be directed by God, who would then become the Teacher. The human role would be to listen and to obey. Contrasts of child and adult, wise or foolish, practical or impractical, by ordinary human standards, would be overcome, and superseded by sole devotion to the divine will.

Regardless of the means by which God's creative power is considered to operate, the divine creation view gives to education a distinctively new aspect. The process of development is seen not as a self-contained and self-justifying series of events but as related to a greater and more profound process and reality. This adds a note of momentousness and imports a depth of meaning which to those who experience it greatly intensifies the significance of the educational enterprise.

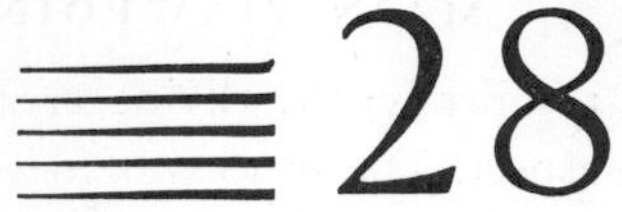

28 The Ultimate Nature of Things

THE PHILOSOPHER is not content to consider only some things or certain restricted aspects of things. Many would regard it as the essence of his enterprise to ask the most comprehensive questions and to seek the most inclusive possible understanding of reality. A philosophic inquiry into the ultimate questions of education must therefore go on from the definitions and analyses of human nature and development to inquire about their place in the total scheme. This will include such questions as these: Are man and education special cases or particular manifestations of some more basic reality? Are they part of a larger system, and if so, what is the character of that in which they participate? Is there some property or essence which all things have in common? Is there an ultimate nature which all the special natures exemplify, some primordial process of which each particular process is a special case?

The practical importance of asking questions like these is that the answers given to them may make a great deal of difference in the views taken about more limited and specialized concerns. In particular, one's conceptions of the ultimate nature of reality will tend to be reflected in his ideas about education, and implicit in every educational outlook is some conception about the ultimate nature of things.

Metaphysics

The philosophical task of inquiring about the ultimate nature of things is called *metaphysics*. The application of such inquiries to educational concerns constitutes the "metaphysical foundations of education."

Some thinkers look with disfavor upon metaphysics. They regard it as a futile, idle, and pretentious enterprise. They believe that nothing of value comes from seeking answers to such general questions as "What is the nature of anything and everything?" They contend that progress in understanding can be made only by careful step-by-step analysis of particular problems, especially in the manner of the scientists. Anyone who attempts more than this is substituting fanciful speculation for reliable methods of investigation. Knowledge of the nature of things is gained only at the price of careful, long-term experimental inquiry by whole communities of investigators. It is absurd to expect that by mere reflection, however profound, a philosopher can comprehend the nature of things entire.

The proponents of metaphysics agree that metaphysical inquiry is no substitute for the step-by-step study of particular things. But they also affirm that there is no necessary conflict between the two kinds of inquiry and that it is impossible to escape *some* metaphysical position. The purpose of metaphysical discussion is to criticize and clarify what is already assumed about the ultimate nature of things. The detailed investigation of particular areas presupposes certain pervasive and fundamental attitudes and concepts. For example, it is a metaphysical postulate that the real world is material and that everything must be analyzed with respect to physical principles. Again, it is a metaphysical question whether the world is made up of substances or of processes.

Perhaps the subject becomes clearer and the anti-metaphysicians' objections subside if one regards metaphysics not as an attempt to find a single formula for everything that is and to comprehend all reality in one speculative sweep, but rather as an enterprise of analyzing the most general possible ways of talking about things and as the clarification of the concepts involved in organizing the experience we have in any realm whatsoever. Metaphysical inquiry then becomes a task of analyzing the most general forms of thought and language. The question next arises whether or not these forms reflect the nature of the "real" world. This question takes one into the problem of knowledge and more particularly into the problem of how language is related to the real nature of things. (See Chapter 17.)

Suffice it to say at this point that to speak of the "real" world or the nature of "reality"—which is frequently regarded as the business of metaphysics—implies that there is an *apparent* world and that it is possible to get behind or beneath the appearances to the true nature of things. Thus the objective of metaphysics is to get beyond what the world *seems* to be to what it truly *is*. Those who reject metaphysics or who insist that it is at most the analysis of the most general thought forms do so largely because they cannot make good sense out of this contrast between "appearance" and "reality." They say that as far as human beings are concerned the only reality there is is defined by how things appear, that it is meaningless to talk about anything behind, beyond, or deeper, that appearance *is* reality.

In what follows we shall consider some of the important modes of thought concerning things in general—basic metaphysical concepts which may be employed in discourse about the most pervasive and universal characteristics of things. In each case reference will also be made to some inferences from these modes of thought for the problems of education.

Substance and Process

Two somewhat contrasting but not mutually exclusive concepts for dealing with the ultimate nature of things are *substance* and *process.*

The substance approach is deeply imbedded in common-sense views of the world. In considering any ordinary object such as a desk or a book, it is natural to ask what it is made of, what is the stuff from which it has been fashioned, or the ingredients of which it is composed. The apparent nature of the thing is the shape or arrangement imparted to the more basic nature, which is the underlying substance. The word "substance" itself implies that which "stands under" or forms the foundation of a thing.

There may, of course, be many different kinds of substance—or there may be few or only one. But whether one or many, the question about the nature of everything and anything is answered by references to substance. The search for ultimate reality is the exploration of underlying ground-stuff. Physical objects are made of various kinds of material substance. Dreams and ideals are made of mind-stuff. Religious inspiration is produced out of some basic spiritual sources or ground. The material substances are the simplest to conceive, and the other kinds are interpreted somewhat by analogy, but in all cases the manner of formulation is the same.

The chief advantages of the substance concept are its simplicity, adaptability, and its immediate appeal to common sense. It provides a way of drastically reducing the variety of things which enter into human experience by identifying common substrata beneath outward forms and changing conditions. Substance is thus based essentially on a static conception of the ultimate nature of things. The alteration of an entity in time is a process which the enduring substance undergoes. Substance itself stands fast while changes and modifications of it take place.

It is precisely with respect to this static character of the substance idea that the most basic objection can be raised. Is it possible to separate the nature of a thing from the changes which take place in it? Is there an independent and unmoved stuff which merely suffers modification? Or is the dynamic process by which things change an inseparable aspect of the real nature of things?

In order to avoid such difficulties the concept of *process* may be used in place of substance. In this case the fundamental reality is not conceived as an underlying stuff but as a ceaselessly flowing stream. To understand the meaning of this we need to consider the relation of the ideas of space and time to the conception of reality. The substance idea is essentially a space-like concept; a substance is regarded as occupying space, being spread out, and having dimensions. Time is incidental; it is not of the essence of substance. From time to time the arrangement of substance may be altered, but the substance itself is free of temporal modification. The process idea is just the opposite of this. It is a time-like concept; process is temporal advance, the inexorable onflow of events. The spatial arrangements of things are incidental. To be sure, there are things which occupy space, but these spatial components are subordinate and derivative features of the true inner reality, which is process.

Thus, in contrast to substance, process is a dynamic concept of reality. One does not analyze an entity with respect to a stuff which undergoes change; the fact and manner of change now become the center of interest. Nothing is fixed and settled. Everything is what it is by virtue of its participation in the flow of time.

It might seem that the process approach would be appropriate primarily for living things but not suitable for inanimate objects. It is true that growth and development do best illustrate the meaning of process. Yet the modern analysis of matter, by which it is explained as a complex of dynamic energy distributions, shows that the idea of process is also applicable to the inanimate. Apparently unchanging things can be regarded as relatively stable process configurations. An example would be a company of fast-moving dancers performing a figure whose general outline remained stationary.

Despite the clear advantage of the process concept in understanding the dynamic nature of reality, one may still feel the need for the substance idea. It is difficult to avoid the intuitive conviction that there is a primary stuff (such as energy) which is in process, that there has to be something which changes, and thus that change cannot itself be primary. Perhaps what is needed is a concept of substance-in-process.

From our basic definition of education as a kind of process it is clear that a process approach to the ultimate nature of things would be especially useful in considering the ultimate questions of education. It is often desirable, however, to use both substance and process approaches in dealing with education. We have already noted the difference between a substance and a process approach to personality. If persons are regarded as changing substance, the educational process becomes one of fashioning or molding a largely passive stuff. If personality is regarded as in itself a process, then educational methods must take due account of the inner dynamic of the developing person. Again, one may take an essentially substance-view of study materials; knowledge may be regarded as "intelligible stuff," and the student may be supposed to swallow, digest, and assimilate it. On the other hand, one may regard learning as a coordination of processes, and knowledge as essentially a mode of activity. In this case there can be no accumulation and storing of knowledge in the person; the evidence of knowledge-in-possession is the nature of the processes in which the person can actively engage.

Structure and Function

A pair of concepts parallel and closely related to substance and process are *structure* and *function*. Again, these are two contrasting approaches to the nature of anything and everything. They reflect different ways of thinking and talking about reality. In a sense they are not quite as fundamental as substance and process because they depend on a prior application of those concepts. Both structure and function have to do with form, shape, or configuration in the ultimate nature of things, and these aspects presuppose a substance or process to which they apply. In general, structure refers to substance and function refers to process; a substance has a certain structure, and a process entails certain functions. Structure involves the "what" of an entity, while function involves the "how." The structural approach is concerned with a recognition of patterns and relationships between parts; the functional approach is concerned with modes of operation.

Suppose one were to describe the nature of a pencil. According to one approach—the structural—a pencil is a slender cylinder of wood substance with a thin central core of graphite substance. According to the functional approach, the first and most important thing to say about a pencil is that it is an instrument for writing. But what kind of an instrument? Must we revert to the structural viewpoint and describe this writing instrument as before? No, replies the functionalist, we can elaborate the definition by describing how one would make a pencil, i.e., by relating the operations or functions necessary to produce it. But would this not lead back to wood and graphite as structural substances? Not necessarily, because "wood" and "graphite" may in turn be defined functionally. Wood refers to something combustible, which usually floats, etc. Similarly for graphite, there are ways of functioning which define it. Thus it is possible to achieve a thoroughly functional description of a pencil.

The structural approach is essentially static, while the functional approach is dynamic. Structure implies a state or arrangement which, at least for the moment, is fixed. Function implies an on-going activity, in which change is of the very essence.

There is no necessary opposition between structure and function. In fact, just as some would say that process requires a substance substratum, so it may be claimed that the ability of anything to function depends upon certain basic structures. Thus, a human being can think (function) only because he has a nervous system (structure). To this the strict functionalist would reply that the only satisfactory way of describing the meaning of the human nervous system is by the way it functions, including among other things the activity called thinking. In saying this he would not be denying structure but simply insisting that function is more fundamental. Therefore, it is not a question of structure or function, but rather one of primacy and emphasis. Everyone grants that it makes sense to talk of structures and of functions, but some would claim that structures must be defined with reference to their functions and others that functions depend on structures. Probably there are some purposes for which one mode of thought is the more useful and other purposes better served by the other approach. However that may be, the contrast of structure and function is an important metaphysical distinction. It makes a great difference in total outlook and approach which of the two is regarded as the most basic in the nature of reality.

Specifically, the distinction appears clearly in the approach to education. Structurally conceived, the school curriculum would consist of certain patterns of materials to be learned, logically organized according to a scheme determined by the natures of the various subjects. The functional approach, on the other hand, would require primary consideration of how learning takes place and of the uses to which the learner can put his knowledge. In fact, the only measure of what anyone knows, according to the functionalist, is what he can do. A structural approach to school administration would place the emphasis upon the patterns of relationship within the organization—salary, work schedules, school hours, plant requirements, etc.—and by these features the operation of the school would be determined. The functionalist would not begin with a concept of how a school should be organized. He would consider first what processes need to be carried on and what activities engaged in, and from this he would determine what arrangements need to be made to accomplish those purposes. A structural view of the family is concerned with the status and priorities of husband and wife, parents and children. These are embodied in various rules and customs which regulate the life of the family. The actual operation of the family is considered successful or unsuccessful in the degree to which the rules are obeyed. A functional approach to the family is concerned primarily with how the persons who compose it actually function, and the regulations for ordering the family's life are evaluated with respect to these actual effects.

Because a functional view makes the fact of change an integral aspect of the real nature of anything, it is likely to lead in practical applications to a greater flexibility than the structural view. For the same reason the functionalist tends to recognize individuality and variety more vividly than does the structuralist. Functionalism is also frequently more concrete and specific than structuralism, which is more concerned with abstract relationships and generalities.

Things and Events

We can combine the considerations of the two preceding sections in the distinction between *things* and *events*. By a "thing" we generally mean a structured substance, and by an "event" we mean a functioning process. It is possible to look at whatever we experience either as things enduring in time and undergoing change or as events, which as "happenings" incorporate time and change within their very being.

This distinction has become particularly important since the development of the relativity theory in twentieth-century physics, as explained in Chapter 20. A thing-view presupposes that the world is spread out in space and endures through time and that the spatial and the temporal are two independent modes or aspects of existence. The theory of relativity showed that such a common-sense view, while adequate for many ordinary purposes, cannot withstand careful analysis and leaves unexplained certain important experimental observations. It was found necessary, therefore, to introduce the concept of four-dimensional space-time and to regard physical occurrences not as spatial entities existing in independent time, but as space-time events. While the technical development of physical science made this view imperative in that field, there has been a tendency to extend its influence and use to other fields of study and thus to employ it as a basic concept in a comprehensive world view. This broader use of the event-idea has not involved a direct application of its precise technical meaning in physics; what has been carried over is the general approach to reality wherein specific occasions and particular happenings are regarded as the basic units of existence.

In the discussion about personal identity in the previous chapter this contrast between thing and event is well illustrated. The argument for personal identity rests upon the thing approach, grounded in the concept of structured person-substance. The contrary argument exemplifies the event approach, based upon the concept of personality as functional process. The thing-view of personality is that there is a real entity called the person who engages in such and such activities. According to the opposed event-view, the person *is* what he *does,* and there is no personal reality apart from the manifold happenings ascribed to him. Or more precisely, what happens *is* the person; there is no person "behind" or "in" the designated life events. As pointed out in the earlier discussion, possibly the strongest support for the reality of personal identity is in the human power of transcending time through memory and anticipation. It would then appear that serious consideration of these characteristics indicates the need for a thing concept and the insufficiency in some respects of the event concept.

Object and Field

Another pervasive contrast in ways of looking at reality is indicated by the pair of concepts, *object* and *field*. By an "object" here is meant a thing-in-itself, an independent, self-contained entity. This is an obvious, simple, common-sense notion. The idea of a field is not quite so immediately understood. Let us again take an example from physics, where the concept was first extensively used and from which it has been generalized for wider application. A magnet is said to produce a "field of force," the nature of which can be indicated by the direction and intensity of magnetic attraction exerted on a small iron test particle at any desired point in the space surrounding the magnet. Suppose one should seek to describe the nature of this magnet. He could say that it is a piece of iron which has the property of attracting other pieces of iron. That is to say, a magnet is a certain kind of *object*. Such a description might be criticized as omitting the most important fact—namely, the nature of the field of force. It could be argued that the magnet *is* primarily its field of force and certainly not solely the visible bar of iron. The essential nature of a magnet can then be fully stated only by specifying the influence it is capable of exerting in its surroundings. In principle this influence extends throughout all space, though the significant part of the field of force is in the vicinity of the magnet. Thus in principle a magnet is not strictly localized but must be defined as a field distribution coextensive with all of space.

Speaking generally, the field associated with any entity is the entire array of influences which it is capable of exerting upon other entities. The essence of the field approach is that an entity can be defined only with respect to this extended environing effectiveness and never entirely by reference to the isolated, independent object. Thus, a human being can be understood only in relation to the interactions experienced with surrounding entities, particularly other persons. The expressions "sphere of influence" and "magnetic personality" suggest the existence of a kind of field of force around a person. It is a matter of common experience that any person, as it were, "charges the atomosphere" about him with gloom or optimism, suspicion or confidence, deceit or sincerity, thus establishing a "personality field."

The field concept is generally employed not to describe the extended influence of a single entity but to analyze the resultant influence distribution in situations with several interacting entities. Thus, a family is a complex of two or more interacting persons, producing a total field with certain tensions, pressures, expectations, and attractions. The behavior of an individual in relation to this family cannot be understood merely by analyzing the nature of that individual but only by also taking account of these influences by which the nature of the family is constituted.

The object and field approaches reflect different ways of asking questions about the ultimate nature of things. The concept of object presupposes questions of the type "What is it?". The concept of field relates to questions like "What happens in this situation?" These general question-types indicate that the object approach is akin to the substance-structure-thing modes of thought and that the idea of fields is closer to the process-function-event approaches. However, perhaps the most important contrast of object and field—and one not found in the previously discussed pairs—is between the description of things-in-themselves and the description of things-in-relationship.

These alternative approaches are clearly reflected in educational thought and practice. For example, one who thinks in terms of objects is likely to expect a more direct and immediate effect of instruction on the developing person than one who uses the field concept. The reason for this is that the former approach tends to take little account of the pervasive and often decisive influences acting upon the student apart from the obvious teaching situation. The teaching of poetry may fail miserably in the case of a boy, otherwise able and interested, whose peer group regards such matters with contempt. How the person develops depends not entirely, perhaps not even largely, upon the conscious direction given to learning but upon the complex interplay of forces in his environment, i.e., upon the field in which his growth occurs. Another way of putting this is to say that in contrast with the object approach in education the field concept puts the emphasis on the total context and the manifold relationships within which development takes place.

Essence and Existence

In speaking of the nature of anything it is often thought useful to distinguish between *essence* and *existence*. These are two different ways of approaching anything and everything and hence are categories relevant to the ultimate nature of things. To understand this pair of terms consider the nature of a clock. If one should ask what the clock *essentially* is, the reply might be that in essence a clock is a mechanical device for measuring time. Nothing would be said about whether it was run by electricity, by weights, or by springs, nor about its size, shape, or color. These properties would not be of the essence, since the instrument would be a clock regardless of these particular physical characteristics; difference in size or in method of powering would make it no less a clock. To state the essence of a clock is to describe those properties which it has in common with all other clocks. The essence is thus a description not of one particular clock but defines the entire class of instruments called clocks.

Now what of the *existence* of the clock? Stating the essence involves disregarding all "non-essentials," ignoring particular qualities which not every clock has. These special characteristics are a necessary part of the "existential" nature of the clock. The clock as existent consists of everything that it actually *is,* including its particular size, shape, color, and source of power. A complete description of the clock's existence would even need to include its location in space and time.

Generally speaking, the essential nature of anything is that set of properties which it shares with all other entities designated by the same class name. The existential nature consists of all properties of the entity, whether or not shared with anything else. Those properties which are not part of the essence of an entity may be called *accidents* or *accidental properties.* Using this terminology, existence equals essence plus accidents. That is to say, we can state the existential nature of something by adding to the essential nature its particular accidental features, or we can obtain the essence from the existential nature by neglecting all non-essential or accidental properties.

It may be noted that essence and existence are identical in the case where the entity in question is the only one of its kind. Of special interest is the case of a person. Consider someone named John Smith. Though there are many other persons with this name, it is not a class name, but a *proper* name intended to designate one individual person. The existential nature of John Smith is whatever he is as a particular unique person, and since he is unique it might be argued that there are no accidents in his nature and hence that his essence is the same as his existence.

On the other hand, it could be argued that there is an essential John Smith, different from all other persons, but not the same as the existential John Smith, who changes from moment to moment. The essence of the person would then be the set of personal characteristics which endure through changing existential circumstances. This would lead to the idea, previously discussed, of the "soul" as the essence of the person. The idea of personal identity rests on some such designation of personal essence, and the difference between essence and existence has to do with the factors which change in the course of time. Those who deny any definite meaning to personal identity in effect insist upon an existential rather than an essential approach to personality.

Quite apart from the problem of personal identity and the essence associated with it, there is a more general essence simply in being human. To belong to the class of beings called human is to have certain special characteristics. An approach to the definition of this human essence was given in Chapter 26. Perhaps each person has his individual essence, but much more obviously he is essentially human. Existentially, a person is what he is in all his individuality and particularity. Essentially, he is a member of the species *homo sapiens.*

As suggested earlier, essence is general, while existence is particular and individual. Essence is shared with other members of the same class of entities, and is thus a general property of the entire set. Existence is unique and is not shared with any other entity. It is the entity in all its unrepeatable singularity.

Essence is timeless and static, while existence is time-bound and dynamic. There are two ways in which this can be interpreted. It may mean that the essence is independent of any existing entities of that class so that, for example, the essence "chair" would survive the destruction of all existing chairs and would also precede the construction of any particular chair. This interpretation would presuppose a kind of realm of essential being not dependent on the world of existential realities. By the other interpretation, the essence would be an invariable property of any and all existing members of the class of entities but would have no being independent of them. In this latter sense the essence would be time-bound in that it would disappear when particular things embodying this essence were so altered as no longer to belong to the class—as when a chair is smashed beyond recognition so that it is not worthy even of being called a broken chair.

This question of the relation between essence and existence, and particularly of the dependence or independence of essence with respect to existence, is one of the classic problems of philosophy, to which anyone who reflects on basic issues will return again and again in various contexts. One persistent view is that essence is prior to existence and that individual things can exist only by virture of participation in the real and powerful essence. The other view affirms the priority of existence, on the ground that the essence is derived from real entities by selecting, for purposes of classification, certain properties which other similar entities happen to have.

An educational system based on the primacy of essence would tend to place a high value on the so-called perennial truths and the essential human qualities and to be less concerned about the particular conditions, special needs, and individual peculiarities of unique persons. There would be more interest in the likenesses among people than in their differences and hence a tendency toward standardization of the learning processes. The effort would constantly be made to secure conformity to the essential pattern without much concern for the specific ways in which this would be done.

An existential approach would emphasize the individual and specific. Methods and materials would be determined to meet special needs in each situation. General principles would be subordinate to the examination of particular circumstances and contexts. Nothing would be assumed permanent or final, and the program would continually be adjusted and reconstructed to meet emerging needs.

Ideal and Actual

Closely akin to the contrast of essence and existence is that of *ideal* and *actual.* The actual is used here as synonymous with the existent. It means the reality of the complete concrete particular entity. The ideal, on the other hand, is conceptual or intellectual in nature, differing from the actual entity in designated respects. The ideal entity is regarded as bearing some immediate and distinctive relation to the actuality of which it is the ideal and the actual is supposed to exemplify with more or less faithfulness the ideal associated with it.

There are two kinds of ideal that need to be distinguished. The first is the ideal as perfection and the second is the ideal as simplification. By an ideal parent one may mean either the idea of a perfect parent or some particular qualities of parenthood which for simplicity of description are singled out as representative but are never actually encountered in pure form. The essence of an entity is an ideal in the latter of these two senses. The essence of a parent is that set of characteristics—a simplification of the complex reality of the actual parent—which are common to all called "parent." An "ideal community" might mean the essence of community or some other simplified picture which would represent important features of actual communities, or it might mean an imagined perfect community.

Whichever meaning is attached to the ideal, the point is that the ideal and the actual reflect two different approaches to the ultimate nature of things. Those who emphasize the ideal are not content to accept at face value the actual entities which confront them, but regard them ultimately and in the last analysis as reflections or embodiments of a deeper reality. They tend to regard the ideal as primary and the world of actuality as derivative and subordinate. Those who equate reality with actuality do not deny the ideal, but they regard it as dependent on the actual and as a partial and incomplete picture of the true nature of things.

These alternative approaches are reflected in attitudes toward persons. The idealist parent is convinced that his child is not "really" this intractable, unpredictable, immature organism. The real child is the one his dreams, hopes, and expectations portray. The evidence for this is that his behavior toward the child is so largely based upon the ideal picture. The actualist parent takes the child to be really what he specifically and immediately is. The immature person is accepted and enjoyed for what he actually is and not for what he promises to become in maturity.

In practice, of course, both the actual and the ideal must be taken into account. Ideals of personality can only become effective in relation to the given actuality, and ideals are means of guiding the progressive changes in the actual. Despite the need for both factors in the practical situation, it is still true that there are significant differences in emphasis and that the conduct of education is related to the predominance of the ideal or the actual in the conception of reality.

Abstract and Concrete

Two contrasting concepts having a major role in the most general descriptions of things are *abstract* and *concrete*. The word abstract means literally "drawn from," implying a more complete something of which the abstraction is a part or aspect. The word concrete means literally "grown together," implying wholeness or completeness within itself. The abstract is therefore partial and incomplete as compared with the concrete. Any concept describing an entity is an abstraction. The weight, color, or shape of an object is a partial aspect of it and hence an abstraction. A trait of personality is an abstraction. Any scientific law is an abstraction because it summarizes the behavior, in certain respects, of a certain class of entities. The concrete reality is the actual unity of the entity, from which the various abstractions are derived.

Essence is abstract and existence is concrete since essence is derived from existence by neglecting accidental characteristics. But essence is only a special case of the abstract. All essences are abstract (except in the case of unique entities) but not all abstractions are essences; accidental features are abstractions also. The abstract, like the essence, is general, while the concrete is particular and individual. Abstraction is an analytical process; concretion is synthetic. The abstract deals with parts or perspectives; the concrete concerns the whole in its undivided and integral character.

The abstract and the concrete are not mutually exclusive; abstraction presupposes the concrete. Again, it is a question of emphasis. There are interpretations of the nature of things which stress the concrete; there are others which concentrate on the abstract. Each involves a different approach to answering the question about ultimate reality. According to the first, the true character of anything is its unique wholeness. According to the second, the most important reality of an entity is its participation in certain general qualities and relationships.

With respect to education, the implications of the abstract and concrete approaches correspond closely to those of essence and existence and of ideal and actual, respectively. Interest in the abstract would be associated with education by principle and precept; interest in the concrete would lead to emphasis on case study and examples. The former would encourage theoretical, analytical, and verbal competences; the latter would stress the practical and constructive activity of the whole person.

The One and the Many

Some thinkers believe that reality at the deepest levels is *one,* while others are convinced that it is *many*. This difference in outlook has been important in the history of human thought, and it has ramifications in every area of life. Those who believe in the one-ness of reality are usually called *monists,* while those who believe in the ultimate many-ness of things are called *pluralists*. The monists hold that ultimately reality is simple, while the pluralists consider that the nature of things is irreducibly complex. Monists are convinced that each thing is fundamentally identical with everything else. Pluralists believe that there are real differences which cannot be overcome at any level of analysis.

Common sense is pluralistic. It is obvious to ordinary perception that the world is composed of many different things, and the average person would regard as nonsense any statement to the effect that everything is really one. Monism is therefore a sophisticated view. A monist does not deny that there are differences among things; he recognizes the obvious variety of the world of experience. What he insists is that if one looks beneath the superficial appearances the differences will disappear and an underlying identity will be discerned. The pluralist, on the other hand, though agreeing in conclusion with the common-sense view, arrives at it only after having explored the possibility of a deeper unity and having found a persisting variety.

The pluralist may criticize the monist for overlooking necessary distinctions and imposing his preferred scheme in the face of contrary evidence. The monist may regard the pluralist as lacking in the courage or imagination to probe to the deepest nature of things. The actual course of human culture lends weight in certain respects to each side of the argument. As man has learned more about his world, the immense richness, variety, and complexity of things have become more and more obvious. On the other hand, the growth of understanding has been achieved by discovering similarities, relationships, and laws which subsume many different things under one class or principle. The pluralist must then grant that there is in human history at least a strong drive toward simplicity, and the monist would have to admit that despite the alleged unity of things there is an increasing complexity in the world revealed to inquiry.

Perhaps it is fair to say that the monist has a vision—a hope, a faith, a confident expectation—that the manifest variety of things can progressively and without limit be reduced to simplicity. The pluralist thinks this vision is an illusion, this hope vain, and this expectant faith misplaced. He believes it is better to take a sober, realistic view of things, and he thinks the experience of mankind clearly suggests the limitations of the drive toward simplification.

For our purposes it is sufficient to observe that reflective persons employ these two contrasting ways of looking at the nature of anything and everything. One way is to see the many in all their discreteness and separateness. The other is to seek, and presumably to find, similarities and relationships which tend to make the many into one. The intensity and predominance of one or the other of these convictions may be reflected in any area of human concern.

Extreme monists would tend to see the process of education as directed to some single goal, to the attainment of which everything should contribute. Special circumstances and interests would be judged in relation to the one basic ideal. Since it would be assumed that everyone should develop in the light of the same ultimate objectives, educational practices would tend to become consistent and uniform. Monists are also tempted to be intolerant and partisan since they cannot admit a variety of ultimate truths. There is one true way, which they hope and expect that they have discovered, and hence other ways must be false. In order to ensure the most effective progress of the young, it is necessary to guide them into the way of truth and to guard them against falsehood. Instruction thus tends to be by assertion and demonstration rather than by free experimentation. Emphasis is upon the unchanging and universal principles which embody the one truth and not upon the particular applications of the rule in differing situations.

The pluralist educator has opposite tendencies. For him there is no single goal of the learning process. Education has many possible aims, and there is no way ultimately of judging between them. Every situation is different from every other and no two persons are alike, and hence no general rule will suffice. Every case must be considered on its own merits and every need met in its own way. There is no single truth. There are many ways of believing and doing, and hence tolerance and generosity toward those who differ are desirable. The practical social necessity for some agreement about rules of conduct does not invalidate this basic ideal of tolerance. Since ultimate reality is manifold, the educator is in no position to dictate the correct path to his students. It is his job to make suggestions and to encourage individual explorations, using his authority only to prevent what the learner would himself recognize as the serious errors of inexperience and to enforce necessary minimal rules of social conduct. Finally, the pluralist would subordinate principles to applications and would encourage his students to think specifically and concretely in particular contexts. He would thus prepare them to live effectively in a world of constant change and endless variety.

Mind and Matter

Of all metaphysical contrasts one of the most time-honored is that of *mind* and *matter*. Those who believe in the ultimacy of mind are commonly called *idealists,* while those who affirm the primacy of matter are designated *materialists*. We have already considered this contrast and some of its implications in Chapter 26 in discussing the uniqueness of man.

Idealists believe that the content of man's mental life—his thoughts, feelings, ideals, purposes—are the best clue to the ultimate nature of things. This belief comes from the observation that the entire content of human experience is mental. For man there is nothing else besides this inner experience. One might object that a rock is certainly not mental. To this the idealist would reply that we do not really know anything about a rock except such mental experiences as the feeling of hardness, heaviness, etc., conventionally associated with the idea of a rock. As far as man is concerned, then, the only world there is is the world of inner experience. The reality of material things is wholly defined by reference to this world of ideas.

The viewpoint directly opposed to this basic argument of idealism is called *realism,* of which materialism is one form. The realist says that the idealist confuses *knowing* with *being,* that just because our experience of the world is mental, there is no reason to say that the world itself is mental. Realists hold that there is a real world independent of our thinking about it and that ideas about that world provide clues to its nature, but that that nature is not itself necessarily ideal in character.

Materialism is a kind of realism in which the primacy and ultimacy of matter is affirmed. Nothing exists which is not material. The differences in things are due to different kinds or organizations of matter. In particular, mind is simply one mode of activity of matter. The materialist does not deny what is called mental experience, but he insists that it is wholly derivative from the modes of physical existence. Matter is a reality independent of our experience of it; in fact our thoughts about matter are simply one kind of material process.

It appears that materialism can include ideas more easily than idealism can include matter. For idealism insists on the ideal nature of everything, while materialism necessarily involves the concept of arrangement or patterns of organization of matter, and this element of form or structure is precisely what may be meant by the idea of a thing.

It is noteworthy also that the character and credibility of materialism depend upon the view of matter involved. The contemporary scientific conception of matter as a complex of energy distributions is a far cry from the common-sense view of matter as tangible, visible stuff. The world of electrons, neutrons, mesons, and quanta, whose organization is expressed by complicated mathematical equations, results in a far different kind of materialism than did the older world of impenetrable atoms striking one another like billiard balls. The new materialism differs from the old primarily in the far greater emphasis given to the structural or formal principles, and this change in emphasis makes it much more hospitable to the kinds of experiences the idealists consider fundamental.

In the process of human development the idealist tends to emphasize the "inner" life—the world of intellect, imagination, and feeling. He believes in the power of ideas to govern the life of man and to fashion the world and that nothing is more important than to improve the quality of inner experience. He thinks ideas control practice, and he tends to teach by direct presentation of principles, generally in verbal form.

The materialist is more concerned with the "outer" world of action. He regards ideas as reflections of material demands and as tools for overcoming obstacles to the smooth functioning of the human mechanism. He is especially interested in the material supports and conditions of human life and believes that the quality of experience is directly dependent on these factors.

He thinks that practical considerations generate ideas, and he is inclined to teach by arranging concrete situations in which the students will be confronted with problems to be solved for the satisfaction of their own vital needs.

Nature and Supernature

Finally, it is possible to distinguish between the views of ultimate reality as *natural* and as *supernatural,* respectively. The naturalist holds that there is only one world which contains all that is. This entire reality he calls "nature." Whatever there is is therefore entirely natural. To call everything natural is merely synonymous with saying that what is *is*. In a sense, then, the idea of nature does not assert anything new. Its chief function is to emphasize the unreality of anything that is not natural. The supernaturalist takes the position that there are two realities, nature and supernature, of which the latter is the more fundamental. Nature is grounded in supernature, emanates from it, or participates in it. Affirming these two realms of being, the supernaturalist may be called a *dualist.*

Most often supernaturalism is associated with systems of religious belief. Supernature may then refer to God the creator in contrast to the natural world which he has made. Or supernature may refer to the abode of the souls before or after death of the natural body. With such a view the soul while still in the body would participate in the supernatural, though also conditioned by natural factors. Again, supernature may be taken to mean the "spiritual" mode of being, as contrasted with the lower mundane existence. Or it may even stand for the realm of ideal essences which give form to all actual entities.

Each conception of supernature is associated with a particular view of the relation between the natural and the supernatural. In some cases the two are quite separate, and supernature may only occasionally break through into nature. In other cases supernature is closely knit with nature, being embodied in all actual entities.

The naturalist would claim that insofar as the alleged supernatural does not enter into nature it has no meaningful existence and that to talk about it is to speak nonsense. He would add that to the extent that it does enter nature it is natural and not supernatural. The naturalist holds that the supernaturalist in effect takes nature in all its richness, including ideas, values, and inspirations as well as things of sense, and renames some aspects of it "supernature," reserving the name "nature" for a partial and impoverished kind of reality.

The supernaturalist in reply would say that the naturalist confuses thought about reality by treating two basically different modes of being as though they were the same. He would also claim that the naturalist needs a more ultimate principle to explain nature and hence that naturalism is a superficial and unreflective view of things.

Education within a naturalistic framework tends to emphasize the scientific and factual approach, is concerned with immediate problems, and takes account of the differing factors in each person and situation. Supernaturalism underscores ideals, seeks ultimate goals, and tends to subordinate particular individuals and circumstances to absolute principles. The naturalist seeks to direct the development of persons through the use of natural intelligence operating in the world of tangible and testable realities. The supernaturalist seeks guidance also from higher sources, believing that man's life cannot be fully realized in nature but requires the illumination and transformation of the divine. For this reason it is often said that the supernaturalist takes a more exalted view of human possibilities and of man's ultimate worth than the naturalist, though he has less confidence in man's *unaided* natural powers.

29 The Cosmic Process

IN CHAPTER 28 we considered some of the concepts by which the ultimate nature of things may be described. The question next arises: How did the world come to be what it is? By what means did the whole nature of things develop to its present condition? This is the problem of cosmic process, which is the topic of the present chapter. Our objective is to suggest answers to questions about the origins of things and about the basic causes of change in the world order. The purpose of such an analysis in the philosophy of education is to discover, if possible, a comprehensive process of which the process of education may be seen as a special illustration. If it can be shown that education has its foundations in some universal process, it may be possible to draw certain inferences for the conduct of education. In any case, an understanding of the largest possible context of education is an important goal of any serious philosophic inquiry into the subject.

The Orders of Being

We begin with a description of the general structure of the world in the light of the several orders or levels of being. This description rests on the possibility of analyzing the universe into interrelated levels of increasing complexity, each order incorporating and depending upon the one next below it in the series. Any such comprehensive world picture, of which this is one kind, is a *cosmology*. The analysis of how the orders of being were generated is the subject of *cosmogony,* which we shall examine in later sections of this chapter. The grand title of our present inquiry might therefore be "the cosmology and cosmogony of education." Such considerations are the most speculative and wide ranging of any in our entire study of the philosophy of education. They ought, however, to be as far as possible based on the best available scientific knowledge as well as upon the best-attested insights from other realms of thought.

Elementary particles. If we consider all of the different kinds of things that go to make up the universe as we know it, it appears possible to arrange them in levels according to the complexity of organization attained. Starting at the lowest level, with the simplest and most elementary entities, these are the various types of particles which enter into the basic structure of matter. These particles have been discovered for the most part in the field of modern atomic physics. Most familiar is the electron, an incredibly small particle of negative electric charge which plays an important role in the transmission of electrical energy and vacuum tube technology. There are also positively charged particles, the protons, which are many times heavier than the electrons. Another type of particle, the neutron, is without electrical charge. In addition to these three primary particles, others such as the positron and the meson have been more recently discovered.

Atoms. The primary organized units, the atoms, are compounded from the elementary particles. The hydrogen atom, the simplest of all atoms, consists of one proton and one electron, the latter being related to the former somewhat as a planet to the central sun. More complicated patterns are built on the same general scheme, with a central nucleus and surrounding layers of orbital electrons in such number that their combined negative charge exactly balances the positive charge of the nucleus. In this manner the entire periodic table of chemical elements may be described. The limit of increasing complexity is reached at the level of the heaviest element in the series, uranium, which has the heaviest nucleus and the maximum number of orbital electrons which can be arranged in a more or less stable patterned relationship. When size and complexity exceed a certain limit (and often also for other reasons of structure), the atoms become unstable and break down into simpler and more stable forms. Such disintegration is the explanation of the phenomena of radioactivity and of the fact that there is an upper limit to the table of elements.

Molecules. The fact that atomic complexity cannot exceed a certain point does not prevent further organization on a new level. At this next higher level the constituent entities are no longer the elementary particles, but the atoms themselves. The organized patterns of atomic elements are molecules. At this level the principles of organization are not expressed as laws of atomic structure but as laws of chemical combination. The molecular type of organization is such as to increase enormously the range and variety of material entities. To see this it is only necessary to compare the relatively small number of elements in the periodic table with the thousands upon thousands of molecular forms (compounds) known to the chemists.

Crystals. The molecular entities form the basis for all larger material structures. In some cases they enter as constituents of new entities with a different system of organization, such as crystals. A crystal is an organization of molecules arranged in definite geometric form as determined by the binding forces operating between the given types of molecules. The principles of crystal structure permit the growth of organized entities whose size far exceeds that of any molecule. This indicates that a new level of organization, above that of the molecules, has been reached.

Colloids. Another kind of organization of molecules makes up the class colloids, whose characteristic is that though apparently soluble they will not pass through a membrane. The constituent molecules of colloids are organized in some way quite different from that of crystals, so as to resist the breach in their unity which passage through the membrane would require.

Larger aggregates. However, molecules are not always or even most frequently further organized on higher levels. Just as there are free electrons and other elementary particles not involved in atomic structures, so there are atoms and molecules which exist in relative independence or which are heaped together in amorphous (relatively non-structured) substances like gases, liquids, and non-crystalline solids.

Yet material aggregates form the basis for the great organized patterns that furnish the large-scale features of the physical world. The more or less balanced contrasts of earth, water, and air, of mountains, rivers, and tides, represent modes of correlation among the gross physical constituents of the earth. Here the principles of organization are no longer the microscopic ones of atomic and molecular binding-forces, but such macroscopic ones as gravitation, inertia, temperature, and pressure. Then beyond these terrestrial patterns there are the vast coordinations of the solar system, of stars and galaxies of stars. These are organized entities on the grand scale, whose constituents are planets, suns, moons, and stars and whose principles of organization are the laws of universal gravitation, the beauty and clarity of which are witnessed to by the refinement and precision of astronomical science.

Life. But the stellar communities, marvelous as they are, do not represent the highest level of organization. Paradoxically, they are, in a sense, on a lower level than some of the atom and molecule structures. Though greater in extent, the intricacy of design and the achievement of balanced contrast is not so striking in stellar systems as in atomic and molecular entities. The next genuinely higher level of organization is that of living substances. The line between the living and the non-living has never been sharply drawn. There are complex chemical compounds which are scarcely distinguishable from the most elementary living substances. But it is clear that in the realm of living things certain new modes of organization rise into dominance. It is these new modes which make possible a vast extension of the possible ways of organizing things. The characteristic feature of living beings is their capacity for such functions as growth, assimilation, and reproduction. All of these functions represent a new flexibility and versatility, whereby the form or pattern remains relatively independent of the precise material entities which make up the living substance. For example, growth represents the capacity to enlarge the body by the addition of new matter according to the ruling structural principle of the organism. Assimilation is the incorporation of appropriate outside material substance into the organism, either to replace other materials which have been lost or to permit growth. Reproduction is the capacity to generate a new and distinct organism with essentially the same pattern of organization as the parent organism. Here again, there is persistence of structural form despite changing material constitution.

The study of living things reveals the most extraordinary variety of organized forms. The seemingly endless possibilities begin with the simplest living substances—colloidal masses of complex organic compounds. Then there are single cells, each with nucleus, cell body, and cell wall organized for systematic growth and reproduction processes. Cells are further organized into many-celled bodies with specialized organs giving new powers for achieving security and efficiently employing the resources of the environment.

In ascending the scale of living things from simple to complex there are two dominant general features which govern the procession. One is the principle of differentiation and the other is a correlative principle of coordination. Differentiation means that certain types of living substance, certain cells, or certain groups of cells or organs specialize in particular functions. Thus, the differentiation between cell wall and cell nucleus makes possible the cell and its activities as opposed to the limitations of relatively amorphous living matter. Similarly, the complex activities of a plant or of an animal are possible only because of the differentiation of cells into the various organs. But along with this differentiation necessarily goes coordination. Each differentiated part performs its special function only by virtue of its sustained relationships with other parts. There can be no functioning cell nucleus without a cell wall, nor can the eye of an animal function without the continuing support of heart and lungs.

Societies. Just as inorganic substances may enter into larger patterns such as those of terrestrial and astronomical formations, so whole organisms may enter into larger communities of living things, forming *societies.* A society is a grouping of distinct organisms according to some principle of organization. Societies are particularly important among the animals, whose characteristic function is locomotion. This mobility clearly makes a great variety of coordinations not only possible but also necessary, if the activities of the animals are not to be frustrated in random collisions. The insect societies, such as those of the ants and the bees, are perhaps the most striking forms of social coordination below man. The marvelous achievements of human society are—despite serious deformities and frequent breakdowns—the supreme example of the possibilities of social community. It is noteworthy that all social orders, whether human or subhuman, depend, as with the hierarchy of organisms, upon differentiation and coordination. The activities of the queen bee and of the worker bee represent specializations of function within a larger whole, just as do the multiple occupations of human society.

Mind. One of the most important sets of functions of living things is designated by the word "mind." In general, mind functions enable the organism to become actively related to its environment. The minded organism is not self-contained and indifferent to the surrounding events. Inorganic bodies, to be sure, are linked to their environment, but in an entirely different way. The changes produced in inorganic substances by energy intake from the environment are in general of the same order as the amount of energy absorbed. Thus, a billiard ball struck by a cue responds to the blow simply by acquiring an amount of momentum equal to that lost by the cue. In the case of minded organisms, on the other hand, the effect of stimuli from the environment on the organism is not in direct relation to the energy input, but to the form of the stimulus, previous experience of the organism with similar stimuli, etc. Thus, if the billiard cue had been aimed at the head of a man instead of at the ball, it is likely that the blow would call forth an energetic response out of all proportion to the energy input. Mind is the means by which living things establish peculiarly sensitive and intimate relationships with their environment. It is particularly important in societies, for it is by virtue of mind that individual organisms can quickly and efficiently relate themselves to other individuals in the group, thus ensuring that flexibility of mutual adjustment which any social order demands.

Human mentality. It is when human mental activity is involved that the appearance of a really new order of being becomes clear. In Chapter 26 the uniqueness of man has already been discussed. It is the special characteristics of man pointed out there—rationality, self-transcendence, use of symbols, memory, imagination, spirituality—that define this next higher level. The distinctively human powers are the basis for a vast expansion in possible structures and modes of organizing entities. The limits imposed by the laws of ordinary inorganic or organic existence are transcended in the boundless realm of cultural creation, in which man by taking thought can remake the world. It is, of course, at this distinctively human level that the process called education takes place. This process is the means whereby the inhabitants of that level from generation to generation make good their title to this high estate.

Education and the levels of being. Having now arrived at education, one may ask what bearing the previous analysis of the subhuman levels of being has on the subject. The answer is that through such a survey it is possible to understand education as rooted in a comprehensive process which may be discerned at every level of being and as an extension of that process at the conscious human level. What is the common factor which is found at every level? Each new order of being is defined by certain new principles of coordination in which the organized entities of the next lower level enter as constituent elements. These new patterns of organization make it possible to increase the complexity and harmonious variety of existence beyond the limits present at the lower levels.

According to this cosmology, there is a universal principle, operating at every level of being, whereby the possibilities of existence are fulfilled by means of hierarchically arranged patterns of coordination. Human development is part of this total scheme, and the process of education may be seen as the means of effecting the required coordinations at the human level. The cosmic picture suggests the general principle that education should direct human development toward the achievement of inclusive harmonious organization of contrasting entities. This is the basic rule of advance from lower to higher levels in the cosmic order as described above. In short, this cosmology of education seems to suggest that education may be defined and conducted in such a way as to advance and fulfill a universal trend toward organization.

The infant begins life with a mass of largely random and uncoordinated movements and impulses. As he begins to interact with his environment, he becomes aware of a not-self, including people and objects, with which he must enter into relationship. His early education helps him achieve adjustment to what is given in his surroundings. This adjustment is the step-by-step fashioning of harmonious patterns of coordination between himself and that which is around him. In later years this elemental process of pattern-creation is elaborated into the complex arrangements of social life. All social organization, with its myriad expectations and demands, is but the exemplifying of possible forms of organized behavior, and all education for social participation involves the orderly construction of successively complex levels of habit and response.

The same is true of growth in knowledge. To know is to establish harmonious cognitive relationships with what is known, and knowledge is deeper and more complete to the extent that ideas are not simply isolated items, but enter into organized schemes of mutual support and relevance. Furthermore, as we have seen in earlier chapters, knowledge is confirmed and established through the creation of communities of discourse, in which persons, together with intelligible objects, enter into mutually affirming relationships.

All cultural creation, whether in social life, in the realm of knowledge, or in the skilled work of artist, inventor, or craftsman, manifests the realization of such successive levels of coordination. No step can be taken without the prior accomplishment of the more basic steps. Consequently, the clue to the educative process would seem to be the discovery and application of the possible ways of building personal-cultural complexes. Each type of coordination presupposes certain earlier organized competences at its basis. The attempt to learn anything without taking thought for the necessary prior accomplishments is folly. True education, on the other hand, is to recognize and work in accord with the principles of possible succession of patterns. According to this view, then, by the very nature of things, education can succeed only insofar as it is directed toward the production of increasingly inclusive complexes.

Superhuman levels. Before leaving the subject of orders of being one further question needs to be considered, namely, whether human beings represent the highest of all levels. This question has direct bearing on the problem of cosmic development, as will be shown in later sections of this chapter. There are influential systems of idealistic and religious thought in which the existence of these higher orders is affirmed. The common characteristic attributed to the higher beings is that they are not bound by material substance but have the freedom of pure spirituality. Some views hold that the higher level is a realm of Absolute Idea. Others believe in *God* as an infinite creative Spirit. Between God and man there may be intermediate levels inhabited by angels or demonic powers or by the immortal souls of men who have died.

One difficulty with these beliefs is that they are not consistent with the hierarchical arrangement of the lower orders, in which each level is built upon and includes all the lower levels. Thus, there could be no human communities apart from the subordinate organized patterns of living substances, colloids, molecules, and atoms. The existence of pure spirits would entail relinquishing this basic principle of subordination and hierarchical dependence. The only type of higher-level conception which would avoid this difficulty would be that of *embodied* spirits or deities as coordinating agencies for groups of actual material-living-thinking entities. For example, one could regard the universe as in some degree an organic whole and God as the new level of being, containing in himself as his "body" all lower orders, including man, God's "mind" then being the ordering principle of the whole.

On the other hand, if one is willing to accept a dualistic world-view, with a clear break in the rule of ascent between man and the higher orders, then the hypothesis of pure spirits becomes credible—though many would consider the evidence in their favor far from convincing.

The Process of Cosmic Development

What follows from this picture of the universe as a hierarchy of orders of beings? Is it simply to be accepted as a general description of the structure of things with no further explanation? Some would be content with such a description. Others would seek for a more satisfying explanation. One line of argument might go like this: It is obvious that in the course of time things undergo change. We know from history the vast transformations that have taken place in human culture. All living things grow and develop. It is clear also that rocks, planets, and stars are continually changing, though usually at a slower rate than living things. Now may it not be that the levels of being are also involved in this process of development—that not only plants and cultures and rocks but the whole cosmos undergoes transformation? And may not the character of the successive orders of being provide some clue to the nature of the cosmic process?

These are crucial questions for the cosmology and cosmogony of education, for if the cosmos does not develop, then there is no cosmic process in which educational process is rooted and from which it may take its direction and derive its impetus. On the other hand, to affirm a cosmic process would provide an analogue and prototype for the process of education.

In the following sections a number of different positions regarding the ultimate explanation of the cosmic order will be considered, together with their possible relevance for education.

Special Creation

One of the standard explanations for the origin of the world is the religious doctrine of special creation. This is the belief that the first cause of everything was a deity or deities by whose wisdom and power the various orders of being were produced. The natural universe is regarded as derivative from and dependent upon a supernatural source. Particular types and levels of entities are explained not by reference to any developmental process but as consequences of the primordial divine decision.

The accounts of special creation are often regarded as mythological in nature, i.e., as dramatic portrayals of the life and activities of the divine powers, in terms drawn from human life. This method is used to make the meaning vivid and to render accessible what must in its full reality transcend human comprehension. On the other hand, religious literalists regard the creation stories as detailed factual accounts, of the same nature as scientific explanations.

There are two different ways in which the creation can be regarded as taking place. One way is for the deity to fashion a pre-existing and unformed stuff into the desired forms. God plays the role of a cosmic artisan fabricating the world according to his special plan and purpose. The other and more sophisticated view is that God created the world out of nothing, bringing it into being simply by his divine command. In this latter form the deity is more omnipotent and self-sufficient than in the former, where he requires an independent world-stuff upon which to work.

The doctrine of special creation in effect denies the existence of cosmic process. It does not deny that growth and development of individual creatures takes place: this is so universally evident that no widely held theory could deny it. Nor does it deny change within the longer-term historic process—e.g., the rise and fall of civilizations. What it does deny is that the total world order, with its various levels of being, from electrons to man or angels, has come into existence through a process of development.

The special-creation hypothesis has the advantage of simplicity and directness. In one vivid picture it explains the whole complex scheme of existence. Its critics would say that herein lies its great fault, that what is proposed as an explanation is no explanation at all but merely a dismissal of the problem by reference to the unfathomable will and wisdom of God.

Under a special-creation theory the function of education is to insure that the primordial and permanent orders of creation shall be recognized and respected. Man has a definite and fixed nature and a pre-established relation to every other creature. Obedience to the will of God requires that man conform to the given fundamental order. The corresponding educational program is essentially conservative, authoritarian, and static. Such changes as occur in man and society are superficial adjustments which do not alter the true nature of things. Insofar as education reflects the cosmic plan, it is not a developmental process at all, but an imposition of order by fiat or by training immature human beings according to certain pre-ordained structures of being.

An Uncreated Static Universe

Those who cannot accept a special creation hypothesis may simply regard the world as itself the primordial reality, never created and always in essential features the same. It may be argued, as stated above, that it really explains nothing to invoke a special creative agency, and that one might with better reason seek no answers beyond the universe itself. For if the deity is introduced as primal cause one might ask for an explanation of the deity's nature and will. If it were replied that this explanation cannot be provided since nothing is prior to God, the response might be that one might then just as well remain content with the world as ultimate principle and not introduce the concept of God, which adds nothing to our understanding.

In relation to education, the point of main concern is whether the universe undergoes a process of development at least analogous to what occurs in human learning. Is the world essentially static or dynamic? Are the orders of existence eternal or have they come into being by cosmic development?

Quite apart from any theological creation hypothesis, the evidence against a static universe seems overwhelming and incontrovertible. Most striking are the abundant indications of organic evolution—particularly in the study of fossils and in the comparative study of plant and animal structures. The mass of available evidence weighs heavily in favor of the theory that these living things came into being through a long process of organic development, that they have not always existed in their present forms, and that they have not even existed thus since some remote creation event.

Additional evidence against the static view comes from recent studies in physical cosmogony—i.e., from theories of the origin and development of the physical world. There is now considerable evidence that not only have living things evolved but that the physical universe itself may have had a similar history. The striking thing is that there are several independent lines of inquiry which all lead to essentially the same result. For example, it is possible to calculate approximately the age of the earth by finding out the relative quantities of various radioactive elements in its crust, since some of these elements decay at different rates than others. Again, it can be shown that the interaction of the earth and the moon is such as to produce a gradual increase in the size of the moon's orbit around the earth. It is then possible to calculate back to the time when the earth and moon were together, i.e., to determine the age of the moon. Still further, astronomers are able from a study of the differences in motion of stars in a stellar cluster to calculate by statistical means the approximate age of this cluster. Each of these methods, and a number of others as well, lead to the same conclusion: that the physical universe is presumed to be several billion years old. It follows from this that modern physical cosmogony lends support to a dynamic world view. It also reopens the question of creation, for if there is a beginning from which the age of the universe can be dated, what preceded the beginning?

The result of all these considerations is to cast into serious doubt the idea of an uncreated static universe and thus to confirm the belief that in the cosmos at large there is a process, which may have some bearing upon the process called education.

Continuous Creation

The two previous views have been based upon the belief that the universe in its main features has always been as it is now. We turn now to two positions in which cosmic development is affirmed. These two parallel the two preceding static views with respect to whether or not the universe has been created. According to the dynamic-creation position, the universe was not created at a particular time, as in the special-creation hypothesis, but has been and is being produced through a process of *continuous creation*. The making of the world is never finished, and the task of making is the continuing responsibility of the creator.

As in the case of special creation, there are two different kinds of continuous creation: One kind is the fashioning or molding of existing material into new forms. The agent in creation is generally conceived of as a deity or deities, or more vaguely as spiritual powers. These powers may be considered either as essentially transcendent (i.e., having their being beyond or above the natural world) or as immanent (i.e., having their being within the natural world). The latter position would tend to relate the cosmic process more closely to the ordinary processes of growth and development than would the former.

The doctrine of continuous creation has the merit of providing an explanation for the fact of cosmic development. It is a flexible explanation in that there is no fixed and determined pattern to which the world order must conform. Continuing creation allows for an indefinite variety of new beings and forms of existence. There is psychological appeal in the belief that the creative powers are always on the job, that there are support and guidance for tasks to be done, and that an endless procession of new and unimagined possibilities lie in store for the universe.

Against the hypothesis of continuous creation it may be urged that it is an explanation in name but not in fact. What does it really mean to assert that the cause of cosmic development is a creative power or powers?

Does that assertion throw any light on how or why the process of world development takes place? Does it add to our knowledge or merely to our vocabulary? Furthermore, what help is it to ascribe the cosmic order to creative powers which then go unexplained themselves? If we must stop somewhere in our explanations, why not come to rest in the developing world itself and gives up the useless attempt to find either immanent or transcendent agencies which must themselves remain a mystery?

The continuous-creation hypothesis lends powerful support to a dynamic view of education. The process of education can be regarded as the focal point of creation in the human sphere. The impulse to learn and the pervasive tendencies toward growth and maturity are seen as evidence of the creative powers at work in human life and the direction of human development as governed by the intention of the creating power. This is usually conceived in theological terms, as the voice or will of God. The right direction for human development is then defined in relation to the divine wisdom or purpose.

But how is the creative purpose made effective in the cosmic process, and more particularly in the development of human beings? In the lower orders of being the divine intention would be seen in the fields of force which are reflected in the coordination of elementary particles, atoms, molecules, crystals, colloids, and other material configurations. At the level of living things creation would be seen in the new forces of cohesion permitting organic persistence through reproduction, nutrition, and repair and in the new powers of sensitivity to stimuli. At the human level the divine purpose would be revealed through such unique human capacities as reason, imagination, self-awareness, and memory. Thus, logical thinking would be considered not merely as a human activity but as a reflection of the divine rationality. The imaginative consideration of the world (e.g., in the arts) would be regarded not only as the free play of the human creative spirit but as a channel for the divine creativity.

From this standpoint, then, education is a means, at the human level, of fulfilling the purposes of the creator as he continues the work of creation. Such activities as careful reflection, experimental inquiry, conscientious self-criticism, and artistic appreciation may be considered as reliable approaches to the discernment of the creator's intention. More particularly, the practices of meditation, prayer, and worship may provide especially favorable occasions for becoming aware of the divine will and responding to it. Group discussion and careful review of past social experience may also be valuable sources of such insight.

The decisive point is that education within the framework of continuous creation is guided by reference to a prior creative purpose, made evident in a variety of ways. The educator's task is to respond gladly to that purpose and to make maximum use of the means available to discern it. The attitude of the educator is that of an elder pupil, attentive to the voice of the great Teacher, in order that he may assist those less experienced to fulfill the creator's plan for them.

Emergence

The basic presupposition of the creation hypothesis—either special or continuous—is that there must be an adequate explanation for everything by reference to a prior agency. It is taken as self-evident and indisputable that no thing can come out of nothing, and thus that whatever exists must be referable to some prior reality. To imagine otherwise, it is held, would be to abandon hope for rational understanding.

It is the denial of this fundamental premise that marks the view of cosmic development as a process of *emergence*. According to this position, new things progressively emerge either by genuine origination or by novel combinations and arrangements of prior entities. There is no agency which produces the emergent entities. They simply arise of themselves in the course of natural interaction. It does no good to invoke as explanation of changes some mysterious creative power, since nothing is known beyond the observed effects in the natural order. It is more reasonable, then, simply to organize what does occur naturally and to seek no explanation elsewhere.

The emergence hypothesis rests on the conception that the higher forms come from the lower forms—that the more complex orders of being are derived from the simpler ones by a natural process of development. The creation hypothesis, on the other hand, regards it as axiomatic that the river cannot rise higher than its source, and thus that the production of the successive levels of being requires the existence of a higher level of being which includes all the lower ones.

The proponent of the creation view would claim that the emergence view leaves the world process unexplained, that the latter hypothesis is actually a confession of ignorance in order to avoid a difficult problem, and that it gives undue importance to the world as it is, without recognition of the ideal sources of the world of the future. To this the proponent of emergence replies that the creation idea is based on an essentially static outlook since nothing genuinely new ever occurs because it is already present in the creator, that this static viewpoint is an outmoded and unfruitful way of looking at things, and that an explicitly and thoroughly dynamic standpoint is needed. Emergence is the view which results from taking the inherent dynamism of reality seriously. The emergence of novel entities is of the very nature of things. Thus, we do not explain changes in things by reference to existing static realities, but we take as fundamental the idea of a world in ceaseless change, in which any apparently static realities are due to a relatively stable balance of dynamic forces.

There are the same two general types of emergence as of creation, namely, emergence of new entities out of nothing and emergence of new forms. The former corresponds to creation by divine fiat, the latter to creation as molding or formation. Besides this distinction, there are at least three different conceptions about the mechanism of emergence.

Chance. The first of these is that emergence happens by chance. There is a considerable degree of unpredictability or lawlessness in the nature of things. Occurrences are frequently random and disorderly, and as a result of the immense numbers of combinations of things in the long ages of cosmic existence the various so-called higher forms accidentally came into being, just as in the random shuffling and reshuffling of a pack of cards one might eventually turn up an arrangement in any desired order of suits and card values. This is a mechanical type of explanation, in which emergence is conceived of only as rearrangement. It has the appeal of a grand simplification in which the vast complexity of the world process is reduced to the blind and unintelligent mechanism of the game of chance. Herein also lies its weakness, for to many it seems an incredible over-simplification, if not pure nonsense. The relative continuity and stability of the world order do not seem to accord with the conception of random arrangement. The complexity of actual structures far exceeds what would be even remotely conceivable by chance, despite the vast stretches of time available for the shuffling process.

Selection. The second type of emergence mechanism assumes some inherent principle of selectivity in things by which chance variations are judged and those which are suitable are conserved, while those which are less fit tend to disappear. Thus chance is still a factor, but there are other factors which eliminate the necessity of beginning again at each reshuffling. Chance is still the basis for the production of the new, but once the new has come into being its persistence or disappearance is determined by some inherent principle of correlation with other things. This view overcomes the most serious objection to the pure chance theory, but it raises questions about the nature of the selection principle and as to whether or not this in effect reverts to a kind of creation hypothesis, since the criteria of acceptance or rejection of emergents would seem to have some reality prior to the rise of the new forms themselves.

Vitalism. A third type of mechanism is to assume that novel entities do not arise by chance but by the operation of some basic vital principle, an inner dynamism of all reality, identical or analogous to human will or intention. The immediate appeal of this view is that it does justice to the progressive character of cosmic process far better than a pure chance theory. On the other hand, it may be objected that the concept of vital principle is too vague, that it illegitimately applies to nonliving things a concept drawn from the animate realm, and that it is inadequate to account for the characteristic dynamics of the higher levels such as that of human consciousness. The vital force theory may be supplemented, as in the chance theory, by a principle of selectivity through which the appropriate novel productions are conserved and further built upon. The comments made about such a selection principle apply here also. The idea of a vital force is, in effect, a compromise between an extreme matter-rearrangement theory of emergence and a theory of immanent creative mind or spirit. Like many such compromises, while it may appear to have the merits of both extremes, it also seems to many an illegitimate obscuring of the real issue by verbal ambiguity.

Education and emergence. What, now, of education within the context of cosmic emergence? Under this hypothesis, the emphasis would tend to be on originality and inventiveness. While the learners would usually be expected to tread familiar paths, emergence might lead one to be alert for the appearance of really creative personalities from whose activities important new suggestions could come. The world would be viewed as wide open to fresh possibilities. No one knows in advance what these are, hence the importance of the experimental method. It is only as a variety of approaches is tried that the emergent possibilities become clearly evident. A philosophy of emergence places man at the top of the cosmic scheme and gives him no superhuman powers upon which to depend. Thus upon education rests the heavy obligation of developing persons who are mature, self-governing, and responsible. The most important of all educational objectives is to develop competence in making decisions. Since no creator makes man, man must learn to make himself and to remake his world according to his own will and desire.

The educational outlook associated with the philosophy of emergence depends to some extent on the type of emergence mechanism one accepts. The theory of chance is hardly consonant with education of any kind, for the whole point of directing human development is to avoid purely haphazard influences. The belief in chance would then mean that education has nothing to do with cosmic development. It would also tend to rob human attainment of any special dignity and would fail to provide any basis for preferring one condition of things over another, since every state of being would be only a random combination of world-elements.

The chance position is so difficult to entertain that it is natural to supplement it with an idea of selection mechanisms. Education fits more easily into this scheme. According to this view, it is important to discover which processes will lead to adjustment, persistence, and endurance of the human organism. Education is thus to be guided by a success objective. The development of persons is to be directed so as to maximize human survival and to open up further possibilities of human achievement.

A vital force mechanism tends toward a view of education in which emotional factors and organic hungers are given special attention. Unless it also is supplemented by a principle of selection between desirable and undesirable impulses, this type of education is likely to become irrational, chaotic, and directionless and hence cease to be education in any proper sense.

The conclusion appears to be that education within the context of a philosophy of emergence must presuppose some basic pattern or structure in the nature of things which favors some directions of human development over others. The task of the educator is to discover and make use of that pattern.

Cosmic Development as Restoration

One function of philosophy is to break the hold of habitual modes of thought by suggesting orientations drastically different from the customary ones. To this end it may be of value to present briefly a view of cosmic development based on a completely different outlook from any discussed thus far. This is not merely a speculative exercise; the view now to be presented may be seriously entertained, and there is a long tradition which makes use of it in one form or another.

The dynamic positions discussed previously have taken for granted that the complex forms on higher levels of being have been somehow built up by the addition and combination of the simpler forms on the lower levels. Suppose this assumption were to be abandoned and replaced by one in which the priority and primacy of the highest forms were affirmed and in which the lower forms were regarded as fragments or degenerate states of the higher ones. Then cosmic development could be understood as a process of *restoration* of a primordial order. The hypothesis is that there was an original cosmic order in which maximum harmony and fitness prevailed, on the basis of certain immanent laws of coordination, that this order has been violently shaken by some cosmic disturbance, destroying the higher and more delicate coordinations of life and mind (or conceivably even higher functions), and that as the disturbance has receded the immanent coordinating principles have progressively restored the primal order. Thus what appears to be the production of new forms of being is actually only the removal of perturbing influences, allowing the original harmony to prevail.

A mechanical analogy may serve to clarify this picture of the universe. Consider a rigid frame containing a number of small hard spheres arranged in a certain pattern by means of a network of elastic bands linking the balls to each other and to the frame. If this assemblage is left undisturbed, the established pattern will prevail. But if the frame is struck or vigorously shaken, the spheres will move about in an apparently random fashion and their original pattern will no longer be discernible. If the frame is then permitted to rest quietly, the elastic bands will soon bring the spheres to rest in their proper positions and the original order will be restored.

Another analogy would be the process of solution and recrystallization of crystalline substances. When a crystal of salt is immersed in water, the binding forces holding the salt molecules in the crystal pattern are overcome by the more or less random water molecules which take captive the salt molecules. When the water is dispelled by evaporation, the original binding forces are no longer overwhelmed by water molecules and the organized salt structure is restored.

The three basic elements in the restoration theory of cosmic development are (1) a primal state of high order, (2) certain permanent immanent forces of cohesion or tendencies toward organization, and (3) a cosmic disturbance. For the first of these there can of course be no direct evidence. One can at most infer it on the basis of the known levels of being. Concerning the second, the "laws of nature" discovered by scientific research would indicate the presence and character of some immanent organizing principles. As for the third, there seems to be increasing evidence that the world process began by some cataclysmic explosion and that subsequent developments have taken place in the course of a cooling-off period. For these reasons a restoration hypothesis would appear at least consistent with some of the available empirical evidence.

Education and the restoration hypothesis. This theory as applied to education would tend to produce a high degree of confidence in the inherent drive toward health and fulfillment in persons, given favorable external conditions. The task of education would be to minimize obstacles to effective realization of persons. The teacher's attitude would be analogous to that of the doctor, who knows that by his healing art he can only give the inner restorative powers a better opportunity to do their work—he cannot himself create health. So the educator would recognize that he can only provide favorable circumstances wherein the immanent cosmic tendency toward restoration works through the learners' personalities. He would not regard it as his task to "make something" of the persons under his direction. Rather would he recognize and welcome the existing forces of personal growth whereby each individual inwardly strives to become his proper self and the social group also tends to achieve harmony and balance.

The restoration view would lead the educator to take seriously the interests, feelings, hopes, fears, and enthusiasms of the learner, for these may be clues to the direction in which fulfillment lies. On the other hand, they may if not properly employed operate as perturbing influences. The right employment of interests is judged by whether or not these dynamic forces lead to further constructive possibilities or to eventual disorganization. Consider, for example, a teacher who is faced with the problem of a student with a powerful impulse to throw objects in the classroom. This leads to disorganization. However, that student might be encouraged to satisfy the throwing interest constructively on the baseball field. In this instance the interest is an indication of a direction in which personal fulfillment lies, and the teacher's search for a satisfying outlet for it could be based upon the conviction that there is an implicit harmony of things in which both personal interest and social well-being may be realized.

The restoration view generally tends to favor an attitude of quiet reflection rather than busy activism. Rush and confusion belong to the perturbing agencies which hinder the process of restoration. Overanxious concern for getting things done and willful insistence on one's own way of doing things betray lack of faith in the persistent natural pattern which seeks realization. Hence education would be dominated by a spirit of patient watchfulness and sensitive awareness rather than one of determined efficiency.

Critics of the restoration view may consider that it is too speculative and that it deals too vaguely with the nature and source of the perturbing influences. Educationally they might object to the implied conservatism of a theory which presupposes a pre-existent goal or intended structure of things. This might seem to rob man of his genuine creativity and freedom, giving him only the option of being either a rebel or a conformist.

The Problem of Causality

In the preceding four sections several positions regarding the process of cosmic development have been outlined. In this and the two following sections three fundamental philosophical problems related to the analysis of cosmic development will be considered. These are actually metaphysical questions in that they concern modes of thought of the widest generality. They are discussed here rather than in Chapter 28 because of their direct bearing on questions of cosmogony.

The first of these problems is that of *causality*. It is a deeply rooted habit of thought that every happening has a cause, that nothing occurs without good and sufficient reason. This is a basic axiom of thinking, the very ground upon which the search for understanding rests. To find the causes of things is to make them intelligible. Failure in causal analysis results in irrationality and obscurity.

What is a cause? It is a thing or event which has direct relevance and productive efficacy in relation to the happening of which it is a cause. The effect incorporates something that previously belonged to the cause. Thus, to say that the cause of motion of a baseball is a swinging bat is to identify the momentum possessed by the ball with at least some of the momentum previously belonging to the bat. Again, to say that a painter is the cause of a picture is to identify the form of the picture with an idea of the picture antecedently in the mind of the painter.

So far everything seems clear. The difficulty arises when one asks whether every happening or entity is completely intelligible in the light of its causes. Is it possible, in theory, to find causes which fully account for any given occurrence? If it were, then would not the present condition of things be identical with the past, since each aspect of every entity would be identified with a corresponding aspect of some antecedent entity? Or if not identical, the present would still contain nothing that the past did not contain, though the past might conceivably have contained more than the present. The question of causality is whether or not every event is fully accounted for by its causes. To this problem there are three possible solutions, and these solutions are represented in the major views on cosmic development previously discussed.

The first position is that there is more in the causes than in the effects. This is generally the implication of the creation theories. The creative powers are usually considered as perfect beings from whom a less-than-perfect universe has come. The things that happen are fully accounted for by reference to omnipotent and omniscient deity, and in this primal cause there are further perfections without limit above and beyond those reflected in the created world.

The opposite position is that the effects are greater than the causes. This is the standpoint of the emergence hypothesis. Emergence means simply that genuinely new entities or forms which are not contained in any antecedent reality come forth. The present state of things is not wholly accounted for by reference to prior states. There are perfections and achievements which exceed those of the earlier stages of universal development.

Between these two is the position that causes exactly equal effects. Strictly speaking, this would apply only to a changeless universe, since any change, even of arrangement, implies either an addition or subtraction of being. In a sense it applies to the restoration theory also, since everything is in principle explained by the primordial order of things, which the essentially irrational and random disturbing forces have for the time being obscured.

These three basic positions on causality represent three pervasive outlooks or orientations which may be reflected in the educational process. The first and third views indicate a firm insistence on completeness and settledness. The role of education is then the somewhat passive one of recognizing and uncovering what already really is. The second view emphasizes novelty, incompleteness, and openness. Then education is concerned with active origination, whereby the universe-that-is-to-be is progressively made anew, without benefit of prior higher wisdom.

The Problem of Possibility

Closely related to the problem of causality is the problem of *possibility*. This is a somewhat broader version of the previously discussed question of the actual and the potential. (See Chapter 27.) Possibility refers to what might conceivably be but which may or may not actually exist. Not only do growing persons have in the early years possibilities which may later be realized, but the cosmic process is a continual actualizing of what were hitherto only possibilities. Furthermore, there are possible modes of being which may never become actual in any determinate entity.

The status of possibility. Possibility becomes a problem when one goes beyond the obvious facts of descriptive analysis to the deeper question of the status of possibility. What kind of reality does possibility have? Does possibility exert any power? Where is the possible before it becomes actualized? Is it just an idea in somebody's mind? If so, what about possibilities before there were men, or possibilities of which no one thinks?

One position is that the possible has some sort of independence and priority. The opposing position is that the possible is wholly derivative from the actual. In the latter view possibilities which are not yet embodied in actual things still depend on the actual state of mind of the person who imagines them. Possibility is then an abstraction from the actuality of existing things.

Possibility and development. This question of the status of possibility becomes particularly crucial in the analysis of development. Do possibilities have power to influence the direction of development? Since it would seem that they could have power only if they had priority, the facts of development appear to weigh in favor of the first of the two positions stated in the preceding paragraph. Development presupposes the realization of some possibilities rather than others and hence some governing principle of selection and relevance. In the emergence theory it seemed necessary to postulate some selective factor even in the case of changes introduced by chance. In the creation theory the creator's mind, will, or intention would be the source of discrimination among possibilities. In the restoration hypothesis the favored possibilities would be embodied in the immanent forces drawing the disordered universe back to its primordial order.

Possibility and education. In education there are three distinct orientations with respect to the status of possibility. The first is that possibility is subordinate and derivative and that man can create what he will. Man thus controls possibility and defines it according to his own intentions. The direction of human development is then not subject to any inherent law or limitation. Hence education must proceed either by letting the learner alone so that he may create and realize his own possibilities or by directing him along lines which are essentially arbitrary. Emphasis in either case will tend to be on the boundlessness of human freedom and creativity.

Second, education may be based on the recognition of a definite structure of possibility which limits what man can do yet still presents him with an infinite variety of possibilities among which he may at will and without fear or favor freely choose. There are then definite paths along which human development may proceed, and it is important to learn the boundaries and conditions of these paths, but there is no one path for all to tread. Emphasis will be on knowledge of principle, law, and structure in the natural and social order, but with particular attention to the variety of possibilities among which to choose.

Third, education may proceed on the basis of the assumption of preferred possibility patterns. Not only is there inherent law and limitation in existence, but there are powers and structures which favor one or several paths over others or which may even dictate a single path of development. The directing power may be conceived as mechanical necessity, in which case education is simply the grinding out of an inexorable determinate sequence. Or the preference may be regarded as the will of a deity who governs by force, by reward and punishment, or by persuasion. Or the directing agency may not be regarded as such a personalized entity but as an immanent moral law or built-in tendency toward restoration. In the case of deity or of immanent principle the objective of education would be to discern the preferred ways and then to direct development as far as possible along those lines.

Possibility and causality. It should be observed that the problem of possibility is closely linked with that of causality. The question just now discussed concerned the causal efficacy of possibility. Do possibilities have power to influence development prior to their actual embodiment in things, and if not, are there entities (e.g., deities) in which the possibilities reside and through which they exercise their power? The classical formulation of this problem has been in the distinction between efficient cause and final cause. An efficient cause is a fully embodied agency which gives form to succeeding entities or events, as in the case of a hand which throws a ball. A final cause is a possibility which as future goal or purpose helps to determine the form of things, as when the growth of justice in civilization is regarded as the consequence of a persistent cosmic lure or persuasion toward justice. Many would deny such a thing as final cause, on the ground that goals and ideals are simply a somewhat different kind of efficient cause, involving imagination and thought. The question would then arise whether there are goals influencing development apart from those entertained by human minds. Opponents of final causation would doubt or deny such purposes and would accuse the proponents of final cause of projecting or reading into the cosmic process their human intentions and attitudes.

Education predicated solely upon efficient causation will tend to emphasize local, particular, individual circumstances, and to see ideals as tentative indications of direction arising out of these situations. The future is thus regarded as an outgrowth of the past, and it would appear that in the long run education by these lights would tend to be provincial, uncritical, and stagnant. Education predicated upon a belief in final causation would, on the other hand, in the long run tend to be universal, critical, and dynamic. However, everything depends upon the quality of the final causes envisioned. They may be conceived narrowly and provincially, in which case they may become the basis for fanatical and exclusive systems of belief with their corresponding impoverished and divisive educational programs. When this happens, there would seem to be ample indication that the ideals in question do not actually reflect any fundamental purposes of cosmic development.

The Problem of Continuity

One of the most basic of all general ideas is that of *continuity*. Anything is continuous of it does not have gaps, jumps, or breaks in it. A pencil tracing a line without leaving the paper makes a continuous figure. If, instead, the pencil is successively raised so as to produce a set of dots, the resulting figure will be discontinuous. The concept of continuity is clearly relevant to the analysis of any process of change. Change is continuous if it proceeds from stage to stage uninterruptedly and smoothly, without complete abruptness. The word "complete" is important, because there can be changes like explosions or sudden collapses which are extremely rapid and yet may still be continuous in that they take place in a sequence of stages without interruption or break. On the other hand, there are processes which may seem to be continuous but actually are not, as, for example, a motion picture or a television image. In such cases the human viewer through his perceptual mechanism in effect supplies the missing links and thus imputes continuity to what is actually discontinuous.

Now an important question about the world process generally is whether it takes place continuously or discontinuously. The view which prevailed almost universally until only a few decades ago, was in favor of continuity, except perhaps for occasional supernatural or miraculous interventions in which many believed. Each state of the world was conceived as an immediate outgrowth of an only slightly different state just preceding it. In fact, this idea of continuity is basic to the concept of causality. To be the cause of anything includes the notion of being related to it in a continuous fashion so that one can trace back from effect to cause in a smooth and unbroken chain of connection. Thus the continuity view of world development implies that each state or condition of things is caused by the immediately preceding state.

Discoveries in the natural sciences, such as quantum phenomena and biological mutations, have cast doubt upon the continuity of processes in the realm of the very small. Large-scale changes which appear to be continuous may, upon extremely minute analysis, turn out to be discontinuous. There seems to be a kind of "grain" in the ultimate nature of things rather than smooth and uniform progression.

Continuity and education. What difference does it make in one's view of education whether the world process is regarded as continuous or discontinuous? The continuity view tends to direct attention to the special contexts in which education takes place, and emphasizes the importance of starting where the learner is and taking direction from prior developments. The conviction prevails that nothing happens effectively without the requisite preparation and the proper sustaining conditions. Growth is seen as a natural extension of what already exists, and ideals or goals are regarded as reflecting actual circumstances.

A discontinuity view tends to emphasize absolutely new developments which could not have been expected from past conditions. Persons are seen as developing in surprising ways and as being in the last analysis unpredictable. Hence the readiness to consider radically new insights and to entertain possibilities hitherto undreamed of. The realms of invention, of artistic and scientific creation, and of moral and religious intuition may be regarded as the special spheres of discontinuous development at the human level. Continuity is given its due, in recognizing the importance of favorable conditions for development, but it is not assumed that in the last analysis these are the sole or even the chief concern of the educator.

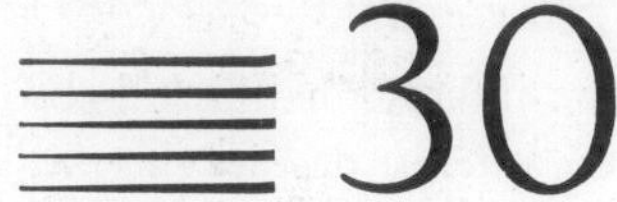

30

The Aims of Education

SINCE EDUCATION involves directing the development of persons, it follows that the central problem of education is the choice of direction, or of *aims*. The aims of education are the directions in which educators seek to guide the development of those under their care. The purpose of the present chapter is to state the nature and kinds of educational aims and to point out standards or criteria for the preference of one aim over another.

Value

The problem of aims is a problem of *values*. Because education requires the selection of direction, it is deeply concerned with values. Value concerns preferences, discrimination in favor of one possibility as against other possibilities. To choose one direction of development rather than another requires a scale of values whereby the relative worth of the two ways may be assessed. There is a problem of values because one cannot always take a neutral position with respect to alternatives. Only if everything were equally acceptable or unacceptable, would there be no need for choice and hence no scale of values.

The way in which values become apparent in human experience is in interest and desire. The value of anything for a person is measured by his interest in it and desire for it. There is something in his nature which finds the valued thing congenial, so that he wishes to affirm and continue the relationship established with it. The measure of the value is the intensity of the affirmative response to the valued entity, the degree to which the interest in it is all-absorbing and all-controlling, and the persistence of the interest despite the passage of time and the threat of opposing influences. Food is a value, or is valuable, because the organism is of such a nature that nourishing substances are congenial to it, so much so that continued existence depends upon an adequate supply. Food is a *primary* value in that the organism cannot live without it, but hunger is quickly satisfied and food then ceases to be an immediate object of interest or desire. There are other values, e.g., power or prestige, the need for which in some persons cannot be fully satisfied, as in the case of food. These values are then not primary in the elemental sense that food is, but they may be far more intense, all-controlling, and persistent than food, and hence in practice higher in the scale of values for those persons.

It seems clear that the general basis of value as revealed in interest or desire is a relationship of harmony or fitness between the valuing person and the entity valued. The interest is the attractive bond which establishes and confirms the pattern of coordination made possible by the congruence of person and valued thing. Thus value arises out of a complementary relationship between valuer and what is valued.

Kinds of value. It is customary to distinguish a number of different kinds of value. Because they support physical existence, food, clothing, and shelter have *material* value, although they may have other kinds as well, as when a large house is valued for prestige or when clothing is used to enhance personal beauty. There are *social* values, which arise out of man's need for association with other persons. Parents, children, and friends have social value in that they supply the love, understanding, and emotional support which persons need. From the realm of intellectual life arise *truth* values. The value of truth is great for those who hunger for knowledge, for scientists who seek to discover the laws of nature, for persons to whom inconsistency or obscurity are painful, and for those whose deepest satisfaction lies in discerning relationships among seemingly disconnected events. Another area of value is the *moral.* Justice, fair play, and honesty are moral values. They are the source of the feeling of obligation and responsibility. The promptings of conscience also reflect a persons's moral interests. The appreciation of beauty reflects *esthetic* values. Certain arrangements of sound, color, or of material elements are, by reason of symmetry, contrast or proportion, congenial while others are not. The satisfying patterns of sense perception communicate esthetic value. Finally, there are *spiritual* or *religious* values, which refer to man's longing for the infinite, for perfection, and for completeness. The entities valued in this area are not any determinate objects but some ultimate and essentially unattainable reality sought for by the faithful in acts of prayer and worship.

The above six areas of value by no means exhaust the field. Other kinds might have been described. Nor are the classes indicated independent or mutually exclusive. Esthetic values may be regarded also as having truth value. Moral values are generally also social values. Religious values have social and esthetic dimensions. The above distinctions have been made simply for convenience in later discussions and to accord with customary usage. A somewhat different typology of values, as reflected in certain general educational aims, will be presented below (pp. 559 ff.).

The aims of education depend upon the kinds of values regarded as most important for directing human development. One program of education may rest upon the primacy of material values. Another may emphasize the esthetic experience. For others, the realm of truth may be the key value. Social considerations are fundamental for some people, while others may regard moral or religious values as the paramount concern of education.

Education and the status of values. When it comes to deciding between competing values—and this is essential in the determination of educational aims—the problem of the status of values at once arises. It was said above that values become apparent in human experience through interest and desire. But that does not necessarily mean that interest and desire are the sole criteria of value. There may be values which are desirable but not actually desired by a particular person at a given time. Their desirability may mean that they would be desired under the proper conditions. In this case, values must have a higher status than immediate individual attractiveness. Some would say that society is the creator and conserver of values; consequently, individual desires must be checked against what the social group approves. Others would hold that values have the status of natural law, such that the morally right and the esthetically desirable are in some way part of the nature of things and can be discovered as such by human reason. Still others are convinced that values have their source in a divine being to whose will human desires ought to conform.

The problem of the status of values is crucial in education. If values have no more standing than individual taste, then directing the development of persons becomes a matter of arbitrary imposition by some persons on others. If values are rooted in society, then personal development must be subjected to group decisions. If there is a rational natural law of values, reason becomes sovereign over individuals and groups in the process of guiding growth. If values have their sanction in God, there are resources and judgments for education which lie beyond individuals, groups, and perhaps even beyond human rationality. For a more extended analysis of the status of values see the section on moral sanctions in Chapter 16.

The Nature of Aims

Aims as directions. One way of regarding aims is to consider them as directions for growth. Direction points the way beyond the present situation to the immediately succeeding situation. It is an indication of where to go from here. It does not indicate where the indicated path will lead but only states the path to be taken. For example, the aim of a teacher may consist in his constant appeal to critical intelligence. The direction in which growth is to be guided is given in the process of intelligent behavior. Another teacher might make social competence the aim of learning. This would mean that each learning situation would be so arranged as to enhance the ability to be socially effective.

There are two essential features of aims as directions. First, they are always rooted in the immediate situation. Full account is taken of the conditions in which learning takes place and from which further developments are to occur. Second, such aims are framed in terms of methods or procedures by which one is to advance from this point to the next. Aims as directions are ways of proceeding, and directing development is accomplished by giving directions on how to go on to the next stage. Consider the example of a parent bringing up a child. The parent's aim for the child is directive in the above sense if two conditions are fulfilled. First, the parent must be sensitive to the child's needs, feelings, and interests and aware at every point of the stage of organic and psychological maturity attained. He must seek to utilize and build upon these facts as the foundation for teaching the child. Second, the parent must try to be as definite and specific as possible about what the child should do to learn desired new patterns of behavior. In accordance with the first criterion the procedures suggested must always be such as to fall within the child's competence and must not be unrealistic demands predicated upon adult standards or even on general standards thought to apply to all children at a given age.

Aims as goals. Instead of direction from the point of departure an aim may be understood as a goal or destination to be reached. Attention is centered upon the objective to be attained rather than upon either the present situation or the path to be taken from that situation. For example, the aim of a teacher may be to produce persons of high moral character, and this aim may be expressed by referring to some model of virtue which the student is expected to emulate. A parent may guide the development of his child by constantly emphasizing the qualities of adult personality which the parent hopes and expects the child will eventually fulfill. Similarly, the aims of teaching skills or intellectual competence may be implemented by the vivid presentation of the final product expected to result from the learning process.

Educational aims conceived in this fashion do not depend on the particular circumstance of the learner nor do they indicate the methods or procedures by which the goal is to be reached. It is only important that mastery be gained, regardless of the method used. Furthermore, those who are strongly committed to aims as goals often regard the procedures as automatically indicated once the final objective is clearly grasped, and they consider it of no importance to take thought about the point of departure, since the entire purpose of education is to move to a different point from that at which the learner now stands.

Means and ends. The contrast between aims as directions and as goals is often expressed by the contrast of means and ends. Directions from the point of departure are the "means" of proceeding. The goal to be reached is the "end" of the process. In the two preceding paragraphs the opposing views of educational aims as means and as ends, respectively, have been presented. Are both views acceptable for certain purposes, or must a decision be made between them? As usual, there is something of value in each extreme, and each has a contribution to make to a balanced view. Means and ends can be brought into fruitful relationship with each other, the means providing effective implements for reaching the ends and the ends supplying vision and motive for using the best means. Goals without methods for reaching them are idle visions, if not actually hindrances to achievement. Directions without goals lack clarity of purpose. Every means may, in fact, be regarded as an immediate goal, and every goal, however distant, does suggest the general direction in which to proceed from the given situation.

In the rearing of a child it is important to start from where he is and to adopt methods appropriate to his age, maturity, abilities, and interests. This does not exclude the consideration of adult goals—parental hopes and ideals of what the child may someday become—provided these goals do not interfere with the realistic concern for next steps and provided the long range goals are held subject to revision as seems warranted by the actual course of development.

The contrast of means and ends underlies the long-standing debate between the advocates of "methods" and "subject matter" in the preparation of teachers. On the one extreme are those who believe that only the process of teaching is important and that the content will take care of itself. On the other extreme are those who care only for the mastery of subject matter, believing that the appropriate methods will be obvious to any teacher with ordinary intelligence. The mediating position would be to recognize the importance of both subject matter and method. Content will be most efficiently learned if the most appropriate techniques of teaching are employed and if due account is taken of the nature and maturity of the learner. Likewise methods serve their legitimate function only if they are appropriate to the subject matter to be learned. Procedures in the study of chemistry are predicated upon the goal of mastering an established body of knowledge and skills, which differs from that applicable in the study of art. Hence the direction of learning in each case must reflect the goals of the respective fields of study. Means need to have ends in view, and ends need to be viewed in the light of the means necessary to reach them.

Ends and means are further related by the fact that in an on-going process any end may be regarded as a means to some further ends. Thus an end is not literally the end, but an opportunity for a new beginning. Means may therefore be regarded as relatively immediate or proximate ends, and ends may be considered as relatively more ultimate means. Hence any sharp distinction between means and ends is unwarranted. For the same reasons it would seem impossible to make a decisive contrast between aims as directions and aims as goals. The more useful distinction is between short-range and long-range aims.

Immediate, mediate, and ultimate aims. Some educational aims are immediate in that they are concerned with what must be done at once and in the situation directly at hand. When a teacher confronts a class in noisy disorder, his immediate educational aim may be to restore some sort of order so that the intended work can continue. But presumably the preservation of order is not the sole aim of teaching; there are further aims which this one is intended to serve. If each aim in this fashion is seen as contributing to the fulfillment of some further aim, the question arises whether there is any aim which has no successor in the series, some final aim to which all prior aims contribute. Such an aim, if it exists, may be called an ultimate aim. Aims which lie between the immediate and the ultimate may be called mediate aims.

No one would dispute the existence of immediate and of mediate aims, but there is no such consensus about the existence of ultimate aims. The critics of ultimate aims believe that the idea of ultimacy implies a fixity and finality of purpose which deny the dynamic and forever unfinished nature of the human enterprise. They hold that no educational aim can so far comprehend the processes of human development as not to be subservient to a still further goal beyond itself. Hence, they think that talk of ultimate aims tends to hinder progress and impede further exploration.

The believers in ultimate aims answer in one of two ways. Some say that there are indeed attainable goals in which one may rest without always pushing on to some further goal, that progress is not the only good or the only truth, that completeness and finality are more basic to human life than continual reformation and reconstruction. Others agree with the critics that every conceivable goal leads on to another, but they also claim that the idea of an ultimate aim is necessary to express precisely this fact about immediate and mediate aims. Accordingly, the ultimate aim is to aspire to an ideal goal to which all mediate goals tend but which they can never attain.

An example of an attainable ultimate aim would be adjustment to an existing social and cultural tradition. The goal of education in such a case would be to direct the young into the habitual practice of the definite and limited customs characteristic of a particular group's life. Social existence in the accepted pattern would be regarded as an end in itself, not requiring justification by reference to any further goals. An example of an unattainable ultimate aim would be the discovery of truth. Each success in the struggle for knowledge would then be merely the prelude to a further attempt at discovery. Since the process is an unending one, the aim of seeking the truth is said to be an ultimate one.

Relative and absolute aims. Do the aims of education depend upon particular circumstances and persons or are they independent of such conditions? Dependent aims are said to be relative to situations. Aims which are unrelated to special circumstances are said to be absolute. Considering the aims which people actually do have, they are certainly relative. The directions and goals by which personal development is guided are of great variety. Some persons seek power or prestige, others are guided by the light of faith. One aspires to technical skill, another to the appreciation of beauty. In the last analysis there are as many educational aims as there are persons.

But may not these aims in all their variety in the last analysis be special forms of some absolute aim? Or may there not be some aims which not all people have but which all *ought* to have, so that though aims are actually relative they are by rights absolute? It is clear that immediate and mediate aims must, by definition, be relative, since they are the differing directions and goals appropriate to different persons in particular situations. Only ultimate aims could then conceivably be absolute. It follows that those who do not admit ultimate aims will necessarily consider all aims as relative.

The answer to the question whether ultimate aims are absolute or relative depends largely upon one's convictions about the status of values. If values are regarded as merely reflecting personal taste or social custom, educational aims will be considered relative. If, on the other hand, values are accorded some objective or cosmic status, educational aims may be considered absolute.

Relativity of aims is reflected in attitudes of flexibility and tolerance of difference but also in the lack of any basis upon which to resolve crucial and intolerable differences. Belief in absolute aims tends toward educational uniformity and inflexibility on the ultimate level as reflected in long-range and comprehensive policy, but it admits variety and flexibility in immediate and mediate aims intended to implement that policy. Such a belief also furnishes in principle a basis for resolving differences, though in practice it often leads to the conflict of contrary absolute aims fanatically espoused.

Variable and constant aims. Educational aims may be regarded as variable because they are subject to revision from time to time or they may be constant. This distinction is another aspect of the contrast between the relative and the absolute. Absolute aims do not vary. But not all constant aims are absolute since there may be aims relative to persons and situations which do not alter in the course of time. Variable aims are always relative.

Educational aims may change for any of three reasons. The first, and by all odds the most frequent, cause is change of circumstances in the course of time. To the degree that aims are an outgrowth and reflection of actual conditions, they will vary with those conditions. There are aims (immediate and mediate) appropriate to a young child but not to the same person in maturity. The direction of learning is quite different for the novice and for the same student at the advanced level. An important task of the educator is to adjust aims in accordance with the changing requirements of the developing personality and to remain sensitive to the new goals which new occasions suggest.

The second reason for changing aims is the clarification of objectives which sometimes takes place with the passage of time. Educational goals are often merely the best possible approximation in what is in many respects an obscure and problematical situation. Many aims are revised in the light of larger experience and more complete knowledge. An educator may with the best of intentions seek the fulfillment of young people through fostering "social adjustment," only to discover after a generation of effort that the personal fulfillment for which he worked requires a set of aims considerably different from social adjustment as he had conceived it. Or again, increasing knowledge of human motivation might cause a teacher to become less exclusively concerned with the mastery of verbal symbols and more interested in emotional maturity.

A third possible basis for variation in aims would be a modification of the very structure of value. That is, there might be something beyond changing circumstances or increasing knowledge—some basic change in the order of values—which would produce different objectives. This third possibility is a remote one, but conceivable in much the same way as would be variable laws in physics and chemistry. It is more likely, however, that variations in aims will be brought about by either of the first two causes.

Immanent and transcendent aims. Aims may be regarded as located within the process of change or as being essentially outside of it. In the former case they are called immanent, in the latter case transcendent. Insofar as aims actually control the process of development they are immanent. If they were not, they could not be relevant to actualities. On the other hand, it is in the nature of aims to point or lead from what is to what might be, and that implies a standpoint beyond the actual, so that in this sense aims are said to be transcendent. Thus interpreted, aims may be at once immanent and transcendent, acting within the process and yet operating from a perspective above the process. Still, there are great differences in emphasis, depending on whether the presentness of aims or their beyondness is considered the more basic.

In general, emphasis on immediacy, relativity, and variability corresponds with immanence, while ultimacy, absoluteness, and invariance parallel transcendence. Furthermore, transcendence suggests a view of values in which they are accorded a status of priority and independence. For example, ideals which are regarded as the will of a supernatural deity may become the basis for a transcendent educational aim. Goals which are considered as merely reflecting the personal desires of the individual or group would, on the other hand, constitute immanent aims.

One or many aims. Are there many aims of education, or is there only one? The answer clearly depends on what kinds of aims one has in mind. There are obviously many immediate and mediate aims. The process of development advances step by step, and at each point along the way a new immediate goal lies ahead. When it comes to ultimate aims, the answer is not so clear. Some would claim that there are many final purposes of education, while others would affirm some single sovereign goal to which all lesser goals should contribute. For example, it might be said that individual happiness is the ultimate objective of all personal development and that every aspect of the teaching and learning process should be tested by this standard. Others might regard the security and power of the state as the highest good, which all lesser goods must serve.

Those who believe in a single ultimate aim generally regard it as absolute and invariable—although there is no obvious reason why different persons might not have different ultimate goals nor why an ultimate objective should always remain the same.

The idea of one sovereign aim leads to the conception of a hierarchy of aims. Every minor goal is seen in its relation to the one major objective. Each preliminary direction is charted in the light of the final destination. Each mediate aim is part of an interrelated scheme of aims whose ruling principle is the one ultimate aim. There is a principle of subordination among goals, their relative position being determined by the degree of generality and directness of relevance to the supreme purpose. Such a principle of hierarchy is important in making decisions in education. Unless there is some principle of appeal, there is no way of judging between alternative immediate educational objectives. Suppose, for example, that it is a question of deciding whether to put students of exceptional ability in special classes or to leave them in the same classes with students of average competence. The decision can be made only in the light of a hierarchy of values in which each alternative aim is seen in relation to its contribution to a larger goal. Thus, individual intellectual attainment might be regarded as less important than fulfillment of the whole person—intellectually and interpersonally—this judgment being made on the basis of the larger principle of democracy. A different comprehensive goal, such as technical efficiency, might make the exploitation of special abilities a higher value than all-around growth.

Implicit and explicit aims. More often than not educational objectives are merely implicit. Those who hold them may be quite unable to state the nature of the goals pursued. This is especially true of the longer-range aims. Immediate purposes are usually more obvious and explicit. Many people never become aware of the fundamental aims which underlie and influence their day-to-day behavior.

Frequently explicitly stated aims are not real aims but merely a form of advertisement to gain approval. A parent may state his objective in the raising of his children as the production of happy mature persons, while his real aim is to create persons after his own image. The former aim wins approval from himself and others, while the latter would not. Hence, the explicit (and untrue) aim differs from the implicit (and true) aim. A school under religious auspices may announce its aim as the nurture of morality and religion and symbolize this aim by erecting a chapel and requiring the students to attend services. Yet the real aim, as evidenced by the methods of faculty selection, by admissions policies, and by curriculum adopted, may be social prestige or intellectual refinement, having little relation to the announced aim.

It is not to be inferred from the previous remarks that differences between explicit and implicit aims indicate intentional deception. This is rarely true. Generally a person who states his aims explicitly does so sincerely, quite oblivious of the fact that the real aims implicit in his actual conduct do not agree with the stated objectives. Explicit aims are framed in such a way as to gain acceptance among those to whom they are announced. Therefore, they are based upon social expectations rather than upon inner realities and the actual dynamics of the learning situation. Such outward acceptance is so important to people that they may hide even from themselves the contrast between real and professed aims, unconsciously adhering to the former while consciously affirming the latter.

Educational aims remain so largely implicit because they involve emotional commitment. To make an aim explicit requires giving it a name, subjecting it to rational scrutiny, and expressing it clearly. Since this process may fail to do full justice to the essential content of the aim, it may seem better to let it remain unanalyzed and unexpressed. The implicit logic of feeling is oftentimes at war with the requirements of explicit discourse.

In spite of what has just been said, it would seem to be the plain duty of intelligent educators to bring to light the hidden assumptions which govern their work. It is an essential function of educational philosophy, in particular, to clarify and criticize aims and to make as fully explicit as possible the goals which are implicit in the teaching process. Only by so doing can the full resources of intelligence be brought to bear in educational planning.

Some General Aims of Education

The educational aims which different individuals and groups have are of considerable variety. This is obviously the case with immediate and mediate goals, which depend on special circumstances. It is also true of the more ultimate aims. One could argue that there is only one goal of human life, which might be called happiness, satisfaction, or fulfillment. But then the questions arise: In what do happiness, satisfaction, and fulfillment consist? What quality of life do they reflect? There are many possible answers to these questions. Happiness for one person may seem misery for another. What satisfies one may appear unsatisfactory to another. What fulfills one may apparently frustrate another. The words "seem," "appear," and "apparently" are used in order to leave open the question of the relativity of ultimate aims. It is possible that what is seemingly misery for a person ought to be or would be in the long run his true happiness.

In the paragraphs that follow several general aims will be discussed.

These describe qualities of life which are considered of prime importance to those who have them as aims. They suggest values which are high and controlling in some persons' scale of values. These dominant values are ones which set the tone and point the direction of the entire educational process. They are not independent or mutually exclusive. Any actual educational effort doubtless combines two or more of these aims in some form and to some degree.

Order. To some people order is the supreme good and disorder the greatest evil. They believe that the direction in which life should develop is toward increasing order, that conflict and disorganization must be progressively overcome by harmony and coordination. To be happy is to be well ordered, to have a place for everything and everything in its place.

The young child at first engages in random and disorganized movement but quickly learns the appropriate coordinations by participation in an organized social environment. The provision of such a carefully ordered environment would thus be an important basis for the education of the child. Care must be taken, however, not to require patterns of behavior too quickly, before the child is capable of practicing them. It is also important to be sensitive to the special modes of organization which the growing individual discovers as his own and not to impose an arbitrary and perhaps essentially alien pattern upon the child. On the other hand, since every person must live in society, the criterion of order forbids anarchic individualism and requires the discovery of individual modes of behavior which will be as far as possible compatible and harmonious.

The supremacy of order underscores the importance of habit in personal development. A well-ordered personality must rest upon a highly developed system of relatively automatic responses. Education must then provide for considerable practice of activities which are to become habitual. Included in such habituation must be opportunities for various kinds of group participation in order that social coordination may be solidly based. There should also be emphasis upon the development of competence in the various well-tested intellectual disciplines, which represent organized bodies of knowledge.

Intensity. Instead of harmony and order, the ultimate goal of education may be intensity and vividness of experience. Some would think of order as a rather cold and unattractive goal and would value much more highly the warmth, color, and excitement of an intense life experience. With this aim feeling is of primary importance. Whatever cannot be inwardly and directly experienced is worth little. The real failures are those who cannot feel deeply. The basic evils are boredom, a sense of meaninglessness, apathy, and emptiness. The highest goods are vitality, interest, conviction, and fullness of life. Even pain is better than emptiness, since it is one kind of intensity and since inability to suffer is accompanied by incapacity for joy.

Education for intensity of life is tolerant of individual peculiarities. Though the social group may contribute to vividness of experience, the ultimate test of value is not social conformity but individual sense of fulfillment. As far as possible, society is for the service of the individual; the individual is not to be sacrificed for the sake of social order. Depth of feeling is hindered by the repeated restriction of a person's impulses by the demands of social convention. Education for intensity therefore requires maximum freedom of expression and minimum arbitrary restraint of natural drives. The restrictions that are imposed should be such as to protect the individual from ultimately destructive and mutually contradictory impulses. This suggests that some considerations of order are relevant to the attainment of maximum intensity.

The aim of vividness in experience requires that all education be conceived in relation to inward effect and not outward conformity. The test of any educational activity is not how it fits some prescribed or preconceived pattern but what it will mean inwardly and personally to those for whom it is intended. No system of education is right unless it is in the long run felt to be right by those who undergo it. Actually this kind of education does not come by "system" at all, but by the influence of sensitive persons who themselves feel deeply and live intensely and who know how to release the secret springs of creative vitality in others.

Security. Life is a dangerous adventure, and threats of disaster beset every pilgrim on his journey. Thus it is easy to understand why many place the highest value on security and subordinate all other goods to that end. For such people the purpose of education is conservation and preservation of life and of social and cultural values. The evil to be avoided is the destruction of the good things attained by centuries of human effort, which constitute the rightful heritage of each new generation. For the individual, the goal is a life as free as possible from interference with normal growth and the reasonable enjoyment of cultural goods. And since death must come to all, the task of education is to insure the faithful handing on from generation to generation of the cultural inheritance, secure from dilution or contamination.

There are different kinds of security which education may aim to insure, corresponding to the various kinds of value. One type of security is material, consisting of bodily safety and steady supply of goods. Another is social, whereby the established patterns of social organization are maintained. A third is intellectual, requiring faithfulness to systems of ideas which have proven their worth. A fourth is emotional security, providing protection against threats to self-esteem and permitting the maintenance of the habitual image of the self. A fifth is moral, consisting of adherence to modes of conduct which have minimized the sense of guilt and anxiety. A sixth is religious security, gained by appropriate acts of commitment, of right belief, and of cultic observance.

Education whose chief aim is security inevitably tends to look to the past since it is there that the achievements to be conserved may be found. There is no disposition for change or experimentation except as these may suggest ways of life which are more stable and less susceptible to dissolution than ones formerly practiced. It is rather a paradox that too much concern for security may actually produce insecurity, since life is intrinsically dynamic and will lose its vigor if constrained within a fixed mold. Hence, the very aim of ultimate security may require the acceptance of the immediate insecurity involved in adventuring into uncharted waters.

Variety. The highest good may be conceived as the enrichment of life by the greatest possible variety of experiences. According to this view, the ultimate evils are repetition, sameness, and uniformity. Contrast and even conflict are welcomed as contributing to a rich and complete life. The differences in persons and in cultures are considered beneficial because they increase the range and scope of possible understanding and appreciation. Restrictions on conduct should be minimized and codes of required behavior should be abandoned. Moral judgments should be replaced by the simple recognition of differences in custom, and esthetic judgments should give way to acceptance of variety in tastes.

Variety as an ultimate aim rests upon a pluralistic view of the world according to which it is neither possible nor desirable to reduce everything to one or a few laws, substances, or processes. Granted the practical value of ordering and classifying things, real satisfaction consists in the experience of things in their irreducible individuality and difference. Granted the utility of explaining the effect by its causes, the real center of interest is not this causal perseverance of the past into the present but the radical novelty which each moment brings forth—the new occasions, new opportunities, new appreciations which continually present themselves from the cornucopia of time.

Education for variety is essentially forward-looking. The new is not of itself better than the old, but it is better that the new be added to the old to increase the richness of the human store. Breadth of learning is better for the individual than specialization, but specialization is socially necessary to permit the more extensive development of new fields of knowledge and skill. Experimentation is encouraged and unorthodox ways of thinking are welcomed. Tolerance and tentativeness are prevailing attitudes. Each person is permitted to be himself and as far as possible to express his unique being in ways of his own choosing without the strictures of social conformity or tradition.

Intelligence. The ultimate aim of education is often said to be rational understanding. The highest goal of human endeavor is then to gain knowledge, and man's accumulated knowledge is his most precious cultural treasure. The greatest respect and honor are due the scholar, the scientist, and the philosopher, since these are the creators and conservers of the intellectual tradition. All other human concerns are considered subordinate to the development of intelligence. Feelings should be under rational control and should have as their highest function the emotional support of intellectual endeavor. Action should be guided by intelligence and must be justified on the grounds of providing occasions for further understanding.

The assumptions underlying this view are that the world has a definite rational structure, that human intelligence is competent to comprehend that structure, and that rationality is the essence of being human. Thus man fulfills his true being by the development of his intelligence, and in so doing he relates himself harmoniously to the ultimate nature of things. It is further assumed that intelligence is in its nature good and that increase in knowledge will promote human felicity and suffice to solve human problems.

Education for intelligence places emphasis on language and other symbolic tools whereby knowledge is gained and communicated. It is concerned both with the mastery of established and well-tested bodies of knowledge and with the acquisition of methods for the further discovery and criticism of knowledge. Of special importance is the study of science, which consists both of accumulated facts and theories and of certain principles of inquiry that have proven successful in research. But perhaps even more important is the wide diffusion of a critical and inquiring outlook on the problems of everyday life, especially those arising from human relationships. Only by thus exalting and refining intelligence, it is believed, can man overcome superstition and prejudice and attain his true birthright of freedom.

Activity. Another view is that man's chief good is not to know but to do, that activity is his true happiness. Man is by nature a dynamic creature, and he can only be fulfilled in creative and constructive activity. The one evil is stagnation. The essence of life is to move ahead; to be idle is to die. Rest has its place, but only as the basis for further activity. The kind of activity is not of primary importance, except that it must be such as to generate and support further activity. Thus, activities which endanger physical health are generally not good because they threaten the possibility of future effective action. However, some sacrificial acts may be good because they stimulate greater activity by those for whose sake the sacrifices are made.

From this standpoint knowledge is justified only in the act; knowledge which is not effective in guiding conduct is worthless. Emotional life also has its value only as a basis for action, providing tone and energy; feeling which is undirected and unapplied leads to confusion and conflict.

Education aimed at activity stresses the relevance to the learner of whatever is learned. Knowledge and skills are taught through the actual participation of the student in useful projects. Passive reception of ideas is discouraged. The meaning of concepts is not imparted by simple precept but by placing the learner in situations where the ideas are needed for the solution of problems. A problem arises when intended activity is frustrated by obstacles, and the solution of the problem is the discovery of ways of circumventing or overcoming the obstacles so that activity may continue. When activity is the ultimate aim of education, there is no separation between theoretical or "pure" studies and practical or "applied" studies. Theory and practice are united in the concrete act. "Vocational" education is as much honored as the "classical" type; it is even preferred if the latter is conceived without reference to its application to life.

Peace. Rather different in emphasis but not necessarily opposed to activity is the ultimate aim which may perhaps best be called peace. Activity tends to suggest haste and unsettlement, and there are many who regard these as evil rather than as good. For them the highest good is an unhurried serenity which rests upon a basic confidence and settledness. The ideal is not always to move on to something else but to reach a state of contentment with what one has and is. The highest good is not to overcome obstacles but to arrive at a condition of maximum harmonious adjustment to existing reality. One should not forever dwell upon the incompleteness of things but should at every point rest in the satisfying goodness of what has been achieved. Human ambitions and desires are deceitful tyrants. They drive men to goals ever beyond, keeping them so enslaved to activity that the promised satisfaction which is the essence of goals is never enjoyed.

When peace is the ultimate aim, the learner is encouraged to find some immediate satisfaction in whatever he does. Care is taken to avoid pressure on the learner. As far as possible he is allowed to grow at his own pace and in his own way in an atmosphere of quiet acceptance and genuine interest. The student is protected against the excessive multiplication of competing demands on his time. It is better, from this viewpoint, to learn a few things well and enjoyably than to aspire to know and do a great many things. While competition may in some situations have certain values, the educational program should not be based upon it. Each person should be encouraged to be and to accept himself and not to compare his achievements with those of others, striving to imitate or to surpass them. Parents and teachers should not disturb children by making excessive demands on them or by holding before them unattainable ideals. If the person at every stage is regarded as enjoyable and intrinsically valuable in his own way, his development will proceed in the best possible fashion and he will learn immediately and well the ultimate lesson of being at peace with himself and with others.

Power. The ultimate aim of education is considered by some to be power. For them, the highest good is to control things and people. The one thing to be avoided is weakness and dependence. Whatever leads to increase of resources at one's disposal is good; whatever makes one subject to the bounty or authority of others is evil. The attainment of power does, of course, require a measure of cooperation with nature and other persons. It is only by satisfying the conditions imposed by the laws of the natural world that natural powers become available to man. Likewise, it is only through obedience to certain requirements of the social order that power over, through, or with other persons may be gained. These requirements of apparent subordination to obtain dominance do not contradict the fact that power is the ultimate objective and that obedience and cooperation are only means to that end.

Power may be defined as the ability to achieve the object of desire, whatever that may be. It might then seem that power is only a mediate aim, the ultimate aim being the desired object. This may sometimes be the case, but it is not so necessarily, for the objects desired may simply be the occasions for the exercise of the truly ultimate and intrinsic power impulse. This becomes clear when the satisfaction of one desire merely leads to the adoption of a new object of desire which in its turn is replaced by another, and so on indefinitely. The true and persistent goal is then not the objects themselves but the ability to satisfy whatever wants one feels.

Infancy is the crucial period in education for power. The newborn child is totally dependent on others for the satisfaction of his wants; he is powerless. If his needs are poorly and tardily supplied, he will tend to become confirmed in his feeling of powerlessness. If his needs are well and promptly supplied, he will tend to gain a sense of his own power. As the infant develops, he must be more and more acquainted with the realities, both natural and social, which condition and implement the exercise of power. At each stage of growth, learning situations will as far as possible be arranged to make use of the individual's capacities and interests. Frustration and conflict will be minimized. The person will be encouraged and praised for successful accomplishment of tasks which he has adopted as his own. Achievements will be appropriately rewarded in order that a lasting taste for successful attainment may be developed.

Love. Love is another value which may serve as an ultimate aim. Here the ideal is not one of power but of service. The loving person is one whose greatest satisfaction is in bringing satisfaction to others. It may in some respects conflict with the ideal of power, which can be self-centered rather than other-centered. Love does not seek dominance. It avoids competition and comparison. Yet love does presuppose a kind of power; it does not proceed from weakness but from strength. Love is power to support, understand, and appreciate others.

It is interesting that love largely incorporates and encompasses not only power but all of the previously discussed aims. By love ordered relationships are established and conflicts and contradictions are overcome. In love there is a quality of intensity in which feelings become deeply engaged. The goal of love is to help others feel secure and to affirm and conserve the values which have been created by others. The loving person is also open to new possibilities. He is sensitive to the changing needs which altered circumstances bring. Love at its best is not blind but welcomes the light of intelligence and gives warmth, purpose, and personal relevance to the intellectual pursuit. Love is active, outgoing, moving. It does not take its ease when there is service to be rendered. Yet in love one may find a profound peace, a quiet confidence which is far from all hurry and anxiety, a restful activity whose power comes from the realization of shared life.

When love is the ultimate aim of education, considerations of personal relationship are all-controlling. Intellectual mastery, the acquisition of skills, the development of appreciations are never to be promoted in and for themselves but only as they clearly contribute to the capacity to care for other persons. Attention is given to the role of feelings and to inward meaning rather than merely to outward performance. The basic method of education for love is by actual participation in loving relationships. Only the parent or teacher who genuinely cares for the child and whose major concern is to serve his needs can effectively guide the growing personality into ways of love. Love is a golden chain whose successive links are the passing generations of those who, loved in their youth, in turn love their young.

Holiness. Holiness is a religious conception of ultimate aim. It has two components. One is moral perfection, and the other is a quality of exaltation or of transcendence which excites feelings of reverence and wonder. The holy person is not only righteous in conduct but is also regarded in some sense as inhabiting a higher sphere of being, as having a kind of spirituality which elevates him above the plane of ordinary existence. The ideal of holiness is typified in the person of the saint. A saint is one who is considered by a particular religious group to have attained a high degree of moral excellence and by wonderful works has given evidence of unusual spiritual power.

Holiness as an aim in general presupposes the existence of moral values which have a higher status than human preferences. It also assumes that there are real spiritual powers in which persons may participate.

In education based on the ideal of holiness the standard of perfection is constantly held in view. Moderate achievement and comfortable "adjustment" are never accepted as sufficient. The saints are cited as examples of what every person ought to be, and toward this goal all are urged strenuously to move. Yet the character of the goal differs essentially from any of the others previously discussed. It is not orderliness, intensity, intelligence, efficiency, or even love which is the measure of holiness. The measure is the presence of a spiritual dimension which inspires wonder and invites reverence. And this quality is generally regarded as a gift rather than as a purely human achievement. Hence the most that can be done in education is to hold fast the vision of the ideal and as far as possible to provide conditions which experience has shown conducive to its realization. Beyond that everything depends upon direct inspiration by the higher powers in whom holiness is grounded.

Education for holiness is frequently other-worldly in orientation. The present life is considered but a preparation for a more perfect one beyond. Therefore, one can take a long-range view, not demanding that the fruits of learning be harvested at once, and not despairing over difficulties here and now, which may but lend greater luster to the glories yet to come. But as the prize for the faithful is rich, and the struggle in learning the way to it well worth while, so may the penalty be great for those who refuse the way. Education for holiness thus often depends upon the powerful motivations of ultimate reward and punishment—for the faithful, the vision of God and everlasting happiness, for the faithless, estrangement, isolation, and perhaps everlasting punishment.

31

Good and Evil in Education

IN NEARLY ALL that has been said thus far about the ultimate problems of education there has been an essentially affirmative outlook. Attention has been directed to the reality of change, the heights of human attainment and potentiality, and the possibility of cosmic support for the processes of human development. Little has been said about the negative factors which may operate at any point. Yet these cannot be ignored. There is failure as well as success, stagnation as well as advance. Potentialities more often than not go unactualized. Incompleteness and frustration are abundantly evident. There is guidance which is misdirection, and there are aims which are based on illusion. It is by no means certain that the universe always cooperates with the learning process or that there is any cosmic order from which man may take his cues.

Were there no such negative realities there would be no education. What is the gaining of knowledge but the conquest of ignorance? What is growth but the defeat of stagnation? What is development but the progressive overcoming of incompleteness? Thus the full meaning of education can be seen only if those factors which negate human aspirations as well as those which affirm them are weighed. It is the purpose of this chapter to raise some of the major questions about good and evil and to indicate their bearing on the problems of education.

What Is Evil?

In simplest terms, evil is a negative value or a dis-value. Something appears evil to a person if he desires not to have it. Just as desire is the indication of apparent value, so avoidance is the sign of apparent evil. The word "apparent" is used because an avoidance reaction may by further consideration or experience change to acceptance, and what is rejected by one person may be desired by another. A bitter pill will be an apparent evil until its goodness is understood in the light of its curative function. Practicing the piano may be an apparent evil to a child but a good to the parent who sees more clearly the possibilities of musical accomplishment, and the child may in later years himself regard the erstwhile evil as having been really good.

It was pointed out in the preceding chapter that value represents a relationship of congruence or fitness between valuer and what is valued. In like manner evil reflects a lack of fitness—an incongruity or disharmony—between the person and that which he regards as evil. Education is in part a process of transmuting apparent evil into good by so guiding the development of persons that what were once incongruities become congruent with one's nature. Thus, the manipulation of mathematical symbols may at first be considered a distasteful and meaningless chore, but by good teaching may become a matter of intense interest. Again, one may by education learn to enjoy music which to the untutored ear was objectionable.

Evil by what standard? To speak intelligibly of evil always requires some standard of value in relation to which the evil is measured. To assert that sickness is evil implies a standard of health by which the extent and seriousness of sickness may be judged. When one says that death is evil, it is assumed that life is good. If life were considered a burden, then death might not be thought of as evil but as welcome release from suffering. Ignorance is evil only on the assumption that knowledge is a value. It is possible to have a system of values in which knowledge is considered a threat or a snare, in which case ignorance would be bliss rather than evil. In short, good and evil—value and dis-value—are correlative terms. If a scale of values is given, the corresponding scale of dis-values is automatically given. Conversely, if one knows what is evil, his concept of the good is directly implied. Hence to talk about evil in education is to cover the same topics and discuss the same problems as in the analysis of educational values, but now from a different perspective. Instead of attainment of values, education is seen as a process of overcoming evils. Instead of directing development, it may be regarded as a way of avoiding stagnation or of shunning false pathways. In each case attention is devoted to the evil to be defeated rather than to the correlative value to be achieved.

Kinds of evil. It is convenient to classify evils into various types, as in the case of values. *Material* evil is the failure to achieve material good. Weakness, poverty, hunger, and disease are examples of material evils. Education requires the defeat of these evils. Persons cannot develop when basic material resources are lacking. None of the so-called "higher" values can be realized as long as the elemental material wants go unsatisfied. It is not necessary to believe, as some do, that the problem of material supply completely determines all other problems in order to take seriously the significance of material needs in education.

Social evil is conflict, disharmony, and frustration within society. It is the failure of persons to develop satisfactory ways of relating themselves to one another. War, tyranny, divorce, and loneliness are examples of social evils. Education clearly has much to do with overcoming such problems. The teaching of manners, while not of the greatest importance, is an example of social education in which minor irritations and misunderstandings are reduced through a definite set of social conventions. Another important function of social education is to gain insight into one's own emotions. Much social evil arises because persons do not recognize their own deep impulses and because they develop mechanisms with which to appear to themselves and others as something other than what they are.

Intellectual evil takes such forms as error, ignorance, or illusion. Education which, positively considered, is the teaching of truth and the development of intellectual competence may negatively be regarded as a means of combating error and dispelling ignorance. When truth is supreme as a value, error becomes the principal evil.

Moral evil arises from mistaken or perverse human choice. In some quarters moral evil is identified with social evil; in others it is believed to be the transgression of a moral law not derived from social consent or usage. In the religious tradition moral evil is often called *sin*. A primary objective of education is to develop in persons the power to choose wisely. Some would claim that the whole purpose of learning is to overcome moral blindness. In religious terminology, it might be said that a major function of education is to make clear the nature and consequences of sin and to show how one can be saved from its power.

Corresponding to the *esthetic* values are the forms of esthetic evil. Included in these are the ugly, the grotesque, the discordant, the clumsy. They represent patterns of sense perception which are repugnant to the sensibilities of the beholder. Education of the tastes is directed against the production and persistence of such esthetic evils. It is also responsible for creating that refinement of perception which will make persons aware of esthetic contradictions and distortions which would otherwise have gone unnoticed. From this it follows that education apparently increases evil by creating more exacting standards by which experience is judged. The person of refined taste sees the drabness and ugliness of what once seemed satisfactory. The same observation also holds for some of the other forms of evil. Education creates conscience and with it a sense of moral evil. Sensitivity to truth produces an awareness of error and with it an increase in the apparent range and intensity of intellectual evils.

Finally there is *religious* evil, which may take such forms as faithlessness, blasphemy, idolatry, or irreverence. Wherever religious values are considered important, it is one task of education to struggle against religious evils. This is partly a matter of dealing with sin, as mentioned above, but it is more than that, since religion is more than morality. The development of a sense of reverence and of wonder in the presence of an infinite reality presupposes an education which is directed against the evils of self-satisfaction and of complete absorption in the world of finite things.

Three Aspects of Educational Evil

In the process of education there are three distinct ways in which evil appears.

Stagnation. The most fundamental element in education is change. This is implicit in its very definition. All learning requires change. Education as a "process" must "proceed" or move ahead. Stagnation is therefore directly and fundamentally opposed to education. It is the basic evil for education.

The failure to develop may have inner or outer causes, or both. There are persons who are poorly endowed with inner drives. When the life impulses are too weak, the organism dies. Growth and development depend upon a preponderance of positive and constructive forces and an ample supply of energy. Development also fails when the available environmental resources are insufficient. Most obvious are the destructive consequences of material privation. Inadequate provision of necessary food, shelter, and protection undermine the growth process. It is beside the point to advocate education among people who because of famine, flood, pestilence, disease, overpopulation, or poor social planning can maintain at best a precarious hold on life.

In many respects even more important is an adequate social environment. A human organism without benefit of a nurturing society could never develop truly into a human being. The very essence of person-hood is bound up with social participation. Hence, the absence or inadequacy of social environment will prevent the proper development of persons.

The person who fails to develop is typically lacking in purpose or motive. He is without interest or concern for achievement. He has no definite aims in life, and simply drifts with the tide of events. His behavior remains immature, and he frequently resorts to infantile patterns of conduct in response to the demands made upon him. He adopts standardized, habitual patterns of life, resisting change and showing no ability to modify conduct in ways appropriate to new situations.

Frustration. A second aspect of evil in education is the frustration or defeat of aims. Granted a sufficient supply of basic energy, high motivation, and well-grounded impulses, granted also adequate environmental resources, both material and social, a person may still fail to attain the goals of the educative process, through the intervention of strong opposing forces. These forces may operate either from within or from outside the person. Consider first the inner forces. A person may have firm convictions about how he wishes to develop and he may have every encouragement and assistance from those around him, and yet he may fail because there are antithetical inner impulses which nullify his best efforts and intentions. The opposing forces are as often as not unrecognized as such. When this is the case, the first step in overcoming the evil is to make the opposition conscious and explicit by therapeutic techniques. When opposing inner forces are fully recognized, they may frequently be brought under rational control and sometimes even turned to constructive use.

Another way of considering frustration of aims from within is as the conflict of inconsistent aims. A person may have a prestige goal which in a certain social setting is incompatible with an intellectual objective. Each aim will then tend to interfere with the full realization of the other. The solution is to eliminate one of the aims in favor of the other, to eliminate both in favor of a single third aim, or to discover a way in which the antithetical aims may be harmonized—as, for example, by finding a situation in which prestige might be gained through intellectual achievement.

Second, there are forces outside the person which defeat educational aims. Though one may set for himself the goal of security, the tide of events may inexorably uproot him and drive him out from settled and dependable existence. A person may seek intellectual competence only to find himself in a society where intellectual achievement is not honored. All too frequently a child will entertain hopes for his career which run directly counter to parental hopes and intentions for him. It should be noted that these external opposing forces are of two essentially different kinds. One kind (e.g., the unsettling factors in contemporary life) operates without regard for education or in active hostility to it. The other kind (e.g., the solicitous parents) acts ostensibly in the interests of education but in such a way as to conflict with other existing aims. Education often fails because of anti-educational barriers, but it may also be defeated by the mutually annulling interplay of incompatible educational aims.

Misdirection. The third way in which evil appears in education is in giving wrong direction to the development of persons. Assuming ample inner and outer resources, and freedom from inner and outer opposition and conflict, personal development may proceed efficiently and fruitfully. Growth may occur without hindrance, and potentialities may be actualized in abundance. But this very process may in fact be efficient in producing evil. The fruit of development may be poisonous. The luxuriant growth may be malignant, and the potentialities actualized may be diabolic. Persons may be well-educated for criminality as well as for social usefulness, for prejudice as well as for understanding.

At this point a crucial issue arises. It can be argued that this third type of evils is really a special case of the other two, in that an evil educational aim is simply one which will lead in the long run, if not immediately, to conflict, opposition, or stagnation. Thus the education of a criminal is evil only because eventually and on the whole it will lead to conflict within the self and with others and will ultimately block the full development of potentialities. Against this position it can be urged that there are kinds of being which are in themselves evil and that these may well thrive and prosper indefinitely without for that reason being adjudged any less evil. From this standpoint education in criminality is to be regarded as evil not because it will lead to ultimate conflict and frustration (if such is actually the case) but because it is bad intrinsically and of itself, whether successful or unsuccessful, opposed or unopposed, efficient or inefficient. The view one takes on this disputed issue has significant implications for the conduct of education. When judgment is rendered on the basis of long-run outcomes, the planning of education will depend upon extensive experimentation and careful observation of the consequences of alternative learning experiences. When one holds the intrinsic-evil view, education will not look primarily to consequences, but will be governed by a precise and firmly held moral code.

Good and Evil in Human Nature

The approach to education is intimately related to conceptions of human nature. In particular, it is important to consider the problem of human nature with respect to good and evil. There are four possible positions.

Man is essentially good. It is difficult to deny that there is evil in the world, but there is no agreement concerning the focus of that evil, and especially as to whether or not it centers in human nature. One position is that in its essence human nature is good and that the focus of evil is outside of man. This does not mean that people are universally good or even that in man the good in fact exceeds the evil. It is not easy to dismiss the obvious perversions and shortcomings to which people are actually subject. To affirm the essential goodness of man is simply to claim that the evil which he manifests is not inherent in his true nature but is a denial and contradiction of that nature. From this viewpoint a human being is less human when he is evil than when he is good. The evil is subhuman or anti-human. The true selfhood of a person is good, and whatever is evil is not one's real self. If a person is unhappy, it is because he has not "found himself." If he is ignorant, he has not fulfilled his nature. If he is dishonest or uncooperative, he is not true to himself. Within the most vicious and depraved there is a spark of essential goodness that can always be appealed to and with care be fanned into full flame.

According to this position, there is within personality an unfailing tendency toward good, and much of what is accounted evil is simply a misdirection of that tendency. Hate, for example, is held to be the result of frustrated love. A person wants desperately to establish a relationship of affectionate mutuality with other persons but circumstances prevent it, and the disappointment felt at this failure finds expression in the angered response called hate. There would be no hate were there not a prior and continuing concern to become related to others. The opposite of love is not hate but unconcern and estrangement.

Again, the many forms of dishonesty can be regarded as misguided attempts to attain the good. A student who cheats on an examination may consciously or unconsciously justify his action to himself or others on any of a number of grounds, such as making a protest against arbitrary and unjust adult authority, as a rejection of a relatively meaningless academic procedure, or as a particularly efficient way of attaining the real objective, which is to pass the course and secure a diploma. This psychological mechanism (called rationalization) may be thus interpreted as evidence of the intrinsic impulse toward the good, as an attempt to guide conduct in ways which appear constructive. Another way of stating this is to say that the conduct of man is always governed by the apparent good. No one knowingly chooses evil. Man is fundamentally good at heart, and it is only necessary, if evil is to be minimized, that he be well informed. If the right is clearly evident to a person, he will do it.

If human nature is essentially good, the function of education is to recognize and encourage that goodness. If only the right conditions are provided, the innate striving toward fulfillment and self-realization can succeed. The native impulses and desires of persons can be trusted and should be respected. What are seemingly bad intentions must be understood as mistaken ways of expressing good intentions. Thus, above all, education must be built upon the sympathetic understanding of motives, in oneself and in others. The good core in all conduct, however unwelcome, must be discerned and then employed for the improvement of behavior. The fundamental rule of education is the acceptance of persons. Such acceptance is grounded in the essential human goodness and is a necessary condition for the effective development of personality in fulfillment of the inner potential. The acquisition of knowledge is also an important objective of education since only the informed person will be able to avoid mistaken ways of carrying out his good intentions.

Man is essentially evil. A second point of view is that the many and obvious evils of life are not merely accidents or mistakes but are integrally rooted in the very nature of man. This is not to deny that there is some goodness in human beings. The manifest virtues in such qualities as love, sacrifice, creativity, and devotion to truth are too obvious to permit a wholly adverse judgment. But it may be argued that such goodness is not of man's own nature; it is grafted upon him from without, either by social experience or by some superhuman agency. To be human is essentially to be evil. To become good is to become social or superhuman. The real self must be overcome since it is selfish, cruel, and domineering. It must be replaced by a new other-self or super-self in which the native egocentric and destructive tendencies will be held in check or transcended.

Unfortunately, it may be that even much of what seems good in persons is disguised evil. Benevolence is frequently a device for ingratiating oneself with those from whom one later hopes to profit. Mother-love may in the last analysis only be disguised self-gratification. The saints and the martyrs may be merely exhibitionists, and the most fervent religious devotion is perhaps only a desperate and illusion-bound attempt to make oneself secure. The supposedly disinterested search for truth may really be a competitive struggle to gain power or prestige.

From this standpoint, human virtue is either purely external or hypocritical. It may be external in the sense that morality is an imposed code whose purpose is to check and channel the evil impulses of men. It is hypocritical to the extent that persons represent goodness as their own, using virtue as a mask for their evil designs. Thus the professing of high ideals is sometimes simply a way of putting up a good front, of representing oneself as better than he really is. Honesty may be practiced not because it is good in itself but because it is the best policy—the best way to "get ahead." The mechanism of rationalization, far from being a sign of good intentions, is perhaps merely another example of the hypocritical tendency to invent acceptable reasons for basically unacceptable conduct.

Knowledge then merely tends to entrench and confirm the evil. It supplies means for furthering man's unwholesome designs. Especially does it provide him with devices for excusing and camouflaging his evil so as to present an innocent front to the world. Even more important is the deception of oneself. If one is able in the face of evil within to convince himself of his own goodness, then it will be easy to convince others. Such are the devious ways of essentially evil men.

The whole aim of education, if men are intrinsically evil, must be to suppress the natural tendencies and replace them as far as possible by more acceptable ones. The education of the young must proceed by curbing their natural destructiveness through the imposition of restraints and through a well-developed scheme of rewards and punishments. Self-centeredness must give way to socialized behavior, and this can be effected only by making the approved social conduct appear to serve self-interest best or to damage it least. It follows from this that the task of education is to provide persons with the means of covering up their innate evil with a show of good. To be educated is to appear to be what one really is not.

According to this view, educated man is still at heart a predatory beast and his civilization and culture are but a thin veneer, artifices created to make coexistence possible, fictions through which alone that armed truce called human society can be maintained. It should occasion no surprise, then, that among civilized people there are still wars, tyrannies, persecutions, and all manner of crimes, both individual and collective, against mankind. The best that education can do is to provide precarious ways of holding the raging forces in partial check and keeping the ugliness as well hidden as possible. Such education must consider the highly ambiguous role of knowledge. Insofar as it contributes to effective social control it is valuable, but to the degree that it provides power to transgress it becomes itself evil. In the education of evil men, then, knowledge cannot be freely given, and it cannot be entrusted to all, but only to those who have proven themselves submissive to the restraints put upon their own evil tendencies.

Man is essentially both good and evil. A third view of human nature combines the first two. To say that man in his essence is both good and evil is not the same as saying that he is essentially good but has fallen into some evil ways nor that he is essentially evil but has developed some good qualities. It is not simply to affirm that in some respects or at one time a person is good and in other respects or at other times evil or that he is a mixture of good and evil characteristics. It is rather to affirm that at the core man is at one and the same time and in the same respects both evil and good. Man is thus essentially *ambiguous.* There is no generosity which does not contain elements of pride. Devotion to truth is never free of bias and special pleading. Moral strictness is inseparable from imperiousness. Love and hate are inextricably intermixed. Thus, it is man's very goodness which may be the occasion for evil in him. His essential goodness becomes captive to his essential evil. There is within his nature a deep cleft, an inescapable contradiction.

Education cannot eliminate the essential ambiguity of human nature. The good and evil tendencies will grow and develop together. There are deep resources of creativity to which appeal may be made, but these are also sources of danger against which there must be protection. Laws, rewards, and punishments, and other measures of control are necessary to minimize the destructive tendencies and to permit the constructive forces to operate more effectively. The educator must be at the same time wise as a serpent, ready to recognize and counteract the manifestations of evil, and gentle as a dove, equally ready to welcome and promote the stirrings of goodness. In every evil tendency he must endeavor to see and utilize the implicit good and in every good be alert to the implicit evil.

Human nature is neutral. A fourth view of human nature is that it is neither good nor evil in essence but is capable of becoming either or both. If one considers mankind in all its variety, it seems clear that one cannot label all people either good or bad. There are some who are vicious and depraved and there are others who are saintly. Most people lie between the extremes, with some good qualities and some evil tendencies. According to the neutral view, there is nothing innately good or evil about man. His nature depends on his experience, taking account of his inherited potentialities. Since human nature can become any of an almost infinite variety of things, it makes no sense to talk about man as either essentially good or evil.

Furthermore, the conception of man as good or evil depends upon the standards adopted by a particular society. A person who would be called evil in one society might be good by the standards of another society. Competition is approved in one culture, while cooperation is the ideal in another culture. Meekness is valued among some peoples, while aggressiveness is prized among others. Each society has its own traditional standards of good and evil, and each succeeds more or less well in molding personalities according to these standards.

Those who consider men as essentially good or evil or both differ from the neutral position on one or both of the two main points made above. They believe, first, that while there are great differences in individuals and in cultures, there is an underlying human nature which is common to all but which operates variously in differing situations. Second, they believe that there is a universally applicable standard—derived from natural law or from deity—by which human beings can be judged. In contrast, the view that human nature is neutral affirms the plasticity of human nature and denies any universal standard of value.

If human nature is neutral, education becomes of basic importance in making a person what he is to become. Given some standard of value, the task of education is to produce persons who are good by that standard. Good people are the products of good education and evil people result from bad education. Since there is no innate evil to be suppressed, the methods of education may be positive and direct. Since there is no innate goodness to be expressed, the educator cannot merely encourage inherent creative powers, but must explicitly demonstrate and inspire desired outcomes. Natural impulses are not to be rejected nor are they to be uncritically accepted. They are neutral resources of personality to be directed into whatever channels are considered desirable. Knowledge also is neither good nor bad in itself but derives its worth from its use for valued ends. Hence, while there will be no such deep concern over the inevitable misuse of knowledge as when man is considered essentially evil, nor such serene confidence in the automatically liberating power of knowledge as when man is considered essentially good, it will be recognized that knowledge is one important aspect of the equipment of men and that it will be used for good or ill according as education has or has not been effective in creating good personality.

Sources of Evil in Man

The conduct of education depends not only upon the view taken of the nature of man with respect to good and evil, but also upon beliefs about the source or cause of evil in man. Four chief sources must be distinguished. From emphasis on one or another of these sources characteristic inferences for education can be suggested.

The body. It is often said that the evil in man results from his having a body. If he were free of this troublesome weight of material substance, it is said, his worst problems would disappear. The body is subject to disease, is the focus of pain, and at death returns to the dust whence it came. Throughout life it is the cause of all manner of temptation. Its hungers for food, for comfort, and for sexual gratification underlie our myriad economic and social problems. The body's inertia is the cause of our laziness, its irritability the basis for our anger and destructiveness. We spend our energies trying to satisfy its seemingly endless demands, keeping its impulses under some degree of control, and arbitrating between the competing and conflicting pressures to which it gives rise.

Given these beliefs, the function of education is to subjugate the body. The obvious instrument for doing this is the "mind" or the "will." The slogans for such education are "mind over matter" and "will power." The classical method of achieving this goal is rigorous physical discipline, including corporal punishment. If the body's demands for pleasure are regularly answered by inflicting pain or privation, the seeking for pleasure will soon be cured. Strict discipline of children by adults is expected to develop habits of abstinence and renunciation which will give the desired self-control in later life. It is the further conviction of many that the ultimate goal of man is a happy immortality after the death of the physical body and that the earthly pilgrimage is a testing ground for the soul. The successful person is one who learns to subject the body to the soul and thus to realize even in this life the spiritual freedom which is the reward of the faithful in the life to come.

The view that the body is the source of evil in man rests upon the assumption of a duality of mind and matter or of spirit and body. Its opponents would point to the extensive evidence for the unity of personality, the intimate relation of mental and bodily functions, and the demonstrated importance of respecting bodily needs in the young. They would cite the many studies which indicate the destructiveness and ineffectiveness of purely repressive and punitive methods of child training. They would affirm the basic goodness of the body and argue that all of the so-called "higher" human functions if they are to prosper must have an adequate bodily foundation. To be sure, control of body impulses is necessary, but this can be done in such a way as to confirm and fulfill them rather than to deny and frustrate them.

Spirit. Another view is that human evil is caused not by man's body but by his spiritual nature. By "spirit" is here meant all of the distinctively human capacities such as reason, imagination, power of speech, freedom, and self-transcendence. From this standpoint, greed is not primarily a bodily hunger; it is a spiritual disease born of the desire to justify one's own existence or to escape from the recognition of its emptiness. Lust is not basically a biological urge; it is a spiritual craving for dominance and possession. While bodily desires are easily satisfied, spiritual demands are unlimited. The striving for power is only accentuated by the acquisition of power. Preeminence augments rather than subdues ambition.

If evil in man has its source in spirit, human beings are capable of deeper degradation than the other animals. Other animals may kill one another, but they do not murder. Only intelligent man can do that. The other animals do not engage in the mutual mass destruction which humans call war. That activity requires the spiritual qualities of pride and fanatical devotion to an "ideal." Other animals act in accordance with the implicit law of their nature. Man alone has within him a principle of contradiction such that his highest endowments may become the cause and occasion of his worst transgressions. That man is free means he can choose the better or the worse. Freedom is a spiritual endowment. Hence, it is by spirit that man becomes his worst (as well as his best) self. The products of his magnificent intellect can be employed to heal or to kill. His unique and marvelous power of speech can be used to bless or to curse, to hearten or to dismay. Thus by spirit man can rise higher than the animals, but by the same endowment he can fall immeasurably lower.

If the source of human evil is conceived as spirit, education must be dedicated to spiritual discipline. Emphasis will be placed on well-trained intelligence, on high ethical standards, and on refined esthetic sensitivity. Logical cogency, moral discrimination, and imaginative insight will be encouraged. The educator will be concerned above all with the quality of the student's inner life, with the purity and fitness of thought, emotion, and intention. If evil has its source in spirit, so does good. Therefore, the evils will be dispelled by the persuasive power and attractive example of persons with good minds, high ideals, and noble affections.

Society. Instead of locating the source of human evil in the individual, either in his bodily or in his spiritual nature, it is asserted by some that evil comes from society. Proponents of this view contend that man as an individual is fundamentally good. He becomes evil only because of the adverse and degrading influences of his social environment. A person learns his prejudices from his group. Naturally peaceful, he learns by social experience that he must strive against others. The simple, unaffected child of nature becomes corrupted by society with all sorts of vain and deceitful customs and manners. The high ideals of the individual degenerate into the second-best compromises required for corporate existence. Social pressures keep originality and individual excellence at a minimum, make the preservation of refined tastes and pure truth precarious, and readily convert prophets, seers, and saints into martyrs. Society is the great monster which devours goodness and institutionalizes evil.

This is not necessarily to say that society is wholly evil. It may also be the source of good. But whatever evil enters human life, so the argument goes, comes from social sources. The individual person is either good or morally neutral, and it is by society's influence that he becomes evil. Social institutions may also contribute important elements of positive value, but these are in whole or in part counteracted by the negative tendencies.

If society is the source of evil, the extreme logic of the case would call for the abandonment of all except self-education. Since any directing of personal development by other persons would be social influence, the only way to avoid the evil effects of society would be to allow the individual to develop naturally from within, unspoiled by social convention. Such a view of education is completely untenable, because it has been amply demonstrated that personality can develop only within the context of human association. The picture of the pure uncompromised child of nature, who has grown without human intervention, is romantic fantasy wholly out of accord with fact.

If, then, society is necessary to education, the only way to minimize socially caused evils is to insure that the society which is educatively effective is as good as possible. This may require a relatively ideal educative society operating within the larger social order. Presumably this is the function of such social institutions as the home, the school, and the church. These institutions provide intimate social environments in which the evils of the general social milieu may be minimized. If the accepted standard of conduct is to destroy one's rivals, the home may be a counteractive influence teaching forebearance and mutuality. If the accepted practice of society is to use language in such a way as to gain personal or group advantage, the school may provide a contrary social influence in favor of truth rather than mere propaganda. If society at large teaches one to measure value by the degree of prestige and power attained, the church may constitute an educative society where humility, love, and forgiveness are the higher values. When society is regarded as the source of human evil, it is of primary importance that education be so organized as to take account of social factors and that as far as necessary special social institutions be provided in which persons can grow with minimum corruption by society.

Demonic powers. Finally, the cause of evil in human life may be assigned neither to individual persons nor to society but to demonic powers. In pre-scientific ages and still among unsophisticated people this view has found favor. Illness of body or mind, social disorder, and all manner of calamities have been regarded as the work of malevolent spirits—devils, demons, or ghosts. The modern mind characteristically rejects this outlook, relegating the demonic to the realm of outmoded superstition. Despite this trend, there are serious and competent thinkers today who consider some conception of the demonic necessary. By this conception they would mean a spirit or spirits of evil having in some sense objective reality, becoming evident in the evil inclinations of individuals and groups. For example, a persistent and all-devouring hatred or the fanatical fury of a lynch mob would be considered as evidences of demonic possession.

Belief in demonic powers is ordinarily associated with a corresponding faith in benign spiritual agencies. Good education would then invoke these helpful powers in the fight against the malevolent ones. Personal development would need to proceed under the direction and protection of the good powers and with the use of methods which would countract the evil ones. Prayers, affirmations of faith, and sacramental acts of various kinds within the religious community are examples of means traditionally used to deal with the demonic powers. It is not that man thereby subjects them to his control, but that he sets up conditions wherein the powers of good may gain mastery over the evil ones.

Evil and Reality

In Chapters 28 and 29 the nature and development of the cosmos were considered, and their bearing on the concerns of education was suggested. Little was said about the flaws, failures, and contradictions within the cosmic scene. It is now time to remedy that deficiency by discussing the nature and place of evil in the larger scheme of things and indicating some inferences for education.

Evil as non-being. One basic position concerning evil and reality is that evil is simply non-being. The real is the good, and evil is the absence of the good. Evil is deficiency; it has no reality of its own. Ignorance is lack of knowledge, vice is deficiency of virtue, ugliness is absence of beauty. Whatever *is* is good; actual things are evil to the degree that they are partial or one-sided. Fullness of being is the highest good.

Since the world is good to the extent that it is complete, and since evil is incompleteness, the right direction of development is toward increase of being. Whatever frustrates the realization of a being, whatever prevents a process from moving ahead to completion, is evil. The world is evil insofar as it is still incomplete. It will remain evil to a degree because by the very nature of things the totality of possibility can never be realized. Since the passage of time brings new things into being and simultaneously ushers old things out, the world process is not a mere accumulation of reality but has debits as well as credits to the account of reality.

From this standpoint the ultimate good is infinitude or perfection, and the world is evil because it is finite. The successive levels in the cosmic scheme described in Chapter 29 are not only increasingly complex; they are progressively better because they are more and more comprehensive. The level of human mentality is particularly noteworthy because here infinitude comes into its own. There are in principle no bounds to the range or penetration of intelligence, imagination, and spiritual creativity. Through the power of reason man in a sense comprehends reality in its fullness; he participates in completeness and perfection. An inorganic object, on the other hand, has far more limited reality, since in no sense does it partake of the infinite, but it merely occupies its own limited and finite position in space and time and has highly restricted relationships to the rest of reality.

These considerations indicate the basis for the ascription of a higher value to the more complex forms emerging from the cosmic process. They provide a reason for saying that cosmic development is progressive. The progress consists in the production of entities which are more complete or less partial. From this viewpoint living beings are higher than the non-living and human beings are superior to plants and animals. The hierarchy of being is also a hierarchy of value because value is identified with fullness of being.

In this theory the function of education is to direct the development of persons toward maximum fulfillment of their being. Variety and richness of experience, breadth of outlook, integrity of insight, versatility in the exercise of skill, catholicity of tastes would be some of the major goals of education. The basic good is growth itself—not just quantitative increase, but enlargement of interests, development of new capacities, deepening of convictions. Education is seen as a life-long process, or even as continuing in an after-life. It is a constant seeking for completeness, a striving for infinitude and perfection, a hunger for ever more knowledge and ever greater sensitivity.

Evil as conflict. To the view of evil as non-being it may be objected that this in effect denies the existence of any evil. Perhaps ignorance is merely the absence of knowledge, but what about error? Error is a real contradiction between what is asserted and what actually is; it is not merely the absence of truth. War is an evil, but the reality of that evil can hardly be described in such mild terms as "the absence of peace." War is evil because it is a state of contradiction in the pursuit of human affairs. Ugliness is evil not simply because beauty is absent but because there are opposing and mutually destructive relationships in the perceived object and between object and perceiver.

Such considerations lead to the view that evil, in essence, is *conflict.* It is not non-being; it is the conflict of beings. It is not incompleteness; it is incompatibility. It is not finitude; it is discord between finite entities. The highest good is not fullness of being but harmony of being. By the former view evil consists in unfinishedness; by the present view it inheres in relationships, and these relationships are real. To understand evil as a conflict relationship is to do justice to the sharpness and insistent actuality which evil has in common experience.

The conflicts may appear in different forms, corresponding to the various kinds of evil, such as physical, social, moral, intellectual, esthetic, and religious. Some disease may be owing to lack of food or of vitamins or of fresh air, but much more often it is evidence of conflict, as between healthy tissues and the bacteria causing an infection. In the intellectual sphere an important kind of evil is the apparent irrationality of things which resist conceptual coordination through reliable laws. A world operating chaotically, not reducible to intelligible order, a world whose events transpire by chance rather than by rule, is to that extent evil. It reflects a discordant relationship among things and between the world and the persons who seek to understand it.

When evil is seen as conflict, the cosmic process is not necessarily regarded as progress to higher levels of being. Increase in complexity may increase correspondingly the number and intensity of conflicts. From the point of view of harmony of existence man is hardly the equal of the lower creatures. On the other hand, it must be granted that the more complex beings do manage to bring together into a workable unity a greater variety of materials and functions than do the simpler beings. If, then, it is assumed that in the long run the conflict-ridden entities will tend to disappear in favor of those in which harmony prevails, the more complex beings would also be "better" or "higher" than the simpler ones. However, this reasoning implicitly introduces the concept of fullness of being as an aspect of harmony and thus combines the criteria of the present section and the preceding one.

When evil is conceived as conflict, the aim of education is to produce the maximum harmony of personal existence. The direction in which persons should grow is such as to eliminate conflicts, both inner and outer. The presence of any obstacle to harmonious functioning provides an opportunity for learning, the outcome of which is the discovery of a way to overcome or circumvent the obstacle and re-establish harmony. From this standpoint education is a process of problem solving, and the solutions of the successive problems are the possible ways of rearranging things so as to remove conflict.

If conflict is evil, it would seem to follow that the right approach is simply to avoid contradictions. This would lead to prescriptions such as the following: Do not prevent a child from doing what he wants to do. Never contradict or frustrate him. Be permissive, as far as humanly possible. There are some who take this stand. The trouble with it is that the person cannot be indefinitely protected from conflicts, and if he is indulged as a child, he will not be prepared to deal with the problems which will inevitably come in later years. In good education, therefore, one should not seek too immediately to remove obstacles but should judiciously employ them as opportunities for learning how to surmount them. The position of extreme permissiveness has the merit of reminding one that the ultimate goal is harmony and of cautioning against the opposite extreme wherein conflict is glorified as an end in itself and the value of education is measured by the rigor of the difficulties which are imposed upon the learner.

Similar considerations apply to the conception of education as "life adjustment." The ideal of adjustment is based upon the assumption that evil is conflict and harmony is good. The learner's goal is therefore to "adjust" to his physical and social environment so as to minimize frustration and destructive conflict. But suppose that the inner integrity of the person requires some protest against the environment, or suppose that his primary duty be to speak out against his society and to seek its reformation. Then continuing conflict and not harmonious adjustment would be the right objective. Ideally such conflict would eventually result in changes both in the person and in his environment (perhaps long after his death) which would bring about a greater harmony of existence. Short-range maladjustment may therefore help to bring about long-range adjustment. Hence, while a literal and immediate conception of education as adjustment seems undesirable, a long-range educational goal of maximum harmonious functioning of persons in their environments may be tenable. Temporary discordances can be skillfully employed to produce the greatest possible ultimate accord.

Evil as malevolent power. A third view takes evil more seriously and gives it a more substantial place in reality than does either of the first two views. According to the first, evil is merely deficiency, and according to the second, it is a discordant relationship. The third position is that evil is malevolent power. This is directly opposed to the conception of evil as non-being; malevolent power is actual being, though not of a desirable kind. The exponents of this view would hold that only such a definite and realistic conception can do justice to the active nature and destructive power of evil forces. Such forces cannot be called non-being; what does not exist can exert no effective influence, as evil does. Furthermore, to holders of this view conflict seems scarcely adequate as a conception of evil. There may be conflicts which are good. In fact, part of the zest and flavor of life comes from conflict. Also the absence of conflict is not necessarily good. In fact, the worst evils may exist in the most harmonious relationships; consistent and well-organized evil is more dangerous than discordant evil.

The alleged inadequacy of both non-being and conflict to account for evil points to the need for a concept of malevolent powers. These powers may be variously conceived. They are not necessarily devils or evil spirits. They may be seen in catastrophes of nature whereby laboriously created things of beauty and use are utterly destroyed. On the human scene they are especially apparent in the evil designs of cruel and selfish men. According to this view, men do not always act in the light of the apparent good. They frequently behave in ways they know are wrong. And even if intentions are good, the power exerted may be evil. The malevolent powers are particularly evident in man's corporate life, in the passions of the mob, the hysteria of war, or in the ruthlessness of the nation that seeks to glorify itself at the expense of other peoples.

It may be argued that education becomes a fully moral enterprise only when evil is conceived in such realistic terms as these. If evil is merely incompleteness, the educational task is the enrichment and enlargement of life, but without any sense, all along the way, that there are good fulfillments and bad fulfillments between which decisive choices must be made. If evil is merely conflict, the goal of education is to produce harmony, but without any consideration for whether the harmony is good or bad. It seems important, then, to recognize the malevolent powers in all their forms and to teach how to do battle with them for the sake of the good. The primary question is not how to become complete, but what kind of fulfillment is achieved. The basic objective is not to become adjusted but to grow in strength to stand firm for the right.

From the realistic view of evil it cannot be inferred that one can know fully what is good and what is evil. The problem of knowing evil is different from that of the reality of evil. To affirm that evil is malevolent power does not imply a knowledge of which powers are evil and which are good. This poses a difficulty for education, the successful conduct of which depends upon such knowledge. Despite this problem, the deeply moral quality of education remains. Using whatever resources of moral insight are available for guidance, the educator sees his work as an important part of man's continuing struggle on behalf of the forces of light against the powers of darkness.

Optimism and Pessimism Concerning Education

There are four possible views concerning the long-term and short-term balance of good and evil in the cosmos and four corresponding positions on optimism and pessimism about education. The first view reflects both proximate and ultimate optimism. According to it, evil is really not a problem. The world is essentially good and is constantly improving. Education shares in this inevitable and unlimited progress. There are no difficulties which cannot with patience and intelligence be satisfactorily solved. The present is better than the past, and the future will be better than the present. It is in the very nature of things to get better. Hence the educator can rely on nature, human and otherwise, to support and direct development toward the unfolding goals of an ever more abundant life.

The directly opposite view is one of proximate and ultimate pessimism. According to it, evil is a real and insuperable problem. The world is essentially bad and is constantly deteriorating. Education is caught in the decline and only serves to accelerate it. The attempt to solve problems only involves man in deeper perplexities. There was a time when life was more serene and more secure because more innocent, but now at a faster and faster pace all things head toward catastrophe. Education is one of the corrupting factors, human and non-human nature conspiring through it to exhaust at last all the resources of good.

An intermediate view is optimistic for the short run but pessimistic about the ultimate outcome. A fortunate combination of circumstances have made it possible for human life to appear for a season upon the earth, but this very exceptional condition does not prevail in the cosmos generally. Thus man and his works are doomed to extinction as soon as the delicate and precarious balance is upset. Education has temporary utility for making the most of this brief interlude, before man and all his works are ushered off the cosmic stage. Chaos and death are kings, though it may seem for the time being that the earth is fair and full of promise. Education thus finds no ultimate sanction in the cosmic scheme. It merely reflects the feeble and transient spark of light and life which flashes momentarily in a universe of darkness and death.

A final view is pessimistic about the short run but optimistic for the long run. According to it, evil is real and powerful. All men must die, nations and cultures rise and fall, men often use their knowledge for evil ends, and the powers of man and nature are turned to destructive purposes. Yet in and through all of this there is a redemptive power at work. Out of the endless succession of deaths new life constantly springs. Beyond the tragedy of earthly existence the eye of faith can discern a triumphant consummation. Within the apparent meaninglessness of the cosmic process there is a hidden thread of purpose. Education, though capable of being used for evil ends by evil men, may also be an instrument of good, but only if those who participate in it constantly seek forgiveness and aim to direct human development in the light of the ultimate good, which is never fully realized in human history but may be a source of present inspiration to those who have the vision to discern it, though from afar.

Bibliography

Bibliography

Chapter 1

Berkson, I. B., *Preface to Educational Philosophy*. New York: Columbia University Press, 1940.

Bode, Boyd H., *Fundamentals of Education*. New York: The Macmillan Company, 1931.

Brameld, Theodore, *Patterns of Educational Philosophy*. Yonkers-on-Hudson, N. Y.: World Book Company, 1950.

———, *Philosophies of Education in Cultural Perspective*. New York: Dryden Press, 1955.

Broudy, Harry S., *Building a Philosophy of Education*. New York: Prentice-Hall, Inc., 1954.

Brubacher, John S., *Eclectic Philosophy of Education*. New York: Prentice-Hall, Inc., 1951.

———, *A History of the Problems of Education*. New York: McGraw-Hill Book Company, Inc., 1947.

———, *Modern Philosophies of Education*. New York: McGraw-Hill Book Company, Inc., 1950.

Butler, J. Donald, *Four Philosophies and Their Practice in Education and Religion*. New York: Harper and Brothers, 1951.

Childs, John L., *American Pragmatism and Education*. New York: Henry Holt and Company, 1956.

Cunningham, William F., *Pivotal Problems of Education*. New York: The Macmillan Company, 1940.

Demiashkevich, Michael, *An Introduction to the Philosophy of Education*. New York: American Book Company, 1935.

Dewey, John, *Democracy and Education*. New York: The Macmillan Company, 1916.

———, *Experience and Education*. New York: The Macmillan Company, 1938.

Eby, Frederick, and Arrowood, C. F., *The Development of Modern Education*. New York: Prentice-Hall, Inc., 1940.

———, *The History and Philosophy of Education Ancient and Medieval*. New York: Prentice-Hall, Inc., 1940.

Fitzpatrick, Edward A., *Readings in the Philosophy of Education*. New York: Appleton-Century-Crofts, Inc., 1936.

Henderson, Stella V., *Introduction to Philosophy of Education*. Chicago: University of Chicago Press, 1947.

Horne, Herman H., *The Democratic Philosophy of Education*. New York: The Macmillan Company, 1935.

Kilpatrick, William H., *Source Book in the Philosophy of Education.* New York: The Macmillan Company, 1934.

Lodge, Rupert C., *Philosophy of Education.* New York: Harper and Brothers, 1947.

National Society for the Study of Education, Fifty-Fourth Yearbook, Part I, *Modern Philosophies and Education.* Chicago: The University of Chicago Press, 1955.

———, Forty-First Yearbook, Part I, *Philosophies of Education.* Bloomington, Ill.: Public School Publishing Company, 1942.

Redden, J. D., and Ryan, F. A., *A Catholic Philosophy of Education.* Milwaukee: Bruce Publishing Company, 1942.

Ulich, Robert, *Fundamentals of Democratic Education.* New York: American Book Company, 1940.

———, *History of Educational Thought.* New York: American Book Company, 1945.

Wynne, John P., *Philosophies of Education from the Standpoint of Experimentalism.* New York: Prentice-Hall, Inc., 1947.

Chapter 2

Butts, R. Freeman, *A Cultural History of Western Education,* rev. ed. New York: McGraw-Hill Book Company, Inc., 1955.

———, and Cremin, Lawrence A., *A History of Education in American Culture.* New York: Henry Holt and Company, 1953.

Counts, George S., *Dare the School Build a New Social Order?* New York: John Day Company, 1932.

———, *Education and American Civilization.* New York: Bureau of Publications, Teachers College, Columbia University, 1952.

Cubberley, Elwood P., *Changing Conceptions of Education.* Boston: Houghton Mifflin Company, 1909.

Curti, Merle, *The Social Ideas of American Educators.* New York: Charles Scribner's Sons, 1935.

Dewey, John, *The School and Society,* rev. ed. Chicago: The University of Chicago Press, 1915.

Educational Policies Commission, *Public Education and the Future of America.* Washington: National Education Association, 1955.

Hart, Joseph K., *Education in the Humane Community.* New York: Harper and Brothers, 1951.

Lee, Gordon C., *An Introduction to Education in Modern America,* rev. ed. New York: Henry Holt and Company, 1957.

Mead, Margaret, *The School in American Culture.* Cambridge: Harvard University Press, 1951.

Monroe, Paul, *The Founding of the American Public School System.* New York: The Macmillan Company, 1940.

Reisner, Edward H., *The Evolution of the Common School.* New York: The Macmillan Company, 1930.

Stanley, William O., *et al, Social Foundations of Education.* New York: Dryden Press, 1956.

Chapter 3

Barzun, Jacques, *Teacher in America*. Boston: Little, Brown and Company, 1945.
Baxter, Bernice, *Teacher-Pupil Relationships*. New York: The Macmillan Company, 1941.
Burton, William H., *The Guidance of Learning Activities; A Summary of the Principles of Teaching Based upon the Growth of the Learner*. New York: Appleton-Century-Crofts, Inc., 1952.
Bush, Robert N., *The Teacher-Pupil Relationship*. New York: Prentice-Hall, Inc., 1954.
Cantor, Nathaniel, *The Teaching-Learning Process*. New York: Dryden Press, 1953.
Garrison, Noble L., *The Improvement of Teaching, A Two-Fold Approach*. New York: Dryden Press, 1955.
Highet, Gilbert, *The Art of Teaching*. New York: Alfred A. Knopf, 1950.
Hook, Sidney, *Education for Modern Man*. New York: The Dial Press, 1946.
Horne, Herman H., *The Teacher as Artist; An Essay in Education as an Aesthetic Process*. Boston: Houghton Mifflin Company, 1917.
Kilpatrick, William H., *Foundations of Method*. New York: The Macmillan Company, 1925.
Livingstone, Sir Richard, *Leadership in Education*. New York: Oxford University Press, 1950.
Rugg, Harold, and Brooks, B. Marion, *The Teacher in School and Society; An Introduction to Education*. Yonkers-on-Hudson, N. Y.: World Book Company, 1950.
McCloskey, Gordon, *et al., Introduction to Teaching in American Schools*. New York: Harcourt, Brace and Company, 1954.
Moustakas, Clark E., *The Teacher and the Child; Personal Interaction in the Classroom*. New York: McGraw-Hill Book Company, Inc., 1956.
Mursell, James C., *Successful Teaching, Its Psychological Principles,* 2d. ed. New York: McGraw-Hill Book Company, Inc., 1954.
Simon, Henry W., *Preface to Teaching*. New York: Oxford University Press, 1938.
Valentine, Percy F., *The Art of the Teacher, An Essay in Humanism*. New York: D. Appleton and Company, 1931.
Waller, Willard, *The Sociology of Teaching*. New York: John Wiley and Sons, Inc., 1932.

Chapter 4

Anderson, Vernon E., *Principles and Procedures of Curriculum Improvement*. New York: Ronald Press Company, 1954.
Beck, Robert H., *et al., Curriculum in the Modern Elementary School*. New York: Prentice-Hall, Inc., 1953.
Bestor, Arthur, *The Restoration of Learning*. New York: Alfred A. Knopf, 1955.
Caswell, Hollis L., *et al., Curriculum Improvement in Public School Systems*. New York: Bureau of Publications, Teachers College, Columbia University, 1950.
———, and Campbell, Doak S., *Readings in Curriculum Development*. New York: American Book Company, 1937.

Dewey, John, *Child and Curriculum*. Chicago: The University of Chicago Press, 1912.

Faunce, Roland C., and Bossing, Nelson I., *Developing the Core Curriculum*. New York: Prentice-Hall, Inc., 1951.

Hutchins, Robert M., *The Higher Learning in America*. New Haven: Yale University Press, 1936.

John Dewey Society, Third Yearbook, *Democracy and the Curriculum*. New York: Appleton-Century, 1939.

Kilpatrick, William H., *Remaking the Curriculum*. New York: Newson and Company, 1936.

MacDonald, John, *Mind, School and Civilization*. Chicago: The University of Chicago Press, 1952.

McNerney, T., *The Curriculum*. New York: McGraw-Hill Book Company, Inc., 1953.

Morrison, Henry C., *The Curriculum of the Common School*. Chicago: The University of Chicago Press, 1940.

National Society for the Study of Education, Twenty-Fourth Yearbook, Part II, *Adapting the Schools to Individual Differences*. Bloomington, Ill.: Public School Publishing Company, 1925.

———, Twenty-Sixth Yearbook, Part II, *The Foundations and Technique of Curriculum Construction*. Bloomington, Ill.: Public School Publishing Company, 1930.

Smith, B. Othanel, *et al., Fundamentals of Curriculum Development,* rev. ed. Yonkers-on-Hudson, N. Y.: World Book Company, 1957.

Stratemeyer, Florence, *et al., Developing a Curriculum for Modern Living,* rev. ed. New York: Bureau of Publications, Teachers College, Columbia University, 1957.

Chapter 5

Brown, Kenneth I., *Not Minds Alone*. New York: Harper and Brothers, 1954.

Butts, R. Freeman, *The American Tradition in Religion and Education*. Boston: Beacon Press, 1950.

Committee on Religion and Education, *The Function of the Public Schools in Dealing with Religion*. Washington: American Council on Education, 1953.

———, *The Relation of Religion to Public Education: The Basic Principles*. Washington: American Council on Education, 1947.

Cuninggim, Merrimon, *Freedom's Holy Light*. New York: Harper and Brothers, 1955.

Educational Policies Commission, *Moral and Spiritual Values in the Public Schools*. Washington: National Education Association, 1951.

Fairchild, Hoxie N. (ed.), *Religious Perspectives in College Teaching*. New York: Ronald Press Company, 1952.

Fleming, William S., *God in Our Public Schools*. Pittsburgh: National Reform Association, 1944.

Gauss, Christian F. (ed.), *The Teaching of Religion in Higher Education*. New York: Ronald Press Company, 1951.

Harner, Nevin C., *Religion's Place in General Education*. Richmond, Va.: John Knox Press, 1949.

Henry, Virgil, *The Place of Religion in the Public Schools*. New York: Harper and Brothers, 1950.

Hutchins, Robert M., *Morals, Religion, and Higher Education*. Chicago: The University of Chicago Press, 1950.

John Dewey Society, Seventh Yearbook, *The Public Schools and Spiritual Values*. New York: Harper and Brothers, 1944.

Johnson, F. Ernest (ed.), *American Education and Religion*. New York: Harper and Brothers, 1952.

Madden, Ward, *Religious Values in Education*. New York: Harper and Brothers, 1951.

Moehlman, Conrad H., *School and Church: the American Way*. New York: Harper and Brothers, 1944.

Moberly, Sir Walter, *The Crisis in the University*. New York: The Macmillan Company, 1949.

O'Neill, James M., *Religion and Education Under the Constitution*. New York: Harper and Brothers, 1949.

Pfeffer, Leo, *Church, State, and Freedom*. Boston: Beacon Press, 1953.

Thayer, Vivian T., *The Attack Upon the American Secular School*. Boston: Beacon Press, 1951.

Van Dusen, Henry P., *God in Education*. New York: Charles Scribner's Sons, 1951.

Wilder, Amos N. (ed.), *Liberal Learning and Religion*. New York: Harper and Brothers, 1951.

Williams, J. Paul, *The New Education and Religion*. New York: Association Press, 1945.

Chapter 6

Barnard, Chester I., *The Functions of the Executive*. Cambridge: Harvard University Press, 1947.

Briggs, Thomas H., and Justman, Joseph, *Improving Instruction Through Supervision*. New York: The Macmillan Company, 1952.

Campbell, Clyde M. (ed.), *Practical Applications of Democratic Administration*. New York: Harper and Brothers, 1952.

Chandler, Bobby Joe, and Petty, Paul V., *Personnel Management in School Administration*. Yonkers-on-Hudson, N. Y.: World Book Company, 1955.

Cubberley, Ellwood P., *Public School Administration*, rev. ed. New York: Houghton Mifflin Company, 1929.

Elsbree, Willard S., and Reutter, E. Edmund, Jr., *Staff Personnel in the Public Schools*. New York: Prentice-Hall, Inc., 1954.

Hagman, Harlan L., and Schwartz, Alfred, *Administration in Profile for School Executives*. New York: Harper and Brothers, 1955.

Kelliher, Alice V., *A Critical Study of Homogeneous Grouping*. New York: Bureau of Publications, Teachers College, Columbia University, 1931.

Knight, Edgar W., *Readings in Educational Administration*. New York: Henry Holt and Company, 1953.

Melby, Ernest O., *Administering Community Education*. Englewood Cliffs, N. J.: Prentice-Hall, Inc., 1955.

Miller, Van, and Spalding, Willard, *The Public Administration of American Schools*. Yonkers-on-Hudson, N. Y.: World Book Company, 1952.

Moehlman, Arthur B., *School Administration; Its Development, Principles, and Function in the United States,* 2d ed. Boston: Houghton Mifflin Company, 1951.

Moore, Harold E., and Walters, Newell B., *Personnel Administration in Education*. New York: Harper and Brothers, 1955.

Mort, Paul R., *Principles of School Administration, a Synthesis of Basic Concepts*. New York: McGraw-Hill Book Company, Inc., 1946.

Newlon, Jesse, *Educational Administration as Social Policy*. New York: Charles Scribner's Sons, 1934.

Reavis, William C., *et al., Administering the Elementary School*. New York: Prentice-Hall, Inc., 1953.

Sargent, Cyril G., and Belisle, Eugenie L., *Educational Administration: Cases and Concepts*. Boston: Houghton Mifflin Company, 1955.

Sears, Jesse B., *The Nature of the Administrative Process*. New York: McGraw-Hill Book Company, Inc., 1950.

Yeager, William, *Administration and the Teacher*. New York: Harper and Brothers, 1954.

Chapter 7

Benne, Kenneth D., *A Conception of Authority*. New York: Bureau of Publications, Teachers College, Columbia University, 1943.

Carr, William G., *School Finance*. Stanford, Calif.: Stanford University Press, 1933.

Conant, James B., *Education in a Divided World*. Cambridge: Harvard University Press, 1948.

Counts, George S., *The Social Composition of Boards of Education*. Chicago: The University of Chicago Press, 1927.

Cubberley, Ellwood P., *State School Administration*. Boston: Houghton Mifflin Company, 1927.

Hales, Dawson W., *Federal Control of Public Education*. New York: Bureau of Publications, Teachers College, Columbia University, 1954.

Harris, Seymour E., *How Shall We Pay for Education?* New York: Harper and Brothers, 1948.

Hulburd, David, *This Happened in Pasadena*. New York: The Macmillan Company, 1951.

Melby, Ernest O., and Puner, Morton (ed.) *Freedom and Public Education*. New York: Frederick A. Praeger, Inc., 1953.

Mort, Paul R., *State Support for Public Schools*. New York: Bureua of Publications, Teachers College, Columbia University, 1926.

Norton, John K., and Norton, Margaret A., *Wealth, Children, and Education*. New York: Bureau of Publications, Teachers College, Columbia University, 1938.

Pittenger, Benjamin F., *Introduction to Public School Finance*. Boston: Houghton Mifflin Company, 1925.

Rainey, Homer P., *Public School Finance*. New York: The Century Company, 1929.
Raup, R. Bruce, *Education and Organized Interests in America*. New York: G. P. Putnam's Sons, 1936.

Chapter 8

Bendix, Reinhard, and Lipset, Seymour, *Class, Status, and Power: A Reader in Social Stratification*. Glencoe, Ill.: The Free Press, 1953.
Conant, James B., *The Citadel of Learning*. New Haven: Yale University Press, 1956.
Davis, Allison, *Social-Class Influences Upon Learning*. Cambridge: Harvard University Press, 1948.
Educational Policies Commission, *Education for All American Youth*. Washington: National Education Association, 1941.
Edwards, Newton, *Equal Educational Opportunity for Youth*. Washington: American Council on Education, 1939.
Hollingshead, August R., *Elmtown's Youth*. New York: John Wiley and Sons, Inc., 1949.
Hollinshead, Byron S., *Who Should Go to College?* New York: Columbia University Press, 1952.
Hutchins, Robert M., *The Conflict in Education in a Democratic Society*. New York: Harper and Brothers, 1953.
Lynd, Robert S., and Lynd, Helen M., *Middletown*. New York: Harcourt, Brace and Company, 1929.
———, *Middletown in Transition*. New York: Harcourt, Brace and Company, 1937.
McGuire, Samuel H., *Trends in Principles and Practices of Equalization of Educational Opportunities*. Nashville, Tenn.: George Peabody College for Teachers, 1934.
Myrdal, Gunnar, *An American Dilemma*. New York: Harper and Brothers, 1944.
Warner, W. Lloyd, *American Life: Dream and Reality*. Chicago: The University of Chicago Press, 1953.
———, *et al., Who Shall Be Educated?* New York: Harper and Brothers, 1944.

Chapter 9

American Civil Liberties Union, *Civil Liberties of Teachers and Students*. New York: 1949.
Beale, Howard K., *Are American Teachers Free?* New York: Charles Scribner's Sons, 1936.
Brubacher, Abraham R., *Teaching: Profession and Practice*. New York: Appleton-Century-Crofts, 1927.
Carr-Saunders, Alexander M., and Wilson, P. A., *The Professions*. Oxford: The Clarendon Press, 1933.
Commission on Educational Reconstruction, *Organizing the Teaching Profession*. Chicago: American Federation of Teachers, 1955.

Commission on Teacher Education, *The Improvement of Teacher Education*. Washington: The American Council on Education, 1946.

Elsbree, Willard S., *The American Teacher; Evolution of a Profession in a Democracy*. New York: American Book Company, 1939.

Hofstadter, Richard, and Metzger, Walter P., *The Development of Academic Freedom in the United States*. New York: Columbia University Press, 1955.

John Dewey Society, First Yearbook, *The Teacher and Society*. New York: Appleton-Century Company, 1937.

Landis, Benson Y., *Professional Codes*. New York: Bureau of Publications, Teachers College, Columbia University, 1927.

Lynd, Albert, *Quackery in the Public Schools*. Boston: Little, Brown and Company, 1953.

MacIver, Robert M., *Academic Freedom in Our Time*. New York: Columbia University Press, 1955.

National Commission on Teacher Education and Professional Standards, *The Certification of Teachers, Advancing Public and Professional Welfare*. Washington: National Education Association, 1953.

———, *The Teacher and Professional Organizations*, 2d ed. Washington: National Education Association, 1956.

National Education Association, *Code of Ethics of the National Education Association*. Washington: 1952.

Taeusch, Carl F., *Professional and Business Ethics*. New York: Henry Holt and Company, 1926.

Walsh, Matthew J., *Teaching as a Profession*. New York: Henry Holt and Company, 1926.

Wilson, Logan, *The Academic Man*. New York: Oxford University Press, 1942.

Znaniecki, Florian, *The Social Role of the Man of Knowledge*. New York: Columbia University Press, 1940.

Chapter 10

Bailey, Liberty H., *The Holy Earth*. New York: Charles Scribner's Sons, 1915.

Brown, Harrison, *The Challenge of Man's Future*. New York: Viking Press, 1954.

Burroughs, John, *John Burroughs' America* (ed. by Farida A. Wiley). New York: Devin-Adair Company, 1951.

Darwin, Charles A., *The Next Million Years*. New York: Doubleday and Company, Inc., 1953.

Dewey, John, *Experience and Nature*. New York: W. W. Norton and Company, Inc., 1929.

Galloway, George (ed.), *Planning for America*. New York: Henry Holt and Company, 1941.

Hartshorne, Charles, *Beyond Humanism; Essays in the New Philosophy of Nature*. Chicago: Willett Clark, 1937.

Hatcher, Halene, *Better Living Through Wise Use of Resources*. Washington: Federal Security Agency, Office of Education, 1950.

Krutch, Joseph Wood, *The Great Chain of Life*. Boston: Houghton Mifflin Company, 1956.

Mather, Kirtley, *Enough and To Spare*. New York: Harper and Brothers, 1944.

Mid-Century Conference on Resources for the Future, *The Nation Looks at Its Resources*. Washington: 1954.

Mitchell, Lucy S., *et al., My Country 'tis of Thee*. New York: The Macmillan Company, 1940.

Opdyke, George H., *Art and Nature Appreciation*. New York: The Macmillan Company, 1932.

Osborn, Fairfield, *Limits of the Earth*. New York: Little, Brown and Company, 1953.

———, *Our Plundered Planet*. New York: Little, Brown and Company, 1948.

Renner, George T., *Conservation of National Resources, an Educational Approach to the Problem*. New York: John Wiley and Sons, Inc., 1942.

Stevens, Bertha, *Nature; the Child Goes Forth*. Boston: Houghton Mifflin Company, 1936.

Woytinsky, Wladimir S., and Woytinsky, Emma S., *World Population and Production*. New York: The Twentieth Century Fund, 1953.

Chapter 11

Anshen, Ruth N., *The Family: Its Function and Destiny*. New York: Harper and Brothers, 1949.

Bossard, James H. S., *Parent and Child; Studies in Family Behavior*. Philadelphia: University of Pennsylvania Press, 1953.

Briffault, Robert, *The Mothers, A Study of the Origins of Sentiments and Institutions,* 3 vol. New York: The Macmillan Company, 1927.

Burgess, Ernest W., *The Family, From Institution to Companionship*. 3d ed. New York: American Book Company, 1953.

Davis, Allison, and Havighurst, Robert J., *Father of the Man*. Boston: Houghton Mifflin Company, 1947.

Folsom, Joseph K., *Youth, Family and Education*. Washington: American Council on Education, 1941.

Groves, Ernest R., *The Family and Its Social Functions*. Philadelphia: J. B. Lippincott Company, 1940.

Hart, Hornell, and Hart, Ella B., *Personality and the Family*. Boston: D. C. Heath and Company, 1941.

Hartshorne, Hugh, *Character in Human Relations*. New York: Charles Scribner's Sons, 1932.

Havighurst, Robert J., and Neugarten, Bernice L., *Society and Education*. New York: Allyn and Bacon, Inc., 1957.

Mead, George H., *Mind, Self, and Society*. Chicago: The University of Chicago Press, 1934.

Mead, Margaret, and Wolfenstein, Martha (ed.), *Childhood in Contemporary Cultures*. Chicago: The University of Chicago Press, 1955.

Sirjamaki, John, *The American Family in the Twentieth Century*. New York: Harcourt, Brace and Company, 1953.

Waller, Willard, *The Family, A Dynamic Interpretation,* rev. ed. New York: Dryden Press, 1951.

Chapter 12

Ballou, Richard B., *The Individual and the State: The Modern Challenge to Education.* Boston: Beacon Press, 1953.

Coe, George A., *Educating for Citizenship.* New York: Charles Scribner's Sons, 1938.

Counts, George S., *The Prospects of Democracy.* New York: John Day, 1938.

———, *The Social Foundations of Education.* New York: Charles Scribner's Sons, 1934.

Dewey, John, *The Public and Its Problems.* New York: Henry Holt and Company, 1927.

Huxley, Julian, *UNESCO, Its Purpose and Philosophy.* Washington: Public Affairs Press, 1947.

John Dewey Society, 11th Yearbook, *Education for a World Society: Promising Practices Today.* New York: Harper and Brothers, 1951.

Mannheim, Karl, *Man and Society in an Age of Reconstruction.* New York: Harcourt, Brace and Company, 1940.

Nisbet, Robert A., *The Quest for Community; a Study in the Ethics of Order and Freedom.* New York: Oxford University Press, 1953.

Pierce, Bessie L., *Citizens Organizations and the Civic Training of Youth.* New York: Charles Scribner's Sons, 1933.

Popper, Karl, *The Open Society and Its Enemies.* Princeton: Princeton University Press, 1950.

Smith, T. V., and Lindeman, Eduard C., *The Democratic Way of Life.* New York: New American Library, 1951.

Stanley, William O., *Education and Social Integration.* New York: Bureau of Publications, Teachers College, Columbia University, 1953.

Tawney, R. H., *Equality.* New York: Harcourt, Brace and Company, 1931.

Chapter 13

Caplow, Theodore, *The Sociology of Work.* Minneapolis: University of Minnesota Press, 1954.

Educational Policies Commission, *Manpower and Education.* Washington: National Education Association, 1956.

Ginsberg, Eli, *et al., Occupational Choice, An Approach to a General Theory.* New York: Columbia University Press, 1951.

Gold, Milton, *Working to Learn.* New York: Bureau of Publications, Teachers College, Columbia University, 1951.

Heron, Alexander, *Why Men Work.* Stanford, Calif.: Stanford University Press, 1948.

Hobson, J. A., *Work and Wealth.* London: G. Allen and Unwin, Ltd., 1933.

John Dewey Society, Fifth Yearbook, *Workers Education in the United States.* New York: Harper and Brothers, 1941.

Kähler, Alfred, and Hamburger, Ernest, *Education for an Industrial Age.* Ithaca, N. Y.: Cornell University Press, 1948.

National Manpower Council, *A Policy for Skilled Manpower.* New York: Columbia University Press, 1954.

Peterson, Frederich, *Creative Re-Education*. New York: G. P. Putnam's Sons, 1936.

Reed, Anna, *Occupational Placement*. Ithaca, N. Y.: Cornell University Press, 1946.

Roe, Anne, *The Psychology of Occupations*. New York: John Wiley and Sons, Inc., 1956.

Super, Donald E., *The Psychology of Careers; an introduction to vocational development*. New York: Harper and Brothers, 1957.

Thomas, Lawrence G., *The Occupational Structure and Education*. Englewood Cliffs, N. J.: Prentice-Hall, Inc., 1956.

Chapter 14

Groos, Karl, *The Play of Men* (trans. Elizabeth L. Baldwin). New York: D. Appleton and Co., 1901.

Gulick, Luther H., *Philosophy of Play*. New York: Charles Scribner's Sons, 1920.

Huizinga, Johan, *Homo Ludens: A Study of the Play Element in Culture* (trans. R. F. C. Hull). New York: Roy Publishers, 1950.

Jacks, L. P., *Education Through Recreation*. New York: Harper and Brothers, 1932.

Joad, C. E. M., *Diagnosis; or the Future of Leisure*. London: Kegan Paul, Trench, Trubner, 1929.

Layman, Emma, *Mental Health Through Physical Education and Recreation*. Minneapolis: Burgess Publishing Company, 1955.

Lehman, Harvey, and Witty, Paul A., *Psychology of Play Activities*. New York: A. S. Barnes and Co., 1927.

Lindeman, Eduard C., *Leisure—A National Issue: Planning for the Leisure of a Democratic People*. New York: Association Press, 1939.

Mitchell, Elmer D., and Mason, Barnard S., *The Theory of Play*. New York: A. S. Barnes and Co., 1948.

Nash, Jay Bryan, *Philosophy of Recreation and Leisure*. St. Louis: C. V. Mosby Company, 1953.

National Recreation Association, *The New Leisure Challenges the Schools*. Washington: National Education Association, 1933.

Neumeyer, Martin, and Neumeyer, Esther, *Leisure and Recreation*, rev. ed. New York: A. S. Barnes and Co., 1949.

Piaget, Jean, *Play, Dreams, and Imitation in Childhood* (trans. C. Gattegno and F. M. Hodgson). London: Heinemann, 1951.

Slavson, Samuel R., *Recreation and the Total Personality*. New York: Association Press, 1946.

Wrenn, C. Gilbert, and Harley, D. L., *Time on Their Hands; a Report on Leisure, Recreation and Young People*. Washington: American Council on Education, 1941.

Chapter 15

Anshen, Ruth N. (ed.), *Freedom: Its Meaning*. New York: Harcourt, Brace and Company, 1940.

Bantock, Geoffrey H., *Freedom and Authority in Education.* Chicago: Henry Regnery Company, 1953.

Berger, Morroe, *et al.* (ed.), *Freedom and Control in Modern Society.* New York: D. Van Nostrand Company, Inc., 1954.

Bryson, Lyman (ed.), *Freedom and Authority in Our Time.* New York: Harper and Brothers, 1953.

Conant, James B., *Education and Liberty.* Cambridge: Harvard University Press, 1953.

Dewey, John, *Freedom and Culture.* New York: G. P. Putnam's Sons, 1939.

Fosdick, Dorothy, *What is Liberty?* New York: Harper and Brothers, 1939.

Fromm, Erich, *Escape from Freedom.* New York: Farrar and Rinehart, Inc., 1941.

Griffin, Alan F., *Freedom: American Style.* New York: Henry Holt and Company, 1940.

Guinan, Sister M. Angelica, *Freedom and Authority in Education.* Washington: The Catholic University of America, 1936.

John Dewey Society, Twelfth Yearbook, *Educational Freedom in an Age of Anxiety.* New York: Harper and Brothers, 1953.

Kallen, Horace M., *The Education of Free Men.* New York: Farrar, Strauss and Cudahy, Inc., 1949.

Macmurray, John, *Freedom in the Modern World.* New York: D. Appleton and Company, 1938.

Malinowski, Bronislaw, *Freedom and Civilization.* New York: Roy Publishers, 1944.

Maritain, Jacques, *Freedom in the Modern World.* New York: Charles Scribner's Sons, 1936.

UNESCO, *Freedom and Culture.* New York: Columbia University Press, 1951.

Chapter 16

Bergson, Henri, *The Two Sources of Morality and Religion.* New York: Henry Holt and Company, 1935.

Bower, William C., *Moral and Spiritual Values in Education.* Lexington: University of Kentucky Press, 1952.

Broad, C. D., *Five Types of Ethical Theory.* New York: Harcourt, Brace and Company, 1930.

Childs, John L., *Education and Morals.* New York: Appleton-Century-Crofts, Inc., 1950.

Dewey, John, *Moral Principles in Education.* New York: Houghton Mifflin Company, 1909.

———, and Tufts, James H., *Ethics,* rev. ed. New York: Henry Holt and Company, 1932.

Educational Policies Commission, *Moral and Spiritual Values in the Public Schools.* Washington: National Education Association, 1951.

Everett, Walter G., *Moral Values.* New York: Henry Holt and Company, 1918.

Fromm, Erich, *Man for Himself.* New York: Rinehart and Company, 1947.

Hartshorne, Hugh, and May, Mark, *Studies in the Nature of Deceit,* and *Studies in the Nature of Character.* New York: The Macmillan Company, 1928.

Hill, Thomas E., *Contemporary Ethical Theories.* New York: The Macmillan Company, 1950.

Leys, Wayne A. R., *Ethics for Policy Decisions; the Art of Asking Deliberate Questions*. New York: Prentice-Hall, Inc., 1952.

Mason, Robert E., *Moral Values and Secular Education*. New York: Columbia University Press, 1950.

Otto, Max, *Science and the Moral Life*. New York: New American Library, 1949.

Piaget, Jean, *The Moral Judgment of the Child*. London: Kegan Paul, Trench, and Trubner, 1932.

Stevenson, Charles L., *Ethics and Language*. New Haven: Yale University Press, 1944.

Tead, Ordway, *Character Building and Higher Education*. New York: The Macmillan Company, 1953.

Wieman, Henry N., *The Directive in History*. Boston: Beacon Press, 1949.

Chapter 17

Ayer, Alfred J., *Language, Truth, and Logic*. New York: Dover Publications, Inc., 1952.

Blanshard, Brand, *The Nature of Thought*. London: Allen and Unwin, Ltd., 1939.

Bode, Boyd H., *How We Learn*. Boston: D. C. Heath and Company, 1940.

Dewey, John, *How We Think*. Boston: D. C. Heath and Company, 1910.

———, *Logic: The Theory of Inquiry*. New York: Henry Holt and Company, 1938.

———, and Bentley, Arthur F., *Knowing and the Known*. Boston: Beacon Press, 1949.

Hardie, C. D., *Truth and Fallacy in Educational Theory*. London: Cambridge University Press, 1942.

Highet, Gilbert, *Man's Unconquerable Mind*. New York: Columbia University Press, 1954.

Langer, Suzanne, *Philosophy in a New Key*. Cambridge: Harvard University Press, 1942.

Leary, Lewis, *The Unity of Knowledge*. Garden City, N.Y.: Doubleday and Company, Inc., 1955.

Lewis, Clarence I., *An Analysis of Knowledge and Evaluation*. LaSalle, Ill.: Open Court Publishing Company, 1946.

Martin, William O., *The Order and Integration of Knowledge*. Ann Arbor: The University of Michigan Press, 1957.

Montague, William P., *Ways of Knowing*. New York: The Macmillan Company, 1925.

Morris, Charles, *Six Theories of Mind*. Chicago: The University of Chicago Press, 1932.

Northrop, Filmer S. C., *The Logic of the Sciences and the Humanities*. New York: The Macmillan Company, 1947.

Reichenbach, Hans, *Experience and Prediction*. Chicago: The University of Chicago Press, 1952.

Russell, Bertrand, *Human Knowledge, its Scope and Limits*. New York: Simon and Schuster, Inc., 1948.

Sinclair, William, *The Conditions of Knowing*. New York: Harcourt, Brace and Company, 1951.

Werkmeister, William H., *The Basis and Structure of Knowledge*. New York: Harper and Brothers, 1948.

Chapter 18

Barnard, J. Darrell and Edwards, Lon, *Basic Science*. New York: The Macmillan Company, 1951.

Benjamin, A. Cornelius, *An Introduction to the Philosophy of Science*. New York: The Macmillan Company, 1937.

Black, Max, *Critical Thinking: An Introduction to Logic and Scientific Method*. New York: Prentice-Hall, Inc., 1952.

Campbell, Norman R., *What Is Science?* New York: Dover Publications, Inc., 1952.

Cohen, Morris R., *Reason and Nature*. New York: Harcourt, Brace and Company, 1931.

———, and Nagel, Ernest, *An Introduction to Logic and Scientific Method*. New York: Harcourt, Brace and Company, 1934.

Conant, James B., *On Understanding Science*. New Haven: Yale University Press, 1947.

Feigl, Herbert (ed.), *Readings in the Philosophy of Science*. New York: Appleton-Century-Crofts, Inc., 1953.

Frank, Phillip, *Modern Science and Its Philosophy*. Cambridge: Harvard University Press, 1949.

Newman, James R. (ed.), *What Is Science?* New York: Simon and Schuster, Inc., 1955.

Nokes, Malcolm C., *Science in Education*. London: Macdonald, 1949.

Poincare, Henri, *The Foundations of Science* (trans. G. B. Halsted). New York: Science Press, 1929.

Reichenbach, Hans, *The Rise of Scientific Philosophy*. Berkeley: University of California Press, 1954.

Russell, Bertrand, *The Scientific Outlook*. New York: W. W. Norton and Company, Inc., 1931.

Tennent, Frederick R., *Philosophy of the Sciences*. Cambridge, Eng.: Cambridge University Press, 1932.

Whitehead, Alfred N., *Science and the Modern World*. New York: The Macmillan Company, 1925.

Wiener, Philip P. (ed.) *Readings in Philosophy of Science*. New York: Charles Scribner's Sons, 1953.

Chapter 19

Bell, Eric T., *Mathematics, Queen and Servant of Science*. New York: McGraw-Hill Book Company, Inc., 1951.

Courant, Richard, and Robbins, Herbert, *What Is Mathematics?* New York: Oxford University Press, 1941.

Dantzig, Tobias, *Number, the Language of Science*. New York: The Macmillan Company, 1954.

Freund, John E., *A Modern Introduction to Mathematics*. Englewood Cliffs, N.J.: Prentice-Hall, Inc., 1956.

Kasner, Edward, and Newman, James, *Mathematics and the Imagination.* New York: Simon and Schuster, Inc., 1940.
Keyser, Cassius J., *The Pastures of Wonder.* New York: Columbia University Press, 1929.
Klein, Felix, *Elementary Mathematics from an Advanced Standpoint.* New York: The Macmillan Company, 1932.
National Council of Teachers of Mathematics, 21st Yearbook, *The Learning of Mathematics.* Washington: 1953.
Stabler, Edward R., *Introduction to Mathematical Thought.* Cambridge, Mass.: Addison-Wesley Publishing Company, Inc., 1953.
Titmarsh, Edward C., *Mathematics for the General Reader.* New York: Hutchinson's University Library, 1948.
Whitehead, Alfred N., *An Introduction to Mathematics.* New York: Oxford University Press, 1911.

Chapter 20

Bertalanffy, Ludwig von, *Problems of Life.* New York: John Wiley and Sons, Inc., 1952.
Born, Max, *The Restless Universe.* New York: Dover Publications, Inc., 1951.
Bridgman, Percy W., *The Nature of Physical Theory.* Princeton: Princeton University Press, 1936.
Eddington, Arthur S., *The Nature of the Physical World.* New York: The Macmillan Company, 1929.
———, *The Philosophy of Physical Science.* Cambridge, Eng.: Cambridge University Press, 1939.
Haldane, John S., *The Philosophical Basis of Biology.* New York: Doubleday and Company, Inc., 1931.
Heisenberg, Werner, *Philosophic Problems of Nuclear Science* (trans. F. C. Hayes). New York: Pantheon Books, Inc., 1952.
Jeans, Sir James, *Physics and Philosophy.* New York: The Macmillan Company, 1943.
Margenau, Henry, *The Nature of Physical Reality.* New York: McGraw-Hill Book Company, 1950.
Oppenheimer, J. Robert, *Science and the Common Understanding.* New York: Simon and Schuster, Inc., 1953.
Weyl, Hermann, *Philosophy of Mathematics and Natural Science.* Princeton: Princeton University Press, 1949.

Chapter 21

Allport, Gordon, *Becoming.* New Haven: Yale University Press, 1955.
Bryson, Lyman, *Science and Freedom.* New York: Columbia University Press, 1947.
Chase, Stuart, *The Proper Study of Mankind,* rev. ed. New York: Harper and Brothers, 1956.
Eysenck, H. J., *Uses and Abuses of Psychology.* Baltimore: Penguin Books, 1955.
Fromm, Erich, *Man for Himself.* New York: Rinehart and Company, Inc., 1947.

Gillin, John P. (ed.), *For a Science of Social Man*. New York: The Macmillan Company, 1954.

Kaufmann, Felix, *Methodology in the Social Sciences*. New York: Oxford University Press, 1944.

Keller, Albert G., *Starting Points in Social Science*, 2d ed. New Haven: Yale University Press, 1947.

Krutch, Joseph W., *The Measure of Man*. Indianapolis: Bobbs-Merrill Company, Inc., 1954.

Lynd, Robert S., *Knowledge for What?* Princeton: Princeton University Press, 1939.

Macmurray, John, *The Boundaries of Science*. London: Faber and Faber, Ltd., 1939.

Mannheim, Karl, *Ideology and Utopia* (trans. Louis Worth and Edward Shils). New York: Harcourt, Brace and Company, 1936.

Naftalin, Arthur (ed.), *An Introduction to Social Science*. Philadelphia: J. B. Lippincott Company, 1953.

Sherrington, Sir Charles S., *Man On His Nature*, 2d ed. Cambridge, Eng.: Cambridge University Press, 1951.

Skinner, B. F., *Science and Human Behavior*. New York: The Macmillan Company, 1953.

Sullivan, J. W. N., *The Limitations of Science*. New York: Viking Press, 1934.

Weber, Max, *On the Methodology of the Social Sciences* (trans. and ed. by E. A. Shils and H. A. Finch). Glencoe, Ill.: The Free Press, 1949.

Wootton, Barbara, *Testament for Social Science*. New York: W. W. Norton and Company, Inc., 1950.

Chapter 22

Beard, Charles A., *The Discussion of Human Affairs*. New York: The Macmillan Company, 1936.

Cohen, Morris R., *The Meaning of Human History*. LaSalle, Ill.: The Open Court Publishing Company, 1947.

Collingwood, R. G., *The Idea of History*. Oxford: The Clarendon Press, 1951.

Croce, Benedetto, *History as the Story of Liberty*. New York: W. W. Norton and Company, Inc., 1941.

Frankel, Charles, *The Case for Modern Man*. New York: Harper and Brothers, 1956.

Hunt, Maurice P., and Metcalf, Lawrence E., *Teaching High School Social Studies*. New York: Harper and Brothers, 1955.

Johnson, Earl S., *Theory and Practice of the Social Studies*. New York: The Macmillan Company, 1956.

Lamprecht, Sterling. *Nature and History*. New York: Columbia University Press, 1950.

Miller, Hugh, *History and Science*. Berkeley: University of California Press, 1939.

Muller, Herbert J., *The Uses of the Past*. New York: Oxford University Press, 1953.

Niebuhr, Reinhold, *Faith and History*. New York: Charles Scribner's Sons, 1949.

Toynbee, Arnold, *A Study of History* (abridged). New York: Oxford University Press, 1946.

Whitehead, Alfred N., *Adventures of Ideas.* New York: The Macmillan Company, 1933.

Chapter 23

Bodmer, Frederick, *The Loom of Language.* New York: W. W. Norton and Company, Inc., 1944.
Britton, Karl, *Communication; a Philosophical Study of Language.* London: Kegan Paul, Trench, and Trubner, 1939.
Carroll, John B., *The Study of Language.* Cambridge: Harvard University Press, 1953.
Cassirer, Ernst, *Language and Myth* (trans. S. Langer). New York: Dover Publications, Inc., 1946.
Chase, Stuart, *Power of Words.* New York: Harcourt, Brace and Company, 1954.
Flew, Anthony G. N., *Logic and Language.* Oxford, Eng.: Blackwell and Sons, Ltd., 1953.
Hayakawa, S. I., *Language in Thought and Action.* New York: Harcourt, Brace and Company, 1949.
Jesperson, Otto, *The Philosophy of Grammar.* New York: Henry Holt and Company, 1948.
Laird, Charlton G., *The Miracle of Language.* Cleveland: World Publishing Company, 1953.
Ogden, C. K., and Richards, I. A., *The Meaning of Meaning,* 8th ed. New York: Harcourt, Brace and Company, 1946.
Pei, Mario, *The Story of Language.* Philadelphia: J. B. Lippincott Company, 1949.
Sapir, Edward, *Selected Writings in Language.* Berkeley: University of California Press, 1949.
Urban, Walter M., *Language and Reality.* New York: The Macmillan Company, 1939.
Whatmough, Joshua, *Language: A Modern Synthesis.* New York: St. Martin's Press, Inc., 1956.

Chapter 24

Dewey, John, *Art as Experience.* New York: Minton, Balch and Company, 1935.
———, *et al., Art and Education,* 3d ed. Marion, Pa.: The Barnes Foundation, 1954.
Ducasse, Curt J., *The Philosophy of Art.* New York: Dial Press, Inc., 1931.
Faulkner, Ray N., *et al., Art Today, An Introduction to the Fine and Functional Arts,* 3d ed. New York: Henry Holt and Company, 1956.
Gotshalk, Dilman W., *Art and the Social Order.* Chicago: The University of Chicago Press, 1947.
Lowenfeld, Viktor, *Creative and Mental Growth.* New York: The Macmillan Company, 1949.
Munro, Thomas, *The Arts and their Interrelations.* New York: Liberal Arts Press, 1949.
National Society for the Study of Education, Fortieth Yearbook, *Art in American Life and Education.* Bloomington, Ill.: Public School Publishing Company, 1941.

National Society for the Study of Education, Thirty-Fifth Yearbook, *Music Education*. Bloomington, Ill.: Public School Publishing Company, 1936.

Parker, DeWitt H., *The Principles of Aesthetics,* 2d ed. New York: Appleton-Century-Crofts, Inc., 1946.

Pearson, Ralph M., *The New Art Education,* rev. ed. New York: Harper and Brothers, 1953.

Pepper, Stephen C., *The Basis of Criticism in the Arts*. Cambridge: Harvard University Press, 1945.

Rader, Melvin M., *A Modern Book of Esthetics,* rev. ed. New York: Henry Holt and Company, 1952.

Read, Herbert, *Education Through Art*. London: Faber and Faber, Ltd., 1943.

Chapter 25

Bertocci, Peter A., *An Introduction to the Philosophy of Religion*. New York: Prentice-Hall, Inc., 1951.

Brightman, Edgar S., *Introduction to Philosophy*. New York: Henry Holt and Company, 1925.

———, *A Philosophy of Religion*. New York: Prentice-Hall, Inc., 1940.

Burtt, Edwin A., *Man Seeks the Divine*. New York: Harper and Brothers, 1957.

———, *Types of Religious Philosophy,* rev. ed. New York: Harper and Brothers, 1951.

Butler, J. Donald, *Four Philosophies and Their Practice in Education and Religion*. New York: Harper and Brothers, 1951.

Dewey, John, *A Common Faith*. New Haven: Yale University Press, 1934.

Hocking, William E., *et al., Preface to Philosophy*. New York: The Macmillan Company, 1947.

Houf, Horace T., *What Religion Is and Does*. New York: Harper and Brothers, 1935.

Hutchison, John A., *Faith, Reason, and Existence*. New York: Oxford University Press, 1956.

Joad, C. E. M., *Guide to Philosophy*. New York: Dover Publications, Inc., 1936.

Langer, Suzanne, *Philosophy in a New Key*. Cambridge: Harvard University Press, 1951.

Macmurray, John, *The Structure of Religious Experience*. New Haven: Yale University Press, 1936.

Maritain, Jacques, *An Introduction to Philosophy*. New York: Sheed and Ward, Inc., 1935.

Phenix, Philip H., *Intelligible Religion*. New York: Harper and Brothers, 1954.

Randall, John H., and Buchler, Justus, *Philosophy: An Introduction*. New York: Barnes and Noble, Inc., 1942.

Russell, Bertrand, *The Problems of Philosophy*. New York: Henry Holt and Company, 1912.

Santayana, George, *The Life of Reason*. New York: Charles Scribner's Sons, 1954.

Stace, Walter T., *Religion and the Modern Mind*. Philadelphia: J. B. Lippincott Company, 1952.

Whitehead, Alfred N., *Religion in the Making*. New York: The Macmillan Company, 1926.

Wright, William K., *A Student's Philosophy of Religion*. New York: The Macmillan Company, 1943.

Chapter 26

Brown, James N., *Educational Implications of Four Conceptions of Human Nature*. Washington: The Catholic University of America Press, 1940.
Cassirer, Ernst, *An Essay on Man*. New Haven: Yale University Press, 1948.
Conklin, Edwin G., *Man, Real and Ideal*. New York: Charles Scribner's Sons, 1943.
Dewey, John, *Human Nature and Conduct*. New York: Henry Holt and Company, 1922.
Faris, Ellsworth, *The Nature of Human Nature*. New York: McGraw-Hill Book Company, Inc., 1937.
Frank, Lawrence K., *Nature and Human Nature*. New Brunswick, N. J.: Rutgers University Press, 1951.
Hocking, William E., *Human Nature and Its Remaking*. New Haven: Yale University Press, 1923.
Jennings, Herbert S., *Biological Basis of Human Nature*. New York: W. W. Norton and Co., Inc., 1930.
Kilpatrick, William H., *Selfhood and Civilization*. New York: The Macmillan Company, 1941.
Klubertanz, George P., *The Philosophy of Human Nature*. New York: Appleton-Century-Crofts, Inc., 1953.
LaBarre, Weston, *The Human Animal*. Chicago: The University of Chicago Press, 1955.
Niebuhr, Reinhold, *The Nature and Destiny of Man*. New York: Charles Scribner's Sons, 1941.
Raup, R. Bruce, *Complacency, The Foundation of Human Behavior*. New York: The Macmillan Company, 1930.

Chapter 27

Allport, Gordon W., *Personality: A Psychological Interpretation*. New York: Henry Holt and Company, 1937.
Dewey, John, *Individualism Old and New*. New York: Minton, Balch and Company, 1930.
Dewey, Richard S., and Humber, W. J., *The Development of Human Behavior*. New York: The Macmillan Company, 1951.
Havighurst, Robert J., *Human Development and Education*. New York: Longmans, Green and Company, Inc., 1953.
Hogben, Lancelot T., *Nature and Nurture*. New York: W. W. Norton and Company, Inc., 1933.
Kluckhohn, Clyde, and Murray, Henry A., *Personality in Nature, Society, and Culture*. New York: Alfred A. Knopf, 1949.
Lecky, Prescott, *Self-Consistency, A Theory of Personality*. New York: Island Press, 1945.

Linton, Ralph, *The Cultural Background of Personality*. New York: Appleton-Century-Crofts, Inc., 1945.

Martin, William E., and Stendler, Celia B., *Child Development*. New York: Harcourt, Brace and Company, 1953.

Mowrer, Orval H., *Learning Theory and Personality Dynamics*. New York: Ronald Press Company, 1950.

Murphy, Gardner, *Personality: a Biosocial Approach to Origins and Structure*. New York: Harper and Brothers, 1947.

Plant, James S., *Personality and the Culture Pattern*. New York: Commonwealth Fund, 1937.

White, Robert W., *Lives in Progress*. New York: Dryden Press, 1952.

Witmer, Helen L., and Kotinsky, Ruth, *Personality in the Making*. New York: Harper and Brothers, 1952.

Ulich, Robert, *The Human Career*. New York: Harper and Brothers, 1955.

Chapter 28

Adams, George P., *Man and Metaphysics*. New York: Columbia University Press, 1948.

Burtt, Edwin A., *The Metaphysical Foundations of Modern Physical Science*. New York: Harcourt, Brace and Company, 1927.

Childs, John L., *Education and the Philosophy of Experimentalism*. New York: Appleton-Century-Crofts, Inc., 1931.

Collingwood, R. G., *An Essay on Metaphysics*. Oxford: Clarendon Press, 1940.

Emmet, Dorothy, *The Nature of Metaphysical Thinking*. London: Macmillan and Company, Ltd., 1946.

Gotschalk, Dilman W., *Metaphysics in Modern Times*. Chicago: The University of Chicago Press, 1940.

Hocking, William E., *Types of Philosophy*. New York: Charles Scribner's Sons, 1929.

Hook, Sidney, *The Metaphysics of Pragmatism*. Chicago: Open Court Publishing Company, 1927.

Maritain, Jacques, *A Preface to Metaphysics*. New York: Sheed and Ward, Inc., 1939.

O'Connell, G., *Naturalism in American Education*. Washington: The Catholic University of America Press, 1936.

Parker, DeWitt H., *Experience and Substance*. Ann Arbor: The University of Michigan Press, 1941.

Pepper, Stephen C., *World Hypotheses*. Berkeley: University of California Press, 1942.

Radhakrishnan, Sir Sarvepalli, *An Idealist View of Life*. London: Allen and Unwin, Ltd., 1951.

Stace, Walter T., *The Nature of the World*. Princeton: Princeton University Press, 1940.

Ushenko, Andrew P., *Power and Events*. Princeton: Princeton University Press, 1946.

Whitehead, Alfred N., *Modes of Thought*. New York: The Macmillan Company, 1938.

Wick, Warner A., *Metaphysics and the New Logic*. Chicago: University of Chicago Press, 1942.

Chapter 29

Bagley, William C., *Education and Emergent Man*. New York: Thomas Nelson and Sons, 1934.

Boodin, John E., *God and Creation*. New York: The Macmillan Company, 1934.

Collingwood, R. G., *The Idea of Nature*. Oxford, Eng.: The Clarendon Press, 1945.

Ehrenfels, Christian F. von, *Cosmology*. New York: 1948.

Eliade, Mircea, *The Myth of the Eternal Return*. New York: Pantheon Books, Inc., 1954.

Hoyle, Fred, *The Nature of the Universe*. New York: Harper and Brothers, 1951.

Langdon-Davies, John, *Man and His Universe*. New York: Harper and Brothers, 1930.

Leighton, Joseph A., *Man and the Cosmos*. New York: D. Appleton and Company, 1922.

Lovejoy, Arthur O., *The Great Chain of Being*. Cambridge: Harvard University Press, 1936.

McWilliams, J. A., *Cosmology, A Text for Colleges,* 2d rev. ed. New York: The Macmillan Company, 1938.

Milne, E. A., *Modern Cosmology and the Christian Idea of God*. Oxford, Eng.: Clarendon Press, 1952.

Simpson, George, *The Meaning of Evolution*. New Haven: Yale University Press, 1949.

Weizsäcker, Carl F. von, *The History of Nature*. Chicago: The University of Chicago Press, 1949.

Whitehead, Alfred N., *Process and Reality*. New York: The Macmillan Company, 1929.

Whyte, Lancelot I., *The Next Development in Man*. New York: Henry Holt and Company, 1948.

Younghusband, Sir Francis E., *The Living Universe*. New York: E. P. Dutton and Company, Inc., 1933.

Chapter 30

Brameld, Theodore, *Ends and Means in Education*. New York: Harper and Brothers, 1950.

Bryson, Lyman, *et al.,* Ninth Symposium, Conference on Science, Philosophy, and Religion in their Relation to the Democratic Way of Life, *Goals for American Education*. New York: Harper and Brothers, 1950.

Educational Policies Commission, *The Purposes of Education in American Democracy*. Washington: National Education Association, 1938.

Hutchins, Robert M., *The Higher Learning in America*. New Haven: Yale University Press, 1936.

Hyde, William DeWitt, *The Five Great Philosophies of Life*. New York. The Macmillan Company, 1911.

Jeffries, M. V. C., *Glaucon: An Inquiry into the Aims of Education*. London: Pitman, 1950.

Kandel, I. L., *Conflicting Theories of Education*. New York: The Macmillan Company, 1938.

Kilpatrick, William H. (ed.), *The Educational Frontier*. New York: Century, 1933.

Lepley, Ray (ed.), *Value: A Cooperative Inquiry*. New York: Columbia University Press, 1949.

Livingstone, Sir Richard W., *On Education*. New York: The Macmillan Company, 1945.

Lynd, Robert, *Knowledge for What?* Princeton: Princeton University Press, 1939.

Maritain, Jacques, *Education at the Crossroads*. New Haven: Yale University Press, 1943.

Niblett, W. R., *Education, the Lost Dimension*. New York: William Sloane Associates, Inc., 1955.

Perry, Ralph, *Realms of Value: A Critique of Human Civilization*. Cambridge: Harvard University Press, 1954.

Smith, Huston, *The Purposes of Higher Education*. New York: Harper and Brothers, 1955.

University Committee on the Objectives of a General Education in a Free Society, *General Education in a Free Society*. Cambridge: Harvard University Press, 1945.

Whitehead, Alfred N., *The Aims of Education*. New York: The Macmillan Company, 1929.

Chapter 31

Buber, Martin, *Images of Good and Evil*. London: Routledge and Kegan Paul, Ltd., 1952.

Bury, John B., *The Idea of Progress*. New York: The Macmillan Company, 1932.

Camus, Albert, *The Rebel*. New York: Alfred A. Knopf, 1954.

Carus, Paul, *The History of the Devil and the Idea of Evil*. Chicago: Open Court Publishing Company, 1900.

Ferré, Nels F. S., *Evil and the Christian Faith*. New York: Harper and Brothers, 1947.

Greene, William C., *Moira*. Cambridge: Harvard University Press, 1948.

Joad, C. E. M., *God and Evil*. New York: Harper and Brothers, 1943.

King, A. R., *The Problem of Evil*. New York: Ronald Press Company, 1952.

Leon, Philip, *The Ethics of Power*. London: Allen and Unwin, Ltd., 1935.

Lewis, Clive S., *The Problem of Pain*. New York: The Macmillan Company, 1953.

Niebuhr, Reinhold, *Moral Man and Immoral Society*. New York: Charles Scribner's Sons, 1932.

Rice, Philip B., *On the Knowledge of Good and Evil*. New York: Random House, Inc., 1955.

Shinn, Roger L., *Christianity and the Problem of History*. New York: Charles Scribner's Sons, 1953.

Tsanoff, Radoslav A., *The Nature of Evil*. New York: The Macmillan Company, 1931.

Index

Index

Bibliothèque Champlain
3 9365 00307659 5